APPIAN

I

LCL 2

APPIAN

ROMAN HISTORY

VOLUME I

EDITED AND TRANSLATED BY

BRIAN McGING

.ARVARD UNIVERSITY PRESS

CAMBRIDGE, MASSACHUSETTS

LONDON, ENGLAND

2019

Library of Congress Control Number 2019940172
CIP data available from the Library of Congress

ISBN 978-0-674-99647-2

*Composed in ZephGreek and ZephText by
Technologies 'N Typography, Merrimac, Massachusetts.
Printed on acid-free paper and bound by
Maple Press, York, Pennsylvania*

CONTENTS

PREFACE

Just over a century ago, Appian of Alexandria was only the second author to be incorporated into the new Loeb Classical Library. For a historian who was, on the whole, so ill-regarded at the time, his speedy elevation to Loeb status may seem surprising, but the reason was that his translator, Horace White, had already produced a translation of Appian's *Roman History* in 1899, originally published by George Bell and Sons. This gave White the opportunity to adjust and improve his translation, and his four Loeb volumes (1912–1913), the last two revised and prepared for the press by E. Iliff Robertson of Christ's College Cambridge, became a landmark moment in the story of Appian's reception in the modern world. For they were the first close and widely accessible translation of Appian (with their accompanying Greek text) into the English language, the versions of White's only predecessors, William Barker (1578) and John Davies (1679), being long out of date stylistically and textually, very difficult to find, and incomplete. Those needing to know the state of the text still required their Teubner editions, but for the vast majority of students, interested readers, and indeed, academics, the Loeb of Appian became and remained standard and indispensable. It would be difficult, I imagine, to over-estimate the number of people who have come to Appian

through White's Loeb. As well as his clear and careful (if now inevitably somewhat dated) translation, White, one of the rare Loeb translators who was not a professional classicist, also wrote in his own preface of qualities in Appian's history that few others appreciated until much later in the twentieth century. It is a pleasure, then, to salute and follow in the footsteps of my Loeb predecessor.

I would like to thank my students at Trinity College Dublin, who with open mind, good humor, and considerable acuity embraced Appian as a set text and helped with some knotty problems of translation. My colleagues John Dillon and, particularly, Ashley Clements have also been very generous with their time and philological expertise. I am most grateful to them.

BMcG
Dublin, March 2019

INTRODUCTION

LIFE OF APPIAN

The second-century AD historian Appian of Alexandria is one of our main sources for the history of the Roman Republic, particularly for the second and first centuries BC, but we do not know a great deal about him.[1] He is usually assumed to have been born toward the end of the first century AD, in the midnineties, since a fragment (fr. 19) of his Arabian history (Book 24) records his dramatic escape in Egypt from a party of Jewish insurgents pursuing him in the Nile delta during the revolt of the Jews in AD 115 to 117. He was clearly an adult at the time, but probably only a young man: references in the *Preface* of his work to nine hundred years of Roman history (*Praef.* 9.34) and nearly two hundred years since the beginning of the monarchy (*Praef.* 7.24) seem to indicate that he was writing the *Preface* around 150.

That Appian flourished in this period is also clear from his friendship with the great lawyer and letter-writer Marcus Cornelius Fronto, who became suffect consul in 142. An exchange of letters with Fronto is preserved among Fronto's correspondence, as is a letter from Fronto to the

[1] On Appian's life, see particularly Gowing 1992, 9–18; Brodersen 1993, 352–54; Bucher 2000, 415–16.

emperor Antoninus Pius, with a request, made on a number of previous occasions, that the emperor confer a procuratorship on Fronto's longtime friend Appian, who was now an old man in search of honor rather than position and money.[2]

One other potential source of information about Appian's life and career may be supplied by a sarcophagus in Rome, which, according to the verse inscription on it, a certain Appianos prepared for himself and his wife, Eutychia, while they were both still alive. Given the rarity of the name Appianos in Rome, the learned nature of the verses, and the suitability of a wife named Eutychia for someone who attributed great importance to Rome's good fortune (*eutychia*), a case can be made that the Appianos in question is our historian.[3] If so, we have the additional information that Appian held a priesthood of Tyche at Rome to which he was appointed by the emperor, that he married Eutychia when she was twelve years old, and that Eutychia died when she was forty-three. If it is the historian Appian, however, it is perhaps strange that there is no mention of his Egyptian origins or of his legal career.

As for the date of death, the 160s seem probable. Appian refers to the practice of sending proconsuls to govern parts of Italy as one revived by the emperor Hadrian, but which did not survive his death by very long (*BCiv.* 1.38.172): he does not seem to know that the practice was reintroduced by Marcus Aurelius in 166/7. And his state-

[2] For the letters, see Van den Hout 1988, 168, 242–48; Van den Hout 1999, 550–57. Appian's letter is included in this edition as fragment 25.

[3] As Brodersen (2015) has elegantly argued.

ment that the Euphrates formed the eastern frontier of the Roman empire (*Praef.* 4.14) shows no awareness of the Mesopotamian campaign of Lucius Verus in 165. It is, of course, possible that Appian lived beyond these events and simply failed to correct what he had written earlier.

At the end of the *Preface* to his work (15.62), Appian appends a brief biographical note, in which he mentions that he was well known, he reached the highest position in his own country, pleaded cases before the emperors in Rome, and was thought worthy of their procuratorship; he had published a more detailed account in his autobiography. What exactly any of this means for the details of his career is unclear.[4] If Appian acted as a lawyer in Rome, it seems likely that it was a legal career that had brought him to the top of society in Alexandria. Pleading before the emperors has been taken to mean that Appian held the post of *advocatus fisci*, legal counsel for the imperial treasury, but it is not certain. And did he actually take up the procuratorship of which he was deemed worthy? His own statement is ambiguous, and it is more likely that he was satisfied with the honor of the offer rather than that he accepted the post.[5] Either way, he must have been of equestrian rank to be eligible for the procuratorship.

In spite of the uncertainty about details, it is clear that Appian was at ease in the highest political and literary circles of Alexandrian and Roman society.[6] There was a long history of antagonism between Greeks and Jews in Alexandria, and the story of Appian's escape during the

---

[4] For discussion, see particularly Gowing 1992, 9–18.

[5] As argued by Champlin (1980, 98–100).

[6] For his literary context, see Gowing 1992, 273–87.

Jewish revolt shows that he was a particular target of Jewish hostility.[7] If he was a representative of upper-class Alexandrian Greeks in this respect, in one other he did not share the outlook of some of his Greek fellow citizens. Since the annexation of Egypt into the Roman empire, certain Alexandrian Greeks had grown bitterly resentful of Rome:[8] unlike them, Appian was a great admirer of the Roman empire of his day. To judge from his evident pleasure in detailing the extensive military and financial resources of the Ptolemaic kingdom (*Praef.* 10.39–42), and indeed from the climactic position in his *Roman History* of the four books on Egyptian history (now lost), he was also very proud of his Egyptian homeland.

With Rome and Alexandria providing the intellectual context for his life, it seems probable that these two cities also constituted Appian's main audience. The manner in which he explains basic Roman institutions, such as the equestrian order (e.g., *BCiv.* 1.22.91 and elsewhere), or the triumphal procession of victorious generals (*Lib.* 66.293–99), makes it clear that he was writing Roman history for a Greek audience.[9] Like Polybius, however, he spanned two cultures, and, in spite of his readiness to reprimand the Romans severely when he believed they were behaving badly (see below), his story is ultimately

[7] For the implications of this, see Gowing 1992, 11–16.

[8] As most famously shown by the so-called *Acts of the Pagan Martyrs*, a set of stories preserved on papyrus, telling of the heroic defiance of the emperor by Alexandrian nobles: see Harker 2008.

[9] See Bucher 2000, 438–39.

about the triumph of Rome and Roman virtues, and it is
difficult to imagine that he did not also envisage, to some
extent, a Roman audience.

THE WORK

Appian sets out the plan of his work, or at least his initial
plan, in the *Preface* (12.45–15.61). His theme is the process by which the Roman empire has achieved its present
greatness. It will involve a comparison of Roman qualities
with those of the nations it conquered. The organization
is, as far as we can tell, entirely Appian's own: he will trace
the story of each individual nation's wars with Rome in a
single book, starting from the time they first came into
conflict, right up to their annexation into the Roman empire, and maintaining strict geographical boundaries. This
sometimes has awkward results: most obviously, for example, in the case of the struggle against Carthage in the
Second Punic War, which was treated in four separate
books, the Sicilian, Iberian, Hannibalic, and African. The
overall order of the books is dictated by simple chronology, following the order in which the nations first went to
war with Rome.

Such a structure makes good sense of Rome's con-
quests in the Regal and Republican periods, but perhaps
less sense of the civil wars, when Rome was fighting not
foreign enemies, but itself. In a second preface, however,
at the start of the first book of *Civil Wars* (*BCiv.* 1.1.1–
6.25), Appian movingly summarizes Rome's slide into civil
violence and murderous savagery, and depicts this period
as the final and greatest challenge the Roman state had to

overcome before it "succeeded in establishing harmony and monarchy" (*BCiv.* 1.6.24). The work, then, is a history of Rome's wars against its various enemies—the last and most troublesome of whom was itself[10]—the whole story eventually leading to the glorious imperial prosperity of Appian's own day.[11]

The *Preface* (14.53–15.61) outlines a neat division into foreign wars, organized according to nations, and civil wars according to the major figures involved, the latter breaking up into four main sections: the wars of Marius and Sulla, of Pompey and Caesar, of Antony and Octavian against the assassins of Caesar, and then against each other. It must be the case, however, that Appian wrote the *Preface* when he knew what he was going to do in the early books but had a less certain idea of how he would write up the story of the civil wars. In the event, while the first two books of the *Civil Wars* correspond, more or less, to his initial plan, the structure becomes quite different thereafter. The *Civil Wars* end with the death of Sextus Pompeius in 35, and the final round of what we think of as the civil wars, the battle for supremacy between Antony and Octavian, is, to some extent at least, recast as another foreign war, telling the story of how Egypt came under Roman rule.[12] This was the most detailed part of the whole work—four books covering five years—and presumably

10 Carter 1996, xiv.

11 For the overall plan and purpose of Appian's work, Bucher 2000 is crucial.

12 For the contents, and the relationship of the Egyptian history to the *Civil Wars*, see Luce 1964.

reflects a mixture of Appian's interest in his Egyptian homeland, an abundance of source material, and his conviction that Octavian's victory at the battle of Actium brought Rome's trials to an end, and ushered in the new era of stable, monarchic rule.

We have very little impression of the character of the remaining books, but the Roman empire of Appian's day was much larger than it had been at the time of the battle of Actium, and he must have felt it necessary to change his original plan and bring the story of imperial conquest up-to-date: Augustus and Trajan, in particular, were two of the greatest conquerors Rome ever had; and for someone on whom the horrors of the civil wars of the first century BC had made such an impression, it is difficult to imagine that Appian would have ignored the internecine struggles of the year of the four emperors (AD 68–69).[13] Although he very briefly refers to his intention to cover the imperial period (*Ill.* 30.87), he does not specifically mention any of these last three books, and there is no trace of the only other planned topics he does mention, a Parthian Book (*Syr.* 52.260) and a final one outlining the military and financial resources of Rome (*Praef.* 15.61). At least one possibility must be that he did not write them, and died before he had finished the work.

The *Roman History* does not survive in full, but from what Appian himself says in the *Preface*, from manuscript notations, and from the comments of later authors, par-

---

[13] On the whole, second-century AD historians seem to have steered clear of writing about the Antonine emperors: see Kemezis 2010 (309–12, on Appian).

ticularly the ninth-century scholar and Patriarch of Constantinople, Photius, we can reconstruct the complete work as follows (Photius' titles in Greek):

[14] In the *Preface* (*Praef.* 14.57), Appian calls it simply the Carthaginian Book, but Photius has "African, Carthaginian, and Numidian Book." The most important manuscript gives the title as "Appian's African Book, or the Carthaginian History," others simply as "Appian's African Book."

[15] Photius just calls it the Macedonian Book, but Appian himself (*BCiv.* 5.602) says that he added the Illyrian history to that of Macedon.

[16] No traces of this book survive.

[17] Photius calls it the Syrian and Parthian Book, but the Parthian book that survives under the name of Appian, and that Photius had at his disposal, has long been recognized as a later forgery.

[18] Unlike Photius, the manuscripts tend to assign a separate book, the twelfth, to the Parthian history, making the Mithridatic the thirteenth, and affecting the numeration thereafter. See Goukowsky 2001, cxl–cxlvi.

[19] Photius numbers the Egyptian History as the sixth to ninth books of the *Civil Wars*, but Appian (*Mith.* 114.557; *BCiv.* 1.6.24, 2.90.379) specifically refers to the Egyptian history; and citations in the lexicon, *On Syntax*, show that there were four Egyptian books.

Of this list, only the *Preface* and Books 6 to 9 and 11 to 17 are preserved in full. There are valuable Byzantine excerpts of Books 1 to 5 and 9, and brief citations of words or phrases from Appian's work in the *Suda*, the tenth-century lexicon, and elsewhere, but with the exception of the story from Book 24 of Appian's escape during the Jewish revolt of AD 115 to 117, nothing survives of Books 10 and 18 to 24.

APPIAN'S REPUTATION

Scholarly assessments of Appian's ability as a historian and writer have greatly improved in recent times. When Horace White published his Loeb translation just over a century ago, he would have struggled to find many, or even anyone, who would have agreed with some of the positive things he wrote in his introduction. Of Appian's style, for instance, he says, "Occasionally he rises to the dignity of the best writers of the ancient world. The introduction to the history of the Civil Wars is an example of this kind.

---

[20] Appian himself nowhere mentions a Dacian book: Photius lists it.

Here the events leading up to the tragedies of the Gracchus brothers move forward with a dignified and measured tread which has been imitated by many later historians but surpassed by none."[21]

Perhaps the fact that White was a newspaper editor and a financial expert, not a professional classicist,[22] gave him the independence to reject the decidedly negative assessment of Appian that prevailed among classical scholars of that time: far from ranking in any way among the best writers of the ancient world, Appian attracted accusations, among others, that he was lazy (Dominicus 1844), stupid and third-rate (Nissen 1863), an amateur (Rosenberg 1925), that he wrote historical fiction rather than history (Schwartz 1896).[23] It had not always been that way. Photius included Appian in his assessment of authors he had read (*Bibl.* 57): his judgment was that Appian had a style that was lean (ἰσχνός) and free from redundancies (ἀπέριττος); that as a historian he was truthful (φιλαλήθης), and particularly sound on military matters; and that he was extremely good (ἄριστος) at writing speeches "to encourage dejected soldiers, to calm them when they were too passionate, to depict emotion and represent faithfully anything else in speeches."

[21] White 1912, x.

[22] See Logsdon (1971) for a study of White's interesting career.

[23] See, for instance, Brodersen 1993, 362–63; McGing 1993, 496–97. Welch (2015b) provides a careful assessment of the ways in which scholarly attitudes to Appian have changed over the centuries.

Appian's dramatic fall from grace was most acute in the nineteenth century,[24] but the seeds of his reputational demise may well have been sown, as Goldmann suggests, by Joseph Scaliger in his 1606 study of Eusebius' chronology, where he attacks Appian for his chronological failings.[25] Appian admits his lack of interest in dates (*Praef.* 13.50): "While I regard it as excessive to record dates for everything, from time to time I will mention chronology in the case of particularly important events." This can have appeared to Scaliger and others only as lazy carelessness: how could you not be interested in chronology, if you wanted to be treated as a serious historian? Scaliger also believed that Appian wrote the book of Parthian history that survives under his name, but which has long been recognized as a crude ancient forgery based on Plutarch.[26] This promoted the view that became almost unanimous: Appian did not have a mind of his own, and scarcely even qualified as a historian in his own right, but was little more than a compiler of sections from the works of other ancient authors.

Since it was generally believed that Appian's own role in producing his history was merely to divide up the material at his disposal according to the structure he set out in the *Preface*, there was only one subject worth studying—his sources. Almost a century and a half of Appianic schol-

[24] Welch 2015b, 3.

[25] See Goldmann 1988, 2–3.

[26] The excellent study of Mallan (2017) suggests that it may well have been composed closer to Appian's own lifetime than is usually thought.

arship was devoted solely to source criticism, with a very low return on such a heavy investment of effort.[27] The main problem was the *Civil Wars*, for which Appian is by far the most important source that survives, and at times the only one. The great prize was to be able to extract from Appian information about the accounts he used, but which are now lost. If, as Emilio Gabba argued at considerable length, Asinius Pollio was Appian's most important single source for the *Civil Wars*, and Appian did little more than translate him into Greek, we suddenly had access, otherwise denied, to a new account of Republican history.[28] But Badian did not accept Gabba's arguments, and Westall makes it even more probable that Pollio was not Appian's main source.[29] Perhaps one of the difficulties in identifying Appian's sources, and one not taken into consideration by source critics, is the quality of his prose style, which recent research has given us reason to believe was constructed with great care.[30]

Even where Appian's sources were well known, the disdain for his historical skills had a detrimental effect. No one, for instance, disputed the importance to Appian of Polybius for the period 200 to 146 BC, but when his account diverged from that of Polybius it must have been because he was not using Polybius directly, but through a

[27] Balsdon 1956, 201: "the vast steppes of Appianic *Quellenforschung* are haunted by the ghosts of nameless lost historians."

[28] Gabba 1956.

[29] Badian 1958; Westall (2015), who makes a much better case for the Elder Seneca.

[30] See Hutchinson 2015.

lost intermediary, who will have provided the divergent material in Appian.[31] It was inconceivable that Appian might have adapted his source material in his own way and for his own historical purposes.

The tide of Appianic scholarship turned, however, when classical authors began to benefit from new twentieth-century intellectual trends. The linguistic turn drew attention to language, to historiographical concerns rather than just to the reliability of historical narrative. One of its products in the field of historical studies was the postmodern refusal to prioritize or even evaluate different pieces of evidence, which in its extreme form foundered on the rocks of the Holocaust, but which perhaps also filtered into the consciousness of classical scholarship, and suggested the possibility that authors like Appian, previously regarded as peripheral or low-ranking in the hierarchy of excellence (in comparison with central and brilliant figures such as Thucydides or Tacitus), might repay more careful study.[32]

As soon as attention focused on historiographical matters, rather than on the sources, it became clear that the whole notion of Appian as a cipher was untenable. He did not suddenly become a great historian, but numerous studies have now made it obvious that he had a plan

[31] Schwartz (1896, 217–22) was particularly influential in promoting the cause of a mysterious early imperial intermediary for Appian; the arguments against it, put most forcefully by Rich (2015, esp. 67–69), should be decisive.

[32] For the most robust defense of evidence-based history against the attacks of extreme postmodernism, see Evans 1977.

of his own making, that he fashioned his sources for his own historical and interpretative purposes and developed themes that reflected his own historical emphases rather than simply what he found in his sources.

THE SOURCES

This welcome recognition of Appian as a historian in his own right and the resulting studies of how he wrote, and how he constructed his history, rather than where he got his information, do not alter the fact that in order to assess the likely value of a historian writing mostly about the distant past, the sources remain an important matter. Did he use a single source for particular books or sections of narrative? What range of sources did he consult? Did he show good judgment in picking previous accounts? And, where accounts survive that we know he used, how did he adapt them?

Answers to these questions will, no doubt, continue to differ, but the passion for seeking Appian's sources, particularly for the *Civil Wars*, among authors whose work no longer survives, has abated. For even if we could confidently identify Asinius Pollio, or Posidonius, or Seneca the Elder as Appian's main sources for sections of his work, it might tell us something about those historians, but not much about Appian, since their work does not survive. We could, to be sure, say that Appian chose wisely; and in general there seems to be a growing consensus that this is the case. In the *Mithridateios*, for example, it is highly probable that Appian used, among other works, Sulla's *Memoirs*, and the *Histories* of Rutilius Rufus, Sallust, and

Strabo, as well as Posidonius. His account, then, rested on a solid basis of well-chosen authorities.[33] It would be far more revealing of Appian as a historian, however, if we knew how he adapted these works.

Fortunately, we can study this process in certain parts of the *Roman History*, in particular for the first half of the second century BC when Polybius was Appian's most important source. One recent investigation of Appian's use of Polybius for his narrative of the war between Antiochus III and Rome provides a convincing working model for future investigations.[34] Appian composed his work in two stages, first assembling material nation by nation and making drafts, then writing up the final version largely from these notes (which would explain the mistakes he made). Where he differs from the main sources he was using, the explanation is not that he was blindly reproducing lost intermediary accounts, but that, as Rich argues, he was handling his sources with "a good deal of freedom in reshaping the material and imposing his own interpretation."[35] That is not to say that he did not follow Polybius closely at times; but fundamental to the future study of Appian's working methods must be the recognition that he chose his sources and what to take from them from his own

[33] See the wise comments of Goukowsky (2001, xci–cxx). In general, the introductions to the Budé editions contain some of the most helpful modern analysis of Appian's sources.

[34] Rich 2015.

[35] Rich 2015, 114. Influential analysis of how Plutarch worked, but certainly applicable to Appian too, is provided by Pelling (2002, 1–90).

wide reading, that he had some critical ability and used it to fashion his own composition and depiction of events.[36]

APPIANIC THEMES AND INTERESTS

One of the first themes identified as specifically Appianic was spotted by Karl Marx: Appian's materialistic approach to history.[37] Time and again in the *Roman History*, money, financial and economic considerations, bribery, and corruption come into play.[38] Appian's interest in the subject is evident from the start, in the *Preface*. He makes what appears to be a passing reference to the unprofitability of the province of Britain (5.18), but goes on to say more about the empire's revenues (7.24–28): in the two hundred years since the beginning of the rule of the emperors, Rome's income has increased greatly and the empire has settled into a "stable prosperity." In general, policy has been to maintain what they have and not extend "their power indefinitely over poor and unprofitable barbarian peoples." Even so, they waste resources on some of their subjects, who cost more than they bring in. The description that follows of the military, naval, and financial resources that Ptolemy II Philadelphus of Egypt had at his disposal (10.39–42) and the plan to write a final book outlining "the current size of the Roman army, the revenue they collect from each country, and what they addition-

[36] Goukowsky 2001, xxcvii. For Appian's coverage of the Third Punic War assessed in these terms, see McGing 2018.

[37] For Marx and Appian, see Bonnell 2015.

[38] The theme is carefully traced by Cuff (1983).

ally spend on naval defense or anything else of this kind"
(15.61) show that these matters were of particular concern
to Appian.[39]

Two of the most obvious of Appian's major themes are
warfare and diplomacy. Necessarily, given his chosen subject, there is a great deal of fighting in Appian. He was not
a soldier himself. His own understanding of the realities
of fighting, therefore, can only have been limited, and
the account we get must be dependent on his sources and
his imagination. The same motifs of heroic generals, exhausted (or fresh) troops, starvation, supply lines, ditches,
palisades, defensive walls and attacking mounds, tunnels,
ladders, siege engines, recur with some monotony.[40] Even
here, however, he does rework his sources to create drama
and horror. Appian's account of the destruction of Carthage at the end of the Third Punic War, for example, is
savage and moving, regardless of how closely it follows
Polybius or represents the actual fighting (*Lib*. 128.610–
32.630). And the dramatic nature of the struggle and ulti-
mate victory is very effectively brought home by the air of
disbelief and joyous retelling at Rome of the details of
the fighting, when the news of events is reported (*Lib*.
134.633–37).[41] The same generic, but dramatic, coverage
of sea battles and storms can be seen, particularly in the

39 For how such materialistic concerns affect the *Mithridateios*, for example, see McGing 1993, 513–14.

40 The most important analysis of this theme is Goldmann
1988, 50–84. See also Gowing 1992, 209–23.

41 On this and other instances of how Appian and the charac-
ters in his work imagine the past, see Pitcher 2012.

extensive coverage of the war at sea in Book 5 of the *Civil Wars*.[42]

Appian's abilities as a historian are seen to better effect in his coverage of diplomatic exchanges, whether before Rome's wars against foreign enemies, or in the negotiations of the chief protagonists during the civil wars, especially when the pace of Appian's narrative slows down after the assassination of Julius Caesar and its immediate aftermath at the end of *Civil Wars* Book 2 (Books 3–5 of the *Civil Wars* cover the period 44–35 BC). He devotes considerable attention to some of these situations, in the process revealing his explanation of why events developed as they did. The maneuvering of Rome, Carthage, and Massinissa before the Third Punic War, for instance, takes up nearly a quarter of the whole African Book (*Lib*. 67.302–94.446) and displays similar narrative patterns to the preliminaries of the Third Macedonian War (*Mac*. 11.1–9) and the First Mithridatic War (*Mith*. 10.31–16.58). Based on reports from Roman embassies or neighboring kings, the senate is suspicious of the growing strength of their enemy. Agitators (Eumenes, Massinissa, Nicomedes) make similar accusations against their neighbors, urging Rome to intervene. Rome acts in bad faith, negotiating terms when they have already decided to go to war, but have kept the decision secret. In each case, blame for the war lies squarely with Rome, a judgment reflected in the invariably weaker arguments Appian gives the Romans in the exchange of speeches. This is not the copying of sources,

[42] *BCiv*. 5.81.342–121.503.

but Appian imposing his own interpretative patterns on events.[43]

Scholars will, no doubt, continue to assess Appian's personal take on how the Roman qualities he identifies in the *Preface* (11.43)—sound judgment, good fortune, courage, endurance, hard work—run through the whole work, and on other Appianic themes, such as his somewhat coy, but interested, approach to matters of love and sex,[44] or how deceit plays out in the work,[45] and there remains much work to do on Appian as storyteller, how he actually builds his narrative.[46]

SPEECHES

The same applies to speeches. As with all historians in the ancient world, Appian makes the people of his *Roman History* deliver speeches, not as they were actually spoken, but in his own style and re-creation. They are very unevenly distributed throughout the work. There are, for example, no speeches in the Hannibalic Book, but sixteen in the *Iberike*, which follows it immediately; there are no speeches in Book 1 of the *Civil Wars* (with one brief exception), but a heavy concentration in Books 3 and 4. On past assumption that Appian more or less copied, or trans-

[43] See McGing 2018, 352–53.
[44] Pitcher 2015.
[45] Cowan 2015.
[46] Good examples of this sort of study applied to the *Civil Wars* will be found in Bucher 2007, Stevenson 2015, Welch 2015c.

lated,[47] his sources, the natural explanation was that where there are no speeches, Appian's source had no speeches.[48] It has been demonstrated beyond doubt, however, that as with his narrative, Appian molded his speeches for his own purposes:[49] as Bronwyn Hopwood summarizes, Appian "felt free to embellish and extrapolate speeches from existing models or to create speeches where none existed."[50] The absence of speeches from parts of the *Roman History* is far more likely to be due to Appian's own compositional strategy; or, as already suggested, to the possibility that he died before finishing the work.

Appian's speeches are clustered around important events; they create drama and help to fill out the character of the leading players of his story, but perhaps their most important characteristic is that they are an integral part of the historical narrative and interpretation, not disconnected rhetorical firework displays showing off Appian's ability to compose brilliant orations.[51] In this he conforms with the requirement of Polybius (12.25b.1–2, 12.25i.8) that speeches in historical works must be part of the chain of cause and consequence. It is a quality not to be underestimated. Time and again, Appian's speeches provide dif-

[47] Gabba 1956, 219.

[48] See particularly Hahn 1982.

[49] An important demonstration of this will be found in Gowing 1990.

[50] Hopwood 2015, 307.

[51] The contrast between the two types of speech is brought out effectively in Gowing's comparison of Dio's and Appian's speeches (1992, 225–45).

ferent perspectives on an issue, insights into the motives of the protagonists, and subtle support for his own interpretation of what was happening.

The speeches before the outbreak of the First Mithridatic War, for example (*Mith.* 12.38–16.58), highlight Roman corruption, incompetence, and immediate responsibility for the war, by giving the Pontic side a much better rhetorical case than the Romans. The perspective at this point, however, is largely that of Mithridates. After the war, Sulla provides a very different point of view (*Mith.* 54.215–58.240), showing that Mithridates was by no means an innocent victim (confirming what the Bithynians had argued all along). This is very effective writing, the speeches being an integral part of Appian's explanation for why the war happened and what was going on before it. Similarly, the extensive exchange of speeches between the Romans and the Carthaginians before the outbreak of the Third Punic War (*Lib.* 78.360–90.426), while building tension before the great drama about to unfold, effectively supports Appian's interpretation of events, that Roman duplicity in the face of Carthaginian compliance brought about the war.[52]

APPIAN'S IMPORTANCE

Although derided in the past for his failings, both apparent and real, Appian has always been an important author, if only because he is, at times, all we have. He provides in the first book of *Civil Wars* our only coherent account of the history of the Roman Republic in what White, in his

[52] See McGing 2018.

original Loeb introduction, called the "'twilight period between Polybius and Cicero.'"[53] White also pointed to Appian's value as the only detailed account of the Third Punic War and destruction of Carthage. But his basic informational value stretches a great deal further than that. We could scarcely, for instance, write a history of Roman Spain, or of the Mithridatic Wars, without Appian. And even when there are other sources, Appian cannot suddenly be dismissed. The detailed narrative of the remaining books of *Civil Wars*, and indeed the more fragmentary early books, must be reckoned with by historians at all times.

Providing valuable information, however, is not the same as being a good historian. This is where modern scholarship has at least established Appian as a real historian who fashioned his own interestingly conceived, if idiosyncratic, analysis of Roman history. Opinion may differ on the quality of that analysis, but it must be remembered in assessing Appian's standing that we do not have the central and pivotal books on Egyptian history that bring the destructive civil discord of the Republic to an end, and usher in the new age of monarchic peace and prosperity. We can have good reason to expect that Appian was at his best in this part of the work.

Appian makes bad mistakes[54] and can be inconsistent,[55] but perhaps one of his greatest, and overlooked, qualities is an unusal degree of objectivity. Although gen-

[53] White 1912, xi.

[54] For some of them see Welch 2015b, 12n16.

[55] See, for instance, Tweedie (2015) for Appian's inconsistent treatment of Scipio Aemilianus.

erally regarded as "above all an ardent admirer of Rome,"[56] this is only an ardent admiration for the peace and prosperity that the Roman empire of his own day had brought about. He is highly critical of the brutality of Rome during the civil wars, and, at times, of Roman behavior during its imperial expansion. Scholars have played this down, arguing that it is an occasional discomfort at particular failings rather than a fundamental critique of Roman imperialism.[57] It is certainly the case that Appian has no difficulty accepting the benefits of Roman imperialism (not least to himself), but his criticisms of Roman behavior in the Republican period constitute far more than an occasional discomfort.

As we have seen, Appian blames Rome, and persistent Roman duplicity, for the outbreak of the Third Punic War. The cause of the First Mithridatic War and the Third Macedonian War he lays firmly at Rome's door, and he is highly critical of Roman greed, corruption, and deceit. He is unequivocal, too, in his castigation of the treachery in Spain, for example, of Licinius Lucullus (*Ib*. 52.218–21), who tricked the people of Cauca into admitting a garrison and then massacred all the men; of Servius Sulpicius Galba (*Ib*. 59.249–60.255), who divided the Lusitanians into three groups on the promise that he would assign each group good land but then massacred them separately; and of Quintus Pompeius (*Ib*. 79.338–45) who lied about making an agreement with the people of Numantia. Con-

---

[56] *Oxford Classical Dictionary*² (ed. N. G. L. Hammond and H. H. Scullard, 1970), 130.

[57] See, for instance, Brodersen 1993, 355, 360; Tweedie 2015, 181–82.

versely, he has high praise for the Spaniards, most notably for Viriathus (*Ib*. 75.317–21) and the people of Numantia (*Ib*. 97.419–23).[58] He even has a rather noble summary of the career of Mithridates Eupator, by far Rome's most murderous enemy (*Mith*. 112.540–50), and reports Pompey paying for his funeral and ordering his burial in the royal tombs at Sinope: "For he admired him for his great deeds and regarded him as the best of the kings of his time." The enemies of Rome get an unusually fair hearing in Appian.

This does not amount to a sustained anti-Roman or anti-imperial position on Appian's part, but it is evidence of a refreshingly balanced approach, one in which he is quite prepared to highlight and be severely critical of Roman behavior that fell far short of the standards the Romans set themselves, and by which they claimed to set such store. This is a valuable corrective to the unwaveringly patriotic accounts of the Roman tradition, as, for example, in Livy.

THE TEXT

The translation is based on the Teubner text of Appian: volume 1, Viereck and Roos (1939, corrections and additional notes by Gabba 1962); volume 2, Mendelssohn (1881, revised by Viereck 1905). On the whole, the text of Appian is not very problematic, but in view of the excellent work of the editors of the Budé series, particularly Paul Goukowsky, I have highlighted in a limited *apparatus criticus* textual variants and editorial suggestions that

[58] See especially Espelosín 1993, 420–21.

make more than a minor difference, and I have at times adopted readings different from the Teubner text.

The standard treatment of the manuscript tradition of Appian is Dilts 1971, and Dilts 1990, and the establishment of the text is well explained by Brodersen 1993, 344–52. Some of the sigla used by Viereck-Roos are out of date, or confusing (they used V, for instance, both for Vaticanus graecus 141 and Vaticanus graecus 134), and I have adopted those used by Dilts and the Budé editors. The following are the main sigla and abbreviations:

V	Vaticanus gr. 141 (11th century)
L	Laurentianus gr. LXX-5 (14th century)
P	Vaticanus gr. 2156 (1450)
B	Marcianus gr. 387 (1440)
J	Vaticanus gr. 134 (ca. 1450)
E	Parisinus gr. 1642 (15th century)
F	Parisinus gr. 1672 (14th century)
M	Laurentianus gr. LXX-26 (15th century)
D	Vaticanus Pii II gr. 37 (15th century)
Q	Matritensis 4564 (15th century)

Exc.   *Excerpta Historica iussu imperatoris Constantini Porphyrogeneti confecta*

               Excerpta de legationibus Romanorum ad gentes, vol. 1, ed. C de Boor (Berlin, 1903)

               Excerpta de legationibus gentium ad Romanos, vol. 1, ed. C. de Boor (Berlin, 1903)

               Excerpta de virtutibus et vitiis, vol. 2, part 2, ed. G. Roos (Berlin, 1910)

               Excerpta de sententiis, vol. 4, ed. U. P. Boissevain (Berlin, 1906)

Bekker, Anecd.	I. Bekker, *Anecdota Graeca*, 3 vols. (Berlin, 1814–1821)
On Syntax, Gaillard	Gaillard 2002, Appendix, xlv–liv
Schweig.	Schweighäuser 1785
Mend.	Mendelssohn 1879–1881

There are also occasional references to readings by earlier editors, such as Karl Nipperdey, whose observations were noted by Mendelssohn, or Samuel Musgrave, whose notes Schweighäuser used, and all are fully identified in Viereck-Roos.

GENERAL BIBLIOGRAPHY

Babcock, R. G., and W. A. Johnson. 1994. "The Appian Papyrus from Dura-Europus (*P. Dura* 2)." *Bulletin of the American Society of Papyrologists* 31:85–88.

Badian, E. 1958. "Appian and Asinius Pollio." *Classical Review* 8:159–62.

Balsdon, J. P. V. D. 1956. Review of P. Meloni, *Il valore storico e le fonti del libro Macedonico di Appiano* (Rome, 1955). In *Journal of Roman Studies* 46:199–201.

Bonnell, A. G. "A 'Very Valuable Book': Karl Marx and Appian." In Welch 2015a, 15–21.

Brodersen, K. 1993. "Appian und sein Werk." *Aufstieg und Niedergang der Römischen Welt* II 34.1, 339–63. Berlin/New York.

———. 2015. "Epitaphios: Appianos and His Treasured Eutychia θησαυρίζειν τὴν εὐτυχίαν." In Welch 2015a, 341–50.

Broughton, T. R. S. 1951–1986. *The Magistrates of the Roman Republic.* 3 vols. New York.

Bucher, G. S. 2000. "The Origins, Program, and Composition of Appian's Roman History." *Transactions and Proceedings of the American Philological Association* 130:411–58.

———. 2007. "Towards a Literary Evaluation of Appian's

Civil Wars, Book I." In *A Companion to Greek and Roman Historiography*, ed. J. Marincola, 454–60. Malden, MA, 2011.

Champlin, E. 1980. *Fronto and Antonine Rome.* Cambridge, MA.

Cornell, T. J. 2013. *The Fragments of the Roman Historians.* 3 vols. Oxford.

Cowan, E. 2015. "Deceit in Appian." In Welch 2015a, 185–203.

Cuff, P. J. 1967. "Prolegomena to a Critical Edition of Appian *BC* I." *Historia* 16:177–88.

———. 1983. "Appian's *Romaica*: A Note." *Athenaeum* 61:148–64.

Dilts, M. R. 1971. "The Manuscripts of Appian's *Historia Romana.*" *Revue d' Histoire des Textes* 1:49–71.

———. 1990. "Manuscripts of Appian's *Iberica* and *Annibaica.*" In *Philophronema. Festschrift für Martin Sicherl zum 75 Geburtstag*, ed. D. Harlfinger, 37–42. Paderborn.

Espelosín, F. J. G. 1993. "Appian's 'Iberike.' Aims and Attitudes of a Greek Historian of Rome." *Aufstieg und Niedergang der Römischen Welt* II 34.1, 403–27. Berlin/New York.

Evans, R. J. 1977. *In Defence of History.* London.

Famerie, E. 1998. *Le latin et le grec d'Appien. Contribution à l'étude du lexique d'un historien grec de Rome.* Geneva.

Gabba, E. 1956. *Appiano e la storia delle guerre civili.* Florence.

Gargola, D. J. 1997. "Appian and the Aftermath of the Gracchan Reform." *American Journal of Philology* 118:555–81.

Goldmann, B. 1988. *Einheitlichkeit und Eigenständigkeit der Historia Romana des Appian*. Hildersheim.

Gomez Espelosin, F. J. 1993. "Appian's *Iberike*, Aims and Attitudes of a Greek Historian of Rome." *Aufstieg und Niedergang der Römischen Welt* II 34.1, 403–27. Berlin/New York.

Gowing, A. M. 1990. "Appian and Cassius' Speech Before Philippi." *Phoenix* 44:158–81.

———. 1992. *The Triumviral Narratives of Appian and Cassius Dio*. Ann Arbor.

Hahn, I. 1982. "Appian und seine Quellen." In *Romanitas-Christianitas*, ed. G. Wirth, 251–76. Berlin.

Hahn, I., and G. Nemeth. 1993. "Appian und Rom." *Aufstieg und Niedergang der Römischen Welt* II 34.1, 364–402. Berlin/New York.

Harker, A. 2008. *Loyalty and Dissidence in Roman Egypt. The Case of the* Acta Alexandrinorum. Cambridge.

Hopwood, B. 2015. "Hortensia Speaks: An Authentic Voice of Resistance?" In Welch 2015a, 305–22.

Hutchinson, G. O. 2015. "Appian the Artist: Rythmic Prose and Its Literary Implications." *Classical Quarterly* 65:1–19.

Kemezis, A. 2010. "Lucian, Fronto and the Absence of Contemporary Historiography under the Antonines." *American Journal of Philology* 131:285–325.

König, J. 2009. *Greek Literature in the Roman Empire*. London.

Leidl, C. G. 1993. "Appians *Annibaike*: Aufbau—Darstellungstendenzen—Quellen." *Aufstieg und Niedergang der Römischen Welt* II 34.1, 428–62. Berlin/New York.

Logsdon, J. 1971. *Horace White: Nineteenth Century Liberal*. Westport, CT.

Luce, T. J. 1961. "Appian's Magisterial Terminology." *Classical Philology* 56:21–28.

———. 1964. "Appian's Egyptian History." *Classical Philology* 59:259–62.

Magnino, D. 1993. "Le *Guerre Civili* di Appiano." *Aufstieg und Niedergang der Römischen Welt* II 34.1, 523–54. Berlin/New York.

Mallan, C. 2017. "The *Parthica* of Pseudo-Appian." *Historia* 66: 362–81.

Marasco, G. 1982. *Appiano e la storia dei Seleucidi fino all' ascesa al trono di Antioco III.* Florence.

———. 1988. "Appiano e gli Ebrei." *Studia Historica* 7–19.

McGing, B. C. 1993. "Appian's *Mithridateios.*" *Aufstieg und Niedergang der Römischen Welt* II 34.1, 496–99. Berlin/New York.

———. 2018. "Appian, the Third Punic War and Polybius." In *Polybius and his Legacy*, ed. N. Miltsios and M. Tamiolaki, 341–56. Berlin.

Pelling. C. B. R. 2002. *Plutarch and History.* London.

Pitcher, L. V. 2012. "War Stories: The Uses of the Plupast in Appian." In *Time and Narrative in Ancient Historiography. The "plu-past" from Herodotus to Appian*, ed. J. Grethlein and C Krebs, 199–210. Cambridge.

———. 2015. "The Erotics of Appian." In Welch 2015a, 205–20.

Rich, J. 2015. "Appian, Polybius and the Romans' War with Antiochus the Great: A Study in Appian's Sources and Methods." In Welch 2015a, 65–123.

Schwartz, E. 1896. "Appianus." *Realencyclopädie* II 1, 216–37 (= *Griechische Geschichtsschreiber*, 361–93. Leipzig, 1957).

Stevenson, T. 2015. "Appian on the Pharsalus campaign: *Civil Wars* 2.48–91. In Welch 2015a, 257–75.

Tweedie, F. 2015. "Appian's Characterisation of Scipio Aemilianus." In Welch 2015a, 169–84.

Van den Hout, M. P. J. 1988. *M. Cornelii Frontonis epistulae.* 2nd ed. Leipzig.

———. 1999. *A Commentary on the Letters of M. Cornelius Fronto.* Leiden.

Welch, K., ed. 2015a. *Appian's Roman History. Empire and Civil War.* Swansea, UK.

———. 2015b. "Appian and the *Roman History*: A Reappraisal." In Welch 2015a, 1–13.

———. 2015c. "Programme and Narrative in *Civil Wars* 2.118–4.138." In Welch 2015a, 277–304.

Westall, R. 2015. "The Sources for the *Civil Wars* of Appian of Alexandria." In Welch 2015a, 125–67.

EDITIONS AND COMMENTARIES

Brodersen, K. 1989. *Appians Abriss der Seleukidengeschichte (Syriake 45, 232–70, 369). Text und Kommentar.* Munich.

———. 1991. *Appians Antiochike (Syriake 1, 1–44, 232). Text und Kommentar.* Munich.

Carsana, C. 2007. *Commentario storico al libro II delle Guerre Civili di Appiano (parte I).* Pisa.

Étienne-Duplessis, M. 2013. *Appien. Histoire Romaine, Tome XII, Livre XVII: Guerres Civiles Livre V.* Paris.

Gabba, E. 1967. *Appiani Bellorum Civilium Liber Primus.* 2nd ed. Florence.

———. 1970. *Appiani Bellorum Civilium Liber Quintus.* Florence.

Gaillard, D. 2002. *Appien, Histoire Romaine, Tome III, Livre VII: le Livre d'Annibal*. Paris.

Gaillard-Goukowsky, D. 2015. *Appien, Histoire Romaine, Tome XI, Livre XVI: Guerres Civiles Livre IV*. Paris.

Goukowsky, P. 1997. *Appien, Histoire Romaine, Tome II, Livre VI: L'Ibérique*. Paris.

———. 2001. *Appien, Histoire Romaine, Tome VII, Livre XII: la Guerre de Mithridate*. Paris.

———. 2003. *Appien, Histoire Romaine, Tome IV, Livre VIII: le Livre Africain*. Paris.

———. 2007. *Appien, Histoire Romaine, Livre XI: le Livre Syriaque*. Paris.

———. 2008. *Appien, Histoire Romaine, Tome VIII, Livre XIII: Guerres Civiles Livre I*. Paris.

———. 2010. *Appien, Histoire Romaine, Tome X, Livre XV: Guerres Civiles Livre III*. Paris.

———. 2011. *Appien, Histoire Romaine, Tome V, Livre IX: Le Livre Illyrien—Fragments du Livre Macédonien*. Paris.

Magnino, D. 1984. *Appiani Bellorum Civilium Liber Tertius*. Pavia.

———. 1998. *Appiani Bellorum Civilium Liber Quartus*. Como.

Mendelssohn, L. 1879–1881. *Appiani Historia Romana*. 2 vols. Vol. 2 revised and corrected edition by P. Viereck. Leipzig, 1905.

Petrova, D. 2006. *Das Lexicon Über die Syntax. Untersuchung und kritische Ausgabe des Lexicons in Codex Paris Coisl. gr. 345*. Wiesbaden.

Richardson, J. S. 2000. *Appian. Wars of the Romans in Iberia. Introduction, Commentary and Translation*. Warminster.

GENERAL BIBLIOGRAPHY

Schweighäuser, J. 1785. *Appiani Alexandrini Romanorum Historiarum quae supersunt.* 3 vols. Leipzig.

Viereck, P. M., and A. G. Roos. 1962 [1939]. *Appiani Historia Romana.* Leipzig. (Additions and corrections by E. Gabba.)

TRANSLATIONS

Carter, J. 1996. *Appian. The Civil Wars.* London.

Veh, O., and K. Brodersen. 1987. *Appian von Alexandria. Römische Geschichte, erster Teil: die römische Reichsbildung.* Stuttgart.

Veh, O., and E. Will. 1989. *Appian von Alexandria. Römische Geschichte, zweiter Teil: die Bürgerkriege.* Stuttgart.

White, H. 1899. *The* Roman History *of Appian of Alexandria.* 2 vols. London and New York.

———. 1912–1913. *Appian's Roman History.* 4 vols. Cambridge, MA. (Vols. 3 and 4 revised and prepared for publication by E. Ilif Robson.)

ΑΠΠΙΑΝΟΥ ΡΩΜΑΪΚΗ
ΙΣΤΟΡΙΑ

APPIAN'S ROMAN
HISTORY

ΠΡΟΟΙΜΙΟΝ[1]

1. Τὴν Ῥωμαϊκὴν ἱστορίαν ἀρχόμενος συγγράφειν ἀναγκαῖον ἡγησάμην προτάξαι τοὺς ὅρους, ὅσων 2 ἐθνῶν ἄρχουσι Ῥωμαῖοι. εἰσὶ δὲ οἵδε· ἐν μὲν τῷ ὠκεανῷ Βρεττανῶν τοῦ πλείονος μέρους, διὰ δὲ τῶν Ἡρακλείων στηλῶν ἐς τήνδε τὴν θάλασσαν ἐσπλέοντί τε καὶ ἐπὶ τὰς αὐτὰς στήλας περιπλέοντι νήσων ἄρχουσι πασῶν καὶ ἠπείρων, ὅσαι καθήκουσιν ἐπὶ τὴν 3 θάλασσαν. ὧν εἰσιν ἐν δεξιᾷ πρῶτοι Μαυρουσίων, ὅσοι περὶ τὴν θάλασσαν, ὅσα τε ἄλλα Λιβύων ἔθνη μέχρι Καρχηδόνος καὶ τούτων ὕπερθε Νομάδες, οὓς Ῥωμαῖοι καλοῦσι Νουμίδας καὶ τὴν χώραν Νουμιδίαν, ἕτεροι δὲ Λίβυες, ὅσοι περιοικοῦσι τὰς Σύρτεις μέχρι Κυρήνης, Κυρήνη τε αὐτὴ καὶ Μαρμαρίδαι καὶ

[1] ἀππιανοῦ τῆς ἰταλικῆς ἱστορίας τὸ προοίμιον V; ἀππιανοῦ σοφιστοῦ ἀλεξανδρέως ῥωμαϊκῆς (vel ἰταλικῆς) ἱστορίας προοίμιον O Candidus

---

[1] The oldest manuscript of Appian, V (Vat. Gr. 141), gives the title as "Appian's Italian History. The Preface." Other manuscripts and the fifteenth-century translation of Candidus have: "The Roman (or Italian) History of Appian of Alexandria, scholar. Preface."

PREFACE[1]

1. As I begin the process of writing up my Roman history, I thought I should first set out the boundaries of all the nations under Roman rule. They are as follows. In the 2 Ocean, most of Britain;[2] in this sea, for someone entering through the Pillars of Heracles and taking in its entire circuit all the way round back to the Pillars of Heracles, Rome controls all the islands and all the coastal lands. First, on the right, are the Mauretanians of the coast, and 3 the various other African peoples as far as Carthage.[3] Inland from them are the Nomads (the Romans call them Numidians and their country Numidia). Then come other Africans who live around the Syrtes[4] as far as Cyrene; after them Cyrene itself, and the Marmaridae and Ammonians

---

[2] Appian refers to the Atlantic as "the Ocean." The Mediterranean he calls "this sea" or "the inner sea."

[3] Appian's circumnavigation takes the reader from the straits of Gibraltar (the Pillars of Heracles) along the southern shore of the Mediterranean first, then round the eastern end and across the north coast, back to Gibraltar. "Libya" is the Greek word for Africa: to avoid confusion with the modern state of Libya, I render it as "Africa."

[4] The Gulf of Libya.

Ἀμμώνιοι καὶ οἳ τὴν Μάρειαν λίμνην κατοικοῦσι, καὶ ἡ μεγάλη πόλις, ἣν Ἀλέξανδρος ἔθηκε πρὸ Αἰγύπτου, Αἴγυπτός τε αὐτὴ μέχρι Αἰθιόπων τῶν ἑῴων ἀνὰ τὸν Νεῖλον πλέοντι καὶ μέχρι Πηλουσίου διὰ θαλάσσης.

4   2. Ἐπιστρέφοντι δὲ τὸν πλοῦν καὶ περιιόντι Συρία τε ἡ Παλαιστίνη καὶ ὑπὲρ αὐτὴν μοῖρα Ἀράβων, ἐχόμενοι δὲ τῶν Παλαιστινῶν Φοίνικες ἐπὶ τῇ θαλάσσῃ καὶ Φοινίκων ὕπερθεν ἥ τε Κοίλη Συρία καὶ μέχρι ἐπὶ ποταμὸν Εὐφράτην ἀπὸ θαλάσσης ἄνω Παλμυρηνοί τε καὶ ἡ Παλμυρηνῶν ψάμμος, ἐπ' αὐτὸν Εὐφράτην καθήκουσα, Κίλικές τε Σύρων ἐχόμενοι καὶ Καππαδόκαι Κιλίκων ὅμοροι καὶ μέρος Ἀρμενίων, οὓς καλοῦσιν Ἀρμενίαν βραχυτέραν, παρά τε τὸν Εὔξεινον πόντον ἄλλα ὅσα Ποντικὰ Ῥωμαίων ὑπήκοα γένη.

5 Σύροι μὲν δὴ καὶ Κίλικες ἐς τήνδε τὴν θάλατταν ἀφορῶσιν, Ἀρμένιοι δὲ καὶ Καππαδόκαι ἔς τε τὰ Ποντικὰ γένη καθήκουσι καὶ ἀνὰ τὴν μεσόγαιον ἐπὶ τὴν καλουμένην Ἀρμενίαν μείζονα, ἧς Ῥωμαῖοι οὐκ ἄρχουσι μὲν ἐς φόρου κομιδήν, αὐτοὶ δὲ αὐτοῖς ἀπο-

6 δεικνύουσι τοὺς βασιλέας. ἀπὸ δὲ Καππαδοκῶν καὶ Κιλίκων ἐς τὴν Ἰωνίαν καταβαίνοντι ἔστιν ἡ μεγάλη χερρόνησος· ὅ τε γὰρ πόντος ὁ Εὔξεινος καὶ ἡ Προποντὶς καὶ ὁ Ἑλλήσποντος ἐπὶ δεξιά, [καὶ τὸ Αἰγαῖον],[2] ἐκ δὲ λαιᾶς τὸ Παμφύλιον ἢ Αἰγύπτιον πέλα-

---

[2] καὶ τὸ Αἰγαῖον delere voluit Schweig.

---

[5] Better known as Lake Moeris (mod., Birket Qarun), located

and those who live beside Lake Marea;[5] next the great city Alexander founded at the entrance to Egypt, and Egypt itself, stretching to eastern Ethiopia as you sail up the Nile, and to Pelusium as you go along the coast.

2. When one changes course and goes around to port, there is Syria-Palestine, and beyond it part of Arabia. On the coast the Phoenicians come after the Palestinians, with Coele Syria inland from Phoenicia; then, in the territory up-country from the sea as far as the river Euphrates, Palmyra and its desert lands extending right up to the Euphrates itself. After Syria come the Cilicians and their neighbors the Cappadocians, and the part of Armenia they call Lesser Armenia.[6] Along the coast of the Euxine sea there are all the other Pontic peoples subject to Rome. The Syrians and Cilicians look out over the Mediterranean, while Armenia and Cappadocia border on the Pontic nations, and, in the interior, stretch as far as what is known as Greater Armenia, which Rome does not rule as a tribute-paying subject, but they themselves appoint their own kings. As one comes down[7] from Cappadocia and Cilicia to Ionia there is the great peninsula. For to the right, the Euxine Sea and the Propontis and the Hellespont and the Aegean, and to the left the Pamphylian or

in the Fayum depression of Egypt, about sixty-two miles southwest of modern Cairo. [6] After moving due north along the eastern seaboard of the Mediterranean (with excursions inland), Appian continues straight on northward through the center of modern Turkey and to the Black Sea coast, before he faces left and looks westward to Ionia over Asia Minor, which he calls a peninsula. [7] That is, down from the high plateau of central Anatolia to the Aegean coast.

APPIAN

7 γος (λέγεται γὰρ ἄμφω) ποιεῖ χερρόνησον, καὶ εἰσὶν
αὐτῆς οἱ μὲν εἰς τὸ Αἰγύπτιον πέλαγος ἀφορῶντες,
Πάμφυλοί τε καὶ Λύκιοι καὶ μετ᾽ αὐτοὺς Καρία μέχρι
Ἰωνίας, οἱ δ᾽ ἐπὶ τὸν Εὔξεινον καὶ τὴν Προποντίδα
καὶ τὸν Ἑλλήσποντον, Γαλάται τε καὶ Βιθυνοὶ καὶ
Μυσοὶ καὶ Φρύγες, ἐν δὲ μεσογαίῳ Πισίδαι τε καὶ
Λυδοί. τοσαῦτα ἔθνη τὴν χερρόνησον οἰκοῦσιν, καὶ
πάντων ἄρχουσι Ῥωμαῖοι.

8   3. Περάσαντες δὲ καὶ ἑτέρων ἐθνῶν ἄρχουσιν ἀμφὶ
τὸν Πόντον καὶ Μυσῶν τῶν ἐν Εὐρώπῃ καὶ Θρᾳκῶν
9 ὅσοι περὶ τὸν Εὔξεινον. ἀπὸ δὲ Ἰωνίας κόλπος ἐστὶ
θαλάσσης ὁ Αἰγαῖος καὶ ἕτερος Ἰονίου θαλάσσης καὶ
ὁ Σικελικὸς πορθμὸς καὶ ἡ Τυρρηνικὴ θάλασσα μέ-
10 χρι τῶν Ἡρακλείων στηλῶν. τοῦτο μῆκός ἐστιν ἀπ᾽
Ἰωνίας ἐπὶ τὸν ὠκεανόν, καὶ ἐν τῷδε αὖ τῷ παράπλῳ
Ῥωμαίων ὑπήκοα τοσαῦτα, ἥ τε Ἑλλὰς πᾶσα καὶ
Θεσσαλία καὶ Μακεδόνες καὶ ὅσα πρόσοικα ἄλλα
Θρᾳκῶν καὶ Ἰλλυριῶν καὶ Παιόνων ἔθνη, αὐτή τε
Ἰταλία μακροτάτη δὴ πάντων ἐθνῶν οὖσα καὶ ἀπὸ
τοῦ Ἰονίου παρήκουσα ἐπὶ πλεῖστον τῆς Τυρρηνικῆς
θαλάσσης μέχρι Κελτῶν, οὓς αὐτοὶ Γαλάτας προσ-
11 αγορεύουσι, καὶ Κελτῶν, ὅσα ἔθνη τὰ μὲν ἐς τήνδε
τὴν θάλασσαν, τὰ δὲ ἐς τὸν βόρειον ὠκεανὸν ἀφορᾷ,
τὰ δὲ παρὰ Ῥῆνον ποταμὸν ᾤκηται, Ἰβηρία τε πᾶσα
καὶ Κελτίβηρες, ἐπὶ τὸν ἑσπέριον καὶ βόρειον ὠκε-
12 ανὸν καὶ τὰς Ἡρακλέους στήλας τελευτῶντες. καὶ

Egyptian Sea (both names are used) form a peninsula. Some of its inhabitants, the Pamphylians and the Lycians 7 and after them the Carians up to Ionia, face the Egyptian Sea; others, the Galatians and Bithynians and Mysians and Phrygians, look out over the Euxine Sea, Propontis, and Hellespont. In the interior are the Pisidians and Lydians. These are the peoples who inhabit the peninsula, and Rome rules them all.

3. Across the Hellespont the Romans also rule other 8 nations on the Pontus, the European Mysians and the Euxine Thracians. After Ionia comes the Aegean gulf, 9 then another one, the Ionian,[8] then the Sicilian straits and the Tyrrhenian Sea all the way over to the Pillars of Heracles.[9] This is what lies in the long stretch between Ionia 10 and the Ocean, but as you sail along this coast from one place to the next, the following are subjects of Rome: all of Greece and Thessaly and Macedonia and the other neighboring Thracian and Illyrian and Paeonian peoples, and Italy itself, the longest country of all: it extends from the Ionian Sea along most of the Tyrrhenian as far as the Celts (whom the Romans themselves refer to as Galatians). Some of the Celts overlook this sea, others the 11 Northern Ocean, and others again live on the Rhine. Then come all of Iberia and the Celtiberians, bounded by the Western Ocean, the Northern Ocean and the Pillars of

[8] The Adriatic.
[9] The Tyrrhenian Sea is usually thought of as the waters between the west coast of Italy and the islands of Sardinia, Corsica, and Sicily. Appian pictures it here (also at *Ib.* 1.1) as stretching all the way to the east coast of Spain: he does not seem to know of the Iberian, or Spanish, Sea (see, for example, Pliny, *HN* 3.2.6).

τούτων πέρι καὶ ἐφ' ἑκάστου δηλώσω τὰ ἀκριβέστατα, ὅταν ἐς ἕκαστον ἔθνος ἡ γραφὴ περιίῃ.

13   4. Νῦν δέ, ὅσον ὅροις μεγάλοις τὴν ἀρχὴν περι-
λαβεῖν, κατὰ μὲν θάλασσαν εἴρηται, κατὰ δὲ γῆν
περιοδεύοντι μοῖρά τε Μαυρουσίων ἂν εἴη τῶν παρ'
Αἰθίοψι τοῖς περὶ ἑσπέραν καὶ εἴ τι θερμότερον ἢ θη-
14   ριῶδες ἄλλο Λιβύης μέχρι Αἰθιόπων τῶν ἑῴων. ταῦτα
μὲν Λιβύης Ῥωμαίοις ὅροι, τῆς δὲ Ἀσίας ποταμός τε
Εὐφράτης καὶ τὸ Καύκασον ὄρος καὶ ἡ Ἀρμενίας τῆς
μείζονος ἀρχὴ καὶ Κόλχοι παρὰ τὴν Εὔξεινον θάλασ-
15   σαν ᾠκημένοι καὶ τὰ λοιπὰ τοῦδε τοῦ πελάγους. ἐν δὲ
τῇ Εὐρώπῃ ποταμοὶ δύο, Ῥῆνός τε καὶ Ἴστρος, μάλιστα τὴν Ῥωμαίων ἀρχὴν ὁρίζουσιν, καὶ τούτων Ῥῆ-
νος μὲν ἐς τὸν βόρειον ὠκεανόν, Ἴστρος δὲ εἰς τὸν
Εὔξεινον πόντον καταδιδοῖ. περάσαντες δέ πη καὶ
τούσδε Κελτῶν τῶν ὑπὲρ Ῥῆνον ἄρχουσιν ἐνίων καὶ
16   Γετῶν τῶν ὑπὲρ Ἴστρον, οὓς Δακοὺς καλοῦσιν. ὅροι
μὲν οὗτοι κατ' ἤπειρον, ὡς ἐγγύτατα ἐλθεῖν τοῦ ἀκρι-
βοῦς·

    5. Νῆσοι δὲ πᾶσαι, ὅσαι τῆς ἐντὸς θαλάσσης εἰσίν,
αἵ τε Κυκλάδες καὶ Σποράδες ἢ Ἰάδες ἢ Ἐχινάδες ἢ
Τυρρηνίδες ἢ Γυμνησίαι ἢ ὅσας ἄλλας ὀνομάζουσιν
ἑτέρως περί τε Λιβύην καὶ τὸ Ἰόνιον ἢ Αἰγύπτιον ἢ
Μυρτῷον ἢ Σικελικὸν ἢ ὅσα ἄλλα τῆσδε τῆς θαλάσ-
17   σης ὀνόματα, ὅσαι τε ἐξαιρέτως ὑπὸ τῶν Ἑλλήνων
ὀνομάζονται μεγάλαι νῆσοι, Κύπρος τε καὶ Κρήτη
καὶ Ῥόδος καὶ Λέσβος καὶ Εὔβοια καὶ Σικελία καὶ

Heracles.[10] I will set out the fullest details about these 12
individually when my work comes round to each nation.

4. For now, enough has been said about the major 13
boundaries encompassing the empire for somebody traveling along the coast. When going by land, the following
are the boundaries: the part of Mauretania that borders
on western Ethiopia, then all the rest of tropical Africa
with its wild animals, over as far as eastern Ethiopia. Such 14
are the Roman frontiers in Africa. In Asia they are the
river Euphrates and the Caucasus mountains and the
kingdom of Greater Armenia and the Colchians who live
on the Euxine Sea, and the rest of that seacoast. In Europe 15
two rivers, the Rhine and the Ister, form the main limits
of the Roman empire. The Rhine flows out into the Northern Ocean and the Ister into the Euxine Sea. Having
crossed these rivers in certain places, the Romans also rule
over some of the Celts on the other side of the Rhine, and
some of the Getae (the Dacians, as the Romans call them)
on the other side of the Ister. These are the land boundar- 16
ies, as accurately as I can describe them.

5. All the islands of the inner sea are subject to Rome:
the Cyclades and Sporades and Ionian isles and Echinades
and Tyrrhenian isles and the Balearics; and any others,
differently named, whether in the African Sea or the Ionian or the Egyptian or the Myrtoan or the Sicilian or any
other part of this sea, whatever it is called; also those spe- 17
cifically identified by the Greeks as the major islands, Cyprus and Crete and Rhodes and Lesbos and Euboea and

[10] The Western Ocean is presumably the Atlantic in this case;
the Northern Ocean seems to include the Bay of Biscay, the English Channel, and the North Sea.

Σαρδὼ καὶ Κύρνος καὶ εἴ τις ἄλλη μικροτέρα τε καὶ
18 μείζων, ἄπαντα ταῦτ' ἐστὶ Ῥωμαίοις ὑπήκοα. καὶ τὸν
βόρειον ὠκεανὸν ἐς τὴν Βρεττανίδα νῆσον περάσαντες, ἠπείρου μεγάλης μείζονα, τὸ κράτιστον αὐτῆς
ἔχουσιν ὑπὲρ ἥμισυ, οὐδὲν τῆς ἄλλης δεόμενοι· οὐ
γὰρ εὔφορος αὐτοῖς ἐστιν οὐδ' ἣν ἔχουσι.
19 6. Τούτων τοσούτων καὶ τηλικούτων ἐθνῶν ὄντων
τὸ μέγεθος, Ἰταλίαν μὲν αὐτὴν ἐπιμόχθως τε καὶ μόλις ἐν πεντακοσίοις ἔτεσι κατειργάσαντο βεβαίως.
20 καὶ τούτων τὰ ἡμίσεα βασιλεῦσιν ἐχρῶντο, τὰ δὲ
λοιπὰ τοὺς βασιλέας ἐκβαλόντες καὶ ἐπομόσαντες
οὐκ ἀνέξεσθαι βασιλέων ἀριστοκρατίᾳ τε ἐχρήσαντο
21 ἀπὸ τοῦδε καὶ προστάταις ἄρχουσιν ἐτησίοις. διακο-
σίοις δὲ μάλιστα ἑξῆς ἐπὶ τοῖς πεντακοσίοις ἐπὶ μέγα
ἦλθεν ἡ ἀρχή, καὶ ξενικῆς τε δυνάμεως ἐκράτησαν
ἀπείρου καὶ τὰ πλεῖστα τῶν ἐθνῶν τότε ὑπηγάγοντο.
22 Γάιός τε Καῖσαρ, ὑπὲρ τοὺς τότε δυναστεύσας καὶ
τὴν ἡγεμονίαν κρατυνάμενός τε καὶ διαθέμενος ἐς φυλακὴν ἀσφαλῆ, τὸ μὲν σχῆμα τῆς πολιτείας καὶ τὸ
ὄνομα ἐφύλαξεν, μόναρχον δ' ἑαυτὸν ἐπέστησε πᾶσι.
23 καὶ ἔστιν ἥδε ἡ ἀρχὴ μέχρι νῦν ὑφ' ἑνὶ ἄρχοντι, οὓς
βασιλέας μὲν οὐ λέγουσιν, ὡς ἐγὼ νομίζω, τὸν ὅρκον
αἰδούμενοι τὸν πάλαι, αὐτοκράτορας δὲ ὀνομάζουσιν,
ὃ καὶ τῶν προσκαίρων στρατηγῶν ὄνομα ἦν· εἰσὶ δὲ
ἔργῳ τὰ πάντα βασιλεῖς.

---

[11] Livy 2.1.9 reports the story that after the expulsion of the
kings, Lucius Iunius Brutus made the Romans swear an oath

Sicily and Sardinia and Corsica, and any other island there may be, whether smaller or bigger. Crossing the Northern   18
Ocean to the island of Britain, which is even bigger than a large continent, the Romans have taken possession of the best part of it, more than half, but have no wish for the rest: even what they have is unprofitable for them.

6. Although the size of their empire now encompasses   19
so many and such great nations as these, it took the Romans five hundred years of toil and difficulty to reduce Italy itself securely. For half this time they employed   20
kings; for the rest, when they had expelled the kings and sworn an oath not to endure kings in the future, from then on they adopted aristocratic government and annual officials to rule them.[11] In the two hundred years, roughly   21
speaking, that followed this half millenium, their empire expanded greatly and they acquired unparallelled power abroad: it was in this period that they brought most of the nations under their rule. When Gaius Caesar[12] established   22
dominance over his contemporaries, he consolidated and safeguarded his political leadership; and although he preserved the form and name of the constitution, he set himself up as sole ruler over everyone. This government of   23
theirs has remained to the present day under the control of a single ruler, but, in my opinion, out of respect for their ancient oath, they do not call the rulers kings, but emperors, which was also a name they used, on occasions, for their generals.[13] In reality they are kings in every respect.

never to accept the rule of a king again. Appian refers to it again in *BCiv.* 2.119. See too Plutarch, *Publ.* 2.   [12] The emperor Augustus.   [13] The Latin word for "emperor," *imperator*, was also a special acclamation for victorious generals.

24 7. Καὶ ἔστι καὶ τοῖσδε τοῖς αὐτοκράτορσιν ἐς τὸν παρόντα χρόνον ἐγγυτάτω διακοσίων ἐτῶν ἄλλων, ἐν οἷς ἥ τε πόλις μάλιστα κατεκοσμήθη καὶ ἡ πρόσοδος ἐπὶ πλεῖστον ηὐξήθη καὶ πάντα ἐν εἰρήνῃ μακρᾷ καὶ

25 εὐσταθεῖ προῆλθεν εἰς εὐδαιμονίαν ἀσφαλῆ. καί τινα καὶ τοῖς προτέροις ἔθνεσιν οἵδε οἱ αὐτοκράτορες ἐς τὴν ἡγεμονίαν προσέλαβον καὶ ἀφιστάμενα ἄλλα

26 ἐκρατύναντο. ὅλως τε δι᾽ εὐβουλίαν τὰ κράτιστα γῆς καὶ θαλάσσης ἔχοντες αὔξειν[3] ἐθέλουσι μᾶλλον ἢ τὴν ἀρχὴν ἐς ἄπειρον ἐκφέρειν ἐπὶ βάρβαρα ἔθνη πενιχρὰ καὶ ἀκερδῆ, ὧν ἐγώ τινας εἶδον ἐν Ῥώμῃ πρεσβευομένους τε καὶ διδόντας ἑαυτοὺς ὑπηκόους εἶναι καὶ οὐ δεξάμενον βασιλέα ἄνδρας οὐδὲν αὐτῷ χρησί-

27 μους ἐσομένους. ἔθνεσί τε ἄλλοις, ἀπείροις τὸ πλῆθος, αὐτοὶ διδόασι τοὺς βασιλέας, οὐδὲν αὐτῶν ἐς τὴν ἀρχὴν δεόμενοι· καὶ τῶν ὑπηκόων ἐνίοις προσαναλίσκουσιν, αἰδούμενοι καίπερ ἐπιζημίους ὄντας ἀπο-

28 θέσθαι. τήν τε ἀρχὴν ἐν κύκλῳ περικάθηνται μεγάλοις στρατοπέδοις καὶ φυλάσσουσι τὴν τοσήνδε γῆν καὶ θάλασσαν ὥσπερ χωρίον.

29 8. Ἀρχή τε οὐδεμία προῆλθέ πω μέχρι νῦν εἰς τοσοῦτο μεγέθους καὶ χρόνου. οὔτε γὰρ τὰ Ἑλλήνων, εἴ τις ὁμοῦ τὰ Ἀθηναίων καὶ Λακεδαιμονίων καὶ Θηβαίων, δυναστευσάντων παρὰ μέρος, ἀπὸ τῆς Δαρείου στρατείας, ὅθεν αὐτοῖς ἐστιν ἐλλαμπρύνεσθαι

---

[3] αὔξειν codd.; σώζειν edd.

7. These emperors have had nearly another two centu- 24
ries up to the present time, a period in which the city has
developed substantially, its revenues have risen hugely
and the whole state has availed of the long and tranquil
period of peace to progress into stable prosperity. These 25
emperors have also annexed some nations to the empire
in addition to the previous ones, and overpowered others
when they revolted, but, on the whole, they have been 26
satisfied with exercising sound judgment to strengthen[14]
what they have—which is the best part of the world both
by land and sea—rather than extending their power indefinitely over poor and unprofitable barbarian peoples. I
have seen ambassadors of some of these nations in Rome
offering themselves as subjects, but the emperor refusing
to accept men who would be of no use to him. In countless 27
other countries, of which they have no need for their empire, the Romans themselves install kings; and they waste
resources on some of their subjects, as they are embarrassed to get rid of them, even though they are financially
loss-making. They have stationed large armies all round 28
the empire, and they guard this great stretch of land and
sea like a single bastion.

8. No empire down to the present day has ever become 29
so large or lasted so long. In Greek history, for example, if
you add up together the period starting from the campaign
of Darius (on which they customarily take particular
pride), include the successive domination of Athens and
Sparta and Thebes, and go up to the leadership of Greece

---

[14] Editors mostly prefer to read "preserve" (*sozein*), rather
than "strengthen" (*auxein*), as recorded in all the manuscripts,
but there is no pressing need to do so.

μάλιστα, ἐς τὴν Φιλίππου τοῦ Ἀμύντου τῆς Ἑλλάδος
30 ἡγεμονίαν συναγάγοι, πολλὰ ἂν ἔτη φανείη. οἵ τε
ἀγῶνες αὐτοῖς ἐγένοντο οὐκ ἐπὶ ἀρχῆς περικτήσει
μᾶλλον ἢ φιλοτιμίᾳ πρὸς ἀλλήλους, καὶ οἱ λαμπρότα-
τοι περὶ τῆς αὐτῶν ἐλευθερίας πρὸς ἀρχὰς ἄλλας
ἐπιούσας. οἱ δέ τινες αὐτῶν ἐς Σικελίαν πλεύσαντες
ἐπὶ ἀρχῆς ἑτέρας ἐλπίδι προσέπταισαν, ἤ, εἴ τις ἐς
τὴν Ἀσίαν διῆλθεν, μικρὰ καὶ ὅδε δράσας εὐθὺς
31 ἐπανήει. ὅλως τε ἡ Ἑλληνικὴ δύναμις, καίπερ ἐκθύμως ὑπὲρ ἡγεμονίας ἀγωνισαμένων, οὐ προῆλθεν
ὑπὲρ τὴν Ἑλλάδα βεβαίως, ἀλλὰ δεινοὶ μὲν ἐγένοντο
ἀδούλωτον αὐτὴν καὶ ἀήττητον κατασχεῖν ἐπὶ πλεῖστον, ἀπὸ δὲ Φιλίππου τοῦ Ἀμύντου καὶ Ἀλεξάνδρου
τοῦ Φιλίππου καὶ πάνυ μοι δοκοῦσι πρᾶξαι κακῶς καὶ
ἀναξίως αὐτῶν.

32   9. Ἥ τε τῆς Ἀσίας ἀρχὴ ἔργων μὲν πέρι καὶ ἀρε-
33 τῆς οὐδ᾽ ἐς τὰ σμικρότατα τῶν Εὐρωπαίων παραβάλ-
λεται δι᾽ ἀσθένειαν καὶ ἀτολμίαν τῶν ἐθνῶν. καὶ
τοῦτο δηλώσει καὶ ἥδε ἡ γραφὴ προϊοῦσα· ὀλίγαις
γὰρ μάχαις Ῥωμαῖοι τοσούτων τῆς Ἀσίας ἐθνῶν κατέσχον, ὅσων ἔτι νῦν ἐπικρατοῦσι, καὶ ταῦτα Μακεδόνων αὐτῶν ὑπερμαχομένων, τὰ δὲ πολλὰ περὶ τὴν
34 Λιβύην καὶ τὴν Εὐρώπην ἐξετρίφθησαν. Ἀσσυρίων
τε αὖ καὶ Μήδων καὶ Περσῶν, τριῶν τῶνδε μεγίστων
ἡγεμονιῶν εἰς Ἀλέξανδρον τὸν Φιλίππου, συντιθεμένων οὔτ᾽ ἂν ὁ χρόνος ἐφίκοιτο τῶν ἐνακοσίων ἐτῶν,

---

15 Philip II of Macedon, father of Alexander the Great.

by Philip, son of Amyntas,[15] it would clearly not amount
to many years. Their contests arose more out of mutual   30
rivalry than a desire to acquire empire, and their most
brilliant struggle was in defense of their liberty against
invading foreign powers. The expedition of those who
sailed to Sicily hoping to win another empire was a failure;
and anyone who crossed into Asia also achieved little and
soon returned home.[16] In short, the Greeks, although they 31
fought among themselves enthusiastically for dominance,
never securely extended their power beyond Greece.
They were good at keeping themselves free and unde-
feated for a very long time, but after Philip, son of Amyntas, and Alexander his son, they seem to me to have performed extremely poorly and unworthily of themselves.

9. As regards the achievements and courage of Asia's   32
empire, so feeble and cowardly are their peoples that it is
not to be compared with even the smallest of the European nations. This work, as it progresses, will also make   33
this clear. For in a few battles the Romans subdued the
many Asian nations they still control now, even with the
Macedonians joining the resistance, whereas the conquest
of Africa and Europe in many cases exhausted them.
Again, if the Assyrians and Medians and Persians, the   34
three greatest empires before Alexander, son of Philip,
were to be counted together, their duration would not

[16] Appian is referring to the Athenian attempt to conquer
Sicily in 415–413 during the Peloponnesian War, and, rather more
vaguely, to Greek involvement in Persia after the Peloponnesian
War, such as the march of the Ten Thousand under the command
of Xenophon (in 401–400) and the Persian campaigns of the Spar-
tan king Agesilaus in 396–395.

35 ὅσα ἐστὶ Ῥωμαίοις ἐς τὸν παρόντα χρόνον, τό τε μέγεθος τῆς ἀρχῆς τῆς ἐκείνων οὐδὲ ἐς ἥμισυ νομίζω
τῆσδε τῆς ἡγεμονίας ἀπαντᾶν, τεκμαιρόμενος, ὅτι
Ῥωμαίοις ἀπό τε δύσεων καὶ τοῦ πρὸς ἑσπέραν ὠκεανοῦ ἐπὶ τὸ Καύκασον ὄρος καὶ ποταμὸν Εὐφράτην
καὶ ἐς Αἰθίοπας τοὺς ἄνω Αἰγύπτου καὶ δι᾽ Ἀράβων
ἐπὶ τὸν ἑῷον ὠκεανὸν ἡ ἀρχὴ διεξέρχεται, καὶ ὅρος
ἐστὶν αὐτοῖς ὁ ὠκεανὸς ἀνερχομένου τε καὶ δυομένου
τοῦ θεοῦ, θαλάσσης τε πάσης ἡγεμονεύουσι τῆς ἐντὸς οὔσης καὶ νήσων ἁπασῶν καὶ ἐν τῷ ὠκεανῷ Βρετ-
36 τανῶν. Μήδοις δὲ καὶ Πέρσαις ἥ τε πλείστη θάλασσα
ἢ ὁ Παμφύλιος κόλπος ἦν καὶ μία νῆσος ἡ Κύπρος
ἢ εἴ τί που ἄλλο σμικρὸν τῆς Ἰωνίας ἐν θαλάσσῃ·
τοῦ τε Περσικοῦ κόλπου (καὶ γὰρ τοῦδε ἐκράτουν)
πόσον τι καὶ τὸ τούτου πέλαγός ἐστιν;

37   10. Τὰ δὲ δὴ Μακεδόνων, τὰ μὲν πρὸ Φιλίππου τοῦ
Ἀμύντου καὶ πάνυ σμικρὰ ἦν, καὶ ἔστιν ὧν ὑπήκου-
σαν· τὰ δὲ αὐτοῦ Φιλίππου πόνου μὲν καὶ ταλαιπω-
ρίας ἔγεμεν οὐ μεμπτῆς, ἀλλὰ καὶ ταῦτα περὶ τὴν
38 Ἑλλάδα καὶ τὰ πρόσχωρα μόνα ἦν. ἐπὶ δὲ Ἀλεξάνδρου μεγέθει τε καὶ πλήθει καὶ εὐτυχίᾳ καὶ ταχυεργίᾳ
διαλάμψασα ἡ ἀρχὴ καὶ ὀλίγου δεῖν εἰς ἄπειρον καὶ
ἀμίμητον ἐλθοῦσα διὰ τὴν βραχύτητα τοῦ χρόνου
προσέοικεν ἀστραπῇ λαμπρᾷ· ἧς γε καὶ διαλυθείσης
ἐς πολλὰς σατραπείας ἐπὶ πλεῖστον ἐξέλαμπε τὰ
39 μέρη. καὶ τοῖς ἐμοῖς βασιλεῦσι μόνοις ἦν στρατιά τε
πεζῶν μυριάδες εἴκοσι καὶ μυριάδες ἱππέων τέσσαρες
καὶ ἐλέφαντες πολεμισταὶ τριακόσιοι καὶ ἅρματα ἐς

16

come to nine hundred years, while the Romans have 35
reached that figure in the present era, and the extent of
Asiatic rule would, I believe, not even be half that of
Rome's empire. I draw this conclusion from the fact that
Roman rule stretches from where the sun sets in the Western Ocean to the Caucasus mountains and river Euphrates, to the Ethiopians of upper Egypt and across Arabia to
the Eastern Ocean. So, where the sun god rises and goes
down, the ocean is their frontier. They also rule the whole
of the inner sea and all its islands, as well as Britain in the
Ocean. The largest area of sea controlled by the Medes 36
and Persians was the gulf of Pamphylia,[17] and they had one
island, Cyprus, and possibly other small Ionian islands in
the Mediterranean. They also controlled the Persian Gulf,
but how much of that is open sea?

10. And indeed Macedonian history before Philip son 37
of Amyntas was also very insignificant; they were even at
times a subject people. The reign of Philip himself was
characterized by war and no mean hardship, but even this
was limited to Greece and neighboring lands. In Alexan- 38
der's time the Macedonian empire was conspicuous for its
extent, the number of its inhabitants and its success and
speed of action, but although it was all but boundless and
unparalleled, because it was so short-lived it seems like a
brilliant flash of lightning. Even when it was broken up
into several satrapies, however, its parts were very splen-
did. The kings of my own country alone had an army of 39
two hundred thousand infantry, forty thousand cavalry,
three hundred war elephants, two thousand battle chari-

[17] The waters of the Mediterranean off the south coast of
Turkey.

17

μάχας δισχίλια καὶ ὅπλα ἐς διαδοχὴν μυριάσι τρι-
40 άκοντα. καὶ τάδε μὲν αὐτοῖς ἦν ἐς πεζομαχίαν, ἐς δὲ
ναυμαχίας κοντωτὰ καὶ ὅσα σμικρότερα ἄλλα, δισχίλια, τριήρεις δὲ ἀπὸ ἡμιολίας μέχρι πεντήρους πεν-
τακόσιαι καὶ χίλιαι καὶ σκεύη τριηρτικὰ διπλότερα
τούτων θαλαμηγά τε χρυσόπρυμνα καὶ χρυσέμβολα
ἐς πολέμου πομπήν, οἷς αὐτοὶ διαπλέοντες ἐπέβαινον
οἱ βασιλεῖς, ὀκτακόσια, χρημάτων δ' ἐν τοῖς θησαυ-
ροῖς τέσσαρες καὶ ἑβδομήκοντα μυριάδες ταλάντων
41 Αἰγυπτίων. ἐς γὰρ δὴ τοσοῦτο παρασκευῆς τε καὶ
στρατιᾶς ἐκ τῶν βασιλικῶν ἀναγραφῶν φαίνεται
προαγαγών τε καὶ καταλιπὼν ὁ δεύτερος Αἰγύπτου
βασιλεὺς μετ' Ἀλέξανδρον, ὃς καὶ πορίσαι δεινότατος
ἦν βασιλέων καὶ δαπανῆσαι λαμπρότατος καὶ κατα-
42 σκευάσαι μεγαλουργότατος. φαίνεται δὲ καὶ πολλὰ
τῶν ἄλλων σατραπῶν οὐ πολὺ τούτων ἀποδέοντα.
ἀλλὰ πάντα ἐπὶ τῶν ἐπιγόνων αὐτῶν συνετρίφθη,
φθαρέντων ἐς ἀλλήλους, ᾧ μόνως ἀρχαὶ μεγάλαι
καταλύονται, στασιασάντων.[4]
43   11. Τὰ δὲ Ῥωμαίων μεγέθει τε καὶ χρόνῳ διήνεγκε
δι' εὐβουλίαν καὶ εὐτυχίαν ἔς τε τὴν περίκτησιν
αὐτῶν ἀρετῇ καὶ φερεπονίᾳ καὶ ταλαιπωρίᾳ πάντας
ὑπερῆραν, οὔτε ταῖς εὐπραγίαις ἐπαιρόμενοι, μέχρι

----

[4] ἀλλὰ πάντα ἐς τοὺς ἐπιγόνους αὐτῶν συνετρίφθη, φθαρέντων ἐς ἀλλήλους, ᾧ δὴ μόνως ἀρχαὶ μεγάλαι καταλύονται, στασιάσασαι codd.; ἀλλὰ πάντα ἐπὶ τῶν ἐπιγόνων
αὐτῶν συνετρίφθη, στασιασάντων ἐς ἀλλήλους· ᾧ δὴ μόνως
ἀρχαὶ μεγάλαι καταλύονται Mend.

ots, and armaments in reserve for three hundred thousand
men. These were their forces for fighting on land. For   40
naval service they had two thousand barges and smaller
vessels; one thousand five hundred warships, ranging from
one and a half banks of oars to five, and warship equipment for twice that number; and eight hundred cabinned
vessels with both stern and ram gilded for battle formation—the kings themselves used to be on board these
while at sea. They also had in their treasury seven hundred
and forty thousand Egyptian talents. For such was the   41
extent of military readiness that the royal accounts show
was achieved and left by the second king of Egypt after
Alexander, who was the most skilled of kings in raising
money, the most lavish in spending it, and the most successful at public building.[18] It appears that many of the   42
resources of the other satraps were not much less than
Egypt's. But it was all wasted in the time of their successors who were ruined by conducting civil violence against
each other, which alone destroys great empires.[19]

11. With their sound judgment and good fortune, the   43
Romans have excelled in the size and longevity of their
empire, and in acquiring this position they have proved
themselves superior to all others in courage, endurance,
and hard work. Never exultant in times of success, they

[18] Ptolemy II Philadelphus ("Brother-loving") (b. 308–d. 246).

[19] This is a highly problematic sentence in the manuscripts, although its general meaning seems to be reasonably clear.

βεβαίως ἐκράτησαν, οὔτε συστελλόμενοι ταῖς συμ-
φοραῖς· ὧν γε καὶ δύο μυριάδες ἀνδρῶν ἐνίοτε μιᾶς
ἡμέρας καὶ ἑτέρας τέσσαρες ἀπώλλυντο καὶ ἄλλης
44 πέντε. καὶ περὶ τῆς πόλεως αὐτῆς πολλάκις ἐκινδύ-
νευον, καὶ λιμοί τε καὶ λοιμοὶ συνεχεῖς καὶ στάσεις,
ὁμοῦ πάντα ἐπιπίπτοντα, οὐκ ἀπέστησε τῆς φιλοτι-
μίας, ἕως ἑπτακοσίοις ἔτεσιν κακοπαθοῦντές τε καὶ
κινδυνεύοντες ἀγχωμάλως τὴν ἀρχὴν ἐς τόδε προή-
γαγον καὶ τῆς εὐτυχίας ὤναντο διὰ τὴν εὐβουλίαν.

45 12. Καὶ τάδε πολλοὶ μὲν Ἑλλήνων, πολλοὶ δὲ Ῥωμαίων συνέγραψαν, καὶ ἔστιν ἡ ἱστορία τῆς Μακεδο-
νικῆς, μεγίστης δὴ τῶν προτέρων οὔσης, πολὺ μεί-
46 ζων. ἀλλ' ἐντυγχάνοντά με καὶ τὴν ἀρετὴν αὐτῶν
ἐντελῆ καθ' ἕκαστον ἔθνος ἰδεῖν ἐθέλοντα ἀπέφερεν ἡ
γραφὴ πολλάκις ἀπὸ Καρχηδόνος ἐπὶ Ἴβηρας καὶ ἐξ
Ἰβήρων ἐπὶ Σικελίαν ἢ Μακεδονίαν ἢ ἐπὶ πρεσβείας
ἢ συμμαχίας ἐς ἄλλα ἔθνη γενομένας, εἶτ' αὖθις ἐς
Καρχηδόνα ἀνῆγεν ἢ Σικελίαν ὥσπερ ἀλώμενον καὶ
πάλιν ἐκ τούτων ἀτελῶν ἔτι ὄντων μετέφερεν, ἕως οὗ
47 τὰ μέρη συνήγαγον ἐμαυτῷ, ὁσάκις ἐς Σικελίαν
ἐστράτευσαν ἢ ἐπρέσβευσαν ἢ ὁτιοῦν ἔπραξαν ἐς Σικελίαν, μέχρι κατεστήσαντο αὐτὴν ἐς τὸν κόσμον τὸν
παρόντα, ὁσάκις τε αὖ Καρχηδονίους ἐπολέμησαν ἢ
ἐσπείσαντο ἢ ἐπρέσβευσαν ἐς αὐτοὺς ἢ πρεσβείας
ἐδέξαντο παρ' ἐκείνων ἢ ἔδρασαν ὁτιοῦν ἢ ἔπαθον

---

[20] Appian does not name the disasters, but he records the
capture of fifty thousand Romans at the battle of the Caudine

eventually firmly secured their power. Nor were they depressed by disaster, although from time to time they lost twenty thousand men in a single day—forty thousand on one occasion, and even fifty thousand on another—and the city of Rome itself was often in danger.[20] Neither famine nor successive plagues nor civil strife, even when they all occurred together, made them abandon their ambition, until after seven hundred years of suffering hardship and facing danger, with the outcome uncertain, they have advanced their empire to its present greatness and enjoyed the prosperity won by their prudence.

12. Many Greek and Roman authors have written about these matters, and this is a much more important history than that of Macedon, which was previously the most important. While I was reading up on the topic, however, and wanted to get a comprehensive view of Roman excellence in their dealings with each nation, the written account often took me from Carthage to Iberia, from Iberia to Sicily or Macedonia, or on embassies and alliance negotiations to other countries and back again, like an outcast, to Carthage or Sicily; and on other occasions it took me away from these events while they were still unfinished, until I brought the different elements together for myself: how often Rome had sent armies or embassies to Sicily, or whatever else they had done in relation to Sicily until they brought it to its present state of order. Again, I established how often they fought against, or made treaties with, Carthage; how often they sent embassies there or received them from the Carthaginians; what damage

Forks in 321 BC (*Sam.* 4.5), as well as the deaths of fifty thousand Roman troops at the battle of Cannae in 216 BC (*Hann.* 25.109).

APPIAN

πρὸς αὐτῶν, ἕως Καρχηδόνα κατέσκαψαν καὶ τὸ Λιβύων ἔθνος προσέλαβον καὶ αὖθις ᾤκισαν αὐτοῖς
Καρχηδόνα καὶ Λιβύην κατέστησαν ἐς τὰ νῦν ὄντα.
48 καὶ τόδε μοι κατὰ ἔθνος ἕκαστον ἐπράχθη, βουλο-
μένῳ τὰ ἐς ἑκάστους ἔργα Ῥωμαίων καταμαθεῖν, ἵνα
τὴν τῶν ἐθνῶν ἀσθένειαν ἢ φερεπονίαν καὶ τὴν τῶν
ἑλόντων ἀρετὴν ἢ εὐτυχίαν ἢ εἴ τι ἄλλο συγκύρημα
συνηνέχθη, καταμάθοιμι.
49   13. Νομίσας δ' ἄν τινα καὶ ἄλλον οὕτως ἐθελῆσαι
μαθεῖν τὰ Ῥωμαίων, συγγράφω κατὰ ἔθνος ἕκαστον·
ὅσα δὲ ἐν μέσῳ πρὸς ἑτέρους αὐτοῖς ἐγένετο, ἐξαίρω
50 καὶ εἰς τὰ ἐκείνων μετατίθημι. τοὺς δὲ χρόνους ἐπὶ
μὲν πᾶσιν περισσὸν ἡγούμην καταλέγειν, ἐπὶ δὲ τῶν
51 ἐπιφανεστάτων ἐκ διαστήματος ὑπομνήσω. καὶ τὰ
ὀνόματα Ῥωμαίοις πάλαι μὲν ἦν ἕν, ὥσπερ ἀνθρώποις ἅπασιν, ἑκάστῳ, μετὰ δὲ ἐγένοντο δύο· καὶ οὐ
πολὺς χρόνος, ἐξ οὗ καὶ τρίτον ἤρξατό τισιν ἐς ἐπί-
γνωσιν ἐκ πάθους ἢ ἀρετῆς προστίθεσθαι, καθὰ καὶ
τῶν Ἑλλήνων τισὶν ἐπὶ τὰ ὀνόματα ἦσαν ἐπικλήσεις.
52 ἐγὼ δὲ ἔστι μὲν ὅπου καὶ πάντων ἐπιμνήσομαι, καὶ
μάλιστα ἐπὶ τῶν ἐπιφανῶν, ἐς γνώρισμα τῶν ἀνδρῶν·
τὰ δὲ πολλὰ καὶ τούτους καὶ τοὺς ἄλλους, ἃ κυριώ-
τατα ἡγοῦνται, προσαγορεύσω.

---

21 With regard to Roman names, this translation generally
imitates Appian's own practice as stated here. Roman forms pre-
dominate, with the exception of the more familiar Anglicized
forms for especially well-known individuals: thus Marc Antony
(rather than Marcus Antonius) and Pompey the Great (rather

they inflicted on Carthage or suffered at its hands, until they razed it to the ground and annexed the African nation, then refounded Carthage and brought Africa to its present condition. I did this in the case of each nation, as 48 I wanted to find out the relationship of Rome with each of them, in order to establish the weakness or endurance of the nations, and the courage and good fortune of their conquerors—or indeed any other contributory factors in their success.

13. In the belief that others too would want to learn 49 about Roman history in this way, I am writing up my work nation by nation: Rome's dealings with other states that took place at the same time, I am extracting and transferring to the relevant place. While I regard it as excessive to 50 record dates for everything, from time to time I will mention chronology in the case of particularly important events. With reference to personal names, in times past 51 the Romans, like everyone else, used to have just one, then afterward two; not much later, for purposes of recognition, some men began to add a third name—derived from an experience, or quality they had demonstrated—just as some Greeks added surnames to their nomenclature. To 52 distinguish between people I will sometimes record all three names, especially when dealing with the famous; but mostly, whether for famous people or others, I will use the names by which they are best known.[21]

than Pompeius Magnus). This has the advantage of distinguishing such figures from less famous members of the same family. I also follow modern convention in using the name Octavian for the future emperor Augustus, whom Appian and other ancient authors tend (somewhat confusingly for contemporary readers) to call "Caesar."

53 14. Τριῶν δὲ βίβλων οὐσῶν, αἳ τὰ ἐς τὴν Ἰταλίαν
ὄντα αὐτοῖς πολλὰ πεπραγμένα συνάγουσιν, τὰς μὲν
τρεῖς ἡγητέον εἶναι Ῥωμαϊκῶν Ἰταλικάς, διὰ δὲ πλῆ-
54 θος ἔργων διῄρηνται. καὶ δηλοῦσιν ἡ μὲν πρώτη τὰ
τῶν βασιλέων ἑπτὰ γενομένων ἔργα, ἐφεξῆς ἅπαντα
55 ἐφ᾽ ἑαυτῶν, ὡς ἐγένετο· καὶ αὐτὴν ἐπιγράφω Ῥωμαϊκῶν βασιλικήν. ἡ δ᾽ ἑξῆς τὰ ἐς τὴν ἄλλην Ἰταλίαν,
χωρίς γε τῆς παρὰ τὸν κόλπον τὸν Ἰόνιον· ἐς δὲ σύγκρισιν τῆς προτέρας ἥδε λέγεται [ἡ ἑξῆς] Ῥωμαϊκῶν⁵
56 Ἰταλική. τελευταίῳ δὲ ἔθνει, Σαυνίταις, οἳ παρὰ τὸν
Ἰόνιον ᾤκηνται, μεγάλῳ τε καὶ χαλεπῷ, ὀγδοήκοντα
ἔτεσι συνεπλάκησαν, μέχρι καὶ τούσδε καὶ ὅσα σφίσιν ἐγγὺς ἔθνη συνεμάχει, καὶ Ἕλληνας, ὅσοι ὑπὸ
τὴν Ἰταλίαν εἰσίν, ὑπηγάγοντο· καὶ ἔστιν ἥδε, τῶν
57 προτέρων εἰς σύγκρισιν, Ῥωμαϊκῶν Σαυνιτική. τὰ δὲ
λοιπά, τούτων ἑκάστη κατὰ λόγον ἐπιγράφονται, Ῥωμαϊκῶν Κελτική τε καὶ Σικελικὴ καὶ Ἰβηρικὴ καὶ Ἀν-
νιβαϊκὴ καὶ Καρχηδονιακὴ καὶ Μακεδονικὴ καὶ ἐφε-
58 ξῆς ὁμοίως. τέτακται δ᾽ αὐτῶν ἄλλη μετ᾽ ἄλλην ὡς
ἑκάστῳ πολέμῳ τὴν ἀρχὴν πρὸ ἑτέρου λαβεῖν συν-
έπεσεν, εἰ καὶ τὸ τέλος τῷ ἔθνει μετὰ πολλὰ ἕτερα
59 γεγένηται. ὅσα δ᾽ αὐτοὶ Ῥωμαῖοι πρὸς ἀλλήλους
ἐστασίασάν τε καὶ ἐπολέμησαν ἐμφύλια, φοβερώτερα
σφίσι ταῦτα μάλιστα γενόμενα, ἐς τοὺς στρατηγοὺς
τῶν στάσεων διῄρηται, τὰ μὲν ἐς Μάριόν τε καὶ Σύλλαν, τὰ δ᾽ ἐς Πομπήιόν τε καὶ Καίσαρα, τὰ δὲ ἐς
Ἀντώνιόν τε καὶ τὸν ἕτερον Καίσαρα, τὸν Σεβαστὸν
ἐπίκλην, πρὸς τοὺς ἀνδροφόνους τοῦ προτέρου Καί-

14. The work includes three books recounting Rome's 53
many dealings with Italy—I have divided them into three
because so much happened—and they should be regarded
as the Italian books of Roman history. The first sets out the 54
events of the seven kings, everything narrated in succession in their respective reigns, as it happened: this I call 55
"Roman History, the Book of Kings." The next covers the
rest of Italy apart from the coast along the Ionian gulf: to
distinguish it from the first, I call it "Roman History, the
Italian Book." With the last people, the Samnites, who 56
lived along the Ionian gulf, the Romans were locked in a
serious and difficult war for eighty years, until they subjected these too, along with their neighboring allies, and
the Greeks of southern Italy. To mark it out from the
previous two, I call this "Roman History, the Samnite
Book." The remainder are named after their subject: "Ro- 57
man History, the Celtic Book" and the "Sicilian" and the
"Iberian" and the "Hannibalic" and the "Carthaginian"
and the "Macedonian," and so on. They are arranged in 58
chronological order according to when their war with
Rome began, even if a particular nation met its end after
much else had happened. The faction-fighting and civil 59
wars among the Romans themselves, which they found
particularly terrible, are divided according to the military
leaders of the factions: the wars of Marius and Sulla, for
instance, or Pompey and Caesar; those of Antony and the
other Caesar, called Augustus,[22] against the murderers of

---

[22] That is, Octavian.

---

[5] ἡ ἑξῆς ante Ῥωμαικῶν codd; del. Zerdik

σαρος, τὰ δὲ ἐς τὰ πρὸς ἀλλήλους, αὐτῶν Ἀντωνίου
60 τε καὶ Καίσαρος στασιασάντων. ᾧ τινι τελευταίῳ τῶν
ἐμφυλίων ὄντι καὶ Αἴγυπτος ὑπὸ Ῥωμαίους ἐγένετο
καὶ τὰ Ῥωμαίων εἰς μοναρχίαν περιῆλθεν.
61   15. Ὧδε μὲν ἐς βίβλους ἕκαστα τῶν ἐθνῶν ἢ στρατηγῶν τὰ ἐμφύλια διῄρηται· ἡ δὲ τελευταία καὶ τὴν
στρατιὰν αὐτῶν, ὅσην ἔχουσιν, ἢ πρόσοδον, ἣν καρ-
ποῦνται καθ᾽ ἕκαστον ἔθνος, ἢ εἴ τι προσαναλίσκουσιν εἰς τὰς ἐπινείους φρουρὰς ὅσα τε τοιουτότροπα
ἄλλα ἐπιδείξει. ἁρμόζει δὲ ἀπὸ τοῦ γένους ἄρξασθαι
62 τὸν περὶ τῆς ἀρετῆς αὐτῶν συγγράφοντα. τίς δὲ ὢν
ταῦτα συνέγραψα, πολλοὶ μὲν ἴσασι καὶ αὐτὸς προ-
έφηνα, σαφέστερον δ᾽ εἰπεῖν, Ἀππιανὸς Ἀλεξανδρεύς,
ἐς τὰ πρῶτα ἥκων ἐν τῇ πατρίδι καὶ δίκαις ἐν Ῥώμῃ
συναγορεύσας ἐπὶ τῶν βασιλέων, μέχρι με σφῶν ἐπι-
τροπεύειν ἠξίωσαν. καὶ εἴ τῳ σπουδὴ καὶ τὰ λοιπὰ
μαθεῖν, ἔστι μοι καὶ περὶ τούτου συγγραφή.

the first Caesar, and, after Antony and Octavian them-
selves fell to faction fighting, against each other. With this,   60
the last of the civil wars, Egypt came under Roman rule,
and Rome reverted to monarchy.

15. Thus a division has been made into books for each   61
of the nations and for the civil wars according to generals.
The last book will set out the current size of the Roman
army, the revenue they collect from each country, and
what they additionally spend on naval defense or anything
else of this kind. It is only proper that an author writing
about Rome's excellence should start by saying something
about his family. Many people know who I, the author of   62
this work, am, and I myself have made it clear before. To
speak more plainly, I am Appian of Alexandria. I reached
the highest rank in my native country, and practiced as an
advocate in cases before the emperors, until they thought
me worthy of being made their procurator. If anyone
would like to know the rest about me, I have written a
work on this subject too.

I

ΕΚ ΤΗΣ ΒΑΣΙΛΙΚΗΣ

1. Ἄρχεται τῆς ἱστορίας ἀπὸ Αἰνείου τοῦ Ἀγχίσου τοῦ Κάπυος, ὃς ἐν τῷ Τρωικῷ ἤκμαζε πολέμῳ, μετὰ δὲ τὴν ἅλωσιν τῆς Τροίας ἔφυγε καὶ μετὰ μακρὰν πλάνην κατέπλει ἔς τινα τῆς Ἰταλίας αἰγιαλόν, Λώρεντον ἐπικαλούμενον, ἔνθα καὶ στρατόπεδον αὐτοῦ δείκνυται, καὶ τὴν ἀκτὴν ἀπ᾽ ἐκείνου Τροίαν καλοῦσιν. ἦρχε τότε Ἀβοριγίνων τῶν τῇδε Ἰταλῶν Φαῦνος ὁ τοῦ Ἄρεως, ὃς καὶ ζεύγνυσιν Αἰνείᾳ τὴν θυγατέρα αὐτοῦ Λαουινίαν, καὶ γῆν δίδωσιν ἐκ περιόδου σταδίων τετρακοσίων. ὃ δὲ πόλιν ἔκτισε καὶ ἀπὸ τῆς γυ-
2 ναικὸς Λαουίνιον ἐπωνόμασε. τρίτῳ δὲ ἔτει τοῦ Φαύνου τελευτήσαντος ἐκδέχεται τὴν ἀρχὴν ὁ Αἰνείας κατὰ τὸ κῆδος καὶ τοὺς Ἀβοριγίνας ἀπὸ τοῦ κηδεστοῦ Λατίνου Φαύνου Λατίνους ἐπωνόμασε. τρίτῳ δὲ

---

1 In Roman tradition Lavinia was the daughter of Latinus, king of the Latins. The intrusion of the name Faunus here is almost certainly due not to Appian but to the ninth-century Byzantine scholar, Photius, in whose work, *The Library*, this excerpt is

BOOK I

FROM THE BOOK OF KINGS

1. Appian begins his history with Aeneas, Anchises' son, grandson of Capys, who was in his prime during the Trojan War. After the capture of Troy, when he had wandered far and wide, he landed on a part of the Italian coast called Laurentum, where his camp is still pointed out; they call it the Trojan shore after him. At the time, Faunus, the son of Ares, ruled the Aborigines, the inhabitants of that part of Italy, and he marries his daughter Lavinia to Aeneas and gives him land measuring four hundred stades around the perimeter.[1] Aeneas founded a town, calling it Lavinium after his wife. Three years later, when Faunus died, Aeneas inherits his kingdom, through this marriage connection, and named the Aborigines Latins, after his father-in-law, Latinus Faunus. Three years later again, Aeneas is

2

preserved. Faunus was a god of the woods who became almost indistinguishable from the Greek god Pan. In Virgil (*Aen.* 7.47–49), Latinus is said to have been the son of Faunus—which is what will have given rise to the mistake. Photius perseveres with his error two sentences later, finding it necessary to give Faunus the additional name Latinus. Appian's version is more accurately preserved in the fragment of an anonymous Byzantine excerptor translated below as 1a.

ἔτει πάλιν διὰ Λαουινίαν τὴν γυναῖκα ὑπὸ Ῥουτούλων
τῶν Τυρρηνῶν, προμνηστευθεῖσαν αὐτῶν τῷ βασιλεῖ,
3 ἀναιρεῖται πολέμου νόμῳ ὁ Αἰνείας, καὶ τὴν ἀρχὴν
διεδέξατο Εὐρυλέων, Ἀσκάνιος μετονομασθείς, ὃς
ἐγεννήθη τῷ Αἰνείᾳ ἐκ Κρεούσης τῆς Πριάμου, τῆς
ἐν Ἰλίῳ γενομένης αὐτῷ γυναικός. οἱ δὲ ἐκ τῆς Λαου-
ινίας Ἀσκάνιον αὐτῷ γεννηθῆναί φασι, τὸν διάδοχον
τῆς ἀρχῆς. Ἀσκανίου δὲ τελευτήσαντος ἔτει τετάρτῳ
μετὰ τὴν Ἄλβης οἴκισιν (καὶ γὰρ οὗτος ἔκτισε πόλιν,
Ἄλβην καλέσας, καὶ ἀπὸ Λαουινίου τὸν λαὸν μετῴκι-
4 σεν) ἐκδέχεται τὴν ἀρχὴν Σίλουιος. καὶ Σιλουίου
παῖδα Αἰνείαν Σιλουιόν φασιν, Αἰνείου δὲ Λατῖνον
Σίλουιον, τοῦ δὲ Κάπυν, Κάπυος δὲ Κάπετον γενέσθαι, Καπέτου δὲ Τιβερῖνον, τοῦ δὲ Ἀγρόπαν,[1] τοῦ δὲ
Ῥωμύλον· καὶ τόνδε μὲν βληθῆναι κεραυνῷ· οὗ γενέσθαι παῖδα Ἀουεντῖνον, Ἀουεντίνου δὲ Πρόκαν γενέσθαι. καὶ πᾶσι δὲ τὸν Σίλουιον ἐπώνυμον εἶναι. τῷ δὲ
Πρόκᾳ δύο ἐγενέσθην υἱοί, πρεσβύτερος μὲν Νεμέτωρ,
5 νεώτερος δὲ Ἀμούλιος. λαβόντος δὲ τοῦ πρεσβυτέρου
παρὰ τοῦ πατρὸς τελευτῶντος τὴν ἀρχὴν ὁ νεώτερος
ὕβρει καὶ βίᾳ κατέσχεν ἀφελόμενος. καὶ τὸν μὲν
παῖδα τοῦ ἀδελφοῦ Ἔγεστον κτείνει, τὴν θυγατέρα δὲ
Ῥέαν Σιλουίαν ἱέρειαν, ἵνα ἄπαις διαμείνῃ, καθί-
στησι· τὸν μέντοι Νεμέτορα τῆς εἰς τὸ σῶμα ἐπι-
βουλῆς ἡ τῶν ἠθῶν ἐξεῖλε πρᾳότης καὶ ἡ πολλὴ ἐπι-
6 είκεια. ἀλλ' ἡ Σιλουία ἔκυε παρὰ τὸν νόμον. καὶ τὴν
μὲν Ἀμούλιος ἐπὶ κολάσει συνελάμβανε, δύο δὲ παῖδας ἐκ τῆσδε γενομένους ποιμέσιν ἔδωκεν, εἰς τὸν

killed in action by the Etruscan Rutuli because of his wife
Lavinia, who had previously been betrothed to their king.
Euryleon, renamed Ascanius, took over the kingdom; he   3
was the son of Aeneas and Creusa, Priam's daughter, to
whom Aeneas had been married in Troy. Some say that his
successor as ruler, Ascanius, was his son by Lavinia. Ascanius died four years after the foundation of Alba—for Ascanius also founded a town, naming it Alba, and transferred the population there from Lavinium—and Silvius
receives the power next. The say that Aeneas Silvius was   4
Silvius' son, that Latinus Silvius was his son, Capys was
Latinus' son, Capetus was son of Capys, Tiberinus was son
of Capetys, Agropas[2] was son of Tiberinus and Romulus
was Agropas' son. Romulus, so the story continues, was
struck by lightning and had a son, Aventinus, father of
Procas. All of these have the additional name, Silvius.
Procas had two sons, the elder named Nemetor, the younger Amulius. On the death of his father, the elder son took   5
over the kingdom, but the younger insolently removed
him by force and held power. He also murders his nephew,
Egestus, and makes his niece Rhea Silvia a priestess, so
that she would remain childless. Nemetor, however, was
saved from an assassination attempt by the gentleness of
his character and great virtue; and Silvia became pregnant   6
in contravention of the law, Amulius punishing her with
imprisonment. The two sons she bore he gave to shep-

[2] Many editors have often assumed that the well-known
name, Agrippa, is intended.

---

[1] Ἀγρίππαν vett.

πλησίον ποταμὸν ἐμβαλεῖν τὰ βρέφη· Θύβρις ἦν ὄνομα τῷ ποταμῷ, Ῥῶμος δὲ καὶ Ῥωμύλος οἱ παῖδες, ἐξ Αἰνείου ἕλκοντες μητρόθεν τὸ γένος· τὸ γὰρ τοῦ φύντος ἄδηλον. (Phot. Bibl. I p. 46 Henry)

1a. Περὶ Ῥώμου καὶ Ῥωμύλου. Ἁλούσης Τροίας ὀγδόῃ τοῦ Δεκεμβρίου μηνὸς φεύγων Αἰνείας εἰς τὴν Ἴδην διῆλθε τοὺς Ἀχαιοὺς συγχωροῦντας αὐτῷ βαστάζοντι εἴδωλα καὶ γένος. οἱ δὲ λέγουσιν ὡς οὐ τὴν ὄψιν αὐτῶν συνενεγκεῖν, ἀλλ' ὅτι πολλάκις εἰσηγήσατο τοῖς βαρβάροις ἀποδοῦναι τὴν Ἑλένην τοῖς Ἀχαιοῖς. ἐκεῖ δὲ Φρυγῶν χεῖρα συλλέξας ἀπῆλθεν εἰς Λωρεντὸν καὶ ἐγγυησάμενος τὴν Λαουίνιαν, θυγατέρα Λατίνου βασιλέως τῶν Ἀβοριγίνων, κτίζει πόλιν
2 καὶ ὀνομάζει αὐτὴν Λαουίνιον ἐκ τῆς γυναικός· καὶ τρίτῳ ἔτει τελευτήσαντος Λατίνου διαδεξάμενος τὴν ἀρχὴν ἀπὸ τοῦ κηδεστοῦ ὀνομάζει τοὺς Ἀβοριγίνας Λατίνους. καὶ τρίτῳ δ' αὖ πάλιν ἔτει Ῥουτούλων βασιλεὺς Μεζέντιος συμβαλὼν μετ' αὐτοῦ πόλεμον διὰ τὸ προεγγεγυῆσθαι αὐτῷ τὴν Λαουίνιαν ἀναιρεῖ Αἰ-
3 νείαν. βασιλεύει οὖν ἀντ' αὐτοῦ Ἀσκάνιος. καὶ τὸ Λαουίνιον ὑπεριδὼν ὡς εὐτελὲς ἑτέραν ᾤκισεν ὑπὸ τὸ ὄρος τὸ Ἀλβανὸν ὀνομάσας Ἄλβην, ἣν δυναστεύσασαν ἔτη τριακόσια ἀνεῖλον Ῥωμαῖοι ὡς μηδὲ οἰκόπεδον αὐτῆς καταλειφθῆναι. διαδέχεται δὲ τοῦτον
4 Σίλουιος τρίτον· εἶτα τέταρτον Αἰνείας ἄλλος· τοῦτον πέμπτον Λατῖνος· τὸν δὲ ἕκτον Κάπυς· εἶτα ἕβδομον Κάπετος· μεθ' ὃν ὄγδοον Τιβερῖνος. ἔνατον μετὰ τοῦτον Ἀγρόπας· δέκατον μετ' αὐτὸν Ῥωμύλος. ἑνδέκα-

herds with instructions to throw the babies into the nearby
river; the Thyber was the name of the river, and the boys
were called Romus and Romulus. They were descended
on their mother's side from Aeneas, but their father's lin-
eage is unclear. (Phot. *Bibl.* I p. 46 Henry)

1a. Concerning Romus and Romulus. When Troy was
captured on the eighth of December, Aeneas fled to Mt.
Ida, making his way through the ranks of the Achaeans
who yielded to him as he was carrying images of the gods
and his own kin. Others maintain that it was not the sight
of these things that helped him, but the fact that he had
often proposed to the barbarians that they give Helen
back to the Achaeans. At Ida he collected a band of Phrygians and went off to Laurentum, where he was betrothed
to Lavinia, daughter of Latinus, king of the Aborigines,
and founds a town which he calls Lavinium after his wife.
Three years later, when Latinus died, he inherited the 2
throne from his father-in-law, and renames the Aborigines
Latins. Three years later again, Mezentius, king of the
Rutuli, because he himself had previously been betrothed
to Lavinia, makes war on Aeneas and kills him. Ascanius 3
rules as king in Aeneas' place. He despised Lavinium,
regarding it as insignificant, and founded a new town under the Alban mount, named Alba. This was the seat of
power for three hundred years, until the Romans destroyed it, so that not even a trace of the town was left.
Silvius succeeds him as the third king, another Aeneas the 4
fourth, Latinus the fifth, Capys the sixth, Capetus then the
seventh, Tiberinus after him as the eighth, then Agropas
the ninth, Romulus the tenth, Aventinus the eleventh,

τον εἶτα Αὐεντῖνος· μεθ᾽ ὃν δωδέκατον Πρόκας καὶ
5 τρισκαιδέκατον Νεμέτωρ καὶ Ἀμούλιος. τούτων ὁ πατὴρ Νεμέτορι ὡς πρεσβυτέρῳ τὴν ἀρχὴν κατέλιπεν·
Ἀμούλιος δὲ ὁ ἀδελφὸς παρωσάμενος αὐτὸν ἐβα-
σίλευσεν· ὑποπτεύων δὲ τὴν τίσιν Ἔγεστον μὲν τὸν
υἱὸν τοῦ ἀπωσμένου ἀναιρεῖ ἐν κυνηγεσίῳ, τὴν δὲ
ἀδελφὴν αὐτοῦ δεδιὼς παῖδα εἰ τεκνογονήσοι, ἱέρειαν
6 καθίστησιν. ἡ δὲ ἔγκυος γενομένη, ὡς ἔφη, ὑπὸ
Ἄρεως ἐν τῇ πηγῇ αὐτοῦ ὑδρευομένη, γεννᾷ Ῥῶμον
καὶ Ῥωμύλον. ταύτην οὖν καθείρξας ὁ Ἀμούλιος τοὺς
παῖδας δίδωσι ῥιφῆναι εἰς τὸν Τίβεριν, τηνικάδε Θύ-
7 βριν ὀνομαζόμενον. φερόντων δὲ τῶν παραλαβόντων
τοὺς παῖδας εἰς τὸν ποταμόν—οὗτοι δὲ ποιμένες
ἦσαν—καὶ θεμένων τὸν γαυλὸν εἰς τὸ πρῶτον ἐν ποσὶν ὕδωρ, ἐκλιμνιάσαντος τοῦ ποταμοῦ, καὶ ἀναχω-
ρησάντων ὑπέρρει τὸ ὕδωρ, καὶ ἦν ἐπὶ τοῦ ξηροῦ τὰ
βρέφη, καὶ λύκαινα εἰς τὸν γαυλὸν ἐμβᾶσα ἔτρεφεν·
8 ἡ Λαυρεντία γυνὴ Φαιστύλου ποιμένος ‹...› τούτων
ἀνδρουμένων ἐπὶ λῃστείᾳ καὶ τὸν Ῥῶμον ἐπιχει-
ροῦντα χωρίοις Νεμέτορος συλλαβόντες ἀνῆγον πρὸς
τὸν Ἀμούλιον, ὁ δὲ Νεμέτορι τῷ ἀδελφῷ ὡς ὑπ᾽ αὐτοῦ
λῃστευθέντι ἀπέστειλεν, ὡς ἂν καταγνωσθέντα κολά-
σαι· ἀλλ᾽ ὁ μὲν ἐς τὴν ὄψιν τοῦ μειρακίου ἰδὼν καὶ
τὸν χρόνον τῆς ἐκθέσεως συγκρίνων καὶ τὰ ἄλλα εἰς
ὑποψίαν τοῦ ἀληθοῦς γενόμενος ἐξήταζεν αὐτὸν περὶ
9 τῆς ἀνατροφῆς. ὁ δὲ Ῥωμύλος φοβηθεὶς καὶ παρὰ
Φαιστύλου μαθὼν τὰ περὶ ἑαυτοῦ καὶ τοῦ ἀδελφοῦ
τῆς τε μητρός, ὡς εἴη καθειργμένη, χεῖρα ποιμένων

Procas the twelfth, Nemetor and Amulius the thirteenth. The father of Nemetor and Amulius left the throne to 5 Nemetor as he was the elder, but Amulius, his brother, ousted him and ruled as king. Suspecting there would be an attempt to take revenge, he murders Egestus, son of the ousted Nemetor, on a hunting expedition, and makes Egestus' sister a priestess, afraid she might have a son. But 6 she did become pregnant, by Ares, so it was said, when she was drawing water at his well; and she gives birth to Romus and Romulus. So Amulius imprisoned her and orders the children to be thrown into the Tiber, or Thyber, as it was then called. The men who received the children— 7 they were shepherds—took them to the river and placed the vessel close by at the edge of the water. But the river was in flood, and when they had gone, the water receded and the babies were left on dry land; and a wolf came across the vessel and nursed them. Laurentia, wife of the shepherd Faustulus ⟨. . .⟩ they had turned to banditry on 8 reaching manhood, they arrested Romus for raiding the estate of Nemetor and took him before Amulius; but Amulius sent him to Nemetor his brother for conviction and punishment, as he was the one who had been robbed by him. Nemetor, however, looking at the appearance of the boy and working out the date when the children were exposed and the other matters, began to suspect the truth and questioned him about his upbringing. Romulus was 9 alarmed, and learning from Faustulus the story of himself and his brother and how his mother had been imprisoned,

APPIAN

ἁλίσας ἐπιπίπτει σὺν αὐτοῖς, καὶ τὸν Ἀμούλιον ἀπο-
κτείναντες ἀποφαίνουσιν Ἀλβανοῖς Νεμέτορα βασιλέα, αὐτοὶ δὲ πόλιν ἔκτισαν ἐπὶ τοῦ ποταμοῦ, παρ᾽ ὃν
ἐκτεθέντες ἐτρέφοντο καὶ τραφέντες ἐλῄστευον, ἣν καὶ
ὠνόμασαν Ῥώμην, τὸ τηνικάδε τετράγωνον λεγομένην, ὅτι δέκα ἐξ σταδίων ἦν αὐτῆς ἡ περίμετρος,
ἑκάστης πλευρᾶς τέσσαρα στάδια ἐχούσης. (Excerpta
anonymi Byzantini ed. Treu 1880, pp. 36.10–37.29)

2. Ὁ μὲν πρῶτος τόμος τῶν ἑπτὰ βασιλέων, Ῥωμύλου, Νουμᾶ Πομπιλίου, Ἄγκου Ὁστιλίου καὶ Ἄγκου ἑτέρου τοῦ καὶ Μαρκίου, ἐπιγόνου Νουμᾶ, Ταρκυνίου, Σερουίου Τυλλίου καὶ Ταρκυνίου Λευκίου τοῦ
Ταρκυνίου, τούτων τῶν ἑπτὰ ἔργα τε καὶ πράξεις
περιέχει. ὧν ὁ πρῶτος κτίστης τε Ῥώμης καὶ οἰκι-
στὴς γεγονὼς ἄρξας τε πατρικῶς μᾶλλον ἢ τυραννι-
κῶς ὅμως ἐσφάγη ἤ, ὡς ἄλλοι φασίν, ἠφανίσθη. ὁ δὲ
δεύτερος, οὐδὲν ἧττον βεβασιλευκώς, εἰ μὴ καὶ μᾶλλον, τὸν ἑαυτοῦ βίον ἐτελεύτησε ζήσας ‹. . .› ὁ δὲ
τρίτος ἐκεραυνώθη. νόσῳ δὲ τὸν βίον ὁ τέταρτος ὑπ-
εξῆλθεν. ὁ δὲ πέμπτος ὑπὸ ποιμένων ἐσφάγη, καὶ ὁ
ἕκτος ὁμοίως σφαγῇ κατέστρεψε τὸν βίον. ὁ δὲ ἕβδο-
μος καὶ τῆς πόλεως καὶ τῆς βασιλείας παρανομῶν
ἐξηλάθη. ἐξ οὗ τῆς βασιλείας καταλυθείσης εἰς τοὺς
ὑπάτους τὰ τῆς ἀρχῆς μετετέθη. (Phot. Bibl. I p. 46
Henry)

3. Ἡ δὲ τὸν πατέρα φυλάξασα ἀποδημοῦντα ὑπ-
ισχνεῖται Τατίῳ προδώσειν τὸ φρούριον. (Suda, τ 150)

36

he collected a band of shepherds and joins them in launching their attacks. They killed Amulius and declare Nemetor king of the Albans. Romus and Romulus founded a town beside the river where they had been exposed, nursed and had turned to banditry. They called it Rome, the word for "square" at that time, as it had a perimeter of sixteen stades, each side four stades long. (*Excerpta anonymi Byzantini* ed. Treu 1880, pp. 36.10–37.29)

2. The first book contains a history of the works and deeds of the seven kings: Romulus, Numa Pompilius, Ancus Hostilius,[3] another Ancus also called Marcius (a descendant of Numa), Tarquinius, Servius Tullius, and Lucius Tarquinius son of Tarquinius. The first of these founded and built Rome, and although he ruled more in a paternal than in a tyrannical way, he was murdered; or, as others maintain, he disappeared. The second king lived no less royally, indeed more so, and died at the age of ‹. . .› the third was struck by lightning. The fourth died of disease. The fifth was murdered by shepherds. Similarly the sixth lost his life as a result of murder. The seventh was driven from the city and his throne for breaking the laws. From that time the monarchy was dissolved, and government was transferred to the consuls. (Phot. *Bibl.* I p. 46 Henry)

3. Keeping a careful eye on her father's absence, she promises to betray the garrison to Tatius.[4] (*Suda, τ* 150)

---

[3] A mistake for Tullus Hostilius.

[4] This (also section 4) refers to Tarpeia, who betrayed the Capitol to Titus Tatius in the war between Rome and the Sabines. When she asked for what the soldiers wore on their left arms (expecting gold bracelets), she was crushed to death by their shields.

4. Κελεύσαντος δὲ Τατίου τὸν χρυσὸν ἐς τὴν παῖδα ἐλίθαζον, ἔστε τιτρωσκομένη κατεχώσθη. (Suda, λ 512)

5. Περὶ πρέσβεων. Ἐκ τῆς ἱστορίας Ἀππιανοῦ τῆς ἐπιγραφομένης Βασιλικῆς. ὅτι τὸν πόλεμον τὸν πρὸς Ῥωμύλον Τατίου αἱ Ῥωμαίων γυναῖκες καὶ Σαβίνων θυγατέρες διῄτησαν, αὐταὶ τῷ χάρακι τῶν γονέων προσελθοῦσαι χεῖράς τε προτείνουσαι καὶ βρέφη τὰ ἤδη σφίν ἐκ τῶν ἀνδρῶν γενόμενα ἐπιδεικνύουσαι καὶ τοῖς ἀνδράσι μαρτυροῦσαι μηδὲν ὑβριστικὸν ἐς αὐτὰς ἁμαρτεῖν ἐδέοντό τε λαβεῖν τινα οἶκτον τοὺς Σαβίνους σφῶν τε αὐτῶν καὶ κηδεστῶν καὶ ἐκγόνων καὶ θυγατέρων καὶ φείσασθαι συγγενοῦς καὶ μιαροῦ πολέμου ἢ πρώτας ἀνελεῖν, αἳ τὴν αἰτίαν ἔχουσι τοῦ

2   πολέμου. οἱ δὲ τῶν τε παρόντων ἀπορίᾳ καὶ οἴκτῳ τῶν γυναικῶν, συγγινώσκοντες ἤδη μὴ καθ᾽ ὕβριν εἰργά-σθαι ταῦτα Ῥωμαίους, ἀλλὰ ὑπὸ χρείας, ἐς τὰς διαλ-λαγὰς ἐνεδίδουν, καὶ συνελθόντες Ῥωμύλος τε καὶ Τάτιος ἐς τὴν ἐξ ἐκείνου γενομένην ἱερὰν ὁδὸν ἐπὶ τοῖσδε συνέβησαν, βασιλεύειν μὲν ἄμφω, Τάτιόν τε καὶ Ῥωμύλον, Σαβίνους δὲ τοὺς τότε τῷ Τατίῳ συ-στρατεύσαντας καί, εἴ τινες ἄλλοι τῶν Σαβίνων ἐθέλοιεν, ἐς τὸ Ῥωμαίων μετοικίσασθαι ἐπ᾽ ἴσῃ καὶ ὁμοίᾳ. (Exc. de leg. gent. 1, p. 516 de Boor)

6. Ὁ δὲ στρατηγὸς αἰσθόμενος παρ᾽ ἰδιοξένων ἐξήγγειλεν Ὁστιλίῳ. (Suda, ι 104)

---

5 The story in sections 6 and 7 concerns Mettus Fufetius, ruler of Alba Longa when Tullus Hostilius was king of Rome. In combat

4. When Tatius gave the order, they "stoned" the girl with gold, until she was buried under the pile and overcome by her wounds. (*Suda,* λ 512)

5. Concerning embassies. From the part of Appian's history entitled the Book of Kings. It was the wives of the Romans—that is, the daughters of the Sabines—who arbitrated in the war of Tatius against Romulus. They went up to the encampment of their parents, stretched out their hands in supplication and showed them the children already born to them and their husbands; and they bore witness that their husbands had committed no violent wrong against them. They asked the Sabines to take pity on them, on their sons-in-law, their grandchildren and daughters, and put an end to this war defiled by the blood of relatives, or first kill the women who were the reason for the war. The Sabines, finding themselves at a loss in the circumstances and sympathetic to the women, agreed to reconciliation, as they recognized now that the Romans had acted as they did out of need rather than lustful violence. Romulus and Tatius met in what became thereafter the *Via Sacra*, and concluded the following treaty: Romulus and Tatius were both to be kings, and the Sabines then serving with Tatius, and any others who wanted to, would be allowed to migrate to Rome on fair and equal terms with the Romans. (*Exc. de leg. gent.* 1, p. 516 de Boor)

6. When he learned this from one of his personal friends, the general informed Hostilius.[5] (*Suda,* ι 104)

between the champions of the two cities, the Horatii triplets overcame the Alban triplets of the Curatii and won the day for Rome. Later, Mettus betrayed the Romans in battle and was torn asunder by horses driven in different directions. For the story, see Dion. Hal. 3.8.1, 3.22.1; Livy 1.27.1.

7. Οἳ δὲ ἐβλασφήμουν αὐτὸν ὡς κακῶς ἐπὶ τρισὶν ἀνδράσι τὰ πάντα θέμενον. (Suda, β 233)

8. Ξυμβάσεις ποιεῖν, ἐφ᾽ οἷς ἂν Γάβιοι δικαιῶσιν. (Suda, δ 1078)

9. Ὠνεῖται τὰ τρία βιβλία τῆς τιμῆς τῶν ἐννέα. (Anecd. Bekker p. 180.15 = Περὶ Συντάξεως No. 35 Gaillard)

10. Ὁ δὲ Ὁράτιος λελωβημένος ἦν τὰ σκέλη ὑπατείας τε οὐκ ἔτυχεν οὔτε ἐν πολέμῳ οὔτε ἐν εἰρήνῃ διὰ τὴν ἀχρηστίαν τῶν ποδῶν. (Suda, α 4717, ο 16)

11. Οἱ ὕπατοι τὰ ὅρκια προύτεινον καὶ ἐς πάντα ἔφασαν ἐνδώσειν μᾶλλον ἢ Ταρκύνιον προσήσεσθαι. (Suda, π 2690)

12. Ἐκ τῆς ἱστορίας Ἀππιανοῦ τῆς ἐπιγραφομένης Βασιλικῆς. Περὶ ἀρετῆς καὶ κακίας. ὅτι Ταρκύνιος Σαβίνους κατὰ Ῥωμαίων ἠρέθιζε. Κλαύδιος δέ, ἀνὴρ Σαβῖνος ἐκ Ῥηγίλλου πόλεως δυνατός, οὐκ εἴα τοὺς Σαβίνους παρασπονδεῖν, ἕως κρινόμενος ἐπὶ τῷδε ἔφυγεν ἐς Ῥώμην μετὰ συγγενῶν καὶ φίλων καὶ δούλων πεντακισχιλίων· οἷς πᾶσι Ῥωμαῖοι χώραν ἐς οἰκίας ἔδοσαν καὶ γῆν ἐς γεωργίαν καὶ πολίτας

---

6 For Tarquinius Superbus' treaty with Gabii, see Dion. Hal. 4.54.3.

7 This refers to the famous story of Tarquinius Priscus buying the Sibylline Books. When the Cumaean Sibyl offered Tarquinius nine books of prophecies, he refused, as the price was too high. She burned three books and then offered the remaining six for

7. They blamed him for wrongly staking everything on three men. (*Suda, β* 233)

8. To make a treaty on the terms thought fair by the people of Gabii.[6] (*Suda, δ* 1078)

9. He buys the three books for the price of the nine.[7] (*Anecd.* Bekker p. 180.15 = *On Syntax* No. 35 Gaillard)

10. Horatius was lame, and because of this handicap to his feet, he failed to win the consulship, either in war or peace.[8] (*Suda, α* 4717, *o* 161)

11. The consuls cited the oath and said they would agree to anything rather than take back Tarquinius.[9] (*Suda, π* 2690)

12. From the part of Appian's history entitled the Book of Kings. Concerning virtue and vice. When Tarquinius provoked the Sabines against Rome, Claudius, a Sabine man of influence from the town of Regillus, opposed any violation of the treaty. Eventually he was convicted for this and fled to Rome with five thousand of his relations, associates and slaves. The Romans gave all of them a place to live and land to farm, and made them citizens. They

the same price, but he again refused. When she burned another three, he finally accepted the last three, but had to pay the original price. Dion. Hal. 4.62 reports the story.

[8] Horatius Cocles and two companions held the Sublician bridge at Rome against the invading Etruscan forces of Lars Porsenna long enough for the bridge to be demolished. In Polybius (6.55) he drowns; in Livy (2.10.11) he swims to safety.

[9] The consuls were P. Valerius Poplicola and M. Horatius Pulvillus, supposedly in 509: Dion. Hal. 5.26–27. The oath is that mentioned in the *Preface* (6.20) that Rome would never again be ruled by kings.

ἔθεντο. τὸν δὲ Κλαύδιον καὶ ἐς τὸ βουλευτήριον κατ-
έλεξαν, ἀποδεικνύμενον ἔργα λαμπρὰ κατὰ τῶν Σαβί-
νων· καὶ φυλὴν ἐπώνυμον αὐτοῦ κατέστησαν. (Exc. de
virt. 1, p. 216 Roos)

13. Λατῖνοι ἔνσπονδοι Ῥωμαίοις ὄντες ἐστράτευον
ἐπ᾽ αὐτούς. (Suda, ε 1439)

Οἱ δὲ Λατῖνοι ἐγλήματα εἰς Ῥωμαίους ἐποιοῦντο
τήν τε πάρεσιν αὐτῶν τὴν ἐπὶ σφᾶς, ὄντας ἐνσπόνδας
καὶ συγγενεῖς. (Suda, π 568)

14. Πᾶσιν ἀπαντῶν. (Anecd. Bekker p. 130.13 = Περὶ
Συντάξεως No. 5 Gaillard)

15. Οὐκ εἰσακουόντων οὐδέτερα Ῥωμαίων. (Anecd.
Bekker p. 146.3 = Περὶ Συντάξεως No. 10 Gaillard)

16. Τὸ μὲν πρῶτον ἔριδες ἦν καὶ ἀψιμαχίαι σμι-
κραί, μετὰ δὲ συμβολαί τε ‹καὶ ἐσβολαὶ›[2] ἐς τὴν
ἀλλήλων. (Suda, α 4732)

17. Πιπράσκων χρημάτων πολλῶν. (Anecd. Bekker
p. 170.28 = Περὶ Συντάξεως No. 24 Gaillard)

[2] ‹καὶ ἐσβολαὶ› add. Roos

enrolled Claudius as a senator in recognition of his brilliant exploits against the Sabines; and they established a tribe named after him. (*Exc. de virt.* 1, p. 216 Roos)

13. Although the Latins had a treaty with the Romans, they still made war on them. (*Suda*, ε 1439)

The Latins blamed the Romans for showing contempt toward them, even though they were related and had a treaty with them. (*Suda*, π 568)

14. Going to meet all of them. (*Anecd.* Bekker p. 130.13 = *On Syntax* No. 5 Gaillard)

15. The Romans refused to listen in either case. (*Anecd.* Bekker p. 146.3 = *On Syntax* No. 10 Gaillard)

16. At first there were quarrels and minor skirmishing, later battles and invasions of each other's territory. (*Suda*, α 4732)

17. On sale for a great deal of money. (*Anecd.* Bekker p. 170.28 = *On Syntax* No. 24 Gaillard)

II

ΕΚ ΤΗΣ ΙΤΑΛΙΚΗΣ

1. Ὁ δὲ δῆμος τὸν Μάρκιον μετιόντα τὴν ὑπατείαν οὐκ ἐχειροτόνησεν, οὐ τὸν ἄνδρα ἀπαξιῶν, ἀλλὰ τὸ φρόνημα δεδιὼς αὐτοῦ. (*Suda*, α 2909)

2. Ὁ Μάρκιος, πιμπράμενος ἐπὶ Ῥωμαίοις φυγὴν κατὰ δικασθεὶς καὶ μικρὸν ἐς αὐτοὺς οὐδὲν ἐπινοῶν, ἐς Βολούσκους ἐτράπετο. (*Suda*, π 1607)

3. Ὅτι πατρίδα καὶ γένος ἀλλαξάμενος ἥκοι, ταῦτα τὸ μηδὲν ἡγησάμενος καὶ τὰ τῶν Οὐολούσκων ἀντὶ τῆς πατρίδος αἱρήσεσθαι βουληθείς. (*Suda*, α 1069)

4. Βολοῦσκοι δὲ τοῖς πταίσμασι τῶν γειτόνων οὐ καταπλαγέντες ἐστράτευον ἐπὶ Ῥωμαίους καὶ ἐπολιόρκουν τοὺς αὐτῶν κληρούχους. (Suda, κ 1788)

5. Περὶ πρέσβεων Ῥωμαίων πρὸς ἐθνικούς. Ἐκ τῆς ἱστορίας Ἀππιανοῦ τῆς ἐπιγραφομένης Ἰταλικῆς. ὅτι τοῦ Μαρκίου φυγαδευθέντος καὶ ἐς Βολούσκους καταφυγόντος καὶ κατὰ Ῥωμαίων ἐκστρατεύσαντος καὶ μ´ σταδίους ἀποσχόντος ἀπὸ τοῦ ἄστεος καὶ στρατοπεδεύσαντος ὁ δῆμος ἠπείλει τῇ βουλῇ παραδώσειν τὰ τείχη τοῖς πολεμίοις, εἰ μὴ πρεσβεύσοιντο περὶ διαλ-

BOOK II

FROM THE ITALIAN BOOK

1. When Marcius stood for the consulship the people did not vote for him, not because they thought he did not deserve it, but because they were afraid of his arrogance.[1] (*Suda, α* 2909)

2. Marcius was enraged at the Romans when they condemned him to exile, and making no small plans against them, he went over to the side of the Volsci. (*Suda, π* 1607)

3. He had come leaving country and kin, holding them of no importance, and intended to take up the cause of the Volsci rather than Rome. (*Suda, α* 1069)

4. The Volsci were not frightened by the failure of their neighbors, but campaigned against Rome and laid siege to her colonists. (Suda, *κ* 1788)

5. Concerning Roman embassies to foreign nations. From the part of Appian's history entitled the Italian Book. On being condemned to exile, Marcius took refuge with the Volsci and made war on Rome. When he was encamped forty stades from the city, the people threatened to surrender the walls to the enemy if the senate did

---

[1] This is the famous Marcius Coriolanus, who in the early fifth century BC deserted Rome to fight for the Volscians.

2 λαγῶν πρὸς Μάρκιον. ἡ δὲ μόλις ἐξέπεμψεν αὐτοκράτορας εἰρήνης πέρι ῥωμαίοις πρεπούσης, οἱ παρ-
ελθόντες εἰς τὸ Βολούσκων στρατόπεδον Μαρκίῳ
μετὰ Βολούσκων ἀκροωμένῳ προύτειναν ἀμνηστίαν
καὶ κάθοδον, εἰ καταλύσει τὸν πόλεμον, τῆς τε βουλῆς
3 αὐτὸν ὑπεμίμνησκον ὡς οὐχ ἁμαρτούσης ἐς αὐτόν. ὁ
δὲ πολλὰ τοῦ δήμου κατηγορήσας περὶ ὧν ἐς αὐτὸν
καὶ Βολούσκους ἐξημαρτήκεσαν, ἐπηγγέλλετο ὅμως
Βολούσκους αὐτοῖς διαλλάξειν, ἂν ἥν τε γῆν ἔχουσι
Βολούσκων καὶ τὰς πόλεις ἀποδῶσι καὶ ποιήσωνται
πολίτας ὥσπερ Λατίνους· ἕως δ᾽ ἂν ἔχωσι τὰ τῶν
κρατούντων οἱ κρατούμενοι, οὐχ ὁρᾶν, τίνες αὐτοῖς
4 ἔσονται διαλύσεις. ταῦτα μετοίσοντας ἀπέλυε τοὺς
πρέσβεις καὶ λ᾽ ἡμέρας ἐς τὴν σκέψιν ἐδίδου. τραπεὶς
δ᾽ ἐπὶ τοὺς ἄλλους Λατίνους ἑπτὰ πόλεις αὐτῶν εἷλε
ταῖς λ᾽ ἡμέραις καὶ ἧκεν ἐπὶ τὰς ἀποκρίσεις. οἱ δὲ
ἀπεκρίναντο, ἐὰν ἐκ τῆς Ῥωμαίων γῆς ἀπαγάγῃ τὸν
στρατόν, πέμψειν τοὺς συνθησομένους αὐτῷ τὰ πρέ-
5 ποντα. πάλιν δ᾽ ἀντειπόντος ἔπεμπον ἑτέρους ι᾽ δεη-
σομένους μηδὲν ἀνάξιον ποιεῖν τῆς πατρίδος μηδ᾽ ἐξ
ἐπιτάγματος, ἀλλ᾽ ἑκουσίους ἐᾶν γίγνεσθαι τὰς συνθήκας, αἰδούμενόν τε τὴν πατρίδα καὶ τὸ τῶν προγόνων ἀξίωμα τιμῶντα τῶν ἐς αὐτὸν οὐχ ἁμαρτόντων.
6 ὁ δὲ τοσοῦτον αὐτοῖς ἀπεκρίνατο, τριῶν ἄλλων ἡμερῶν ἥκειν βουλευσαμένους τι κάλλιον. οἱ μὲν δὴ τοὺς
ἱερέας ἔπεμπον ταῖς ἱεραῖς ἐσθῆσιν ἐσταλμένους,
ταὐτὰ τοῦ Μαρκίου δεησομένους· ὁ δὲ καὶ τούτοις ἔφη
δεῖν ἢ τὰ κελευόμενα ποιεῖν ἢ μηδ᾽ ἂν ἀφικνεῖσθαι

not send an embassy to negotiate with Marcius. Reluc- 2
tantly they dispatched representatives with full powers to
make a peace worthy of the Roman people. They came to
the Volscian camp, and with Marcius and the Volsci in attendance, they offered him an amnesty and a recall from
exile if he would stop the war, reminding him that the
senate had done him no wrong. Although he accused the 3
people of committing many wrongs against himself and
the Volsci, nevertheless he proclaimed that the Volsci
would make peace with them, on condition that they gave
back all the Volscian land and towns they held, and made
them Roman citizens on the same terms as the Latins. But
as long as the defeated held onto what belonged to the
victors, he did not see how they could reach a settlement.
He dismissed the ambassadors to report these terms, and 4
gave the Romans thirty days to consider them. He then
turned against the other Latins, captured seven of their
towns in the thirty days, and came back to hear the Roman
answer. They responded that if he would withdraw his
army from Roman territory, they would send people to
make a suitable agreement. But he turned them down 5
again. So they sent another ten ambassadors to beg him
not to do anything unworthy of his country: and to allow
them, if he respected Rome and honored the reputation
of his ancestors who had done him no wrong, to make
peace willingly, not at his command. In reply, he merely 6
said they had three more days to come up with something
better. To be sure, they sent their priests dressed in the
sacred garments with the same demands, but he told them
too either to do what he had ordered, or not to approach
him again. So they organized themselves for a siege, piling

πρὸς αὐτόν. ἐς οὖν πολιορκίαν καθίσταντο καὶ τὸ τεῖχος ἐπλήρουν λίθων καὶ βελῶν ὡς ἄνωθεν ἀμυνούμε-
7 νοι Μάρκιον. Βαλερία δ᾽, ἡ Ποπλικόλα θυγάτηρ, πολλὰς ἀγομένη γυναῖκας ἐπί τε τὴν μητέρα τοῦ Μαρκίου
Βετουρίαν καὶ ἐπὶ τὴν γυναῖκα Βολουμνίαν, πένθιμα
ἠμφιεσμέναι πᾶσαι καὶ τὰ παιδία ταῖς ἱκεσίαις ἐπι-
φέρουσαι, συνεξελθεῖν αὐταῖς πρὸς Μάρκιον ἠξίουν
αὐτὰς καὶ δεηθῆναι φείσασθαι σφῶν τε αὐτῶν καὶ
8 τῆς πατρίδος. αἱ μὲν δὴ τῆς βουλῆς ἐπιτρεπούσης
ἐξῄεσαν, μόναι γυναῖκες, ἐς ἐχθρῶν στρατόπεδον. ὁ
δὲ Μάρκιος, θαυμάζων τῆς εὐτολμίας τὴν πόλιν, οἷα
Ῥωμαίων ἐστὶ καὶ τὰ γύναια, προσιούσαις ἀπήντα
καὶ τὰς ῥάβδους καθήρει καὶ τοὺς πελέκεας διὰ τὴν
μητέρα προσδραμών τε ἠσπάζετο καὶ ἦγεν ἐπὶ τὸ
συνέδριον τῶν Βολούσκων καὶ λέγειν ἐκέλευσεν, ὅ τι
9 χρῄζοι. ἡ δὲ συνηδικῆσθαι μὲν ἐξελαυνομένῳ τῆς
πόλεως οὖσα μήτηρ ἔφη, ὁρᾶν δ᾽, ὅτι Ῥωμαῖοι πολλὰ
πρὸς αὐτοῦ πεπόνθασιν ἤδη καὶ τίσιν ἔτισαν ἱκανήν,
ὧν χώρα τε τοσαύτη διέφθαρται καὶ πόλεις ἀπο-
λώλασι πολλαὶ καί, τὸ Ῥωμαίοις ἔσχατον, παρακα-
λοῦσι καὶ πρέσβεις πέμπουσιν ὑπάτους καὶ ἱερέας
καὶ μητέρα καὶ γυναῖκα τό τε ἀδίκημα ἰῶνται ἀμνη-
10 στίᾳ καὶ καθόδῳ. "Σὺ δὲ μὴ ἀνιάτῳ κακῷ τὸ κακὸν
ἰῶ μηδὲ συμφοραῖς ἐπιχείρει κοιναῖς αὐτοῦ τε σοῦ
καὶ τῶν ἀδικούντων. ποῖ φέρων οἴσεις τὸ πῦρ; μετὰ

---

2 The rods and axes (in Latin, *fasces*) carried by lictors were
the symbols of magisterial authority in Rome. Perhaps Appian

up stones and missiles on the wall to defend themselves against Marcius from their elevated position. But Valeria, 7 the daughter of Publicola, collected a large number of women, all wearing mourning clothes and accompanied as petitioners by their children, and brought them to Veturia, Marcius' mother, and Volumnia, his wife, whom they asked to go with them to Marcius, to beg him to spare both themselves and their country. With the agreement of the 8 senate, they set out for the enemy camp, a group of women all on their own. Marcius, admiring the city for its courage, displayed even by Roman women, went out to meet them as they approached. He removed the rods and axes[2] out of respect for his mother whom he ran to embrace, and brought into the council of the Volsci, telling her to say what she wanted. She said that as his mother she had 9 shared the wrong done to him when he had been exiled from the city. But she saw that the Romans had suffered greatly at his hands and had paid a sufficient price in the ravaging of so much land and destruction of so many towns. Now, reduced to what was for Romans a last resort, they were beseeching him, sending as ambassadors consuls and priests and a mother and a wife; and they were seeking to rectify the wrong done by offering an amnesty and recall from exile. "As for you, do not cure evil with an 10 evil that is itself incurable, or make an attempt that would be a common disaster both for yourself and those who wrong you. Where will you bring the fire of destruction?

thought that Volscian leaders used the same symbols of power; or, more probably, Coriolanus had retained his Roman lictors, although he is not listed among the magistrates of the Roman Republic.

49

τὴν χώραν ἐπὶ τὴν πόλιν; μετὰ τὴν πόλιν ἐπὶ τὴν
ἑστίαν τὴν σήν; μετὰ τὴν ἑστίαν ἐπὶ τὰ ἱερά; δὸς
χάριν, ὦ παῖ, κἀμοὶ καὶ τῇ πατρίδι παρακαλούσαις."

11 ἢ μὲν δὴ τοσαῦτα εἶπεν, ὁ δὲ Μάρκιος οὐκ εἶναι πατρίδα τὴν ἐκβαλοῦσαν, ἀλλὰ τὴν ὑποδεδεγμένην· οὐδὲν γὰρ εἶναι φίλιον, ἂν ἀδικῇ, οὐδὲ ἐχθρὸν εὖ ποιοῦν.
καὶ τὸ τῶν παρόντων ἐκέλευεν ὁρᾶν, πίστιν τε δόντων
αὐτῷ καὶ λαβόντων καὶ πολίτην πεποιημένων καὶ
στρατηγὸν ἀποφηνάντων καὶ τὰ ἴδια ἐπιτρεψάντων,
τιμάς τε, ὅσων ἠξίωτο, καὶ ὅρκους, οὓς ὤμοσεν
αὐτοῖς, ἐπεξῄει καὶ παρεκάλει τὴν μητέρα τοὺς αὐτοὺς

12 ἐκείνοις τίθεσθαι πολεμίους καὶ φίλους. ἢ δὲ ἔτι λέγοντος ἀγανακτήσασα καὶ τὰς χεῖρας εἰς τὸν οὐρανὸν
ἀνασχοῦσα θεοὺς γενεθλίους ἐμαρτύρατο δύο μὲν
ἤδη πρεσβείας γυναικῶν ἀπὸ Ῥώμης ἐν μεγάλοις
ἐστάλθαι κακοῖς, ἐπὶ Τατίου βασιλέως καὶ Γαΐου
Μαρκίου, τούτοιν δὲ Τάτιον μὲν ὄντα ξένον καὶ ἀληθῆ
πολέμιον ἐνδοῦναι ταῖς γυναιξὶν αἰδούμενον, Μάρκιον
δ' ὑπερορᾶν πρεσβείας γυναικῶν τοσῶνδε, καὶ τῆς
γεγαμημένης καὶ μητρὸς ἐπὶ ταύταις. "Ἄλλη μὲν
οὖν," ἔφη, "Μηδεμία μήτηρ, ἀτυχοῦσα παιδός, ἐς
ἀνάγκην ἀφίκοιτο προσπεσεῖν αὐτῷ· ἐγὼ δ', εἰ καὶ
τοῦτο ὑφίστασαι, προκυλίσομαί σου." καὶ λέγουσα ἐς

13 τὸ ἔδαφος ἑαυτὴν ἐρρίπτει. ὁ δὲ ἐδάκρυσέ τε καὶ ἀνε-
πήδα καὶ ἀντείχετο αὐτῆς ὑπό τε τοῦ πάθους ἐξεφώ-
νησεν· "νικᾷς, ὦ μῆτερ, ἀλλὰ νίκην, ἐξ ἧς τὸν υἱὸν
ἀπολεῖς." ταῦτα εἰπὼν ἀπῆγε τὴν στρατιὰν ὡς λόγον
ἀποδώσων Βολούσκοις καὶ τὰ ἔθνη συναλλάξων· ἐλ-

From the country to the city? From the city to your own hearth? From your hearth to the temples? Show favor, my son, both to me and your country, we beg you." This is 11 what she said, but Marcius refused to recognize as his own a country that had expelled him; his own country was rather the one that took him in. For nothing was friendly if it did you wrong, nor hostile if it was good to you. He asked Veturia to observe the present company who had exchanged mutual pledges of loyalty with him, and had made him a citizen, appointed him general and entrusted their private welfare to him. He described the honors he had received and the oaths he had sworn to them, and he invited his mother to regard their friends and enemies as her friends and enemies. He was still speaking when in a 12 fury she raised her hands to heaven and called on the gods of the family to bear witness that two embassies of women had set out from Rome in the midst of great troubles, one in the time of king Tatius, the other in the time of Gaius Marcius. Of these, Tatius, although a stranger and outright enemy, yielded out of respect for the women; but Marcius despised the embassy of such prominent women, including even his own wife and mother. "May no other mother," she said, "unfortunate in her son, be reduced to the necessity of throwing herself down before him. But even this I endure: I will prostrate myself before you." And with these words she threw herself on the ground. At this he burst 13 into tears, leaped up and took her in his arms, exclaiming with emotion, "You win, mother, but it is a victory with which you will destroy your son." With these words he led the army back, intending to offer an explanation to the Volsci and to make peace between the two nations. It was

51

πίς τε ἦν, ὅτι καὶ ταῦτα πείσει Βολούσκους. κατελεύ-
σθη δὲ φθονούμενος παρὰ τοῦ στρατηγοῦ Ἀττιδίου.
(*Exc. de leg. Rom.* 1, p. 65 de Boor)

5b. Ὁ δὲ Μάρκιος ἀντιλέγειν μὲν πρὸς οὐδὲ ἐν
αὐτῶν ἐδικαίου. (*Suda*, ε 237)

6. Ἐλεεινοὶ τοῦ πάθους, ἀξιέπαινοι τῆς ἀρετῆς
γενόμενοι. μέγα γὰρ πάθος Ῥωμαίοις τοῦτο ἐγένετο,
καὶ πλήθους ἕνεκα καὶ ἀξιώματος εὐγενοῦς οἴκου καὶ
πανωλεθρίας. καὶ τὴν ἡμέραν ἀποφράδα τίθενται.
(*Suda*, ε 781)

7. Τῷ δὲ στρατηγῷ στρατὸς δυσπειθὴς ἦν ὑπὸ
μνησικακίας, ἐθελοκάκως τε ἠγωνίζοντο καὶ ἔφευγον
ἐπιδησάμενοι τὰ σώματα ὡς τετρωμένοι καὶ τὰς σκηνὰς διέλυον καὶ ἀναχωρεῖν ἐπεχείρουν, ἀπειρίαν ἐπι-
καλοῦντες τῷ στρατηγῷ. (*Suda*, ε 304)

8. Ὅτι σημείων γενομένων ἐκ Διὸς ἀηδῶν μετὰ τὴν
Βηϊεντίας ἅλωσιν οἱ μάντεις ἔλεγον ἐκλειφθῆναί τινα
πρὸς εὐσέβειαν, καὶ ὁ Κάμιλλος ἀνήνεγκεν, ὅτι τὴν
δεκάτην τῆς λείας ἐκλάθοιτο τῷ θεῷ τῷ χρήσαντι
2 περὶ τῆς λίμνης ἐξελέσθαι. ἡ μὲν οὖν βουλὴ τοὺς
λαβόντας ὁτιοῦν ἐκ τῆς Βηϊέντης ἐκέλευσεν ἀποτιμή-
σασθαι καθ' αὑτοὺς καὶ σὺν ὅρκῳ τὸ δέκατον ἐσενεγκεῖν, ὑπὸ δὲ εὐσεβείας οὐκ ὤκνησεν καὶ τῆς γῆς ἤδη

---

[3] This extract refers to the Fabian gens, three hundred of
whom were killed at the river Cremera in 477 when Rome clashed
with Veii, the southernmost city of the Etruscans: see Dion. Hal.
9.23.2.

hoped that he would be able to win over the Volsci, even on this matter, but their general Attidius was jealous of him and he was executed. (*Exc. de leg. Rom.* 1, p. 65 de Boor)

5b. Marcius did not think it right to oppose even a single one of their demands (*Suda, ε 237*)

6. They were worthy both of pity for their misfortune and praise for their courage.[3] Their fate was a great disaster for Rome, in view of the huge number involved, the noble reputation of their clan and its complete destruction. And they still hold the anniversary of the battle as a day of ill omen. (*Suda, ε 781*)

7. But the army was reluctant to obey their commander as they bore him a grudge and fought badly on purpose: they fled and put bandages on their bodies pretending to be wounded; and they set about breaking camp and trying to retreat, blaming the general's inexperience.[4] (*Suda, ε 304*)

8. When Jupiter sent bad omens after the capture of Veii, the seers said that some aspect of piety had been omitted, and Camillus reported that he had forgotten to reserve a tithe of the booty for the god who had issued the oracle about the lake.[5] So the senate issued an order that those who had taken anything from Veii should make a personal valuation of it and pay ten percent on oath. Such was their piety that they did not hesitate to dedicate ten percent even of the land that had already been sold, as well

[4] The general was Appius Claudius Sabinus, consul in 471.
[5] Veii was captured by M. Furius Camillus in 396.

3 πεπραμένης ὡς λαφύρου τὸ δέκατον ἀναθεῖναι. κρα-
τήρ τε ἀπὸ τῶνδε τῶν χρημάτων ἐν Δελφοῖς ἔκειτο
χρύσεος ἐπὶ χαλκῆς βάσεως ἐν τῷ Ῥωμαίων καὶ
Μασσαλιητῶν θησαυρῷ, μέχρι τὸν μὲν χρυσὸν Ὀνό-
μαρχος ἐν τῷ Φωκικῷ πολέμῳ κατεχώνευσε, κεῖται δ'
4 ἡ βάσις. αὐτὸν δὲ Κάμιλλον ἐν τῷ δήμῳ τις ἐδίωκεν
ὡς αἴτιον γεγονότα τῇ πόλει φασμάτων καὶ τεράτων
χαλεπῶν, καὶ ὁ δῆμος ἐκ πολλοῦ τὸν ἄνδρα ἀποστρε-
φόμενος ἐζημίωσε πεντήκοντα μυριάσιν, οὐκ ἐπικλα-
5 σθεὶς οὐδ' ὅτι πρὸ τῆς δίκης αὐτῷ παῖς ἐτεθνήκει. τὰ
μὲν οὖν χρήματα οἱ φίλοι συνήνεγκαν, ἵνα μὴ ὑβρι-
σθείη τὸ σῶμα τοῦ Καμίλλου· αὐτὸς δὲ βαρυθυμῶν
ἐς τὴν Ἀρδεατῶν πόλιν μετῴκησεν, εὐξάμενος τὴν
Ἀχίλλειον εὐχήν, ἐπιποθῆσαι Ῥωμαίους Κάμιλλον ἐν
6 καιρῷ. καὶ ἀπήντησεν αὐτῷ καὶ τόδε οὐ πολὺ ὕστε-
ρον· Κελτῶν γὰρ τὴν πόλιν καταλαβόντων ὁ δῆμος
ἐπὶ Κάμιλλον κατέφυγεν καὶ δικτάτωρα αὖθις εἵλετο,
ὡς ἐν ταῖς Κελτικαῖς πράξεσιν συγγέγραπται. (Exc.
de virt. 2, p. 216 Roos)

9. Ὅτι Μᾶρκος Μάλλιος εὐπατρίδης, Κελτῶν ἐπ-
ελθόντων τῇ Ῥώμῃ, ταύτην περιέσωσε καὶ τιμῶν μεγίστων ἠξιώθη. ὕστερον δὲ πρεσβύτην πολλάκις
ἐστρατευμένον ἀγόμενον ἐς δουλείαν ὑπὸ τοῦ δανει-
στοῦ γνωρίσας ἀπέδωκε τὸ χρέος ὑπὲρ αὐτοῦ καὶ ἐπὶ
τῷδε εὐφημούμενος πᾶσιν ἡφίει τοῖς ἑαυτοῦ χρήσταις
2 τὰ ὀφλήματα. προϊὼν δὲ τῇ δόξῃ καὶ ὑπὲρ ἄλλων

as of the spoils. A gold mixing bowl made from these funds 3
sat on a bronze stand at Delphi in the treasury of Rome and
Massilia until Onomarchus melted down the gold during
the Phocian war;[6] but the stand is still there. Camillus 4
himself was publicly accused of being responsible for the
portents and unfavorable omens experienced by the city,
and the populace, who had turned against him some time
before and were not moved to pity, even by the fact that
shortly before the case a son of his had died, fined him five
hundred thousand sesterces. His associates jointly paid 5
the money, so that his person would not be subject to
physical abuse. Deeply insulted, he himself emigrated to
the town of Ardea, praying, like Achilles,[7] that a time
would come when the Romans would miss Camillus. And 6
indeed shortly after, this did in fact happen to him: for
when the Celts captured Rome the people fled to Camillus
and reappointed him dictator (as described in my Celtic
history). (*Exc. de virt.* 2, p. 216 Roos)

9. Marcus Manlius, a patrician, saved the city when the
Celts attacked Rome, and was awarded the highest honors.[8] On a later occasion, when he found out that an old
man who had served in the army on many occasions was
being dragged off to slavery by a moneylender, he paid his
debt for him. He was much applauded for this, and can-
celed what was owed to him by his own debtors. His rep- 2

[6] The Third Sacred War, in which Phocis seized Delphi and
plundered its rich dedications to pay for mercenaries, ran from
356 to 346. Onomarchus was one of the great Phocian generals.

[7] Homer, *Il.* 1.240–44.   [8] M. Manlius Capitolinus was
supposed to have saved the Capitol in 390 from the Gauls, after
Juno's sacred geese alerted him.

ἀπεδίδου καὶ ταῖς δημοκοπίαις ἐπαιρόμενος ἐβούλευ-
σεν ἤδη χρεῶν ἀποκοπὰς κοινὰς ἢ τὸν δῆμον ἠξίου
τοῖς δανείσασιν ἀποδοῦναι, τὴν γῆν ἐς τοῦτο ἀποδό-
μενον, ἔτι οὖσαν ἀνέμητον. (Suda, μ 218)

10. Ἀπέδοτο εὐτελεστάτης τιμῆς. (Anecd. Bekker
p. 120.19 = Περὶ Συντάξεως No. 1 Gaillard)

11. Λιμὸς ὁμοῦ καὶ λοιμὸς ἐπέλαβε Ῥωμαίους.
(Anecd. Bekker p. 146.7 = Περὶ Συντάξεως No. 12
Gaillard)

12. Ἀναπείθει θανάτῳ ζημιοῦσθαι. (Anecd. Bekker
p. 146.7 = Περὶ Συντάξεως No. 14 Gaillard)

13. Ἀμφοτέροις τοῖς γονεῦσι θάλλοντες. (Anecd.
Bekker p. 149.5 = Περὶ Συντάξεως No. 16 Gaillard)

14. Πραθῆναι πάντα τοσοῦδε, ὅσου τὸν ἐκ Τυρρηνίας[1] ἐώνητο. (Anecd. Bekker p. 170.29 = Περὶ Συντάξεως No. 24 Gaillard)

15. Ὅθεν ἐσπάνιζε τροφῶν. (Anecd. Bekker p. 174.7
= Περὶ Συντάξεως No. 27 Gaillard)

---

[1] Τυρρηνίας Gaillard; τυρρανίας codd.

utation grew as he began to pay other people's debts. Encouraged by the success of these populist measures, he now proposed a general cancellation of debt; or at any rate he suggested that the people repay the moneylenders by giving back for this purpose the land which was still undistributed. (*Suda*, μ 218)

10. He sold it for the cheapest price. (*Anecd.* Bekker p. 120.19 = *On Syntax* No. 1 Gaillard)

11. Hunger along with pestilence gripped the Romans. (*Anecd.* Bekker p. 146.7 = *On Syntax* No. 12 Gaillard)

12. He persuades them to impose the death penalty. (*Anecd.* Bekker p. 146.7 = *On Syntax* No. 14 Gaillard)

13. Prospering along with both their parents. (*Anecd.* Bekker p. 149.5 = *On Syntax* No. 16 Gaillard)

14. The whole thing had been sold for as much as the Etruscan had paid for it. (*Anecd.* Bekker p. 170.29 = *On Syntax* No. 24 Gaillard)

15. This was the reason he was short of food. (*Anecd.* Bekker p. 174.7 = *On Syntax* No. 27 Gaillard)

III

ΕΚ ΤΗΣ ΣΑΥΝΙΤΙΚΗΣ

1. Ὅτι οἱ Ῥωμαίων στρατηγοὶ Κορνήλιος καὶ Κορβῖνος καὶ Δέκιος δημότης Σαυνίτας νικήσαντες ὑπέλι-
πον Καμπανοῖς φύλακας πρὸς τὰς Σαυνιτῶν ἐπιδρο-
μάς. οἱ δὲ φύλακες οἵδε Καμπανοῖς ἁβροδιαίτοις καὶ
πολυτελέσιν οὖσι κοινωνοῦντες ἐφθείροντο τὰς γνώ-
μας καὶ ἐφθόνουν ὧν ἔχουσι ἀγαθῶν, αὐτοὶ πενόμενοι
2 καὶ τὰ χρέα δεδιότες τὰ ἐν Ῥώμῃ. τέλος δὲ ἐπεβού-
λευον τοὺς ξένους ἑαυτῶν ἀνελόντες ἕκαστοι τὴν περιουσίαν κατασχεῖν καὶ τὰς γυναῖκας ἐς γάμον προσ-
3 αγαγέσθαι. καὶ τάχα ἂν ἔπραξαν αἰσχρὸν οὕτω
μῦσος, εἰ μὴ Μάμερκος, ἕτερος Ῥωμαίων στρατηγός,
ἐπὶ Σαυνίτας ὁδεύων ἔμαθε τὸ βούλευμα τῶν φυλάκων
καὶ ἐπικρύψας τοὺς μὲν αὐτῶν ἐξώπλισε καὶ ἀφῆκεν
οἷα κεκμηκότας, τοὺς δὲ πονηροτέρους ἐκέλευσεν ἐς
Ῥώμην ἐπί τινα χρείαν ἐπείγεσθαι χιλίαρχόν τε αὐτοῖς συνέπεμψεν, ᾧ εἴρητο ἀφανῶς αὐτοὺς φυλάσ-

---

[1] A. Cornelius Cossus and M. Valerius Corvinus were the
consuls of 343 (Publius Decius was a military tribune) during the
First Samnite War.

BOOK III

FROM THE SAMNITE BOOK

1. On defeating the Samnites, the Roman generals Cornelius and Corvinus, and the plebeian Decius, left a garrison in Campania against the Samnite raids.[1] Because these garrison troops shared the luxurious and extravagant life of the Campanians, their judgment became impaired. They themselves were poor and frighteningly in debt at Rome, and they began to envy the wealth of the Campanians. Finally they developed a plan to kill their hosts, take 2 possession of their estates and marry their wives. And they 3 might have carried out such a shameful crime, if Mamercus, another Roman general, who was marching against the Samnites, had not learned of the garrison's plot.[2] Disguising his knowledge, he disarmed and discharged some of them, supposedly on grounds of long service; and he ordered the more depraved to hurry to Rome on some mission, and sent a military tribune with them, with secret instructions to watch them closely. Both groups began to 4

[2] Appian, or his source, has probably got the wrong person: he should be referring to C. Marcius Rutilus, consul in 342 (Dion. Hal. 15.3.10), but has confused him with L. Aemilius Mamercus, who was deputy (*magister equitum*) to M. Valerius Corvus, dictator in the same year (Livy 7.39.17).

4 σειν. ἑκάτεροι δ' ὑπώπτευον μεμηνῦσθαι καὶ περὶ
Ταρρακίνην ἀφίστανταί τε τοῦ χιλιάρχου καὶ τοὺς
ἐπὶ τῶν ἔργων ἐν τοῖς ἀγροῖς δεδεμένους ἐκλύσαντες
καὶ ὁπλίσαντες, ὡς ἐδύναντο, ἤλαυνον ἐς Ῥώμην,
5 ὁμοῦ δισμύριοι γεγονότες. ἔτι δ' αὐτῶν ὁδὸν ἡμέρας
μιᾶς ἀπεχόντων ὑπήντα Κορβῖνος καὶ παραστρατο-
πεδεύσας ἐν τοῖς ὄρεσι τοῖς Ἀλβανῶν ἠρέμει, περισκοπῶν τε τὸ ἔργον ἔτι καὶ μέγα ἡγούμενος ἀπεγνω-
6 κόσι μάχεσθαι. οἱ δὲ ἐπεμίγνυντο ἀλλήλοις κρύφα,
καὶ ὀδυρμοὶ καὶ δάκρυα τῶν φυλάκων ἦν, ὡς ἐν οἰκείοις καὶ φίλοις ἁμαρτεῖν μὲν ὁμολογούντων, τὴν δὲ
7 αἰτίαν ἐς τὰ χρέα φερόντων τὰ ἐν Ῥώμῃ. ὧν ὁ Κορβῖνος αἰσθανόμενος καὶ ὀκνῶν ἅψασθαι πολιτικοῦ
καὶ τοσούτου φόνου συνεβούλευσε τῇ βουλῇ τὰ χρέα
τοῖς ἀνδράσι μεθεῖναι, τόν τε πόλεμον ἐξαίρων ἐπὶ
μέγα, εἰ τοσῶνδε ἀνδρῶν δύναιτο κρατῆσαι μαχομένων ἐξ ἀπογνώσεως, καὶ τὰς συνόδους αὐτῶν καὶ
ἐπιμιξίας ἐν ὑπονοίᾳ τιθέμενος, μὴ οὐδ' ὁ ἴδιος αὐτῷ
στρατὸς ἐς πάντα ᾖ πιστός, ἅτε συγγενεῖς ὄντες
ἐκείνων καὶ οὐχ ἧσσον αὐτῶν αἰτιώμενοι τὰ χρέα.
8 σφαλέντα δὲ κινδυνεύσειν ἔφη περὶ μειζόνων· καὶ τὴν
νίκην, εἰ κρατήσειεν, ἀτυχεστάτην ἔσεσθαι τῇ πόλει
9 κατ' οἰκείων τοσῶνδε. οἷς ἡ βουλὴ πεισθεῖσα τὰς μὲν
τῶν χρεῶν ἀποκοπὰς ἐψηφίσατο πᾶσι Ῥωμαίοις, τοῖς
δὲ τότε ἐχθροῖς καὶ ἄδειαν. οἱ μὲν δὴ τὰ ὅπλα ἀποθέ-
μενοι κατῄεσαν ἐς τὴν πόλιν. (Exc. de virt. 4, p. 217
Roos)

2. Ὅτι Μάλλιος Τορκουᾶτος ὁ ὕπατος τοιοῦτος ἦν

suspect that they had been betrayed, and near the town of
Tarracina, they break away from the tribune. They freed
the agricultural slaves, armed them as best they could and
marched on Rome. Their total number was twenty thousand. When they were still a day's journey from Rome,   5
Corvinus intercepted them, but after encamping opposite
them in the Alban hills, he took no action except to continue keeping an eye on the situation, as he thought it a
serious matter to engage desperate men in battle. The two   6
forces began to mix with each other in private, and the
garrison troops, now among relatives and friends, admitted with tears and regrets that they had been in the wrong,
but blamed the debts they had incurred at Rome. When   7
Corvinus heard this, he was reluctant to cause such extensive civil bloodshed, and advised the senate to release the
men from their debts. He greatly exaggerated the difficulty of the war, questioning whether he could actually
defeat so many men fighting out of desperation, and using
the meetings and dealings of the men with each other to
raise suspicions about the general reliability of his own
soldiers, who were, after all, related to these men and no
less critical of their own debts. The danger, he said, would   8
increase greatly if he were defeated; and if he won, the
victory, achieved against so many of their own people,
would be a most unfortunate one for Rome. The senate   9
were won over by these arguments, and voted both a cancellation of debt for all Romans and immunity for those
who were at the time public enemies. The latter laid down
their arms and returned to the city. (*Exc. de virt.* 4, p. 217
Roos)

2. The following incident demonstrates the great virtue

τὴν ἀρετήν. τούτῳ πατὴρ γεγένητο μικρολόγος καὶ
ἀμελὴς ἐς αὐτὸν καὶ ἐν ἀγροῖς αὐτὸν εἶχε μετὰ τῶν
2 θεραπόντων ἐργαζόμενόν τε καὶ τρεφόμενον. γρα-
ψαμένου δὲ αὐτὸν ἐπὶ πολλοῖς ἀδικήμασι Πομπωνίου
δημάρχου καὶ μέλλοντος ἐρεῖν τι καὶ περὶ τῆς ἐς τὸν
παῖδα κακώσεως ὁ παῖς ὅδε Μάλλιος ἧκεν, ἐπικρύ-
πτων ξιφίδιον, ἐς τὴν οἰκίαν τοῦ δημάρχου καὶ τυχεῖν
ἠξίωσεν αὐτοῦ μόνου, ὡς δή τι λέξων χρήσιμον ἐς
3 τὴν δίκην. ὑποδεχθεὶς δὲ καὶ λέγειν ἀρχόμενος
ἐπέκλεισε τὰς θύρας καὶ τὸ ξίφος ἐπισπάσας ἠπείλει
τῷ δημάρχῳ κτενεῖν αὐτόν, εἰ μὴ ὀμόσειεν, ὅτι λύσει
τῷ πατρὶ τὴν δίκην. καὶ ὁ μὲν ὤμοσε καὶ διέλυσεν,
ἐκθέμενος τῷ δήμῳ τὸ συμβάν. ὁ δὲ Μάλλιος ἐξ ἐκείνου λαμπρὸς ἦν, ἐπαινούμενος, ὅτι τοιόσδε ἐς τοιόνδε
πατέρα ἐγεγένητο. (Exc. de virt. 5, p. 219 Roos)

3. Ὁ δὲ αὐτὸν εἰς μονομαχίαν προὐκαλεῖτο σκώ-
πτων ἐς αὐτόν. ὃ δὲ τέως μὲν αὐτοῦ κατεῖχε· μετὰ δὲ
οὐ φέρων ἔτι τὸ ἐρέθισμα ἀντήλασε τὸν ἵππον. (Suda,
ε 2926)

4. Ὅτι Σαυνῖται ἐς τὴν Φρεγελλανῶν ἐμβαλόντες
ἐπόρθουν, Ῥωμαῖοι δὲ Σαυνιτῶν καὶ Δαυνίων ὀγδοήκοντα κώμας καὶ μίαν εἷλον καὶ ἄνδρας ἐξ αὐτῶν
χιλίους καὶ δισμυρίους ἀνελόντες ἀπανέστησαν αὐτοὺς ἀπὸ τῆς Φρεγέλλης. καὶ πάλιν ἐς Ῥώμην ἐπρέσβευον οἱ Σαυνῖται, νεκρὰ σώματα ἀνδρῶν σύροντες,
ὡς αἰτίους τοῦδε τοῦ πολέμου γεγονότας ἀνῃρηκότες,

of the consul Manlius Torquatus.[3] His father was petty-minded and negligent toward him, and kept him in the fields, working and eating with the slaves. When the tribune Pomponius indicted the father for his many wrong-doings, and intended to mention the ill-treatment of his son among them, the young Manlius, concealing a dagger, went to the house of the tribune and asked to see him alone, on the pretext of giving him information relevant to the case. He was admitted and had just begun talking when he locked the doors, drew his sword and threatened to kill the tribune unless he swore an oath that he would withdraw the case against his father. He did swear the oath and withdrew the case, and explained to the people what had happened. Manlius became famous from the affair, and was praised for being such a son to such a father. (*Exc. de virt.* 5, p. 219 Roos)

3. He jeered at him and challenged him to single combat. The other controlled himself for a time, but eventually could no longer stand the provocation and drove his horse at him.[4] (*Suda*, ϵ 2926)

4. While the Samnites were raiding and plundering Fregellan territory, the Romans captured eighty-one villages belonging to them and the Daunii, killing twenty-one thousand of their men, and forcing them to withdraw from Fregellae. The Samnites once again sent ambassadors to Rome, who dragged with them the corpses of those they had executed as being responsible for this war; they

---

[3] T. Manlius Imperiosus Torquatus, consul for the third time in 340.

[4] The story is in Livy 8.7: Gemmius Maecius issued the challenge to Titus Manlius, son of the consul of 340.

καὶ χρυσίον, ὡς ἀπὸ τῆς ἐκείνων περιουσίας πεπο-
2 ρισμένον. ἐφ᾽ οἷς αὐτοὺς ἡ βουλὴ πάνυ νομίζουσα
τετρῦσθαι προσεδόκα κακοπαθοῦντας ἐνδώσειν περὶ
τῆς ἡγεμονίας. οἱ δὲ τὰ μὲν ἄλλα ἐδέχοντο καί, εἴ τῳ
καὶ ἀντέλεγον, ἢ παρῃτοῦντο καὶ παρεκάλουν ἢ ἐς τὰς
πόλεις ἀνετίθεντο· περὶ δὲ τῆς ἡγεμονίας οὐκ ἀνα-
σχόμενοι πάλιν οὐδ᾽ ἀκοῦσαι, οὐκ ἐκδωσόμενοι δὴ
τὰς πόλεις ἔφασαν ἥκειν, ἀλλὰ ἐς φιλίαν συνάξοντες.
λυσάμενοι δὴ τοῦ χρυσίου τοὺς αἰχμαλώτους ἀπῇε-
σαν ὀργῇ καὶ τὴν πεῖραν ἔχοντες τὴν περὶ τῆς ἡγε-
3 μονίας. καὶ Ῥωμαῖοι μὲν ἐψηφίζοντο μηδὲ πρεσβείας
ἔτι παρὰ Σαυνιτῶν προσίεσθαι, ἀλλὰ ἄσπονδον καὶ
ἀκήρυκτον πόλεμον αὐτοῖς πολεμεῖν, ἕως κατὰ κράτος
ἐξέλωσιν, θεὸς δὲ ἐνεμέσησε τῆς μεγαληγορίας, καὶ
ὕστερον ἡττήθησαν ὑπὸ Σαυνιτῶν καὶ ὑπὸ ζυγὸν
4 ἤχθησαν οἱ Ῥωμαῖοι. ἐς γὰρ στενότατον χῶρον τούτους συγκλείσαντες οἱ Σαυνῖται, τοῦ Ποντίου σφῶν
στρατηγοῦντος, καὶ λιμῷ πιεζομένων Ῥωμαίων, οἱ
στρατηγοὶ σφῶν πρεσβευσάμενοι παρεκάλουν τὸν
Πόντιον καταθέσθαι Ῥωμαίοις χάριν, ἣν οὐ πολλοὶ
παρέχουσι καιροί. ὁ δὲ ἀπεκρίνατο μὴ δεῖν μηδὲ πρεσβεύειν ἔτι πρὸς αὐτόν, εἰ μὴ τὰ ὅπλα καὶ αὐτοὺς
5 παραδιδοῖεν. θρῆνος οὖν ἦν οἷα πόλεως ἁλούσης. καὶ
οἱ στρατηγοὶ διέτριψαν μὲν ἔτι ἄλλας ἡμέρας, ὀκνοῦν-
τες ἀνάξιόν τι τῆς πόλεως ἐργάσασθαι· ὡς δ᾽ οὔτε

---

5 This was the so-called battle of the Caudine Forks in 321, a
famous incident of the Second Samnite War. Commanding the

also brought gold, supposedly provided from the estates
of these men. As a result of this, the senate believed they 2
were completely worn down, and expected that in their
distress they would yield supremacy to Rome. But the
Samnites, although they accepted everything else—and if
they objected to something, they either asked to be ex-
cused and made their appeal, or referred the matter to
their towns—on the subject of supremacy they refused
even to hear it discussed again: they had not come, they
said, to surrender their towns, but to foster friendship.
Using the gold to ransom their prisoners, they went away
angry and determined to dispute the political leadership. The Romans for their part voted not even to receive 3
any further embassies from the Samnites, but to wage war
on them without treaties or truces, until they had destroyed them by force of arms. The gods resented this
arrogant bravado, and subsequently the Romans were defeated by the Samnites and forced to pass under the yoke.[5]
For the Samnites, under the command of their general 4
Pontius, shut the Romans up in a narrow defile. With hunger pressing, the consuls sent an embassy to Pontius urging him to win a degree of gratitude with Rome that not
many opportunities provided. He replied telling them that
they should send no further embassies to him, unless they
were prepared to surrender themselves and their weapons. This caused the same sort of dismay as when a city is
captured, and the generals delayed several more days, 5
hesitating to take action unworthy of Rome. But when it

Roman army trapped in a narrow defile and eventually forced into
humiliating surrender were the consuls of the year, T. Veturius
Calvinus and Sp. Postumius Albinus.

μηχανὴ σωτηρίας ἐφαίνετο ὅ τε λιμὸς ἐπίεζεν αὐτοὺς
καὶ νεότης ἦν πέντε μυριάδων, ἣν ὤκνουν φθειρο-
μένην ὑπεριδεῖν, ἐπέτρεψαν ἑαυτοὺς τῷ Ποντίῳ καὶ
παρεκάλουν, εἴτε κτείνειν εἴτε πωλεῖν εἴτε φυλάττειν
ἐπὶ λύτροις ἕλοιτο, μηδὲν ἐς σώματα ἀνδρῶν ἀτυχούν-
των ὑβρίσαι.

6   Ὁ δὲ τῷ πατρὶ συνεβουλεύετο, μεταπεμψάμενος
αὐτὸν ἐκ τοῦ Καυδίου, φερόμενον ὑπὸ γήρως ἁμάξῃ.
καὶ ὁ πρεσβύτης ἔφη· "Ἓν ἔστιν, ὦ παῖ, μεγάλης
ἔχθρας φάρμακον, εὐεργεσίας ἢ κολάσεως ὑπερβολή.
αἱ μὲν οὖν κολάσεις καταπλήσσουσιν, αἱ δὲ εὐεργε-
σίαι προσάγονται. ἴσθι νίκην τήνδε πρώτην καὶ μεγίστην, θησαυρίζειν τὴν εὐτυχίαν, καὶ πάντας ἀπόλυ-
σον ἀπαθεῖς μήτ' ἐνυβρίσας μήτ' ἀφελόμενος μηδέν,
7 ἵνα σῷον ᾖ σοι τὸ μέγεθος τῆς εὐεργεσίας. εἰσὶ δ',
ὡς ἀκούω, φιλότιμον κακόν, ἀλλὰ μόναις εὐεργεσίαις
ἡττώμενον, διαγωνιοῦνταί τε σοι περὶ τῆσδε τῆς
χάριτος. ἔχεις ἐνέχυρον τήνδε τὴν εὐεργεσίαν εἰρήνης
8 ἀθανάτου λαβεῖν. ἢν δέ σε ταῦτα μὴ πείθῃ, κτεῖνον
ἅπαντας ὁμαλῶς, μηδ' ἄγγελον ὑπολιπών. λέγω δ'
ἐκεῖνα μὲν αἱρούμενος, ταῦτα δ' ὡς ἀναγκαῖα. Ῥωμαῖοι γὰρ ὁτιοῦν ὑβρισθέντες ἀμυνοῦνταί σε πάντως·
ἀμυνεῖσθαι δὲ μέλλοντας αὐτοὺς προκατάβλαπτε.
μεῖζον δ' οὐκ ἂν εὕροις βλάβος νέων ὁμοῦ πέντε μυριάδων."

9   Ὁ μὲν τοσαῦτα εἶπεν, ὁ δὲ παῖς ἀντέλεξεν· "Ὅτι
μέν, ὦ πάτερ, ἐναντιώτατα εἶπας ἀλλήλοις, οὐ θαυ-

was clear that there was no other way of reaching safety, and hunger pressed them hard—there were fifty thousand young men whom they were reluctant to see slaughtered—they surrendered to Pontius, begging him, whether he chose to execute them, sell them, or keep them for ransom, not to commit an outrage upon the persons of unfortunate men.

Pontius decided to consult with his father and sent a 6 wagon to fetch him from Caudium, as he was an old man. "My son," he said, "there is only one cure for a great hatred—an act of extreme kindness, or an act of extreme severity. Severity strikes terror, kindness brings reconciliation. You should know that the first and greatest victory is to store up good fortune as a treasure. To secure for yourself the full benefit of your kindness, release them all without punishment, insult or any loss at all. I hear that 7 the Romans are competitive to a fault, but are overcome with kindness alone, and they will try to outdo you in respect of this favor. With such an act of kindness you will be able to guarantee permanent peace. If you are not 8 persuaded by this argument, then kill every last one of them; don't even leave one to bring the news. I would choose and advise the former course of action, otherwise the latter is a necessity. For the Romans will certainly avenge themselves on you for any outrage you do to them. So, as they are going to take their revenge, you should strike first; and you won't get an opportunity to inflict a heavier blow than killing fifty thousand of their young men at one time."

In reply to these words, his son spoke as follows: "I am 9 not surprised, father, that you have proposed two com-

μάζω· προεῖπας γὰρ ἐρεῖν ὑπερβολὰς ἑκατέρων. ἐγὼ
δὲ οὐ κτενῶ μὲν ἄνδρας τοσούτους, νέμεσίν τε θεοῦ
φυλασσόμενος καὶ φθόνον ἀνθρώπων αἰδούμενος, καὶ
τὰ ἔθνη τὰς ἐς ἀλλήλους ἐλπίδας οὐκ ἀφαιρήσομαι
δι' ἀνηκέστου κακοῦ. περὶ δὲ τῆς ἀφέσεως οὐδ' αὐτῷ
μέν μοι δοκεῖ, Ῥωμαίων πολλὰ καὶ δεινὰ δεδρακότων
ἡμᾶς καὶ χωρία καὶ πόλεις ἡμετέρας ἔτι νῦν ἐχόντων,
τούσδε τοὺς εἰλημμένους ἀπολύειν παντὸς ἀπαθεῖς.
10 οὐ ποιήσω· ἐμπληξία γὰρ ἡ ἄλογος φιλανθρωπία.
ἐπισκόπει δέ, παρεὶς ἐμέ, καὶ τὸ Σαυνιτῶν, ὧν παῖδες
καὶ πατέρες καὶ ἀδελφοὶ τεθνᾶσιν ὑπὸ Ῥωμαίων καὶ
κτήματα καὶ χρήματα ἀφηρημένοι χρῄζουσι παραμυ-
θίας. φύσει δὲ γαῦρον ὁ νενικηκώς, καὶ τὰ κέρδη
περιβλέπονται. τίς οὖν ἀνέξεταί μου τούσδε μὴ κτείνειν μήτε πωλεῖν μηδὲ ζημιοῦν, ἀλλ' ὡς εὐεργέτας
ἀπαθεῖς προπέμπειν; διὰ μὲν δὴ ταῦτα παρῶμεν τὰς
ὑπερβολάς, ἐπεὶ τῆς μὲν οὐ κύριος ἐγώ, τῆς δ' ἀπαν-
11 θρωποτέρας οὐκ ἀνέχομαι. ὡς δ' ἂν καὶ Ῥωμαίων τι
τοῦ φρονήματος περιέλοιμι καὶ τὰ πρὸς τοὺς ἄλλους
ἀδιάβλητος εἴην, ὅπλα μὲν αὐτούς, οἷς ἐχρήσαντο ἀεὶ
καθ' ἡμῶν, ἀφαιρήσομαι καὶ χρήματα (καὶ γὰρ ταῦτ'
ἔχουσι παρ' ἡμῶν), ἐκπέμψω δ' ὑπὸ ζυγὸν σώους, ᾗ
12 τινι αἰσχύνῃ καὶ αὐτοὶ κατ' ἄλλων ἐχρήσαντο· καὶ
εἰρήνην εἶναι τοῖς ἔθνεσι συνθήσομαι τῶν τε ἱππέων
ἐπιλέξομαι τοὺς ἐπιφανεστάτους ὅμηρα τῶνδε τῶν
συνθηκῶν, ἕως ἅπας ὁ δῆμος ἐπιψηφίσῃ. καὶ τάδε

pletely opposite courses of action, as you said at the beginning that one way or another you would be suggesting extreme measures. But I will not kill such a large number of men, both to protect myself from divine retribution and avoid the shame of human indignation; and I will not deprive the Roman and Samnite nations of their mutual hopes by committing an act of irreparable wickedness. On the matter of releasing them, not even I think we should let these prisoners off with no punishment at all, as the Romans have done many terrible things to us, and even still hold lands and towns that belong to us. No, I won't do it. For irrational generosity is madness. Leaving my own 10 case aside, just look at the situation the Samnites find themselves in. Their sons, fathers and brothers have died at the hands of the Romans, their estates and wealth have been taken from them; and they want satisfaction. Victors are by nature arrogant, and turn their minds to material gain. So, who would stand for it if I fail to kill, sell or even fine these men, but send them off unscathed as if they were our benefactors? On these grounds let us disregard the extremes: I don't have the power to be merciful, and I refuse to adopt the more inhuman alternative. But in 11 order to strip away some of the arrogance of the Romans and avoid censure at the hands of the rest of the world, I am going to confiscate their weapons which they have been using against us the whole time, and take their money (for even this they get from us); and I will make them go under the yoke unharmed, a form of dishonor they themselves impose on others. I will build peace be- 12 tween our nations and select the most distinguished of their knights as hostages to be guarantors of this agreement until the whole people ratify it. I believe that in

69

ποιῶν ἡγοῦμαι νενικηκότος τε ἔργα ποιήσειν καὶ φι-
λανθρώπου Ῥωμαίους τε ἀγαπήσειν, ὅσα καὶ αὐτοί,
φάσκοντες ἀρετῆς ἀντιποιεῖσθαι, πολλάκις ἐς ἄλλους
ἔδρασαν."

13 Ταῦτα τοῦ Ποντίου λέγοντος ὁ πρεσβύτης ἐδάκρυσέ
τε καὶ ἐπιβὰς τῆς ἀπήνης εἰς τὸ Καύδιον ἀπήλαυνεν.
ὁ δὲ Πόντιος τοὺς πρέσβεις καλέσας ἤρετο, εἴ τις
εἰρηνοδίκης αὐτοῖς παρείη. τοῖς δὲ παρῆν οὐδεὶς ὡς
ἐπὶ ἄσπονδον καὶ ἀκήρυκτον πόλεμον ἐστρατευκόσι.

14 τοῖς οὖν ὑπάτοις καὶ τοῖς ἄλλοις ἄρχουσι τῆς στρατιᾶς καὶ παντὶ τῷ πλήθει λέγειν ἐκέλευε τοὺς πρέ-
σβεις· "Ἡμεῖς ἀεὶ Ῥωμαίοις ἐσπενδόμεθα φιλίαν, ἣν
αὐτοὶ διελύσατε, Σιδικηνοῖς τοῖς ἡμετέροις ἐχθροῖς
συμμαχοῦντες· εἶτ᾽ αὖθις αὖ φιλίας ἡμῖν γενομένης
Νεαπολίταις ἐπολεμεῖτε, τοῖς ἡμετέροις γείτοσιν. καὶ
οὐκ ἠγνοοῦμεν, ὅτι ταῦτ᾽ ἦν ὑμῖν παρασκευὴ πλεονε-

15 ξίας ἐπὶ ὅλην τὴν Ἰταλίαν. ἔν τε ταῖς προτέραις μάχαις πολλὰ παρὰ τὴν ἀπειρίαν τῶν ἡμετέρων στρατηγῶν προλαβόντες οὐδὲν ἐπεδείξασθε μέτριον ἐς
ἡμᾶς οὐδ᾽ ἠρκεῖσθε τὴν χώραν πορθοῦντες καὶ χωρία
καὶ πόλεις ἔχοντες ἀλλοτρίας καὶ κληρούχους ἐς αὐτὰ
πέμποντες, ἀλλὰ καὶ πρεσβευσαμένων ἡμῶν δὶς πρὸς
ὑμᾶς καὶ πολλὰ συγχωρούντων ὑπερήφανα ἡμῖν ἄλλ᾽
ἐπετάσσετε, τὴν ἀρχὴν ὅλην ἀποθέσθαι καὶ ὑμῶν
ὑπακούειν, ὥσπερ οὐ σπενδομένους, ἀλλὰ ἑαλωκότας.

---

6 The *fetiales* at Rome oversaw the elaborate procedures for
declaring war and making treaties. When these procedures were

doing this I will be acting like a victor and a humane person, and that the Romans will approve: they themselves have often done the same sort of thing to others, claiming to be champions of virtue."

While Pontius was still speaking, the old man burst into 13 tears, got into his carriage and drove back to Caudium. Pontius summoned the Roman ambassadors and asked them if they had any Fetial priests with them. But none was in their company, as they had embarked on a truceless and undeclared war.[6] So he ordered the ambassadors to 14 make the following proclamation to the consuls, other army officers, and to the whole body of men: "We always used to live in formally agreed friendship with you Romans, but you dissolved it when you allied yourselves to our enemies, the Sidicini. Then again, although friendship was renewed with us, you made war on our neighbors, the Neapolitans. We were well aware that this was part of your greedy preparations against the whole of Italy. In the early 15 battles, when the inexperience of our generals gave you a big advantage, you showed us no moderation. Not content with laying waste the land, occupying estates and towns that did not belong to you and sending colonists into them, on two occasions when we sent embassies to you and offered substantial concessions, you made the additional arrogant demand of us that we give up our whole empire and submit to your rule, as if we were prisoners of war not

properly observed, the consequence was that a war so declared could be regarded as a "just war." Appian unjustifiably deduces from the absence of Fetials in this case that the army trapped in the Caudine Forks had not properly declared war, which was therefore not a just war.

71

16 καὶ ἐπὶ τοῖσδε τὸν πόλεμον τόνδε ἄσπονδον καὶ ἀκήρυκτον ἐψηφίσασθε κατ' ἀνδρῶν ποτε φίλων, κατὰ
17 Σαβίνων ἐκγόνων τῶν ὑμῖν συνοικούντων. ἕνεκα μὲν
οὖν τῆς ὑμετέρας πλεονεξίας ἔδει καὶ τὰ παρ' ἡμῶν
ὑμῖν ἄσπονδα εἶναι, ἐγὼ δὲ νέμεσίν τε θεῶν αἰδούμενος, ἣν ὑμεῖς ὑπερείδεσθε, καὶ συγγενείας καὶ φιλίας
τῆς ποτὲ μνημονεύων δίδωμι ἕκαστον ὑμῶν σὺν ἱμα-
τίῳ σῶον ὑπὸ ζυγὸν ἀπελθεῖν, ἣν ὀμόσητε τήν τε γῆν
καὶ τὰ χωρία πάνθ' ἡμῖν ἀποδώσειν καὶ τοὺς κληρούχους ἀπὸ τῶν πόλεων ἀπάξειν καὶ μηδέ ποτ' ἐπὶ Σαυνίτας στρατεύσειν."

18   Ἀπαγγελθέντων δὲ τούτων ἐς τὸ στρατόπεδον ὀλο-
φυρμὸς ἦν καὶ θρῆνος ἐπὶ πλεῖστον· θανάτου γὰρ
ἡγοῦντο εἶναι χείρονα τὴν ὕβριν τὴν ὑπὸ τῷ ζυγῷ.
ὡς δὲ καὶ περὶ τῶν ἱππέων ἐπύθοντο, αὖθις ἐθρήνουν
ἐπὶ πλεῖστον, ὑπὸ δὲ ἀπορίας αὐτὰ ἐδέχοντο καὶ τοὺς
ὅρκους ὤμνυον ὅ τε Πόντιος καὶ οἱ Ῥωμαίων ὕπατοι,
δύο ὄντες, Ποστούμιός τε καὶ Βετούριος, καὶ ταμίαι
δύο καὶ ταξιάρχαι δ' καὶ χιλίαρχοι δώδεκα, σύμπαν-
19 τες ὅσοι μετὰ τοὺς διεφθαρμένους ἦρχον. γενομένων
δὲ τῶν ὅρκων ὁ μὲν Πόντιος παραλύσας τι τοῦ δια-
τειχίσματος καὶ δυσὶ δόρασιν ἐς τὴν γῆν ἐμπεπηγό-
σιν ἐπικάρσιον ἄλλο ἐπιθεὶς ἐξέπεμπε Ῥωμαίων ἕκαστον ὑπὸ τούτῳ καί τινα ὑποζύγια ἔδωκεν αὐτοῖς ἐς
τοὺς ἀρρωστοῦντας καὶ τροφήν, ἄχρι τῆς Ῥώμης
φέρεσθαι. δύναται δ', ἐμοὶ δοκεῖν, τὸ εἶδος τῆς ἀφέσεως, ὃ καλοῦσιν οἱ τῇδε ζυγόν, ὀνειδίζειν ὡς δορι-
αλώτοις.

peace negotiators. And to that end you voted to undertake   16
this truceless and undeclared war against former friends,
against descendants of your fellow settlers, the Sabines. In   17
view of your greed we too should make no truce with you.
But out of respect for the gods' righteous anger, something
you disdained, and keeping in mind our former friendship
and kinship, I have decided to allow every one of you to
leave unharmed and with your cloak, passing under the
yoke, if you swear to return all our land and estates, and
to withdraw the colonies from our towns, and never again
make war on the Samnites."

When the army were told of these terms they wept and   18
grieved at length, for they regarded the disgrace of going
under the yoke as worse than death. There was further
extensive grieving when they learned about the knights.
But necessity forced them to accept the terms, and they
swore the oaths, Pontius on one side, on the other the two
Roman consuls, Postumius and Veturius, two quaestors,
four legionary commanders and twelve military tribunes,
that is, all the surviving officers. With the oaths taken,   19
Pontius opened a section of the retaining fence, fixed two
spears in the ground with one across the top and made
each Roman pass under it. He provided transport animals
for their wounded and sufficient provisions to get them to
Rome. In my opinion this form of release, which the Romans call "a yoke," functions as a reproach for those captured by the spear.

20 Ἀπαγγελθείσης δὲ τῆς συμφορᾶς ἐς τὴν πόλιν
οἰμωγὴ καὶ θρῆνος ἦν ὡς ἐπὶ πένθει, καὶ αἱ γυναῖκες
ἐκόπτοντο τοὺς αἰσχρῶς περισεσωσμένους ὡς ἀπο-
θανόντας, ἥ τε βουλὴ τὴν ἐπιπόρφυρον ἐσθῆτα
ἀπέθετο, καὶ θυσίαι καὶ γάμοι καὶ ὅσα ἄλλα τοιουτότροπα ἐπέσχητο ἐπὶ τὸ ἔτος ὅλον, ἕως τὴν συμ-
21 φορὰν ἀνέλαβον. τῶν δὲ ἀφειμένων οἱ μὲν ἐς τοὺς
ἀγροὺς διέφευγον ὑπὸ αἰδοῦς, οἱ δὲ νυκτὸς ἐς τὴν
πόλιν ἐσῄεσαν. οἱ δὲ ἄρχοντες ἡμέρας μὲν ἐσῆλθον
ὑπ᾽ ἀνάγκης, καὶ τὰ σημεῖα τῆς ἀρχῆς ἐπέκειτο
αὐτοῖς, ἔπρασσον δὲ οὐδέν. (Exc. de leg. gent. 2, p. 517
de Boor)

5. Δεντάτῳ κατὰ ζῆλον ἀρετῆς εἵπετο νέων λογά-
δων πλῆθος ὀκτακοσίων, ἐπὶ πάντα τὰ ἔργα ἕτοιμοι·
καὶ βαρὺς ἦν τῇ βουλῇ παρὰ τὰς ἐκκλησίας. (Suda,
ζ 57)

6. Ἐκ τῆς Σαυνιτικῆς ἱστορίας. ὅτι Κελτῶν Σενόνων
πολὺ πλῆθος Τυρρηνοῖς συνεμάχουν κατὰ Ῥωμαίων.
Ῥωμαῖοι δ᾽ ἐς τὰς Σενόνων πόλεις ἐπρέσβευον καὶ
ἐνεκάλουν, ὅτι ὄντες ἔνσπονδοι μισθοφοροῦσι κατὰ
2 Ῥωμαίων. τούσδε τοὺς πρέσβεις Βριτόμαρις μετὰ
τῶν κηρυκείων καὶ τῆς ἱερᾶς στολῆς κατέτεμεν ἐς
πολλὰ καὶ διέρριψεν ἐγκαλῶν, ὅτι αὐτοῦ ὁ πατὴρ ἐν
3 Τυρρηνίᾳ πολεμῶν ἀνήρητο ὑπὸ Ῥωμαίων. Κορνήλιος δὲ ὁ ὕπατος τοῦ μύσους ἐν ὁδῷ πυθόμενος τὰ μὲν

When news of the disaster reached Rome there was   20
wailing and weeping like public grief. The women
mourned for those who had survived in such shameful
circumstances as if they had died; the senators took off
their purple-bordered togas; and festivals, weddings and   21
all similar events were banned for the whole year, until
they put the disaster right. Some of the released soldiers
fled to the country out of shame, others entered the city
at night. The consuls were required to enter by day, and
they wore the insignia of office, but they conducted no
business. (*Exc. de leg. gent.* 2, p. 517 de Boor)

5. In admiration of his courage, a crowd of eight hundred chosen young men used to accompany Dentatus,
ready to do any deed.[7] He proved a burden for the senate
at its meetings.[8] (Suda, ζ 57)

6. From the Samnite history. A large force of the Celtic
Senones were fighting as allies of the Etruscans against
Rome. A Roman embassy sent to the towns of the Senones
accused them of fighting as mercenaries against Rome,
although they were her allies. These ambassadors, along   2
with their heralds' staffs and sacred robes, Britomaris cut
up into small pieces and threw away, because, so he
claimed, his father had been killed by the Romans while
on campaign in Etruria. The consul Cornelius[9] learned   3
of this vile act on the road, and abandoned his campaign

---

[7] Manius Curius Dentatus, consul four times between 290
and 274, was a hero of Rome's wars against the Samnites, Sabines,
and others.   [8] The meaning is not obvious. The Adler Suda
translates, "and he was inflexible on the advice coming from the
comitia."   [9] The consuls of the year 283 were P. Cornelius
Dolabella and Cn. Domitius.

Τυρρηνῶν εἴασεν, ἐς δὲ τὰς Σενόνων πόλεις συντόνῳ
σπουδῇ διὰ Σαβίνων καὶ Πικεντίνων ἐσβαλὼν πάντα
καθῄρει καὶ ἐνεπίπρη καὶ τὰς μὲν γυναῖκας καὶ τὰ
παιδία ἠνδραποδίζετο, τοὺς δὲ ἡβῶντας πάντας ἔκτεινε πλὴν Βριτομάριος, ὃν δεινῶς αἰκισάμενος ἦγεν
4 ἐς τὸν θρίαμβον. οἱ δὲ Σενόνων, ὅσοι ἦσαν ἐν Τυρρηνίᾳ, πυθόμενοι ἀνῃρῆσθαι, Τυρρηνοὺς ἦγον ἐπὶ
Ῥώμης. καὶ—πολλῶν μεταξὺ γενομένων—οἱ Σένονες,
οὔτε πατρίδας ἔχοντες, ἐς ἃς διαφύγωσιν, ὀργιζόμε-
νοί τε τῶν γεγονότων, ἐνέπιπτον τῷ Δομιτίῳ, καὶ
διεφθάρησαν πολλοί, τὸ δὲ λοιπὸν σφᾶς αὐτοὺς διεχρῶντο μανικῶς. καὶ δίκη μὲν ἥδε παρανομίας ἐς
πρέσβεις ἐγένετο Σένοσιν. (Exc. de leg. Rom. 2, p. 68 de
Boor)

7. Ὅτι Κορνήλιος ἐπὶ καταφράκτων δέκα νεῶν
ἐθεᾶτο τὴν μεγάλην Ἑλλάδα. καί τις ἐν Τάραντι δη-
μαγωγὸς Φιλόχαρις, αἰσχρῶς τε βεβιωκὼς καὶ παρὰ
τοῦτο καλούμενος Θαΐς, παλαιῶν τοὺς Ταραντίνους
ἀνεμίμνησκε συνθηκῶν, μὴ πλεῖν Ῥωμαίους πρόσω
Λακινίας ἄκρας, παροξύνας τε ἔπεισεν ἐπαναχθῆναι
2 τῷ Κορνηλίῳ. καὶ τέσσαρας μὲν αὐτοῦ ναῦς κατέδυσαν οἱ Ταραντῖνοι, μίαν δὲ ἔλαβον αὐτοῖς ἀνδράσιν.
ἔς τε Θουρίους ἐγκλήματα ποιούμενοι, ὅτι Ἕλληνες
ὄντες ἐπὶ Ῥωμαίους κατέφυγον ἀντὶ σφῶν καὶ παρελθεῖν αὐτοὺς ἐπέκεινα αἴτιοι μάλιστα ἐγεγένηντο, τοὺς

---

10 The colonization of Sicily and southern Italy by Greek

against the Etruscans: advancing with extreme speed against the towns of the Senones through Sabine territory and Picenum, he destroyed or burned everything. He enslaved the women and children and killed all the adult males, except Britomaris, whom he tortured horribly and led in his triumph. When the Senones in Etruria heard of 4 this destruction, they led the Etruscans against Rome. Eventually—and much happened in between—without a homeland to offer them refuge, and angry at the way things had developed, the Senones attacked Domitius. Many were killed and the rest committed suicide in a frenzy. Such was the punishment suffered by the Senones for their crime against the ambassadors. (*Exc. de leg. Rom.* 2, p. 68 de Boor)

7. While Cornelius was reconnoitering Magna Graecia[10] with a squadron of ten decked ships, a certain demagogue in Tarentum called Philocharis (a man of shameful lifestyle and for that reason given the nickname Thais[11]) reminded the Tarentines of an old treaty in which the Romans were not to sail beyond the headland at Lacinium. He roused their passions and persuaded them to put to sea against Cornelius, and the Tarentines sank four of his ships 2 and captured one with all its crew. They also accused the people of Thurii of ignoring the fact that they were Greeks and looking to Rome rather than Tarentum for refuge; and, holding them largely responsible for the Roman in-

mainland states starting in the early eighth century led to the designation of the area as *Magna Graecia* (Greater Greece).

[11] Thais was a famous courtesan in the entourage of Alexander the Great, who was instrumental in persuading him to burn the Persian royal palace at Persepolis: see Diod. Sic. 17.20–22.

μὲν ἐπιφανεῖς αὐτῶν ἐξέβαλον, τὴν δὲ πόλιν διήρπα-
σαν καὶ τοὺς Ῥωμαίων φρουροὺς ὑποσπόνδους ἀφῆ-
3 καν. Ῥωμαῖοι δὲ τούτων πυθόμενοι πρέσβεις ἐς
Τάραντα πέμπουσι τοὺς μὲν αἰχμαλώτους κελεύοντες,
οὓς οὐ πολεμοῦντας, ἀλλὰ θεωμένους ἔλαβον, ἀποδοῦναι, Θουρίων δ', οὓς ἐξέβαλον, ἐς τὴν πόλιν κατ-
αγαγεῖν, ἅ τε διηρπάκεσαν αὐτούς, ἀποκαταστῆσαι ἢ
τὴν ζημίαν τῶν ἀπολομένων ἀποτῖσαι, σφίσι δ' ἐκδοῦναι τοὺς αἰτίους τῆς παρανομίας, εἰ Ῥωμαίων
4 ἐθέλουσιν εἶναι φίλοι. οἱ δὲ τοὺς πρέσβεις μόλις ποτὲ
ἐπὶ τὸ κοινὸν ἐπήγαγον καὶ ἐπελθόντας ἐχλεύαζον, εἴ
τι μὴ καλῶς ἑλληνίσειαν· ἔσκωπτον δὲ καὶ τὴν στο-
5 λὴν αὐτῶν καὶ τὸ ἐπιπόρφυρον. Φιλωνίδης δέ τις,
ἀνὴρ γελοῖος καὶ φιλοσκώμμων, Ποστουμίῳ τῷ τῆς
πρεσβείας ἡγουμένῳ προσελθὼν ἀπεστράφη τε καὶ
ἐπικύψας τὴν ἐσθῆτα ἀνεσύρατο τὴν ἑαυτοῦ καὶ τοῦ
6 πρεσβευτοῦ κατησχημόνησεν. καὶ τὸ μὲν θέατρον
ἔπαιζεν ὡς ἐπὶ γελοίῳ, Ποστούμιος δὲ προτείνας
τὸ μεμολυσμένον "Ἐκπλυνεῖτ'," ἔφη, "Τοῦτο αἵματι
πολλῷ, τοιούτοις ἀρεσκόμενοι γέλωσιν." καὶ οὐδὲν
τῶν Ταραντίνων ἀποκριναμένων ἀπῆλθον οἱ πρέ-
7 σβεις. ὁ δὲ Ποστούμιος τὴν ὕβριν ἐκ τῆς ἐσθῆτος οὐκ
ἀποπλύνας ἐπέδειξε Ῥωμαίοις, καὶ ὁ δῆμος ἀγανακτῶν Αἰμιλίῳ πολεμοῦντι Σαυνίταις ἐπέστειλε τὰ μὲν
Σαυνιτῶν ἐν τῷ παρόντι ἐᾶν, ἐς δὲ τὴν Ταραντίνων
ἐσβάλλειν καὶ αὐτούς, ἐφ' οἷς ἠξίουν οἱ πρέσβεις, ἐς
διαλλαγὰς προκαλέσασθαι, ἂν δ' ἀπειθῶσι, πολεμεῖν
8 κατὰ κράτος. ὁ μὲν δὴ τάδε προύτεινε τοῖς Ταραντί-

cursion, the Tarentines exiled their leading citizens, destroyed Thurii itself and got the Roman garrison to leave
under a truce. When the Romans heard of these events   3
they send ambassadors to Tarentum to demand the return
of the prisoners: these had been captured, they claimed,
while on reconnaissance, not engaged in open war. They
also required them to bring back to the town the Thurians
they had expelled, restore the property seized from them
(or compensate them for what they had lost) and hand
over to Rome those responsible for this criminal behavior.
This is what they had to do if they wanted to remain
friends of the Romans. But it was only with great reluc-   4
tance that the Tarentines admitted the Roman ambassadors to their council at all, and when they did, they mocked
the Romans for the mistakes they made in the Greek language. They also mocked their toga with its purple border.
Indeed a man called Philonides, a comic and joker, went   5
up to Postumius, the leader of the Roman embassy, and
turning his back to him hitched up his own clothes, bent
over and defecated on the ambassador. Those watching   6
treated this as a joke, something to laugh at, but Postumius
held out the soiled garment and said, "You may find this
sort of thing funny, but you will wash this out in a bath of
blood." The Tarentines made no reply and the ambassadors left. Postumius showed the toga to the Romans with-   7
out cleaning the filth off it. The people were furious and
ordered Aemilius,[12] who was fighting the Samnites, to
suspend that campaign for the moment, and attack Tarentum: he should invite them to make peace on the same
conditions as the embassy had offered, and if they refused,
he was to wage full-out war against them. So he made   8

---

[12] L. Aemilius Barbula was consul in 281.

νοις, οἳ δὲ οὐκ ἐγέλων ἔτι τὴν στρατιὰν ὁρῶντες, ἀλλ᾽
ἐγίνοντο ταῖς γνώμαις ἀγχώμαλοι, μέχρι τις ἀπο-
ροῦσι καὶ βουλευομένοις ἔφη τὸ μὲν ἐκδοῦναί τινας
ἤδη δεδουλωμένων εἶναι, τὸ δὲ πολεμεῖν μόνους ἐπι-
9 σφαλές. "Εἰ δὲ καὶ τῆς ἐλευθερίας ἐγκρατῶς ἐξόμεθα
καὶ πολεμήσομεν ἐξ ἴσου, Πύρρον ἐξ Ἠπείρου τὸν
βασιλέα καλῶμεν καὶ στρατηγὸν ἀποφήνωμεν τοῦδε
τοῦ πολέμου." ὃ καὶ γέγονεν. (Exc. de leg. Rom. 3, p. 68
de Boor)

8. Ὅτι μετὰ τὸ ναυάγιον ὁ Πύρρος, ὁ βασιλεὺς τῆς
Ἠπείρου, ἐς τὸν Τάραντα κατήγετο, καὶ οἱ Ταραντῖνοι τότε μάλιστα τοὺς βασιλικοὺς ἐβαρύνοντο,
ἐσοικιζομένους τε παρὰ σφᾶς βίᾳ καὶ φανερῶς ἐνυ-
2 βρίζοντας αὐτῶν γυναιξὶ καὶ παισίν. ὡς δὲ καὶ τὰ
συσσίτια σφῶν ὁ Πύρρος καὶ τὰς ἄλλας συνόδους
καὶ διατριβὰς ὡς οὐ πρεπούσας πολέμῳ διέλυε
γυμνάσιά τε ἔνοπλα ἔτασσεν αὐτοῖς καὶ θάνατον τοῖς
ἀμελοῦσιν ὥριζε, τότε δὴ καὶ πάμπαν ἀήθεσιν ἔργοις
καὶ ἐπιτάγμασι κάμνοντες οἱ Ταραντῖνοι ἐκ τῆς πό-
3 λεως ὡς ἀλλοτρίας ἐς τοὺς ἀγροὺς ἀπεδίδρασκον. καὶ
ὁ βασιλεὺς τὰς θύρας ἀπέκλειε καὶ φρουρὰς ἐφίστη.
καὶ οἱ Ταραντῖνοι τῆς ἀβουλίας σφῶν ᾐσθάνοντο σαφῶς. (Exc. de virt. 6, p. 219 Roos)

9. Ὅτι ὅσοι ἐν Ῥηγίῳ Ῥωμαίων ἐπὶ σωτηρίᾳ καὶ
φυλακῇ τῆς πόλεως, μή τι πάθοιεν ὑπὸ τῶν ἐχθρῶν,
παρέμενον, αὐτοί τε καὶ Δέκιος, ὁ ἡγεμὼν αὐτῶν, τοῖς

---

13 Decius Vibellius came from a well-known family in Capua.

them this offer. The Tarentines no longer found it a laugh-
ing matter when they saw his army. But they were divided
in their opinions and at a loss in their deliberations, until
one of them said that while it was only those already enslaved who would hand anyone over, it was also dangerous
to go to war on your own. "If we want to hold fast to our   9
freedom and fight on equal terms, let us invite Pyrrhus,
king of Epirus, and appoint him commander in this war."
And this is what happened. (*Exc. de leg. Rom.* 3, p. 68 de
Boor)

8. After the shipwreck, King Pyrrhus of Epirus landed
at Tarentum. The Tarentines then became very distressed
at the behavior of the royal troops who billeted themselves
on them by force and openly insulted their wives and children. Furthermore Pyrrhus closed the Tarentine public   2
halls and banned all their other gatherings and amuse-
ments, on the grounds that they were not conducive to
war: he ordered them to conduct military exercises and
decreed a sentence of death for those who disobeyed. The
Tarentines at the time were completely unfamiliar with
such exercises and orders, and growing weary of them,
abandoned the city as if it did not belong to them and ran
away to the countryside. But they recognized with clarity   3
their own foolishness when the king locked the gates and
put guards over them. (*Exc. de virt.* 6, p. 219 Roos)

9. The Roman soldiers who stayed behind in Rhegium
for the safety and protection of the town, to make sure it
did not suffer at the hands of its enemies, became jealous,
they and their leader, Decius,[13] of the good life enjoyed by

Appian seems to think he was protecting the city against Pyrrhus,
as does Polybius (1.7.6); Dionysius of Halicarnassus (20.4) speci-
fies local Italian enemies.

ἀγαθοῖς τοῖς Ῥηγίνων φθονήσαντες καὶ φυλάξαντες
αὐτοὺς εὐωχουμένους ἐν ἑορτῇ διέφθειραν καὶ ταῖς
2 γυναιξὶν ἀκουσίαις συνῆσαν. πρόφασιν δὲ τῆς παρανομίας ἔφερον, ὅτι Ῥηγῖνοι τὴν φρουρὰν προεδίδο-
σαν Πύρρῳ. καὶ Δέκιος μὲν ἀντὶ φρουράρχου τύραν-
νος ἦν καὶ φιλίαν ἔθετο Μαμερτίνοις, τοῖς ἐπὶ τοῦ
πορθμοῦ τοῦ Σικελικοῦ κατῳκημένοις, οὐ πρὸ πολλοῦ
3 κἀκείνοις ἐς ἰδίους ξένους ὅμοια δεδρακόσιν. ἀλγή-
σαντα δ᾽ αὐτὸν τοὺς ὀφθαλμοὺς καὶ τοῖς ἐν Ῥηγίῳ
ἰατροῖς ἀπιστοῦντα μετάπεμπτος ἀπὸ Μεσσήνης ἐθε-
ράπευε Ῥηγῖνος ἀνήρ, μετῳκηκὼς ἐς Μεσσήνην πρὸ
πολλοῦ, ὅτι Ῥηγῖνος ἦν ἀγνοούμενος. οὗτος αὐτὸν
ἔπεισεν, ἐπὶ ἀπαλλαγῇ συντόμῳ, φαρμάκων ἀνασχέσθαι θερμῶν καὶ χρίσας ἰοῖς κατακαίουσι καὶ δα-
πανῶσιν ἐκέλευσεν ἀνασχέσθαι τοῦ πόνου, μέχρι
αὐτὸς ἐπανέλθοι· καὶ λαθὼν ἔπλευσεν ἐς Μεσσήνην.
ὁ δ᾽ ἐς πολὺ τῆς ὀδύνης ἀνασχόμενος ἀπενίψατο καὶ
4 εὗρε τοὺς ὀφθαλμοὺς δεδαπανημένους. Φαβρίκιος δὲ
ὑπὸ Ῥωμαίων ἐπὶ διορθώσει τῶνδε πεμφθεὶς τήν τε
πόλιν τοῖς ἔτι Ῥηγίνων λοιποῖς ἀπεδίδου καὶ τῶν
φρουρῶν τοὺς αἰτίους τῆς ἀποστάσεως ἐς Ῥώμην
5 ἔπεμψεν· οἱ μαστιγωθέντες ἐν ἀγορᾷ μέσῃ τὰς κε-
φαλὰς ἀπεκόπησαν καὶ ἐξερρίφησαν ἄταφοι. Δέκιος
δὲ φυλασσόμενος ἀμελῶς, οἷα πηρός, ἑαυτὸν διεχρή-
σατο. (Exc. de virt. 7, p. 219 Roos)

---

14 The straits of Messina.   15 According to Dionysius of
Halicarnassus (20.5.2), his name was Dexicrates.

the people of Rhegium; and waiting for a holiday when the citizens were feasting, they murdered the men and raped the women. As an excuse for this crime they claimed that 2 the Rhegians were about to betray the garrison to Pyrrhus. So, instead of a garrison commander, Decius became a tyrant, and made an alliance of friendship with the Mamertines who had settled on the other side of the Sicilian straits,[14] and not long before had behaved in a similar fashion toward their own hosts. When his eyes became 3 sore, distrusting the doctors in Rhegium, Decius sent for someone from Messena to treat him. This man was himself a Rhegian, but had emigrated to Messena so long before that no one knew he was originally from Rhegium.[15] He persuaded Decius that for a quick cure he would have to put up with hot drugs, and having applied burning and corrosive ointments to his eyes, he told him to tolerate the pain until he returned, but then secretly sailed off to Messena. Decius did endure the pain for a long time, but eventually washed the ointment off and discovered that he had been blinded. Fabricius was dis- 4 patched from Rome to put the situation right.[16] He re- stored the city to the remaining Rhegians and sent those responsible for the revolt of the garrison off to Rome, where they were whipped and beheaded in the middle of 5 the Forum, and their bodies thrown out unburied. Be- cause he was blind, Decius was not carefully guarded and he committed suicide. (*Exc. de virt.* 7, p. 219 Roos)

[16] C. Fabricius Luscinus, consul in 282 and 278 and censor in 275, was a man of famously austere lifestyle and one of Rome's heroes in the wars against its Italian enemies, for which he was awarded triumphs in 282 and 278.

10. Ὅτι ὁ Πύρρος, ὁ βασιλεὺς τῆς Ἠπείρου, νικήσας τοὺς Ῥωμαίους καὶ ἀναλαβεῖν χρῄζων τὴν στρατιὰν ἐκ μάχης ἐντόνου καὶ Ῥωμαίους ἐλπίζων ἐς διαλύσεις τότε μάλιστα ἐνδώσειν ἔπεμπεν ἐς Ῥώμην Κινέαν τὸν Θεσσαλόν, δόξαν ἐπὶ λόγοις ἔχοντα μι-
2 μεῖσθαι τὴν Δημοσθένους ἀρετήν. καὶ παρελθὼν ὁ Κινέας ἐς τὸ βουλευτήριον ἄλλα τε πολλὰ περὶ τοῦ βασιλέως ἐσεμνολόγει καὶ τὴν ἐπὶ τῷ ἀγῶνι μετριοπάθειαν κατελογίζετο, μήτ᾽ ἐπὶ τὴν πόλιν εὐθὺς ἐλά-
3 σαντος μήτ᾽ ἐπὶ τὸ ἡσσημένον στρατόπεδον· ἐδίδου δ᾽ αὐτοῖς εἰρήνην καὶ φιλίαν καὶ συμμαχίαν πρὸς Πύρρον, εἰ Ταραντίνους μὲν ἐς ταῦτα συμπεριλάβοιεν, τοὺς δ᾽ ἄλλους Ἕλληνας τοὺς ἐν Ἰταλίᾳ κατοικοῦντας ἐλευθέρους καὶ αὐτονόμους ἐῶεν, Λευκανοῖς δὲ καὶ Σαυνίταις καὶ Δαυνίοις καὶ Βρεττίοις ἀποδοῖεν, ὅσα αὐτῶν ἔχουσι πολέμῳ λαβόντες. καὶ γιγνομένων ἔφη τούτων Πύρρον ἀποδώσειν αὐτοῖς τοὺς αἰχμα-
4 λώτους ἄνευ λύτρων. οἱ δ᾽ ἐνεδοίαζον ἐπὶ πλεῖστον, τῇ τε δόξῃ τοῦ Πύρρου καὶ τῷ συμβεβηκότι πάθει καταπλαγέντες, ἕως Ἄππιος Κλαύδιος ὁ Καῖκος ἐπίκλησιν, ἤδη τετυφλωμένος, ἐς τὸ βουλευτήριον τοῖς παι-
5 σὶν αὐτὸν ἀγαγεῖν κελεύσας, "Ἠχθόμην," εἶπεν, "Ὅτι μὴ βλέπω, νῦν δ᾽, ὅτι ἀκούω. τὰ γὰρ τοιαῦτα ὑμῶν βουλεύματα ἠξίουν μήθ᾽ ὁρᾶν μήτ᾽ ἀκούειν, οἳ δι᾽ ἓν ἀτύχημα ἀθρόως οὕτως ἑαυτῶν ἐκλέλησθε καὶ τὸν τοῦτο δράσαντα αὐτόν τε καὶ τοὺς ἐπαγαγομένους

10. After defeating the Romans in battle,[17] Pyrrhus king of Epirus needed time for his army to recover from the fierce fighting and, expecting that the Romans would be strongly disposed to make a settlement at that moment, sent Cineas the Thessalian to Rome. Cineas had a reputation for eloquence that rivaled the brilliance of Demosthenes. Entering the senate, he solemnly praised the king 2 on many counts, emphasizing his restraint after the battle when he refrained from marching straight on the city or on the camp of the defeated. He offered them peace, 3 friendship, and alliance with Pyrrhus if they included Tarentum in the same agreement, allowed the other Greek inhabitants of Italy to remain free and autonomous, and returned to the Lucanians, Samnites, Daunii and Brutii all the property Rome had taken in war and was now holding. If they did this, he said that Pyrrhus would give back the prisoners without ransom. The senators could not 4 make up their minds for a very long time, overawed both by the reputation of Pyrrhus and the disaster they had suffered, until Appius Claudius, surnamed "the blind," since at this stage in his life he had lost his sight, ordered his sons to bring him into the senate.[18] "I used to be de- 5 pressed," he said, "at not being able to see; now I am depressed that I still have my hearing. For I did not expect either to see or hear you make such plans. After a single reverse, you have suddenly so forgotten yourselves that you are proposing to treat as friends rather than enemies

[17] The battle of Heraclea in 280, the first of Pyrrhus' "Pyrrhic" victories.

[18] Ap. Claudius Caecus was unusual in holding the censorship in 312 before the consulship; he was consul in 307 and 296.

αὐτὸν βουλεύεσθε φίλους ἀντὶ πολεμίων θέσθαι καὶ
τὰ τῶν προγόνων κτήματα Λευκανοῖς καὶ Βρεττίοις
δοῦναι. τί τοῦτ᾽ ἐστὶν ἢ Ῥωμαίους ἐπὶ Μακεδόσι γενέσθαι; καὶ ταῦτά τινες εἰρήνην ἀντὶ δουλείας τολμῶσιν
6 ὀνομάζειν." ἄλλα τε πολλὰ ὅμοια τούτοις ὁ Ἄππιος
εἰπὼν καὶ ἐρεθίσας εἰσηγήσατο Πύρρον, εἰ δέοιτο τῆς
Ῥωμαίων φιλίας καὶ συμμαχίας, ἐξ Ἰταλίας ἀπελθόντα πρεσβεύειν, παρόντα δὲ μήτε φίλον ἡγεῖσθαι
μήτε σύμμαχον μήτε Ῥωμαίοις δικαστὴν ἢ διαιτη-
τήν. καὶ ἡ βουλὴ ταῦθ᾽, ἅπερ καὶ Ἄππιος εἶπεν, ἀπε-
7 κρίνατο Κινέᾳ. Λαιβίνῳ δ᾽ ἄλλα δύο τέλη καταλέγοντες ἐκήρυξαν οὕτως, εἴ τις ἀντὶ τῶν ἀπολωλότων
αὐτὸν ἐπιδίδωσιν, ἐς τὴν στρατιὰν ἀπογράφεσθαι.
8 καὶ ὁ Κινέας ἔτι παρὼν καὶ θεώμενος αὐτοὺς ὠθουμένους ἐς τὰς ἀπογραφὰς λέγεται πρὸς τὸν Πύρρον
ἐπανελθὼν εἰπεῖν, ὅτι πρὸς ὕδραν ἐστὶν αὐτοῖς ὁ
πόλεμος. οἱ δὲ οὐ Κινέαν, ἀλλὰ Πύρρον αὐτὸν εἰπεῖν
τοῦτο τὸ ἔπος, ἰδόντα τὴν στρατιὰν τῶν Ῥωμαίων
πολὺ τῆς προτέρας πλείονα. καὶ γὰρ ὁ ἕτερος ὕπατος
τῷ Λαιβίνῳ Κορογκάνιος ἧκεν ἐκ Τυρρηνίας μεθ᾽ ἧς
9 εἶχε παρασκευῆς. λέγεται δὲ καὶ τἆλλα περὶ τῆς
Ῥώμης πυνθανομένῳ Πύρρῳ Κινέας εἰπεῖν, ὅτι πόλις
ἐστὶ στρατηγῶν ὅλη, καὶ τοῦ Πύρρου θαυμάσαντος
μεταλαβὼν φάναι· "Βασιλέων μᾶλλον ἢ στρατηγῶν."
10 Πύρρος δ᾽, ὡς οὐδὲν εἰρηναῖον οἱ παρὰ τῆς βουλῆς
ἀπήντησεν, ἐπὶ τὴν Ῥώμην ἠπείγετο, πάντα δῃῶν,

both the man who did this to you and those who led him against you, and you are planning to give to the Lucanians and Brutii the heritage of your forefathers. What is this but making Rome subject to Macedon? And some of you even dare to call it peace rather than slavery!" Encouraging them with these and many other similar words, Appius proposed that if Pyrrhus wanted friendship and alliance with the Romans he should withdraw from Italy and send an embassy; but that if he stayed, they should regard him as neither friend nor ally, neither judge nor arbitrator for the Romans. And the senate answered Cineas with the very words that Appius had used. They levied two further legions for Laevinus,[19] making an announcement that anyone volunteering to replace those who had been killed would be enlisted in the army. Cineas was still there and saw the crush of men queuing for registration: when he returned to Pyrrhus he is supposed to have said they were fighting a war against a hydra. Others maintain it was not Cineas who made this statement, but Pyrrhus, when he saw that the Roman army was now even larger than before. The reason for this was that the other consul Coruncanius had come from Etruria with his army to join Laevinus. There is also a story that when Pyrrhus made further inquiries about Rome, Cineas said that it was a city made up entirely of generals; but Pyrrhus expressed surprise and Cineas corrected himself by saying, "Well, of kings, perhaps, rather than generals." When Pyrrhus met with no peaceful overtures from the senate, he pressed on to Rome, destroying everything on the way. But arriving first

[19] P. Valerius Laevinus was consul in 280, along with Tiberius Coruncanius.

καὶ φθάνει μὲν ἐς πόλιν Ἀναγνίαν, βαρεῖαν δ' ἔχων
ἤδη τὴν στρατιὰν ὑπὸ λείας καὶ πλήθους αἰχμαλώτων, ἀναθέμενος μάχην, ἀνέστρεφεν ἐπὶ Κα-
μπανίας, ἡγουμένων τῶν ἐλεφάντων, καὶ τὴν στρατιὰν ἐς χειμασίαν κατὰ πόλεις διῄρει.

11   Ῥωμαίων δὲ πρέσβεις αὐτὸν ἠξίουν λύσασθαι τῇ
πόλει τοὺς αἰχμαλώτους ἢ ἀντιλαβεῖν, ὅσους ἔχουσι
Ταραντίνων καὶ τῶν ἄλλων συμμάχων αὐτοῦ. ὁ δὲ
σπενδομένοις μὲν ἔφη, καθάπερ προεῖπε Κινέας,
χαριεῖσθαι τοὺς αἰχμαλώτους, πολεμοῦσι δ' οὐ δώσειν ἐφ' ἑαυτὸν ἄνδρας τοιούτους καὶ τοσούτους.
12   ἐξένιζε δ' αὐτοὺς βασιλικῶς καὶ τὸν τῆς πρεσβείας
ἡγούμενον Φαβρίκιον πυνθανόμενος ἐν τῇ πόλει μέγα
δύνασθαι καὶ δεινῶς πένεσθαι καθωμίλει, λέγων, εἰ
πράξειεν αὐτῷ τὰς διαλύσεις, ὑποστράτηγον καὶ κοι-
νωνὸν τῶν παρόντων ἀγαθῶν ἀπάξειν ἐς Ἤπειρον·
χρήματά τε αὐτὸν λαβεῖν ἐντεῦθεν ἤδη παρεκάλει,
πρόφασιν ὡς δώσοντα τοῖς τὴν εἰρήνην ἐργασομέ-
13   νοις. ἐπιγελάσας δ' ὁ Φαβρίκιος περὶ μὲν τῶν κοινῶν
οὐδ' ἀπεκρίνατο, "Τὴν δ' ἐμήν," ἔφη, "Παρρησίαν
οὔτε τῶν σῶν φίλων οὐδεὶς οὔτε αὐτὸς οἴσεις σύ, ὦ
βασιλεῦ, καὶ τὴν πενίαν τὴν ἐμαυτοῦ μακαρίζω μᾶλ-
14   λον ἢ τὸν τῶν τυράννων πλοῦτον ὁμοῦ καὶ φόβον." οἱ
δὲ οὐχ οὕτω φασὶν αὐτὸν εἰπεῖν, ἀλλ' ὅτι, "Μου τῆς
φύσεως Ἠπειρῶται <πεῖραν>[1] λαβόντες ἐμὲ σοῦ προ-
15   θήσουσι." ὁποτέρως δ' οὖν ἀπεκρίνατο, θαυμάσας
αὐτὸν τοῦ φρονήματος ὁ Πύρρος ἑτέραν ὁδὸν ἐς τὰς
διαλλαγὰς ἐπενόει καὶ τοὺς αἰχμαλώτους ἐς τῶν Κρο-

at the city of Anagnia with an army weighed down by booty and a large number of prisoners, he postponed battle and turned back to Campania with his elephants in the van. He put his army into winter quarters by dividing them up among the towns.

Roman ambassadors asked Pyrrhus to return the prisoners to the city for a ransom, or to exchange them for the Tarentines and other allies of his they held captive. In reply, he said that if they were willing to come to terms he would, as Cineas had proposed, release the prisoners without penalty; but if they were to continue the war, he would not hand over so many brave men to fight against him. At any rate he entertained them royally. On learning that the leader of the embassy, Fabricius, was very influential at Rome and also extremely poor, Pyrrhus began to befriend him: if he could bring about the agreement for the king, he said he would take him back to Epirus, and make him his second-in-command and joint owner of all he possessed. He invited him to accept money on the spot, supposedly to give to those who had actually negotiated the peace. Fabricius laughed at him and saying nothing about public affairs, answered, "Neither you yourself, my lord, nor any of your courtiers can take away my freedom to say what I like. As for my poverty, I value it more highly than the wealth of tyrants and the fear that goes with it." Others do not believe he said this, but rather, "If the people of Epirus try out my way of doing things, they will prefer me to you." Whichever way he answered, Pyrrhus admired his spirit and began to devise a new means to bring about a settlement. He sent the Roman prisoners home for the

11

12

13

14

15

---

1 πεῖραν add. Roos

νίων τὴν ἑορτὴν ἔπεμπεν ἄνευ φυλάκων, ἐφ᾽ ᾧ, δεχομένης μὲν τῆς πόλεως, ἃ ὁ Πύρρος προτείνει, μένειν
καὶ τῆς αἰχμαλωσίας ἀπολελύσθαι, μὴ δεχομένης δὲ
16 ἑορτάσαντας ἐπανήκειν ἐς αὐτόν. τούτους ἡ βουλὴ
πάνυ παρακαλοῦντας καὶ ἐνάγοντας ἐς τὰς διαλύσεις
ἐκέλευσεν ἑορτάσαντας Πύρρῳ παραδοῦναι σφᾶς αὑτοὺς ἐν ἡμέρᾳ ῥητῇ καὶ θάνατον ἐπέταξε τοῖς ἀπολει-
φθεῖσι τῆς ἡμέρας. οἱ δὲ αὐτὴν ἅπαντες ἐφύλαξαν,
καὶ Πύρρῳ πολεμητέα πάντως αὖθις ἐδόκει. (Exc. de
leg. gent. 3, p. 520 de Boor)

11. Ὅτι τὸν Πύρρον ἤδη μὲν τὰ Ῥωμαίων κατ-
έπλησσεν, ἐτάρασσε δὲ καὶ τὰ ἐν Μολοσσοῖς θο-
ρυβούμενα, Ἀγαθοκλῆς τε, ἄρχων Σικελίας, ἄρτι
ἐτεθνήκει, οὗ θυγατέρα Λάνασσαν ἔχων ὁ Πύρρος ἐν
ταῖς γυναιξὶ τὴν νῆσον ὡς οἰκείαν ἀντὶ τῆς Ἰταλίας
περιεβλέπετο. ὤκνει δ᾽ ὅμως ἔτι τοὺς ἐπικαλέσαντας
2 ἄνευ τινὸς εἰρήνης καταλιπεῖν. ἄσμενος οὖν τῆς προφάσεως τῆς περὶ τὸν αὐτόμολον ἐπιβὰς ἐμαρτύρει
τοῖς ὑπάτοις καὶ Κινέαν ἔπεμπεν ἐς Ῥώμην χάριν
ὁμολογήσοντα τῆς σωτηρίας τοῦ βασιλέως καὶ τοὺς
αἰχμαλώτους ἀμοιβὴν ἄγοντα εἰρήνην τε, ὅπῃ δύ-
3 ναιτο, πράξοντα. δῶρα δ᾽ ὁ Κινέας ἔφερε πολλὰ μὲν
ἀνδράσι, πολλὰ δὲ γυναικῶν, φιλοχρήματον καὶ φι-
λόδωρον εἶναι τὴν πόλιν πυθόμενος καὶ τὰς γυναῖκας

---

[20] Agathocles (361–289), tyrant and then king of Syracuse,
was one of the major figures of Sicilian history. His attempts to

festival of the Saturnalia without guards; they could stay there and win their freedom on condition that Rome accepted Pyrrhus' terms. If she rejected the terms, the prisoners could celebrate the festival, but would have to return to him afterward. Although the prisoners begged and pressed strenuously for the agreement, the senate ordered them to surrender themselves to Pyrrhus after the festival on the appointed day, and set death as a penalty for anyone left behind on that day. Every one of them kept the appointment, and Pyrrhus again decided that he had no option but to fight. (*Exc. de leg. gent.* 3, p. 520 de Boor)

16

11. While Pyrrhus was still worried about Roman affairs, he was also troubled by a disturbance among the Molossians. As Agathocles, the ruler of Sicily, had died recently, Pyrrhus, whose daughter, Lanassa, was one of his wives, began to think of Sicily rather than Italy as his rightful possession.[20] But he was reluctant to abandon those who had invited him without some sort of peace deal. So he was happy to take advantage of the excuse provided by the deserter to acknowledge the consuls, and he sent Cineas to Rome to convey his thanks to them for saving his life, exchange the prisoners, and make peace in whatever way he could manage it.[21] Cineas was told that Romans loved money and gifts, and that their women had long wielded great influence. So he brought with him

2

3

create an empire in Sicily and southern Italy met with periodic, but not lasting, success.   [21] The story as recorded in Plutarch's *Life of Pyrrhus* (21.1–4) tells of how Pyrrhus' private doctor sent to the consuls of 278, Gaius Fabricius Luscinus and Q. Aemilius Papus, an offer to poison Pyrrhus. They rejected it and informed the king, thus saving his life.

APPIAN

4 ἰσχύειν παρὰ Ῥωμαίοις ἐκ παλαιοῦ. οἱ δὲ περὶ μὲν
τῶν δώρων ἐνεκελεύσαντο ἀλλήλοις, καί φασιν οὐδένα λαβεῖν οὐδὲν οὔτε ἄνδρα οὔτε γυναῖκα, ἀπεκρίναντο δ᾽ αὐτῷ, καθὰ καὶ πρότερον, ἀπελθόντα Πύρρον
ἐξ Ἰταλίας πρεσβεύειν πρὸς αὐτοὺς ἄνευ δώρων·
5 ἀπορήσειν γὰρ οὐδενὸς τῶν δικαίων. τοὺς δὲ πρέσβεις καὶ αὐτοὶ πολυτελῶς ἐξένιζον καὶ Πύρρῳ τοὺς
Ταραντίνων καὶ τῶν ἄλλων αὐτοῦ συμμάχων αἰχμα-
6 λώτους ἀντέπεμπον. ὁ μὲν δὴ Πύρρος ἐπὶ τούτοις ἐς
Σικελίαν διέπλει μετά τε τῶν ἐλεφάντων καὶ ὀκτακι-
σχιλίων ⟨πεζῶν καὶ . . .⟩ ἱππέων, ὑποσχόμενος τοῖς
συμμάχοις ἐκ Σικελίας ἐπανήξειν ἐς τὴν Ἰταλίαν. καὶ
ἐπανῆλθεν ἔτει τρίτῳ, Καρχηδονίων αὐτὸν ἐξελασάν-
των ἐκ Σικελίας. (Exc. de leg. gent. 4, p. 523 de Boor)

12. Ὅτι Πύρρος μετὰ τὴν μάχην καὶ τὰς πρὸς
Ῥωμαίους συνθήκας ἐς Σικελίαν διέπλει, ὑποσχόμενος τοῖς συμμάχοις ἐκ Σικελίας ἐπανήξειν ἐς Ἰταλίαν.
καὶ ἐπανῆλθεν ἔτει τρίτῳ, Καρχηδονίων αὐτὸν ἐξελα-
σάντων ἐκ Σικελίας, ἤδη καὶ τοῖς Σικελιώταις βαρὺν
ἐπί τε ξενίαις καὶ χορηγίαις καὶ φρουραῖς καὶ εἰσφο-
2 ραῖς γενόμενον. ὁ μὲν δὴ πλούσιος ἐκ τῶνδε γεγονὼς
ἐς τὸ Ῥήγιον διέπλει ναυσὶ καταφράκτοις δέκα καὶ
ρ᾽, φορτίσι δὲ καὶ ὁλκάσι πολὺ πλείοσιν. οἱ δὲ Καρχηδόνιοι διαναυμαχήσαντες αὐτῷ κατέδυσαν ναῦς ο᾽
3 καὶ τὰς λοιπὰς ἄπλους ἐποίησαν πλὴν ιβ μόνων. αἷς
ὁ Πύρρος διαφυγὼν ἐτίννυτο Λοκροὺς τοὺς Ἐπιζεφυ-
ρίους, ὅτι φρουρὰν αὐτοῦ καὶ τὸν φρούραρχον αὐτῆς,
4 ὑβρίσαντας ἐς αὐτούς, ἀνῃρήκεσαν. ὅμως δ᾽ αὐτοὺς

92

many gifts both for men and women, but they encouraged   4
each other to refuse, and it is said that not a single person,
either man or women, accepted a gift. The Romans repeated the answer they had given him before: if Pyrrhus
would leave Italy and send them an embassy (without
gifts), he would get thoroughly fair treatment. But they too   5
entertained the ambassadors lavishly and sent back to Pyrrhus the prisoners from Tarentum and his other allies.
After this Pyrrhus sailed off to Sicily with his elephants and   6
eight thousand ⟨infantry and . . .⟩ cavalry, promising his
allies he would return to Italy from Sicily. He did indeed
return three years later when the Carthaginians drove him
out of Sicily. (*Exc. de leg. gent.* 4, p. 523 de Boor)

12. After the battle[22] and peace agreement with the
Romans, Pyrrhus sailed off to Sicily, promising his allies
he would return to Italy from Sicily. He did indeed return
three years later when the Carthaginians drove him out of
Sicily, where he had now proved a heavy burden to the
Sicilians because of the billeting, requisitions, garrisons
and taxes he had imposed. Having become rich from these   2
exactions, he sailed off to Rhegium with one hundred and
ten decked ships and many more merchantmen and cargo
ships. But the Carthaginians attacked him at sea and sank
seventy of his ships, disabling all but twelve of the rest.
Escaping with these, Pyrrhus took vengeance on the Epi-   3
zephyrian Locrians for killing his garrison troops and their
commander (they had mistreated the inhabitants). He   4

---

[22] The battle of Ausculum in 279.

καὶ πικρῶς κτείνων τε καὶ συλῶν ὁ Πύρρος οὐδὲ τῶν
ἀναθημάτων τῆς Φερσεφόνης ἀπέσχετο, ἐπισκώψας
τὴν ἄκαιρον εὐσέβειαν εἶναι δεισιδαιμονίαν, τὸ δὲ
5 συλλέξαι πλοῦτον ἄπονον εὐβουλίαν. ἀναχθέντα δ᾽
αὐτὸν μετὰ τῶν σύλων χειμὼν ὑπέλαβε καὶ τῶν νεῶν
τὰς μὲν κατέδυσε καὶ διέφθειρεν αὐτοῖς ἀνδράσι, τὰς
δ᾽ ἐς τὴν γῆν ἐξέρριψε, τὰ δὲ ἱερὰ πάντα σῶα ὁ κλύ-
6 δων ἐς τοὺς Λοκρῶν λιμένας ἐπανήγαγεν, ὥστε καὶ
Πύρρον ὀψὲ τῆς ἀσεβείας αἰσθόμενον ἀναθεῖναί τε
αὐτὰ ἐς τὸ ἱερὸν τῇ Φερσεφόνῃ καὶ θυσίαις ἱλάσκε-
σθαι τὴν θεὸν πολλαῖς. τῶν δὲ ἱερῶν οὐκ ἀπαντώντων
ἔτι μᾶλλον ἐξεμαίνετο καὶ τοὺς περὶ τῆς ἱεροσυλίας
αὐτῷ συμβουλεύσαντας ἢ λέγοντι συνθεμένους ἢ
διακονησαμένους τὸ ἔργον ἔκτεινεν. ὁ μὲν δὴ Πύρρος
οὕτως ἐπεπράχει κακῶς. (Exc. de virt. 8, p. 220 Roos)

killed and plundered with bitter cruelty, not even keeping his hands off the dedications to Persephone: misplaced piety, he joked, was mere superstition, and it made good sense to get rich without work. But a storm overtook him 5 when he put to sea with this plunder: it destroyed and sank some of the ships, along with their crews, and threw others up on the land. But the current brought all the sacred dedications safely back to Locrian harbors, with the result 6 that even Pyrrhus recognized, too late, his impiety and rededicated the offerings in the temple of Persephone, while trying to propitiate the goddess with multiple sacrifices. But the sacrificial victims proved unfavorable and he became even more maddened, killing those who had either advised him about the sacrilege, or had agreed when he suggested it, or had assisted in carrying out the deed. Such is the story of Pyrrhus' misfortune. (*Exc. de virt.* 8, p. 220 Roos)

IV

ΕΚ ΤΗΣ ΚΕΛΤΙΚΗΣ

1. Κελτοὶ Ῥωμαίοις ἐπεχείρησαν πρῶτοι καὶ τὴν
Ῥώμην εἷλον ἄνευ τοῦ Καπιτωλίου καὶ ἐμπεπρήκασι.
Κάμιλλος δὲ αὐτοὺς ἐνίκησε καὶ ἐξήλασε καὶ μετὰ
χρόνον ἐπελθόντας αὖθις ἐνίκησε καὶ ἐθριάμβευσεν
2 ἀπ᾽ αὐτῶν, ὀγδοήκοντα γεγονὼς ἔτη. καὶ τρίτη δὲ
Κελτῶν στρατιὰ ἐμβέβληκεν ἐς τὴν Ἰταλίαν, ἣν καὶ
αὐτὴν οἱ Ῥωμαῖοι διεφθάρκασιν ὑφ᾽ ἡγεμόνι Τίτῳ
Κοϊντίῳ.

3 Μετὰ δὲ ταῦτα Βοιοί, Κελτικὸν ἔθνος θηριωδέστα-
τον, ἐπῆλθεν Ῥωμαίοις, καὶ αὐτοῖς Γάϊος Σουλπίκιος
δικτάτωρ μετὰ στρατιᾶς ἀπήντα, ὅς τις καὶ στρατη-
γήματι τοιούτῳ χρήσασθαι λέγεται· ἐκέλευσε γὰρ
τοὺς ἐπὶ τοῦ μετώπου τεταγμένους ἐξακοντίσαντας
ὁμοῦ συγκαθίσαι τάχιστα, μέχρι βάλωσιν οἱ δεύτε-
ροι καὶ τρίτοι καὶ τέταρτοι· τοὺς δ᾽ ἀφιέντας αἰεὶ
συνίζειν, ἵνα μὴ κατ᾽ αὐτῶν ἐνεχθείη τὰ δόρατα· βα-

---

1 The passages in 1.1–13 are preserved in the *Epitome Celti-corum* of Vaticanus gr 141.

2 Marcus Furius Camillus held office six times as a consular

BOOK IV

FROM THE CELTIC BOOK

1.[1] The Celts initiated hostilities with the Romans, capturing and burning Rome itself, all except the Capitol. Camillus, however, defeated them and drove them off, and defeated them a second time when they later invaded, celebrating a triumph over them at the age of eighty.[2] When a third army of Celts invaded Italy, it too was defeated by the Romans under the leadership of Titus Quinctius.[3]

The Boii, a particularly savage Celtic people, were the next to attack the Romans. The dictator, Gaius Sulpicius,[4] led an army to confront them and is said to have used the following stratagem. He ordered the troops in the front line to throw their spears at the same time, and then immediately crouch down, until the second, third, and fourth ranks had thrown theirs. In each case those who had thrown their spears were to crouch down so that they

tribune. He was also dictator five times, the last time in 367, when he is supposed to have won his triumph over the Gauls.

[3] Titus Quinctius Pennus Capitolinus Crispinus was consul five times between 364 and 351, censor in 366, and dictator in 361, when he defeated the Gauls.

[4] Gaius Sulpicius Peticus was dictator in 358.

λόντων δὲ τῶν ὑστάτων ἀναπηδᾶν ἅπαντας ὁμοῦ καὶ
σὺν βοῇ τάχιστα εἰς χεῖρας ἰέναι· καταπλήξειν γὰρ
ὧδε τοὺς πολεμίους τοσῶνδε δοράτων ἄφεσιν καὶ ἐπ᾽
αὐτῇ ταχεῖαν ἐπιχείρησιν. τὰ δὲ δόρατα ἦν οὐκ ἐοικότα[1] ἀκοντίοις, ἃ Ῥωμαῖοι καλοῦσιν ὑσσούς, ξύλου
τετραγώνου τὸ ἥμισυ καὶ τὸ ἄλλο σιδήρου, τετραγώνου καὶ τοῦδε καὶ μαλακοῦ χωρίς γε τῆς αἰχμῆς. καὶ
οἱ Βοιοὶ οὖν ὑπὸ Ῥωμαίων τότε ἐφθάρησαν πανστρα-
τιᾷ.

4   Ἄλλους δὲ πάλιν Κελτοὺς ἐνίκα Ποπίλλιος, καὶ
μετ᾽ ἐκεῖνον τοὺς αὐτοὺς Κάμιλλος, ὁ τοῦ Καμίλλου
υἱός. ἔστησε δὲ κατὰ Κελτῶν καὶ Παῦλος Αἰμίλιος
τρόπαια.

5   Πρὸ δὲ τῶν τοῦ Μαρίου ὑπατειῶν πλεῖστόν τι καὶ
μαχιμώτατον τῇ τε ἡλικίᾳ μάλιστα φοβερώτατον
χρῆμα Κελτῶν ἐς τὴν Ἰταλίαν τε καὶ Γαλατίαν εἰσ-
έβαλε καί τινας ὑπάτους Ῥωμαίων ἐνίκησε καὶ στρατόπεδα κατέκοψεν· ἐφ᾽ οὓς ὁ Μάριος ἀποσταλεὶς
ἅπαντας διέφθειρε.

6   Τελευταῖα δὲ καὶ μέγιστα τῶν ἐς Γαλάτας Ῥωμαίοις πεπραγμένων ἐστὶ τὰ ὑπὸ Γαΐῳ Καίσαρι
στρατηγοῦντι γενόμενα· μυριάσι τε γὰρ ἀνδρῶν

---

[1] οὐκ ἐοικότα codd; οὐκ ⟨ἀπ⟩εοικότα edd. vett.

---

[5] Editors disagree on whether Appian intended to say that the
spears of the Boii were similar to, or not similar to, the Roman
pila.

[6] The Romans mentioned are Marcus Popillius Laenas (con-

would not be hit by the spears from behind. When the last rank had hurled their weapons they were all to jump up together and with a roar very swiftly engage the enemy in hand-to-hand fighting. The discharge of so many spears like this, followed very quickly by a charge, would terrify the enemy. These spears were not similar[5] to javelins (*pila*, as the Romans call them), but had half the shaft made of squared off wood, the other half of iron, also squared off and pliable, except for the point. So, the entire army of the Boii was destroyed by the Romans on this occasion.

Popillius again defeated other Celts, and after him Camillus, son of Camillus, the same ones. Paulus Aemilius also set up a victory monument over the Celts.[6]   4

Before the consulships of Marius, a very large, warlike and physically frightening force of Celts invaded Italy and Gaul,[7] defeated certain Roman consuls and butchered their armies. Marius was sent against them and destroyed them all.[8]   5

The most recent and greatest of the confrontations between Rome and the Gauls is the campaign under the command of Gaius Caesar.[9] For, in the ten years of his   6

sul 350), Lucius Furius Camillus (consul 349) and Lucius Aemilius Papus (consul 225). The manuscripts incorrectly refer to the last as Paulus, rather than Papus.

[7] The same Greek words, *Galatia* and *Galatai*, cover both Gaul and the Gauls of Europe, and Galatia and the Galatians of Asia Minor.

[8] Gaius Marius, consul six times in a row from 105 to 100, defeated the invading northern tribes at the battles of Aquae Sextiae (102) and Vercellae (101).

[9] The Gallic campaigns of Gaius Julius Caesar took place in the years 58 to 49.

ἀγρίων ἐν τοῖς δέκα ἔτεσιν, ἐν οἷς ἐστρατήγησεν, εἰς χεῖρας ἦλθον, εἴ τις ὑφ᾽ ἓν τὰ μέρη συναγάγοι, τετρακοσίων πλείοσιν καὶ τούτων ἑκατὸν μὲν ἐζώγρησαν, ἑκατὸν δ᾽ ἐν τῷ πόνῳ κατέκανον, ἔθνη δὲ τετρακόσια καὶ πόλεις ὑπὲρ ὀκτακοσίας, τὰ μὲν ἀφιστάμενα σφῶν, τὰ δὲ προσεπιλαμβάνοντες, ἐκρατύναντο.

7   Πρὸ δὲ τοῦ Μαρίου καὶ Φάβιος Μάξιμος ὁ Αἰμιλιανός, ὀλίγην κομιδῇ στρατιὰν ἔχων, ἐπολέμησε τοῖς Κελτοῖς καὶ δώδεκα μυριάδας αὐτῶν ἐν μιᾷ μάχῃ κατέκανε, πεντεκαίδεκα μόνους τῶν ἰδίων ἀποβαλών. καὶ ταῦτα μέντοι ἔπραξε πιεζόμενος ὑπὸ τραύματος ὑπογύου καὶ τὰ τάγματα ἐπιὼν καὶ παραθαρρύνων καὶ διδάσκων, ὅπως τοῖς βαρβάροις πολεμητέον, τὰ μὲν ἐπ᾽ ἀπήνης φερόμενος, τὰ δὲ καὶ βάδην χειραγωγούμενος.

8   Καῖσαρ δὲ πολεμήσας αὐτοῖς πρῶτον μὲν Ἐλουητίους καὶ Τιγυρίους, ἀμφὶ τὰς εἴκοσι μυριάδας ὄντας, ἐνίκησεν. οἱ Τιγύριοι δ᾽ αὐτῶν χρόνῳ ἔμπροσθεν Πίσωνος καὶ Κασσίου τινὰ στρατὸν ἑλόντες ὑπὸ ζυγὸν ἐξεπεπόμφεσαν, ὡς ἐν χρονικαῖς συντάξεσι δοκεῖ Παύλῳ τῷ Κλαυδίῳ. τοὺς μὲν οὖν Τιγυρίους ὑποστράτηγος αὐτοῦ Λαβιηνὸς ἐνίκησε, τοὺς δὲ ἄλλους

9   ὁ Καῖσαρ, καὶ Τρικούρους ἀμύνοντας σφίσιν, ἔπειτα τοὺς μετ᾽ Ἀριοβίστου Γερμανούς, οἳ καὶ τὰ μεγέθη

---

[10] Quintus Fabius Maximus Allobrogicus, son of the famous Scipio Aemilianus, was consul in 121 and campaigned in Gaul.

[11] Lucius Calpurnius Piso Caesoninus was consul in 112 and

command, Roman armies fought against more than four million fierce opponents (if you count them all together), captured a million of them, and killed another million in battle. They subjected four hundred tribes and more than eight hundred towns, some of which had revolted from us, others were new acquisitions.

Even before Marius, Fabius Maximus Aemilianus campaigned against the Celts with a very small army, killing one hundred and twenty thousand of them in a single battle and losing only fifteen of his own men.[10] He managed this even though he was suffering from a recent wound. He went up and down the lines encouraging them and instructing them how they should fight the barbarians, riding in a chariot some of the time and walking with assistance the rest.

Caesar opened his campaigns with a victory over some two hundred thousand of the Helvetii and Tigurini. At an earlier date the Tigurini had captured an army of Piso and Cassius, and had made them walk under the yoke,[11] as Paulus Claudius believes in his annals.[12] Caesar's legate, Labienus,[13] defeated these Tigurini, while Caesar himself defeated the others, who were assisted by the Tricorii, and then the Germans under Ariovistus. In terms of their size,

served as legate for the consul of 107, Lucius Cassius Longinus; they were both killed in battle against the Tigurini.

[12] Some scholars have identified Paulus Clodius (*FRH* 16 F2) with Q. Claudius Quadrigarius, the first-century BC Roman annalist, but it remains unclear who Appian, or his epitomator, had in mind.

[13] Titus Labienus was Tribune of the People in 63. In 49 he abandoned Caesar and went over to Pompey's side; he died in 45.

μείζους τῶν μεγίστων ὑπῆρχον καὶ τὸ ἦθος ἄγριοι
καὶ τὴν τόλμαν θρασύτατοι καὶ θανάτου καταφρονη-
ταὶ δι' ἐλπίδα ἀναβιώσεως, καὶ κρύος ὁμοίως ἔφερον
θάλπει καὶ πόᾳ ἐχρῶντο παρὰ τὰς ἀπορίας τροφῇ,
καὶ ὁ ἵππος ξύλοις. ἦσαν δέ, ὡς ἔοικεν, οὐ φερέπονοι
ἐν ταῖς μάχαις οὐδὲ λογισμῷ ἢ καὶ ἐπιστήμῃ τινί,
ἀλλὰ θυμῷ χρώμενοι καθάπερ θηρία· διὸ καὶ ὑπὸ τῆς
Ῥωμαίων ἐπιστήμης καὶ φερεπονίας ἡσσῶντο. οἱ μὲν
γὰρ μετὰ ὁρμῆς βαρυτάτης ἐπεπήδων αὐτοῖς καὶ
ὅλην ὁμοῦ τὴν φάλαγγα ἀνεώθουν, Ῥωμαῖοι δ' ὑπέμενον ἐν τάξει καὶ κατεστρατήγουν αὐτοὺς καὶ ὀκτα-
κισμυρίους αὐτῶν τελευτῶντες ἀπέκτειναν.

10 Μετὰ τούτους ὁ Καῖσαρ τοῖς καλουμένοις Βέλγαις
ἐπιπεσών, ποταμόν τινα περῶσι, τοσούτους ἀπέκτεινεν ὡς τὸν ποταμὸν γεφυρωθέντα τοῖς σώμασι περᾶ-
11 σαι. Νέρβιοι δὲ αὐτὸν ἐτρέψαντο, ἄρτι στρατόπεδον
ἐξ ὁδοιπορίας κατασκευάζοντι αἰφνιδίως ἐπιπεσόντες,
καὶ παμπόλλους ἐφόνευσαν, τοὺς δὲ ταξιάρχους καὶ
λοχαγοὺς ἅπαντας· καὶ αὐτὸν ἐκεῖνον εἰς λόφον τινὰ
μετὰ τῶν ὑπασπιστῶν πεφευγότα περιέσχον κύκλῳ,
ὑπὸ δὲ τοῦ δεκάτου τάγματος αὐτοῖς ἐξόπισθεν ἐπι-
πεσόντος ἐφθάρησαν, ἑξακισμύριοι ὄντες. ἦσαν δὲ
τῶν Κίμβρων καὶ Τευτόνων ἀπόγονοι. ἐκράτησε καὶ
12 Ἀλλοβρίγων ὁ Καῖσαρ. Οὐσιπετῶν δὲ καὶ Ταγχαρέων
τεσσαράκοντα μυριάδες, στρατεύσιμοί τε καὶ ἀστρά-
τευτοι, συνεκόπησαν. Σούκαμβροι δὲ πεντακοσίοις
ἱππεῦσι τοὺς πεντακισχιλίους ἱππεῖς τοῦ Καίσαρος

the Germans were huge, larger than the largest of men, and in character fierce and exceptionally brave and audacious. They disdained death, as they believed in an afterlife, they were equally tolerant of heat and cold, and when food was short they ate grass, while their horses ate trees. It appears, however, that they lacked endurance in battle and fought with fury, like wild animals, but without calculation or any technical skill. This is why they were overwhelmed by Roman skill and endurance. For although the Germans launched a violent charge against them and pushed back the whole line together, the Romans held their ranks, counterattacked and ended up killing eighty thousand of them.

After them, Caesar attacked the so-called Belgae as 10 they were in the process of crossing a river, and killed so many of them that he crossed the river on a bridge of their bodies. The Nervii, however, routed him by attacking un- 11 expectedly as he was making camp just after a march. They killed a large number, including all the tribunes and centurions, and surrounded Caesar himself on a hill where he had taken refuge with his bodyguard. But they were attacked in the rear by the tenth legion and destroyed, although they numbered sixty thousand men. The Nervii were descendants of the Cimbri and Teutones. Caesar also conquered the Allobroges, and cut to pieces four hundred 12 thousand of the Usipites and Tencteri, both soldiers and civilians. The Sigambri, however, with their five hundred cavalry, unexpectedly attacked Caesar's five thousand cav-

ἔτρεψαν, ἐξαίφνης ἐπιπεσόντες, καὶ δίκην ἔδοσαν ἡττηθέντες μετὰ ταῦτα.

13   Ἐπέρασε καὶ τὸν Ῥῆνον πρῶτος Ῥωμαίων ὁ Καῖσαρ καὶ ἐς τὴν Βρεττανίδα νῆσον, ἠπείρου τε μείζονα οὖσαν μεγίστης καὶ τοῖς τῇδε ἀνθρώποις ἄγνωστον ἔτι. ἐπέρασε δὲ κατὰ τὸν καιρὸν τῆς ἀμπώτεως· ἄρτι γὰρ τὸ πάθος ἥπτετο τῆς θαλάσσης, καὶ ὁ στόλος ἐσαλεύετο, ἠρέμα πρῶτον, εἶτα ὀξύτερον, μέχρι σὺν βιαίῳ τάχει διέπλευσεν ὁ Καῖσαρ ἐς τὴν Βρεττανίαν.

2. Ὅτι Ὀλυμπιάδων τοῖς Ἕλλησιν ζ΄ καὶ Ϙ΄ γεγενημένων, τῆς γῆς τῶν Κελτῶν οὐκ ἀρκούσης αὐτοῖς διὰ τὸ πλῆθος, ἀνίσταται μοῖρα Κελτῶν τῶν ἀμφὶ τὸν Ῥῆνον ἱκανὴ κατὰ ζήτησιν ἑτέρας γῆς· οἳ τό τε Ἄλπειον ὄρος ὑπερέβησαν καὶ Κλουσίνοις εὐδαίμονα

2   γῆν ἔχουσι Τυρρηνῶν ἐπολέμουν. οὐ πάλαι δὲ οἱ Κλουσῖνοι Ῥωμαίοις ἔνσπονδοι γεγονότες ἐπ᾽ αὐτοὺς κατέφυγον. καὶ οἱ Ῥωμαῖοι πρέσβεις συνέπεμψαν αὐτοῖς Φαβίους τρεῖς, οἳ τοῖς Κελτοῖς ἔμελλον προαγορεύσειν ἀνίστασθαι τῆς γῆς, ὡς Ῥωμαίων φίλης,

3   καὶ ἀπειλήσειν ἀπειθοῦσιν. ἀποκριναμένων δὲ τῶν Κελτῶν, ὅτι ἀνθρώπων οὐδένα δεδίασιν οὔτε ἀπειλοῦντα σφίσιν οὔτε πολεμοῦντα, χρήζοντες δὲ γῆς οὔπω τὰ Ῥωμαίων πολυπραγμονοῦσιν, οἱ πρέσβεις οἱ Φάβιοι τοὺς Κλουσίνους ἐνῆγον ἐπιθέσθαι τοῖς Κελ-

4   τοῖς, τὴν χώραν λεηλατοῦσιν ἀπερισκέπτως. καὶ συνεκδημοῦντες αὐτοῖς ἀναιροῦσι τῶν Κελτῶν πολὺ πλῆθος ἐν προνομῇ· καὶ τὸν ἡγούμενον ἐκείνου τοῦ μέρους αὐτὸς ὁ Ῥωμαίων πρεσβευτὴς Κόιντος Φάβιος ἀνεῖλέ

alry and put them to flight, but they paid the penalty when defeated at a later date.

Caesar was the first Roman to cross the Rhine and the first to reach Britain, an island bigger than the largest continent and still unkown to the people of that region.[14] He made the crossing by using the ebb tide. For as soon as it began to take effect on the sea, the fleet was carried along, gently at first, then more rapidly, until eventually Caesar sailed across to Britain with headlong speed.

2. In the 97th Olympiad of the Greek calendar,[15] a large section of the Celtic people who lived by the river Rhine sets off in search of new land as their own territory was not sufficient for them because of the size of their population. They crossed the Alps and made war on the people of Clusium who possessed fertile land in Etruria. Not long before, the Clusians had made a treaty with the Romans and now took refuge with them. Rome sent three members of the Fabian family with the Clusians as ambassadors to order the Celts publicly to withdraw from the land, as it belonged to friends of Rome; they were to threaten them if they disobeyed. The Celts replied that whether under threat or actual attack they feared no man; they needed land and so far were not interfering with the interests of Rome. The Fabian ambassadors, having urged the Clusians to attack the Celts while they were plundering the land without due caution, joined the expedition and killed a large number of the Celts out foraging. Indeed the ambassador Quintus Fabius himself killed the leader

[14] As Appian is dealing with the Gallic wars, he presumably means the people of Gaul.

[15] 392 to 388 BC.

APPIAN

τε καὶ ἐσκύλευε καὶ τὰ ὅπλα φορῶν ἐπανῆλθεν ἐς
Κλούσιον. (Exc. de leg. Rom. 4, p. 70 de Boor)

3. Ὅτι ὁ τῶν Κελτῶν βασιλεὺς Βρέννος, τῶν Φα-
βίων τῶν Ῥωμαίων πολλοὺς ἀνελόντων Κελτῶν, μὴ
δεξάμενος τοὺς Ῥωμαίων πρέσβεις, ἐπὶ τούτοις
πρέσβεις ἐπιλεξάμενος ἐς κατάπληξιν, οἳ Κελτῶν
ἁπάντων μεγάλων τὰ σώματα ὄντων ὑπερέβαλλον,
ἐξέπεμπεν ἐς Ῥώμην, αἰτιώμενος τοὺς Φαβίους, ὅτι
πρεσβεύοντες παρὰ τοὺς κοινοὺς νόμους ἐπολέμησαν,
ᾔτει τε τοὺς ἄνδρας ἐς δίκην ἐκδότους οἱ γενέσθαι, εἰ
2 μὴ θέλουσι Ῥωμαῖοι κοινὸν αὐτῶν εἶναι τὸ ἔργον. οἱ
δὲ Ῥωμαῖοι συνεγίνωσκον μὲν τοὺς Φαβίους ἁμαρτεῖν, αἰδοῖ δὲ οἴκου διαφέροντος χρήματα τοὺς Κελ-
3 τοὺς πράξασθαι παρὰ σφῶν παρεκάλουν. οὐ πειθο-
μένων δὲ χειροτονοῦσι τοὺς Φαβίους ἐπὶ τὴν ἐτήσιον
ἀρχὴν χιλιάρχους καὶ τοῖς πρεσβεύουσι τῶν Κελτῶν
ἔφασαν οὐ δύνασθαι νῦν οὐδὲν ἐς τοὺς Φαβίους ἄρχοντας ἤδη, τοῦ δὲ ἐπιόντος ἔτους ἥκειν αὐτούς, ἂν
4 ἔτι μηνίωσιν, ἐκέλευον. Βρέννος δὲ καὶ ὅσοι Κελτῶν
ἦσαν ὑπ᾽ ἐκείνῳ, νομίσαντες ὑβρίσθαι καὶ χαλεπῶς
ἐνεγκόντες, ἐς τοὺς ἄλλους Κελτοὺς περιέπεμπον, ἀξι-
οῦντες αὐτοὺς συνεφάψασθαι τοῦδε τοῦ πολέμου. καὶ
πολλῶν ἀφικομένων ἄραντες ἤλαυνον ἐπὶ τὴν Ῥώμην.
(Exc. de leg. gent. 5, p. 523 de Boor)

of that detachment, stripped his body and returned to Clusium carrying his weapons.[16] (*Exc. de leg. Rom.* 4, p. 70 de Boor)

3. As the Fabii, that is Romans, had killed many Celts, Brennus, king of the Celts, refused to receive the Roman ambassadors. Then, to cause consternation, he picked as his own ambassadors men who were even bigger than usual—and Celts are all large men—and sent them off to Rome to accuse the Fabii of waging war while serving on an embassy, in contravention of international law. He demanded that the men be surrendered to him for punishment, if the Romans did not want to be accessories to the crime. The Romans acknowledged that the Fabii were in the wrong, but asked the Celts to accept a monetary settlement from them out of respect for such a distinguished family. As the request was refused, the Romans appointed the Fabii to the annual office of military tribune[17] and told the Celtic ambassadors that no action was now possible against the Fabii as they were already magistrates; but they should come back next year, if they were still angry. Brennus and the Celts under his leadership took this badly, regarding it as an insult, and sent round to the other Celts inviting them to join him in this war. When many had come, they set out and marched on Rome. (*Exc. de leg. gent.* 5, p. 523 de Boor)

[16] The role of Quintus Fabius Ambustus and his two brothers in aggravating the Gauls and thus bringing about the Gallic sack of Rome in 390 is probably a patriotic fiction.

[17] The three Fabii were appointed military tribunes with consular power in 390.

4. Ὁ δὲ ὑφίσταται γράμματα διοίσειν διὰ τῶν ἐχθρῶν ἐς τὸ Καπιτώλιον. (*Suda,* υ 736)

5. Ὅτι ὁ Καιδίκιος γράμμα φέρων ἀπὸ τῆς βουλῆς περὶ τῆς ὑπάτου ἀρχῆς παρεκάλει τὸν Κάμιλλον μη-
2 δὲν ἐν τῷ παρόντι μηνῦσαι τῇ πατρίδι τῆς ζημίας. ὁ δὲ ἐπισχὼν αὐτὸν ἔτι λέγοντα εἶπεν· "Οὐκ ἂν εὐξάμην ἐπιποθῆσαί με Ῥωμαίους, εἰ τοιαύτην ἤλπισα τὴν ἐπιπόθησιν αὐτοῖς ἔσεσθαι. νῦν δὲ δικαιοτέραν εὐχὴν εὔχομαι, γενέσθαι τῇ πατρίδι χρήσιμος ἐς τοσοῦτον ἀγαθοῦ, ἐς ὅσον κακοῦ περιελήλυθεν." (*Exc. de virt.* 9, p. 221 Roos)

6. Ὅτι Κελτοὶ μηδεμιᾷ μηχανῇ δυνηθέντες ἐπι-βῆναι τῆς ἀκροπόλεως ἠρέμουν ὡς λιμῷ τοὺς ἔνδον παραστησόμενοι. καί τις ἀπὸ τοῦ Καπιτωλίου κατ-έβαινεν ἱερεύς, ὄνομα Δόρσων, ἐπὶ ἐτήσιον δή τινα ἱερουργίαν ἐς τὸν τῆς Ἑστίας νεὼν στέλλων τὰ ἱερὰ
2 διὰ τῶν πολεμίων εὐσταθῶς· τὸν δὲ νεὼν ἐμπεπρη-σμένον ἰδὼν ἔθυσεν ἐπὶ τοῦ συνήθους τόπου καὶ ἐπανῆλθεν αὖθις διὰ τῶν πολεμίων αἰδεσθέντων ἢ καταπλαγέντων αὐτοῦ τὴν τόλμαν ἢ τὴν εὐσέβειαν ἢ
3 τὴν ὄψιν ἱερὰν οὖσαν. ὁ μὲν δὴ κινδυνεύειν ὑπὲρ τῶν ἱερῶν ἑλόμενος ὑπ' αὐτῶν ἐσώζετο τῶν ἱερῶν. καὶ τόδε φησὶν ὧδε γενέσθαι Κάσσιος[2] ὁ Ῥωμαῖος. (*Exc. de virt.* 10, p. 221 Roos)

[2] Καύσιος P; Κάσσιος edd.

---

[18] The story of Pontius Cominius floating down the Tiber to

4. He promised to carry a letter through the enemy lines to the Capitol.[18] (*Suda*, *v* 736)

5. When Caedicius brought the letter from the senate concerning the office of consul, he urged him in view of the present circumstances not to be angry with his countrymen for the punishment they had imposed on him. Camillus interrupted him and said, "I would not have prayed for Rome to need me, if I thought her need would be this great. So now I pray a more righteous prayer, that I may serve my country sufficiently well to match the disaster she has suffered." (*Exc. de virt.* 9, p. 221 Roos)

6. When the Celts could find no way to get up onto the Capitol, they took no further action, intending to starve the defenders into submission. A priest called Dorson[19] came down from the Capitol to conduct some annual religious service in the temple of Vesta, steadfastly carrying the sacred objects through the enemy ranks. Finding that the temple had been burned down, he sacrificed at the customary place and made his way back up through the enemy, who let him pass either out of respect for, or astonishment at, his courage, piety, and holy appearance. Having chosen to put himself at risk to carry out his sacred duty, he was saved by that same sacred duty. The Roman writer Cassius reports that this is how it happened.[20] (*Exc. de virt.* 10, p. 221 Roos)

bring a message to the Capitol concerning the recall of Camillus is recorded in Livy 5.46 and Plutarch, *Cam.* 25.

[19] Gaius Fabius Dorsuo appears in Livy's story (5.46).

[20] The manuscript of this excerpt gives the name of the Roman author as Kausios, which is usually emended to Kassios and thought to refer to the second-century BC historian L. Cassius Hemina, one of the earliest to write in Latin.

7. Ὅτι τοῦ οἴνου καὶ τῶν ἄλλων ἄδην ἐνεπίμπλαντο οἱ Κελτοί, τήν τε φύσιν ὄντες ἀκρατεῖς καὶ χώραν ἔχοντες, ὅτι μὴ πρὸς δημητριακοὺς καρπούς, τῶν ἄλλων ἄγονον καὶ ἀφυᾶ. τά τε σώματα αὐτοῖς, μεγάλα ὄντα καὶ τρυφηλὰ καὶ σαρκῶν ὑγρῶν μεστά, ὑπὸ τῆς ἀδηφαγίας καὶ μέθης ἐς ὄγκον καὶ βάρος ἐξεχεῖτο καὶ πρὸς δρόμους καὶ πόνους ἀδύνατα πάμπαν ἐγίγνετο, ὑπό τε ἱδρῶτος καὶ ἄσθματος, ὅπου τι δέοι κάμνειν, ἐξελύοντο ταχέως. (Exc. de virt. 11, p. 222 Roos; Suda, α 463)

8. Ἀππιανὸς περὶ τῶν Κελτῶν φησιν· οὓς γυμνοὺς ἐπεδείκνυε Ῥωμαίοις· "Οὗτοί εἰσιν οἱ τὴν βοὴν τὴν βαρεῖαν ἱέντες ὑμῖν ἐν ταῖς μάχαις καὶ τὰ ὅπλα παταγοῦντες καὶ ξίφη μακρὰ καὶ κόμας αἰωροῦντες, ὧν τὸ ἄτολμον ὁρῶντες καὶ τὸ σῶμα μαλακὸν καὶ ἄτονον πρόσιτε τῷ ἔργῳ." (Suda, ι 152)

9. Τὸν δὲ δῆμον ἀπὸ τοῦ τείχους ὁρᾶν καὶ τοῖς πονουμένοις ἑτέρους νεαλεῖς ἐπιπέμπειν ἀεί. οἱ δὲ Κελτοὶ κεκμηκότες ἀκμῆσι συμπλεκόμενοι ἔφευγον ἀτάκτως. (Suda, ν 104)

10. Ὁ δὲ Κελτὸς ἀγανακτῶν καὶ λιφαιμῶν ἐδίωκε τὸν Βαλέριον, συγκαταπεσεῖν ἐπειγόμενος· ὑπὸ δὲ τοὺς πόδας ἀναχωροῦντος ἀεὶ τοῦ Βαλερίου κατέπεσε πρηνὴς ὁ Κελτός. καὶ δεύτερον τοῦτο μονομάχιον ἐπὶ Κελτοῖς ἐμεγαλαύχουν οἱ Ῥωμαῖοι. (Suda, λ 627)

---

21 Marcus Furius Camillus.

22 This seems to refer to the Gallic invasion of Rome in 361 (App. Celt. 1.2); Livy (7.11) talks of a battle outside the Colline

7. The Celts lived on land that could only produce grains, and was unsuited to, and unproductive of anything else and, by nature lacking self-control, they used to take their fill of wine and other things. Their bodies were big, soft and flabby, and overindulgence in wine and food made them fat and heavy, and entirely incapable of running or hard work: whenever they needed to exert themselves at all, they poured sweat, ran out of breath and quickly became exhausted. (*Exc. de virt.* 11, p. 222 Roos; *Suda* α 463)

8. Appian says the following about the Celts. He[21] showed them naked to the Romans and said: "these are the men who let out their great roar against you in battle, who beat their shields, swing their long swords and shake their hair. Now that you see how timid they are, how soft and unfit their bodies, apply yourselves to the task." (*Suda*, ι 152)

9. The people looked out from the walls, and constantly sent in fresh replacements for those who were tiring. And the Celts, exhausted troops engaging with fresh ones, fled in disorder.[22] (*Suda*, ν 104)

10. The Celt was furious and bleeding to death, but chased Valerius, determined to die with him in battle. But Valerius kept on retiring in front of him and the Celt fell flat on his face. And the Romans bragged about this second single combat against the Celts.[23] (*Suda*, λ 627)

Gate in which the Romans fought in full view of their parents, wives, and children.

[23] This comes from the campaign of Lucius Furius Camillus in 349, in which Marcus Valerius, a young military tribune, defeated a Gaul in single combat, matching the earlier achievement of the famous Titus Manlius Torquatus; see, among other sources, Livy 7.26.

11. Ὅτι τὸ τῶν Σενόνων ἔθνος ἔνσπονδον ἦν Ῥωμαίοις, καὶ ἐμισθοφόρουν κατὰ Ῥωμαίων. ἡ δὲ βουλὴ
πρέσβεις ἔπεμψεν ἐγκαλέσοντας, ὅτι ὄντες ἔνσπονδοι
2 μισθοφοροῦσι κατὰ Ῥωμαίων. τούτους Βριτόμαρις ὁ
Κελτὸς ἀγανακτῶν ὑπὲρ τοῦ πατρός, ὅτι συμμαχῶν
Τυρρηνοῖς ὑπὸ Ῥωμαίων ἐν τῷδε τῷ πολέμῳ δι-
έφθαρτο, τά τε κηρύκεια φέροντας καὶ τὴν ἄσυλον
ἐσθῆτα περικειμένους κατέτεμεν ἐς πολλὰ καὶ τὰ
3 μέρη τῶν σωμάτων διέρριψεν ἐς τὰ πεδία. καὶ τοῦ
μύσους ὁ Κορνήλιος ἐν ὁδῷ πυθόμενος, ἐς τὰς
Σενόνων πόλεις συντόνῳ σπουδῇ διὰ Σαβίνων καὶ
Πικεντίνων ἐσβαλών, ἅπαντα καθῄρει καὶ ἐνεπίμπρη
τῶν τε ἀνθρώπων τὰς μὲν γυναῖκας καὶ τὰ παιδία
ἠνδραποδίζετο, τοὺς δ' ἐν ἥβῃ πάντας ἔκτεινεν
ὁμαλῶς καὶ τὴν χώραν ἐλυμαίνετο ποικίλως καὶ ἄοι-
κον ἐς τὸ λοιπὸν ἐποίει· Βριτόμαριν δὲ μόνον ἦγεν
4 αἰχμάλωτον ἐπὶ λύμῃ. ὕστερον δὲ Σένονες, οὐκ ἔχοντες οὐκέτι πατρίδας, ἐς ἃς διαφύγωσιν, συνέπεσον εἰς
χεῖρας ὑπὸ τόλμης τῷ Δομετίῳ καὶ ἡττώμενοι σφᾶς
αὐτοὺς ὑπὸ ὀργῆς διεχρῶντο μανικῶς. καὶ δίκη μὲν
ἤδη παρανομίας ἐς πρέσβεις ἐγένετο Σένοσιν. (Exc.
de leg. Rom. 5, p. 70 de Boor)

12. Ὅτι οἱ Σαλύων ⟨δυνάσται⟩,[3] τοῦ ἔθνους ἡττη-
θέντος ὑπὸ Ῥωμαίων, ἐς Ἀλλόβριγας κατέφυγον. καὶ
αὐτοὺς ἐξαιτοῦντες οἱ Ῥωμαῖοι στρατεύουσιν ἐπὶ τοὺς
Ἀλλόβριγας οὐκ ἐκδιδόντας, ἡγουμένου σφῶν Γναίου

---

[3] δυνάσται add. Schweig.

11. While still under treaty with the Romans, the Senonan people were hiring themselves out as mercenaries against Rome. The senate sent an embassy to complain that in spite of being under treaty, the Senones were hiring themselves out as mercenaries against Rome. Britomaris 2 the Celt was angry that his father, an ally of the Etruscans, had been killed by the Romans in this very war, and cut up the senatorial ambassadors into small pieces, even though they were carrying the herald's staff and wearing the sacrosanct robes; he scattered their body parts in the fields. Cornelius[24] learned of this vile act on the road, and 3 advancing with extreme speed against the towns of the Senones through Sabine territory and Picenum, he destroyed and burned everything. Of their people, he enslaved the women and children, killed all the adult males indiscriminately, and thoroughly laid waste to the land and made it uninhabitable for the future. Britomaris was the only one he took prisoner so he could torture him. Later, 4 no longer having a homeland to offer them refuge, the Senones bravely engaged Domitius, but were defeated and committed suicide in a frenzy of anger. Such was the punishment suffered by the Senones for their crime against the ambassadors. (*Exc. de leg. Rom.* 5, p. 70 de Boor)

12. When their people had been defeated by the Romans, the leaders of the Salyi fled for refuge to the Allobroges. The Romans demanded they be handed over, but since the Allobroges refused, they took to the field against

[24] P. Cornelius Dolabella, consul with Gnaeus Domitius in 283.

2 Δομετίου. ᾧ παροδεύοντι τὴν τῶν Σαλύων ἐντυγχάνει
πρεσβευτὴς Βιτοίτου βασιλέως τῶν Ἀλλοβρίγων,
ἐσκευασμένος τε πολυτελῶς, καὶ δορυφόροι παρεί-
ποντο αὐτῷ κεκοσμημένοι καὶ κύνες· δορυφοροῦνται
3 γὰρ δὴ καὶ πρὸς κυνῶν οἱ τῇδε βάρβαροι. μουσικός
τε ἀνὴρ εἵπετο, βαρβάρῳ μουσικῇ τὸν βασιλέα Βι-
τοῖτον, εἶτ᾽ Ἀλλόβριγας, εἶτα τὸν πρεσβευτὴν αὐτὸν
ἔς τε γένος καὶ ἀνδρείαν καὶ περιουσίαν ὑμνῶν· οὗ δὴ
καὶ μάλιστα ἕνεκα αὐτοὺς οἱ τῶν πρεσβευτῶν ἐπιφανεῖς ἐπάγονται. ἀλλ᾽ ὃ μὲν συγγνώμην αἰτῶν τοῖς
Σαλύων δυνάσταις ἀπέτυχεν. (Exc. de leg. gent. 6,
p. 524 de Boor)

13. Ὅτι τῶν Τευτόνων μοῖρα ληστεύουσα πολύαν-
δρος ἐς τὴν γῆν τῶν Νωρικῶν ἐσέβαλεν, καὶ ὁ Ῥωμαίων ὕπατος Παπίριος Κάρβων δείσας, μὴ ἐς τὴν
Ἰταλίαν ἐσβάλοιεν, ἐφήδρευε τοῖς Ἀλπείοις, ᾗ μάλι-
2 στά ἐστιν ἡ διάβασις στενωτάτη. οὐκ ἐπιχειρούντων
δὲ ἐκείνων αὐτὸς ἐπέβαινεν αὐτοῖς αἰτιώμενος ἐς Νω-
ρικοὺς ἐσβαλεῖν Ῥωμαίων ξένους ὄντας. ἐποιοῦντο δ᾽
οἱ Ῥωμαῖοι ξένους, οἷς ἐδίδοσαν μὲν εἶναι φίλοις,
3 ἀνάγκη δ᾽ οὐκ ἐπῆν ὡς φίλοις ἐπαμύνειν. οἱ μὲν δὴ
Τεύτονες πλησιάζοντι τῷ Κάρβωνι προσέπεμπον
ἀγνοῆσαί τε τὴν ἐς Ῥωμαίους Νωρικῶν ξενίαν καὶ
αὐτῶν ἐς τὸ μέλλον ἀφέξεσθαι· ὁ δ᾽ ἐπαινέσας τοὺς
πρέσβεις καὶ δοὺς αὐτοῖς ὁδῶν ἡγεμόνας κρύφα τοῖς

---

25 Gnaeus Domitius Ahenobarbus was consul in 122 and defeated the Allobroges and Arverni in 121.

them under the command of Gnaeus Domitius.[25] He was passing through Salyan territory when an ambassador of Bituitus, king of the Allobroges, had a meeting with him.[26] The ambassador was expensively robed and attended by bodyguards in elaborate dress, and by dogs: for the barbarians of this region also use dogs as guards. A musician was in attendance too, celebrating in foreign strain the ancestry, courage, and wealth of king Bituitus, of the Allobroges, and of the ambassador himself. Indeed, it is particularly for this purpose that distinguished ambassadors bring musicians with them. This one, however, failed in his appeal to win pardon for the leaders of the Salyi. (*Exc. de leg. gent.* 6, p. 524 de Boor)

13. A large force of the Teutones made an incursion into the territory of Noricum to plunder it, and the Roman consul Papirius Carbo was afraid they would invade Italy.[27] So he occupied the narrowest point of the route across the Alps. When the Teutones made no attack, Carbo marched against them himself, blaming them for their assault on the people of Noricum, who were guest-friends of Rome. The Romans used to make people guest-friends whom they allowed to be friendly, but whom they felt no compulsion to defend as friends. When Carbo approached, the Teutones sent a deputation to him saying that they had been unaware of Noricum's relationship with Rome and would keep their hands off it in future. Carbo praised the envoys and gave them guides for their journey,

[26] Bituitus was king of the Arverni, not the Allobroges. Domitius captured him by treachery (Val. Max. 9.6.3) and led him in his triumph at Rome (Flor. 1.37).

[27] Gaius Papirius Carbo was consul in 113.

ἡγουμένοις ἐνετείλατο μακροτέραν αὐτοὺς περιάγειν,
τῇ βραχυτέρᾳ δὲ αὐτὸς διαδραμών, ἀδοκήτως ἀνα-
παυομένοις ἔτι τοῖς Τεύτοσιν ἐμπεσών, ἔδωκε δίκην
4 ἀπιστίας πολλοὺς ἀποβαλών. τάχα δ᾽ ἂν καὶ πάντας
ἀπώλεσεν, εἰ μὴ ζόφος καὶ ὄμβρος καὶ βρονταὶ βα-
ρεῖαι τῆς μάχης ἔτι συνεστώσης ἐπιπεσοῦσαι διέστησαν αὐτοὺς ἀπ᾽ ἀλλήλων καὶ ὁ ἀγὼν ὑπὸ τῆς ἄνωθεν
ἐκπλήξεως διελύθη. σποράδες δὲ καὶ ὡς ἐς ὕλας οἱ
Ῥωμαῖοι διαφυγόντες τρίτῃ μόλις ἡμέρᾳ συνῆλθον.
καὶ Τεύτονες ἐς Γαλάτας ἐχώρουν. (Exc. de leg. gent. 7,
p. 524 de Boor)

14. Ὁ δὲ τοῖς σώμασι τῶν Κίμβρων ἀψαυστεῖν
ἐκέλευεν, ἕως ἡμέρα γένηται, πολύχρυσα εἶναι δοκῶν.
(Suda, α 4725, κ 1615)

15. Ὅτι ἔθνη δύο Τιγύριοι καὶ Ἑλουήτιοι ἐς τὴν
Ῥωμαίων Κελτικὴν ἐσέβαλον, καὶ τούτων τὸν στόλον
ὁ Καῖσαρ Γάϊος πυθόμενος διετείχισεν, ὅσα περὶ
Ῥοδανόν ἐστι ποταμὸν ἐς ἑκατὸν καὶ πεντήκοντα
2 σταδίους μάλιστα. καὶ πρεσβευσαμένοις ἐπὶ δια-
πείρᾳ τοῖς πολεμίοις ὑπὲρ σπονδῶν ἐκέλευεν ὅμηρα
δοῦναι καὶ χρήματα. ἀποκριναμένων δ᾽ εἰθίσθαι
ταῦτα λαμβάνειν, οὐ διδόναι, βουλόμενος φθάσαι τὴν
ὁμαιχμίαν αὐτῶν, ἐπὶ μὲν τοὺς Τιγυρίους ἐλάσσους
ὄντας ἔπεμπε Λαβινόν, αὐτὸς δὲ ἐπὶ τοὺς Ἑλουη-
τίους ἐχώρει προσλαβὼν Γαλατῶν τῶν ὀρείων ἐς δισ-
3 μυρίους. καὶ γίνεται Λαβιηνῷ τὸ ἔργον εὐμαρές, ἀδο-
κήτοις Τιγυρίοις περὶ τὸν ποταμὸν ἐπιπεσόντι καὶ

but secretly instructed the guides to lead them around by a longer route. He himself took a shortcut, and fell on the Teutones unexpectedly while they were still resting. He paid for his treachery, however, with heavy losses. He probably would have lost his whole army if darkness and rain and thunder had not separated the combatants when the battle was still raging. So, the battle came to an end because of terror from on high, but even as it was, the Romans escaped to the woods only in scattered groups and had difficulty in coming together three days later. The Teutones advanced against the Gauls. (*Exc. de leg. gent.* 7, p. 524 de Boor)

14. He gave orders that the bodies of the Cimbri were to be left untouched until dawn, in the belief that they had been carrying a lot of gold on them.[28] (*Suda, α* 4725, *κ* 1615)

15. Two nations, the Tigurini and the Helvetii, invaded the Roman province of Gaul. On hearing of their expedition, Gaius Caesar fenced off about one hundred and fifty stades of land along the river Rhone. When enemy ambassadors tried to negotiate a truce, he ordered them to hand over hostages and money, but they replied that they were more accustomed to receive rather than give such things. Caesar, wishing to take action before the two nations joined forces, sent Labienus against the lesser force of the Tigurini, while he himself went after the Helvetii, taking twenty thousand Gauls from the mountains with him. It proves an easy task for Labienus, who launched an assault on the unsuspecting Tigurini beside the Rhone, routed

---

[28] The subject of the sentence may be Gaius Marius after his victory over the Cimbri at the battle of Vercellae in 101.

τρεψαμένῳ καὶ σκεδάσαντι τοὺς πολλοὺς ἐν ἀσυν-
ταξίᾳ. (Exc. de leg. gent. 8, p. 525 de Boor)

16. Ὅτι Ἀριούιστος, Γερμανῶν βασιλεὺς τῶν ὑπὲρ
Ῥῆνον, ἐπιβαίνων τῆς πέραν Αἰδούοις ἔτι πρὸ τοῦ
Καίσαρος ἐπολέμει, φίλοις οὖσι Ῥωμαίων. τότε μὲν
δὴ τοῖς Ῥωμαίοις κελεύουσι πεισθεὶς ἀνέζευξεν ἀπὸ
τῶν Αἰδούων καὶ φίλος ἠξίωσε Ῥωμαίοις γενέσθαι·
καὶ ἐγένετο, ὑπατεύοντος αὐτοῦ Καίσαρος καὶ ψηφι-
σαμένου. (Exc. de leg. gent. 9, p. 525 de Boor)

17. Ὅτι Ἀριούιστος, ὁ Γερμανῶν βασιλεύς, φίλος
γενόμενος Ῥωμαίων ἐς λόγους ἦλθε τῷ Καίσαρι καὶ
διαχωρισθέντων ἀπ᾽ ἀλλήλων αὖθις συνελθεῖν ἐς
λόγους ἠξίωσεν. τοῦ δὲ Καίσαρος οὐ συνελθόντος,
ἀλλὰ τοὺς πρωτεύοντας Γαλατῶν ἀποστείλαντος,
ἔδησε τοὺς πρέσβεις. καὶ ὁ Καῖσαρ ἐστράτευεν ἐπ᾽
αὐτὸν μετὰ ἀπειλῆς. δέος δ᾽ ἐμπίπτει τῷ στρατῷ κατὰ
κλέος τῶν Γερμανῶν. (Exc. de leg. Rom. 6, p. 71 de Boor)

17a. Ἀλλόβριγες, Γαλατῶν ἔθνος. δύσμαχοι δ᾽
αὐτῶν ἦσαν αἱ πόλεις, ὑπὸ τῆς ἀμπώτεως ἐφ᾽ ἡμέραν
ἠπειρούμεναί τε καὶ νησούμεναι· οἱ δὲ πλοίοις ἐπολέμουν. τοῦ δὲ Καίσαρος Γαΐου περὶ τὰς πόλεις σταυροὺς πηξαμένου ὑψηλοὺς καὶ τοῖς σταυροῖς ἐπιθέντος
γεφυρώματα ὁ μὲν κλύδων ἐχώρει διὰ τῶν σταυρω-
μάτων ὑπὸ τοῖς γεφυρώμασι, Ῥωμαίοις δὲ ἀδεὲς καὶ
ἐπίμονον ἦν τὸ ἔργον. (Suda, η 408)

---

[29] Julius Caesar's defeat of these tribes occurred in 58. On
Labienus, see above, note 13.

them and scattered the majority in disarray.[29] (*Exc. de leg. gent.* 8, p. 525 de Boor)

16. Ariovistus, king of the Germans on the other side of the Rhine, crossed over to this side while Caesar had still not arrived, and attacked the Aedui who were friends of Rome. But then, in obedience to Roman orders, he broke off contact with the Aedui and asked to become a friend of the Romans. And so it happened, while Caesar himself was consul and had the measure put to the vote.[30] (*Exc. de leg. gent.* 9, p. 525 de Boor)

17. Ariovistus, king of the Germans, who had become a friend of Rome, entered discussions with Caesar, and after they had parted from each other, asked for another meeting. Caesar did not turn up, but sent off a delegation of leading Gauls. When Ariovistus threw the ambassadors in chains, Caesar marched off against him menacingly, although the reputation of the Germans causes fear in his army. (*Exc. de leg. Rom.* 6, p. 71 de Boor)

17a. The Allobroges, a Gallic nation. It was difficult to storm their towns on account of the tides which turned them into both mainland and islands each day.[31] And they used boats for fighting. So Gaius Caesar fixed high stakes around their towns and built a bridge on the stakes so that the water flowed between the stakes, but under the bridge. The work posed no danger for the Romans and had lasting effect. (*Suda*, η 408)

[30] Julius Caesar was consul in 59. Ariovistus in fact conquered the Aedui and was recognized as a friend of Rome, but he was later defeated by Caesar. The main source is Caesar himself (*B Gall.* 1.31–53).   [31] Caesar (*B Gall.* 3.12) says the same thing about the towns of the Veneti.

18. Ὅτι Οὐσιπέται, ἔθνος Γερμανικόν, καὶ Ταγχρεῖς δοκοῦσι πρότεροι σφετέροις ἱππεῦσιν ὀκτακοσίοις τρέψασθαι τῶν Καίσαρος ἱππέων ἐς πεντακισχιλίους, ὁ δὲ Καῖσαρ αὐτοῖς πρεσβευομένοις ἐς αὑτὸν ἐπιθέσθαι τοὺς πρέσβεις κατασχών, καὶ τὸ πάθος ἐκείνοις ἐς τέλος αἰφνίδιον οὕτω συνενεχθῆναι
2 ὡς τεσσαράκοντα μυριάδας τούτων συγκοπῆναι. Κάτωνά τε ἐν Ῥώμῃ τῶν τις συγγραφέων φησὶ γνώμην ἐσενεγκεῖν ἐκδοῦναι τοῖς βαρβάροις τὸν Καίσαρα ὡς
3 ἐναγὲς ἔργον ἐς διαπρεσβευσαμένους ἐργασάμενον. ὁ δὲ Καῖσαρ ἐν ταῖς ἰδίαις ἀναγραφαῖς τῶν ἐφημέρων ἔργων φησὶ τοὺς Οὐσιπέτας καὶ Ταγχρέας, κελευομένους ἐκπηδᾶν ἐς τὰ ἀρχαῖα σφῶν, φάναι πρέσβεις ἐς τοὺς ἐκβαλόντας Σουήβους ἀπεσταλκέναι καὶ τὰς ἀποκρίσεις αὐτῶν ἀναμένειν καὶ ἐν ταῖσδε ταῖς διαπρεσβεύσεσιν ἐπιθέσθαι τοῖς ὀκτακοσίοις καὶ παρ'
4 αὐτὸ τρέψαι τοὺς Ῥωμαίων πεντακισχιλίους. ἐπιπρεσβευομένων δ' αὐτῶν καὶ περὶ τοῦ παρασπονδήματος ἀπολογουμένων, ὑποτοπήσας ἐνέδραν ὁμοίαν ἐπιθέσθαι πρὸ τῶν ἀποκρίσεων. (Exc. de leg. gent. 10, p. 525 de Boor)

19. Εὐθὺς ἠρέθιζον τοὺς Βρεττανοὺς παρορκῆσαι, ἔγκλημα ἔχοντας, ὅτι σπονδῶν σφίσι γενομένων ἔτι παρῆν τὸ στρατόπεδον. (Suda, π 700)

18. The Usipetes, a German people, and the Tencteri are said to have earlier put to flight with eight hundred of their own cavalry about five thousand of Caesar's. But then Caesar, when they sent a delegation to him, detained the ambassadors and attacked: the disaster that overtook them was so sudden and complete that about four hundred thousand of them were slaughtered.[32] According to the report of one historian,[33] at Rome Cato proposed that Caesar should be handed over to the barbarians for carrying out an accursed deed against people who were in the process of negotiation. But in his own diaries Caesar says that the Usipites and Tencteri, when ordered to move back immediately to their former homes, claimed that they had sent ambassadors to the Suebi (who had expelled them) and were waiting for their reply; and it was in the middle of these negotiations that they had attacked with their eight hundred cavalry and thereby put to flight the five thousand Romans. When they sent a second embassy to explain their breach of faith, Caesar suspected a similar trap and launched his attack before giving an answer. (*Exc. de leg. gent.* 10, p. 525 de Boor)

19. They immediately pressed the Britons to break the oath on the grounds of their complaint that while there was a treaty with them in operation, the army was still present. (*Suda*, π 700)

[32] Caesar (*B Gall.* 4.12–15) tells the story in detail himself.

[33] This is usually thought to be the little known, but anti-Cesarean, historian of the late first century BC, Tanusius Geminus.

20. Δείσας ὁ Καῖσαρ περὶ τῷ Κικέρωνι ὑπέστρεφεν εἰς τοὐπίσω. (*Suda*, δ 367)

21. Ὅτι ὁ Βριτόρης διέφθειρεν Αἰδούους Ῥωμαίων ἀποστῆναι· καὶ τοῦ Καίσαρος ὀνειδίσαντος αὐτοῖς φιλίαν παλαιὰν ἔφασαν ἐφθακέναι. (*Exc. de sent.* 6, p. 66 Boissevain)

22. Πρεσβεύειν εἰς Καίσαρα. (*Anecd.* Bekker p. 170.31 = Περὶ Συντάξεως No. 25 Gaillard)

23. Τὸ γενόμενον ὑποτοποῦντες. (*Anecd.* Bekker p. 179.1 = Περὶ Συντάξεως No. 32 Gaillard)

24. Οἱ δὲ Κελτοὶ ἐς Ῥωμαίους τι μήνιμα ἐκ πολλοῦ διέφερον. (*Suda*, δ 979)

20. Fearing for Cicero, Caesar turned back.[34] (*Suda*, δ 367)

21. Britores bribed the Aedui into revolting from Rome. When Caesar criticized them for this, they said that an ancient friendship had precedence.[35] (*Exc. de sent.* 6, p. 66 Boissevain)

22. To send an embassy to Caesar. (*Anecd.* Bekker p. 170.31 = *On Syntax* No. 25 Gaillard)

23. Suspecting what had happened. (*Anecd.* Bekker p. 179.1 = *On Syntax* No. 32 Gaillard)

24. The Celts harbored a resentment against Rome for a long time. (*Suda*, δ 979)

---

[34] In 54 BC Quintus Cicero, brother of the famous orator, was a legate of Julius Caesar in Gaul and held out bravely against the winter attack of the Nervii: Caesar, *B Gall.* 40–52.

[35] In *B Gall.* 7.37–42 Caesar refers to a prince by the name of Litovicus who persuades the Aedui to revolt from Rome.

V

ΕΚ ΤΗΣ ΣΙΚΕΛΙΚΗΣ ΚΑΙ
ΝΗΣΙΩΤΙΚΗΣ

1. Ὅτι ἀποροῦντες Ῥωμαῖοί τε καὶ Καρχηδόνιοι χρημάτων, οἳ μὲν οὐκ ἔτι ἐναυπήγουν, τετρυμένοι διὰ τὰς εἰσφοράς, ἀλλὰ πεζὴν στρατιὰν καταλέγοντες ἐξέπεμπον ἐς Λιβύην καὶ ἐς Σικελίαν ἀνὰ ἔτος ἕκαστον, Καρχηδόνιοι δ' ἐς Πτολεμαῖον ἐπρεσβεύοντο, τὸν Πτολεμαίου τοῦ Λάγου, βασιλέα Αἰγύπτου, δισχίλια
2 τάλαντα κιχρώμενοι. τῷ δ' ἦν ἔς τε Ῥωμαίους καὶ Καρχηδονίους φιλία, καὶ συναλλάξαι σφᾶς ἐπεχείρησεν ἀλλήλοις. οὐ δυνηθεὶς δ' ἔφη χρῆναι φίλοις κατ' ἐχθρῶν συμμαχεῖν, οὐ κατὰ φίλων. (Exc. de leg. gent. 11, p. 526 de Boor; Exc. de sent. 7, p. 66 Boissevain)

2. Ὅτι οἱ Καρχηδόνιοι δὶς ἐν τῇ γῇ τοῦ αὐτοῦ χρόνου καὶ δὶς ἐν τῇ θαλάσσῃ παθόντες, ἐν ᾗ δὴ καὶ πάνυ προύχειν ἐνόμιζον, καὶ χρημάτων ἀποροῦντες ἤδη καὶ νεῶν καὶ ἀνδρῶν, ᾔτουν ἀνοχὰς παρὰ τοῦ Λουτατίου καὶ λαβόντες ἐπρεσβεύοντο εἰς Ῥώμην

---

[1] The passage seems to refer to the period in the First Punic War after 249, when the Romans suspended naval operations for

BOOK V

FROM THE SICILIAN AND
ISLAND BOOK

1. The Romans and the Carthaginians were both lacking funds. So the Romans stopped building ships, worn out as they were by taxation, but they did levy an infantry force every year and sent them off to Africa and Sicily.[1] The Carthaginians on the other hand sent an embassy to Ptolemy, son of Ptolemy, grandson of Lagus, the king of Egypt, to ask for a loan of two thousand talents.[2] Ptolemy was a 2 friend of both Carthage and Rome, and tried to reconcile them, but failed and said that friends should form alliances against enemies, not against friends. (*Exc. de leg. gent.* 11, p. 526 de Boor; *Exc. de sent.* 7, p. 66 Boissevain)

2. The Carthaginians had been defeated twice on land in the same period, and twice at sea (where they regarded themselves as completely superior); and they were now running out of money and ships and men. So they requested an armistice from Lutatius, and on getting it, they sent an embassy to Rome to negotiate a treaty on very

a number of years. The Romans sent troops to Africa only from 256 to 255.

[2] Ptolemy II Philadelphus ("Brother-loving") ruled Egypt from 282 to 246.

περὶ διαλλαγῶν ἐπὶ βραχυτέροις συνέπεμπόν τε τοῖς
πρέσβεσιν Ἀτίλιον Ῥῆγλον τὸν ὕπατον, αἰχμάλωτον
ὄντα σφῶν, δεησόμενον τῆς πατρίδος ἐπὶ τοῖσδε
2 συνθέσθαι. ὁ δὲ ἧκε μὲν ὡς αἰχμάλωτος ἐσταλμένος
φοινικικῶς, ὑπολειφθεὶς δὲ τῶν πρέσβεων ἐν τῷ
βουλευτηρίῳ τετρῦσθαι τὰ Καρχηδονίων ἐδήλου καὶ
παρήνεσεν ἢ πολεμεῖν ἐγκρατῶς ἢ ἐπὶ πλείοσι συν-
3 θέσθαι. καὶ τόνδε μὲν ἐς Καρχηδόνα ἑκόντα ἐπανελ-
θόντα ἔκτειναν οἱ Καρχηδόνιοι, κέντρα σιδήρεα σανί-
σιν ἐνηρμοσμένα πάντοθεν ἑστῶτι περιθέντες, ἵνα
μηδαμόσε δύναιτο ἐπικλίνεσθαι, αὐτοὶ δὲ τὴν εἰρήνην
4 ἐπὶ πλέοσι συνέθεντο. καὶ ἦν, ἐφ᾽ οἷς συνέθεντο, τὰ
μὲν αἰχμάλωτα Ῥωμαίων καὶ τοὺς αὐτομόλους, ὅσοι
παρὰ Καρχηδονίοις εἰσί, Ῥωμαίοις εὐθὺς ἀποδοῦναι
καὶ Σικελίας Ῥωμαίοις ἀποστῆναι καὶ τῶν βραχυ-
τέρων νήσων ὅσαι περὶ Σικελίαν, Συρακουσίοις δὲ ἢ
Ἱέρωνι, τῷ Συρακουσῶν τυράννῳ, πολέμου Καρχηδονίους μὴ κατάρχειν μηδὲ ἐκ τῆς Ἰταλίας ξενολογεῖν,
ποινὴν δὲ τοῦ πολέμου Ῥωμαίοις ἐνεγκεῖν τάλαντα
Εὐβοϊκὰ δισχίλια ἐν ἔτεσιν εἴκοσι, τὸ μέρος ἑκάστου
ἔτους ἐς Ῥώμην ἀναφέροντας. ἔχει δὲ τὸ Εὐβοϊκὸν
5 τάλαντον Ἀλεξανδρείους δραχμὰς ἑπτακισχιλίας. ὁ
μὲν δὴ πρῶτος περὶ Σικελίας Ῥωμαίοις καὶ Καρχηδονίοις πόλεμος, ἔτεσιν εἴκοσι καὶ τέσσαρσιν αὐτοῖς
γενόμενος, ἐς τοῦτο ἐτελεύτα. καὶ ἀπώλοντο νῆες ἐν
αὐτῷ Ῥωμαίων ἑπτακόσιαι, Καρχηδονίων δὲ πεντα-
6 κόσιαι. Σικελίας δὲ οὕτω τοῦ πλέονος Ῥωμαῖοι κατ-

limited terms.[3] Along with their own ambassadors they sent the consul, Atilius Regulus, whom they had taken prisoner, to urge his countrymen to agree to these terms.[4] Atilius arrived dressed as a prisoner of war in Phoenician clothing and when the ambassadors left him in the senate, he made clear how exhausted Carthage really was, and advised that Rome should either conduct the war with determination or make peace on more demanding conditions. Although he returned to Carthage of his own accord, the Carthaginians executed him by placing him standing up in a box fitted with iron spikes which completely prevented him from lying down. Nevertheless, Carthage agreed to the more demanding terms. The terms of the agreement were as follows. The Carthaginians were to return all Roman prisoners and deserters held by them immediately. They were to concede Sicily and the smaller islands around it to Rome. The Carthaginians were not to begin a war against Syracuse or its tyrant Hiero, or even recruit mercenaries in Italy. They were required to pay the Romans a war indemnity of two thousand Euboic talents within twenty years, and to deliver each annual installment in Rome (there are seven thousand Alexandrian drachmas to the Euboic talent). So this was how the first war between Rome and Carthage over Sicily came to an end. It lasted twenty-four years and in its course Rome lost seven hundred ships, Carthage five hundred. In this way Rome took possession of most of Sicily, which had been

3 Gaius Lutatius Catulus was consul in 242 .

4 Marcus Atilius Regulus, consul in 267 and 256, led the Roman expedition to Africa in 256 but was defeated and captured in 255.

APPIAN

ἔσχον, ὅσου Καρχηδόνιοι κατεῖχον, φόρους τε αὐτοῖς
ἐπέθεσαν καὶ τέλη τὰ θαλάσσια ταῖς πόλεσι μερισάμενοι στρατηγὸν ἐτήσιον ἔπεμπον ἐς Σικελίαν.
Ἱέρωνα δέ, τὸν Συρακουσίων τύραννον, ἀνθ᾽ ὧν αὐτοῖς
ἐς τόνδε τὸν πόλεμον συνεπεπράχει, φίλον καὶ σύμμαχον ἔθεντο.

7   Καταλυθέντος δὲ τοῦ πολέμου τοῦδε Κελτοὶ Καρχηδονίους τόν τε μισθὸν ᾔτουν τὸν ἔτι ὀφειλόμενον
σφίσιν ἐκ Σικελίας καὶ δωρεάς, ὅσας ὑπέσχητο
8   αὐτοῖς δώσειν Ἀμίλχας. ᾔτουν δὲ καὶ Λίβυες, ὑπήκοοι
μὲν ὄντες οἵδε Καρχηδονίων, ἀπὸ δὲ τῆς ἐν Σικελίᾳ
στρατείας ἐπὶ φρονήματος γεγονότες καὶ τοὺς Καρχηδονίους ἀσθενεῖς καὶ ταπεινοὺς ὁρῶντες, ἐχαλέπαι-
νόν τε αὐτοῖς τῆς ἀναιρέσεως τῶν τρισχιλίων, οὓς
ἐσταυρώκεσαν τῆς ἐς Ῥωμαίους μεταβολῆς οὕνεκα.
9   διωθουμένων δὲ τῶν Καρχηδονίων ἑκατέρους, κατέλαβον ἄμφω, Τύνητα πόλιν καὶ Ἰτύκην, ἣ μεγίστη Λιβύης ἐστὶ μετὰ Καρχηδόνα· ὅθεν ὁρμώμενοι τήν τε
ἄλλην ἀφίστανον καὶ τῶν Νομάδων τινὰς ἔπειθον καὶ
δούλων πολὺ πλῆθος ἀποδιδρασκόντων ὑπεδέχοντο
10   τά τε Καρχηδονίων πάντα ἐλεηλάτουν. οἱ δὲ πανταχόθεν πολεμούμενοι συμμάχους ἐπὶ τοὺς Λίβυας Ῥωμαίους ἐπεκαλοῦντο. καὶ Ῥωμαῖοι στρατιὰν μὲν
αὐτοῖς οὐκ ἔπεμψαν, ἀγορὰν δὲ ἔκ τε Ἰταλίας καὶ
Σικελίας ἐπάγεσθαι καὶ ξενολογεῖν ἐκ τῆς Ἰταλίας ἐς
11   μόνον τόνδε τὸν πόλεμον ἐπέτρεψαν, ἔπεμψαν δὲ καὶ
πρέσβεις ἐς Λιβύην, εἰ δύναιντο διαλῦσαι τὸν πόλε-
μον· οἱ ἐπανῆλθον ἄπρακτοι. καὶ Καρχηδόνιοι ἐγκρα-

128

held by Carthage, and imposed tribute on it; they assigned naval taxes among the towns and sent a governor to Sicily each year. But they made Hiero, tyrant of Syracuse, a friend and ally, in return for his cooperation with them in this war.

No sooner had this war come to an end than the Celts 7 demanded payment from the Carthaginians both of the money still owed to them from Sicily and of the donatives Hamilcar had promised them. Even though they were 8 subjects of Carthage, the Africans made the same demand, having become presumptuous as a result of their service in Sicily and their observation of Carthage's weakness and humbled position. They were also annoyed at them for killing the three thousand whom they crucified for changing sides to Rome. The Carthaginians rejected 9 both demands and together the Celtic and African mercenaries captured the town of Tunis and Utica (Utica is the largest town of Africa after Carthage).[5] Using these as their base they began to stir revolt in the rest of the country, persuading some of the Numidians to join them and taking in a large number of runaway slaves, and they plundered all Carthaginian possessions. Attacked on all sides, 10 the Carthaginians invited Rome to join them as allies against the Africans. The Romans did not send them an army, but allowed them to get supplies from Italy and Sicily and to recruit mercenaries in Italy just for this war. They also sent envoys to Africa to try to bring the war to 11 an end, but they failed and returned home. The Cartha-

[5] The war of Carthage against her mercenaries ran from 241 to 237.

τῶς εἴχοντο τοῦ πολέμου. (*Exc. de leg. gent.* 12, p. 526 de Boor)

3. Ὅτι Ἱπποκράτης καὶ Ἐπικύδης, ἀδελφὼ μὲν ἀλλήλων, στρατηγὼ δὲ Συρακουσίων, Ῥωμαίοις ἐκ πολλοῦ δυσχεραίνοντες, ἐπεὶ τὰς Συρακούσας οὐκ ἴσχυον ἐκπολεμῶσαι, κατέφυγον ἐς Λεοντίνους, διαφερομένους τοῖς Συρακουσίοις, καὶ κατηγόρουν τῆς πατρίδος, ὅτι τὰς σπονδὰς Ἱέρωνος ἐφ' ὅλῃ Σικελίᾳ πεποιημένου μόνοι Συρακούσιοι σφίσιν αὐτοῖς ἀνα-
2 καινίσειαν. οἳ δὲ ἠρεθίζοντο, καὶ Συρακούσιοι μὲν ἐπεκήρυσσον, εἴ τις Ἱπποκράτους ἢ Ἐπικύδους κομίσειε τὴν κεφαλήν, ἰσόσταθμον αὐτῷ χρυσίον ἀντιδώσειν, Λεοντῖνοι δὲ αὐτὸν Ἱπποκράτη στρατηγὸν ᾑροῦντο. (*Exc. de virt.* 12, p. 222 Roos; *Suda*, ε 2426)

4. Ὅτι Σικελοί, καὶ τέως ἀγανακτοῦντες ἐπὶ τῇ ὠμότητι Μαρκέλλου τοῦ στρατηγοῦ, μᾶλλόν τι καὶ τῷδε τῷ ἔργῳ συνεταράσσοντο, ἐφ' ᾧ κατὰ προδοσίαν ἐς Συρακούσας ἐσῆλθεν, καὶ πρὸς Ἱπποκράτη μετετίθεντο καὶ συνώμνυντο μὴ διαλύσασθαι χωρὶς ἀλλήλων ἀγοράν τε αὐτῷ καὶ στρατιὰν ἔπεμπον, ἐς δισμυρίους πεζοὺς καὶ ἱππέας πεντακισχιλίους. (*Exc. de virt.* 13, p. 222 Roos)

5. Ὅτι διαβεβλημένῳ τῷ Μαρκέλλῳ οὐκ ἐπίστευον χωρὶς ὅρκων. διὸ καὶ Ταυρομενίων προσχωρούντων οἳ συνέθετο καὶ ὤμοσε μήτε φρουρήσειν τὴν πόλιν

---

6 Appian seems to be referring to the treaty that Hieronymus (not his father, Hiero) had made with the Carthaginians, by

ginians continued to prosecute the war vigorously. (*Exc. de leg. gent.* 12, p. 526 de Boor)

3. Hippocrates and Epicydes, two brothers, were Syracusan generals and had long hated the Romans, but were not sufficiently influential to persuade the Syracusans to go to war, and took refuge in Leontini, which was quarreling with Syracuse. The brothers accused their Syracusan countrymen of unilaterally renewing in their own interests the treaty that Hiero had made to include the whole of Sicily:[6] they were angry about this. While the Syracusans made a public proclamation that anyone bringing them the head of either Hippocrates or Epicydes would be paid its weight in gold, the people of Leontini chose Hippocrates as their general. (*Exc. de virt.* 12, p. 222 Roos; *Suda*, ε 2426)

4. The Sicilians had been angry for some time at the cruelty of Marcellus, the commander in chief, and they were even more disturbed at the fact that he had effected entry into Syracuse by means of treachery.[7] So they changed sides to Hippocrates and swore an oath to make no treaty without mutual agreement; and they sent him supplies and an army of twenty thousand infantry and five thousand cavalry. (*Exc. de virt.* 13, p. 222 Roos)

5. Marcellus was so discredited that they refused to trust him without the swearing of oaths. For this reason, when Tauromenium went over to him, he agreed under

which, after the defeat of Rome, he would be ruler of the whole island. The story is in Polybius 7.2–5 and Livy 24.6.

[7] Marcus Claudius Marcellus was consul in 222, 216, 214, 210, and 208. During the Second Punic War he commanded Roman forces in Sicily from 214 to 211, capturing Syracuse in 212.

μήτε στρατολογήσειν ἀπ' αὐτῆς. (Exc. de virt. 14,
p. 223 Roos)

6. Ὅτι Κρήτη ἐξ ἀρχῆς εὐνοϊκῶς ἔχειν ἐδόκει Μι-
θριδάτῃ βασιλεύοντι Πόντου καὶ αὐτῷ μισθοφορῆσαι
πολεμοῦντι Ῥωμαίοις ἐλέγετο. ἔδοξε δὲ καὶ τοῖς πλε-
ονάσασι τότε λῃσταῖς ἐς χάριν τοῦ Μιθριδάτου
συλλαβεῖν καὶ συμμαχῆσαι σαφῶς διωκομένοις ὑπὸ
Γαΐου Ἀντωνίου, πρεσβευσαμένου δὲ τοῦ Ἀντωνίου
πρὸς αὐτοὺς ὑπεριδεῖν καὶ ὑπερηφάνως ἀποκρίνα-
2 σθαι. καὶ πολεμῆσαι μὲν αὐτοῖς εὐθὺς ἐπὶ τῷδε Ἀν-
τώνιος καὶ οὐ πρᾶξαι καλῶς, χρηματίσαι δ' ὅμως διὰ
τὴν πρᾶξιν Κρητικός. καὶ ἦν ὅδε πατὴρ Μάρκου
Ἀντωνίου τοῦ πολεμήσαντος ὕστερον Καίσαρι τῷ
3 κληθέντι Σεβαστῷ περὶ Ἄκτιον. ψηφισαμένων δὲ Ῥωμαίων Κρησὶ πολεμεῖν διὰ τάδε, οἱ Κρῆτες ἐπρέσβευ-
4 σαν ἐς Ῥώμην περὶ διαλλαγῶν. οἱ δὲ αὐτοὺς ἐκέλευον
ἐκδοῦναί τε αὐτοῖς Λασθένη τὸν πολεμήσαντα Ἀντω-
νίῳ καὶ τὰ σκάφη τὰ λῃστικὰ πάντα παραδοῦναι καὶ
ὅσα Ῥωμαίων εἶχον αἰχμάλωτα καὶ ὅμηρα τριακόσια
5 καὶ ἀργυρίου τάλαντα τετρακισχίλια. οὐ δεξαμένων
δὲ ταῦτα Κρητῶν ᾑρέθη στρατηγὸς ἐπ' αὐτοὺς Μέτελλος καὶ νικᾷ μὲν ὁ Μέτελλος ἐν Κυδωνίᾳ Λασθένη,
καὶ φυγόντος ἐς Κνωσσὸν Πανάρης Μετέλλῳ τὴν
Κυδωνίαν παρέδωκεν ἐπὶ συνθήκῃ μηδὲν παθεῖν αὐτός. Μετέλλου δὲ Κνωσσὸν περικαθημένου, ὁ Λασθέ-

oath not to garrison the town or draft troops from it. (*Exc. de virt.* 14, p. 223 Roos)

6. It appears that the Cretans were well disposed to Mithridates, king of Pontus, from the beginning, and when he was at war with Rome they are said to have provided mercenaries for him. It seems they also helped the pirates, of whom there were at the time very large numbers, and made open alliance with them when they were pursued by Gaius Antonius, in order to oblige Mithridates.[8] And when Antonius dispatched a mission to the Cretans, they treated him with disdain and replied arrogantly. He immediately thereafter made war on them, and   2 although he did not enjoy success, he was still given the title "Creticus" for what he had done. He was father of the Marc Antony who later fought against Caesar Augustus at Actium. Because of these events in Crete the Romans   3 voted for war, but the Cretans sent to Rome to sue for peace. They were ordered to hand over Lasthenes, who   4 had fought against Antonius, to surrender all pirate ships and all Roman prisoners of war and to provide three hundred hostages and four thousand silver talents. The Cre-   5 tans refused these terms and Metellus was appointed commander of the Roman forces sent against them.[9] Metellus defeats Lasthenes at Cydonia, and while he fled to Cnossus, Panares, in exchange for his own personal safety, agreed to hand Cydonia to Metellus. Lasthenes escaped

[8] Marcus (not Gaius) Antonius Creticus, father of the famous Marc Antony, was praetor in 74 and received a special command against the pirates. Diodorus (40.1) reports his defeat.

[9] Quintus Caecilius Metellus Creticus was consul in 69 and was given proconsular command in Crete, which he subdued.

νης τὴν οἰκίαν χρημάτων πλήσας κατέφλεξε καὶ διέ-
6 φυγεν ἀπὸ τῆς Κνωσσοῦ. καὶ οἱ Κρῆτες ἐς Πομπήιον
Μάγνον, στρατηγοῦντα τοῦ λῃστικοῦ καὶ Μιθριδα-
τείου πολέμου, πέμψαντες ἔφασαν ἑαυτοὺς ἐλθόντι
ἐπιτρέψειν. ὁ δὲ ἀσχόλως τότε ἔχων ἐκέλευε τὸν
Μέτελλον, ὡς οὐ δέον ἔτι πολεμεῖν τοῖς ἑαυτοὺς ἐπι-
τρέπουσιν, ἐξανίστασθαι τῆς νήσου· παραλήψεσθαι
7 γὰρ αὐτὸς αὐτὴν ἐπελθών. ὁ δὲ οὐ φροντίσας ἐπέμεινε
τῷ πολέμῳ, μέχρι ὑπηγάγετο αὐτὴν Λασθένει συνθέμενος ὅμοια Πανάρει, καὶ ἐθριάμβευσε καὶ Κρητικὸς
ἐκλήθη ὅδε δικαιότερον Ἀντωνίου τὴν νῆσον ἐξεργα-
σάμενος. (Exc. de leg. Rom. 7, p. 71 [§§1–3] de Boor; Exc.
de leg. gent. 13, p. 527 [§§3–7] de Boor)

7. Ὅτι Κλώδιος ὁ πατρίκιος, ὁ Πούλχερ ἐπίκλην,
τοῦτ' ἔστιν εὐπρεπής, τῆς Γαΐου Καίσαρος γυναικὸς
ἤρα. καὶ ἁρμόσασθαι αὐτὸν ἐς γυναῖκα ἐκ κεφαλῆς
ἐς ἄκρους πόδας, ἔτι ὄντα ἀγένειον, καὶ ἐς τὴν οἰκίαν
τοῦ Γαΐου παρελθεῖν οἷα γυναῖκα νυκτός, ὅτε μόναις
γυναιξὶν ἐξῆν ἐσελθεῖν, μυστηρίων ἀγομένων. πλανη-
θέντα δὲ τῆς ὁδηγούσης, κατάφωρον ὑπ' ἄλλων ἐκ
τῆς φωνῆς γενόμενον, ἐξελαθῆναι. (Exc. de virt. 15,
p. 223 Roos)

---

10 Pompey was given a special three-year command to deal
with the pirates in 67 but needed only three months to do the job.
In 66 his powers were transferred to the command of the war
against Mithridates.

from Cnossus when it was under siege by Metellus, having filled his own house with money and set fire to it. The Cretans then approached Pompey the Great, who had command of the war against the pirates and against Mithridates, saying that they would turn themselves over to him, if he came.[10] Pompey was too busy at the time, but considering it not right to continue fighting against people who had offered to surrender, he ordered Metellus to withdraw from the island: he said he would come and take it over himself. Metellus ignored the order and pressed on with the war until he reduced the island and made the same arrangement with Lasthenes as he had with Panares. He was awarded a triumph and given the title "Creticus," this time rather more justifiably than in the case of Antonius, as he had actually conquered it. (*Exc. de leg. Rom.* 7, p. 71 [§§1–3] de Boor; *Exc. de leg. gent.* 13, p. 527 [§§3–7] de Boor)

7. The patrician Claudius, surnamed Pulcher (Pulcher means "the handsome one"), was in love with the wife of Gaius Caesar. Dressing up as a woman from head to toe (he was still only a youth), he gained entry to Caesar's house as if he were a woman, on the night when the mysteries were being celebrated and only women were supposed to be admitted.[11] He lost his guide and was chased away by others who recognized him from his voice. (*Exc. de virt.* 15, p. 223 Roos)

[11] The mysteries were those of the Bona Dea, celebrated in Caesar's residence in December 62. The discovery of P. Clodius Pulcher at the sacred rites caused a public scandal. Clodius was prosecuted, but acquitted.

VI

ΙΒΗΡΙΚΗ[1]

1. Ὄρος ἐστὶ Πυρήνη διῆκον ἀπὸ τῆς Τυρρηνικῆς
θαλάσσης ἐπὶ τὸν βόρειον ὠκεανόν, οἰκοῦσι δ᾽ αὐτοῦ
πρὸς μὲν ἕω Κελτοί, ὅσοι Γαλάται τε καὶ Γάλλοι νῦν
προσαγορεύονται, πρὸς δὲ δύσεων Ἴβηρές τε καὶ
Κελτίβηρες, ἀρχόμενοι μὲν ἀπὸ τοῦ Τυρρηνικοῦ
πελάγους, περιιόντες δ᾽ ἐν κύκλῳ διὰ τῶν Ἡρακλείων
στηλῶν ἐπὶ τὸν βόρειον ὠκεανόν. οὕτως ἐστὶν ἡ Ἰβηρία περίκλυστος, ὅτι μὴ τῇ Πυρήνῃ μόνῃ, μεγίστῳ
τῶν Εὐρωπαίων ὀρῶν καὶ ἰθυτάτῳ σχεδὸν ἁπάντων.
2 τοῦ δὲ περίπλου τοῦδε τὸ μὲν Τυρρηνικὸν πέλαγος
διαπλέουσιν ἐπὶ τὰς στήλας τὰς Ἡρακλείους, τὸν δ᾽
ἑσπέριον καὶ τὸν βόρειον ὠκεανὸν οὐ περῶσιν, ὅτι μὴ
πορθμεύεσθαι μόνον ἐπὶ Βρεττανούς, καὶ τοῦτο ταῖς
3 ἀμπώτεσι τοῦ πελάγους συμφερόμενοι. ἔστι δ᾽ αὐτοῖς
ὁ διάπλους ἥμισυ ἡμέρας, καὶ τὰ λοιπὰ οὔτε Ῥωμαῖοι
4 οὔτε τὰ ἔθνη τὰ ὑπὸ Ῥωμαίοις πειρῶνται τοῦδε τοῦ
ὠκεανοῦ. μέγεθος δὲ τῆς Ἰβηρίας, τῆς Ἰσπανίας νῦν
ὑπό τινων ἀντὶ Ἰβηρίας λεγομένης, ἐστὶ πολὺ καὶ

---

[1] Ἀππιανοῦ Ῥωμαικῶν Ἰβερική VM

BOOK VI

THE IBERIAN BOOK

1. The Pyrenees mountains stretch from the Tyrrhenian Sea to the Northern Ocean.[1] Starting at the Tyrrhenian Sea and going all the way round through the Pillars of Heracles and into the Northern Ocean, Celts (now called Galatians or Gauls) inhabit the eastern part, and Iberians and Celtiberians the western. Iberia is thus entirely surrounded by water, except for the Pyrenees, which are the highest mountains in Europe and probably the steepest. Of this circuit, they sail through the Tyrrhenian Sea as far as the Pillars of Heracles, but they do not cross the Western and Northern Ocean, unless they are making their way over to Britain, a journey facilitated by the tides which takes them half a day. Otherwise no one plies this ocean, neither Romans nor any of their subject peoples. Iberia, or, as it is now called by some people, Spain, rather than Iberia, is huge, almost unbelievably so for a single country:

---

[1] As in *Praef.* 3.9, Appian calls the whole stretch of the Mediterranean between Italy and Spain the Tyrrhenian Sea; others limit it to the waters enclosed by Italy and the islands of Corsica, Sardinia, and Sicily. See above, *Praef.* 3.9 n. 9.

ἄπιστον ὡς ἐν χώρᾳ μιᾷ, ὅπου τὸ πλάτος μυρίους
σταδίους ἀριθμοῦσι, καὶ ἔστιν αὐτῇ τὸ πλάτος ἀντὶ
μήκους. ἔθνη τε πολλὰ καὶ πολυώνυμα αὐτὴν οἰκεῖ,
καὶ ποταμοὶ πολλοὶ ῥέουσι ναυσίποροι.

5   2. Οἵ τινες δ' αὐτὴν οἰκῆσαι πρῶτοι νομίζονται καὶ
οἳ μετ' ἐκείνους κατέσχον, οὐ πάνυ μοι ταῦτα φροντί-
ζειν ἀρέσκει, μόνα τὰ Ῥωμαίων συγγράφοντι, πλὴν
ὅτι Κελτοί μοι δοκοῦσί ποτε, τὴν Πυρήνην ὑπερβάντες, αὑτοῖς συνοικῆσαι, ὅθεν ἄρα καὶ τὸ Κελτιβήρων
6 ὄνομα ἐρρύη. δοκοῦσι δέ μοι καὶ Φοίνικες, ἐς Ἰβηρίαν ἐκ πολλοῦ θαμινὰ ἐπ' ἐμπορίᾳ διαπλέοντες,
οἰκῆσαί τινα τῆς Ἰβηρίας Ἕλληνές τε ὁμοίως, ἐς
Ταρτησσὸν καὶ Ἀργανθώνιον Ταρτησσοῦ βασιλέα
7 πλέοντες, ἐμμεῖναι καὶ τῶνδέ τινες ἐν Ἰβηρίᾳ. ἡ γὰρ
Ἀργανθωνίου βασιλεία ἐν Ἴβηρσιν ἦν, καὶ Ταρτησ-
σός μοι δοκεῖ τότε εἶναι πόλις ἐπὶ θαλάσσης, ἣ νῦν
8 Καρπησσὸς ὀνομάζεται. τό τε τοῦ Ἡρακλέους ἱερὸν
τὸ ἐν στήλαις Φοίνικές μοι δοκοῦσιν ἱδρύσασθαι· καὶ
θρησκεύεται νῦν ἔτι φοινικικῶς, ὅ τε θεὸς αὐτοῖς οὐχ
ὁ Θηβαῖός ἐστιν, ἀλλ' ὁ Τυρίων.

9   3. Ταῦτα μὲν δὴ τοῖς παλαιολογοῦσιν μεθείσθω·
τὴν δὲ γῆν τήνδε εὐδαίμονα οὖσαν καὶ μεγάλων ἀγαθῶν γέμουσαν Καρχηδόνιοι πρὸ Ῥωμαίων ἤρξαντο

---

2 A stade was a unit of length containing six hundred feet, but
the length of a foot was not standard, and so precision about the
stade depends on the context. Allowing nine stades to the mile
gives an approximate idea of what Appian intended (i.e., Spain
was about 1,100 miles wide).

estimates put its breadth at ten thousand stades, and it is as long as it is wide.[2] It is inhabited by a large number of peoples with different names, and many navigable rivers flow through it.

2. As I am only writing about Roman history, I have 5 decided to pay no attention at all to the question who the original inhabitants of the country are thought to have been, and who held it after them—except to say that I believe the Celts crossed the Pyrenees at some stage in the past and settled with the Iberians, this, of course, being the origin of the name Celtiberian. I also believe that a 6 long time ago Phoenicians sailed frequently to Iberia for trading purposes and settled parts of it. Similarly the Greeks sailed to Tartessus and its king Arganthonius, and some of them stayed in Iberia: for Arganthonius' kingdom 7 was located among the Iberians.[3] In my opinion, Tartessus was at that time a city on the coast now called Carpessus, and the temple of Heracles at the Pillars was, I believe, 8 founded by Phoenicians; at least, the religious ceremonies conducted there now are still Phoenician and their god is the Tyrian, not the Theban, Heracles.

3. But let us leave these matters to the antiquarians. 9 This was a rich land full of great blessings when the Carthaginians began to interfere in it, followed by the Ro-

---

[3] Arganthonius is an obscure figure, best known in antiquity for living to a great age. According to both Strabo (3.2.14 C151) and Pliny the Elder (*HN* 7.49), the lyric poet Anacreon said that Arganthonius ruled Tartessus for 150 years. Pliny dismisses this, but accepts that he ruled for 80 years and lived to the age of 120, figures first presented by Herodotus (1.163).

πολυπραγμονεῖν καὶ μέρος αὐτῆς τὸ μὲν εἶχον ἤδη,
10 τὸ δ' ἐπόρθουν, μέχρι Ῥωμαῖοι σφᾶς ἐκβαλόντες, ἃ
μὲν εἶχον οἱ Καρχηδόνιοι τῆς Ἰβηρίας, ἔσχον αὐτίκα,
τὰ δὲ λοιπὰ σὺν χρόνῳ πολλῷ καὶ πόνῳ λαμβανό-
μενά τε ὑπὸ σφῶν καὶ πολλάκις ἀφιστάμενα χειρω-
σάμενοι διεῖλον ἐς τρία καὶ στρατηγοὺς ἐς αὐτὰ
11 πέμπουσι τρεῖς. ὅπως δὲ εἶλον ἕκαστα καὶ ὅπως Καρχηδονίοις τε περὶ αὐτῶν καὶ μετὰ Καρχηδονίους
Ἴβηρσι καὶ Κελτίβηρσιν ἐπολέμησαν, δηλώσει τόδε
τὸ βιβλίον, μοῖραν μὲν ἐς Καρχηδονίους τὴν πρώτην
12 ἔχον· ὅτι δὲ καὶ τοῦτο περὶ Ἰβηρίας ἦν, ἀνάγκη μοι
συνενεγκεῖν ἐς τὴν Ἰβηρικὴν συγγραφὴν ἐγένετο, ᾧ
λόγῳ καὶ τὰ περὶ Σικελίας Ῥωμαίοις καὶ Καρχηδονίοις ἐς ἀλλήλους γενόμενα, ἀρξάμενα Ῥωμαίοις τῆς
ἐς Σικελίαν παρόδου τε καὶ ἀρχῆς, ἐς τὴν Σικελικὴν
συνενήνεκται γραφήν.

13   4. Πρὸς γὰρ δὴ Καρχηδονίους Ῥωμαίοις πρῶτος
ἐγένετο πόλεμος ἔκδημος περὶ Σικελίας ἐν αὐτῇ Σικελίᾳ καὶ δεύτερος ὅδε περὶ Ἰβηρίας ἐν Ἰβηρίᾳ, ἐν ᾧ
καὶ ἐς τὴν ἀλλήλων μεγάλοις στρατοῖς διαπλέοντες
14 οἱ μὲν τὴν Ἰταλίαν, οἱ δὲ τὴν Λιβύην ἐπόρθουν. ἤρξαντο δὲ αὐτοῦ μεθ' ἑκατὸν καὶ τεσσαράκοντα ὀλυμ-
πιάδας μάλιστα, ὅτε τὰς σπονδὰς ἔλυσαν, αἳ ἐπὶ τῷ
Σικελικῷ πολέμῳ σφίσιν ἦσαν γενόμεναι. ἔλυσαν δ'
15 ἐκ τοιᾶσδε προφάσεως. Ἀμίλχαρ ὁ Βάρκας ἐπίκλησιν, ὅτε περ ἐν Σικελίᾳ Καρχηδονίων ἐστρατήγει,
Κελτοῖς τότε μισθοφοροῦσίν οἱ καὶ Λιβύων τοῖς συμ-

mans. Part of it the Carthaginians already held, part they
plundered, until the Romans expelled them and took im-   10
mediate possession of the Carthaginian holdings in Iberia;
the rest of it was acquired by them with great difficulty
over a long period. They put down many revolts, divided
the land into three parts and now send a praetor to each.[4]
This book will show how they annexed each of the parts   11
and how they fought over them with Carthage, and after
Carthage with the Iberians and Celtiberians. Although the
first section deals with the Carthaginians, the subject mat-   12
ter was still Iberia, and so I was obliged to include it in the
Iberian history. By the same logic, the relations between
Rome and Carthage with respect to Sicily, beginning from
when the Romans arrived in Sicily and started to rule,
have been included in the Sicilian account.

4. Rome's first overseas war was against Carthage. The   13
issue at stake was Sicily and the conflict took place in Sicily. This second war was fought over Iberia in Iberia itself,
although the combatants also transported large armies to
each other's country and ravaged both Italy and Africa.
They began the war, approximately speaking, in Olympiad   14
one hundred and forty,[5] when they broke the treaty made
at the end of the Sicilian war. The reason alleged for breaking the treaty was as follows. When Hamilcar, the one   15
known as Barca, was commanding the Carthaginian forces
in Sicily, he promised to give many rewards to the Celts

[4] The eastern part of Spain was divided into Hispania Citerior
(Nearer) and Hispania Ulterior (Farther) in 197. Lusitania, the
western part, was added by the emperor Augustus, who reorga-
nized and renamed the other two, Tarraconensis in the east and
north, Baetica in the southwest.   [5] 220 to 216.

μαχοῦσιν πολλὰς δωρεὰς ὑπέσχητο δώσειν, ἅς,
ἐπειδὴ ἐπανῆλθεν ἐς Λιβύην, ἀπαιτούντων ἐκείνων ὁ
Λιβυκὸς Καρχηδονίοις ἐξῆπτο πόλεμος, ἐν ᾧ πολλὰ
μὲν πρὸς αὐτῶν Λιβύων ἔπαθον οἱ Καρχηδόνιοι, Σαρδόνα δὲ Ῥωμαίοις ἔδοσαν ποινὴν ὧν ἐς τοὺς ἐμπόρους
αὐτῶν ἡμαρτήκεσαν ἐν τῷδε τῷ Λιβυκῷ πολέμῳ.
16 ὑπαγόντων οὖν ἐπὶ τοῖσδε τὸν Βάρκαν τῶν ἐχθρῶν ἐς
κρίσιν, ὡς αἴτιον τῇ πατρίδι τοσῶνδε συμφορῶν
γενόμενον, θεραπεύσας ὁ Βάρκας τοὺς πολιτευομέ-
νους, ὧν ἦν δημοκοπικώτατος Ἀσρούβας, ὁ τὴν αὐτοῦ
Βάρκα θυγατέρα ἔχων, τάς τε δίκας διεκρούετο καὶ
Νομάδων τινὸς κινήματος γενομένου στρατηγὸς
ἔπραξεν ἐπ᾽ αὐτοὺς αἱρεθῆναι μετὰ Ἄννωνος τοῦ Μεγάλου λεγομένου, ἔτι τὰς εὐθύνας τῆς προτέρας
στρατηγίας ὀφείλων.

17   5. Παυομένου δὲ τοῦ πολέμου καὶ Ἄννωνος ἐπὶ
διαβολαῖς ἐς Καρχηδόνα μεταπέμπτου γενομένου,
μόνος ὢν ἐπὶ τῷ στρατῷ καὶ τὸν κηδεστὴν Ἀσρούβαν
ἔχων οἱ συνόντα, διῆλθεν ἐπὶ Γάδειρα καὶ τὸν
πορθμὸν ἐς Ἰβηρίαν περάσας ἐλεηλάτει τὰ Ἰβήρων
οὐδὲν ἀδικούντων, ἀφορμὴν αὑτῷ ποιούμενος ἀποδη-
18 μίας τε καὶ ἔργων καὶ δημοκοπίας (ὅσα γὰρ λάβοι,
διῄρει καὶ τὰ μὲν ἐς τὸν στρατὸν ἀνάλισκεν, ἵνα προ-
θυμότερον αὑτῷ συναδικοῖεν, τὰ δ᾽ ἐς αὑτὴν ἔπεμπε
Καρχηδόνα, τὰ δὲ τοῖς ὑπὲρ αὑτοῦ πολιτευομένοις
19 διεδίδου), μέχρι Ἰβήρων αὐτὸν οἵ τε βασιλεῖς συ-

then fighting as mercenaries for him and to his African allies. On his return to Africa, they demanded these rewards, thus sparking the outbreak of Carthage's African war, during which Carthage suffered badly at the hands of the Africans, and ceded Sardinia to Rome as compensation for the crimes they had committed against Roman merchants in the course of this African war. His enemies 16 blamed Barca for the scale of the Carthaginian disaster and indicted him, but he escaped punishment by cultivating the leading politicians, among them the archpopulist Hasdrubal, who was married to the daughter of Barca himself. And when there was a disturbance in Numidia, he got himself appointed general against them along with Hanno, the one called "the Great," even though an official audit of his previous command was still outstanding.[6]

5. At the end of this conflict, Hanno was recalled to 17 Carthage to answer charges made against him, leaving Barca in sole command of the army. With his son-in-law, Hasdrubal, in attendance on him, he crossed the straits to Iberia, to Gadeira,[7] and began to plunder the territory of the Iberians, although they had committed no offense. This gave him the opportunity to fight and court popularity away from home. For he shared all the plunder he took: 18 some he spent on the army—to make it a more enthusiastic partner in his misdeeds—some he sent to Carthage itself, and some he distributed to his own political partisans. Eventually the individual Iberian kings and other 19

[6] Appian seems to think that there was a separate conflict with the Numidians after the Mercenary War, but Polybius makes no mention of it (1.65–88).

[7] Modern Cadiz.

στάντες οἱ κατὰ μέρος καὶ ὅσοι ἄλλοι δυνατοί, κτείνουσιν ὧδε· ξύλων ἁμάξας ἄγοντες, αἷς βοῦς ὑπέζευ-
20 ξαν, εἵποντο ταῖς ἁμάξαις ὡπλισμένοι. τοῖς δὲ
Λίβυσιν ἰδοῦσιν εὐθὺς μὲν ἐνέπιπτε γέλως, οὐ συνι-
εῖσι τοῦ στρατηγήματος· ὡς δ' ἐν χερσὶν ἐγένοντο, οἱ
μὲν Ἴβηρες αὐταῖς βουσὶν ἐξῆψαν τὰς ἁμάξας καὶ
ἐξώτρυναν ἐς τοὺς πολεμίους, τὸ δὲ πῦρ σκιδναμένων
τῶν βοῶν πάντῃ φερόμενον ἐτάρασσε τοὺς Λίβυας.
21 καὶ τῆς τάξεως διαλυθείσης οἱ μὲν Ἴβηρες αὐτοῖς
ἐπιδραμόντες αὐτόν τε τὸν Βάρκαν καὶ πολὺ πλῆθος
ἀμυνομένων ἐπ' αὐτῷ διέφθειραν.

22   6. Οἱ δὲ Καρχηδόνιοι, τοῖς κέρδεσιν ἤδη τοῖς ἐξ
Ἰβηρίας ἀρεσκόμενοι, στρατιὰν ἄλλην ἔπεμπον ἐς
Ἰβηρίαν καὶ στρατηγὸν ἁπάντων ἀπέφηναν Ἀσρού-
23 βαν, τὸν τοῦ Βάρκα κηδεστήν, ὄντα ἐν Ἰβηρίᾳ.[2] ὁ δὲ
Ἀννίβαν, τὸν οὐ πολὺ ὕστερον ἀοίδιμον ἐπὶ στρατη-
γίαις παῖδά τε ὄντα τοῦ Βάρκα καὶ τῆς γυναικός οἱ
γιγνόμενον ἀδελφόν, ἔχων ἐν Ἰβηρίᾳ, νέον ὄντα καὶ
φιλοπόλεμον καὶ ἀρέσκοντα τῷ στρατῷ, ὑποστράτη-
24 γον ἀπέφηνε. καὶ τῆς τ' Ἰβηρίας τὰ πολλὰ πειθοῖ
προσήγετο, πιθανὸς ὢν ὁμιλῆσαι, ἔς τε τὰ βίας δεό-
μενα τῷ μειρακίῳ χρώμενος προῆλθεν ἀπὸ τῆς
ἑσπερίου θαλάσσης ἐς τὸ μεσόγεων ἐπὶ Ἴβηρα ποταμόν, ὃς μέσην που μάλιστα τέμνων τὴν Ἰβηρίαν

___

2 ὄντα ἐν Ἰβηρίᾳ om. Exc.

strongmen got together and kill him in the following manner. They loaded some wagons with wood, yoked oxen to them and drove them along with armed men following behind. The Africans failed to detect the ambush and immediately broke out in laughter at the sight. But when the two sides engaged, the Iberians set fire to their wagons, oxen and all, and drove them into the enemy. The oxen scatterd in all directions bringing the fire with them and terrifying the Africans. With this break in the Carthaginian ranks, the Iberians charged in and killed Barca himself and a large number of those fighting in his defense.[8]

6. The Carthaginians sent another army to Iberia, as they were pleased with the gains they had already won there, and they appointed Hasdrubal, Barca's son-in-law, who was in Iberia, to the overall command. He had with him in Iberia Hannibal, who was soon to become famous for his generalship, and appointed him his second-in-command. Hannibal was the son of Barca and brother of Hasdrubal's wife, a young man who delighted in war and was admired by the army. Hasdrubal was a convincing speaker and won over much of Iberia by persuasion, but used the young Hannibal when force was needed. Advancing from the Western Sea, Hasdrubal made his way into the interior up to the river Ebro, which more or less cuts

---

[8] Polybius (3.10.7, 2.1.7–8) says that Hamilcar died, fighting bravely in battle, ten years before the beginning of the Second Punic War, that is, in 229. According to Diodorus (25.10.3–4), Hamilcar drowned when fleeing the siege of Helice.

καὶ τῆς Πυρήνης ἀφεστὼς ὁδὸν ἡμερῶν πέντε ἐξίησιν
ἐς τὸν ἑσπέριον³ ὠκεανόν.

25   7. Ζακανθαῖοι δέ, ἄποικοι Ζακυνθίων, ἐν μέσῳ τῆς
τε Πυρήνης καὶ τοῦ ποταμοῦ τοῦ Ἴβηρος ὄντες, καὶ
ὅσοι ἄλλοι Ἕλληνες περί τε τὸ καλούμενον Ἐμπόριον
καὶ εἴ πῃ τῆς Ἰβηρίας ᾤκουν ἀλλαχοῦ, δείσαντες
26 ὑπὲρ σφῶν ἐπρέσβευον ἐς Ῥώμην. καὶ ἡ σύγκλητος
οὐκ ἐθέλουσα τὰ Καρχηδονίων ἐπαίρεσθαι πρέσβεις
27 ἐς Καρχηδόνα ἔπεμπε. καὶ συνέβησαν ἀμφότεροι
ὅρον εἶναι Καρχηδονίοις τῆς ἀρχῆς τῆς ἐν Ἰβηρίᾳ
τὸν Ἴβηρα ποταμὸν καὶ μήτε Ῥωμαίους τοῖς πέραν
τοῦδε τοῦ ποταμοῦ πόλεμον ἐκφέρειν, Καρχηδονίων
ὑπηκόοις οὖσι, μήτε Καρχηδονίους ἐπὶ πολέμῳ τὸν
Ἴβηρα διαβαίνειν, Ζακανθαίους δὲ καὶ τοὺς ἄλλους
ἐν Ἰβηρίᾳ Ἕλληνας αὐτονόμους καὶ ἐλευθέρους εἶναι. καὶ τάδε ταῖς συνθήκαις ταῖς Ῥωμαίων καὶ Καρχηδονίων προσεγράφη.

28   8. Ἀσρούβαν δ᾽ ἐπὶ τοῖσδε Ἰβηρίαν τὴν ὑπὸ Καρχηδονίοις καθιστάμενον ἀνὴρ δοῦλος, οὗ τὸν δεσπότην ὠμῶς διεφθάρκει, λαθὼν ἐν κυνηγεσίοις ἀναιρεῖ.
29 καὶ τόνδε μὲν Ἀννίβας ἐλεγχθέντα δεινῶς αἰκισάμε-

---

³ βόρειον VM: ἑσπέριον Exc.

9 The Ebro flows into the Mediterranean about one hundred
miles south of Barcelona. In this chapter, by the Western Sea (or
Ocean), Appian seems to intend the western part of the Mediterranean. The manuscript reading, "the Northern Ocean," makes
no sense at all.

Iberia in two, and, at a distance of five days march from the Pyrenees, issues into the Western Ocean.[9]

7. Fearing for their own welfare, the people of Sagun- 25 tum, a colony of Zacynthus, situated half way between the Pyrenees and the river Ebro,[10] and all other Greeks living in the vicinity of what is known as Emporium or indeed anywhere else in Iberia, sent an embassy to Rome. The 26 senate, not wishing to see the advance of Carthaginian interests, sent envoys to Carthage. Both sides agreed that 27 the river Ebro should form the boundary of Carthaginian rule in Iberia: the Romans were not to wage war on those south of this river, as these were Carthaginian subjects; and the Carthaginians were not to cross the Ebro for the purpose of conducting war; the Saguntines and other Greeks in Iberia were to be free and autonomous. These terms were added to the existing treaty between Rome and Carthage.

8. Later on, while Hasdrubal was governing the part of 28 Iberia under Carthaginian control, a slave ambushes and kills him on a hunt; Hasdrubal had cruelly killed the slave's master. Hannibal had the man examined, horribly tor- 29

[10] Appian's location of Saguntum to the north of the river Ebro is incorrect. In fact it was about ninety-three miles south of the river. As Appian explains, the Carthaginians agreed not to cross the Ebro in arms. In order to lay the blame for the Second Punic War on Carthage, some patriotic Roman historians placed it north of the river, thus making an attack on Saguntum a breach of that agreement. Appian is reflecting that invented tradition. Emporium is modern Ampurias, about sixty-two miles northeast of Barcelona.

APPIAN

νος διέφθειρε· ἡ στρατιὰ δὲ τὸν Ἀννίβαν, καίπερ ὄντα
κομιδῇ νέον, ἀρέσκοντα δ' ἰσχυρῶς, στρατηγὸν ἀπέ-
δειξαν αὐτῶν· καὶ ἡ Καρχηδονίων βουλὴ συνέθετο.
30 ὅσοι δὲ τοῦ Βάρκα διαπολιτευταὶ τὴν Βάρκα τε καὶ
Ἀσρούβα δύναμιν ἐδεδοίκεσαν, ὡς ἔμαθον αὐτοὺς
τεθνεῶτας, Ἀννίβα κατεφρόνουν ὡς νέου καὶ τοὺς
ἐκείνων φίλους τε καὶ στασιώτας ἐδίωκον ἐπὶ τοῖς
31 ἐκείνων ἐγκλήμασιν. ὅ τε δῆμος ἅμα τοῖς κατηγοροῦ-
σιν ἐγίγνετο, μνησικακῶν τοῖς διωκομένοις τῆς βαρύ-
τητος τῆς ἐπὶ Βάρκα τε καὶ Ἀσρούβα· καὶ τὰς δωρεὰς
ἐκέλευον αὐτούς, ὅσας μεγάλας Ἀσρούβας τε καὶ
Βάρκας αὐτοῖς ἐπεπόμφεσαν, ἐς τὸ κοινὸν ἐσενεγκεῖν
32 ὡς ἐκ τῶν πολεμίων πεπορισμένας. οἳ δ' ἐπέστελλον
τῷ Ἀννίβᾳ, σφίσιν τε ἐπικουρεῖν δεόμενοι καὶ διδά-
σκοντες, ὅτι καὶ αὐτὸς ἔσοιτο τοῖς πατρῴοις ἐχθροῖς
εὐκαταφρόνητος, εἰ τοὺς ἐν τῇ πατρίδι συνεργεῖν
αὐτῷ δυναμένους ὑπερίδοι.
33   9. Ὁ δὲ καὶ ταῦτα προεώρα καὶ τὰς ἐκείνων δίκας
ἀρχὴν τῆς ἐφ' ἑαυτὸν οὖσαν ἐπιβουλῆς· οὐδ' ἠξίου
τὴν ἔχθραν, ὥσπερ ὁ πατὴρ καὶ ὁ κηδεστής, ἐσαεὶ
καὶ μετὰ φόβου διαφέρειν οὐδ' ἐπὶ τῷ Καρχηδονίων
κουφόνῳ μέχρι παντὸς εἶναι, ῥᾳδίως ἐς εὐεργέτας
34 πρὸς ἀχαριστίαν τρεπομένων. ἐλέγετο δὲ καὶ παῖς ὢν
ἔτι ὑπὸ τοῦ πατρὸς ὁρκωθῆναι ἐπὶ ἐμπύρων ἄσπει-
στος ἐχθρὸς ἔσεσθαι Ῥωμαίοις, ὅτε ἐς πολιτείαν
παρέλθοι. διὰ δὴ ταῦτ' ἐπενόει, μεγάλοις καὶ χρονίοις
πράγμασι τὴν πατρίδα περιβαλὼν καὶ καταστήσας
ἐς ἀσχολίας καὶ φόβους, τὸ ἑαυτοῦ καὶ τὰ τῶν φίλων

tured, and executed. Although he was very young, Hannibal was extremely popular with the soldiers, who now appointed him their commander in chief. The Carthaginian
senate confirmed the appointment. But all the political   30
opponents of Barca, who had feared both his and Hasdrubal's power, when they heard that both were dead,
began to dismiss Hannibal as a youth and attack the
friends and partisans of Barca and Hasdrubal on the same
charges as they had used against them before. The people   31
supported the accusers, bearing a grudge against the de-
fendants for their oppressive behavior when Barca and
Hasdrubal were still alive, and they ordered the accused
to pay into the treasury the large gifts Barca and Hasdrubal had sent them, on the grounds that these were
public spoils taken from the enemy. They also appealed to   32
Hannibal asking for his help and pointing out that he too
would become contemptible to his father's enemies if he
ignored those in his homeland who were in a position to
help him.

9. For his part, Hannibal had foreseen these matters   33
and knew that the prosecution of those men was the first
act of a plot against himself. In contrast to his father and
brother-in-law, he decided he would not put up with the
constant fear of this threat, nor remain permanently at the
mercy of Carthaginian whims, which only too easily turned
to ingratitude toward benefactors. There was also a story   34
that when he was still a child, Hannibal was made to swear
an oath by his father at a sacrifice to the effect that when
he was old enough to enter political life, he would be an
implacable enemy of Rome. For these reasons he planned
to make his own and his friends' position safe by engaging
his country in serious and time-consuming affairs and

35 ἐν ἀδεεῖ θέσθαι. Λιβύην μὲν οὖν εὐσταθοῦσαν ἑώρα
καὶ Ἰβήρων, ὅσα ὑπήκοα ἦν· εἰ δὲ πρὸς Ῥωμαίους
πόλεμον αὖθις ἀναρριπίσειεν, οὗ μάλιστα ἐπεθύμει,
ἐδόκει Καρχηδονίους μὲν ἐν φροντίσι καὶ φόβοις ἔσεσθαι μακροῖς, αὐτὸς δέ, εἴτε κατορθώσειεν, ἐπὶ κλέους
ἀθανάτου γενήσεσθαι, τὴν πατρίδα τῆς οἰκουμένης
[γῆς]⁴ ἄρχουσαν ἀποφήνας (οὐ γὰρ εἶναί τινας ἀντι-
μάχους αὐτοῖς ἔτι ἐπὶ Ῥωμαίοις), εἴτε καὶ πταίσειε,
μεγάλην καὶ ὡς τὸ ἐγχείρημα αὐτῷ δόξαν οἴσειν.

36   10. Ἀρχὴν δ᾽ ὑπολαμβάνων ἔσεσθαι λαμπράν, εἰ
τὸν Ἴβηρα διαβαίη, Τορβολήτας, οἳ γείτονές εἰσι
Ζακανθαίων, ἀνέπεισε τῶν Ζακανθαίων παρὰ οἷ κατα-
βοᾶν ὡς τήν τε χώραν αὐτῶν ἐπιτρεχόντων καὶ πολλὰ
37 σφᾶς ἄλλα ἀδικούντων. οἳ δ᾽ ἐπείθοντο. καὶ πρέσβεις
αὐτῶν ὁ Ἀννίβας ἐς Καρχηδόνα ἔπεμπεν αὐτός τε
ἐν ἀπορρήτοις ἔγραφε Ῥωμαίους τὴν ὑπὸ Καρχηδονίοις Ἰβηρίαν ἀναπείθειν ἀπὸ Καρχηδονίων ἀφίστα-
σθαι καὶ Ζακανθαίους Ῥωμαίοις ταῦτα συμπράσσειν.
ὅλως τε τῆς ἀπάτης οὐ μεθίει πολλὰ τοιαῦτα ἐπιστέλ-
λων, ἕως ἡ βουλὴ προσέταξεν αὐτῷ πράσσειν ἐς Ζα-
38 κανθαίους, ὅ τι δοκιμάσειεν. ὁ δ᾽ ἐπεὶ τῆς ἀφορμῆς
ἐλάβετο, Τορβολήτας αὖθις ἔπραξεν ἐντυχεῖν οἱ κατὰ
τῶν Ζακανθαίων καὶ Ζακανθαίων μετεπέμπετο πρέσβεις. οἳ δὲ ἀφίκοντο μέν, κελεύοντος δὲ τοῦ Ἀννίβου
λέγειν ἑκατέρους ἐφ᾽ ἑαυτοῦ, περὶ ὧν διαφέρονται,
39 Ῥωμαίοις ἔφασαν ἐπιτρέψειν τὴν δίκην. ὁ μὲν δὴ
ταῦτ᾽ εἰπόντας ἀπέπεμπεν ἀπὸ τοῦ στρατοπέδου καὶ
τῆς ἐπιούσης νυκτὸς παντὶ τῷ στρατῷ τὸν Ἴβηρα

busying it with fears. But he saw that there were stable   35
conditions in Africa and among the Carthaginian subjects
of Iberia. If only he could rekindle a war against Rome—
and that is what he particularly wanted—he thought the
Carthaginians would be distracted by their great concerns
and fears, while he himself, if successful, would win im-
mortal fame for making his country ruler of the whole
world; for the Carthaginians had no other challengers after the Romans. And if he failed, even the attempt itself
would bring him great glory.

10. Thinking that it would be a brilliant start if he   36
crossed the Ebro, Hannibal set about persuading the Turbuletes, neighbors of Saguntum, to complain to him that
the Saguntines were overrunning Turbuletan territory and
doing them many other injuries. They duly complied.   37
Hannibal sent their ambassadors to Carthage, while he
himself secretly wrote that the Romans were trying to
persuade the people of Carthaginian Iberia to revolt from
Carthage and the Saguntines were helping them in this.
He persisted with this deceit, sending many similar mes-
sages, until the council ordered him to take whatever action against the Saguntines he saw fit. Once he had the   38
impetus, he again got the Turbuletes to appeal to him
against the Saguntines, and summoned ambassadors from
Saguntum. When they arrived, although Hannibal ordered both sides to set out the grounds of their dispute
before him, the Saguntines said they would refer the case
to Rome. In view of this statment, Hannibal dismissed   39
them from his camp, and the following night crossed the

---

4 γῆς del. Viereck-Roos

διαβὰς τὴν χώραν ἐπόρθει καὶ τῇ πόλει μηχανήματα
ἐφίστη. ἑλεῖν δ' οὐ δυνάμενος ἀπετάφρευε καὶ περι-
ετείχιζε καὶ φρούρια πολλὰ περιθεὶς ἐκ διαστημάτων
ἐπεφοίτα.

40   11. Ζακανθαῖοι δὲ αἰφνιδίῳ κακῷ καὶ ἀκαταγγέλτῳ
συμπεσόντες ἐπρέσβευον ἐς Ῥώμην. καὶ ἡ σύγκλητος αὐτοῖς συνέπεμπε πρέσβεις, οἳ πρῶτον μὲν Ἀννίβαν ἔμελλον ὑπομνήσειν τῶν συγκειμένων, οὐ πει-
θομένου δὲ ἐς Καρχηδόνα πλευσεῖσθαι κατ' αὐτοῦ.

41   τούτοις τοῖς πρέσβεσι πλεύσασιν ἐς Ἰβηρίαν καὶ
ἐς τὸ στρατόπεδον ἀπὸ θαλάσσης ἀναβαίνουσιν ὁ
Ἀννίβας ἀπηγόρευσε μὴ προσιέναι. καὶ οἱ μὲν ἀπέ-
πλευσαν ἐπὶ Καρχηδόνος σὺν τοῖς πρέσβεσιν τοῖς
Ζακανθαίων καὶ τῶν συνθηκῶν ἀνεμίμνησκον αὐτούς·
Καρχηδόνιοι δὲ ᾐτιῶντο τοὺς Ζακανθαίους πολλὰ

42   τοὺς ὑπηκόους σφῶν ἀδικεῖν. καὶ Ζακανθαίων οἱ πρέσβεις ἐς δίκην αὐτοὺς προυκαλοῦντο ἐπὶ Ῥωμαίων
κριτῶν· οἳ δ' οὐκ ἔφασαν χρῄζειν δίκης, ἀμύνεσθαι

43   δυνάμενοι. ὧν ἐς Ῥώμην ἀπαγγελθέντων, οἱ μὲν ἐκέλευον ἤδη συμμαχεῖν τοῖς Ζακανθαίοις, οἳ δ' ἐπεῖχον
ἔτι, λέγοντες οὐ συμμάχους αὐτοὺς ἐν ταῖς συνθήκαις
σφῶν, ἀλλ' αὐτονόμους καὶ ἐλευθέρους ἀναγεγρά-
φθαι, ἐλευθέρους δὲ ἔτι καὶ τοὺς πολιορκουμένους εἶναι. καὶ ἐκράτησεν ἡ γνώμη.

44   12. Ζακανθαῖοι δέ, ἐπειδὴ τὰ Ῥωμαίων ἀπέγνωσαν
καὶ ὁ λιμὸς σφᾶς ἐπίεζε καὶ Ἀννίβας περιεκάθητο
συνεχῶς (εὐδαίμονα γὰρ καὶ πολύχρυσον ἀκούων εἶναι τὴν πόλιν οὐκ ἀνίει τῆς πολιορκίας), τὸν μὲν χρυ-

Ebro with his entire force, ravaged the land and brought up his war engines to assault the town. As he proved unable to take it, he invested it with a ditch and a wall, and after setting up numerous guard posts around it, made intermittent attacks.

11. Plunged into this sudden crisis without diplomatic 40
warning, the Saguntines sent a mission to Rome. The senate dispatched their own ambassadors along with those of Saguntum with instructions first to remind Hannibal of what had been agreed and then, if he paid no attention, to sail to Carthage and lay a complaint against him. These 41
ambassadors sailed to Iberia, but as they were coming up from the sea to his camp, Hannibal refused to let them approach. So they and the Saguntine mission sailed off to Carthage where they reminded the Carthaginians of the treaty. The latter accused Saguntum of committing many injustices against Carthaginian subjects, and the Saguntine 42
envoys invited them to refer the case to Roman arbitration: they did not need a legal process, they said, as they were quite capable of defending themselves. When news 43
of this reached Rome, some recommended that they immediately send help to the Saguntines, while others continued to prevaricate, arguing that the Saguntines had been registered in the treaty not as allies, but as free and autonomous agents, and even people under siege were still free. This latter opinion prevailed.

12. At Saguntum they had given up on Rome. Hunger 44
pressed them, and Hannibal persevered with the blockade unremittingly: he had heard that the city was prosperous and rich in gold, and for that reason maintained his grip on the siege. By public order, the Saguntines collected all

σὸν καὶ ἄργυρον, ὅσος ἦν δημόσιός τε καὶ ἰδιωτικός,
ἀπὸ κηρύγματος ἐς τὴν ἀγορὰν συνήνεγκαν καὶ μο-
λύβδῳ καὶ χαλκῷ συνεχώνευσαν, ὡς ἀχρεῖον Ἀννίβᾳ
45 γενέσθαι, αὐτοὶ δ', ἐν χερσὶν ἑλόμενοί τι παθεῖν μᾶλλον ἢ ὑπὸ τοῦ λιμοῦ, ἐξέδραμον ἔτι νυκτὸς ἐπὶ τὰ
φρούρια τὰ τῶν Λιβύων, ἀναπαυομένων ἔτι καὶ οὐδὲν
τοιοῦτον οὐδ'[5] ὑπονοούντων· ὅθεν αὐτοὺς ἀνισταμέ-
νους τε ἐξ εὐνῆς καὶ σὺν θορύβῳ μόλις ὁπλιζομένους,
ἔστι δ' οὓς ἤδη καὶ μαχομένους, διέφθειρον. μακροῦ
δὲ τοῦ ἀγῶνος γενομένου, Λιβύων μὲν ἀπώλοντο πολ-
46 λοί, Ζακανθαῖοι δὲ πάντες. αἱ δὲ γυναῖκες, ἀπὸ τοῦ
τείχους ὁρῶσαι τὸ τέλος τῶν ἀνδρῶν, αἱ μὲν ἐρρίπτουν ἑαυτὰς κατὰ τῶν τεγῶν, αἱ δ' ἀνήρτων, αἱ δὲ
καὶ τὰ τέκνα προκατέσφαζον. καὶ τοῦτο τέλος ἦν Ζα-
47 κανθαίοις, πόλει τε μεγάλῃ καὶ δυνατῇ γενομένῃ. Ἀννίβας δ', ὡς ἔμαθε περὶ τοῦ χρυσοῦ, τοὺς μὲν ὑπολοίπους καὶ ἔτι ἡβῶντας αὐτῶν αἰκιζόμενος διέφθειρεν
ὑπὸ ὀργῆς, τὴν δὲ πόλιν ὁρῶν ἐπὶ θάλασσόν τε καὶ
Καρχηδόνος οὐ μακρὰν καὶ χώρας ἄρχουσαν ἀγαθῆς
ᾤκιζεν αὖθις καὶ Καρχηδονίων ἄποικον ἀπέφαινεν· ἣν
νῦν οἶμαι Καρχηδόνα καλεῖσθαι τὴν Σπαρταγενῆ.

48   13. Ῥωμαῖοι δὲ πρέσβεις ἐς Καρχηδόνα ἔπεμπον,
οἷς εἴρητο ἐξαιτεῖν παρὰ Καρχηδονίων Ἀννίβαν ὡς ἐς
τὰς συνθήκας ἁμαρτόντα, εἰ μὴ κοινὸν ἡγοῦνται τὸ
ἔργον· ἦν δὲ μὴ διδῶσιν, εὐθέως αὐτοῖς πόλεμον προ-
49 αγορεύειν. καὶ οἱ μὲν ἔπραξαν ὧδε καὶ τὸν πόλεμον

_____
[5] οὐδ' Goukowsky: δ' (erasa) V

gold and silver, both state owned and private, in the market place, where they melted it down with lead and bronze to make it unusable for Hannibal. They themselves, pre- 45 ferring to die in action rather than starve to death, made a sortie during the night against the African guard posts—who were still asleep and not expecting such a maneuver—thereby killing some as they were getting out of bed and finding it difficult in the melée to arm themselves, and others already fighting. The battle lasted a long time, and many of the Africans were killed, but all the Saguntines. From the walls, the women could see their husbands die, 46 and some threw themselves down onto the buildings, others hanged themselves, others even killed their children first. Such was the end of Saguntum, a great and powerful town. When he heard about the gold, Hannibal was furi- 47 ous and tortured and executed all the surviving adults. But he could see that the town was on the coast not far from Carthage and that it controlled rich land. So he resettled it and declared it to be a Carthaginian colony. I believe it is now called Espartan Carthage.[11]

13. The Romans sent ambassadors to Carthage with 48 instructions to demand that Hannibal be handed over by the Carthaginians for violating the treaty, unless they regarded his actions as official policy. If they did not give him up, the ambassadors were immediately to declare war. They followed orders and when the Carthaginians refused 49

[11] Appian seems to be confusing Saguntum with the city of New Carthage (modern Cartagena) some 150 miles south of it. The name Carthago Spartaria is known in later times (e.g., Pliny, *HN* 31.31), as is the abundance of esparto grass in the area (Plin. *HN* 19.7; Livy 22.20.6).

αὐτοῖς, οὐκ ἐκδιδοῦσι τὸν Ἀννίβαν, ἐπήγγειλαν· λέγεται δ᾽ οὕτω γενέσθαι. ὁ μὲν πρεσβευτὴς αὐτοῖς γελώ-
μενος ἔφη, τὸν κόλπον ἐπιδεικνύς· "Ἐνταῦθ᾽ ὑμῖν, ὦ
Καρχηδόνιοι, καὶ τὴν εἰρήνην καὶ τὸν πόλεμον φέρω·
50 ὑμεῖς δ᾽, ὁπότερα αἱρεῖσθε, λάβετε." οἳ δ᾽ ἔφασαν· "Σὺ
μὲν οὖν, ἃ βούλει, δίδου." προτείναντος δὲ τὸν πόλεμον ἐξεβόησαν ὁμοῦ πάντες· "Δεχόμεθα." καὶ εὐθὺς
ἐπέστελλον τῷ Ἀννίβᾳ πᾶσαν ἤδη τὴν Ἰβηρίαν
51 ἀδεῶς ἐπιτρέχειν ὡς τῶν σπονδῶν λελυμένων. ὁ μὲν
δὴ τὰ ἔθνη τὰ ἀγχοῦ πάντα ἐπιὼν ὑπήγετο, ἢ πείθων
ἢ δεδιττόμενος ἢ καταστρεφόμενος, καὶ στρατιὰν
πολλὴν συνέλεγεν, τὴν μὲν χρείαν οὐχ ὑποδεικνύς,
52 ἐς δὲ τὴν Ἰταλίαν ἐπινοῶν ἐμβαλεῖν, Γαλάταις τε
διεπρεσβεύετο καὶ τὰς διόδους τῶν Ἀλπείων ὁρῶν
κατεσκέπτετο καὶ ‹τὴν Πυρήνην›[6] διῆλθεν, Ἀσρούβαν τὸν ἀδελφὸν ἐν Ἰβηρίᾳ ‹καταλιπὼν . . .
53   14. . . .› σφίσι[7] καὶ Λιβύη τὸν πόλεμον ἔσεσθαι (οὐ
γὰρ δὴ μὴ Λίβυές ποτε ἐς τὴν Ἰταλίαν ἐσβάλωσιν,
οὐδ᾽ ὑπενόουν), Τιβέριον μὲν Σεμπρώνιον Λόγγον ἐπὶ
νεῶν ἑκατὸν ἑξήκοντα σὺν δύο στρατοῦ τέλεσιν ἐς
Λιβύην ἐξέπεμπον (καὶ ὅσα Λόγγος τε καὶ οἱ λοιποὶ
Ῥωμαίων στρατηγοὶ περὶ Λιβύην ἔπραξαν, ἐν τῇ
54 Καρχηδονικῇ βύβλῳ συγγέγραπται), Πούπλιον δὲ
Κορνήλιον Σκιπίωνα ἔστελλον ἐς Ἰβηρίαν ἐπὶ νεῶν

----

[6] τὴν Πυρήνην add. Goukowsky
[7] Steph. explevit lacunam: ἐν Ἰβηρίᾳ ‹καταλιπὼν· οἱ δὲ
Ῥωμαῖοι προορῶντες καὶ ἐν Ἰβηρίᾳ › σφίσι

to hand over Hannibal, duly declared war on them. The story of what happened runs as follows. The Roman spokesman was being mocked, but pointing to the fold of his cloak, said, "In here, men of Carthage, I bring you both war and peace: take whichever one you choose." But they 50 said, "No, give us the one you want." When he offered them war, they all roared in agreement, "We accept!" And they immediately wrote to Hannibal with instructions now to overrun the whole of Iberia without fear as the treaty was dissolved. He moved against all the neighboring peo- 51 ples and subjected them, using a mixture of persuasion, fear, and military force; and he began to collect a large army, without revealing his purpose, as he intended to use it to invade Italy. He also began to establish diplomatic 52 links with the Gauls and reconnoiter the Alpine passes. He then set out across the Pyrenees, leaving his brother Hasdrubal in Iberia ‹. . .

14. The Romans, foreseeing›[12] that the war would take 53 place in Iberia and Africa—for they did not even imagine that Africans would ever invade Italy—dispatched Tiberius Sempronius Longus to Africa with one hundred and sixty ships and two legions (I have recorded in my Carthaginian Book what Longus and the other Roman generals accomplished in Africa),[13] and they posted Pub- 54 lius Cornelius Scipio to Iberia with sixty ships, ten thou-

---

[12] I have followed Stephanus' suggestion for what has been lost from the text.   [13] Appian does not mention Sempronius Longus in the Carthaginian Book, nor indeed, in his separate work on the Hannibalic War. Longus campaigned in Sicily to prepare for an invasion of Africa, but it did not take place. Scipio Africanus eventually crossed to Africa in 204.

ἑξήκοντα μετὰ πεζῶν μυρίων καὶ ἱππέων ἑπτακοσίων καὶ πρεσβευτὴν αὐτῷ συνέπεμπον Γναῖον Κορνήλιον
55 Σκιπίωνα τὸν ἀδελφόν. τούτοιν ὁ μὲν Πόπλιος παρὰ Μασσαλιωτῶν ἐμπόρων πυθόμενος Ἀννίβαν διὰ τῶν Ἀλπείων ὀρῶν ἐς τὴν Ἰταλίαν ὑπερβάντα, δείσας, μὴ ἀδοκήτως τοῖς Ἰταλιώταις ἐπιπέσοι, παραδοὺς Γναίῳ τῷ ἀδελφῷ τὴν ἐν Ἰβηρίᾳ στρατιὰν διέπλευσεν ἐπὶ
56 πεντήρους ἐς Τυρρηνίαν. καὶ ὅσα ἔπραξεν ἐν τῇ Ἰταλίᾳ οὗτός τε καὶ ὅσοι μετ' αὐτὸν ἄλλοι στρατηγοὶ τοῦδε τοῦ πολέμου ἐγένοντο, ἕως Ἀννίβαν ἑκκαιδεκάτῳ μόλις ἔτει τῆς Ἰταλίας ἐξήλασαν, ἡ ἑξῆς βίβλος ὑποδείκνυσιν, ἣ τὰ ἔργα Ἀννίβου τὰ ἐν Ἰταλίᾳ πάντα περιλαμβάνει καὶ παρ' αὐτὸ λέγεται Ῥωμαϊκῶν Ἀννιβαϊκή.[8]
57   15. Γναῖος δὲ οὐδέν, ὅ τι καὶ εἰπεῖν, ἔπραξεν ἐν τοῖς Ἴβηρσι, πρὶν αὐτῷ Πόπλιον τὸν ἀδελφὸν ἐπανελθεῖν· Ῥωμαῖοι γάρ, ληγούσης τῆς ἀρχῆς τῷ Ποπλίῳ, πρὸς μὲν Ἀννίβαν ἐς τὴν Ἰταλίαν τοὺς μετὰ τὸν Πόπλιον ὑπάτους ἐξέπεμψαν, αὐτὸν δ' ἀνθύπα-
58 τον ἀποφήναντες ἐς Ἰβηρίαν αὖθις ἔστειλαν. καὶ ἀπὸ τοῦδε οἱ δύο Σκιπίωνες τὸν ἐν Ἰβηρίᾳ πόλεμον διέφερον, Ἀσρούβου σφίσιν ἀντιστρατηγοῦντος, μέχρι Καρχηδόνιοι μὲν ὑπὸ Σύφακος, τοῦ τῶν Νομάδων δυνάστου, πολεμούμενοι τὸν Ἀσρούβαν καὶ μέρος τῆς ὑπ' αὐτῷ στρατιᾶς μετεπέμψαντο, τῶν δ' ὑπολοίπων
59 οἱ Σκιπίωνες εὐμαρῶς ἐκράτουν. καὶ πολλαὶ τῶν

[8] Ἀννιβιακή VM

sand infantry and seven hundred cavalry. They also sent
his brother, Gnaeus Cornelius Scipio, with him as his legate.[14] Of the two, when Publius Scipio learned from Mas-   55
siliot merchants that Hannibal had crossed the Alps into
Italy, he was afraid that his attack would take the Italians
by surprise; and transferring the command in Iberia to his
brother Gnaeus, he sailed on a quinquireme to Etruria.
The next book will describe what Publius Scipio and the   56
other the generals who succeeded him accomplished in
Italy during this war, until fifteen years later they just
about managed to drive Hannibal out of Italy: it contains
all Hannibal's actions in Italy and is named the Hannibalic
Book of Roman History for this reason.

15. Gnaeus on the other hand achieved nothing worth   57
noting in Iberia before his brother Publius returned to join
him. When Publius' year of office was running out, the
senate appointed him proconsul and sent him back to Iberia, while dispatching Publius' successors in the consulship against Hannibal in Italy. From then on, the two   58
Scipios ran the war in Iberia, with Hasdrubal as the opposing commander, until the Carthaginians were attacked
by Syphax, prince of the Numidians, and sent for Hasdrubal and part of the army under his command. The
Scipios easily defeated the rest. Indeed many towns   59

---

[14] Publius Cornelius Scipio (father of Scipio Africanus) was
consul with Tiberius Sempronius Longus in 218. Gnaeus Cornelius Scipio Calvus, brother of the consul of 218, had himself been
consul in 222.

πόλεων ἐς αὐτοὺς ἑκοῦσαι μετετίθεντο· καὶ γὰρ ἤστην
πιθανωτάτω στρατηγῆσαί τε καὶ προσαγαγέσθαι.

60   16. Θέμενοι δ' οἱ Καρχηδόνιοι πρὸς Σύφακα εἰρήνην
αὖθις ἐξέπεμπον εἰς Ἰβηρίαν Ἀσρούβαν μετὰ πλέονος στρατοῦ καὶ ἐλεφάντων τριάκοντα καὶ σὺν αὐτῷ
ἄλλους δύο στρατηγούς, Μάγωνά τε καὶ Ἀσρούβαν
ἕτερον, ὃς Γέσκωνος ἦν υἱός. καὶ χαλεπώτερος ἦν τοῖς
Σκιπίωσιν ὁ πόλεμος ἀπὸ τοῦδε, ἐκράτουν δὲ καὶ ὥς.

61   καὶ πολλοὶ μὲν τῶν Λιβύων, πολλοὶ δὲ τῶν ἐλεφάντων ἐφθάρησαν, μέχρι χειμῶνος ἐπιλαβόντος οἱ μὲν
Λίβυες ἐχείμαζον ἐν Τυρδιτανίᾳ, τῶν δὲ Σκιπιώνων ὁ
μὲν Γναῖος ἐν Ὀρσῶνι, ὁ δὲ Πούπλιος ἐν Καστολῶνι.

62   ἔνθα αὐτῷ προσιὼν ὁ Ἀσρούβας ἀπηγγέλθη· καὶ
προελθὼν τῆς πόλεως μετ' ὀλίγων ἐς κατασκοπὴν
στρατοπέδου ἔλαθε πλησιάσας τῷ Ἀσρούβᾳ, καὶ
αὐτὸν ἐκεῖνος καὶ τοὺς σὺν αὐτῷ πάντας ἱππεῦσι

63   περιδραμὼν ἀπέκτεινεν. ὁ δὲ Γναῖος οὐδέν ἔτι[9] προμα-
θὼν ἐς τὸν ἀδελφὸν ἐπὶ σίτον ἔπεμπε στρατιώτας, οἷς
ἕτεροι Λιβύων συντυχόντες ἐμάχοντο. καὶ πυθόμενος
ὁ Γναῖος ἐξέδραμεν, ὡς εἶχεν, μετὰ τῶν εὐζώνων ἐπ'
αὐτούς. οἱ δὲ τούς τε προτέρους ἀνῃρήκεσαν ἤδη καὶ
τὸν Γναῖον ἐδίωκον, ἕως ἐσέδραμεν ἔς τινα πύργον.
καὶ τὸν πύργον ἐνέπρησαν οἱ Λίβυες, καὶ ὁ Σκιπίων
κατεκαύθη μετὰ τῶν συνόντων.

64   17. Οὕτω μὲν οἱ Σκιπίωνες ἀπέθανον ἄμφω, ἄνδρες
ἐς πάντα ἀγαθοὶ γενόμενοι· καὶ αὐτοὺς ἐπεπόθησαν

[9] ἔτι Goukowsky: τι VM

changed to the Roman side of their own accord, for the two brothers inspired a high level of confidence both in their command of armies and their ability to win friends.

16. When the Carthaginians made peace with Syphax,   60 they again sent out Hasdrubal to Iberia with a bigger army and thirty elephants, and along with them two other generals, Mago and a second Hasdrubal, who was the son of Gisco. After this, the war became more difficult for the Scipios, but they continued to dominate nonetheless. Many Africans were killed and many elephants, until with   61 the onset of winter the Africans went into winter quarters in Turditania, Gnaeus Scipio in Orso and Publius in Castolo, where he was informed of Hasdrubal's advance.[15]   62 Advancing out of the town with a small force to reconnoiter the Carthaginian camp, Publius failed to notice that he had approached too close to Hasdrubal, who surrounded him and his men with cavalry and killed them all. Gnaeus still knew nothing of this and sent some soldiers   63 to Publius to collect grain, but they encountered another force of Africans who engaged with them. When he heard this, Gnaeus rushed out against the enemy without delay with his light-armed troops. The Africans had already destroyed the first Roman force and now put Gnaeus to flight, until he escaped to a tower. But they set fire to the tower, and Scipio and his men were burned to death.

17. So died the two Scipios, good men in every respect,   64 and sorely missed by all the Iberians who, because of

---

[15] Castulo, modern Cazlona (near Linares, sixty-two miles northeast of Córdoba). Appian's Orso should be ancient Urso, modern Osuna (about fifty miles east of Seville), but that would have put Gnaeus some 125 miles away from Publius.

65 Ἴβηρες, ὅσοι δι᾽ αὐτοὺς ἐς Ῥωμαίους μετέθεντο. πυθόμενοι δ᾽ οἱ ἐν ἄστει βαρέως τε ἤνεγκαν καὶ Μάρκελλον ἐκ Σικελίας ἄρτι ἀφιγμένον καὶ σὺν αὐτῷ Κλαύδιον ἐπὶ νεῶν <...> ἐξέπεμπον ἐς Ἰβηρίαν μετὰ χιλίων ἱππέων καὶ πεζῶν μυρίων καὶ χορηγίας ἱκανῆς.

66 οὐδενὸς δὲ λαμπροῦ παρὰ τῶνδε γιγνομένου τὰ Λιβύων ὑπερηύξητο, καὶ πᾶσαν σχεδὸν Ἰβηρίαν εἶχον, ἐς βραχὺ Ῥωμαίων ἐν τοῖς ὄρεσι τοῖς Πυρηναίοις

67 κατακεκλησμένων. πάλιν οὖν οἱ ἐν ἄστει πυνθανόμενοι μᾶλλον ἐταράσσοντο· καὶ φόβος ἦν, μὴ Ἀννίβου πορθοῦντος τὰ πρόσω τῆς Ἰταλίας καὶ οἵδε οἱ Λίβυες ἐς τὰ ἕτερα αὐτῆς ἐσβάλοιεν. ὅθεν οὐδ᾽ ἀποσχέσθαι τῆς Ἰβηρίας βουλομένοις αὐτοῖς δυνατὸν ἦν, δέει τοῦ μὴ καὶ τόνδε τὸν πόλεμον ἐς τὴν Ἰταλίαν ἐπαγαγέσθαι.

68 18. Προύγραφον οὖν ἡμέραν, ἐν ᾗ χειροτονήσουσιν στρατηγὸν εἰς Ἰβηρίαν. καὶ οὐδενὸς παραγγέλλοντος ἔτι πλείων ἐγίγνετο φόβος, καὶ σιωπῇ σκυθρωπὸς ἐπεῖχε τὴν ἐκκλησίαν, ἐς οὗ Κορνήλιος Σκιπίων, ὁ Ποπλίου Κορνηλίου τοῦ ἀναιρεθέντος ἐν Ἴβηρσιν υἱός, νέος μὲν ὢν κομιδῇ (τεσσάρων γὰρ καὶ εἴκοσιν ἐτῶν ἦν), σώφρων δὲ καὶ γενναῖος εἶναι νομιζόμενος, ἐς τὸ μέσον ἐλθὼν ἐσεμνολόγησεν ἀμφί τε τοῦ πατρὸς καὶ ἀμφὶ τοῦ θείου καὶ τὸ πάθος αὐτῶν ὀδυράμενος ἐπεῖπεν οἰκεῖος εἶναι τιμωρὸς ἐκ πάντων πατρὶ

16 Gaius Claudius Nero held Spain until Scipio Africanus arrived in 210. Claudius was consul in 207, and with his fellow

them, had gone over to the Roman side. At Rome, they   65
took the news with dismay, and sent off to Iberia Marcellus, who had just arrived from Sicily, and Claudius too,
with < . . .> ships, one thousand cavalry, ten thousand infantry and sufficient supplies.[16] With neither of them   66
achieving any brilliant success, Carthaginian power grew
enormously to embrace nearly the whole of Iberia; Roman
forces were restricted to a small part of the Pyrenees.
Again, when this news got to Rome the people were even   67
more troubled. They were afraid that while Hannibal was
ravaging the south of Italy, these Africans would invade
the rest of it. And so, although they wanted to evacuate
Iberia, they could not do so out of fear that the war there
would be transferred to Italy.

18. They fixed a day, therefore, to choose a commander   68
for Iberia. The fact that nobody put himself forward for
the job greatly increased the anxiety, and a sullen silence
held the assembly until Cornelius Scipio, son of the Publius Cornelius Scipio killed in Iberia, who although very
young (he was twenty-four years old), was well regarded
as a man of moderation and nobility, came forward and
spoke inspiringly about his father and uncle.[17] Lamenting
their death, he emphasized how he of all men was the right

consul defeated and killed Hasdrubal in Italy at the battle of the
Metaurus. Other sources know nothing of a Marcellus at this
point: Livy 25.37–39 gives a dramatic version of how a Roman
equestrian L. Marcius saved the day after the death of the Scipios.

[17] Publius Cornelius Scipio Africanus, consul in 205 and 194,
was the hero of Rome's victory over Hannibal in the Second Punic
War.

69 καὶ θείῳ καὶ πατρίδι. ἄλλα τε πολλὰ ἀθρόως καὶ λάβρως ὥσπερ ἔνθους ἐπαγγειλάμενος, οὐκ Ἰβηρίαν
λήψεσθαι μόνην, ἀλλ᾽ ἐπ᾽ αὐτῇ καὶ Λιβύην καὶ Καρχηδόνα, τοῖς μὲν ἔδοξε κουφολογῆσαι νεανικῶς, τὸν
δὲ δῆμον ἀνέλαβε κατεπτηχότα (χαίρουσι γὰρ ἐπαγ-
γελίαις οἱ δεδιότες) καὶ ᾑρέθη στρατηγὸς ἐς Ἰβηρίαν
70 ὡς πράξων τι τῆς εὐτολμίας ἄξιον. οἱ πρεσβύτεροι
δ᾽ αὐτὴν οὐκ εὐτολμίαν, ἀλλὰ προπέτειαν ἐκάλουν.
καὶ ὁ Σκιπίων αἰσθόμενος ἐς ἐκκλησίαν αὖθις αὐτοὺς
71 συνεκάλει τε καὶ ἐσεμνύνετο ὅμοια· καὶ τὴν ἡλικίαν
εἰπὼν οὐδὲν ἐμποδὼν οἱ γενήσεσθαι προυκαλεῖτο
ὅμως, εἴ τις ἐθέλοι τῶν πρεσβυτέρων τὴν ἀρχὴν
72 παραλαβεῖν ἑκόντος αὐτοῦ παραδιδόντος. οὐδενὸς δ᾽
ἑλομένου μᾶλλον ἐπαινούμενός τε καὶ θαυμαζόμενος
ἐξῄει μετὰ μυρίων πεζῶν καὶ ἱππέων πεντακοσίων· οὐ
γὰρ ἐνεχώρει πλέονα στρατὸν ἐξάγειν, Ἀννίβου δη-
οῦντος τὴν Ἰταλίαν. ἔλαβεν δὲ καὶ χρήματα καὶ
παρασκευὴν ἄλλην καὶ ναῦς μακρὰς ὀκτὼ καὶ εἴκοσι,
μεθ᾽ ὧν ἐς Ἰβηρίαν διέπλευσε.

73 19. Παραλαβών τε τὴν ἐκεῖ στρατιὰν καὶ οὓς ἦγεν
ἐς ἓν συναγαγὼν ἐκάθηρε καὶ διελέχθη καὶ τοῖσδε
μεγαληγόρως. δόξα τε διέδραμεν ἐς ὅλην αὐτίκα τὴν
Ἰβηρίαν, βαρυνομένην τε τοὺς Λίβυας καὶ τῶν Σκιπιώνων τὴν ἀρετὴν ἐπιποθοῦσαν, ὅτι στρατηγὸς αὐτοῖς
ἥκοι Σκιπίων ὁ Σκιπίωνος κατὰ θεόν. οὗ δὴ καὶ αὐτὸς
αἰσθανόμενος ὑπεκρίνετο πάντα ποιεῖν πειθόμενος
74 θεῷ. πυνθανόμενος δ᾽, ὅτι οἱ ἐχθροὶ σταθμεύουσι μὲν
ἐν τέσσαρσι στρατοπέδοις, μακρὰν διεστηκότες ἀπ᾽

one to avenge his father, uncle, and country. He spoke   69
fluently and passionately like a man possessed, promising
among many other things to take not just Iberia, but Africa
and Carthage too. Some thought that this was the giddy
talk of youth, but the people were dejected and he raised
their hopes (those in a state of fear are cheered by promises). He was duly elected to the Iberian command as a
man who was expected to accomplish something worthy
of his daring. The older men, however, were saying that   70
this was more rashness than courage. When Scipio heard
this he summoned them again to a meeting and spoke with
gravity on the same sort of topic as before. Although his   71
youth would not, he said, prove any hindrance, nevertheless he invited any older man who wanted it to take over
the command, as he would willingly give it up. When no-   72
body accepted the invitation, he was even more highly
praised and admired, and set off with ten thousand infantry and five hundred cavalry. For since Hannibal was ravaging Italy, it was not possible to take a larger army with
him. He did get money and other equipment and twenty-
eight warships, with which he sailed off to Iberia.

19. After taking over the Roman forces there and unit-   73
ing them with the expedition he had brought with him, he
performed a ceremony of purification and addressed these
men too in lofty terms. Word had raced around the whole
of Iberia, oppressed by the Africans and missing the excellence of the Scipios, that it was divinely ordained that
Scipio's son, Scipio, had arrived to take command of them.
When he heard this himself he pretended that he was doing everything in obedience to heaven's will. Reports came   74
to him that the enemy, in total twenty-five thousand infan-

ἀλλήλων, ἀνὰ δισμυρίους καὶ πεντακισχιλίους πεζοὺς καὶ ἱππέας πεντακοσίους ἐπὶ δισχιλίοις, τὴν δὲ
παρασκευὴν τῶν τε χρημάτων καὶ σίτου καὶ ὅπλων
καὶ βελῶν καὶ νεῶν καὶ αἰχμαλώτων καὶ ὁμήρων τῶν
ἐξ ὅλης Ἰβηρίας ἔχουσιν ἐν τῇ πρότερον μὲν Ζα-
κάνθῃ, τότε δὲ ἤδη Καρχηδόνι, καὶ φρουρὸς αὐτῶν
75 ἐστι Μάγων μετὰ μυρίων Καρχηδονίων, ἔκρινε πρῶτον ἐς τούτους ἐπιδραμεῖν διά τε τὴν ὀλιγότητα τοῦ
στρατοῦ τοῦ μετὰ Μάγωνος καὶ τὸ μέγεθος τῆς παρασκευῆς καὶ ὡς ὁρμητήριον ἀσφαλὲς ἐκ γῆς καὶ θαλάσσης ἕξων ἐπὶ ὅλην τὴν Ἰβηρίαν πόλιν ἀργυρεῖα
καὶ χώραν εὐδαίμονα καὶ πλοῦτον πολὺν ἔχουσαν καὶ
τὸν διάπλουν ἐς Λιβύην βραχύτατον.

76   20. Ὁ μὲν δὴ τοσοῖσδε λογισμοῖς ἐπαιρόμενος,
οὐδενὶ προειπών, ὅπῃ χωρήσειν ἔμελλεν, ἡλίου δύναν-
τος ἦγε τὴν στρατιὰν δι᾽ ὅλης τῆς νυκτὸς ἐπὶ τὴν
Καρχηδόνα. καὶ αὐτὴν ἅμα ἕῳ τῶν Λιβύων καταπλαγέντων περιταφρεύσας ἐς τὴν ἐπιοῦσαν ἡμέραν ἡτοι-
μάζετο, κλίμακάς τε καὶ μηχανὰς πάντῃ περιτιθεὶς
χωρὶς ἑνὸς μέρους, ᾗ τὸ μὲν τεῖχος ἦν βραχύτατον,
ἕλος δ᾽ αὐτῷ καὶ θάλασσα προσέκλυζε καὶ δι᾽ αὐτὸ
77 καὶ οἱ φύλακες ἀμελῶς εἶχον. νυκτὸς δὲ πάντα πληρώ-
σας βελῶν καὶ λίθων καὶ τοῖς λιμέσι τῆς πόλεως
ναῦς ἐπιστήσας, ἵνα μὴ αἱ νῆες αὐτὸν αἱ τῶν πολεμίων διαφύγοιεν (ὑπὸ γὰρ δὴ μεγαλοψυχίας ἤλπιζε
πάντως αἱρήσειν τὴν πόλιν), πρὸ ἕω τὴν στρατιὰν

try and two thousand five hundred cavalry, were quartered in four camps situated a long way from each other, while they kept all their supplies of money, grain, weapons, missiles, ships, prisoners, and hostages, from all over Iberia, in the town formerly known as Saguntum, but then called Carthage.[18] It was garrisoned by Mago with ten thousand Carthaginians. Because of the small force with Mago and the huge quantity of supplies, Scipio decided to make it his first objective: it would provide a secure base for land and sea operations against the whole of Iberia; it was a town with silver mines, fertile territory and great wealth; and it afforded the shortest crossing to Africa.

75

20. Excited by these plans and telling no one where he was intending to go, he led his army out at sunset and marched through the night against New Carthage.[19] He arrived at dawn, much to the astonishment of the Carthaginians, and invested the town with a ditch. Making preparations for the following day, he brought up ladders and war engines everywhere around the town, except at one point where the wall was at its lowest, but where a lagoon of the sea washed up right against it and for that reason it was carelessly guarded. He loaded all the artillery with bolts and stones during the night, and stationed ships in the town's harbors to make sure that the enemy vessels would not escape him (for his great spirit gave him complete confidence that he would capture the town). Before

76

77

[18] See above, 13.47, where Appian also confuses Saguntum with New Carthage. He continues to use the name Carthage for New Carthage, but to avoid confusion with the Carthage in Africa, I refer to it as New Carthage.

[19] The date was the spring of 209.

ἀνεβίβαζεν ἐπὶ τὰς μηχανάς, τοὺς μὲν ἄνωθεν ἐγχειρεῖν κελεύων τοῖς πολεμίοις, τοὺς δὲ κάτω τὰς μη-
78 χανὰς ὠθεῖν ἐς τὸ πρόσω. Μάγων δὲ τοὺς μὲν μυρίους ἐπέστησεν ταῖς πύλαις ὡς ἐκπηδήσοντας, ὅτε
καιρὸς εἴη, μετὰ μόνων ξιφῶν (οὐ γὰρ εἶναι δόρασιν
ἐν στενῷ χρῆσθαι), τοὺς δ' ἄλλους ἐς τὰς ἐπάλξεις
ἀνῆγε. καὶ πολλὰ καὶ ὅδε μηχανήματα καὶ λίθους
καὶ βέλη καὶ καταπέλτας ἐπιστήσας εἴχετο τοῦ ἔργου
79 προθύμως. γενομένης δὲ βοῆς καὶ παρακελεύσεως
ἑκατέρωθεν, οὐδέτεροι μὲν ὁρμῆς καὶ προθυμίας ἐν-
έλειπον, [καὶ] λίθους τε καὶ βέλη καὶ ἀκόντια ἀφιέντες, οἳ μὲν ἀπὸ χειρῶν, οἳ δ' ἀπὸ μηχανῶν, οἳ δ' ἀπὸ
σφενδόνης, εἴ τέ τις ἦν ἄλλη παρασκευὴ καὶ δύναμις,
ἐχρῶντο προθύμως ἅπασιν·
80   21. Ἐκακοπάθει δὲ τὰ τοῦ Σκιπίωνος, καὶ οἱ μύριοι
Καρχηδονίων, οἳ περὶ τὰς πύλας ἦσαν, ἐκδραμόντες
σὺν τοῖς ξίφεσι γυμνοῖς ἐνέπιπτον ἐς τοὺς τὰ μηχανήματα ὠθοῦντας καὶ πολλὰ μὲν ἔδρων, οὐχ ἥσσω
δ' ἀντέπασχον, μέχρι τῷ φιλοπόνῳ καὶ ταλαιπώρῳ τὰ
81 Ῥωμαίων ὑπανίστατο. καὶ μεταβολῆς γενομένης οἵ τε
ἐπὶ τῶν τειχῶν ἔκαμνον ἤδη, καὶ αἱ κλίμακες αὐτοῖς
προσεπέλαζον. οἱ δὲ ξιφήρεις τῶν Καρχηδονίων ἐς
τὰς πύλας ἐσέτρεχον καὶ ἀποκλήσαντες αὐτὰς ἀνεπή-
82 δων ἐπὶ τὰ τείχη. καὶ τοῖς Ῥωμαίοις αὖθις ἦν ὁ πόνος
πολύς τε καὶ χαλεπός, ἐς οὗ Σκιπίων ὁ στρατηγὸς
πάντῃ περιθέων τε καὶ βοῶν καὶ παρακαλῶν εἶδε περὶ
μεσημβρίαν, ᾗ τὸ βραχὺ τεῖχος ἦν καὶ τὸ ἕλος προσέκλυζε, τὴν θάλασσαν ὑποχωροῦσαν· ἄμπωτις γὰρ

dawn he mounted his soldiers on the war engines, ordering the men on top to engage with the enemy and those below to push the machines forward. Mago stationed his   78
ten thousand men at the gates with orders to make a sortie at the right moment, but only using swords, as the space was too narrow for spears; the others he ordered to the battlements. He too brought up many engines and stones and missiles and catapults, and enthusiastically set about the task. There was shouting and encouragement on both   79
sides and neither lacked effort or eagerness, but they fired off stones and missiles and javelins, some throwing by hand, others from engines, others again using slings: indeed they enthusiastically employed any other part of the armament and means in their power.

21. Scipio's men were having a tough time of it, as the   80
ten thousand Carthaginians at the gates were making sorties with swords drawn to attack the men pushing the war engines. They were inflicting much damage, but were also taking heavy casualties themselves, until eventually Roman application and perseverance began to get the upper hand. With this change, the defenders on the walls now   81
began to tire and ladders were brought up against them, but the Carthaginian swordsmen ran back to the gates, locked them and climbed onto the battlements. Once   82
again the Romans were faced with great effort and difficulty, until their commander, Scipio, who had been running around everywere shouting enouragement, noticed about midday that the sea was going out at the place where the wall was low and washed by the water of the lagoon. For there is an ebb tide every day: when the tide was in,

ἐφήμερός ἐστιν. καὶ ὁ κλύδων ἐπῄει μὲν ἐς μαστούς,
83 ὑπεχώρει δ' ἐς μέσας κνήμας. ὅπερ ὁ Σκιπίων τότε
ἰδὼν καὶ περὶ τῆς φύσεως αὐτοῦ πυθόμενος, ὡς ἔχοι
τὸ λοιπὸν τῆς ἡμέρας, πρὶν ἐπανελθεῖν τὸ πέλαγος,
ἔθει πάντῃ βοῶν· "Νῦν ὁ καιρός, ὦ ἄνδρες, νῦν ὁ
σύμμαχός μοι θεὸς ἀφῖκται. πρόσιτε τῷ μέρει τῷδε
τοῦ τείχους. ἡ θάλασσα ἡμῖν ὑποκεχώρηκε. φέρετε
τὰς κλίμακας, ἐγὼ δ' ἡγήσομαι."

84   22. Καὶ πρῶτος ἁρπάσας τινὰ τῶν κλιμάκων μετέ-
φερέν τε καὶ ἀνέβαινεν, οὔπω τινὸς ἀναβάντος ἄλλου,
μέχρι περισχόντες αὐτὸν οἵ τε ὑπασπισταὶ καὶ ἡ
ἄλλη στρατιὰ τόνδε μὲν ἐπέσχον, αὐτοὶ δὲ πολλὰς
85 ὁμοῦ κλίμακας προσετίθεσάν τε καὶ ἀνεπήδων. βοῆς
δὲ καὶ ὁρμῆς ἑκατέρωθεν γεγομένης καὶ ποικίλων ἔργων καὶ παθῶν, ἐκράτησαν ὅμως οἱ Ῥωμαῖοι καὶ
πύργων τινῶν ἐπέβησαν ὀλίγων, οἷς ὁ Σκιπίων σαλπικτὰς καὶ βυκανιστὰς ἐπιστήσας ἐξοτρύνειν ἐκέλευσε καὶ θορυβεῖν ὡς τῆς πόλεως εἰλημμένης ἤδη.
86 ἕτεροί τε περιθέοντες ὁμοίως διετάρασσον, καὶ καθ-
αλόμενοί τινες ἀνέῳξαν τῷ Σκιπίωνι τὰς πύλας· ὁ δ'
εἰσεπήδησε μετὰ τῆς στρατιᾶς δρόμῳ. καὶ τῶν ἔνδον
οἱ μὲν ἐς τὰς οἰκίας ἀπεδίδρασκον, ὁ δὲ Μάγων τοὺς
87 μυρίους ἐς τὴν ἀγορὰν συνεκάλει. ταχὺ δὲ καὶ τούτων
κατακοπέντων ἐς τὴν ἄκραν σὺν ὀλίγοις ἀνεχώρει.
τοῦ δὲ Σκιπίωνος καὶ ἐπὶ τὴν ἄκραν εὐθὺς ἐπιόντος,
οὐδὲν ἔτι δρᾶν σὺν ἡττημένοις τε καὶ κατεπτηχόσιν
ἔχων ἐνεχείρισεν ἑαυτὸν τῷ Σκιπίωνι.

88   23. Ὁ δὲ τόλμῃ καὶ τύχῃ πόλιν εὐδαίμονα καὶ

the water came up to chest level, when it was out, it only
reached the middle of the leg. This was what Scipio now   83
saw, and having been told about the nature of the tide and
that the situation would last for the rest of the day, before
the sea came back in, he ran everywhere shouting, "Now
is the time, men. Now the god has come to assist me. Attack this part of the wall. The sea has retired for us. Bring
up the ladders and I will lead the way."

22. Scipio was the first to seize one of the ladders,   84
transfer it across the lagoon and begin to climb the wall
when no one else had yet gone up, but his bodyguards and
other soldiers gathered round and held him back, while
they themselves placed many ladders against the wall and
climbed up. There was shouting and eagerness on both   85
sides, and manifold actions and experiences, but the Romans got the upper hand and mounted a small number of
towers, on which Scipio placed trumpeters and buglers
with orders to give encouragement and make a noise as if
the town had already been captured. Others ran around   86
causing similar confusion, and some jumped down to open
the gates for Scipio, who burst into the town with his army
at speed. Some of the defenders escaped into the houses,
but Mago called his ten thousand together in the market-
place. These were quickly cut down, and he retreated to   87
the citadel with just a few men. When Scipio immediately
attacked the citadel, Mago could do no more with his
beaten and dejected men, and surrendered to Scipio.

23. With daring and good fortune Scipio had captured   88

APPIAN

δυνατὴν ἑλὼν ἡμέρᾳ μιᾷ, τετάρτῃ τῆς ἐπ' αὐτὴν ἀφί-
ξεως, ἐπῆρτο μεγάλως καὶ μᾶλλον ἐδόκει κατὰ θεὸν
ἕκαστα δρᾶν· αὐτός τε οὕτως ἐφρόνει καὶ οὕτως ἐλο-
γοποίει καὶ τότε καὶ ἐς τὸν ἔπειτα βίον, ἀρξάμενος ἐξ
89   ἐκείνου. πολλάκις γοῦν ἐς τὸ Καπιτώλιον ἐσῄει μόνος
καὶ τὰς θύρας ἐπέκλειεν ὥσπερ τι παρὰ τοῦ θεοῦ μαν-
θάνων. καὶ νῦν ἔτι τὴν εἰκόνα τὴν Σκιπίωνος ἐν ταῖς
πομπαῖς μόνου προφέρουσιν ἐκ τοῦ Καπιτωλίου, τῶν
90   δ' ἄλλων ἐξ ἀγορᾶς φέρονται. τότε δ' εἰρηνικὸν ὁμοῦ
καὶ πολεμικὸν ταμιεῖον παραλαβὼν ὅπλα τε πολλὰ ἐν
αὐτῷ καὶ βέλη καὶ μηχανήματα καὶ νεωσοίκους καὶ
ναῦς μακρὰς τρεῖς καὶ τριάκοντα καὶ σῖτον καὶ
ἀγορὰν ποικίλην καὶ ἐλέφαντα καὶ χρυσὸν καὶ ἄργυρον, τὸν μὲν ἐν σκεύεσι πεποιημένον, τὸν δὲ ἐπί-
σημον, τὸν δὲ ἀσήμαντον, ὅμηρά τε Ἰβήρων καὶ
αἰχμάλωτα καὶ ὅσα Ῥωμαίων αὐτῶν προείληπτο,
ἔθυε τῆς ἐπιούσης καὶ ἐθριάμβευε καὶ τὴν στρατιὰν
ἐπῄνει καὶ ⟨πρὸς τοὺς ἐν⟩[10] τῇ πόλει μετὰ τὴν στρατιὰν ἐδημηγόρει τῶν τε Σκιπιώνων αὐτοὺς ἀναμνήσας
ἀπέλυε τοὺς αἰχμαλώτους εἰς τὰ ἴδια, θεραπεύων τὰς
91   πόλεις. ἀριστεῖα δ' ἐδίδου τῷ μὲν ἐς τὸ τεῖχος ἀνα-
βάντι πρώτῳ μέγιστα, τῷ δ' ἑξῆς τὰ ἡμίσεα τούτων,
τῷ δὲ τρίτῳ τὰ τρίτα καὶ τοῖς ἄλλοις κατὰ λόγον. τὰ
δὲ λοιπὰ ἐς Ῥώμην ἔπεμψεν ἐπὶ τῶν εἰλημμένων νεῶν,
92   ὅσα χρυσὸς ἢ ἄργυρος ἦν ἢ ἐλέφας. ἡ μὲν δὴ πόλις
ἔθυεν ἐπὶ τρεῖς ἡμέρας, ὡς τῆς πατρῴας εὐπραξίας ἐκ
πόνων πολλῶν αὖθις ἀνακυπτούσης, ἡ δὲ Ἰβηρία καὶ

172

a rich and powerful town in a single day, four days after his arrival there. This greatly encouraged him, and it seemed even more that heaven inspired all his actions. He began to think this himself and it was the story he would promote both then and for the rest of his life, but starting then. For instance, he often used to go into the Capitol on his own and close the doors behind him, as if he was getting information from the god. Even still today in public processions they bring out only Scipio's image from the Capitol; all the others are carried from the Forum. On that day, however, he captured a whole store of military and civil supplies, that is to say, many weapons, missiles and war engines, shipsheds with thirty-three warships, grain and varous provisions, ivory, gold and silver (some of it fashioned into silverware, some coined, some in bullion), Iberian hostages and prisoners of war, including those taken before from the Romans themelves. The following day Scipio offered sacrifice and organized a triumphal procession. He praised his troops, and when he was finished talking to the army, he addressed the inhabitants of the town, telling them to remember the Scipios. He released the prisoners back to their families in an attempt to win favor among the towns. He also awarded prizes for bravery, the most valuable to the man who had been first to scale the walls, half that amount to the second, a third to the next, and proportionately to the others. What remained of the gold, silver, and ivory he dispatched to Rome on the captured ships. For three days the city conducted sacrifices to celebrate the recovery of its traditional success after such difficult times. Iberia and the

89

90

91

92

---

[10] πρὸς τοὺς ἐν add. Goukowsky

οἱ ἐν αὐτῇ Φοίνικες κατεπεπλήγεσαν τῷ μεγέθει καὶ τάχει τοῦ τολμήματος.

93 24. Ὁ δὲ φρουρὰν μὲν Καρχηδόνι ἐπέστησε καὶ τὸ τεῖχος ἐκέλευσε τὸ παρὰ τὴν ἄμπωτιν ἐς ὕψος ἐγεῖραι· τὴν δ' ἄλλην Ἰβηρίαν αὐτός τε ἐπιὼν καὶ τοὺς φίλους ἐς ἕκαστα περιπέμπων ὑπήγετο καὶ τἆλλα τὰ ἀντέ-
94 χοντα ἐβιάζετο. Καρχηδονίων δ' οἱ στρατηγοί, δύο ὄντε λοιπὼ καὶ δύο Ἀσρούβα, ὁ μὲν τοῦ Ἀμίλχαρος πορρωτάτω παρὰ Κελτίβηρσιν ἐξενολόγει, ὁ δὲ τοῦ Γέσκωνος ἐς μὲν τὰς πόλεις τὰς ἔτι βεβαίους περι-έπεμπεν, ἀξιῶν Καρχηδονίοις ἐμμένειν ὡς στρατιᾶς ἐλευσομένης αὐτίκα ἀπείρου τὸ πλῆθος, Μάγωνα δ' ἕτερον ἐς τὰ πλησίον περιέπεμπεν ξενολογεῖν, ὁπόθεν δυνηθείη, καὶ αὐτὸς ἐς τὴν Ἰλεργητῶν[11] ἀφισταμένων ἐνέβαλεν καί τινα αὐτῶν πόλιν ἔμελλεν πολιορκήσειν.
95 ἐπιφανέντος δ' αὐτῷ τοῦ Σκιπίωνος ἐς Βαιτύκην ὑπ-εχώρει καὶ πρὸ τῆς <Βαικύλης>[12] πόλεως ἐστρατοπέ-δευεν· ἔνθα τῆς ἐπιούσης εὐθὺς ἡσσᾶτο, καὶ τὸν χάρακα αὐτοῦ καὶ τὴν Βαικύλην[13] ἔλαβεν ὁ Σκιπίων.
96 25. Ὁ δὲ τὴν στρατιὰν τὴν Καρχηδονίων τὴν ἔτι οὖσαν ἐν Ἰβηρίᾳ συνέλεγεν ἐς Καρμώνην πόλιν, ὡς ὁμοῦ πᾶσιν ἀμυνούμενος τὸν Σκιπίωνα. καὶ αὐτῷ συνῆλθον πολλοὶ μὲν Ἰβήρων, οὓς Μάγων ἦγεν, πολ-
97 λοὶ δὲ Νομάδων, ὧν ἦρχε Μασσανάσσης. καὶ τούτων

[11] ἐς τὴν λέρσα γῆν V: ἐς τὴν Ἰλεργητῶν Goukowsky
[12] Βαικύλης add. Goukowsky
[13] Βαιτύκην VM: Βαικύλην Goukowsky

Carthaginians there were astonished at the scale and speed of Scipio's daring.

24. After installing a garrison in New Carthage and ordering the wall where the ebb tide had its effects to be built to its full height, Scipio himself set out against the rest of Iberia: he sent his officials to all parts and brought them under control, subduing by force others that held out against him. There were two Carthaginian generals left, both called Hasdrubal. One of them, the son of Hamilcar, was recruiting mercenaries far away in Celtiberia. The other, the son of Gisco, was sending missions round to the towns that were still loyal, urging them to stand firm with Carthage, as a huge army was just about to arrive. He also sent another Mago to recruit mercenaries closer by from wherever he could get them, while he himself attacked the territory of the Ilergetes, who had revolted. He intended to besiege one of their towns, but instead withdrew to Baetica when Scipio appeared, and camped in front of the town of Baecula. Next day, he was defeated there swiftly, and Scipio captured his camp and Baecula itself.

25. Hasdrubal collected all remaining Carthaginian forces in Iberia at the town of Carmona to present a united defense against Scipio.[20] Assembling there for him were many Iberians under the command of Mago, and a large number of Numidians led by Massinissa. Of these gener-

93

94

95

96

97

---

[20] The modern town of Carmona lies about twenty miles northeast of Seville. The battle Appian recounts here is what Polybius (11.20–24) calls the battle of Ilipa. It took place probably in early 206.

ὁ μὲν Ἀσρούβας μετὰ τῶν πεζῶν ὑπὸ χάρακι ἐστρατοπέδευεν, ὁ δὲ Μασσανάσσης καὶ ὁ Μάγων ἱππαρ-
98 χοῦντες αὐτῷ προηυλίζοντο τοῦ στρατοπέδου. ὧδε δὲ
ἔχουσιν αὐτοῖς ὁ Σκιπίων τοὺς ἰδίους ἱππέας ἐπιδι-
ήρει καὶ Λαίλιον μὲν ἐπὶ Μάγωνα ἔπεμπεν, αὐτὸς δ᾽
99 ἐπὶ Μασσανάσσην ἐτράπετο. μέχρι μὲν οὖν τινος ἦν
ἐν ἀγῶνι καὶ πόνῳ δυσχερεῖ, τῶν Νομάδων αὐτὸν
ἀκοντιζόντων τε καὶ ὑποχωρούντων, εἶτ᾽ αὖθις ἐπελαυ-
νόντων· ὡς δὲ παρήγγειλεν ὁ Σκιπίων ἀμεταστρεπτὶ
διώκειν αὐτούς, τὰ δόρατα προβαλόντας, οὐκ ἔχοντες
ἀναστροφὴν οἱ Νομάδες κατέφυγον ἐς τὸ στρατόπεδον. καὶ ὁ Σκιπίων ἀποσχὼν δέκα σταδίους ἐστρατο-
100 πέδευσεν εὐσταθῶς, ᾗπερ ἐβούλετο. ἦν δὲ ἡ μὲν τῶν
ἐχθρῶν σύμπασα δύναμις ἑπτακισμύριοι πεζοὶ καὶ
ἱππεῖς πεντακισχίλιοι καὶ ἐλέφαντες ἓξ καὶ τριάκοντα·
Σκιπίωνι δὲ τούτων οὐδὲ τριτημόριον ἦν. διὸ καὶ μέχρι τινὸς ἐνεδοίαζε καὶ μάχης οὐ κατῆρχε, ἀλλ᾽ ἀκρο-
βολισμοῖς ἐχρῆτο μόνοις.

101   26. Ἐπεὶ δ᾽ ἐπέλειπεν αὐτὸν ἡ ἀγορὰ καὶ λιμὸς
ἥπτετο τοῦ στρατοῦ, ἀναζεῦξαι μὲν οὐκ εὐπρεπὲς
ἡγεῖτο εἶναι Σκιπίων· θυσάμενος δὲ καὶ εὐθὺς ἐπὶ ταῖς
θυσίαις τὴν στρατιὰν ἐς ἐπήκοον ἐλάσας καὶ τὸ
βλέμμα καὶ τὸ σχῆμα διαθεὶς πάλιν ὥσπερ ἔνθους,
ἔφη τὸ δαιμόνιον ἥκειν τὸ σύνηθες αὐτῷ καὶ καλεῖν
ἐπὶ τοὺς πολεμίους· χρῆναι δὲ θαρρεῖν θεῷ μᾶλλον ἢ
πλήθει στρατοῦ· καὶ γὰρ τῶν πρότερον ἔργων κατὰ
102 θεόν, οὐ κατὰ πλῆθος κρατῆσαι. ἔς τε πίστιν τῶν
λεγομένων τὰ ἱερὰ παραφέρειν ἐς τὸ μέσον ἐκέλευε

als, Hasdrubal camped with the infantry inside the palisade, while the cavalry commanders, Massinissa and Mago, bivouacked infront of it. Against this Carthaginian setup Scipio divided his own cavalry, sending Laelius against Mago, while he himself confronted Massinissa. For some time he found himself in a difficult and troublesome fight, as the Numidians would throw their javelins, then retire, before attacking again. But when Scipio ordered his men to pursue them relentlessly, spears to the front, the Numidians were unable to wheel round and fled into the camp. He then retired ten stades to camp in a secure location of his own choosing. The enemy force numbered in full seventy thousand infantry, five thousand cavalry and thirty-six elephants. Scipio scarcely had a third this number.[21] With this in mind, he hesitated for a time and held back from battle, and engaged only in skirmishing.

26. When his supplies began to run out and hunger was affecting the army, thinking it improper to withdraw, Scipio sacrificed and immediately afterward summoned the troops to a meeting. He again adopted the appearance and character of a man divinely inspired, telling them that his customary divinity had come to him, calling on him to attack the enemy. They should put their trust in god, he said, rather than the size of their army: for it was not their numbers that had led to victory on previous occasions, but divine assistance. To add conviction to his words he ordered the seers to bring the sacrificial victims into the

98

99

100

101

102

---

[21] This reflects a Roman patriotic exaggeration to boost Scipio's reputation: Polybius (11.20.8–9) says that Scipio had forty-five thousand infantry and three thousand cavalry.

τοὺς μάντεις. καὶ λέγων ὁρᾷ τινας οἰωνοὺς πετομέ-
νους, οὓς μεθ᾽ ὁρμῆς καὶ βοῆς αὐτόθεν ἐπιστραφεὶς
ἐδείκνυέν τε καὶ ἔλεγεν, ὅτι οἱ σύμβολα νίκης οἱ θεοὶ
καὶ τάδε ἔπεμψαν. συνεκινεῖτο δὲ πρὸς αὐτὰ ἐνθέως
103 ὁρῶν καὶ βοῶν· καὶ ἡ στρατιὰ πᾶσα ἐς τὰς ἐκείνου
φαντασίας, περιφερομένου δεῦρο κἀκεῖσε, συνεπε-
στρέφετο, καὶ πάντες ὡς ἐπὶ νίκην ἕτοιμον ἠρεθί-
104 ζοντο. ὁ δ᾽ ἐπεὶ πᾶν εἶχεν, ὅσον τι καὶ ἐβούλετο, οὐκ
ἀνέθετο οὐδ᾽ εἴασε τὴν ὁρμὴν ἐκλυθῆναι, ἀλλ᾽ ὡς ἔτι
ὢν θεόληπτος ἔφη δεῖν ἐπὶ τοῖσδε τοῖς σημείοις εὐθὺς
ἀγωνίσασθαι. καὶ φαγόντας ἐκέλευεν ὁπλίσασθαι καὶ
ἐπῆγεν ἀδοκήτως τοῖς πολεμίοις, τοὺς μὲν ἱππέας Σι-
λανῷ, τοὺς δὲ πεζοὺς Λαιλίῳ καὶ Μαρκίῳ παραδούς.
105   27. Ἀσρούβας δὲ καὶ Μάγων καὶ Μασσανάσσης,
ἐπιόντος αὐτοῖς τοῦ Σκιπίωνος ἄφνω, σταδίων ὄντων
ἐν μέσῳ δέκα μόνων, ἄσιτον οὖσαν ἔτι τὴν στρατιὰν
106 ὥπλιζον μετὰ σπουδῆς καὶ θορύβου καὶ βοῆς. γενομένης δὲ ὁμοῦ πεζομαχίας τε καὶ ἱππομαχίας οἱ μὲν
ἱππῆς οἱ τῶν Ῥωμαίων ἐκράτουν ὑπὸ τῆς αὐτῆς μηχανῆς, ἀμεταστρεπτὶ τοὺς Νομάδας διώκοντες, ὑπο-
χωρεῖν εἰθισμένους καὶ ἐπελαύνειν· οἷς τὰ ἀκόντια διὰ
τὴν ἐγγύτητα οὐδὲν ἦν ἔτι χρήσιμα· οἱ πεζοὶ δ᾽ ἐπο-
νοῦντο ὑπὸ τοῦ πλήθους τῶν Λιβύων καὶ ἡττῶντο δι᾽
107 ὅλης ἡμέρας. οὐδὲ τοῦ Σκιπίωνος αὐτοὺς ἐπιθέοντός

---

22 M. Iunius Silanus was praetor in 212 and accompanied
Scipio Africanus to Spain in 210, where he took over the forces

meeting. While he was speaking he sees some birds in the sky, and with a rapid movement and a shout turned on the spot to point them out, saying that these too were omens of victory sent to him by the gods. He followed their movement, looking and shouting in an inspired manner. As his   103
attention was carried one way and then another, the whole army turned with him imitating the physical shapes he adopted; and they were all roused to think of victory as a certainty. When he had arranged everything as he wanted,   104
he held to his purpose and, refusing to let the momentum diminish, he continued to act as a man possessed and told them that with such omens as these they had to fight immediately. He ordered them to eat and arm themselves, and then led them unexpectedly against the enemy. He gave command of the cavalry to Silanus and the infantry to Laelius and Marcius.[22]

27. With only ten stades separating the two sides,   105
Scipio's attack came suddenly, and in the confusion and noise Hasdrubal, Mago and Massinissa rapidly armed their troops, even though they had not eaten yet. Both   106
infantry and cavalry joined battle. The Roman cavalry were victorious by using the same tactics as before: that is, by relentlessly pursuing the Numidians, who were used to falling back and then attacking again, they rendered the Numidian missiles ineffective because there was no room to fire them. The infantry, on the other hand, were hard pressed by the sheer numbers of Carthaginians and took a beating the whole day. Their situation did not improve,   107

of C. Claudius Nero (see above, 17.65). L. Marcius Septimus was a legate. C. Laelius, consul in 190, was a close friend of Scipio Africanus (see Polyb. 10.3).

τε καὶ παρακαλοῦντος μετετίθεντο, μέχρι τὸν ἵππον
Σκιπίων τῷ παιδὶ παραδοὺς καὶ παρά τινος ἀσπίδα
λαβὼν ἐξέδραμεν, ὡς εἶχε, μόνος ἐς τὸ μεταίχμιον,
κεκραγώς· "Ἐπικουρεῖτε, ὦ Ῥωμαῖοι, κινδυνεύοντι
108 <ὑπερ>[14] ὑμῶν τῷ Σκιπίωνι." τότε γὰρ οἱ μὲν ἐγγὺς
ὁρῶντες, οἳ κινδύνου φέρεται, οἳ δὲ πόρρω πυνθανόμενοι καὶ πάντες ὁμοίως αἰδούμενοί τε καὶ περὶ τῷ
στρατηγῷ δεδιότες ἐσέδραμον ἐς τοὺς πολεμίους μετ'
ἀλαλαγμοῦ καὶ βίας, ἣν οὐκ ἐνεγκόντες οἱ Λίβυες
ἐνέδωκαν, ἐπιλειπούσης αὐτοὺς ἅμα τῆς δυνάμεως
ὑπὸ τῆς ἀσιτίας περὶ ἑσπέραν· καὶ πολὺς αὐτῶν δι'
109 ὀλίγου τότε φόνος ἐγίγνετο. τοῦτο μὲν δὴ τέλος ἦν
Σκιπίωνι τῆς περὶ Καρμώνην μάχης, ἐπισφαλοῦς ἐς
πολὺ γενομένης. ἀπέθανον δ' ἐν αὐτῇ Ῥωμαίων μὲν
ὀκτακόσιοι, τῶν δὲ πολεμίων μύριοι καὶ πεντακισχίλιοι.

110   28. Μετὰ δὲ τοῦθ' οἱ μὲν Λίβυες ὑπεχώρουν ἀεὶ
μετὰ σπουδῆς, ὁ δὲ Σκιπίων αὐτοῖς εἵπετο, βλάπτων
111 τι καὶ λυπῶν, ὁσάκις καταλάβοι. ὡς δ' οἱ μὲν ὀχυρόν
τι χωρίον προύλαβον, ἔνθα καὶ ὕδωρ ἦν ἄφθονον καὶ
ἀγορὰ καὶ οὐδὲν ἄλλο ἢ πολιορκεῖν αὐτοὺς ἔδει, Σκιπίωνα δ' ἤπειγον ἕτεραι χρεῖαι, Σιλανὸν μὲν ἀπέλιπε
τούσδε πολιορκεῖν, αὐτὸς δ' ἐπῄει τὴν ἄλλην Ἰβηρίαν
112 καὶ ὑπήγετο. Λιβύων δὲ τῶν ὑπὸ Σιλανοῦ πολιορ-
κουμένων αὖθις ὑποχωρούντων, ἕως ἐπὶ τὸν πορθμὸν
ἀφικόμενοι ἐς Γάδειρα ἐπέρασαν, ὁ Σιλανός, ὅσα δυνατὸν ἦν, βλάψας ἀνεζεύγνυεν ἐς Καρχηδόνα πρὸς
113 Σκιπίωνα. Ἀσρούβαν δὲ τὸν Ἀμίλχαρος περὶ τὸν

even though Scipio galloped about everywhere giving encouragement, until he handed his horse to his slave, took someone's shield and ran straight out alone into the space between the two lines, shouting, "Scipio risks his life for you, men of Rome: go and help him." At that moment, 108 those who were close could see he was in danger, and those further away were told, so that all alike out of shame and in fear for their commander gave a loud roar and launched a violent attack on the enemy. The Africans were unable to resist it and fell back about evening just as their strength failed them for want of food; and in a short time then many of them were massacred. Although the result 109 had long been in doubt, this was how the battle of Carmona ended for Scipio. In the course of it eight hundred Romans died, fifteen thousand of the enemy.

28. After this, the Africans continued to retreat at 110 speed, with Scipio following them and inflicting damage and injury as often as he could catch them. But when they 111 stole a march on him and managed to occupy a stronghold where there were plentiful supplies and water—making a siege the only option—Scipio was pressed by other urgent priorities and, leaving Silanus to conduct the siege, he himself moved against the rest of Iberia and set about subduing it. The Carthaginians besieged by Silanus again 112 withdrew, eventually reaching the straits and making their way to Gadeira, and Silanus inflicted as much damage on them as he could, before withdrawing to join Scipio at New Carthage. As for Hasdrubal, the son of Hamilcar, 113

---

14 ὑπέρ add. Goukowsky

βόρειον ὠκεανὸν στρατιὰν ἔτι συλλέγοντα ὁ ἀδελφὸς
Ἀννίβας ἐκάλει κατὰ σπουδὴν ἐς τὴν Ἰταλίαν ἐσβαλεῖν. ὁ δέ, ἵνα λάθοι τὸν Σκιπίωνα, παρὰ τὸν βόρειον
ὠκεανὸν τὴν Πυρήνην ἐς Γαλάτας ὑπερέβαινεν, μεθ᾽
ὧν ἐξενολογήκει Κελτιβήρων.

114   29. Καὶ ὁ μὲν Ἀσρούβας ὧδε ἐς τὴν Ἰταλίαν τῶν
Ἰταλῶν ἀγνοούντων ἠπείγετο· Λεύκιος δ᾽ ἀπὸ Ῥώμης
ἐπανιὼν ἔφραζε τῷ Σκιπίωνι, ὅτι αὐτὸν οἱ ἐν ἄστει
Ῥωμαῖοι διανοοῦνται στρατηγὸν ἐς Λιβύην ἀποστέλ-
115 λειν. ὁ δὲ τοῦδε αὐτοῦ μάλιστα ἐπιθυμῶν ἐκ πολλοῦ
καὶ ἐλπίζων ὧδε ἔσεσθαι Λαίλιον ἐπὶ νεῶν πέντε
προύπεμπεν ἐς Λιβύην πρὸς τὸν δυνάστην Σύφακα,
δωρεάς τε φέροντα καὶ τῶν Σκιπιώνων ὑπόμνησιν τῆς
ἐς αὐτὸν Σύφακα φιλίας καὶ δέησιν Ῥωμαίοις, ἂν
ἐπίωσι, συλλαμβάνειν. ὁ δὲ ὑπέσχετό τε ποιήσειν καὶ
116 τὰ δῶρα ἔλαβεν καὶ ἀντέπεμψεν ἕτερα. αἰσθανόμενοι
δὲ τούτων οἱ Καρχηδόνιοι καὶ αὐτοὶ περὶ συμμαχίας
ἐπρεσβεύοντο παρὰ τὸν Σύφακα. καὶ ὁ Σκιπίων, πυν-
θανόμενός τε καὶ μέγα ποιούμενος ἐπὶ Καρχηδονίοις
προλαβεῖν καὶ βεβαιώσασθαι Σύφακα, ᾔει πρὸς αὐτὸν ἐπὶ νεῶν δύο σὺν τῷ Λαιλίῳ.

117   30. Καὶ αὐτῷ καταγομένῳ οἱ πρέσβεις τῶν Καρχηδονίων, ἔτι ὄντες παρὰ τῷ Σύφακι, ναυσὶν αἷς εἶχον
118 μακραῖς ἐπανήγοντο, λαθόντες τὸν Σύφακα. ἀλλ᾽ ὁ
μὲν ἱστίῳ χρώμενος παρέπλευσεν αὐτοὺς ἀδεῶς καὶ
κατήχθη, ὁ δὲ Σύφαξ ἐξένιζεν ἀμφοτέρους καὶ τῷ
Σκιπίωνι συνθέμενος ἰδίᾳ καὶ πίστεις παρασχὼν ἀπέ-

who was still collecting an army on the coast of the Northern Ocean, his brother Hannibal called on him to hurry up and invade Italy. To avoid Scipio's attention, he crossed the Pyrenees into Gaul beside the Northern Ocean, bringing with him the Celtiberian mercenaries he had hired.

29. In this way Hasdrubal pressed on to Italy without the Italians knowing. When Lucius[23] returned from Rome, he told Scipio that in Rome they were proposing to send him in command of an expedition to Africa. Scipio, who had long been particularly keen on this very idea, in the hope that the expedition would take place now sent Laelius ahead with five ships to Africa to visit prince Syphax. He brought gifts, reminded him of the friendship between the Scipios and himself, and asked for his assistance if Rome invaded. Syphax promised to do so, accepted the gifts and sent others in return. When the Carthaginians learned of this, they too sent a mission to him seeking an alliance. On being informed of this, and regarding it as a matter of great importance to win the support of Syphax against the Carthaginians and confirm his resolve, Scipio took two ships along with Laelius and visited him.

30. As he was approaching land, the Carthaginian ambassadors, who were still with Syphax, put to sea in their warships against Scipio without Syphax's knowledge. But Scipio spread his sails and, safely outsailing them, made port. Although he entertained both groups, Syphax made a private agreement with Scipio and sent him off with as-

114

115

116

117

118

[23] L. Cornelius Scipio Asiagenes was the brother of Africanus and served with him in Spain, Sicily, and Africa during the Hannibalic War. While consul in 190, he defeated the Seleucid king Antiochus III at the battle of Magnesia.

πεμπε καὶ τοὺς Καρχηδονίους ἐφεδρεύοντας αὖθις
αὐτῷ κατεῖχεν, ἕως ἐν βεβαίῳ τῆς θαλάσσης γένοιτο
119 ὁ Σκιπίων. παρὰ μὲν δὴ τοσοῦτον ἦλθε κινδύνου Σκιπίων, καταγόμενός τε καὶ ἀναπλέων· λέγεται δ' ἐν
Σύφακος ἑστιώμενος συγκατακλιθῆναι τῷ Ἀσρούβᾳ
καὶ αὐτὸν ὁ Ἀσρούβας περὶ πολλῶν ἐρόμενος κατα-
πλαγῆναι τῆς σεμνότητος καὶ πρὸς τοὺς φίλους εἰπεῖν, ὅτι μὴ μόνον πολεμῶν οὗτος ὁ ἀνήρ, ἀλλὰ καὶ
ἑστιώμενος φοβερὸς εἴη.

120   31. Τῷ δ' αὐτῷ χρόνῳ Μάγωνί τινες Κελτιβήρων
καὶ Ἰβήρων ἔτι ἐμισθοφόρουν, ὧν αἱ πόλεις ἐς Ῥωμαίους μετετέθειντο· καὶ ὁ Μάρκιος αὐτοῖς ἐπιθέμενος
χιλίους μὲν καὶ πεντακοσίους διέφθειρεν, οἱ δὲ λοιποὶ
121 διέφυγον αὐτὸν ἐς τὰς πόλεις. ἑτέρους δὲ ἑπτακοσίους
ἱππέας καὶ πεζοὺς ἑξακισχιλίους, Ἄννωνος αὐτῶν
ἡγουμένου, συνήλασεν ἐς λόφον, ὅθεν ἀποροῦντες
ἁπάντων ἐπρεσβεύοντο πρὸς τὸν Μάρκιον περὶ σπον-
122 δῶν. ὁ δ' ἐκέλευεν αὐτοὺς Ἄννωνα καὶ τοὺς αὐτομόλους ἐκδόντας αὐτῷ τότε πρεσβεύειν. οἱ μὲν δὴ καὶ
τὸν Ἄννωνα στρατηγὸν ὄντα σφῶν συναρπάσαντες,
ἔτι τῶν λεγομένων ἀκροώμενον, καὶ τοὺς αὐτομόλους
123 παρέδοσαν· ὁ δὲ Μάρκιος ᾔτει καὶ τὰ αἰχμάλωτα. λαβὼν δὲ καὶ ταῦτ' ἐκέλευεν αὐτοὺς τακτὸν ἀργύριον
κατενεγκεῖν ἅπαντας ἔς τι τοῦ πεδίου χωρίον· οὐ γὰρ
ἁρμόζειν τὰ ὑψηλότερα τοῖς παρακαλοῦσιν. καταβάν-
124 των δ' ἐς τὸ πεδίον ἔφη· "Ἄξια μὲν θανάτου δε-
δράκατε, οἳ τὰς πατρίδας ἔχοντες ὑφ' ἡμῖν εἵλεσθε
μετὰ τῶν ἐχθρῶν ἐπ' αὐτὰς στρατεύειν· δίδωμι δ'

surances of good faith. The Carthaginians were again planning to ambush Scipio, but Syphax held them back until Scipio was securely on the open sea. Such was the great danger Scipio encountered at sea both departing and arriving. It is said that he dined beside Hasdrubal at a feast in Syphax's residence, and that Hasdrubal, after questioning him on many issues, was struck by his dignity, and told his associates that Scipio was formidable not just as a warrior, but also as a fellow diner. 119

31. About the same time, some Celtiberians and Iberians were still fighting for Mago as mercenaries, even though their hometowns had changed sides to Rome. Marcius attacked them killing one thousand five hundred; the rest got away from him to their towns. Another eight hundred cavalry and six thousand infantry under the command of Hanno, he drove onto a hill where they ran short of all supplies, and sent a delegation to Marcius to ask for a truce. He ordered them to surrender Hanno and the deserters first, then send an embassy. So they did indeed seize Hanno, even though he was their commander and was still listening to what was being said, and they handed over the deserters too. When Marcius demanded the prisoners of war as well, he got them too, and then ordered everyone to bring a fixed amount of money down to a place in the plain. For, he said, high places were not fitting for suppliants. When they came down to the plain, he said, "You deserve death for what you have done. Your hometowns are under Roman rule, but you have chosen to fight on the side of the enemy against them. If you lay down 120 121 122 123 124

125 ὑμῖν, τὰ ὅπλα καταθεῖσιν, ἀπαθέσιν ἀπιέναι." ἀγανα-
κτησάντων δ' εὐθὺς ὁμοῦ πάντων καὶ ἀνακραγόντων
οὐκ ἀποθήσεσθαι τὰ ὅπλα μάχη γίγνεται καρτερά.
καὶ τὸ μὲν ἥμισυ τῶν Κελτιβήρων πολλὰ δρασάντων
126 κατεκόπη, τὸ δ' ἥμισυ πρὸς Μάγωνα διεσώθη. ὁ δ'
ἄρτι μὲν ἐς τὸ στρατόπεδον τὸ Ἄννωνος κατεπεπλεύ-
κει ναυσὶν ἑξήκοντα μακραῖς, μαθὼν δὲ τὴν Ἄννωνος
συμφορὰν ἐς Γάδειρα διέπλει καὶ λιμῷ κακοπαθῶν
περιεσκόπει τὸ μέλλον.

127   32. Καὶ Μάγων μὲν ἐπὶ ἀργίας ἦν, Σιλανὸς δ'
ἀπέσταλτο μὲν ὑπὸ τοῦ Σκιπίωνος Κάστακα πόλιν
προσαγαγέσθαι, πολεμικῶς δ' αὐτῷ τῶν Καστακαίων
ἐχόντων παρεστρατοπέδευε· καὶ τοῦτο ἐμήνυε τῷ Σκι-
128 πίωνι. ὁ δὲ προπέμψας τινὰ παρασκευὴν πολιορκίας
εἵπετο· καὶ παροδεύων ἐνέβαλλεν ἐς Ἰλυργίαν πόλιν,
ἢ Ῥωμαίων μὲν ἦν φίλη κατὰ τὸν πρότερον Σκιπίωνα,
ἀναιρεθέντος δ' ἐκείνου κρύφα μετετέθειτο καὶ στρατιὰν ὑποδεξαμένη Ῥωμαίων ὡς ἔτι φίλη Καρχηδο-
129 νίοις ἐκδεδώκει. ὧν χάριν ὁ Σκιπίων σὺν ὀργῇ τέσσαρσιν ὥραις ἐξεῖλεν αὐτήν, τρωθεὶς μὲν τὸν αὐχένα,
τῆς δὲ μάχης οὐκ ἀνασχών, ἕως ἐκράτησεν. καὶ ἡ
στρατιὰ δι' αὐτόν, οὐδενὸς ἐπικελεύσαντος, ὑπερι-
δοῦσα τῆς ἁρπαγῆς ἔκτεινον ὁμαλῶς καὶ παιδία καὶ
γυναῖκας, μέχρι καὶ τὴν πόλιν αὐτοῖς ἐπικατέσκαψαν.
130 ἀφικόμενος δ' ἐς τὴν Κάστακα ὁ Σκιπίων τὸν μὲν
στρατὸν ἐς τρία διεῖλε καὶ τὴν πόλιν ἐφρούρει, μάχης

your weapons, however, I will allow you to leave without punishment." As they were all immediately furious at this, shouting that they would not surrender their weapons, a fierce battle ensues. After a brave resistance, about half of the Celtiberians were cut down, while the other half found safety with Mago, who had recently put in at the camp of Hanno with sixty warships. When he learned of the disaster suffered by Hanno, he sailed off to Gadeira and awaited future events, suffering badly from shortage of food. 125 126

32. While Mago remained inactive, Silanus was sent by Scipio to bring the town of Castax over to the Roman side, but the townspeople offered armed resistance; so Silanus camped infront of it and informed Scipio. Scipio sent some siege machinery ahead and set out to follow, but changed his route to attack the town of Ilurgia.[24] The Ilurgians had been friends of Rome in the time of the elder Scipio, but had changed sides secretly when he was killed; and pretending that they were still allies, they had given refuge to a Roman army which they then betrayed to the Carthaginians. Scipio was outraged by this and stormed the town in four hours. Even though wounded in the neck he refused to withdraw from the battle until he had won it. On his account, but with nobody issuing an order, the soldiers did not bother to plunder the town, but instead slaughtered everyone indiscriminately, including women and children, eventually destroying the town and its inhabitants. When Scipio arrived at Castax, he divided his army into three sections and blockaded the town. He did 127 128 129 130

[24] Castax can hardly be the town of Castulo, which Appian calls by its correct name in chapter 16 (see n. 15, above). Ilurgia is presumably the modern town of Lorqui, about fifty miles west of New Carthage.

δ' οὐκ ἦρχε, διδοὺς ἔτι τοῖς Καστακαίοις μεταγνῶναι·
καὶ γὰρ ἤκουεν αὐτοὺς οὕτω φρονεῖν. οἱ δὲ τοῖς φρου-
ροῦσι σφᾶς ἐμποδὼν οὖσιν ἐπιθέμενοι καὶ κρατήσαν-
131 τες ἐνεχείρισαν τὴν πόλιν τῷ Σκιπίωνι. καὶ τοῖσδε
μὲν φρουρὰν ὁ Σκιπίων ἐπέστησε καὶ τὴν πόλιν
ἐπέτρεψεν ἑνὶ τῶν Καστακαίων ἐπὶ δόξης ὄντι ἀγα-
θῆς· αὐτὸς δ' ἐς Καρχηδόνα ἀνεζεύγνυε, Σιλανὸν καὶ
Μάρκιον περιπέμψας ἐπὶ τὸν πορθμὸν δῃοῦν, ὅσα
δύναιντο.

132   33. Ἀσταπὰ δ' ἦν πόλις Καρχηδονίοις αἰεὶ διαμεί-
νασα ὁμαλῶς· οἱ τότε τοῦ Μαρκίου σφᾶς περικαθημένου συγγιγνώσκοντες, ὅτι Ῥωμαῖοι λαβόντες αὐτοὺς ἀνδραποδιοῦνται, τὴν περιουσίαν σφῶν ἐς τὴν
ἀγορὰν συνήνεγκαν καὶ ξύλα περιθέντες αὐτῇ τὰ
133 τέκνα καὶ τὰ γύναια ἐπέβησαν ἐπὶ τὴν ὕλην. πεντήκοντα δὲ σφῶν ὥρκωσαν τοὺς ἀρίστους, ὅταν ἡ πόλις
ἁλίσκηται, τὰ γύναια καὶ τοὺς παῖδας ἀνελεῖν καὶ τὸ
134 πῦρ ἅψαι καὶ ἑαυτοὺς ἐπικατασφάξαι. οἱ μὲν δὴ μάρ-
τυρας τῶνδε ποιησάμενοι τοὺς θεοὺς ἐξέδραμον ἐπὶ
τὸν Μάρκιον οὐχ ὑφορώμενον οὐδέν, ὅθεν αὐτοῦ τοὺς
135 ψιλοὺς καὶ τοὺς ἱππέας ἐτρέψαντο. ὁπλισαμένης δὲ
τῆς φάλαγγος τὰ μὲν τῶν Ἀσταπαίων ἦν ἄριστα, ἐξ
ἀπογνώσεως μαχομένων, Ῥωμαῖοι δ' ὅμως ἐκράτουν
αὐτῶν διὰ τὸ πλῆθος· οὐ γὰρ δὴ τῇ γε ἀρετῇ χείρους
136 ἦσαν οἱ Ἀσταπαῖοι. πεσόντων δ' ἁπάντων οἱ πεντήκοντα τὰς γυναῖκας καὶ τὰ παιδία κατέσφαξαν καὶ τὸ
πῦρ ἐγείραντες ἑαυτοὺς ἐπέρριψαν, ἀκερδῆ τοῖς πολεμίοις τὴν νίκην ἐργασάμενοι. ὁ δὲ Μάρκιος τὴν

not initiate battle, but gave the inhabitants an opportunity to change their mind, as he had heard they were minded to do so. For their part, they attacked and overpowered the guards in their way and handed the town to Scipio. He 131 stationed a garrison there and placed the town in the hands of one of its own citizens, a man of good reputation, before returning to New Carthage and sending Silanus and Marcius out to the straits to cause as much damage as they could.

33. The people of the town of Astapa had always re- 132 mained unfailingly loyal to Carthage, and when Marcius besieged it, they realized then that he would capture it and enslave them.[25] So they brought their possessions into the place of assembly, piled wood all around and put their wives and children on top. They made fifty of their leading 133 men swear an oath to kill the women and children when the town was captured, set fire to the wood and kill them- selves over the flames. Then, calling on the gods to witness 134 their actions, they sortied from the town and, with Marcius not expecting it, routed his light armed troops and cavalry. When the legionaries, however, armed themselves, al- 135 though the men of Astapa fought with exceptional bravery in their desperation, the Romans overwhelmed them due to their numbers, certainly not because the men of Astapa were inferior in courage. When they had all fallen, the 136 select fifty slaughtered the women and children, lit the fire and threw themselves on it, leaving the enemy with a profitless victory. Marcius was very impessed at the cour-

[25] Astapa is modern Estepa, about sixty-two miles east of Seville.

ἀρετὴν τῶν Ἀσταπαίων καταπλαγεὶς οὐκ ἐνύβρισεν
ἐς τὰ οἰκόπεδα αὐτῶν.

137   34. Μετὰ δὲ τοῦθ᾽ ὁ μὲν Σκιπίων ἐς ἀρρωστίαν
ἐνέπεσεν, καὶ ὁ Μάρκιος αὐτῷ διῴκει τὸ στρατόπεδον·
ὅσοι δὲ τῶν στρατιωτῶν ὑπ᾽ ἀσωτίας ἀναλώκεσαν τὰ
πεπορισμένα, ἡγούμενοι τῶν μὲν πόνων οὐδὲν ἄξιον
εὑρῆσθαι παρὰ τὸ μηδὲν ἔχειν, σφετερίζεσθαι δ᾽
αὐτῶν τὰ ἔργα καὶ τὴν δόξαν Σκιπίωνα, ἀφίσταντο
138   ἀπὸ τοῦ Μαρκίου καὶ ἐφ᾽ ἑαυτῶν ἐστρατοπέδευον. ἔκ
τε τῶν φρουρίων αὐτοῖς πολλοὶ συνέτρεχον, καὶ παρὰ
Μάγωνός τινες ἀργύριον φέροντες ἔπειθον αὐτοὺς
ἐς τὸν Μάγωνα μεταθέσθαι. οἳ δὲ τὸ μὲν ἀργύριον
ἔλαβον, στρατηγοὺς δ᾽ ἀπὸ σφῶν ἑλόμενοι καὶ ταξιάρχους καὶ τἆλλα διακοσμηθέντες ἐφ᾽ ἑαυτῶν ἐτάσ-
139   σοντο καὶ συνώμνυον ἀλλήλοις. πυθόμενος δ᾽ ὁ
Σκιπίων ἐπέστελλεν ἐν μέρει μὲν τοῖς ἀφεστηκόσιν,
ὅτι διὰ τὴν νόσον αὐτοὺς οὐκ ἀμείψαιτό πω, ἐν μέρει
δὲ τοῖς ἄλλοις, ἵνα μεταπείθωσιν αὐτοὺς πλανωμέ-
νους, κοινῇ δ᾽ ἅπασιν ἐπιστολὴν ἄλλην ὡς ἤδη συν-
ηλλαγμένοις, ὅτι αὐτοὺς αὐτίκα ἀμείψεται. καὶ ἐκέλευεν εὐθὺς ἥκειν ἐπὶ σῖτον ἐς Καρχηδόνα.

140   35. Ἀναγινωσκομένων δὲ τούτων οἳ μὲν ὑπώπτευον,
οἳ δὲ πιστεύειν ἠξίουν καὶ συνετίθεντο, καὶ πάντες
141   ὥδευον ἐς τὴν Καρχηδόνα ὁμοῦ. προσιόντων δ᾽ αὐτῶν
ὁ Σκιπίων προσέταξε τοῖς συνοῦσίν οἱ βουλευταῖς
ἕκαστον τῶν ἐξάρχων τινὰ τῆς στάσεως προσεταιρί-
σασθαι προσιόντα καὶ ὡς ἀπ᾽ εὐνοίας διορθοῦντα
142   ὑποδέξασθαί τε καὶ δῆσαι λαθόντα. προσέταξεν δὲ

age of Astapa and refrained from doing violence to its dwellings.

34. After this, Scipio fell ill and Marcius took over com- 137 mand of the army from him. Those of the soldiers who had spent all their wages wastefully thought that, because they had nothing, they had not been properly rewarded for their efforts, while Scipio was claiming all the glory of their hard work for himself. So they mutinied against Marcius and set up camp by themselves. They were joined by 138 many garrison troops, and when messengers came from Mago bringing money and trying to persuade them to come over to his side, the mutineers accepted the money, appointed generals and company commanders from their own number and put everything else in order on their own authority, before arraying themselves on parade and exchanging oaths with each other. When he was told of this, 139 Scipio sent separate word, first to the mutineers that he had not been able to pay them yet because of his illness, then to the others that they should try to win back the waverers. Lastly, he wrote another letter to them all jointly, as if they were already reconciled, saying that he would pay them immediately and ordering them to go straight to New Carthage for provisions.

35. Some men were suspicious of what they read, oth- 140 ers thought it trustworthy, but they came to an agreement, and all marched to New Carthage together. When they 141 were near, Scipio ordered each of the senators in his entourage to welcome one of the ringleaders of the mutiny as they came in, and after admonishing them in an apparently kindly way, to take them home and detain them without anyone knowing. He also ordered all military tribunes 142

191

καὶ τοῖς χιλιάρχοις τοὺς πιστοτάτους ἕκαστον ἀφανῶς ἅμα ἕῳ ξιφήρεις ἔχειν καὶ τὰ εὔκαιρα τῆς ἐκκλησίας ἐκ διαστημάτων καταλαβόντας, ἤν τις ἐπαν-
ιστῆται, κατακεντεῖν καὶ κατακαίνειν αὐτίκα ἄνευ
143 παραγγέλματος. αὐτὸς δ᾽ ἄρτι φαινομένης ἡμέρας ἐπὶ
τὸ βῆμα ἐκομίζετο καὶ τοὺς κήρυκας ἐς ἐκκλησίαν
ἐποτρύνειν περιέπεμπεν. οἳ δέ, αἰφνιδίου μὲν αὐτοῖς
τοῦ κηρύγματος γενομένου, αἰδούμενοι δ᾽ ἔτι νο-
σοῦντα τὸν στρατηγὸν σφῶν παρακρατεῖν καὶ νομίζοντες ἐπὶ τὰς ἀμοιβὰς καλεῖσθαι, συνέθεον ὁμοῦ
πάντοθεν, οἱ μὲν ἄζωστοι τὰ ξίφη, οἱ δὲ καὶ ἐν χιτῶσι
μόνοις, οὐ φθάσαντες οὐδὲ τὴν ἐσθῆτα πᾶσαν ἐπιθέσθαι.

144   36. Σκιπίων δέ, φρουρὰν ἔχων ἀμφ᾽ αὑτὸν ἀφανῆ,
πρῶτα μὲν αὐτοῖς ἐπεμέμφετο τῶν γεγονότων, εἶτ᾽ ἔφη
τὴν αἰτίαν ἀναθήσειν μόνοις τοῖς ἄρξασιν, "Οὓς ἐγὼ
145 κολάσω δι᾽ ὑμῶν." καὶ λέγων ἔτι προσέταξε τοῖς ὑπη-
ρέταις διαστῆσαι τὸ πλῆθος. οἱ μὲν δὴ διίστανον, οἱ
δὲ βουλευταὶ τοὺς αἰτίους παρῆγον ἐς τὸ μέσον. ἀνα-
βοησάντων δ᾽ αὐτῶν καὶ τοὺς συστρατιώτας βοηθῆσαι σφίσι παρακαλούντων, τοὺς ἐπιφθεγγομένους
146 εὐθὺς ἔκτεινον οἱ χιλίαρχοι. καὶ τὸ μὲν πλῆθος, ἐπειδὴ τὴν ἐκκλησίαν φρουρουμένην εἶδεν, ἐφ᾽ ἡσυχίας
ἦν σκυθρωποῦ· ὁ δὲ Σκιπίων, τοὺς εἰς τὸ μέσον
παραχθέντας αἰκισάμενος, καὶ μᾶλλον αὐτῶν τοὺς
ἐκβοήσαντας, ἐκέλευσε τοὺς αὐχένας ἁπάντων ἐς τοὔ-
δαφος παττάλοις προσδεθέντας ἀποτμηθῆναι καὶ τοῖς
ἄλλοις ἀμνηστίαν ἐκήρυξεν διδόναι.

to have their most reliable swordsmen ready at dawn, without attracting attention, but armed, and to station them at intervals around the most strategic parts of the assembly: if anyone caused trouble they were to run them through and kill them immediately without receiving specific orders. Scipio himself was carried to the tribunal just 143 after dawn and sent the heralds around to summon the men to assembly. They were not expecting the summons, but, ashamed to keep their still unwell commander waiting, and expecting that they were being called to receive what they were owed, they came running together from everywhere, some without having buckled on their swords, others just in their cloaks, not having had time even to put on all their clothes.

36. Surrounded unobtrusively by guards, Scipio first 144 berated the men for what had happened, then said that he would lay the blame only on the ringleaders: "With your help," he added, "I will personally punish them." Even 145 before he finished speaking he instructed his assistants to move the crowd back, and when they had done so, the senators brought those responsible for the mutiny into the assembly. These shouted out and called on their fellow soldiers to help, but the military tribunes immediately killed anyone who uttered a word. When the crowd saw 146 that there was heavy security at the meeting, they fell into a sullen silence. As for Scipio, he had the men who had been brought into the public place tortured, especially those who had cried out for help, and then ordered that they should all have their neck pegged to the ground and their head cut off; he proclaimed the granting of an amnesty to the others.

147   37. Ὧδε μὲν τὸ στρατόπεδον καθίστατο τῷ Σκι-
πίωνι· Ἰνδίβιλις δέ, τῶν συνθεμένων τις αὐτῷ δυνα-
στῶν, στασιαζούσης ἔτι τῆς Ῥωμαϊκῆς στρατιᾶς κα-
148 τέδραμέν τι τῆς ὑπὸ τῷ Σκιπίωνι γῆς. καὶ αὐτῷ τοῦ
Σκιπίωνος ἐπελάσαντος ὑπέστη μὲν τὸν ἀγῶνα γενναίως καὶ χιλίους καὶ διακοσίους Ῥωμαίων διέφθειρεν, ἀπολομένων δ᾽ αὐτῷ δισμυρίων ἐδεῖτο προσ-
πέμψας. καὶ ὁ Σκιπίων αὐτὸν χρήμασι ζημιώσας
149 συνηλλάσσετο. λαθὼν δὲ καὶ Μασσανάσσης Ἀσρούβαν ἐπέρασε τὸν πορθμὸν καὶ φιλίαν τῷ Σκιπίωνι
συνθέμενος ὤμοσε συμμαχήσειν, ἂν ἐς Λιβύην στρα-
τεύῃ. ἔπραξεν δὲ τοῦτο ἀνὴρ ἐς πάντα βέβαιος διὰ
150 τοιάνδε αἰτίαν. Ἀσρούβου τοῦ τότε οἱ συνόντος στρατηγοῦ θυγάτηρ ἐς γάμον ἐγγεγύητο Μασσανάσσῃ·
Σύφακα δ᾽ ἄρα τὸν δυνάστην ἔρως ἔκνιζε τῆς παιδός,
καὶ οἱ Καρχηδόνιοι, μέγα ποιούμενοι Σύφακα ἐπὶ
Ῥωμαίους προσλαβεῖν, ἔδωκαν αὐτῷ τὴν παῖδα, οὐδὲν τοῦ Ἀσρούβου πυθόμενοι. καὶ τῶνδε πραχθέντων
ὁ μὲν Ἀσρούβας αὐτὰ ἐπέκρυπτε, τὸν Μασσανάσσην
αἰδούμενος, ὁ δὲ αἰσθόμενος συνέθετο τῷ Σκιπίωνι.
151 Μάγων δ᾽ ὁ ναύαρχος, ἀπογνοὺς ἀπὸ τῶν παρόντων
τὰ ἐν Ἰβηρίᾳ, πλεύσας ἐς Λίγυας καὶ Κελτοὺς ἐξενολόγει.

152   38. Καὶ ὁ μὲν περὶ ταῦτ᾽ ἦν, καὶ τὰ Γάδειρα ἐκλει-
φθέντα ὑπὸ τοῦ Μάγωνος οἱ Ῥωμαῖοι παρέλαβον·
στρατηγοὺς δὲ Ἰβηρίας ἐτησίους ἐς τὰ ἔθνη τὰ
εἰλημμένα ἔπεμπον ἀπὸ τοῦδε ἀρξάμενοι, μικρὸν πρὸ
τῆς τετάρτης καὶ τεσσαρακοστῆς καὶ ἑκατοστῆς

37. This was how Scipio restored order in his army.   147
While the Roman army was still in a state of mutiny, however, a certain Indibilis, one of the princes with whom
Scipio had made an agreement, overran some territory
under Scipio's control. When Scipio marched against him,   148
he resisted bravely, killing one thousand two hundred Roman soldiers and losing twenty thousand of his own men,
but then sought a truce from Scipio, who imposed a fine
and agreed terms with him. Massinissa now crossed the   149
straits without Hasdrubal finding out, and established a
formal friendship with Scipio, and swore an oath to give
him military assistance if he campaigned in Africa. His
reasons for doing this and remaining completely loyal
were as follows. At the time he was serving under the com-   150
mand of Hasdrubal, Hasdrubal's daughter had been betrothed to Massinissa. King Syphax, however, fell in love
with the girl, and because the Carthaginians thought it
very important to have Syphax on their side against Rome,
they gave her to him without asking Hasdrubal. He kept
quiet about what had happened, out of respect for Massinissa, but Massinissa found out and made the agreement
with Scipio. As a result, the admiral Mago, despairing of   151
the situation in Iberia, sailed off to Liguria and Gaul to
recruit mercenaries.

38. While he was doing that, the Romans occupied   152
Gadeira, which he had abandoned. It was from this period,
a little before the 144th Olympiad, that the Romans began
to send praetors every year to the conquered peoples

ὀλυμπιάδος, ἁρμοστὰς ἢ ἐπιστάτας αὐτοῖς τῆς εἰρή-
153 νης ἐσομένους. καὶ αὐτοῖς ὁ Σκιπίων ὀλίγην στρατιὰν
ὡς ἐπὶ εἰρήνῃ καταλιπὼν συνῴκισε τοὺς τραυματίας
ἐς πόλιν, ἣν ἀπὸ τῆς Ἰταλίας Ἰταλικὴν ἐκάλεσε· καὶ
πατρίς ἐστι Τραϊανοῦ τε καὶ Ἀδριανοῦ, τῶν ὕστερον
154 Ῥωμαίοις ἀρξάντων τὴν αὐτοκράτορα ἀρχήν. αὐτὸς
δ᾽ ἐς Ῥώμην ἐπὶ στόλου πολλοῦ διέπλει, λαμπρῶς τε
κεκοσμημένου καὶ καταγέμοντος αἰχμαλώτων ὁμοῦ
155 καὶ χρημάτων καὶ ὅπλων καὶ λαφύρων ποικίλων. καὶ
ἡ πόλις αὐτὸν ἐπιφανῶς ἐξεδέχετο μετὰ δόξης ἀοιδίμου τε καὶ παραλόγου διά τε νεότητα καὶ ταχυεργ-
ίαν καὶ μέγεθος εὐπραξίας. οἵ τε φθονοῦντες αὐτῷ
τὴν πάλαι κουφολογίαν ὡμολόγουν ἐς ἔργον ἀποβῆ-
156 ναι. καὶ Σκιπίων μὲν θαυμαζόμενος ἐθριάμβευεν, Ἰνδίβιλις δ᾽ οἰχομένου τοῦ Σκιπίωνος αὖθις ἀφίστατο.
καὶ αὐτὸν οἱ στρατηγοὶ τῆς Ἰβηρίας τὸν στρατὸν
ἀγείραντες, ὅσος αὐτοῖς ἦν περὶ τὰ φρούρια, καὶ
δύναμιν ἄλλην ἀπὸ τῶν ὑπηκόων συναγαγόντες
157 ἔκτειναν. τοὺς δ᾽ αἰτίους τῆς ἀποστάσεως ἐς κρίσιν
παραγαγόντες θανάτῳ μετῆλθον καὶ τὰ ὄντα αὐτοῖς
ἐδήμευσαν. τά τε ἔθνη τὰ συναράμενα αὐτῷ χρήμασιν ἐζημίωσαν καὶ τὰ ὅπλα αὐτῶν παρείλοντο
καὶ ὅμηρα ᾔτησαν καὶ φρουρὰς δυνατωτέρας αὐτοῖς
ἐπέστησαν.
158   39. Καὶ τάδε μὲν ἦν εὐθὺς μετὰ Σκιπίωνα, καὶ ἡ
πρώτη Ῥωμαίων ἐς Ἰβηρίαν πεῖρα ἐς τοῦτο ἔληγε·

of Iberia as their governors and superintendents of the
peace.[26] Scipio left a small force for them, suitable for a   153
peaceful situation, and settled his wounded in a town
which he named Italica, after Italy.[27] This is the hometown
of Trajan and Hadrian, who later exercised imperial rule
over the Romans. Scipio himself sailed off to Rome with   154
a large fleet brilliantly arrayed and loaded with prisoners,
money, arms, and all sorts of booty. On account of his   155
youthfulness, speed and great success, the city received
him in fine fashion, with both glorious and unexpected
splendor. Even those who resented him admitted that the
boastful promises he issued in the past had come true.
Admired as he was, Scipio was awarded a triumph.[28] In his   156
absence, however, in Iberia Indibilis again revolted. The
commanders there collected an army from the garrisons
available to them, and raising another force from their
Iberian subjects, they killed Indibilis. Those responsible   157
for the revolt were put on trial, punished with death, and
their estates confiscated. Rome fined and disarmed the
peoples who had assisted Indibilis, demanded hostages
from them and imposed stronger garrisons over them.

39. These were the events that took place immediately   158
after Scipio's departure, bringing to an end Rome's first

[26] Olympiad 144 ran from 204 to 201.

[27] Italica was near the modern town of Santiponce, about six
miles from Seville.

[28] There is a dispute in the ancient sources over whether
Scipio celebrated a triumph in 206: Polybius (11.33.7) and Appian
say that he did, Livy (28.38.4–5) and Valerius Maximus (2.8) say
that his request was refused by the senate on the grounds that he
was not holding a magistracy at the time of the victory.

Χρόνῳ δ' ὕστερον, ὅτε Ῥωμαῖοι Κελτοῖς τε τοῖς περὶ
Πάδον ἐπολέμουν καὶ Φιλίππῳ τῷ Μακεδόνι, ἐνεωτέ-
159 ρισαν αὖθις ἐς τὴν ἀσχολίαν αὐτῶν οἱ Ἴβηρες. καὶ
αὐτοῖς ἐπεπέμφθησαν ἐκ Ῥώμης στρατηγοὶ τοῦδε
τοῦ πολέμου Σεμπρώνιός τε Τουδιτανὸς καὶ Μᾶρκος
160 Ἕλουιος, μετὰ δ' ἐκείνους Μινούκιος. καὶ ἐπὶ τούτῳ
μείζονος ἔτι τῆς κινήσεως γιγνομένης μετὰ πλέονος
δυνάμεως ἐπέμφθη Κάτων, νέος μὲν ὢν ἔτι πάμπαν,
αὐστηρὸς δὲ καὶ φιλόπονος συνέσει τε γνώμης καὶ
δεινότητι λόγων ἀριπρεπής, ὥστε αὐτὸν ἐπὶ τοῖς λόγοις ἐκάλουν οἱ Ῥωμαῖοι Δημοσθένη, πυνθανόμενοι
τὸν ἄριστον ἐν τοῖς Ἕλλησι ῥήτορα γεγενῆσθαι Δημοσθένη.
161 40. Ὡς δὲ κατέπλευσε τῆς Ἰβηρίας ἐς τὸ καλούμενον Ἐμπόριον ὁ Κάτων, οἱ μὲν πολέμιοι πάντοθεν ἐπ'
αὐτὸν ἐς τετρακισμυρίους ἀγηγέρατο, ὁ δ' ἐπὶ μέν τι
162 τὴν στρατιὰν ἐγύμναζεν, ὡς δ' ἔμελλε συνενεχθήσε-
σθαι μάχῃ, τὰς ναῦς, ἃς εἶχεν, ἐς Μασσαλίαν ἀπέ-
πεμψεν καὶ τὸν στρατὸν ἐδίδασκεν οὐ τοῦτ' εἶναι φο-
βερόν, ὅτι πλήθει προύχουσιν οἱ πολέμιοι (τὴν γὰρ
εὐψυχίαν αἰεὶ τοῦ πλέονος ἐπικρατεῖν), ἀλλ' ὅτι "Νεῶν
ἀποροῦμεν, ὡς οὐκ ἔχειν, εἰ μὴ κρατοῖμεν, οὐδὲ σω-
163 τηρίαν." ταῦτα εἰπὼν αὐτίκα συνέβαλλεν, οὐκ ἐπελπί-
σας ὥσπερ ἕτεροι τὸν στρατόν, ἀλλὰ φοβήσας. γενομένης δ' ἐν χερσὶν τῆς μάχης ἐς πάντα μετεπήδα

29 C. Sempronius Tuditanus and Marcus Helvius were among
the praetors elected in 197: Sempronius was assigned the prov-

venture into Iberia. Later, when the Romans were fighting both the Celts around the river Po and Philip of Macedon, the Iberians again revolted, taking advantage of Rome's other preoccupations. Sempronius Tuditanus and Marcus   159
Helvius were sent out to assume command of this war, and later Minucius.[29] As the revolt then spread, Cato was dis-   160
patched with a more substantial army. He was still a very young man, but strict and hardworking, and he enjoyed such a distinguished reputation for intelligent views and eloquent speaking, that the Romans used to call him Demosthenes on account of his speeches: for they had heard that Demosthenes had been the best orator among the Greeks.

40. When Cato landed in Iberia at the place called   161
Emporium, up to forty thousand of the enemy had gathered against him from all around. He spent some time   162
training the army, but when he was about to join battle, he sent the ships he had with him off to Massilia. He explained to the soldiers that what was frightening was not the superior numbers of the enemy—for courage, he told them, is always mightier than mere numbers—but the fact that "we have no ships, so that we will not even have the possibility of saving ourselves, unless we are victorious." With these words he immediately joined battle, having   163
instilled not hope in his army, like other generals, but fear. When the fighting started, Cato rushed all over the battle-

ince of Nearer Spain, Helvius Further Spain. Sempronius was killed on campaign against the Spaniards and was replaced by Q. Minucius Thermus, praetor in 196, who was awarded a triumph (he reached the consulship in 193). M. Porcius Cato was sent out to Spain as consul in 195.

164 παρακαλῶν καὶ παροξύνων. ἀκρίτου δ᾽ αὐτῆς ἐς δεί-
λην ἑσπέραν ἔτι οὔσης καὶ πολλῶν πιπτόντων ἑκατέρωθεν ἔς τινα λόφον ὑψηλὸν μετὰ τριῶν τάξεων
ἐφέδρων ἀνέδραμεν, τὸ ἔργον ὁμοῦ πᾶν ἐποψόμενος.

165 ὡς δὲ εἶδε τοὺς μέσους τῶν ἰδίων μάλιστα ἐνοχλουμέ-
νους, ὥρμησεν ἐς αὐτοὺς προκινδυνεύων ἔργῳ τε καὶ
βοῇ συνετάραξε τοὺς ἐχθροὺς καὶ πρῶτος κατῆρξε

166 τῆς νίκης. διώξας τε νυκτὸς ὅλης ἐκράτησεν αὐτῶν
τοῦ στρατοπέδου καὶ πολλοὺς ἀπέκτεινεν. ἐπανιόντι
δ᾽ ὡς ἡγεμόνι τῆς νίκης συνήδοντο συμπλεκόμενοι.
καὶ μετὰ τοῦτο ἀνέπαυε τὴν στρατιὰν καὶ τὰ λάφυρα
ἐπίπρασκεν.

167   41. Πρεσβευόντων δ᾽ ἐς αὐτὸν ἁπάντων ὅμηρά τε
ᾔτησεν ἄλλα καὶ βιβλία ἐσφραγισμένα ἐς ἑκάστους
περιέπεμπε καὶ τοὺς φέροντας ἐκέλευεν ἡμέρᾳ μιᾷ
πάντας ἀποδοῦναι· καὶ ὥριζε τὴν ἡμέραν τεκμηράμενος, ὅτε μάλιστα ἐς τὴν πορρωτάτω πόλιν ἀφίξονται.

168 ἐκέλευεν δ᾽ ἡ γραφὴ ταῖς ἀρχαῖς τῶν πόλεων ἁπάσαις
καθαιρεῖν τὰ τείχη σφῶν αὐτῆς ἡμέρας, ᾗ τὰ γράμματα λάβοιεν· εἰ δὲ ἀνάθοιντο τὴν ἡμέραν, ἀνδραπο-

169 δισμὸν ἠπείλει. οἱ δ᾽ ἄρτι μὲν ἡττημένοι μεγάλῃ
μάχῃ, ὑπὸ δ᾽ ἀγνοίας, εἴτε μόνοις, εἴθ᾽ ἅπασι ταῦτα
προσετάχθη, φοβούμενοι μόνοι μὲν ὡς εὐκαταφρόνη-
τοι, μετὰ δὲ τῶν ἄλλων, μὴ μόνοι βραδύνωσι, καιρόν
τε οὐκ ἔχοντες περιπέμψαι πρὸς ἀλλήλους καὶ τοὺς
στρατιώτας τοὺς ἐληλυθότας μετὰ τῶν γραμμάτων
ἐφεστῶτας σφίσιν εὐλαβούμενοι, τὸ σφέτερον ἀσφαλὲς ἕκαστοι προὔργου τιθέμενοι, τὰ τείχη καθῄρουν

field encouraging and urging on his men. The battle 164
was evenly fought with heavy casualties on both sides until late afternoon, when Cato took three reserve companies
and climbed a high hill to get a view of the whole battle.
When he saw that his own center was under particular 165
pressure, he rushed to them, and exposing himself to great
danger scattered the enemy with his yelling and courage,
and personally initiated the victory. Pressing the pursuit 166
throughout the night, he captured the enemy camp and
killed large numbers of them. When he returned to his
lines the soldiers embraced him and congratulated him on
instigating the victory. After this Cato rested the army and
sold the spoils.

41. Everyone now sent him embassies and Cato de- 167
manded more hostages. He also sent round sealed letters
to everyone, and ordered the men carrying them to deliver
them all on the same day, which he fixed by calculating
how long they would take to get to the most distant town.
What he had written was an order to all the town leaders 168
to tear down their walls on the very day they got the letter.
If they tried to postpone the day, he threatened to sell
them into slavery. As they had just been defeated in a great 169
battle and did not know whether the instructions had been
sent just to them or to everyone, they were afraid that if it
was just to them, they would be easy to treat with disdain,
but if the others were all included, they were afraid of
being the only ones to delay. They had no time to send
round and ask each other, as the soldiers who had come
with the letter were attentively standing over them, so
they each prioritized their own safety and speedily demol-

μετὰ σπουδῆς. ἐν ᾧ γὰρ ἅπαξ ὑπακούειν ἐδόκει,
καὶ τὸ ταχέως εἰργάσθαι προσλαβεῖν ἐφιλοτιμοῦντο.

170 οὕτω μὲν αἱ πόλεις αἱ περὶ Ἴβηρα ποταμὸν μιᾶς ἡμέρας ὑφ᾽ ἑνὸς στρατηγήματος αὐταὶ τὰ τείχη τὰ ἑαυτῶν καθῄρουν καὶ Ῥωμαίοις ἐς τὸ μέλλον εὐέφοδοι
γενόμεναι διέμειναν ἐς πλεῖστον ἐπὶ εἰρήνης.

171   42. Ὀλυμπιάσι δ᾽ ὕστερον τέσσαρσιν, ἀμφὶ τὰς
πεντήκοντα καὶ ἑκατόν, πολλοὶ τῶν Ἰβήρων γῆς ἀποροῦντες ἀπέστησαν ἀπὸ Ῥωμαίων, ἄλλοι τε καὶ Λού-

172 σονες, οἳ περὶ τὸν Ἴβηρα ᾤκηνται. στρατεύσας οὖν
ἐπ᾽ αὐτοὺς ὕπατος Φούλβιος Φλάκκος ἐνίκα μάχῃ.
καὶ πολλοὶ μὲν αὐτῶν κατὰ πόλεις διελύθησαν· ὅσοι
δὲ μάλιστα γῆς ἠπόρουν καὶ ἐξ ἄλης ἐβιότευον, ἐς
Κομπλέγαν πόλιν συνέφυγον, ἣ νεόκτιστός τε ἦν καὶ

173 ὀχυρὰ καὶ ηὔξετο ταχέως. ὅθεν ὁρμώμενοι τὸν Φλάκ-
κον ἐκέλευον, καταθέντα σφίσιν ὑπὲρ τῶν ἀνῃρημέ-
νων ἑκάστου σάγον τε καὶ ἵππον καὶ ξίφος, ἀποτρέ-
χειν ἐξ Ἰβηρίας, πρίν τι κακὸν παθεῖν. ὁ δὲ πολλοὺς
αὐτοῖς ἔφη σάγους οἴσειν καὶ τοῖς πρέσβεσιν αὐτῶν

174 ἑπόμενος τῇ πόλει παρεστρατοπέδευσεν. οἳ δὲ ἀνο-
μοίως ταῖς ἀπειλαῖς σφῶν αὐτίκα ἀπεδίδρασκον καὶ
τὰ τῶν ἐγγὺς βαρβάρων ἐλήζοντο. χρῶνται δὲ δι-
πλοῖς ἱματίοις παχέσιν, ἀντὶ χλαμύδων αὐτὰ περι-
πορπώμενοι, καὶ τοῦτο σάγον ἡγοῦνται.

---

30 180 to 176.   31 Q. Fulvius Flaccus was praetor in 182
and was posted to Further Spain, where he won a triumph in 180.
He was consul in 179 and was awarded another triumph for his

ished their walls. For, once they had decided to submit, they were ambitious to get the job done quickly. In this way the towns along the river Ebro demolished their walls themselves in one day as a result of a single plan, and having become more accessible to the Romans for the future, they remained at peace for a very long time. 170

42. Four Olympiads later, that is in about the 150th Olympiad,[30] land shortage forced many Iberians—among others the Lusones who lived on the Ebro—to revolt from Rome. The consul Fulvius Flaccus campaigned against them, therefore, and defeated them in battle, many of them dispersing among the towns.[31] Those who were particularly short of land and living a nomadic life took refuge in the town of Complega, a new and secure foundation that was growing rapidly.[32] With this as their base they instructed Flaccus to present them with a cloak, a horse, and a sword in recompense for every one of those who had been killed, and to get out of Iberia fast, before anything bad happened to him. Flaccus replied that he would bring them a large number of cloaks,[33] and following their ambassadors he encamped before the town. But they failed to live up to their threats and ran away immediately, plundering the neighboring barbarians on their way. Instead of a military mantle, they wear a thick double garment which they fasten around themselves with a clasp. This is what they call a *sagum*. 171 172 173 174

campaigns in Liguria (south of France). The incorrect description of him as consul while he was in Spain may be a mistake by Appian, or by his source.   [32] The site of Complega is not known.   [33] That is, he would bring a large number of his own (cloak-wearing) troops.

175   43. Φλάκκῳ μὲν οὖν διάδοχος ἦλθεν ἐπὶ τὴν στρατηγίαν Τιβέριος Σεμπρώνιος Γράκχος. Κάραουιν δὲ
πόλιν, ἣ Ῥωμαίων ἦν φίλη, δισμύριοι Κελτιβήρων
ἐπολιόρκουν· καὶ ἐπίδοξος ἦν ἁλώσεσθαι, Γράκχου
σφόδρα μὲν ἐπειγομένου βοηθῆσαι τῇ πόλει, περιιόν-
τος δ᾽ ἐν κύκλῳ τοὺς πολεμίους καὶ οὐκ ἔχοντος οὐδὲ
176 μηνῦσαι τῇ πόλει περὶ ἑαυτοῦ. τῶν οὖν τις ἰλάρχων,
Κομίνιος, ἐνθυμηθεὶς πρὸς ἑαυτὸν καὶ Γράκχῳ τὸ
τόλμημα ἀνενεγκών, ἐνεπορπήσατο σάγον Ἰβηρικῶς
καὶ λαθὼν ἀνεμίχθη τοῖς χορτολογοῦσιν τῶν πολεμίων συνεισῆλθέ τε αὐτοῖς ὡς Ἴβηρ ἐς τὸ στρατόπεδον καὶ εἰς τὴν Κάραουιν διαδραμὼν ἐμήνυσεν, ὅτι
177 Γράκχος ἐπίοι. οἱ μὲν δὴ διεσώθησαν, ἐγκαρτερήσαν-
τες τῇ πολιορκίᾳ, μέχρι Γράκχος αὐτοῖς ἐπῆλθε μετὰ
τρίτην ἡμέραν καὶ οἱ πολιορκοῦντες ἀπανέστησαν·
178 δισμύριοι δ᾽ ἐκ τῆς Κομπλέγας διέτρεχον ἐς τὸ Γράκχου στρατόπεδον σὺν ἱκετηρίαις καὶ πλησιάσαντες
ἀδοκήτως ἐπέθεντο αὐτῷ καὶ συνετάραξαν. ὁ δ᾽ εὐμηχάνως ἐξέλιπεν αὐτοῖς τὸ στρατόπεδον καὶ ὑπεκρίνατο φεύγειν· εἶτα διαρπάζουσιν ἐπιστραφεὶς ἐπέπε-
σέν τε καὶ πλείστους ἔκτεινεν καὶ τῆς Κομπλέγας
179 κατέσχε καὶ τῶν περιοίκων. τοὺς δὲ ἀπόρους συνῴκιζε
καὶ γῆν αὐτοῖς διεμέτρει καὶ πᾶσιν ἔθετο τοῖς τῇδε
συνθήκας ἀκριβεῖς, καθ᾽ ἃ Ῥωμαίων ἔσονται φίλοι·
ὅρκους τε ὤμοσεν αὐτοῖς καὶ ἔλαβεν, ἐπιποθήτους ἐν

---

34 Tiberius Sempronius Gracchus, father of the famous tribunes Tiberius and Gaius Gracchus, was praetor in Spain from

43. Tiberius Sempronius Gracchus came as successor   175
to Flaccus in the command.[34] Twenty thousand Celtiberians were besieging the town of Caravis, a friend of Rome,
and its capture was expected.[35] Gracchus pressed with
great haste to relieve the town, but he was only able to
circle around behind the besiegers, and could not even get
information to the town about his presence. One of his   176
cavalry officers, however, called Cominius, considered the
matter carefully and proposed his daring plan to Gracchus. And so, buckling on a cloak in the Iberian manner
and secretly mixing with the enemy foragers, Cominius
got into the camp with them as if he were an Iberian, and
rapidly making his way through to Caravis, told them that
Gracchus was coming. And they were indeed rescued,   177
having endured the siege until Gracchus arrived three
days later, and the besieging forces withdrew. Twenty   178
thousand men of Complega then came to Gracchus' camp
with the olive branches of suppliants, but when they got
near they unexpectedly attacked him and caused great
confusion. He cleverly abandoned the camp to them and
pretended to flee, but turned and fell on them as they were
plundering, and after killing most of them, took possession
of Complega and the surrounding district. He settled the   179
economically deprived together and distributed land to
them, and drew up detailed agreements with all the inhabitants of the region, setting out the terms on which they
would be friends of Rome. Oaths were exchanged, only to

180 to 178, and he also won a triumph there. He was consul in
177 and censor in 169.
[35] Caravis has been identified with the modern town of Ma-
gallón, some thirty-seven miles northwest of Saragossa.

τοῖς ὕστερον πολέμοις πολλάκις γενομένους. δι᾿ ἃ καὶ
ἐν Ἰβηρίᾳ καὶ ἐν Ῥώμῃ διώνυμος ἐγένετο ὁ Γράκχος
καὶ ἐθριάμβευσε λαμπρῶς.

180   44. Ἔτεσιν δὲ οὐ πολλοῖς ὕστερον πόλεμος ἄλλος
ἠγέρθη περὶ Ἰβηρίαν χαλεπὸς ἐκ τοιᾶσδε προφάσεως. Σεγήδη πόλις ἐστὶ Κελτιβήρων τῶν Βελλῶν
λεγομένων μεγάλη τε καὶ δυνατὴ καὶ ἐς τὰς Σεμ-
181   πρωνίου Γράκχου συνθήκας ἐνεγέγραπτο. αὕτη τὰς
βραχυτέρας πόλεις ἀνῴκιζεν ἐς αὑτὴν καὶ τεῖχος ἐς
τεσσαράκοντα σταδίους κύκλῳ περιεβάλετο Τίτθους
182   τε ὅμορον γένος ἄλλο συνηνάγκαζεν ἐς ταῦτα. ἡ δὲ
σύγκλητος πυθομένη τό τε τεῖχος ἀπηγόρευε τειχίζειν καὶ φόρους ᾔτει τοὺς ὁρισθέντας ἐπὶ Γράκχου
στρατεύεσθαί τε Ῥωμαίοις προσέτασσε· καὶ γὰρ
183   τοῦθ᾿ αἱ Γράκχου συνθῆκαι ἐκέλευον. οἱ δὲ περὶ μὲν
τοῦ τείχους ἔλεγον ἀπηγορεῦσθαι Κελτίβηρσιν ὑπὸ
Γράκχου μὴ κτίζειν πόλεις, οὐ τειχίζειν τὰς ὑπαρχού-
σας· τῶν δὲ φόρων καὶ τῆς ξεναγίας ὑπ᾿ αὐτῶν ἔφασαν Ῥωμαίων ἀφεῖσθαι μετὰ Γράκχον. καὶ τῷ ὄντι
ἦσαν ἀφειμένοι, δίδωσι δ᾿ ἡ βουλὴ τὰς τοιάσδε δωρεὰς ἀεὶ προστιθεῖσα κυρίας ἔσεσθαι, μέχρι ἂν αὐτῇ
καὶ τῷ δήμῳ δοκῇ.

184   45. Στρατηγὸς οὖν ἐπ᾿ αὐτοὺς Νωβελίων ἐπέμπετο
μετὰ στρατιᾶς οὐ πολὺ τρισμυρίων ἀνδρῶν ἀποδεού-
σης· ὃν ἐπειδὴ σφίσιν οἱ Σεγηδαῖοι προσιόντα ἔγνω-

---

36 Segeda was located near modern Saragossa in northeastern
Spain.

be found wanting on many occasions in the wars that followed. Gracchus became very famous for these actions both in Iberia and Rome, and he held a magnificent triumph.

44. Not many years later another troublesome war 180 broke out in Iberia for which the following was the stated reason. Segeda is a large and powerful town of those Celtiberians known as the Belli, and it was a signatory to the agreements made with Sempronius Gracchus.[36] It now 181 forced the smaller towns to migrate to Segeda, and built a wall forty stades long around the town, also forcing another neighboring people, the Titthi, to take part in the venture. When the senate heard about the wall they for- 182 bade its completion, demanded the tribute agreed in the time of Gracchus, and ordered the people to provide troops for Rome: for this too was a requirement of the Gracchan treaty. Concerning the wall, however, the Belli 183 said that the Celtiberians had been forbidden by Gracchus from building new towns, not from fortifying existing ones; and as for the tribute and military service, they had been exempted from them by the Romans themselves in the time after Gracchus. They had in fact been exempted, but the senate always adds a rider to concessions like these that they will remain in operation only as long as the senate and Roman people decide.

45. Consequently Nobilior was sent against them with 184 an army of just under thirty thousand men.[37] When the people of Segeda realized he was coming against them, as

[37] Q. Fulvius Nobilior was consul in 153, when he was sent to Spain.

σαν, οὔπω τὸ τεῖχος ἐκτελέσαντες ἔφευγον ἐς Ἀρουακοὺς μετὰ παίδων καὶ γυναικῶν καὶ σφᾶς ὑποδέχεσθαι
185 τοὺς Ἀρουακοὺς παρεκάλουν. οἳ δ' ὑποδέχονταί τε καὶ
Κάρον αὐτῶν Σεγηδαίων, πολεμικὸν εἶναι νομιζόμε-
νον, αἱροῦνται στρατηγόν. ὁ δὲ τρίτῃ μετὰ τὴν χειρο-
τονίαν ἡμέρᾳ δισμυρίους πεζοὺς καὶ ἱππέας πεντακισχιλίους ἔς τινα λόχμην ἐνεδρεύσας παροδεύουσι
τοῖς Ῥωμαίοις ἐπέθετο καὶ τῆς μάχης ἐπὶ πολὺ ἀγ-
χωμάλου γενομένης ἐκράτει τε λαμπρῶς καὶ Ῥωμαίων τῶν ἐξ ἄστεως ἔκτεινεν ἐς ἑξακισχιλίους, ὡς
186 μέγα τῇ πόλει γενέσθαι τὸ ἀτύχημα. ἀτάκτου δ' αὐτῷ
τῆς διώξεως ἐπὶ τῇ νίκῃ γενομένης οἱ τὰ σκευοφόρα
Ῥωμαίων φυλάσσοντες ἱππῆς ἐπέδραμον καὶ Κάρον
τε αὐτὸν ἀριστεύοντα ἔκτειναν καὶ ἑτέρους ἀμφ' αὐτόν, οὐκ ἐλάσσους καὶ οἵδε τῶν ἑξακισχιλίων, μέχρι
187 νὺξ ἐπελθοῦσα διέλυσεν. ἐγίγνετο δὲ ταῦθ', ὅτε Ῥωμαῖοι τῷ Ἡφαίστῳ τὴν ἑορτὴν ἄγουσιν· ὅθεν οὐδεὶς
ἂν ἑκὼν ἄρξειεν ἐξ ἐκείνου μάχης παρὰ τήνδε τὴν
ἡμέραν.

188   46. Ἀρουακοὶ μὲν οὖν εὐθὺς αὐτῆς νυκτὸς ἐς Νομαντίαν, ἣ δυνατωτάτη πόλις ἦν, συνελέγοντο καὶ στρατηγοὺς Ἄμβωνα καὶ Λεύκωνα ᾑροῦντο· Νωβελίων δ'
αὐτοῖς τρισὶν ἡμέραις ὕστερον ἐπελθὼν παρεστρατο-
189 πέδευσεν ἀπὸ σταδίων τεσσάρων καὶ εἴκοσι. παρα-
γενομένων δέ οἱ Νομάδων ἱππέων τριακοσίων, οὓς
Μασσανάσσης ἐπεπόμφει, καὶ ἐλεφάντων δέκα τὴν
στρατιὰν ἐπῆγε τοῖς πολεμίοις, ἄγων ὀπίσω τὰ θηρία
190 λανθάνοντα. καὶ γενομένης ἐν χερσὶ τῆς μάχης οἱ

they had not yet finished building the wall, they fled to the Arevaci with their women and children and begged to be given refuge. The Arevaci take them in and choose as their 185 commander a man of Segeda called Carus, who had a good reputation as a soldier. Three days after his selection, he set an ambush with twenty thousand infantry and five thousand cavalry in a wooded spot, and attacked the Romans as they marched past. For a long time the outcome of the battle was in doubt, but in the end Carus won a brilliant victory, killing some six thousand Roman citizens, resulting in a great disaster for the city itself. After the 186 victory, however, Carus conducted a disorderly pursuit and the Roman cavalry guarding the baggage train launched an attack, killing Carus himself, who died fighting bravely, and many of his men—no fewer than six thousand, like the Romans. Eventually, night put an end to the fighting. These events occurred at the time the Romans 187 celebrate the festival of Vulcan, and as a result no Roman since then willingly starts a battle on that day.[38]

46. That very same night the Arevaci gathered at Numantia, a most formidable town, and chose as their commanders Ambo and Leuco.[39] Three days later Nobilior advanced toward them and camped twenty four stades away. After he was joined by three hundred Numidian 189 cavalry sent by Massinissa and ten elephants, he led his army against the enemy, keeping the elephants at the rear out of sight. When battle was joined, the men stood aside 190

[38] The Volcanalia was held on August 23.

[39] Numantia lay close to the modern town of Soria, some 125 miles north of Madrid.

μὲν ἄνδρες διέστησαν, τὰ δὲ θηρία ἐξεφαίνετο· καὶ οἱ
Κελτίβηρες αὐτοί τε καὶ οἱ ἵπποι σφῶν, οὐ πρὶν ἑω-
ρακότες ἐλέφαντας ἐν πολέμοις, ἐθορυβοῦντο καὶ κατ-
191 έφευγον ἐς τὴν πόλιν. ὁ δὲ καὶ τοῖς τείχεσιν αὐτοὺς
ἐπῆγε καὶ ἐμάχετο γενναίως, μέχρι τῶν ἐλεφάντων
τις ἐς τὴν κεφαλὴν λίθῳ μεγάλῳ καταπίπτοντι πληγεὶς ἠγριώθη τε καὶ ἐκβοήσας μέγιστον ἐς τοὺς
φίλους ἐπεστρέφετο καὶ ἀνήρει τὸν ἐν ποσίν, οὐ δια-
192 κρίνων ἔτι φίλιον ἢ πολέμιον. οἵ τε ἄλλοι ἐλέφαντες
πρὸς τὴν ἐκείνου βοὴν διαταραχθέντες ὅμοια πάντες
ἔδρων καὶ τοὺς Ῥωμαίους συνεπάτουν τε καὶ ἀνέ-
τεμνον καὶ ἀνερρίπτουν· ὅπερ ἀεὶ θορυβηθέντες οἱ
ἐλέφαντες εἰώθασι πάσχειν καὶ πάντας ἡγεῖσθαι πο-
λεμίους· καί τινες διὰ τήνδε τὴν ἀπιστίαν αὐτοὺς
193 καλοῦσι κοινοὺς πολεμίους. φυγὴ οὖν τῶν Ῥωμαίων
ἐγίγνετο ἄτακτος· ἣν οἱ Νομαντῖνοι κατιδόντες ἀπὸ
τῶν τειχῶν ἐξέθορον καὶ διώκοντες ἔκτειναν ἄνδρας
μὲν ἐς τετρακισχιλίους, ἐλέφαντας δὲ τρεῖς ὅπλα τε
πολλὰ καὶ σημεῖα ἔλαβον. Κελτιβήρων δ᾽ ἀπέθανον
ἐς δισχιλίους.

194 47. Καὶ ὁ Νωβελίων μικρὸν ἐκ τοῦ πταίσματος
ἀναλαβὼν ἀγορᾷ μέν τινι τῶν πολεμίων ἐπεχείρει
περὶ Ἀξείνιον πόλιν σεσωρευμένῃ, οὐδὲν δὲ ἀνύσας,
ἀλλὰ κἀνταῦθα πολλοὺς ἀποβαλὼν ἐπανῆλθε νυκτὸς
195 ἐς τὸ στρατόπεδον. ὅθεν Βήσιον ἵππαρχον ἐπὶ συμμαχίαν ἔς τι γειτονεῦον ἔθνος ἔπεμπεν, ἱππέων δεόμενος. οἱ δὲ συνέπεμψαν αὐτῷ τινας ἱππέας, οὓς ἐρ-
χομένους ἐλόχων οἱ Κελτίβηρες· καὶ τῆς ἐνέδρας

and revealed the elephants. Neither the Celtiberians themselves nor their horses had ever seen elephants in battle before, and they were thrown into confusion and fled to the town. Nobilior took the elephants right up to 191 the walls of the town and was fighting bravely until one of the elephants was hit on the head by a heavy stone. The animal was enraged, let out a terrible roar and turned on the men of his own side, killing anyone in the way and making no distinction between friend and foe. Disturbed 192 by his trumpeting, all the other elephants began to do the same, trampling the Romans under foot, tearing them to pieces and tossing them in the air. This is always what happens when elephants are upset: they regard everyone as hostile. Because they are so unreliable, some people call them the common enemy. At any rate, the Romans fled in disorder. When the Numantines saw this they rushed out 193 from the walls in pursuit and killed about four thousand men and three elephants, as well as capturing many weapons and standards. About two thousand Celtiberians died.

47. Nobilior recovered a little from this setback and 194 attacked a supply depot of the enemy that they had built up at the town of Axeinium, but he accomplished nothing; indeed here too he lost many men, and withdrew by night to his camp. As a result, he sent a cavalry officer named 195 Biesius to seek an alliance with a neighboring people and ask them for cavalry. They agreed to send him some, but the Celtiberians ambushed them on the way. Although the

ἐκφανείσης οἱ μὲν σύμμαχοι διεδίδρασκον, ὁ δὲ Βιή-
σιος μαχόμενος αὐτός τε καὶ σὺν αὐτῷ πολλοὶ Ῥω-
196 μαίων ἀπέθανον. συνεχῶν δὲ τοιῶνδε πταισμάτων
αὐτοῖς ἐπιγιγνομένων πόλις Ὀκιλις, ἔνθα ἡ ἀγορὰ
καὶ τὰ χρήματα ἦν τὰ Ῥωμαίων, μετέθετο ἐς τοὺς
197 Κελτίβηρας. καὶ ὁ Νωβελίων ἀπιστῶν ἅπασιν ἐν τῷ
στρατοπέδῳ διεχείμαζε, στεγάσας, ὡς ἐδύνατο, καὶ
τὴν ἀγορὰν ἔχων ἔνδον καὶ κακοπαθῶν αὐτῆς τε τῆς
ἀγορᾶς τῇ ὀλιγότητι καὶ νιφετοῦ πυκνότητι καὶ κρύους χαλεπότητι, ὥστε πολλοὶ τῶν στρατιωτῶν οἱ μὲν
ἐν τοῖς φρυγανισμοῖς, οἱ δὲ καὶ ἔνδον ὑπὸ στενοχω-
ρίας καὶ κρύους ἀπώλλυντο.

198   48. Τοῦ δ᾽ ἐπιόντος ἔτους Νωβελίωνι μὲν ἐπὶ τὴν
στρατηγίαν ἀφικνεῖται διάδοχος Κλαύδιος Μάρκελλος, ἄγων πεζοὺς ὀκτακισχιλίους καὶ ἱππέας πεντα-
κοσίους· λοχώντων δὲ καὶ τόνδε τῶν πολεμίων διῆλθε
πεφυλαγμένως καὶ σύμπαντι τῷ στρατῷ παρὰ τὴν
199 Ὀκιλιν ἐστρατοπέδευσεν. ἐπιτυχὴς δὲ τὰ πολέμια
ὢν τὴν πόλιν αὐτίκα παρεστήσατο καὶ συγγνώμην
ἔδωκεν, ὅμηρά τινα καὶ ἀργυρίου τάλαντα τριάκοντα
200 λαβών. Νεργόβριγες δ᾽, αὐτοῦ περὶ τῆσδε τῆς μετρι-
οπαθείας πυθόμενοι, πέμψαντες ἠρώτων, τί ἂν πρά-
201 ξαντες εἰρήνης ἐπιτύχοιεν. ὡς δὲ αὐτοὺς ἐκέλευεν
ἑκατὸν ἱππέας δοῦναι συστρατεύσοντας, οἱ μὲν ὑπ-
ισχνοῦντο δώσειν, κατὰ δ᾽ ἄλλο μέρος τοῖς οὐραγοῦ-
202 σιν ἐπετίθεντο καὶ τῶν σκευοφόρων τι περιέσπων. εἶτ᾽
ἀφίκοντο τοὺς ἑκατὸν ἱππέας ἄγοντες ὡς δὴ κατὰ τὸ
συγκείμενον περί τε τῶν ἐπὶ τῆς οὐραγίας γενομένων

ambush was spotted beforehand and the allies escaped,
Biesius himself was killed in battle and many Romans died
with him. As a result of this string of disasters, the town of   196
Ocilis, where the Romans stored their supplies and money,
went over to the Celtiberian side.[40] At this, Nobilior lost   197
all confidence and wintered in camp, roofing it over as
much as possible and keeping his supplies inside. Indeed
he suffered badly from a shortage of supplies, and also
from the heavy snow and severe frost. The result was that
many of his troops died, some while out foraging for fire-
wood and others in the confines of the freezing camp.

48. The following year Claudius Marcellus arrives to   198
take over command from Nobilior, bringing with him
eight thousand infantry and five hundred cavalry.[41] The
enemy laid an ambush for him too, but by exercising due
caution he got through it and camped infront of Ocilis with
his whole army. Marcellus was a successful soldier and he   199
immediately brought the town to terms, granting it a pardon, but taking hostages and thirty talents of silver. The   200
Nergobriges heard how reasonable he was, so they sent
and asked him what they would have to do to achieve
peace. When he ordered them to provide one hundred   201
cavalry to serve in the Roman army, they undertake to do
so, but at the same time they were attacking another section of the army, the rearguard, and stealing some of the
baggage animals. Arriving with the one hundred cavalry,   202
in accordance with the agreement, they said that what had
happened to the rearguard was a mistake made by some

[40] Ocilis is modern Medinaceli, midway between Madrid and
Saragossa.

[41] M. Claudius Marcellus was consul in 166, 155, and 152.

ἔλεγόν τινας ἀγνοοῦντας τὰ ὡμολογημένα ἁμαρτεῖν.
203 ὁ δὲ τοὺς μὲν ἑκατὸν ἱππέας ἔδησε, τοὺς δ' ἵππους
αὐτῶν ἀποδόμενος καὶ τὸ πεδίον καταδραμὼν τὴν
λείαν διεῖλεν τῷ στρατῷ καὶ τῇ πόλει παρεστρατοπέ-
204 δευσε. Νεργόβριγες δέ, προσαγομένων αὐτοῖς μηχα-
νημάτων ἅμα καὶ χωμάτων, κήρυκα πέμψαντες λυκῆν
ἀντὶ κηρυκείου περικείμενον ᾔτουν συγγνώμην. ὁ δὲ
οὐκ ἔφη δώσειν, εἰ μὴ πάντες Ἀρουακοὶ καὶ Βελλοὶ
205 καὶ Τίτθοι δεηθεῖεν ὁμοῦ. ὧν τὰ μὲν ἔθνη πυθόμενα
προθύμως ἐπρεσβεύετο καὶ τὸν Κλαύδιον[15] ἠξίου, ποινὴν αὐτοῖς ἐπιθέντα μετρίαν, ἐς τὰς Γράκχου συνθήκας ἀναγαγεῖν· ἀντέλεγον δ' αὐτοῖς ἐπιχώριοί τινες
ὑπ' ἐκείνων πεπολεμημένοι.
206   49. Καὶ ὁ Μάρκελλος ἐξ ἑκατέρων πρέσβεις ἐς
Ῥώμην ἔπεμπεν ἀντιλέξοντας ἀλλήλοις, ἰδίᾳ δ' ἐπέστελλε τῇ βουλῇ προτρέπων ἐς τὰς διαλύσεις·
ἐβούλετο γὰρ ἐφ' ἑαυτοῦ τὸν πόλεμον ἐκλυθῆναι, δό-
207 ξαν οἱ χρηστὴν καὶ ἀπὸ τοῦδε νομίζων ἔσεσθαι. τῶν
δὲ πρέσβεων οἱ μὲν ἐκ τῆς φιλίας ἐς τὴν πόλιν ἐσελθόντες ἐξενίζοντο, οἱ δὲ ἐκ τῶν πολεμίων, ὡς ἔθος
208 ἐστίν, ἔξω τειχῶν ἐστάθμευον. ἀποδοκιμάζουσα δ' ἡ
βουλὴ τὴν εἰρήνην καὶ χαλεπῶς φέρουσα, ὅτι μή,
καθάπερ αὐτοὺς ἠξίου Νωβελίων, ὁ πρὸ Μαρκέλλου,
Ῥωμαίοις αὐτοὺς ἐπετετρόφεσαν, Μάρκελλον αὐτοῖς
209 ἐξοίσειν ἔφη τὰ δόξαντα. καὶ στρατιὰν εὐθὺς ἐκλήρουν
ἐς Ἰβηρίαν τότε πρῶτον ἀντὶ καταλέξεως· πολλῶν

of their troops who were unaware of the agreement. Mar- 203
cellus, however, arrested the one hundred cavalrymen,
sold their horses, overran the plain, distributed the booty
to his army, and made camp in front of the town. When 204
siege engines were brought up against them and earthworks dug, the Nergobriges sent a herald, dressed in a
wolf skin, rather than carrying the usual herald's staff, to
ask for forgiveness. Marcellus said he would only grant a
pardon if the Arevaci, Belli, and Titthi all asked for it together. On being told, these peoples eagerly sent an em- 205
bassy to Claudius, asking him to impose a reasonable punishment on them and to renew the terms of the Gracchan
treaty. Some natives who had been attacked by these
peoples opposed the request.

49. Marcellus sent representatives from each group to 206
Rome to argue their case with each other, but privately
wrote to the senate urging them to make an agreement.
For he wanted the war to be brought to an end under his
command, thinking that he would thereby win a good
reputation too. The ambassadors who came to Rome from 207
the friendly side entered the city and were entertained as
guests, and, as was customary, the ones from the hostile
side took up quarters outside the walls. The senate turned 208
down the peace proposal and were annoyed that the Celtiberians had not committed themselves to Rome when
asked to do so by Marcellus' predecessor, Nobilior; Marcellus, they said, would communicate the senate's decision
to them. They immediately enlisted an army for Iberia 209
using a random draft for the first time rather than the

---

15 τὸν Κλαύδιον Goukowsky: τὸν Κλαύδιον Μάρκελλον
Exc.

γὰρ αἰτιωμένων τοὺς ὑπάτους ἀδίκως ποιεῖσθαι τὰς
καταγραφὰς καί τινας ἐς τὰς κουφοτέρας στρατείας
210 καταλέγειν ἔδοξεν ἀπὸ κλήρου τότε συναγαγεῖν. ὧν
ἐστρατήγει Λικίνιος Λούκουλλος ὕπατος, πρεσβευτῇ
χρώμενος Κορνηλίῳ Σκιπίωνι, τῷ Καρχηδόνα μετ᾽ οὐ
πολὺ ἑλόντι καὶ Νομαντίαν ὕστερον.

211   50. Ὁ μὲν δὴ Λούκουλλος ᾤδευεν, ὁ δὲ Μάρκελλος
τόν τε πόλεμον προεῖπε τοῖς Κελτίβηρσι καὶ τὰ
ὅμηρα αἰτοῦσιν ἀπέδωκε. τὸν δ᾽ ἐν Ῥώμῃ τοὺς λόγους
διαθέμενον ὑπὲρ τῶν Κελτιβήρων ἰδίᾳ πρὸς αὐτὸν
212 ἀνακαλέσας ἐπὶ πολὺ διέτριβεν· ὑπὲρ ὅτου δὴ καὶ
ὑπωπτεύετο μὲν καὶ τότε, μᾶλλον δ᾽ ἐπιστώθη τοῖς
ὕστερον γενομένοις, ὅτι αὐτοὺς ἀνέπειθεν ἑαυτῷ τὰ
κατὰ σφᾶς ἐπιτρέψαι, ἐπειγόμενος ἄρα πρὸ τοῦ Λου-
213 κούλλου τὸν πόλεμον καταλυθῆναι. μετὰ γὰρ τὴν
συνουσίαν Νεργόβριγα μὲν Ἀρουακῶν πεντακισχίλιοι κατέλαβον, Μάρκελλος δ᾽ ἐπὶ Νομαντίαν ἐχώρει καὶ πέντε σταδίους ἀποσχὼν παρεστρατοπέδευεν
214 αὐτοῖς καὶ συνεδίωκεν ἐς τὴν πόλιν, ἕως ὁ τῶν Νομαντίνων στρατηγὸς Λιτέννων ὑποστὰς ἐβόα βούλεσθαι
Μαρκέλλῳ συνελθεῖν ἐς λόγους καὶ συνελθὼν ἔφη
Βελλοὺς καὶ Τίτθους καὶ Ἀρουακοὺς ἑαυτοὺς ἐπιτρέπειν Μαρκέλλῳ. ὁ δ᾽ ἄσμενος ἀκούσας ὅμηρά τε καὶ
χρήματα πάντας ᾔτησε καὶ λαβὼν ἀφῆκεν ἐλευθέρους.

---

42 L. Licinius Lucullus, consul in 151, was initially arrested by
the tribunes in Rome for enforcing the levy too harshly. The fa-

normal levy. The reason for this was the many complaints that the consuls were conducting the levy unfairly and sending some men to easier theaters of war. So on this occasion they decided to recruit an army using lot. The consul Licinius Lucullus commanded these men, employing as legate Cornelius Scipio, the one who shortly afterward captured Carthage and later on Numantia.[42] 210

50. While Lucullus was on his way, Marcellus declared war on the Celtiberians, and when they asked for the return of their hostages he gave them back. He also summoned the man who had made the Celtiberians' case in Rome to a private meeting, and had a long discussion with him. This gave rise to the suspicion even then—and later events lent it yet greater credibility—that Marcellus was trying to persuade the Celtiberians to entrust their case to him because he was so eager to bring the war to an end before the arrival of Lucullus. At any rate, after the meeting, five thousand of the Arevaci occupied the town of Nergobriga, and Marcellus marched against Numantia, making camp five stades away. Marcellus set about chasing the enemy into the town, until the Numantine commander, Litenno, stopped and shouted that he wanted to negotiate with him. A meeting was arranged and Litenno said that the Belli, Titthi, and Arevaci would surrender to him. Marcellus was delighted to hear this and let them go free after demanding and receiving hostages and money from them all. 211 212 213 214

mous Scipio Aemilianus (consul in 147 and 134) volunteered to serve in Spain to counter the prevailing reluctance of his contemporaries to fight there (Polyb. 35.4).

215   51. Ὁ μὲν δὴ πόλεμος ὁ Βελλῶν τε καὶ Τίτθων καὶ
Ἀρουακῶν ἔληγεν οὕτω πρὸ Λουκούλλου· Ὁ δὲ Λούκουλλος, δόξης τε ἐπιθυμῶν καὶ ἐκ πενίας χρῄζων
χρηματισμοῦ, ἐς Οὐακκαίους, ἕτερον γένος Κελτιβήρων, ἐνέβαλεν, οἳ γείτονες τῶν Ἀρουακῶν εἰσιν,
οὔτε τινὸς αὐτῷ ψηφίσματος γεγονότος οὔτε Οὐακκαίων Ῥωμαίοις πεπολεμηκότων οὐδ᾽ ἐς αὐτόν τι Λού-
216   κουλλον ἁμαρτόντων. περάσας δὲ τὸν ποταμὸν τὸν
καλούμενον Τάγον ἀφίκετο πρὸς Καύκαν πόλιν καὶ
παρεστρατοπέδευσεν. οἱ δ᾽ ἐπύθοντο μὲν αὐτοῦ, τίνος
ἥκοι δεόμενος ἢ τί πολέμου χρῄζων, φήσαντος δέ, ὅτι
Καρπητανοῖς ὑπὸ Καυκαίων[16] ἀδικουμένοις βοηθοίη,
τότε μὲν ἀνεχώρουν ἐς τὴν πόλιν, ξυλευομένῳ δ᾽ αὐτῷ
καὶ χορτολογοῦντι ἐπέκειντο καὶ κτείνουσι πολλοὺς
217   καὶ τοὺς λοιποὺς διώκουσιν ἐς τὸ στρατόπεδον. γενομένης δὲ καὶ παρατάξεως οἱ Καυκαῖοι ψιλοῖς ἐοικότες
ἐκράτουν ἐπὶ πολὺ τοῦ Λουκούλλου, μέχρι σφῶν τὰ
ἀκόντια πάντα ἐξαναλώθη· καὶ τότε ἔφευγον, οὐκ ὄντες μενέμαχοι, περί τε τὰς πύλας αὐτῶν ὠθουμένων
ἀνῃρέθησαν ἀμφὶ τοὺς τρισχιλίους.

218   52. Τῆς δ᾽ ἐπιούσης οἱ πρεσβύτατοι στεφανωσάμε-
νοί τε καὶ φέροντες ἱκετηρίας τὸν Λούκουλλον αὖθις
ἠρώτων, τί ποιοῦντες ἂν εἶεν φίλοι. ὁ δὲ αὐτοὺς ὅμηρά
τε ᾔτει καὶ ἀργυρίου τάλαντα ἑκατὸν καὶ τοὺς ἱππέας
219   αὐτῶν ἐκέλευέν οἱ συστρατεύειν. ὡς δὲ πάντα ἔλαβεν,
ἠξίου φρουρὰν ἐς τὴν πόλιν ἐσαγαγεῖν. δεξαμένων δὲ
καὶ τοῦτο τῶν Καυκαίων ἐσήγαγε δισχιλίους ἀρι-
στίνδην ἐξειλεγμένους, οἷς ἐσελθοῦσιν εἴρητο γίγνε-

51. In this way the war with the Belli, Titthi, and Are-   215
vaci came to an end before Lucullus' arrival. But Lucullus
wanted glory, and because he was poor and needed to
make money, he invaded the territory of the Vaccaei, another Celtiberian people, neighbors of the Arevaci. This
was in spite of the fact he had no authorization from the
senate, and the Vaccaei had not fought against Rome or
given the slightest offense to Lucullus. Crossing what is   216
known as the river Tagus, he arrived at the town of Cauca
and camped in front of it. The townspeople asked him why
he had come and why he wanted war. When he said he was
coming to the assistance of the Carpetani who had been
wronged by the people of Cauca, they then retired into
the town, but attacked the Romans foraging for wood and
supplies and killed many of them and drove the rest back
into their camp. A pitched battle developed in which the   217
Caucaei, who fought in the manner of light-armed troops,
got the better of Lucullus for a long time until they completely ran out of ammunition. At that point, as they were
not frontline fighters, they fled and about three thousand
of them were killed in the crush at the gates.

52. Next day the town elders, wearing garlands and   218
carrying the olive branch of suppliants, again asked Lucullus what they had to do to win his friendship. He demanded hostages and one hundred talents of silver, and
ordered their cavalry to serve with him. When he got all   219
this from them, he demanded the installation of a garrison
in the town. This too the Caucaei accepted. But Lucullus
brought in two thousand men specially chosen for their

---

16 Καυκαίων Goukowsky: Οὐακκαίων edd.

σθαι περὶ τὰ τείχη. καταλαβόντων δ᾽ αὐτὰ τῶν δισχι-
λίων ἐσήγαγε τὴν ἄλλην στρατιὰν ὁ Λούκουλλος καὶ
τῇ σάλπιγγι ὑπεσήμαινε κτείνειν Καυκαίους ἅπαντας
220 ἡβηδόν. οἱ μὲν δὴ πίστεις τε καὶ θεοὺς ὁρκίους ἐπι-
καλούμενοι καὶ Ῥωμαίους ἐς ἀπιστίαν λοιδοροῦντες
διεφθείροντο ὠμῶς, ἐκ δισμυρίων ἀνδρῶν κατὰ πύλας
ἀποκρήμνους διαφυγόντων ὀλίγων· ὁ δὲ Λούκουλλος
τὴν πόλιν διήρπαζε καὶ δόξης Ῥωμαίους ἐνεπίμπλη
221 κακῆς. οἱ δ᾽ ἄλλοι βάρβαροι συνέθεον ἐκ τῶν πεδίων,
οἱ μὲν ἐς τὰ ἀπόκρημνα, οἱ δὲ ἐς τὰς ὀχυρωτέρας
πόλεις, συμφέροντες, ἃ δύναιντο, καὶ ἐμπιμπράντες,
ὅσα λείποιεν, τοῦ μηδὲν ἔτι Λούκουλλον εὑρεῖν.
222   53. Ὁ δὲ πολλὴν γῆν ἔρημον ὁδεύσας ἔς τινα πόλιν
Ἰντερκατίαν ἀφίκετο, ἔνθα πεζοὶ μὲν ὑπὲρ δισμυρίους
συνεπεφεύγεσαν, ἱππῆς δὲ δισχίλιοι. καὶ αὐτοὺς ὁ
Λούκουλλος ἐς συνθήκας ὑπὸ ἀνοίας προυκαλεῖτο· οἱ
δ᾽ ἐπ᾽ ὀνείδει τὰ Καυκαίων αὐτῷ προύφερον καὶ ἐπυν-
θάνοντο, εἰ ἐπὶ τὰς ἐκείνων πίστεις αὐτοὺς καλοίη.
223 ὁ δ᾽, οἷον ἅπαντες οἱ ἁμαρτόντες, ἀνθ᾽ ἑαυτοῦ τοῖς
ὀνειδίζουσιν χαλεπαίνων ἔκειρεν αὐτῶν τὰ πεδία καὶ
περικαθίσας κύκλῳ τὴν πόλιν χώματα ἤγειρε πολλὰ
224 καὶ συνεχῶς ἐξέτασσε προκαλούμενος ἐς μάχην. οἱ δ᾽
οὔπω μὲν ἀντεξέτασσον, ἀλλ᾽ ἦσαν ἀκροβολισμοὶ
μόνοι· θαμινὰ δέ τις τῶν βαρβάρων ἐξίππευεν ἐς
τὸ μεταίχμιον, κεκοσμημένος ὅπλοις περιφανῶς, καὶ

bravery with orders to occupy the town walls when they got there. Once they had control of the walls, Lucullus introduced the rest of his army and signaled the order by trumpet that they were to kill all the adult males of the town. Calling on the guarantees given and the gods who 220 witness oaths, the Caucaei denounced the treachery of the Romans, but were slaughtered mercilessly; out of the total of twenty thousand, only a small number escaped by climbing down the steep gates. Lucullus plundered the town and brought complete disgrace on the Romans. The 221 other barbarians fled from the fields together, some to rocky crags, others to the more secure towns, taking with them what they could carry, and burning all they were leaving, so that Lucullus would find nothing.

53. After a long march through deserted territory, 222 Lucullus arrived at a town called Intercatia, where more than twenty thousand infantry and two thousand cavalry had taken refuge together.[43] When he stupidly invited them to come to terms, by way of reproach they cited the fate of the Caucaei, and asked if he was offering them the same pledges of good faith. Like all people who are in the 223 wrong, he was annoyed with those who criticized him rather than with himself, and ravaged their fields. He invested the town, threw up many earthworks and repeatedly arrayed his men in battle order challenging the enemy to fight. At this point, however, they did not parade 224 in battle order, but engaged only with missiles. And on many occasions, one of the barbarians, decked out in magnificent armor, would ride out into the space between the

[43] Intercatia is the modern town of Villanueva del Campo, about thirty-seven miles south of Léon.

προυκαλεῖτο Ῥωμαίων ἐς μονομαχίαν τὸν ἐθέλοντα,
οὐδενὸς δ᾽ ὑπακούοντος ἐπιτωθάσας καὶ τῷ σχήματι
225 κατορχησάμενος ἀπεχώρει. γιγνομένου δὲ τούτου
πολλάκις ὁ Σκιπίων, ἔτι νέος ὤν, ὑπερήλγησέν τε καὶ
προπηδήσας ὑπέστη τὸ μονομάχιον, εὐτυχῶς δ᾽ ἐκράτησεν ἀνδρὸς μεγάλου σμικρὸς ὤν.

226   54. Καὶ τόδε μὲν ἐπῆρε Ῥωμαίους, νυκτὸς δὲ φόβοι
πολλοὶ κατεῖχον· οἱ γὰρ ἱππῆς, ὅσοι τῶν βαρβάρων,
πρὶν ἀφικέσθαι Λούκουλλον, ἐπὶ χορτολογίαν προ-
εληλύθεσαν, οὐκ ἔχοντες ἐσελθεῖν ἐς τὴν πόλιν Λουκούλλου περικαθημένου, περιθέοντες ἐβόων καὶ συν-
227 ετάρασσον· καὶ συνεπήχουν οἱ ἔνδον αὐτοῖς. ὅθεν ὁ
φόβος ἦν τοῖς Ῥωμαίοις ποικίλος. ἔκαμνον δὲ καὶ τῇ
φυλακῇ δι᾽ ἀγρυπνίαν καὶ ἀήθειαν τροφῶν ἐπιχω-
ρίων· οἴνου γὰρ οὐκ ὄντος οὐδ᾽ ἁλῶν οὐδ᾽ ὄξους οὐδ᾽
ἐλαίου πυροὺς καὶ κριθὰς καὶ ἐλάφων κρέα πολλὰ
καὶ λαγωῶν χωρὶς ἁλῶν ἑψόμενα σιτούμενοι κατερ-
ρήγνυντο τὰς γαστέρας, καὶ πολλοὶ καὶ ἀπώλλυντο,
μέχρι ποτὲ τὸ χῶμα ἠγέρθη καὶ τὰ τείχη τῶν πολεμίων τύπτοντες μηχαναῖς μέρος μέν τι κατέβαλον
228 καὶ ἐσέδραμον ἐς τὴν πόλιν· μετὰ δ᾽ οὐ πολὺ βιασθέν-
τες τε καὶ ἀναχωροῦντες ἐσπίπτουσιν ἔς τινα δεξαμε-
νὴν ὕδατος ὑπὸ ἀγνωσίας, ἔνθα οἱ πλείους ἀπώλοντο.
καὶ νυκτὸς οἱ βάρβαροι τὰ πεσόντα ἀνῳκοδόμουν.
229 πάνυ δ᾽ ἑκατέρων κακοπαθούντων (ὁ γὰρ λιμὸς ἀμ-
φοῖν ἥπτετο) Σκιπίων ἀνεδέχετο τοῖς βαρβάροις οὐδὲν ἔσεσθαι παράσπονδον καὶ πιστευθεὶς κατὰ κλέος
ἀρετῆς διέλυσε τὸν πόλεμον ἐπὶ τοῖσδε, Λουκούλλῳ

armies and challenge any willing Roman to single combat; when nobody took up the challenge he would jeer at the Romans, do a little jig and retire to his lines. After this had happened a number of times, Scipio, although still only a youth, became very annoyed and springing forward to take on the duel, small as he was, successfully overpowered the large man.   225

54. This gave encouragement to the Romans, but at night they were haunted by numerous terrors. The cavalry the barbarians had at their disposal had gone out foraging before Lucullus' arrival, and were not able to get into the town when he surrounded it. So they charged around shouting and causing confusion, while the people in the town shouted back at them. This gave rise to a variety of fears among the Romans. They even struggled to mount guard duty, both because of lack of sleep and because they were not used to the local food. They had no wine, salt, vinegar or oil, but lived on wheat, barley and large quantites of venison and rabbit boiled without salt. This upset their stomachs with dysentery, and many died. Eventually a ramp was erected and after battering the enemy walls with their siege engines they knocked down a section and rushed into the town. But after a short time they were overpowered and while withdrawing, fall into a reservoir they were unaware of, where most of them drowned. And during the night the barbarians rebuilt the damaged part of the wall. With both sides now in a very bad way—for famine gripped the two of them—Scipio gave a guarantee to the barbarians that he would not break any ageement. In view of his honorable reputation, they believed him and he thus brought the war to an end on the following condi-   226   227   228   229

δοθῆναι παρὰ τῶν Ἰντερκατίων σάγους μυρίους καὶ
θρεμμάτων τι πλῆθος ὡρισμένον καὶ πεντήκοντα ἄν-
230 δρας ἐς ὅμηρα. χρυσὸν δὲ καὶ ἄργυρον Λούκουλλος
αἰτῶν, οὗ δὴ χάριν ἡγούμενος ὅλην Ἰβηρίαν πολύχρυσον εἶναι καὶ πολυάργυρον ἐπολέμει, οὐκ ἔλαβεν·
οὐ γὰρ εἶχον, οὐδ᾽ ἐν δόξῃ ταῦτ᾽ ἐκεῖνοι Κελτιβήρων
τίθενται.

231   55. Ἐπὶ δὲ Παλλαντίαν ᾔει πόλιν, ἣ δόξαν τε ἀρετῆς εἶχε μείζω καὶ πολλοὶ συνεπεφεύγεσαν ἐς αὐτήν·
ὅθεν αὐτῷ συνεβούλευόν τινες ἀποχωρεῖν πρὸ πείρας.
ὁ δὲ πολυχρήματον εἶναι πυνθανόμενος οὐκ ἀνεχώρει,
μέχρι σιτολογοῦντα αὐτὸν οἱ Παλλάντιοι συνεχῶς ἱπ-
232 πεῦσιν ἠνώχλουν τε καὶ σιτολογεῖν ἐκώλυον. ἀπορῶν
δὲ τροφῶν ὁ Λούκουλλος ἀνεζεύγνυ, τετράγωνον ἐν
πλινθίῳ τὸν στρατὸν ἄγων, ἑπομένων αὐτῷ καὶ τότε
τῶν Παλλαντίων μέχρι Δορίου ποταμοῦ, ὅθεν οἱ μὲν
Παλλάντιοι νυκτὸς ἀνεχώρουν, ὁ δ᾽ ἐς τὴν Τυρδι-
233 τανῶν χώραν διελθὼν ἐχείμαζε. καὶ τοῦτο τέλος ἦν
τοῦ Οὐακκαίων πολέμου, παρὰ ψήφισμα Ῥωμαίων
ὑπὸ Λουκούλλου γενομένου. καὶ ὁ Λούκουλλος ἐπὶ
τῷδε οὐδὲ ἐκρίθη.

234   56. Τοῦ δ᾽ αὐτοῦ χρόνου μέρος ἄλλο Ἰβήρων αὐ-
τονόμων, οἳ Λυσιτανοὶ καλοῦνται, Πουννίκου σφῶν
ἡγουμένου, τὰ Ῥωμαίων ὑπήκοα ἐλήζοντο καὶ τοὺς
στρατηγοῦντας αὐτῶν, Μανίλιόν τε καὶ Καλπούρνιον
Πείσωνα, τρεψάμενοι κτείνουσιν ἑξακισχιλίους καὶ
235 ἐπ᾽ αὐτοῖς Τερέντιον Οὐάρρωνα ταμίαν. οἷς ἐπαρθεὶς

tions: the people of Intercatia were to hand over to him ten thousand cloaks, a specified number of livestock and fifty men as hostages. Lucullus demanded gold and silver—indeed it was in the belief that the whole of Iberia was rich in gold and silver that he had gone to war—but he got none, because they did not have any: these particular Celtiberians just do not value them. 230

55. Lucullus then advanced on the city of Pallantia,[44] which had a rather better reputation for courage than Intercatia, and where large numbers had taken refuge. As a result, some advised him to withdraw rather than make an attempt on it. But on hearing that it was very rich, Lucullus refused to withdraw, until the people of Pallantia prevented him from collecting supplies by constantly harassing his foraging parties with their cavalry. Lacking provisions he broke camp, marching with his army formed in squares, and even then pursued by the Pallantians as far as the river Douro. From here they withdrew by night, and Lucullus crossed into Turditanian territory where he spent the winter. This marked the end of the Vaccaean War. Lucullus had conducted it in contravention of a decree of the Roman people, but was not even brought to trial for it. 231 232 233

56. At the same time, another group of autonomous Iberians, called the Lusitanians, were ravaging Roman subject areas under the leadership of Punicus. They defeated the Roman praetors Manilius and Calpurnius Piso, killing six thousand, among them the quaestor Terentius 234

[44] The modern city of Palencia, some sixty-two miles southeast of Léon.

ὁ Πούνικος τὰ μέχρι ὠκεανοῦ κατέδραμεν καὶ Οὐέττωνας ἐς τὴν στρατείαν προσλαβὼν ἐπολιόρκει Ῥωμαίων ὑπηκόους τοὺς λεγομένους Βαστουλοφοίνικας,[17] οἷς φασιν Ἀννίβαν τὸν Καρχηδόνιον ἐποικίσαι
τινὰς ἐκ Λιβύης καὶ παρὰ τοῦτο κληθῆναι Βαστου-
236 λοφοίνικας. Πούνικος μὲν οὖν λίθῳ πληγεὶς ἐς τὴν
κεφαλὴν ἀπέθανεν, διαδέχεται δ' αὐτὸν ἀνήρ, ᾧ ὄνομα
ἦν Καίσαρος. οὗτος ὁ Καίσαρος Μομμίῳ, μετὰ
στρατιᾶς ἄλλης ἐπελθόντι ἀπὸ Ῥώμης, ἐς μάχην
237 συνηνέχθη καὶ ἡττώμενος ἔφυγε. Μομμίου δ' αὐτὸν
ἀτάκτως διώκοντος ἐπιστραφεὶς ἔκτεινεν ἐς ἐνακισχι-
λίους καὶ τήν τε λείαν τὴν ἡρπασμένην καὶ τὸ οἰκεῖον
στρατόπεδον ἀνεσώσατο καὶ τὸ Ῥωμαίων προσέλαβέ
τε καὶ διήρπασεν ὅπλα καὶ σημεῖα πολλά, ἅπερ οἱ
βάρβαροι κατὰ τὴν Κελτιβηρίαν ὅλην περιφέροντες
ἐπετώθαζον.

238 57. Μόμμιος δ' ὑπολοίπους ἔχων πεντακισχιλίους
ἐγύμναζεν ἔνδον ἐν τῷ στρατοπέδῳ, δεδιὼς ἄρα προ-
ελθεῖν ἐς τὸ πεδίον, πρὶν τοὺς ἄνδρας ἀναθαρρῆσαι.
φυλάξας δέ, εἴ τι μέρος οἱ βάρβαροι τῆς ἀφῃρημένης
λείας παρέφερον, ἀδοκήτως αὐτοῖς ἐπέθετο καὶ πολλοὺς διαφθείρας ἔλαβε τὴν λείαν καὶ τὰ σημεῖα.
239 Λυσιτανῶν δ' οἱ ἐπὶ θάτερα τοῦ Τάγου ποταμοῦ,
κἀκεῖνοι Ῥωμαίοις πεπολεμωμένοι, Καυκαίνου σφῶν

17 Βλαστοφοίνικας VM; Βαστουλοφοίνικας Schweig.

Varro.[45] Encouraged by these events Punicus overran the   235
land all the way to the ocean, and after adding the Vettones
to his army, blockaded some Roman subjects called Bas-
toulophoenicians.[46] Hannibal the Carthaginian is said to
have brought settlers here from Africa, giving rise to the
name Bastoulophoenician. When Punicus was hit on the   236
head with a stone and died, a man called Caesarus succeeds him. This Caesarus fought a battle with Mummius,
who had come from Rome with another army, but was
defeated and fled.[47] When Mummius pursued him in dis-   237
order, however, he rallied and killed about six thousand;
and not only did he recover his own camp and the booty
seized from him, but he also captured the Roman camp,
along with a large supply of weapons and standards, which
the barbarians mockingly carried all over Celtiberia.

57. Mummius now set about training his remaining five   238
thousand troops inside the camp, as he was afraid to venture out into the plain before restoring his men's morale.
But keeping watch in case the barbarians passed by carrying a part of the captured booty, he attacked them unexpectedly, killed many and recovered the booty and the
standards. Under the leadership of Caucaenus, the Lusita-   239
nians on the other side of the river Tagus—they too had
been treated as enemies by Rome—ravaged the land of

---

[45] Lucius Calpurnius Piso Caesoninus (consul 148) was praetor and governor of Further Spain in 154. Manius Manilius (consul 149) was praetor and governor of Further Spain probably in
the previous year.   [46] Ptolemy (*Geog.* 2.4.6) confirms the
name, against the manuscript reading, Blastophoenicians.

[47] Lucius Mummius (consul 146) was praetor in 153 when he
succeeded Calpurnius Piso as governor of Further Spain.

ἡγουμένου, Κουνέους ἐπόρθουν, οἳ Ῥωμαίοις ἦσαν
ὑπήκοοι, καὶ πόλιν αὐτῶν μεγάλην εἷλον Κονίστορ-
240   γιν. παρά τε τὰς στήλας τὰς Ἡρακλείους τὸν ὠκεανὸν ἐπέρων, καὶ οἳ μὲν τὴν ἄλλην Λιβύην κατέτρε-
241   χον, οἳ δ' Ὀκίλην πόλιν ἐπολιόρκουν. Μούμμιος δ',
ἑπόμενος ἐνακισχιλίοις πεζοῖς καὶ ἱππεῦσι πεντακοσίοις, ἔκτεινε τῶν μὲν δῃούντων ἐς μυρίους καὶ
πεντακισχιλίους, τῶν δ' ἑτέρων τινάς, καὶ τὴν πολι-
242   ορκίαν διέλυσε τὴν Ὀκίλης. ἐντυχὼν δὲ καὶ τοῖς φέρουσιν, ἃ σεσυλήκεσαν, ἔκτεινε καὶ τούσδε πάντας,
ὡς μηδ' ἄγγελον ἀπὸ τοῦ κακοῦ διαφυγεῖν. τὴν δὲ
λείαν διαδοὺς τῷ στρατῷ τὴν δυνατὴν φέρεσθαι τὰ
λοιπὰ τοῖς θεοῖς τοῖς ἐνναλίοις ἔκαυσε.

243   58. Καὶ Μούμμιος μὲν τάδε πράξας ἐπανῆλθεν ἐς
Ῥώμην καὶ ἐθριάμβευσεν, ἐνδέχεται δ' αὐτὸν Μᾶρκος
Ἀτίλιος, ὃς Λυσιτανῶν μὲν ἐς ἑπτακοσίους ἐπιδραμὼν
ἀπέκτεινε καὶ τὴν μεγίστην πόλιν ἐξεῖλεν, ᾗ ὄνομα
Ὀξθράκαι, τὰ δ' ἐγγὺς καταπληξάμενος ἅπαντα ἐπὶ
συνθήκαις παρέλαβε. καὶ τούτων ἦν ἔνια τοῦ Οὐετ-
244   τώνων ἔθνους, ὁμόρου τοῖς Λυσιτανοῖς. ὡς δ' ἀνεζεύ-
γννε χειμάσων ὁ Ἀτίλιος, αὐτίκα πάντες μετετίθεντο
καί τινας Ῥωμαίοις ὑπηκόους ἐπολιόρκουν· οὓς ἐπειγόμενος ἐξελεῖν τῆς πολιορκίας Σέρουιος Γάλβας, ὁ
Ἀτιλίου διάδοχος, ἡμέρᾳ μιᾷ καὶ νυκτὶ πεντακοσίους

---

[48] Conistorgis was in the Algarve in the south of Portugal,
although the site is not known.

the Cunei, who were Roman subjects, and captured one of their big towns, Conistorgis.[48] They crossed the ocean   240
at the Pillars of Heracles, and some of them ravaged the rest of Africa, while others laid siege to the town of Ocile.[49]
Mummius followed with nine thousand infantry and five   241
hundred cavalry, and, killing about fifteen thousand of those doing the plundering and a few of the others, he raised the siege of Ocile. He also encountered some who   242
were taking away what they had pillaged and killed all these too, so that not even a messenger escaped from the disaster to spread the news. All the booty they could carry he distributed to the army, the rest he offered as burnt sacrifice to the gods of war.

58. Such were the achievements of Mummius. He re-   243
turned to Rome where he celebrated a triumph. Marcus Atilius succeeds him.[50] Atilius attacked the Lusitanians, killing about seven hundred of them and capturing their largest town, called Oxthracae.[51] This frightened all the neighboring nations into agreeing terms with Atilius, among them some of the Vettonian people whose land bordered Lusitania. But when Atilius retired to take up   244
winter quarters, they all immediately changed their mind, and laid siege to some Roman subjects. Atilius' successor, Servius Galba, in his rush to relieve them from the siege, covered five hundred stades in a day and a night, and on

[49] It is not known where on the African coast Ocile was located.

[50] Marcus Atilius Serranus was praetor and governor of further Spain in 152. His successor, Servius Sulpicius Galba, was praetor in 151 and reached the consulship in 144.

[51] The location of Oxthracae is not known.

σταδίους διελθὼν ἐπιφαίνεται τοῖς Λυσιτανοῖς καὶ
εὐθὺς ἐς μάχην ἐξέτασσε, κατάκοπον τὸν στρατὸν
245 ἔχων. τρεψάμενος δ' εὐτυχῶς τοὺς πολεμίους ἐπέκειτο
φεύγουσιν ἀπειροπολέμως. ὅθεν ἀσθενοῦς αὐτῷ καὶ
ἀσυντάκτου τῆς διώξεως οὔσης διὰ κόπον οἱ βάρβαροι κατιδόντες αὐτοὺς διεσπασμένους τε καὶ ἀναπαυ-
ομένους κατὰ μέρη συνελθόντες ἐπέθεντο καὶ κτείνου-
246 σιν ἐς ἑπτακισχιλίους. ὁ δὲ Γάλβας μετὰ τῶν ἀμφ'
αὑτὸν ἱππέων κατέφυγεν ἐς Καρμώνην πόλιν, ἔνθα
τοὺς διαφυγόντας ἀνελάμβανε, καὶ συμμάχους ἀθροίσας ἐς δισμυρίους διῆλθεν ἐς Κουνέους καὶ παρεχεί-
μαζεν ἐν Κονιστόργει.

247   59. Λούκουλλος δέ, ὁ τοῖς Οὐακκαίοις ἄνευ ψηφίσματος πολεμήσας, ἐν Τυρδιτανίᾳ τότε χειμάζων
ᾔσθετο Λυσιτανῶν ἐς τὰ πλησίον ἐμβαλόντων καὶ
περιπέμψας τοὺς ἀρίστους τῶν ἡγεμόνων ἔκτεινε τῶν
248 Λυσιτανῶν ἐς τετρακισχιλίους. περί τε Γάδειρα τὸν
πορθμὸν ἑτέρων περώντων ἔκτεινεν ἐς χιλίους καὶ
πεντακοσίους καὶ τοὺς λοιποὺς συμφυγόντας εἴς τινα
λόφον ἀπετάφρευσε πλῆθός τε ἔλαβεν ἀνδρῶν ἄπειρον. καὶ τὴν Λυσιτανίαν ἐπιὼν κατὰ μέρος ἐπόρθει.
249 ἐπόρθει δὲ καὶ Γάλβας ἐπὶ θάτερα. καί τινων πρεσβευομένων ἐς αὐτὸν καὶ θελόντων βεβαιοῦν καὶ ὅσα
Ἀτιλίῳ τῷ πρὸ αὐτοῦ στρατηγῷ συνθέμενοι παρεβε-
βήκεσαν, ἐδέχετο καὶ ἐσπένδετο καὶ ὑπεκρίνετο αὐτοῖς καὶ συνάχθεσθαι ὡς δι' ἀπορίαν λῃστεύουσί τε
250 καὶ πολεμοῦσι καὶ παρεσπονδηκόσιν. "Τὸ γὰρ
λυπρόγεων," ἔφη, "Καὶ πενιχρὸν ὑμᾶς ἐς λῃστείαν

230

making his appearance before the Lusitaninas, immediately deployed for battle, although his army was exhausted. He was lucky to defeat the enemy, but inexperience led him to pursue them as they fled. The result was that the pursuit was weak and disorganized because of fatigue. When the barbarians saw that the Romans were scattered and were stopping to rest in units, they regrouped, counterattacked and kill about seven thousand. Galba fled with his cavalry escort to the town of Carmone, where he retrieved the fugitives and collected about twenty thousand allies. He then crossed into the territory of the Cunei and wintered at Conistorgis.

59. At the time, Lucullus, who had campaigned against the Vaccaei without authorization, was wintering in Turditania. When he heard that the Lusitanians were making incursions in the neighborhood, he sent his best officers and killed about four thousand of them. Others were crossing the straits near Gadeira, and he killed about one thousand five hundred of them. The rest took refuge on a hill which Lucullus surrounded with a ditch, thus capturing huge numbers of prisoners. He then invaded Lusitania, ravaging one part after another; Galba did the same from the opposite direction. When a Lusitanian mission came to him wanting to confirm the very agreement they had made, and then broken, with Atilius his predecessor in the command, Galba accepted, made a truce, and even pretended to sympathize with them on the grounds that it was because of poverty that they had resorted to banditry, warfare, and violating their treaty. "It is poor land and poverty that drive you into banditry," he said, "but you are

245

246

247

248

249

250

ἄγει·[18] δώσω δ' ἐγὼ πενομένοις φίλοις γῆν ἀγαθὴν
καὶ ἐν ἀφθόνοις συνοικιῶ, διελὼν ἐς τρία."

251   60. Οἱ μὲν δὴ τάδε προσδοκῶντες ἀπὸ τῶν ἰδίων
ἀνίσταντο καὶ συνῄεσαν, οἷ προσέτασσεν ὁ Γάλβας·
ὁ δὲ αὐτοὺς ἐς τρία διῄρει καὶ πεδίον ἑκάστοις τι
ὑποδείξας ἐκέλευεν ἐν τῷ πεδίῳ περιμένειν, μέχρι πο-
252   λίσειεν αὐτοὺς ἐπελθών. ὡς δ' ἧκεν ἐπὶ τοὺς πρώτους,
ἐκέλευεν ὡς φίλους θέσθαι τὰ ὅπλα, θεμένους δ' ἀπε-
τάφρευέν τε καὶ μετὰ ξιφῶν τινας ἐσπέμψας ἀνεῖλεν
ἅπαντας, ὀδυρομένους τε καὶ θεῶν ὀνόματα καὶ πί-
253   στεις ἀνακαλοῦντας. τῷ δ' αὐτῷ τρόπῳ καὶ τοὺς δευ-
τέρους καὶ τρίτους ἐπειχθεὶς ἀνεῖλεν, ἀγνοοῦντας ἔτι
τὰ πάθη τὰ τῶν προτέρων, ἀπιστίᾳ μὲν ἄρα ἀπιστίαν
μετιών, οὐκ ἀξίως δὲ Ῥωμαίων μιμούμενος βαρ-
254   βάρους. ὀλίγοι δ' αὐτῶν διέφυγον, ὧν ἦν Οὐρίατθος,
ὃς μετ' οὐ πολὺ ἡγήσατο Λυσιτανῶν καὶ ἔκτεινε πολλοὺς Ῥωμαίων καὶ ἔργα μέγιστα ἐπεδείξατο. ἀλλὰ
255   τάδε μὲν ὕστερον γενόμενα ὕστερον λέξω· τότε δ' ὁ
Γάλβας, Λουκούλλου φιλοχρηματώτερος ὤν, ὀλίγα
μέν τινα τῆς λείας τῇ στρατιᾷ διεδίδου καὶ ὀλίγα τοῖς
φίλοις, τὰ λοιπὰ δ' ἐσφετερίζετο, καίτοι πλουσιώτα-
τος ὢν ὁμοῦ τι Ῥωμαίων· ἀλλ' οὐδὲ ἐν τῇ εἰρήνῃ φασὶν αὐτὸν διαλιπεῖν ψευδόμενόν τε καὶ ἐπιορκοῦντα
διὰ κέρδη. μισούμενος δὲ καὶ κατηγορούμενος διέ-
φευγε διὰ τὸν πλοῦτον.

256   61. Οὐ πολὺ δὲ ὕστερον, ὅσοι διέφευγον ἐκ τῆς

---

[18] λῃστείαν ἄγει Suda; ταῦτα ἀναγκάζει VM

our friends and in your need I myself am going to give you good land and, after dividing you into three separate groups, I will settle you in a rich place."

60. In the expectation that this would be the case, they 251 left their own lands and gathered where Galba told them. He divided them up into three groups, assigned a separate agricultural area for each group and told them to stay there until he came and built towns for them. Coming to 252 the first group, he ordered them to lay down their weapons as they were friends, but when they did so he dug a ditch around them, sent in armed men and massacred them all, even as they cried out and called on the names of the gods and the pledges they had received. In the same way Galba 253 hurried against the second and third groups too and killed them while they still had not learned the fate of the first. This matched treachery with treachery, of course, but copying the way of barbarians was unworthy of Rome. A 254 few of the Lusitanians escaped, among them Viriathus, who soon after became their leader, killed many Romans and accomplished great things. But this happened later and I will speak of it later. At the time, Galba, who was 255 even greedier for money than Lucullus, distributed a small part of the plunder to the army and a small part to his associates, but kept the rest for himself, even though he was just about the richest Roman there was. They say that even in time of peace he never stopped lying and perjuring himself for gain. Although he was hated and charges were brought against him, he got off because of his wealth.

61. Not long after, about ten thousand of those who had 256

Λουκούλλου καὶ Γάλβα παρανομήσεως, ἀλισθέντες
257 ἐς μυρίους τὴν Τυρδιτανίαν κατέτρεχον. καὶ αὐτοῖς
ἀπὸ Ῥώμης ἐπελθὼν Γάιος Οὐετίλιος, ἄγων τέ τινα
στρατὸν ἄλλον καὶ τοὺς ἐν Ἰβηρίᾳ προσλαβών,
ἅπαντας ἔχων ἐς μυρίους, ἐπέπεσε προνομεύουσι καὶ
πολλοὺς ἀνελὼν συνέωσε τοὺς λοιποὺς ἔς τι χωρίον,
οἳ κινδυνεύειν τε μένοντας ἐχρῆν ὑπὸ λιμοῦ καὶ ἀπιόν-
258 τας ὑπὸ Ῥωμαίων· ὧδε γὰρ εἶχε δυσχωρίας. καὶ διὰ
τοῦτο πρέσβεις ἐς τὸν Οὐετίλιον ἔπεμπον σὺν ἱκετηρίαις, γῆν ἐς συνοικισμὸν αἰτοῦντες ὡς ἀπὸ τοῦδε
ἐσόμενοι Ῥωμαίων ἐς πάντα κατήκοοι. ὃ δ' ὑπισχνεῖτο
259 δώσειν καὶ συνετίθετο ἤδη. Οὐρίατθος δ', ὁ ἐκ τῆς
Γάλβα παρανομίας ἐκφυγών, τότε συνὼν αὐτοῖς ὑπ-
εμίμνησκε τῆς Ῥωμαίων ἀπιστίας, ὁσάκις τε αὐτοῖς
ὀμόσαντες ἐπιθοῖντο καὶ ὡς ὅδε πᾶς ὁ στρατὸς ἐκ
τοιῶνδε ἐπιορκιῶν Γάλβα καὶ Λουκούλλου διαφύγοι-
μεν. οὐδ' ἀπορεῖν ἔφη σωτηρίας ἀπὸ τοῦδε τοῦ χωρίου, ἂν ἐθέλωσι πείθεσθαι.

260   62. Ἐρεθισθέντων δ' αὐτῶν καὶ ἐν ἐλπίσι γενομένων ᾑρέθη τε στρατηγὸς καὶ πάντας ἐκτάξας ἐς
μέτωπον ὡς ἐπὶ μάχῃ τοὺς μὲν ἄλλους ἐκέλευσεν,
ὅταν αὐτὸς ἐπιβῇ τοῦ ἵππου, διαιρεθέντας ἐς μέρη
πολλὰ φεύγειν, ὡς δύνανται, κατ' ἄλλας καὶ ἄλλας
ὁδοὺς ἐς Τριβόλαν πόλιν, ἔνθα αὐτὸν περιμένειν,
χιλίους δὲ μόνους ἐπιλεξάμενος ἐκέλευσεν αὐτῷ συν-
261 ίστασθαι. καὶ γιγνομένων τούτων οἱ μὲν εὐθὺς ἔφυ-

escaped the lawlessness of Lucullus and Galba got together and overran Turditania. Gaius Vetilius came out   257
from Rome against them bringing a new army with him: with the addition of the troops already in Iberia, he had about ten thousand men in all.[52] After falling on the foragers and killing many of them, he forced the others into a place where they faced the unavoidable danger of starving if they stayed, and of confronting the Romans if they left. Such was the difficult terrain in which they found them-   258
selves. They therefore sent ambassadors to Vetilius with the olive branch of suppliants, to ask for land to settle, saying that they would henceforth obey all Roman orders. Vetilius promised to give them the land and they now came to an agreement. Viriathus, however, himself a fugi-   259
tive from Galba's treachery, was present at the time and reminded them of how untrustworthy the Romans were, how often they had attacked them having sworn not to, and how "we," every soldier in this army, had escaped the wholesale perjuries of Galba and Lucullus. He told them that if they were willing to obey him they would find a way to safety out of their present position.

62. Roused by this and now with something to hope for,   260
they chose him to take command. He drew them up in battle line as if he was going to fight, but to some he gave orders that, when he mounted his horse, they were to divide up into many groups and flee as best they could by different roads to the town of Tribola, where they were to wait for him, while he chose just one thousand men to stand by him. And in the event, as soon as Viriathus got up   261

---

[52] Vetilius was praetor in 147. Viriathus ambushed and killed him at Tribola.

γον, ἐπειδὴ ὁ Οὐρίατθος τὸν ἵππον ἀνέβη, ὁ δὲ Οὐετίλιος αὐτοὺς δείσας διώκειν ἐς πολλὰ διῃρημένους,
ἐπὶ τὸν Οὐρίατθον ἑστῶτα καὶ ἐφεδρεύοντα τῷ γενη-
262 σομένῳ τραπεὶς ἐμάχετο. ὁ δ᾽ ὠκυτάτοις ἵπποις αὐτὸν
ἐνοχλῶν καὶ ὑποφεύγων καὶ πάλιν ἱστάμενος καὶ
ἐπιὼν ἐκείνην τε τὴν ἡμέραν ἐν τῷ αὐτῷ πεδίῳ καὶ
263 τὴν ἐπιοῦσαν ὅλην διέτριψε περιθέων. ὡς δ᾽ εἴκασεν
ἀσφαλῶς ἔχειν τῆς φυγῆς τοὺς ἑτέρους, τότε νυκτὸς
ὁρμήσας δι᾽ ὁδῶν ἀτριβῶν κουφοτάτοις ἵπποις ἀπέ-
δραμεν ἐς Τριβόλαν, Ῥωμαίων αὐτὸν διώκειν ὁμοίως
οὐ δυναμένων διά τε βάρος ὅπλων καὶ ἀπειρίαν ὁδῶν
264 καὶ ἵππων ἀνομοιότητα. ὧδε μὲν ἐξ ἀέλπτου στρατὸν
ἀπογιγνώσκοντα αὑτοῦ περιέσωσε, καὶ τὸ στρατήγημα τόδε περιφερόμενον ἐς τοὺς τῇδε βαρβάρους
ἐξῆρεν αὐτόν, καὶ πολλοὶ πανταχόθεν αὐτῷ προσ-
εχώρουν.

265   63. Ὁ δ᾽ ἐς ὀκτὼ[19] ἔτη Ῥωμαίοις ἐπολέμει· καί μοι
δοκεῖ τὸν Οὐρίατθου πόλεμον σφόδρα τε ἐνοχλή-
σαντα Ῥωμαίοις καὶ δυσεργότατον αὐτοῖς γενόμενον
συναγαγεῖν, ἀναθέμενον, εἴ τι τοῦ αὐτοῦ χρόνου περὶ
266 Ἰβηρίαν ἄλλο ἐγίγνετο. Οὐετίλιος μὲν δὴ αὐτὸν
διώκων ἦλθεν ἐπὶ τὴν Τριβόλαν, ὁ δ᾽ Οὐρίατθος ἐν
λόχμαις ἐνέδραν ἐπικρύψας ἔφυγε, μέχρι τὰς λόχμας
ὑπερελθόντος τοῦ Οὐετιλίου αὐτός τε ἐπεστρέφετο καὶ
οἱ ἐκ τῆς ἐνέδρας ἀνεπήδων καὶ Ῥωμαίους ἑκατέρωθεν ἔκτεινόν τε καὶ ἐζώγρουν καὶ ἐς τὰς φάραγγας

_____

[19] τρία VM: ὀκτὼ prop. Schweig.

on his horse, the former fled. Vetilius was afraid to pursue so many different groups and instead turned to engage Viriathus who was standing there and waiting on events. He harassed Vetilius with his fastest cavalry and by with-   262 drawing, halting again and advancing, he spent the whole of that day and the next maneuvering round the same ground. When he estimated that the others had safely   263 escaped, he started out by night and slipped away to Tri-bola on unused roads with his quickest horses. The Ro-mans were unable to pursue him at the same pace because their weapons were heavy, they did not know the roads and they had inferior horses. So it was that Viriathus un-   264 expectedly saved an army in despair. As news of this feat of arms circulated among the barbarians in that area it increased his prestige, and many came from all parts to join him.

63. He campaigned against Rome for about eight   265 years.[53] As the war against Viriathus was paticularly trou-blesome and difficult for the Romans, I have decided to draw it together into one account, putting off until later anything else that happened in Iberia at the same time. So, Vetilius pursued him to Tribola, where Viriathus, hav-   266 ing laid an ambush in some thickets, took to flight until Vetilius was passing the thickets, when Viriathus himself wheeled around, the men in the ambush jumped out, and from both directions they began to kill and capture the Romans and push them over the cliffs. Vetilius himself was

[53] The manuscripts say three years, but Appian himself (*Ib.* 75.319) later refers to eight years of fighting, thus justifying Sch-weighaüser's emendation.

APPIAN

ἐώθουν. ἐζωγρήθη δὲ καὶ ὁ Οὐετίλιος· καὶ αὐτὸν ὁ
λαβὼν ἀγνοῶν, γέροντα ὑπέρπαχυν ὁρῶν, ἔκτεινεν ὡς
267 οὐδενὸς ἄξιον. Ῥωμαίων δὲ μόλις ἐκ μυρίων ἑξακισ-
χίλιοι διέδρασαν ἐς Καρπησσόν, ἐπὶ θαλάσσῃ πόλιν,
ἣν ἐγὼ νομίζω πρὸς Ἑλλήνων πάλαι Ταρτησσὸν ὀνο-
μάζεσθαι καὶ Ἀργανθώνιον αὐτῆς βασιλεῦσαι, ὃν ἐς
268 πεντήκοντα καὶ ἑκατὸν ἔτη ἀφικέσθαι φασί. τοὺς μὲν
οὖν ἐς τὴν Καρπησσὸν διαφυγόντας ὁ ταμίας, ὃς εἵπετο τῷ Οὐετιλίῳ, συνέτασσεν ἐπὶ τειχῶν δεδιότας·
παρὰ δὲ Βελλῶν καὶ Τίτθων αἰτήσας πεντακισχιλίους
συμμάχους καὶ λαβὼν προύπεμψεν ἐπὶ τὸν Οὐρίατθον. ὁ δὲ πάντας ἔκτεινεν, ὡς μηδ᾽ ἄγγελον διαφυγεῖν. καὶ ὁ ταμίας ἡσύχαζεν ἐν τῇ πόλει, περιμένων
τινὰ βοήθειαν ἀπὸ Ῥώμης.
269 64. Οὐρίατθος δὲ τὴν Καρπητανίαν, εὐδαίμονα
χώραν, ἐπιὼν ἀδεῶς ἐλεηλάτει, ἕως ἧκεν ἐκ Ῥώμης
Γάιος Πλαύτιος, ἄγων πεζοὺς μυρίους καὶ ἱππέας
270 χιλίους ἐπὶ τριακοσίοις. τότε δ᾽ αὖθις ὑπεκρίνατο
φεύγειν ὁ Οὐρίατθος, καὶ ὁ Πλαύτιος αὐτὸν ἔπεμψε
διώκειν ἐς τετρακισχιλίους, οὓς ἐπιστραφεὶς ὁ Οὐρί-
271 ατθος ἔκτεινε χωρὶς ὀλίγων. καὶ τὸν Τάγον ποταμὸν
διαβὰς ἐστρατοπέδευεν ἐν ὄρει περιφύτῳ μὲν ἐλάαις,
Ἀφροδίτης δ᾽ ἐπωνύμῳ, ἔνθα ὁ Πλαύτιος καταλαβὼν
καὶ τὸ πταῖσμα ἀναλαβεῖν ἐπειγόμενος συνέβαλεν.
ἡττηθεὶς δὲ φόνου πολλοῦ γενομένου διέφυγεν ἀκόσμως ἐς τὰς πόλεις καὶ ἐκ μέσου θέρους ἐχείμαζεν,

238

captured. His capturer, however, did not recognize him, but seeing he was old and very fat, thought he was of no consequence and killed him. Of the ten thousand Romans 267 scarcely six thousand made their escape to Carpessus, a town on the coast which I believe the Greeks formerly called Tartessus and was ruled by king Arganthonius who is said to have reached the age of a hundred and fifty.[54] The quaestor who escorted Vetilius stationed the men who 268 had escaped to Carpessus, frightened as they were, on the walls of the town, and asked for five thousand allied troops from the Belli and Titthi. When he got them, he sent them out against Viriathus, but Viriathus killed them all, so that not even a messenger escaped to spread the news. The quaestor remained inactive in the town awaiting help from Rome.

64. Viriathus invaded Carpetania, a fertile region, and 269 plundered it without fear until Gaius Plautius arrived from Rome with ten thousand infantry and one thousand three hundred cavalry.[55] Once again Viriathus now pretended to 270 flee, but then turned to face and kill all but a few of the approximately four thousand men Plautius sent in pursuit of him. Crossing the river Tagus, Viriathus made camp on 271 what is known as Mt Aphrodite, a mountain heavily planted with olive trees, where Plautius caught up with him. Keen to make up for his reverse, Plautius joined battle, but was defeated with heavy losses and his army fled in disorder to the towns. Although it was the middle of summer, Plautius went into winter quarters and did not

54 For Arganthonius, see above, note 3.

55 Gaius Plautius Hypsaeus, praetor in 146, was prosecuted on his return to Rome, condemned, and exiled (Diod. Sic. 33.2).

272 οὐ θαρρῶν οὐδαμοῖ προϊέναι. ὁ δ᾽ Οὐρίατθος τὴν χώραν ἀδεῶς περιιὼν ᾔτει τοὺς κεκτημένους τιμὴν τοῦ ἐπικειμένου καρποῦ καὶ παρ᾽ ὧν μὴ λάβοι, διέφθειρεν.

273   65. Ὧν οἱ ἐν ἄστει Ῥωμαῖοι πυνθανόμενοι Φάβιον Μάξιμον Αἰμιλιανόν, Αἰμιλίου Παύλου τοῦ Περσέα τὸν Μακεδόνων βασιλέα ἀνελόντος υἱόν, ἔπεμπον ἐς Ἰβηρίαν καὶ στρατιὰν ἑαυτῷ καταγράφειν ἐπέτρεπον.

274 ὁ δέ, Ῥωμαίων ἄρτι Καρχηδόνα καὶ τὴν Ἑλλάδα ἑλόντων καὶ τὸν τρίτον ἐν Μακεδονίᾳ πόλεμον κατωρθωκότων, φειδοῖ τῶν ἀνδρῶν τῶν ἐκεῖθεν ἐληλυθότων κατέλεγεν πρωθήβας, οὐ πρὶν πολέμου πεπειραμένους, ἐς δύο τέλη. καὶ παρὰ τῶν συμμάχων στρατὸν ἄλλον αἰτήσας ἧκεν ἐς Ὄρσωνα τῆς Ἰβηρίας, σύμπαντας ἔχων πεζοὺς μυρίους καὶ πεντακισχιλίους καὶ

275 ἱππέας ἐς δισχιλίους. ὅθεν οὔπω μάχης ἄρχων, μέχρι τὴν στρατιὰν γυμνάσειεν, ἐς Γάδειρα διέπλευσε τὸν πορθμόν, Ἡρακλεῖ θύσων. ὁ δὲ Οὐρίατθος αὐτοῦ τῶν ξυλευομένων τισὶν ἐπιπεσὼν ἔκτεινε πολλοὺς καὶ ἐφό-

276 βησε τοὺς λοιπούς. τοῦ δ᾽ ὑποστρατήγου συντάξαντος αὐτοὺς αὖθις ὁ Οὐρίατθος ἐκράτει καὶ πολλὴν λείαν περιεσύρατο. ἀφικομένου τε τοῦ Μαξίμου συν-

277 εχῶς ἐξέτασσε προκαλούμενος. ὁ δὲ ὅλῳ μὲν οὐ συν-

---

56 Q. Fabius Maximus Aemilianus and his more famous brother, P. Cornelius Scipio Aemilianus, both served under their father, Aemilius Paullus, in the Third Macedonian War (171–167), which was brought to an end by Aemilius' defeat of Perseus

dare to venture out anywhere. Viriathus, on the other 272
hand, moved around the countryside without fear, demanding from the landowners money to the value of their current crops; if they refused, he destroyed the crops.

65. When news of this got to Rome, they sent Fabius 273
Maximus Aemilianus to Iberia—he was the son of Aemilius Paullus who had destroyed Perseus king of Macedon—and ordered him to raise an army for himself. Rome 274
had recently defeated Carthage and Greece, as well as bringing the Third Macedonian War to a successful conclusion.[56] So, in order to spare the men who had recently returned from those campaigns, he enrolled two legions of young recruits who had not been in battle before. Along with the additional forces he demanded from the allies, he arrived at Orso in Iberia with a total force of fifteen thousand infantry and about two thousand cavalry.[57] Given the 275
situation, he refrained from initiating hostilities until he had a chance to train his army, and sailed through the straits to Gadeira, to sacrifice to Heracles. Viriathus, however, attacked some of his wood-gathering parties and killed many of them, while striking fear in the rest; and he 276
defeated them again and seized a great deal of plunder when the Roman legate led his men out to battle. When Maximus arrived, although Viriathus repeatedly deployed in battle formation to challenge him, he declined to en- 277

at the battle of Pydna in 168. Fabius was praetor in 149 and consul in 145, when he went to Farther Spain to face Viriathus. Rome's destruction of Carthage at the end of the Third Punic War (149–146) coincided with its victory in Greece over the Achaean League and destruction of Corinth (146).

[57] For Orso, see above, note 15.

ἐμίσγετο τῷ στρατῷ, γυμνάζων αὐτοὺς ἔτι, κατὰ δὲ
μέρη πολλάκις ἠκροβολίζετο, πεῖράν τε ποιούμενος
τῶν πολεμίων καὶ τοῖς ἰδίοις ἐντιθεὶς θάρσος. χορτο-
λογῶν τε ἐνόπλους ἀεὶ τοῖς γυμνοῖς περιίστη καὶ
περιέτρεχε μεθ' ἱππέων αὐτός, οἷα Παύλῳ τῷ πατρὶ
278 συστρατευόμενος ἐν Μακεδόσιν ἑώρα. μετὰ δὲ χειμῶνα γεγυμνασμένῳ τῷ στρατῷ τρέπεται δεύτερος
ὅδε[20] τὸν Οὐρίατθον καλῶς ἀγωνισάμενον καὶ πόλεις
αὐτοῦ δύο τὴν μὲν διήρπασεν, τὴν δ' ἐνέπρησεν,
αὐτόν τε φεύγοντα ἐς χωρίον, ᾧ ὄνομα ἦν Βαικόρ,
διώκων ἔκτεινε πολλούς. καὶ ἐχείμαζεν ἐν Κορδύβῃ.
279   66. Ἐφ' οἷς ὁ Οὐρίατθος, οὐχ ὁμοίως ἔτι καταφρονῶν, Ἀρουακοὺς καὶ Τίτθους καὶ Βελλούς, ἔθνη μαχι-
280 μώτατα, ἀπέστησεν ἀπὸ Ῥωμαίων. καὶ πόλεμον ἄλλον οἵδε ἐφ' ἑαυτῶν ἐπολέμουν, ὃν ἐκ πόλεως αὐτῶν
μιᾶς Νομαντῖνον ἡγοῦνται, μακρόν τε καὶ ἐπίπονον
Ῥωμαίοις γενόμενον, καὶ συνάξω καὶ τόνδε ἐς ἓν μετὰ
281 Οὐρίατθον. Οὐρίατθος μὲν ἐπὶ θάτερα τῆς Ἰβηρίας
ἑτέρῳ στρατηγῷ Ῥωμαίων Κοΐντῳ[21] συνεπλέκετο καὶ
282 ἡσσώμενος ἐς τὸ Ἀφροδίσιον ὄρος ἀνέστρεφεν. ὅθεν
ἐπιστραφεὶς ἔκτεινε τῶν Κοΐντου ἐς[22] χιλίους καὶ ση-

[20] δεύτερον ἔτος ἤδη στρατηγῶν prop. Schulten.
[21] Κοΐντῳ Goukowsky: Κοϊντίῳ VM
[22] τῶν Κοΐντου ἐς Goukowsky: τοὺς Κοϊντείους VM

[58] Up to this point Appian has mentioned no Roman commander defeating Viriathus. Either he has taken this directly from
his source, who was aware that C. Laelius (praetor 145) defeated

gage with Viriathus' whole army, as he was still in the
process of training his men. Maximus did, however, employ part of his force in frequent skirmishing expeditions,
thereby making trial of the enemy and instilling confidence in his own men. When sending out foragers he
would always station armed men around the unarmed, and
would himself circle around with the cavalry—practices
he had seen while serving with his father in Macedonia.
After the winter, with his army fully trained, he becomes   278
the second Roman to defeat Viriathus,[58] who fought
bravely, plundering one of his towns, burning another and
killing many of his men as he pursued him in his flight to
a place called Baecor. Maximus then wintered in Corduba.

66. After these events, Viriathus became less arrogant   279
than before, and he brought the Arevaci, the Tithi and
Belli—very warlike peoples—into revolt against Rome.
They waged a separate war on their own account, called   280
the Numantine War, after one of their towns, which the
Romans found long and laborious. This one too I will describe in a single account after Viriathus. Viriathus himself   281
engaged another Roman commander Quintus[59] at the
other end of Iberia, but was defeated and retired to Mt.
Aphrodite. Turning back from here, he killed about a   282

Viriathus (Cic. *Brut.* 84), or something has gone wrong with the
text. Perhaps, "in the second year of his command he defeated
Viriathus." Or just, "he defeated Viriathus."   59 The manuscripts have Quinctius at this point, and either this is an otherwise
unknown person or perhaps Appian means Quintus Caecilius
Metellus Macedonicus (consul 143), proconsul in Spain in 142—
although without knowing it, as he is full of praise for Metellus
when he does clearly refer to him below at 76.322–25.

μειά τινα ἥρπασε· τοὺς δὲ λοιποὺς ἐς τὸ στρατόπεδον
αὐτῶν συνεδίωξε καὶ τὴν ἐν Ἰτύκκῃ φρουρὰν ἐξέβαλε
καὶ τὴν Βαστιτανῶν χώραν ἐλήζετο, Κοίντου[23] διὰ
δειλίαν καὶ ἀπειρίαν οὐκ ἐπιβοηθοῦντος, ἀλλ᾽ ἐν Κορδύβῃ χειμάζοντος ἐκ μέσου μετοπώρου καὶ Γάιον
Μάρκιον θαμινὰ ἐπιπέμποντος αὐτῷ, ἄνδρα Ἴβηρα
ἐκ πόλεως Ἰταλικῆς.

283   67. Τοῦ δ᾽ ἐπιόντος ἔτους Κοίντῳ[24] μὲν ὁ ἀδελφὸς
Αἰμιλιανοῦ, Φάβιος Μάξιμος Σερουιλιανός,[25] ἦλθεν
ἐπὶ τὴν στρατηγίαν διάδοχος, δύο ἄλλα τέλη Ῥωμαίων ἄγων καὶ συμμάχους τινάς, ἅπαντας ἐς μυρίους καὶ ὀκτακισχιλίους πεζοὺς καὶ ἱππέας ἑξακοσίους
284 ἐπὶ χιλίοις. ἐπιστείλας δὲ καὶ Μικύψῃ, τῷ Νομάδων
βασιλεῖ, πέμψαι οἱ τάχιστα ἐλέφαντας ἐς Ἰτύκκην
ἠπείγετο, τὴν στρατιὰν ἄγων κατὰ μέρος· καὶ τὸν
Οὐρίατθον ἑξακισχιλίοις ἀνδράσιν ἐπιόντα οἱ μετά τε
κραυγῆς καὶ θορύβου βαρβαρικοῦ καὶ κόμης μακρᾶς,
ἣν ἐν τοῖς πολέμοις ἐπισείουσι τοῖς ἐχθροῖς, οὐδὲν
ὑποπτήξας ὑπέστη τε γενναίως καὶ ἀπεώσατο ἄπρα-
285 κτον. ὡς δέ οἱ καὶ τὸ ἄλλο πλῆθος ἀφῖκτο καὶ ἐκ
Λιβύης ἐλέφαντες δέκα σὺν ἱππεῦσι τριακοσίοις,
στρατόπεδον ὠχύρου μέγα καὶ προεπεχείρει τῷ Οὐ-
286 ριάτθῳ καὶ τρεψάμενος αὐτὸν ἐδίωκεν. ἀτάκτου δὲ τῆς
διώξεως γενομένης, ἰδὼν ἐν τῇ φυγῇ τοῦτο ὁ Οὐρίατθος ἐπανῆλθε καὶ κτείνας ἐς τρισχιλίους τοὺς λοιποὺς

<hr/>

[23] Κοίντου Goukowsky: Κιντίου VM
[24] Κοίντῳ V: Κοϊντίῳ prop. Schweig.

thousand of Quintus' men, seized some standards, and chased the remaining Romans back into their camp. He also expelled the garrison in Itucca and ravaged the territory of the Bastitani. Out of cowardice and inexperience Quintus did not come to their assistance, but went into winter quarters at Corduba in the middle of autumn and sent Gaius Marcius, an Iberian man from the town of Italica, on frequent missions against Viriathus.

67. The following year, Fabius Maximus Servilianus, the brother of Aemilianus, succeeded Quintus in the command.[60] He brought two more Roman legions with him and some allied forces, in total about eighteen thousand infantry and one thousand six hundred cavalry. Having ordered Micipsa, king of Numidia, to send him elephants as quickly as possible, he pressed on to Itucca, marching with his army in separate divisions. Viriathus attacked him with six thousand men, but without success, as Servilianus was not in the least put off by the shouting, barbarian clamor or long hair which they shake at their enemy in battle, and stood his ground bravely and drove him off. When the rest of his army arrived, along with ten elephants and three hundred cavalry from Africa, he fortified a large camp and took the offensive against Viriathus. Although he defeated and pursued him, the pursuit became undisciplined and, noting this while in flight, Viriathus returned to the attack, killed about three thousand Ro-

283

284

285

286

---

[60] Servilianus was consul in 142 when he took over the command in Further Spain.

---

25 Αἰμιλιανός VM: Σερουιλιανός edd.

συνήλασεν ἐς τὸ στρατόπεδον καὶ προσέβαλε καὶ
τῷδε, ὀλίγων μόλις αὐτὸν ὑφισταμένων περὶ τὰς
πύλας, τῶν δὲ πλεόνων ἐς τὰς σκηνὰς καταδύντων
ὑπὸ δέους καὶ μόλις ὑπὸ τοῦ στρατηγοῦ καὶ τῶν χι-
287 λιάρχων ἐξαγομένων. τότε μὲν οὖν Φάνιός τε, ὁ Λαι-
λίου κηδεστής, λαμπρῶς ἠρίστευε, καὶ νὺξ ἐπελθοῦσα
Ῥωμαίους περιέσωσεν· ὁ δὲ Οὐρίατθος, ἢ νυκτὸς ἢ
καύματος ὥρᾳ θαμινὰ ἐπιὼν καὶ οὔ τινα καιρὸν
ἀδόκητον ἐκλείπων, ψιλοῖς ἀνδράσι καὶ ἵπποις ταχυ-
τάτοις ἠνώχλει τοῖς πολεμίοις, μέχρι τὸν Σερουι-
λιανὸν ἐς Ἰτύκκην ἀναστῆσαι.

288   68. Τότε δ᾽ ἤδη τροφῶν τε ἀπορῶν ὁ Οὐρίατθος καὶ
τὸν στρατὸν ἔχων ἐλάττω, νυκτὸς ἐμπρήσας τὸ στρατόπεδον, ἐς Λυσιτανίαν ἀνεχώρει. καὶ αὐτὸν ὁ Σερουιλιανὸς οὐ καταλαβὼν ἐς Βαιτουρίαν ἐνέβαλε καὶ
πέντε πόλεις διήρπαζεν, αἳ τῷ Οὐρίατθῳ συνεπεπρά-
289 χεσαν. μετὰ δὲ τοῦτο ἐστράτευεν ἐς Κουννέους, ὅθεν ἐς
Λυσιτανοὺς ἐπὶ τὸν Οὐρίατθον αὖθις ἠπείγετο. καὶ
αὐτῷ παροδεύοντι δύο λήσταρχοι μετὰ μυρίων ἀνδρῶν ἐπιθέμενοι, Κούριός τε καὶ Ἀπουλήιος, ἐθορύβη-
290 σαν καὶ τὴν λείαν ἀφείλοντο. καὶ Κούριος μὲν ἐν τῷ
ἀγῶνι ἔπεσεν, ὁ δὲ Σερουιλιανὸς τήν τε λείαν μετ᾽ οὐ
πολὺ ἀνέλαβε καὶ πόλεις εἷλεν Εἰσκαδίαν τε καὶ Γέ-
μελλαν καὶ Ὀβόλκολαν, φρουρουμένας ὑπὸ τῶν Οὐριάτθου, καὶ διήρπαζεν ἑτέρας καὶ συνεγίγνωσκεν

mans and drove the rest into their camp, which he also assaulted. A small number just about held him off at the gates, while the majority hid in their tents out of fear and were only with difficulty ejected from them by the general and tribunes. It was at this point that Fannius, the son-in-law of Laelius, fought with particular courage.[61] The onset of night saved the Romans. Viriathus, however, continued to launch frequent attacks at night or in the heat of the day, missing no opportunity to do the unexpected, and using his light armed troops and fastest cavalry, he harrassed the enemy until Servilianus was forced to withdraw to Itucca. 287

68. But even at that time Viriathus was already short of supplies, and with his army dwindling in numbers, he burned his camp one night and retreated to Lusitania. Servilianus failed to catch him, but attacked Baeturia and plundered five towns that had taken Viriathus' side. Next, he campaigned against the Cunei and then pressed on into Lusitania once more against Viriathus. On the way there two bandit leaders, Curius and Apuleius, attacked him with ten thousand men, throwing his army into confusion and making off with his booty. Curius was killed in the fighting and shortly after, Servilianus recovered the booty and captured the towns of Escadia, Gemella, and Obulcula which had been garrisoned by Viriathus' troops. He plundered other towns too, but spared some. He had 288 289 290 291

[61] Gaius Fannius, son-in-law of the famous orator Gaius Laelius (consul in 140 and later anti-Gracchan activist) was consul in 122 when he fell out with G. Sempronius Gracchus. It is not clear whether he is the Fannius who wrote the history referred to by Cicero (*Brut.* 81, 101) and Sallust (*Hist.* 1.4).

291 ἄλλαις. αἰχμάλωτα δ' ἔχων ἀμφὶ τὰ μύρια πεντακο-
σίων μὲν ἀπέτεμεν τὰς κεφαλάς, τοὺς δὲ λοιποὺς ἀπέδοτο. καὶ ἐχείμαζε,[26] δεύτερον ἔτος ἤδη στρατηγῶν
τοῦδε τοῦ πολέμου. καὶ τάδε μὲν ὁ Σερουιλιανὸς ἐργασάμενος ἐς Ῥώμην ἀπῆρε διαδεξαμένου τὴν ἀρχὴν
Κοίντου [Πομπηίου Αὔλου] <τοῦ ἀδελφοῦ>.[27]

292 69. Ὁ δὲ ἀδελφὸς αὐτοῦ Μάξιμος Αἰμιλιανὸς Κον-
νόβαν μέν τινα λήσταρχον ἑαυτὸν ἐγχειρίσαντα λαβὼν καὶ φεισάμενος αὐτοῦ μόνου τοὺς σὺν αὐτῷ πάντας ἐχειροκόπησεν, Οὐρίατθον δὲ διώκων Ἐρισάνην
αὐτοῦ πόλιν ἀπετάφρευεν, ἐς ἣν ὁ Οὐρίατθος ἐσδρα-
μὼν νυκτὸς ἅμα ἕῳ τοῖς ἐργαζομένοις ἐπέκειτο, μέχρι

293 τὰ σκαφεῖα ῥίψαντες ἔφυγον. τήν τε ἄλλην στρατιάν, ἐκταχθεῖσαν ὑπὸ τοῦ Αἰμιλιανοῦ,[28] τρεψάμενος
ὁμοίως Οὐρίατθος ἐδίωκε καὶ συνήλασεν ἐς κρημνούς,

294 ὅθεν οὐκ ἦν τοῖς Ῥωμαίοις διαφυγεῖν. Οὐρίατθος δὲ
ἐς τὴν εὐτυχίαν οὐχ ὕβρισεν, ἀλλὰ νομίσας ἐν καλῷ
θήσεσθαι τὸν πόλεμον ἐπὶ χάριτι λαμπρᾷ συνετίθετο
Ῥωμαίοις, καὶ τὰς συνθήκας ὁ δῆμος ἐπεκύρωσεν,
Οὐρίατθον εἶναι Ῥωμαίων φίλον καὶ τοὺς ὑπ' αὐτῷ

---

[26] ἐχείμαζε . . . Μάξιμος Αἰμιλιανὸς susp. Viereck-Roos
non esse Appiani.

[27] Κοίντου Πομπηίου Αὔλου codd; Πομπηίου Αὔλου del.
Goukowsky; τοῦ ἀδελφοῦ add. Goukowsky.

[28] Αἰμιλιανοῦ Goukowsky cum VM: Σερουιλιανοῦ edd.

about ten thousand prisoners, five hundred of whom he beheaded and sold the rest into slavery. He then went into winter quarters.[62] It was the second year of his command in this war. Having achieved these results, he sailed off to Rome, his brother Quintus succeeding to the command.[63]

69. With regard to Servilianus' brother, Maximus Aemilianus, he captured a bandit leader called Connobas who surrendered himself willingly.[64] Aemilianus spared him alone, but cut off the hands of all the men with him. In pursuit of Viriathus, he set about investing Erisana, one of the towns under his control. Viriathus got into the town during the night and at dawn fell on the Romans doing the work, forcing them to throw away their shovels and flee. In similar fashion, he defeated the rest of the Roman army which had been deployed by Aemilianus, and in the course of his pursuit drove them to the edge of some cliffs, from where there was no escape for the Romans. Rather than abuse his success, however, he regarded it as a fine opportunity to end the war with a display of exceptional goodwill. So he made terms with the Romans and the people ratified the treaty: Viriathus was to be a friend of

292

293

294

[62] Viereck-Roos suspect that from this sentence as far as Maximus Aemilianus (at 69.292) are not Appian's words.

[63] His brother was Quintus Servilius Caepio (consul 140). The text at this point is difficult to establish. I have followed Goukowsky's Budé edition.

[64] The reappearance of Q. Fabius Maximus Aemilianus (last mentioned as wintering in Corduba, above 65.278) is difficult to explain, as he had long left Spain by this date, but there can be little doubt that Appian was confused by four Roman commanders in Spain with the praenomen Quintus (Servilius Caepio, Fabius Servilianus, Fabius Maximus, and Pompeius).

295 πάντας ἧς ἔχουσι γῆς ἄρχειν. ὧδε μὲν ὁ Οὐριάτθου
πόλεμος ἐδόκει πεπαῦσθαι, χαλεπώτατός τε Ῥωμαίοις
γενόμενος καὶ ἐπὶ εὐεργεσίᾳ καταλυθείς, οὐ μὴν ἐπ-
έμεινεν οὐδ᾽ ἐς βραχὺ τὰ συγκείμενα.

296   70. Ὁ γὰρ ἀδελφὸς Αἰμιλιανοῦ[29] τοῦ ταῦτα συν-
θεμένου, Καιπίων, διάδοχος αὐτῷ τῆς στρατηγίας
γενόμενος, διέβαλλε τὰς συνθήκας καὶ ἐπέστελλε
297 Ῥωμαίοις ἀπρεπεστάτας εἶναι. καὶ ἡ βουλὴ τὸ μὲν
πρῶτον αὐτῷ συνεχέρει κρύφα λυπεῖν τὸν Οὐρίατθον,
ὅ τι δοκιμάσειεν· ὡς δὲ αὖθις ἠνώχλει καὶ συνεχῶς
ἐπέστελλεν, ἔκρινε λῦσαί τε τὰς σπονδὰς καὶ φα-
298 νερῶς πολεμεῖν αὖθις Οὐριάτθῳ. ἐψηφισμένου δὴ σαφῶς ὁ Καιπίων Ἄρσαν τε πόλιν ἐκλιπόντος Οὐριάτθου παρέλαβε καὶ αὐτὸν Οὐρίατθον φεύγοντά τε καὶ
τὰ ἐν παρόδῳ φθείροντα περὶ Καρπητανίαν κατέλα-
299 βεν, πολὺ πλείονας ἔχων. ὅθεν ὁ Οὐρίατθος, οὐ δοκιμάζων αὐτῷ συμπλέκεσθαι διὰ τὴν ὀλιγότητα, κατὰ
μέν τινα φάραγγα ἀφανῆ τὸ πλέον τοῦ στρατοῦ περι-
έπεμψεν ἀπιέναι, τὸ δὲ λοιπὸν αὐτὸς ἐκτάξας ἐπὶ λό-
300 φου δόξαν παρεῖχε πολεμήσοντος. ὡς δ᾽ ᾔσθετο τῶν
προαπεσταλμένων ἐν ἀσφαλεῖ γεγονότων, ἐξίππευσεν
ἐς αὐτοὺς μετὰ καταφρονήσεως, ὀξέως οὕτως, ὡς μηδ᾽
αἰσθέσθαι τοὺς διώκοντας, ὅποι διέδραμεν. ὁ δὲ Καιπίων, ἐς Οὐέττωνας καὶ Καλλαίκους τραπείς, τὰ ἐκείνων ἐδῄου.

301   71. Καὶ ζήλῳ τῶν ἔργων Οὐριάτθου τὴν Λυσιτανίαν
ληστήρια πολλὰ ἄλλα ἐπιτρέχοντα ἐπόρθει. Σέξτος

Rome, and all those subject to him were to control the
territory they held. In this way, so it appeared, the war   295
against Viriathus had been brought to an end. The Romans had found it extremely difficult and peace had only
come though a display of goodwill, but the agreement did
not hold, even for a short time.

70. For Caepio, brother of the Aemilianus who negoti-   296
ated the treaty, succeeded him in the command, and began to discredit the terms, and reported back to Rome that
they were extremely demeaning. The senate at first ad-   297
vised him to use his discretion in causing trouble for
Viriathus secretly, but when he renewed his lobbying of
the senate by sending frequent reports, they decided to
break off the treaty and openly make war again on Viriathus. When the war vote was passed publicly, Caepio   298
seized the town of Arsa, abandoned by Viriathus, who had
taken to flight, employing a scorched earth policy on his
way, and caught up with him near Carpetania. As Caepio
enjoyed considerable numerical superiority, Viriathus de-   299
cided not to join battle, given his small numbers. Instead,
he sent off most of his force to retreat through a hidden
ravine, while he himself marshaled the rest on a hill, giving
the impression that he would fight. But when he learned   300
that those he had sent away before were safe, he contemp-
tuously rode off to join them, and with such speed that his
pursuers could not even find out where he had gone.
Caepio turned against the Vettones and Callaeci and ravaged their territory.

71. In trying to match the deeds of Viriathus, many   301
other bandit groups attacked Lusitania and plundered it.

---

29 Αἰμιλιανοῦ Goukowsky cum VM: Σερουιλιανοῦ edd.

δὲ Ἰούνιος Βροῦτος, ἐπὶ ταῦτα πεμφθείς, ἀπέγνω μὲν
αὐτὰ διώκειν διὰ χώρας μακρᾶς, ὅσην ὁ Τάγος τε καὶ
Λήθης καὶ Δόριος καὶ Βαῖνις[30] ποταμοὶ ναυσίποροι
περιέχουσιν, ὀξέως, οἷα δὴ ληστήρια, μεθιπταμένους
δυσεργὲς ἡγούμενος εἶναι καταλαβεῖν καὶ αἰσχρὸν οὐ
302 καταλαβόντι καὶ νικήσαντι τὸ ἔργον οὐ λαμπρόν· ἐς
δὲ τὰς πόλεις αὐτῶν ἐτράπετο, δίκην τε λήψεσθαι
προσδοκῶν καὶ τῇ στρατιᾷ πολὺ κέρδος περιέσεσθαι
καὶ τοὺς λῃστὰς ἐς ἑκάστην ὡς πατρίδα κινδυνεύου-
303 σαν διαλυθήσεσθαι. ὁ μὲν δὴ ταῦτ᾽ ἐνθυμούμενος
ἐδῄου τὰ ἐν ποσὶν ἅπαντα, συμμαχομένων τοῖς ἀνδράσι τῶν γυναικῶν καὶ συναιρουμένων καὶ οὔ
τινα φωνὴν οὐδ᾽ ἐν ταῖς σφαγαῖς ἀφιεισῶν. εἰσὶ δ᾽ οἳ
καὶ εἰς τὰ ὄρη, μεθ᾽ ὧν ἐδύναντο, ἀνεπήδων· καὶ
αὐτοῖς δεομένοις συνεγίγνωσκεν ὁ Βροῦτος καὶ τὰ
ὄντα ἐμερίζετο.

304 72. Καὶ τὸν Δόριον περάσας πολλὰ μὲν πολέμῳ
κατέδραμεν, πολλὰ δὲ παρὰ τῶν αὐτοὺς ἐνδιδόντων
ὅμηρα αἰτήσας ἐπὶ Λήθην μετῄει, πρῶτος ὅδε Ῥω-
305 μαίων ἐπινοῶν τὸν ποταμὸν τόνδε διαβῆναι. περάσας
δὲ καὶ τόνδε καὶ μέχρι Μίνιος,[31] ἑτέρου ποταμοῦ, προ-
ελθών, Βρακάρων αὐτῷ φερομένην ἀγορὰν ἁρπασάν-
των, ἐστράτευεν ἐπὶ τοὺς Βρακάρους, οἵ εἰσιν ἔθνος

30 Βαῖνις Goukowsky: Βαίτης VM
31 Μίνιος Goukowsky: Νίμιος VM

Sextus Iunius Brutus was sent against them, but rejected the idea of pursuing them through the huge area bordered by the navigable rivers Tagus, Lethe, Dorius and Baenis.[65] He thought they would be difficult to catch as they moved swiftly, in the manner of bandit groups, from one place to another; and while it would be a disgrace not to catch them, nor would it be a brilliant achievement to defeat them. So he turned against their towns, expecting to exact   302 punishment on them and acquire large quantities of booty for his army, and that the bandits would scatter to their own hometowns as these came under threat. With this   303 purpose in mind, he began to destroy everything before him. The women fought alongside their men and died with them, making no sound even in death. There were some who reached the mountains with what they could carry. These asked to be pardoned and Brutus did so, but he confiscated their property.

72. Crossing the river Dorius, he brought war and de-   304 struction to many areas, demanding large numbers of hostages from those who surrendered, and reached the river Lethe. He was the first Roman to plan a crossing of this river. He did indeed cross it and advanced to another river   305 called the Minis, and attacked the Bracari for seizing supplies being brought to him. They are a ‹most warlike?›[66]

[65] Decimus (not Sextus) Iunius Brutus Callaicus was consul in 138 and was posted to Further Spain, where he remained until 136, when he returned to Rome and celebrated a triumph. The Lethe is the modern Limia; the Dorius, the Duero; and the Baenis, the Minho.

[66] There is a brief lacuna in the text requiring some such word.

<. . .> καὶ ἅμα ταῖς γυναιξὶν ὡπλισμέναις καὶ οἵδε ἐμάχοντο καὶ προθύμως ἔθνησκον, οὐκ ἐπιστρεφόμενος αὐτῶν οὐδεὶς οὐδὲ τὰ νῶτα δεικνὺς οὐδὲ φωνὴν

306 ἀφιέντες. ὅσαι δὲ κατήγοντο τῶν γυναικῶν, αἱ μὲν αὐτὰς διεχρῶντο, αἱ δὲ καὶ τῶν τέκνων αὐτόχειρες ἐγίγνοντο, χαίρουσαι τῷ θανάτῳ μᾶλλον τῆς αἰχμα

307 λωσίας. εἰσὶ δέ τινες τῶν πόλεων, αἳ τότε μὲν τῷ Βρούτῳ προσετίθεντο, οὐ πολὺ δ᾽ ὕστερον ἀφίσταντο, καὶ αὐτὰς ὁ Βροῦτος κατεστρέφετο αὖθις.

308 73. Ἐπὶ δὲ Ταλάβριγα πόλιν ἐλθών, ἣ πολλάκις μὲν αὐτῷ συνετέθειτο, πολλάκις δ᾽ ἀποστᾶσα ἠνώχλει, παρακαλούντων αὐτὸν καὶ τότε τῶν Ταλαβρίγων καὶ διδόντων αὐτούς, ἐς ὅ τι χρῄζοι, πρῶτα μὲν τοὺς αὐτομόλους Ῥωμαίων ᾔτει καὶ τὰ αἰχμάλωτα καὶ ὅπλα, ὅσα εἶχον, καὶ ὅμηρα ἐπὶ τούτοις, εἶτ᾽ αὐτοὺς ἐκέλευσε σὺν παισὶ καὶ γυναιξὶν ἐκλιπεῖν τὴν

309 πόλιν. ὡς δὲ καὶ τοῦθ᾽ ὑπέστησαν, τὴν στρατιὰν αὐτοῖς περιστήσας ἐδημηγόρει, καταλέγων, ὁσάκις ἀποσταῖεν καὶ ὅσους πολέμους πολεμήσειαν αὐτῷ. φόβον δὲ καὶ δόξαν ἐμφήνας ἐργασομένου τι δεινὸν ἐπὶ τῶν ὀνειδῶν[32] ἔληξε καὶ τοὺς μὲν ἵππους αὐτῶν καὶ τὸν σῖτον καὶ χρήματα, ὅσα κοινὰ ἦν, ἢ εἴ τις ἄλλη δημοσία παρασκευή, πάντα περιεῖλε, τὴν δὲ

310 πόλιν αὖθις οἰκεῖν ἔδωκεν ἐξ ἀέλπτου. τοσάδε μὲν δὴ Βροῦτος ἐργασάμενος ἐς Ῥώμην ἀπῄει. καὶ αὐτὰ ἐς τὴν Οὐριάθου γραφὴν συνήγαγον, ἐν τῷ αὐτῷ χρόνῳ διὰ τὸν ἐκείνου ζῆλον ὑπὸ λῃστηρίων ἄλλων ἀρξάμενα γίγνεσθαι.

people, who also fought with their women under arms and died willingly, not a single one of them turning and showing their back or uttering a sound. Of the women who were subdued, some killed themselves, others also killed their children, preferring death to captivity. There are some towns that sided with Brutus at the time, but revolted soon after, and Brutus subjected them again.

73. When he advanced on the town of Talabriga, often under treaty with him, often a troublesome rebel, on this occasion, as before, the people invited him in and agreed to submit at his discretion. He first demanded the Roman deserters, the prisoners, any weapons the Talabrigans possessed, and, in addition, hostages. He then ordered the inhabitants along with their wives and children to abandon the town. When they submitted even to this, Brutus surrounded them with his troops and delivered a speech enumerating the many occasions on which they had revolted and the many times they had waged war on him. In this way he instilled fear in them and gave the impression that he was going to do something terrible, but in fact he went no further than abuse, and after depriving them of all their horses, grain, communal funds and any other public resources, he unexpectedly allowed them to reoccupy the town. This was the extent of Brutus' achievement before he returned to Rome. I have included these events in my account of Viriathus because it was at the same time that they began to be undertaken by other bandit groups in emulation of Viriathus.

306
307
308
309
310

---

[32] ἐπὶ τῶν ὀνειδῶν VM: ἐπονειδίζων Goukowsky

311   74. Οὐρίατθος δὲ Καιπίωνι περὶ συμβάσεων τοὺς
πιστοτάτους αὑτῷ φίλους ἐπέπεμπεν, Αὔδακα καὶ Δι-
τάλκωνα καὶ Μίνουρον, οἳ διαφθαρέντες ὑπὸ τοῦ Και-
πίωνος δώροις τε μεγάλοις καὶ ὑποσχέσεσι πολλαῖς
ὑπέστησαν αὐτῷ κτενεῖν τὸν Οὐρίατθον. καὶ ἔκτειναν
312   ὧδε· ὀλιγοϋπνότατος ἦν διὰ φροντίδα καὶ πόνους ὁ
Οὐρίατθος καὶ τὰ πολλὰ ἔνοπλος ἀνεπαύετο, ἵνα ἐξ-
εγρόμενος εὐθὺς ἐς πάντα ἕτοιμος εἴη. τοῖς οὖν φίλοις
313   ἐξῆν καὶ νυκτερεύοντι ἐντυγχάνειν. ᾧ δὴ καὶ τότε ἔθει
οἱ περὶ τὸν Αὔδακα φυλάξαντες αὐτὸν ἀρχομένου
ὕπνου παρῆλθον ἐς τὴν σκηνήν, ὡς δή τινος ἐπείγον-
τος, καὶ κεντοῦσιν ὡπλισμένον ἐς τὴν σφαγήν· οὐ
314   γὰρ ἦν ἄλλοθι. οὐδεμιᾶς δ' αἰσθήσεως γενομένης διὰ
τὴν τῆς πληγῆς εὐκαιρίαν διέδρασαν ἐς Καιπίωνα καὶ
τὰς δωρεὰς ᾔτουν. ὁ δὲ αὐτίκα μὲν αὐτοῖς ἔδωκεν
ἀδεῶς ἔχειν, ὅσα ἔχουσι, περὶ δὲ ὧν ᾔτουν, ἐς Ῥώμην
315   αὐτοὺς ἔπεμπεν. οἱ δὲ θεραπευτῆρες Οὐρίατθου καὶ ἡ
ἄλλη στρατιά, γενομένης ἡμέρας, ἀναπαύεσθαι νομίζοντες αὐτόν, ἐθαύμαζον διὰ τὴν ἀήθειαν, μέχρι τινὲς
316   ἔμαθον, ὅτι νεκρὸς κέοιτο ἔνοπλος. καὶ εὐθὺς ἦν οἰ-
μωγή τε καὶ πένθος ἀνὰ τὸ στρατόπεδον, ἀλγούντων
τε ἐπ' ἐκείνῳ καὶ περὶ σφῶν δεδιότων καὶ ἐνθυμου-
μένων, ἐν οἷοις εἰσὶ κινδύνοις καὶ οἵου στρατηγοῦ
στέρονται. μάλιστα δὲ αὐτούς, ὅτι τοὺς δράσαντας
οὐχ εὕρισκον, ὑπερήλγυνεν.
317   75. Οὐρίατθον μὲν δὴ λαμπρότατα κοσμήσαντες
ἐπὶ ὑψηλοτάτης πυρᾶς ἔκαιον ἱερεῖά τε πολλὰ ἐπ-

74. Viriathus sent his most trusted associates, Audax,   311
Ditalco, and Minurus to make an agreement with Caepio,
but they were bribed by Caepio with lavish gifts and many
promises, and undertook to kill Viriathus.[67] This is how
they did it. Due to worry and work, Viriathus slept very   312
little, and what rest he did take was mostly in armor, so
that he would immediately be ready for all eventualities if
woken. For this reason he permitted his associates to call
on him during the night. So, on this occasion too, Audax   313
and his men, relying on this practice, waited for their opportunity, and as soon as he went to sleep, entered his tent
as if on urgent business and, because he was armed, they
stab him in the neck, there being nowhere else they could
do it. It was such an accurate blow that no one noticed   314
anything, and they escaped back to Caepio and demanded
their reward. For the moment, he granted them the security of keeping what they already received, but in relation
to their demands, he referred them to Rome. At daybreak   315
Viriathus' attendants and the rest of the army thought he
was still asleep, an unusual situation which surprised
them, until some made the discovery that he was lying
there dead in his armor. Immediately the camp was filled   316
with weeping and mourning, as people both grieved for
him and feared for themselves, thinking about the severe
dangers they faced and the greatness of the general they
had lost. What particularly upset them was the fact that
they could not find the perpetrators.

75. But they dressed the body of Viriathus in the finest   317
gear and cremated him on the highest of funeral pyres.

---

[67] Appian now returns to where he left the Viriathus story at
section 300.

ἔσφαττον αὐτῷ, καὶ κατὰ ἴλας οἵ τε πεζοὶ καὶ οἱ ἱππῆς ἐν κύκλῳ περιθέοντες αὐτὸν ἔνοπλοι βαρβαρικῶς
ἐπήνουν μέχρι τε σβεσθῆναι τὸ πῦρ παρεκάθηντο
πάντες ἀμφ᾽ αὐτό. καὶ τῆς ταφῆς ἐκτελεσθείσης
ἀγῶνα μονομάχων ἀνδρῶν ἤγαγον ἐπὶ τοῦ τάφου.

318 τοσοῦτον αὐτοῦ πόθον κατέλιπεν Οὐρίατθος, ἀρχι-
κώτατος μὲν ὡς ἐν βαρβάροις γενόμενος, φιλοκινδυ-
νότατος δ᾽ ἐς ἅπαντα πρὸ ἁπάντων καὶ ἰσομοιρότατος
ἐν τοῖς κέρδεσιν. οὐ γάρ ποτε πλέον ὑπέστη λαβεῖν,
αἰεὶ παρακαλούντων· ὃ δὲ καὶ λάβοι, τοῖς ἀριστεύσα-

319 σιν ἐδίδου. ὅθεν αὐτῷ, δυσχερέστατον ἔργον καὶ οὐ-
δενί πω στρατηγῶν εὐμαρῶς ἐγγενόμενον, ἔτεσιν
ὀκτὼ τοῦδε τοῦ πολέμου παμμιγὴς στρατὸς ἀστασί-
αστος ἦν καὶ κατήκοος ἀεὶ καὶ ἐς τοὺς κινδύνους

320 ὀξύτατος. τότε δὲ σφῶν Ταύταλον ἑλόμενοι στρατηγεῖν ἐπὶ Ζάκανθαν ἐφέροντο, ἣν Ἀννίβας καθελὼν
ἔκτισεν καὶ ἀπὸ τῆς αὐτοῦ πατρίδος Καρχηδόνα

321 προσεῖπεν. ἀποκρουσθεῖσι δ᾽ αὐτοῖς ἐκεῖθεν καὶ τὸν
Βαῖτιν ποταμὸν περῶσιν ὁ Καιπίων ἐπέκειτο, μέχρι
κάμνων ὁ Ταύταλος αὐτόν τε καὶ τὴν στρατιὰν τῷ
Καιπίωνι παρέδωκεν ὡς ὑπηκόοις χρῆσθαι. ὁ δὲ ὅπλα
τε αὐτοὺς ἀφείλετο ἅπαντα καὶ γῆν ἔδωκεν ἱκανήν,
ἵνα μὴ λῃστεύοιεν ἐξ ἀπορίας.

322   76. Ὁ μὲν δὴ Οὐριάτθου πόλεμος ἐς τοῦτο ἐτελεύτα,
ἐπάνεισι δ᾽ ἐς τὸν Οὐακκαίων[33] καὶ Νομαντίνων πόλε-

---

[33] Οὐακκαίων Goukowsky cum VM: Ἀρουακῶν edd.

They slaughtered many sacrificial victims over him, and the infantry and cavalry circled the pyre at the double in formation and fully armed, singing his praises in the manner of barbarians; and they all sat round the fire until it went out. When the funeral was finished, they held gladiatorial contests at the tomb. Such was the great longing 318 for him Viriathus left behind. Even allowing for his barbarian origins, he was extraordinarily well suited to command, always ahead of everyone else in facing danger and in dividing the spoils equally. For he never agreed to take more than others, although they always invited him to. And indeed, even what he did accept he distributed to those who had excelled in bravery. The result was—and it 319 is a most difficult task, which no general has ever easily achieved—that in the eight years of this war his army, a very mixed force, never mutinied, always obeyed orders, and faced danger with the keenest enthusiasm. Afterward, 320 they chose Tautalus as their commander and attacked Saguntum, which Hannibal had destroyed and refounded, naming it Carthage after his own hometown.[68] Forced 321 back from Saguntum, they were crossing the river Baetis when Caepio pressed home his attack, until Tautalus in exhaustion surrendered himself and his army to Caepio to be treated as subjects. Caepio confiscated all their weapons, but gave them enough land so they would not resort to banditry for lack of resources.

76. So ended the war against Viriathus. My account 322 now returns to the war against the Vaccaei and Numan-

[68] For Appian's confusion between Saguntum and New Carthage, see above, note 11.

APPIAN

μον ἡ γραφή, οὓς Οὐρίατθος μὲν ἠρέθισεν ἐς ἀπόστασιν, Καικίλιος δ' αὐτοῖς Μέτελλος ἀπὸ Ῥώμης
ἐπιπεμφθεὶς μετὰ πλέονος στρατοῦ Οὐακκοὺς[34] μὲν
ἐχειρώσατο, σὺν ἐκπλήξει καὶ τάχει θερίζουσιν ἐμ-
πίπτων, Τερμεντία δ' αὐτῷ καὶ Νομαντία ἔτι ἔλειπον.
323 ἦν δ' ἡ Νομαντία ποταμοῖς δύο καὶ φάραγξιν ἀπό-
κρημνος, ὗλαί τε αὐτῇ πυκναὶ περιέκειντο, καὶ μία
κάθοδος ἦν ἐς τὸ πεδίον, ᾗ τάφρων ἐπεπλήρωτο καὶ
324 στηλῶν. αὐτοὶ δ' ἦσαν ἄριστοι μὲν ἱππῆς τε καὶ πεζοί, πάντες δ' ἀμφὶ τοὺς ὀκτακισχιλίους· καὶ τοσοίδε
ὄντες ὅμως ὑπ' ἀρετῆς ἐς μέγα ἠνώχλησαν τὰ Ῥω-
325 μαίων. Μέτελλος μὲν δὴ μετὰ χειμῶνα τὴν στρατιὰν
Κοΐντῳ Πομπηΐῳ Αὔλου υἱῷ, διαδόχῳ τῆς στρατηγίας οἱ γενομένῳ, παρέδωκεν, τρισμυρίους πεζοὺς
καὶ δισχιλίους ἱππέας ἄριστα γεγυμνασμένους, ὁ δὲ
Πομπήιος τῇ Νομαντίᾳ παραστρατοπεδεύων ᾤχετό
ποι, καὶ ἱππέας αὐτοῦ μεταθέοντες ἑκατόν οἱ Νο-
326 μαντῖνοι [καταβάντες][35] ἔκτειναν. ἐπανελθὼν οὖν παρ-
έτασσεν ἐς τὸ πεδίον, καὶ οἱ Νομαντῖνοι καταβάντες
ὑπεχώρουν κατ' ὀλίγον οἷα φεύγοντες, μέχρι ταῖς
στήλαις καὶ φάραγξιν ὁ Πομπήιος ⟨ἐνέπεσεν⟩.[36]
327 77. Καὶ καθ' ἡμέραν ἐν ταῖς ἀκροβολίαις ἐλασσού-

34 Οὐακκοὺς Goukowsky cum VM: Ἀρουακοὺς edd.
35 μεταθέοντες ἑκατὸν Goukowsky: μεταθέοντας αὐτὸν VM.
καταβάντες del. Goukowsky
36 ἐνέπεσεν add. Schulten

tines, whom Viriathus had roused to revolt.[69] Caecilius
Metellus was sent against them from Rome with a larger
army and overpowered the Vaccaei, falling on them with
astounding speed as they harvested their crops.[70] He still
faced the problem of Termantia and Numantia.[71] Numan-   323
tia was located on a precipitous height formed by two
rivers and ravines. It was also surrounded by thick woods,
and there was one road down into the plain, which had
been filled with ditches and stone blocks. Their soldiers,   324
both infantry and cavalry, were of the highest quality, although in total they numbered only about eight thousand.
In spite of their small number, their courage made them
extremely troublesome to Rome. After the winter, Me-   325
tellus handed the army over to Quintus Pompeius, son of
Aulus, who succeeded him in the command: there were
thirty thousand infantry and two thousand cavalry, all in
an excellent state of training. Pompeius encamped outside
Numantia, but while he was away elsewhere, the Numantines chased after his cavalry, killing one hundred of them.
Returning, therefore, he drew up his army in the plain,   326
and the Numantines came down to meet him. They withdrew slowly, as if they were intending to flee, until Pompeius crashed into the stone blocks and ravines.[72]

77. As he was getting the worst of it in skirmishes day   327

[69] Appian refers back to section 280.

[70] Quintus Caecilius Metellus Macedonicus (consul 143), famous for defeating the Macedonian pretender, Andriscus, in 148.

[71] For Numantia, see note 39. Termantia, modern Montejo de
Tiermes, is located about ninety-three miles north of Madrid.

[72] The text of sections 325 and 326 is very uncertain, and the
translation reflects a number of conjectures.

μενος ὑπ᾽ ἀνδρῶν πολὺ ἐλασσόνων μετέβαινεν ἐπὶ
328 Τερμεντίαν ὡς εὐχερέστερον ἔργον. ὡς δὲ καὶ τῇδε
συμβαλὼν ἑπτακοσίους τε ἀπώλεσε καὶ τὸν τὴν
ἀγορὰν αὐτῷ φέροντα χιλίαρχον οἱ Τερμεντεῖς ἐτρέψαντο καὶ τρίτῃ πείρᾳ κατὰ τὴν αὐτὴν ἡμέραν ἐς
ἀπόκρημνα τοὺς Ῥωμαίους συνελάσαντες πολλοὺς
αὐτῶν πεζούς τε καὶ ἱππέας αὐτοῖς ἵπποις κατέωσαν
ἐς τὰ ἀπόκρημνα, περιφόβως ἔχοντες οἱ λοιποὶ δι-
ενυκτέρευον ἔνοπλοι. καὶ ἅμα ἕῳ προσιόντων τῶν
πολεμίων ἐκταξάμενοι τὴν ἡμέραν ὅλην ἠγωνίζοντο
329 ἀγχωμάλως καὶ διεκρίθησαν ὑπὸ νυκτός. ὅθεν ὁ Πομπήιος ἐπὶ πολίχνης Μαλίας ἤλασεν, ἣν ἐφρούρουν οἱ
Νομαντῖνοι. καὶ οἱ Μαλιεῖς, τοὺς φρουροὺς ἀνελόντες
330 ἐξ ἐνέδρας, παρέδοσαν τὸ πολίχνιον τῷ Πομπηίῳ. ὁ
δὲ τά τε ὅπλα αὐτοὺς καὶ ὅμηρα αἰτήσας μετῆλθεν
ἐπὶ Σηδητανίαν, ἣν ἐδῄου λήσταρχος ὄνομα Ταγγῖ-
νος· καὶ αὐτὸν ὁ Πομπήιος ἐνίκα καὶ πολλοὺς ἔλαβεν
331 αἰχμαλώτους. τοσοῦτον δ᾽ ἦν φρονήματος ἐν τοῖς λῃσταῖς, ὥστε τῶν αἰχμαλώτων οὐδεὶς ὑπέμεινε δου-
λεύειν, ἀλλ᾽ οἱ μὲν αὑτούς, οἱ δὲ τοὺς πριαμένους
ἀνῄρουν, οἱ δὲ τὰς ναῦς ἐν τῷ διάπλῳ διετίτρων.

332 78. Ὁ δὲ Πομπήιος αὖθις ἐλάσας ἐπὶ Νομαντίαν
ποταμόν τινα μετωχέτευεν ἐς τὸ πεδίον ὡς λιμῷ πι-
έσων τὴν πόλιν. οἱ δὲ ἐργαζομένῳ τε ἐπέκειντο καὶ
σαλπικτῶν χωρὶς ἐκτρέχοντες ἀθρόοι τοὺς ὀχετεύον-
τας ἠνώχλουν. ἔβαλλον δὲ καὶ τοὺς ἀπὸ τοῦ χάρακος
ἐπιβοηθοῦντας, ἕως κατέκλεισαν ἐς τὸ στρατόπεδον.
333 καὶ σιτολογοῦσιν ἑτέροις ἐπιδραμόντες καὶ τῶνδε

after day at the hands of a much smaller force, Pompeius changed the focus of his attack to Termantia, in the hope that it would prove an easier task. But here too in one day   328
he lost seven hundred men in an attack, and the Termantians routed the tribune bringing him supplies; and in a third action on the same day, they drove the Roman forces onto cliffs and pushed many of the foot soldiers and cavalrymen, along with their horses, over the edge, while the rest spent the night in fear and under arms. At dawn, the enemy came out in battle order and an indecisive engagement was fought over the course of the whole day: the sides were only separated by night. From here, Pompeius   329
marched against the township of Malia, which the Numantines were garrisoning. The inhabitants treacherously killed the garrison troops, and handed the township to Pompeius. He demanded they give up their weapons   330
and provide hostages, and then moved against Sedetania, which was being ravaged by a bandit leader called Tanginus. Pompeius defeated him and took many of his men prisoner. But there was such high spirit among the bandits   331
that none of the prisoners would submit to slavery: some killed themselves, others killed the people who had bought them and yet others scuttled the ships in which they were being transported.

78. Returning to the campaign against Numantia,   332
Pompeius set about diverting a river into the plain in order to press the town with famine, but the enemy attacked him while engaged in the task. Without warning from trumpets, they rushed out en masse to harass those working on the channel and threw missiles at the reinforcements sent from the stockade, until eventually they forced them to stay in their camp. The Numantines also attacked others   333

πολλοὺς διέφθειραν Ὄππιόν τε χιλίαρχον ἐπ' αὐτοῖς
ἀνεῖλον. καὶ κατ' ἄλλο μέρος τάφρον ὀρύσσουσι Ῥωμαίοις ἐπιδραμόντες ἔκτειναν ἐς τετρακοσίους καὶ τὸν
334 ἡγούμενον αὐτῶν. ἐφ' οἷς τῷ τε Πομπηίῳ σύμβουλοι
παρῆσαν ἐκ Ῥώμης καὶ τοῖς στρατιώταις (ἐξ γὰρ ἔτη
διεληλύθει στρατευομένοις) διάδοχοι νεοκατάγραφοί
335 τε καὶ ἔτι ἀγύμναστοι καὶ ἀπειροπόλεμοι. μεθ' ὧν ὁ
Πομπήιος, αἰδούμενός τε τὰ ἐπταισμένα καὶ ἐπειγόμενος τὴν αἰσχύνην ἀναλαβεῖν, ἐπέμενε χειμῶνος ἐν
336 τῷ στρατοπέδῳ. καὶ οἱ στρατιῶται, κρύους τε ὄντος
ἐν ἀστέγῳ σταθμεύοντες καὶ πρῶτον ἄρτι πειρώμενοι
τοῦ περὶ τὴν χώραν ὕδατός τε καὶ ἀέρος, κατὰ γα-
337 στέρα ἔκαμνον, καὶ διεφθείροντο ἔνιοι. μέρους δ' ἐπὶ
σῖτον οἰχομένου κρύψαντες ἐνέδραν οἱ Νομαντῖνοι
παρ' αὐτὸ τὸ Ῥωμαίων στρατόπεδον ἠκροβολίζοντο
ἐρεθίζοντες, ἕως οἱ μὲν οὐ φέροντες ἐπεξῆεσαν, οἱ δ'
ἐκ τῆς ἐνέδρας ἀνίσταντο· καὶ Ῥωμαῖοι πολλοὶ μὲν ἐκ
τοῦ πλήθους, πολλοὶ δὲ τῶν ἐπιφανῶν ἀπέθανον. οἱ
δὲ Νομαντῖνοι, καὶ τοῖς τὸν σῖτον φέρουσιν ἀπαντή-
σαντες, ἔκτειναν καὶ τῶνδε πολλούς.

338 79. Καὶ ὁ Πομπήιος, τοσοῖσδε συνενεχθεὶς κακοῖς,
ἐς τὰς πόλεις μετὰ τῶν συμβούλων ἀνεζεύγνυε, χειμάσων τὸ ἐπίλοιπον, τοῦ ἔαρος προσδοκῶν ἥξειν οἱ
διάδοχον. καὶ δεδιὼς κατηγορίαν ἔπρασσεν ἐς τοὺς
339 Νομαντίνους κρύφα τοῦ πολέμου διαλύσεις. οἱ δὲ καὶ
αὐτοὶ κάμνοντες ἤδη φόνῳ τε πολλῷ ἀρίστων καὶ γῆς
ἀργίᾳ καὶ τροφῶν ἀπορίᾳ καὶ μήκει τοῦ πολέμου,
μακροῦ παρὰ προσδοκίαν γεγονότος, ἐπρέσβευον ἐς

out on foraging expeditions and killed many of these too, including the tribune Oppius. Elsewhere, they attacked some Romans who were digging a ditch and killed about four hundred of them, along with their commanding officer. It was at this point that a senatorial commission arrived from Rome with replacements—new recruits, untrained and not yet tested in battle—to take the place of his own troops who had served for six years. Pompeius, embarrassed by his failures and keen to recover from the disgrace, remained in camp for the winter with the new soldiers. But with freezing weather and being quartered in the open, combined with the fact that they were new to the water and air of the region, the soldiers got dysentery, and some of them died. When a detachment went out for grain, the Numantines set an ambush right beside the camp of the Romans, whom they provoked by volleys of missiles. Unable to bear it, the Romans launched a sortie, at which the Numantines rose from their ambush. Many Romans died, both ordinary soldiers and those of high rank. The Numantines also intercepted those bringing the grain and killed many of them too.

79. Having met with so many reverses, Pompeius took the senatorial comissioners with him and withdrew to the towns to spend the rest of the winter there, expecting that his successor would arrive in spring. Afraid he might face prosecution, he secretly negotiated with Numantia to bring the war to an end. The Numantines themselves sent an embassy to Pompeius, as they were now worn out by the death of so many of their best men, by having to leave their land untilled, by food shortages and by the length of the war, which had turned out to be unexpectedly long.

340 Πομπήιον. ὁ δ᾽ ἐς μὲν τὸ φανερὸν ἐκέλευεν αὐτοὺς
Ῥωμαίοις ἐπιτρέπειν (οὐ γὰρ εἰδέναι συνθήκας ἑτέρας
Ῥωμαίων ἀξίας), λάθρᾳ δ᾽ ὑπισχνεῖτο, ἃ ἔμελλεν
341 ποιήσειν. καὶ συνθεμένων ἐκείνων καὶ ἐπιτρεψάντων
ἑαυτοὺς ὅμηρά τε καὶ αἰχμάλωτα ᾔτησε καὶ τοὺς
αὐτομόλους καὶ πάντα ἔλαβεν. ᾔτησε δὲ καὶ ἀργυρίου
τάλαντα τριάκοντα· ὧν μέρος αὐτίκα ἔδοσαν οἱ Νο-
342 μαντῖνοι, καὶ τὰ λοιπὰ ὁ Πομπήιος ἀνέμενεν. παρα-
γενομένου δ᾽ αὐτῷ διαδόχου Μάρκου Ποπιλίου Λαίνα,
οἱ μὲν ἔφερον τὰ λοιπὰ τῶν χρημάτων, ὁ δ᾽, ἀπηλ-
λαγμένος μὲν τοῦ περὶ τοῦ πολέμου δέους τῷ παρεῖ-
ναι τὸν διάδοχον, τὰς δὲ συνθήκας εἰδὼς αἰσχράς τε
καὶ ἄνευ Ῥωμαίων γενομένας, ἠρνεῖτο μὴ συνθέσθαι
343 τοῖς Νομαντίνοις. καὶ οἱ μὲν αὐτὸν ἤλεγχον ἐπὶ μάρ-
τυσι τοῖς τότε παρατυχοῦσιν ἀπό τε βουλῆς καὶ
ἱππάρχοις καὶ χιλιάρχοις αὐτοῦ Πομπηίου, ὁ δὲ
Ποπίλιος αὐτοὺς ἐς Ῥώμην ἔπεμπε δικασομένους τῷ
344 Πομπηίῳ. κρίσεως δ᾽ ἐν τῇ βουλῇ γενομένης Νομαντῖνοι μὲν καὶ Πομπήιος ἐς ἀντιλογίαν ἦλθον, τῇ
345 βουλῇ δ᾽ ἔδοξε πολεμεῖν Νομαντίνοις. καὶ ὁ Ποπίλιος
ἐνέβαλεν ἐς τοὺς γείτονας αὐτῶν Λούσονας, οὐδὲν δ᾽
ἐργασάμενος (ἧκε γὰρ αὐτῷ διάδοχος ἐπὶ τὴν στρατηγίαν Ὁστίλιος Μαγκῖνος) ἀνέζευξεν ἐς Ῥώμην.
346 80. Ὁ δὲ Μαγκῖνος τοῖς Νομαντίνοις συμβαλὼν
ἡττᾶτό τε πολλάκις καὶ τέλος ἀναιρουμένων πολλῶν
ἐς τὸ στρατόπεδον ἔφυγεν. λόγου δὲ ψευδοῦς ἐμπεσόν-

---

[73] Marcus Popillius Laenas was consul in 139, succeeding
Pompeius as governor of Nearer Spain in that year.

In public, Pompeius ordered them to surrender to Rome   340
(for he knew there were no other terms acceptable to
Rome), but in private he made promises about his inten-
tions. When the Numantines agreed and surrendered un-   341
conditionally, Pompeius demanded that they hand over
hostages and return Roman prisoners and deserters. He
got agreement on all points. He also demanded thirty talents of silver. Part of this they paid immediately, and Pompeius waited for the rest. When his successor, Marcus   342
Popillius Laenas, arrived, they paid the rest of the money.[73]
Freed now, however, by his successor's presence from any
fears about the outcome of the war, and aware that the
agreement he had reached was a disgrace and made without authority from Rome, he began to deny that he had
made any agreement with the Numantines. They refuted   343
this on the testimony of witnesses who were there at the
time, the members of the senate and Pompeius' own cavalry commanders and military tribunes. Popillius sent
them to Rome to argue their case with Pompeius. The   344
judgment took place in the Senate where the Numantines
and Pompeius set out their opposing arguments. The Senate decided on war with Numantia. So Popillius attacked   345
the Lusones, neighbors of Numantia, but achieved nothing—Hostilius Mancinus, his successor in the command
had arrived—and returned to Rome.[74]

80. In his engagements with the Numantines, Manci-   346
nus was repeatedly defeated and after suffering heavy
casualties, fled to his camp. Taking fright at a false rumor

[74] Gaius Hostilius Mancinus was consul in 137 with Marcus
Aemilus Lepidus, who replaced him after the treaty he made with
Numantia.

τος, ὅτι Νομαντίνοις ἔρχονται βοηθοῦντες Κάνταβροί
τε καὶ Οὐακκαῖοι, δείσας ἄπυρον τὴν νύκτα διήγαγεν
ὅλην ἐν σκότῳ, φεύγων ἐς ἔρημον τὸ Νωβελίωνός

347 ποτε χαράκωμα. καὶ μεθ᾽ ἡμέραν ἐς αὐτὸ συγκλει-
σθείς, οὔτε κατεσκευασμένον οὔτε ὠχυρωμένον, περι-
εχόντων αὐτὸν τῶν Νομαντίνων καὶ πάντας ἀποκτε-
νεῖν ἀπειλούντων, εἰ μὴ συνθοῖτο εἰρήνην, συνέθετο

348 ἐπὶ ἴσῃ καὶ ὁμοίᾳ Ῥωμαίοις καὶ Νομαντίνοις. καὶ ὁ
μὲν ἐπὶ τούτοις ὤμνυε τοῖς Νομαντίνοις, οἱ δ᾽ ἐν ἄστει
πυθόμενοι χαλεπῶς ἔφερον ὡς ἐπὶ αἰσχίσταις πάνυ
σπονδαῖς καὶ τὸν ἕτερον τῶν ὑπάτων Αἰμίλιον Λέπι-
δον ἐς Ἰβηρίαν ἐξέπεμπον, Μαγκῖνον δ᾽ ἀνεκάλουν ἐς

349 κρίσιν. καὶ τῷδε μὲν ἕσποντο πρέσβεις Νομαντίνων·
ὁ δ᾽ Αἰμίλιος, ἀναμένων καὶ ὅδε τὰς ἐκ Ῥώμης ἀποκρίσεις καὶ τὴν ἀργίαν οὐ φέρων (ὡς γὰρ ἐπὶ δόξαν
ἢ κέρδος ἢ θριάμβου φιλοτιμίαν ἐξῄεσάν τινες ἐς τὰς
στρατηγίας, οὐκ ἐπὶ τὸ τῇ πόλει συμφέρον), Οὐακ-

350 καίων κατεψεύδετο ὡς ἀγορὰν ἐν τῷδε τῷ πολέμῳ
Νομαντίνοις παρασχόντων. καὶ τὴν γῆν αὐτῶν κατ-
έτρεχεν Παλλαντίαν τε πόλιν, ἣ μεγίστη Οὐακκαίων
ἐστίν, οὐδὲν ἐξαμαρτοῦσαν ἐς τὰ συγκείμενα, ἐπολιόρκει καὶ Βροῦτον, ἐφ᾽ ἕτερα τῆς Ἰβηρίας ἀπεσταλ-
μένον, ὥς μοι προείρηται, κηδεστὴν ὄντα οἱ, τοῦδε
τοῦ ἔργου μετασχεῖν ἔπεισεν.

351   81. Κατέλαβον δ᾽ αὐτοὺς ἀπὸ Ῥώμης πρέσβεις
Κίννας τε καὶ Καικίλιος, οἳ τὴν βουλὴν ἔφασαν ἀπο-

---

75 For Quintus Fulvius Nobilior, see above, 45.184.

circulating that the Cantabri and Vaccaei were coming to the assistance of Numantia, he retreated to a remote spot where Nobilior once had a palisade, and spent a whole night in darkness without camp fires.[75] Dawn revealed   347 him to be cut off here, and without equipment, unprotected and surrounded by the Numantines, who threatened to kill all his men if he did not make peace; he agreed on terms of complete equality between Rome and Numantia. Although for his part he swore an oath to the   348 Numantines on these terms, at Rome they took the news badly, regarding the treaty as quite the most shameful, dispatching the other consul, Aemilius Lepidus, to Iberia, and summoning Mancinus to Rome for trial. Ambassadors   349 from Numantia followed him there. As for Aemilius, he too had to wait for the decision from Rome, and grew impatient with his forced inactivity. For some men went out to these Iberian commands for glory or gain or ambitious for a triumph, rather than for the good of Rome. So Aemilius falsely accused the Vaccaei of sending provisions to Numantia during this war. He overran their territory,   350 and began to besiege their largest town, Pallantia, which had done nothing to break the terms of their agreement; and he persuaded Brutus, who was related to him by marriage, to share in the enterprise. As I explained before, Brutus had been sent to Farther Iberia.[76]

81. Envoys from Rome, however, Cinna and Caeci-   351 lius,[77] intercepted them, and expressed the senate's puz-

---

[76] See above, 71.301.   [77] Perhaps L. Cornelius Cinna (consul 125). It is not known which Caecilius is referred to, perhaps one of the four sons of Q. Caecilius Metellus Macedonicus: Baliaricus (consul 123), was proconsul in Spain.

ρεῖν, εἰ τοσῶνδε πταισμάτων σφίσιν ἐν Ἰβηρίᾳ γενομένων ὁ Αἰμίλιος πόλεμον ἕτερον ἀρεῖται, καὶ ψήφισμα ἐπέδοσαν αὐτῷ προαγορεῦον Αἰμίλιον Οὐακκαίοις
352 μὴ πολεμεῖν. ὁ δὲ ἀρξάμενός τε ἤδη τοῦ πολέμου καὶ
τὴν βουλὴν τοῦτ᾽ ἀγνοεῖν ἡγούμενος, ἀγνοεῖν δ᾽, ὅτι
καὶ Βροῦτος αὐτῷ συνεπιλαμβάνει καὶ σῖτον καὶ
χρήματα καὶ στρατιὰν Οὐακκαῖοι τοῖς Νομαντίνοις
παρέσχον, ἔσεσθαι δὲ καὶ τὴν ἀνάζευξιν τοῦ πολέμου
φοβερὰν ὑπολαβὼν καὶ σχεδὸν Ἰβηρίας ὅλης διάλυ-
σιν, εἰ καταφρονήσειαν ὡς δεδιότων, τοὺς μὲν ἀμφὶ
τὸν Κίνναν ἀπράκτους ἀπέλυσεν καὶ τάδε αὐτὰ ἐπέστειλε τῇ βουλῇ, αὐτὸς δ᾽ ὀχυρωσάμενος φρούριον
μηχανὰς ἐν αὐτῷ συνεπήγνυτο καὶ σῖτον συνέφερε.
353 Φλάκκος δ᾽ αὐτῷ σιτολογῶν, ἐνέδρας ἐκφανείσης,
εὐμηχάνως διέδωκεν, ὅτι Παλλαντίαν ἐξεῖλεν Αἰμίλιος·
καὶ τοῦ στρατοῦ συναλαλάξαντος ὡς ἐπὶ νίκῃ, πυθόμενοι τούτων οἱ βάρβαροι καὶ ἀληθῆ νομίσαντες ἀπ-
εχώρουν.

354   82. Φλάκκος μὲν δὴ τὴν ἀγορὰν κινδυνεύουσαν ὧδε
περιέσωζε, μακρᾶς δὲ τῆς ἐπὶ τῇ Παλλαντίᾳ πολιορκίας οὔσης αἱ τροφαὶ Ῥωμαίους ἐπέλειπον, καὶ λιμὸς
ἥπτετο αὐτῶν, καὶ τὰ ὑποζύγια πάντα ἔφθαρτο, καὶ
355 πολλοὶ τῶν ἀνθρώπων ἐξ ἀπορίας ἀπέθνησκον. οἱ
στρατηγοὶ δέ, Αἰμίλιός τε καὶ Βροῦτος, ἐς μὲν πολὺ
διεκαρτέρουν, ἡσσώμενοι δ᾽ ὑπὸ τοῦ κακοῦ νυκτὸς
ἄφνω περὶ ἐσχάτην φυλακὴν ἐκέλευον ἀναζευγνύναι·
χιλίαρχοί τε καὶ λοχαγοὶ περιθέοντες ἐπέσπευδον
356 ἅπαντας ἐς τοῦτο πρὸ ἕω. οἱ δὲ σὺν θορύβῳ τά τε

zlement that Aemilius was stirring up another war, when
there had been such a succession of disasters in Iberia, and
they handed him a decree forbidding him to make war on
the Vaccaei. In fact he had already begun the war, but he   352
thought that the senate did not know this, and that they
were also unaware that Brutus was colluding with him in
the matter, or that the Vaccaei had been supplying food,
money and manpower to Numantia. He reasoned that the
abandonment of the war would be dangerous and would
involve the secession of virtually the whole of Iberia,
should the Romans be treated with contempt as cowards,
and so he dismissed Cinna's delegation, who failed to complete their mission, and wrote to the senate setting out
these very arguments. He himself fortified a stronghold,
and began to assemble artillery in it and collect provisions.
Flaccus went out on a foraging expedition for him and was   353
ambushed, but cleverly spread word that Aemilius had
captured Pallantia. His troops cheered as if there had been
a victory, and when the barbarians heard this they thought
it was true and retreated.

82. This was how Flaccus saved his foraging mission   354
when it ran into danger. With the siege of Pallantia taking
a long time, Roman supplies began to run short and hunger affected them: all the pack animals perished, and
many of the men died from lack of food. The generals,   355
Aemilius and Brutus, persevered for a long time, but,
overwhelmed by the grim situation, suddenly one night,
about the last watch, ordered a retreat. Tribunes and centurions ran around urging everyone to apply themselves
to the task before dawn. In the confusion the Romans   356

271

ἄλλα πάντα καὶ τοὺς τραυματίας καὶ τοὺς νοσοῦντας
ἀπέλιπον, συμπλεκομένους τε σφίσι καὶ δεομένους.
καὶ αὐτοῖς ἀτάκτου καὶ θορυβώδους τῆς ἀναχωρή-
σεως γιγνομένης καὶ φυγῇ μάλιστα ὁμοίας οἱ Παλλάντιοι πανταχόθεν ἐπικείμενοι πολλὰ ἔβλαπτον ἐξ
357 ἠοῦς ἐπὶ ἑσπέραν. νυκτὸς δ' ἐπιλαβούσης Ῥωμαῖοι
μὲν ἐς τὰ πεδία ἑαυτοὺς ἐρρίπτουν ἀνὰ μέρος, ὡς τύ-
χοιεν, ἄσιτοί τε καὶ κατάκοποι, οἱ δὲ Παλλάντιοι θεοῦ
σφᾶς ἀποτρέποντος ἀνεχώρουν.

358 83. Καὶ τάδε μὲν ἦν περὶ τὸν Αἰμίλιον, Ῥωμαῖοι δ'
αὐτὰ πυθόμενοι τὸν μὲν Αἰμίλιον παρέλυσαν τῆς
στρατηγίας τε καὶ ὑπατείας, καὶ ἰδιώτης ἐς Ῥώμην
359 ὑπέστρεφεν καὶ χρήμασιν ἐπεζημιοῦτο· Μαγκίνῳ δ'
ἐδίκαζον καὶ τοῖς πρέσβεσι τοῖς Νομαντίνων. οἱ μὲν
δὴ τὰς συνθήκας, ἃς ἐπεποίηντο πρὸς Μαγκίνον,
ἐπεδείκνυον· ὁ δὲ τὴν αἰτίαν αὐτῶν ἐς Πομπήιον ἀνέ-
φερεν, τὸν πρὸ αὐτοῦ γενόμενον στρατηγόν, ὡς ἀρ-
γὸν καὶ ἄπορον τὸν στρατὸν ἐγχειρίσαντά οἱ καὶ δι'
αὐτὸ κἀκεῖνον ἡσσημένον τε πολλάκις καὶ συνθήκας
ὁμοίας αὑτῷ θέμενον πρὸς τοὺς Νομαντίνους· ὅθεν
ἔφη καὶ τὸν πόλεμον τόνδε, παρὰ τὰς συνθήκας ἐκείνας ὑπὸ Ῥωμαίων ἐψηφισμένον, ἀπαίσιον αὐτοῖς γε-
360 γονέναι. οἱ δ' ἐχαλέπαινον μὲν ἀμφοτέροις ὁμοίως,
ἀπέφυγε δ' ὅμως Πομπήιος ὡς περὶ τῶνδε κριθεὶς καὶ
πάλαι. Μαγκίνον δ' ἔγνωσαν ἐκδοῦναι τοῖς Νομαντί-

---

[78] Appian is unlikely to be right about the removal of Lepidus
from the consulship. Lepidus can hardly have got to Spain until

abandoned everything, including the sick and wounded, who clung to them and begged not to be left. The withdrawal was disorganized and chaotic, very like a flight, with the forces of Pallantia pressing from all directions and inflicting heavy casualties from dawn to dusk. At the 357 onset of night, unfed and exhausted, the Romans threw themselves on the ground in groups wherever they happened to be; some god turned the Pallantii back, and they withdraw.

83. This is what happened to Aemilius. When they 358 heard the news in Rome, they relieved Aemilius of his command and of the consulship,[78] and he returned as a private citizen to the city, where a fine was imposed on him. The dispute between Mancinus and the Numantine ambassadors was still under judicial review. In evidence, 359 the ambassadors presented the treaty they had made with Mancinus, while he tried to lay the responsibility for the treaty on Pompeius, his predecessor in the command, who, he maintained, had handed him a lazy and poorly supplied army, which also explained his many defeats and the similar agreement he had made with Numantia. As a result, he said, they had conducted this war too in unpropitious circumstances, since the Romans had voted for it in violation of these agreements. The senate was equally 360 angry with both of them, but Pompeius was acquitted on the grounds that he had already been tried on these charges beforehand. Mancinus, however, had made a dishonorable agreement without the authority of the senate,

late in his consulship, and the events Appian describes probably belong in the following year, 136, when Lepidus was, as Livy says (*Per.* 56), proconsul.

APPIAN

νοις, ἄνευ σφῶν αἰσχρὰς συνθήκας πεποιημένον, ᾧ
λόγῳ καὶ Σαυνίταις οἱ πατέρες, ὅμοια χωρὶς αὐτῶν
361 συνθεμένους, ἡγεμόνας εἴκοσιν ἐξεδεδώκεσαν. Μαγκῖνον μὲν δὴ Φούριος ἀγαγὼν εἰς Ἰβηρίαν γυμνὸν παρ-
362 εδίδου τοῖς Νομαντίνοις· οἱ δ' οὐκ ἐδέξαντο. στρατηγὸς δ' ἐπ' αὐτοὺς αἱρεθεὶς Καλπούρνιος Πείσων οὐδ'
ἤλασεν ἐπὶ Νομαντίαν, ἀλλ' ἐς τὴν Παλλαντίων γῆν
ἐσβαλὼν καὶ μικρὰ δῃώσας ἐχείμαζεν ἐν Καρπητα-
νίᾳ τὸ ἐπίλοιπον τῆς ἀρχῆς.
363   84. Ἐν δὲ Ῥώμῃ κάμνων ὁ δῆμος ἐπὶ τοῖς Νομαντίνοις, μακροῦ καὶ δυσχεροῦς τοῦ πολέμου σφίσι
παρὰ προσδοκίαν γεγονότος, ᾑροῦντο Κορνήλιον
Σκιπίωνα, τὸν Καρχηδόνα ἑλόντα, αὖθις ὑπατεύειν,
364 ὡς μόνον ἐπικρατῆσαι τῶν Νομαντίνων δυνάμενον. ὁ
δὲ καὶ τότε ἦν ἔτι νεώτερος τῆς νενομισμένης τοῖς
ὑπατεύουσιν ἡλικίας· ἡ οὖν βουλὴ πάλιν, ὥσπερ ἐπὶ
Καρχηδονίοις αὐτοῦ χειροτονουμένου [Σκιπίωνος],[37]
ἐψηφίσατο τοὺς δημάρχους λῦσαι τὸν περὶ τῆς ἡλι-
365 κίας νόμον καὶ τοῦ ἐπίοντος ἔτους αὖθις θέσθαι. οὕτω
μὲν ὁ Σκιπίων αὖθις ὑπατεύων ἐς Νομαντίαν ἠπεί-

[37] Σκιπίωνος del. Nipperdey

[79] After the Battle of the Caudine Forks in 321, in which a
Roman army was forced into a humiliating surrender, those who
had sponsored the agreement were handed over to the Samnites.
Appian (*Sam.* 4) recounts the battle, but his text breaks off before
the end of the account. Livy 9.2–6 has the full story.

[80] L. Furius Philus, consul 136. Mancinus returned to Rome

and they decided to hand him over to the Numantines, in line with the precedent set by the fathers when they had surrendered to the Samnites twenty leaders who had made a similar agreement without senatorial authority.[79] But when Furius brought Mancinus to Iberia and delivered him naked to the Numantines, they refused to take him.[80] Calpurnius Piso was then appointed commander against them, but he did not even march against Numantia, instead invading the territory of Pallantia, were he did some minor damage and then wintered in Carpetania for the rest of his command.[81]

361
362

84. At Rome the people were growing tired of Numantia. The war had turned out unexpectedly long and difficult, and so they decided to reelect to the consulship Cornelius Scipio, who had captured Carthage, as being the only person capable of conquering Numantia. At the time he was still under the required age for election to the consulship, so the Senate voted, as they had done when Scipio was chosen consul to take command against Carthage, to get the tribunes to repeal the law about the age limit, and reenact it the following year.[82] This was how Scipio was elected to the consulship for a second time and hurried off to Numantia. He did not take an army from

363
364
365

and was readmitted to the citizenship, rising to the rank of praetor.   [81] Q. Calpurnius Piso, consul 135.

[82] P. Cornelius Scipio Aemilianus was born in 185/4 and was thus under the required age (forty-two) when elected consul for 147. Appian has confused this suspension of the law with the one needed in 134, when Scipio was clearly old enough, but had now already been consul: in this period you were not supposed to hold the consulship twice.

γετο, στρατιὰν δ᾽ ἐκ καταλόγου μὲν οὐκ ἔλαβεν, πολλῶν τε πολέμων ὄντων καὶ πολλῶν ἀνδρῶν ἐν Ἰβηρίᾳ, ἐθελοντὰς δέ τινας, ἔκ τε πόλεων καὶ βασιλέων
ἐς χάριν ἰδίαν πεμφθέντας αὐτῷ, συγχωρούσης τῆς
βουλῆς, ἐπηγάγετο καὶ πελάτας ἐκ Ῥώμης καὶ φίλους
πεντακοσίους, οὓς ἐς ἴλην καταλέξας ἐκάλει φίλων
366   ἴλην. πάντας δὲ ἐς τετρακισχιλίους γενομένους παραδοὺς ἄγειν ἀδελφιδῷ Βουτεῶνι σὺν ὀλίγοις αὐτὸς
προεξώρμησεν ἐς Ἰβηρίαν ἐπὶ τὸ στρατόπεδον, πυνθανόμενος αὐτὸ γέμειν ἀργίας καὶ στάσεων καὶ τρυφῆς, εὖ εἰδώς, ὅτι μὴ κρατήσει πολεμίων, πρὶν κατασχεῖν τῶν ἰδίων ἐγκρατῶς.

367   85. Ἐλθὼν δὲ ἐμπόρους τε πάντας ἐξήλαυνε καὶ
ἑταίρας καὶ μάντεις καὶ θύτας, οἷς διὰ τὰς δυσπρα-
ξίας οἱ στρατιῶται περιδεεῖς γεγονότες ἐχρῶντο συν-
εχῶς· ἔς τε τὸ μέλλον ἀπεῖπε μηδὲν ἐσφέρεσθαι τῶν
περισσῶν, μηδὲ ἱερεῖον ἐς μαντείαν πεπιασμένον.[38]
368   ἐκέλευσεν δὲ καὶ τὰς ἁμάξας καὶ τὰ περισσὰ τῶν ἐς
αὐτὰς τιθεμένων καὶ τὰ ὑποζύγια, χωρὶς ὧν αὐτὸς
ὑπελείπετο, πραθῆναι. καὶ σκεῦος οὐκ ἐξῆν ἐς δίαιταν
ἔχειν οὐδενὶ πλὴν ὀβελοῦ καὶ χύτρας χαλκῆς καὶ ἐκ-
πώματος ἑνός. τά τε σιτία αὐτοῖς ὥριστο κρέα ζεστὰ
369   καὶ ὀπτὰ εἶναι. κλίνας τε ἀπεῖπεν ἔχειν καὶ πρῶτος
ἐπὶ στιβάδων ἀνεπαύετο. ἀπεῖπεν δὲ καὶ ὁδεύοντας
ἡμιόνοις ἐπικαθέζεσθαι· "Τί γὰρ ἐν πολέμῳ προσ-
δοκᾶν," ἔφη, "Παρ᾽ ἀνδρὸς οὐδὲ βαδίζειν δυναμένου;"

[38] πεπιασμένον Goukowsky: πεποιημένον codd.

276

the service register, as there were many military actions under way at the time and plenty of troops in Iberia.[83] Instead, with the permission of the senate, he brought volunteers sent to him by towns and kings as a personal favor, and in addition five hundred clients and associates from Rome whom he enrolled in what he called the company of friends. All of these—there were about four thousand of them—he gave to his nephew Buteo to bring, while he himself went ahead with a small force to join the army in Iberia. He discovered that it was idle, riven by disagreements and leading a pampered life, and he was well aware that he would not be able to defeat the enemy until he brought his own men under firm control.

85. So when he arrived, he got rid of all merchants and female camp followers—prophets and diviners too, whom the soldiers, grown timid by their lack of success, were constantly consulting. He gave orders that in future nothing superfluous was to be brought into camp, not even an animal fattened for sacrificial divination. He also ordered the wagons, their unnecessary contents, and the draft animals to be sold, apart from those he retained himself. The only cooking utencils anyone was allowed to have were a spit, a bronze pot and a single cup. Food was limited to boiled and roast meat. He refused to let them have beds, and Scipio was the first to sleep on straw. He forbade those on the march to ride on mules. "For when you are at war," he said, "what can you expect from a man who

366

367

368

369

---

[83] The only other major war going on at the time was the First Slave War in Sicily, from 135 to 132 (Livy, *Per.* 56), but there was also fighting in Thrace, where the praetor, M. Cosconius, won victories against the Scordisci (Livy, *Per.* 56).

κἄν τοῖς ἀλείμμασι καὶ λουτροῖς ἑαυτοὺς ἤλειφον,
ἐπισκώπτοντος τοῦ Σκιπίωνος, ὡς αἱ ἡμίονοι, χεῖρας
370 οὐκ ἔχουσαι, χρῄζουσι τριβόντων. οὕτω μὲν αὐτοὺς
ἐς σωφροσύνην μετέβαλλεν ἀθρόως, εἴθιζεν δὲ καὶ ἐς
αἰδῶ καὶ φόβον, δυσπρόσιτος ὢν καὶ δυσχερὴς ἐς
371 τὰς χάριτας, καὶ μάλιστα τὰς παρανόμους. ἔλεγέν
τε πολλάκις τοὺς μὲν αὐστηροὺς καὶ ἐννόμους τῶν
στρατηγῶν τοῖς οἰκείοις, τοὺς δὲ εὐχερεῖς καὶ φιλο-
δώρους τοῖς πολεμίοις εἶναι χρησίμους· τὰ γὰρ στρατόπεδα τοῖς μὲν εἶναι κεχαρμένα τε καὶ καταφρονη-
τικά, τοῖς δὲ σκυθρωπὰ μέν, εὐπειθῆ δὲ καὶ πᾶσιν
ἕτοιμα.

372   86. Οὐ μὴν οὐδ᾽ ὡς ἐτόλμα πολεμεῖν, πρὶν αὐτοὺς
γυμνάσαι πόνοις πολλοῖς. τὰ οὖν ἀγχοτάτω πεδία
πάντα περιιὼν ἑκάστης ἡμέρας ἄλλο μετ᾽ ἄλλο στρατόπεδον ἤγειρέ τε καὶ καθῄρει καὶ τάφρους ὤρυσσε
βαθυτάτας καὶ ἐνεπίμπλη τείχη τε μεγάλα ᾠκοδόμει
καὶ κατέφερεν, αὐτὸς ἐξ ἠοῦς ἐς ἑσπέραν ἅπαντα
373 ἐφορῶν. τὰς δὲ ὁδοιπορίας, ἵνα μή τις ὡς πάλαι δια-
σκιδνῷτο, ἦγεν ἐν πλινθίοις ἀεί, καὶ τὴν δεδομένην
ἑκάστῳ τάξιν οὐκ ἦν ἐναλλάξαι. περιιών τε τὴν ὁδοι-
πορίαν καὶ τὰ πολλὰ οὐραγῶν τοὺς μὲν ἀρρωστοῦντας ἐπὶ τοὺς ἵππους ἀνεβίβαζεν ἀντὶ τῶν ἱππέων, τὰ
δὲ βαροῦντα τὰς ἡμιόνους ἐς τοὺς πεζοὺς διεμέριζεν.
374 εἰ δὲ σταθμεύοι, τοὺς μὲν προφύλακας τῆς ἡμέρας ἐκ
τῆς ὁδοιπορίας ἔδει περὶ τὸν χάρακα ἵστασθαι καὶ
ἱππέων ἑτέραν ἴλην περιτρέχειν· οἱ δ᾽ ἄλλοι τὰ ἔργα
διῄρηντο, καὶ τοῖς μὲν ταφρεύειν ἐτέτακτο, τοῖς δὲ

cannot even walk?" Oiling and bathing they began to do
for themselves: only mules, Scipio quipped, having no
hands, need someone else to rub them. In this way he   370
completely restored them to a state of discipline, and accustomed them to respect and fear him by making himself
inaccessible and ill disposed to requests for favors, especially if they involved a breach of regulations. He often   371
used to say that generals who are strict and stick to the
rules are useful to their own side, while those who are
affable and generous are useful to the enemy; in the latter
case, the troops are happy but disrespectful, in the former
they are sullen but obedient and ready for anything.

86. In spite of this, he still did not dare to engage the   372
enemy until he had put his men through rigorous training.
So, every day he ranged over all the plains in the vicinity,
setting up one camp after another and then taking them
down, digging the deepest ditches and filling them in
again, building high walls and knocking them down. And
from dawn till dusk, he oversaw the whole operation himself. To prevent anyone becoming detached while on the   373
march, as formerly happened, he always had the army
move in squares and everyone was required to stay in the
rank assigned to them. He also took up different positions
in the line of march, often at the rear, where he would
mount the sick on the horses instead of the cavalrymen,
and distribute what the mules were carrying among the
infantry. When making camp, he required those who had   374
been the advanced guard on the march during the day to
take up position around the palisade, and sent another
squadron of cavalry out scouting. The rest were assigned
their various tasks, some ordered to dig the trenches, others to build the walls and others to pitch the tents. He set

τειχίζειν, τοῖς δὲ σκηνοποιεῖν, χρόνου τε μῆκος ὡρίζετο αὐτοῖς καὶ διεμετρεῖτο.

375   87. Ὅτε δ᾽ εἴκασεν ὀξὺ καὶ εὐπειθὲς αὐτῷ καὶ φερέπονον γεγονέναι τὸ στράτευμα, μετέβαινεν ἀγχοῦ τῶν Νομαντίνων. προφυλακὰς δέ, ὥσπερ τινές, ἐπὶ φρουρίων οὐκ ἐποιεῖτο· οὐδὲ διῄρει ποι τὸν στρατὸν ὅλως, τοῦ μή τινος ἐν ἀρχῇ γενομένου πταίσματος εὐκαταφρόνητον τοῖς πολεμίοις αὐτὸν γενέσθαι, καὶ
376 τέως καταφρονοῦσιν. οὐδ᾽ ἐπεχείρει τοῖς ἐχθροῖς, ἔτι περισκοπῶν αὐτόν τε τὸν πόλεμον καὶ τὸν καιρὸν αὐτοῦ καὶ τὴν τῶν Νομαντίνων ὁρμήν, ἐς ὅ τι τρέψοιντο. τὰ δ᾽ ὀπίσω τοῦ στρατοπέδου πάντα ἐχορτολόγει
377 καὶ τὸν σῖτον ἔκειρεν ἔτι χλωρόν. ὡς δὲ αὐτῷ ταῦτα ἐξετεθέριστο καὶ ἐς τὸ πρόσθεν ἔδει βαδίζειν, ὁδὸς μὲν ἦν παρὰ τὴν Νομαντίαν ἐπὶ τὰ πεδία σύντομος, καὶ πολλοὶ συνεβούλευον ἐς αὐτὴν τραπέσθαι. ὁ δ᾽ ἔφη τὴν ἐπάνοδον δεδιέναι, κούφων μὲν τότε τῶν πολεμίων ὄντων, καὶ ἐκ πόλεως ὁρμωμένων καὶ ἐς πόλιν
378 ἀφορμώντων· "Οἱ δ᾽ ἡμέτεροι βαρεῖς ἐπανίασιν ὡς ἀπὸ σιτολογίας καὶ κατάκοποι καὶ κτήνη καὶ ἁμάξας καὶ φορτία ἄγουσιν. δυσχερής τε ὅλως καὶ ἀνόμοιος ὁ ἀγών· ἡσσωμένοις μὲν γὰρ πολὺς ὁ κίνδυνος, νι-
379 κῶσι δὲ οὐ μέγα τὸ ἔργον οὐδὲ ἐπικερδές." εἶναι δ᾽ ἄλογον κινδυνεύειν ἐπὶ ὀλίγοις καὶ στρατηγὸν ἀμελῆ τὸν ἀγωνιζόμενον πρὸ τῆς χρείας, ἀγαθὸν δὲ τὸν ἐν μόναις παρακινδυνεύοντα ταῖς ἀνάγκαις. συγκρίνων δ᾽ ἔφη καὶ τοὺς ἰατροὺς μὴ χρῆσθαι τομαῖς μηδὲ καύ-
380 σεσι πρὸ φαρμάκων. ταῦτ᾽ εἰπὼν ἐκέλευεν τοῖς ἡγεμό-

a time limit for them, and measured how long they were taking.

87. When he thought the army had become sharp, obe- 375
dient to his orders and ready for work, he moved camp near to Numantia. He did not station advanced guards in guard posts, as some commanders do; indeed, he did not divide his army at all, as he was afraid of meeting with a reverse right at the beginning and making himself con- temptible to an enemy who already despised him. Nor did 376 he take the offensive against the enemy, as he was still considering carefully the nature of the war itself, waiting for its decisive moment and assessing the direction of the Numantine attack. To the rear of his camp he foraged ev- erywhere and cut the grain when it was still unripe. When 377 he had exhausted all the available supplies there and was forced to advance, many advised him to take the shortcut that led past Numantia into the plains, but he said it was the return journey he feared. The Numantines would be carrying nothing heavy at that time and would have the city to use as a base for attack and retreat. "Our troops, on 378 the other hand, will be returning heavily burdened and tired from their foraging expedition, leading animals, wag- ons, and crops. It would be an uneven and difficult con- test. Defeat would pose great danger, while victory would be neither a fine achievement nor particularly valuable." He said it did not make sense to take risks for insignificant 379 results, and it was a careless commander who resorted to fighting before he needed to: a good general only took risks when he was forced to. He drew a comparison with doctors who, he said, only cauterize or conduct surgery when they have first tried drugs. After this speech, he 380

281

σιν τὴν μακροτέραν περιάγειν. καὶ συνεξῄει τότε μὲν
ἐς τὸ πέραν τοῦ στρατοπέδου, ὕστερον δ' ἐς τὰ Οὐακκαίων, ὅθεν οἱ Νομαντῖνοι τὰς τροφὰς ἐωνοῦντο,
κείρων ἅπαντα καὶ τὰ χρήσιμα ἐς τὰς ἑαυτοῦ τροφὰς
συλλέγων, τὰ δὲ περιττὰ σωρεύων τε καὶ κατακαίων.

381   88. Ἐν δέ τινι πεδίῳ τῆς Παλλαντίας, ὄνομα Κο-
πλανίῳ, πολλοὺς ἐπὶ τῶν ὁρῶν ὑπὸ λόφοις ἔκρυψαν
οἱ Παλλάντιοι καὶ ἑτέροις ἐς τὸ φανερὸν τοὺς σιτολο-
382   γοῦντας ἠνώχλουν. ὁ δὲ Ῥουτίλιον Ῥοῦφον, συγγραφέα τῶνδε τῶν ἔργων, τότε χιλιαρχοῦντα, ἐκέλευσε
τέσσαρας ἱππέων ἴλας λαβόντα ἀναστεῖλαι τοὺς
ἐνοχλοῦντας. Ῥοῦφος μὲν οὖν ὑποχωροῦσιν αὐτοῖς
ἀμέτρως εἵπετο καὶ φεύγουσιν ἐς τὸν λόφον συνανε-
πήδα, ἔνθα τῆς ἐνέδρας ἐκφανείσης ἐκέλευε τοὺς
ἱππέας μήτε διώκειν μήτε ἐπιχειρεῖν ἔτι, ἀλλ' ἐν προ-
βολῇ τὰ δόρατα θεμένους ἑστάναι καὶ ἐπιόντας ἀμύ-
383   νεσθαι μόνον. ὁ δὲ Σκιπίων εὐθὺ ἀνατρέχοντος αὐτοῦ
παρὰ τὸ πρόσταγμα δείσας εἵπετο κατὰ σπουδὴν καί,
ὡς εὗρε τὴν ἐνέδραν, ἐς δύο διεῖλε τοὺς ἱππέας καὶ
προσέταξεν αὐτῶν ἑκατέροις παρὰ μέρος ἐμπηδᾶν
τοῖς πολεμίοις καὶ ἀκοντίσαντας ὁμοῦ πάντας εὐθὺς
ἀναχωρεῖν, οὐκ ἐς τὸν αὐτὸν τόπον, ἀλλ' αἰεὶ κατ'
384   ὀλίγον προστιθέντας ὀπίσω καὶ ὑποχωροῦντας. οὕτω
μὲν τοὺς ἱππέας ἐς τὸ πεδίον περιέσωσεν· ἀναζευ-
γνύοντι δ' αὐτῷ καὶ ἀναχωροῦντι ποταμὸς ἦν ἐν μέσῳ
δύσπορός τε καὶ ἰλυώδης, καὶ παρ' αὐτὸν ἐνήδρευον
385   οἱ πολέμιοι. ὁ δὲ μαθὼν ἐξέκλινε τῆς ὁδοῦ καὶ μακρο-

ordered his officers to march around by the longer route. He joined them then as they moved beyond the camp, and also later when they invaded the land of the Vaccaei, from whom the Numantines bought their supplies: here he cut all crops, collecting what was useful for his own food supplies, and piling up and burning anything superfluous.

88. In a plain in Pallantia, called Complanium, the Pallantii hid many of their men on the hills below the ridges and used others to harry the foragers openly. For his part, Scipio ordered Rutilius Rufus, who wrote a history of these events, but was at the time a military tribune, to take four squadrons of cavalry and repel those harrying his men.[84] He pursued the enemy as they withdrew in disorder, and chased them closely as they ran up the hill. Here, when the ambush was revealed, Rufus ordered his cavalry not to pursue or attack further, but with spears extended, to hold their position and merely fight off the attackers. As soon as Rutilius began running up the hill, contrary to orders, Scipio became anxious and followed him with speed. When he discovered the ambush he divided his cavalry in two and ordered both groups to take turns in charging the enemy, throwing their missiles all together and then immediately retreating, not to the same spot, but retiring a little further back each time and yielding ground. In this way he brought the cavalry to safety back in the plain. After he broke camp and withdrew, the enemy laid an ambush for him beside a river on his route that was difficult to cross and muddy, but he learned about the ambush and changed his route. This involved a longer

381

382

383

384

385

[84] P. Rutilius Rufus was consul in 105. His trial and conviction in 92 for extortion while legate in Asia was a cause célèbre.

τέραν ἦγε καὶ δυσενέδρευτον, νυκτός τε ὁδεύων διὰ τὸ
δίψος καὶ φρέατα ὀρύσσων, ὧν τὰ πλέονα πικρὰ εὑρί-
σκετο. τοὺς μὲν οὖν ἄνδρας ἐπιμόχθως περιέσωσεν,
ἵπποι δέ τινες αὐτοῦ καὶ ὑποζύγια ὑπὸ τῆς δίψης
ἀπώλοντο.

386 89. Καὶ Καυκαίους δὲ παροδεύων, ἐς οὓς παρεσπόν-
δησε Λούκουλλος, ἐκήρυξε Καυκαίους ἐπὶ τὰ ἑαυτῶν
387 ἀκινδύνως κατέρχεσθαι. καὶ παρῆλθεν ἐς τὴν Νομαν-
τίνην χειμάσων, ἔνθα αὐτῷ καὶ Ἰογόρθας ἐκ Λιβύης
ἀφίκετο, ὁ Μασσανάσσου υἱωνός, ἄγων ἐλέφαντας
δυοκαίδεκα καὶ τοὺς συντασσομένους αὐτοῖς τοξότας
388 τε καὶ σφενδονήτας. αἰεὶ δέ τι δηῶν καὶ τὰ περικεί-
μενα πορθῶν, ἔλαθε περὶ κώμην ἐνεδρευθείς, ἣν ἐκ
τοῦ πλέονος τέλμα πηλοῦ περιεῖχεν, ἐπὶ δὲ θάτερα
φάραγξ ἦν, καὶ ἀφανὴς ἐν ἐκείνῃ λόχος ὑπεκρύπτετο.
389 τῆς οὖν στρατιᾶς τῷ Σκιπίωνι διῃρημένης οἱ μὲν τὴν
κώμην ἐπόρθουν ἐσελθόντες, τὰ σημεῖα ἔξω κατα-
390 λιπόντες, οἱ δὲ περιίππευον οὐ πολλοί. τούτοις οὖν
ἐμπίπτουσιν οἱ λοχῶντες, καὶ οἱ μὲν αὐτοὺς ἀπεμά-
χοντο, ὁ δὲ Σκιπίων (ἔτυχεν γὰρ πρὸ τῆς κώμης παρὰ
τὰ σημεῖα ἑστώς) ἀνεκάλει τῇ σάλπιγγι τοὺς ἔνδον
καί, πρὶν αὐτῷ γενέσθαι χιλίους, τοῖς ἱππεῦσιν
391 ἐνοχλουμένοις ἐπεβοήθει. τοῦδε δὲ τοῦ στρατοῦ τοῦ
πλέονος ἐκ τῆς κώμης ἐκδραμόντος ἐτρέψατο μὲν ἐς
φυγὴν τοὺς πολεμίους, οὐ μὴν ἐδίωκε φεύγοντας, ἀλλ'
ἐς τὸν χάρακα ἀνεχώρει πεσόντων ἑκατέρωθεν ὀλίγων.

march but one less susceptible to ambush. He traveled by night to minimize the need for water, and although he dug wells, most of them were found to be bitter water. So it was only with difficulty that he saved his men, but some of his horses and transport animals died of thirst.

89. While traveling through the territory of the Caucaei, whose treaty with Rome Lucullus had violated,[85] Scipio made an announcement that they could return home under guarantee of safety. Then he went to Numantia to take up winter quarters, where he was joined from Africa by Jugurtha, the grandson of Massinissa, who brought twelve elephants with him and the archers and sling throwers deployed with them. Scipio spent his time ravaging and laying waste the neighboring country, but did not notice an ambush set for him near a village largely surrounded by a muddy swamp; on the remaining side of the village there was a ravine where the soldiers of the ambush were hidden out of sight. So Scipio's forces were now split, some entering the village to plunder it (they left the standards outside), others, although not many, riding round the perimeter. It was these latter who fell victim to the ambush. They set about defending themselves, while Scipio, who happened to be standing outside the village beside the standards, got the trumpeters to recall the troops who had gone inside, and even before he had a thousand men with him, went to help the cavalry out of their difficulty. When most of his force had run out of the village, he put the enemy to flight, but did not follow them in pursuit, instead withdrawing to his palisade. There were a few casualties on both sides.

386

387

388

389

390

391

[85] See above, 52.218–20.

392　　90. Μετ᾽ οὐ πολὺ δὲ ἀγχοτάτω τῆς Νομαντίας δύο
στρατόπεδα θέμενος τῷ μὲν ἐπέστησεν τὸν ἀδελφὸν
Μάξιμον, τοῦ δ᾽ αὐτὸς ἡγεῖτο. Νομαντίνων δὲ θαμινὰ
ἐκτασσόντων καὶ προκαλουμένων αὐτὸν ἐς μάχην
ὑπερεώρα, οὐ δοκιμάζων ἀνδράσιν ἐξ ἀπογνώσεως
μαχομένοις συμπλέκεσθαι μᾶλλον ἢ συγκλήσας αὐ-
393　　τοὺς ἑλεῖν λιμῷ. φρούρια δ᾽ ἑπτὰ περιθείς, πολιορκίαν
<. . .> ἐπιγράψας ἑκάστοις, οὓς ἔδει πέμπειν. ὡς δὲ
ἦλθον, ἐς μέρη πολλὰ διεῖλεν αὐτοὺς καὶ τὴν ἑαυτοῦ
στρατιὰν ἐπιδιεῖλεν· εἶθ᾽ ἡγεμόνας ἐπιστήσας ἑκάστῳ
μέρει προσέταξεν περιταφρεύειν καὶ περιχαρακοῦν
394　　τὴν πόλιν. ἦν δὲ ἡ περίοδος ἡ μὲν αὐτῆς Νομαντίας
τέσσαρες καὶ εἴκοσι στάδιοι, ἡ δὲ τοῦ χαρακώματος
ὑπὲρ τὸ διπλάσιον. καὶ τοῦτο διῃρεῖτο πᾶν οἱ κατὰ
395　　μέρος ἕκαστον. καὶ προείρητο, εἴ τι ἐνοχλοῖεν οἱ πολέμιοι, σημεῖον ἐξαίρειν, ἡμέρας μὲν φοινικίδα ἐπὶ
δόρατος ὑψηλοῦ, νυκτὸς δὲ πῦρ, ἵνα τοῖς δεομένοις
396　　ἐπιθέοντες αὐτός τε καὶ Μάξιμος ἀμύνοιεν. ὡς δὲ
ἐξείργαστο πάντα αὐτῷ καὶ τοὺς κωλύοντας εἶχεν
ἱκανῶς ἀπομάχεσθαι, ἑτέραν τάφρον ὤρυσσεν οὐ μακρὰν ὑπὲρ ἐκείνην καὶ σταυροὺς αὐτῇ περιεπήγνυ καὶ
τεῖχος ᾠκοδόμει, οὗ τὸ μὲν πάχος ἦν πόδες ὀκτώ, τὸ
δὲ ὕψος δέκα χωρὶς τῶν ἐπάλξεων· πύργοι τε παν-
397　　ταχόθεν αὐτῷ διὰ πλέθρου περιέκειντο. καὶ λίμνην
συνάπτουσαν οὐκ ἐνὸν περιτειχίσαι χῶμα αὐτῇ περι-
έθηκεν ἴσον τῷ τείχει καὶ τὸ βάθος καὶ τὸ ὕψος, ὡς
ἂν εἴη καὶ τόδε ἀντὶ τείχους.

90. Not long after, Scipio established two camps very 392
close to Numantia, one under the command of his brother
Maximus,[86] the other commanded by himself. The Numantines repeatedly came out in battle order and challenged him to combat, but he refused, deeming it unwise
to tangle with men fighting out of desperation; his plan was
rather to shut them in and reduce them by starvation. He 393
set up seven forts around the city, he began (?) the siege
⟨. . .⟩ having written to each of them specifying the numbers they were required to send.[87] When they arrived, he
divided them into many units, and further divided his own
army. He appointed a commander for each unit and ordered them to invest the city with a ditch and stockade.
The perimeter of Numantia itself was twenty-four stades, 394
the stockade more than twice that. Each unit was assigned
a part of the whole perimeter, and ordered to signal if the 395
enemy should harass them at all—by raising a red flag on
a long spear during the day, and sending a fire signal at
night—so that he himself and Maximus could hasten to
offer asistance to those who needed it. When he had com- 396
pleted all this work, and had taken sufficient measures to
fight off those trying to hinder him, he dug another ditch
not far behind the first one, fixing it with stakes, and built
a wall eight feet wide, and ten feet high (not including the
parapets), with towers placed along its length at intervals
of one hundred feet. As it was not possible to wall off the 397
adjoining marsh, he dug a rampart around it, as a substi-
tute for the wall, of the same height and thickness as it.

[86] Q. Fabius Maximus Aemilianus, consul 145, was Scipio's
elder brother and his legate in Spain.

[87] It is not clear how much is missing in this lacuna.

398   91. Οὕτω μὲν ὁ Σκιπίων ὅδε πρῶτος, ὡς ἐμοὶ δοκεῖ, περιετείχισε πόλιν οὐ φυγομαχοῦσαν· τόν τε Δόριον ποταμόν, συμφερόμενον τῷ περιτειχίσματι καὶ πολλὰ τοῖς Νομαντίνοις χρήσιμον ἔς τε ἀγορᾶς κομιδὴν καὶ διαπομπὴν ἀνδρῶν, ὅσοι κατ᾿ αὐτὸν κολυμβηταί τε καὶ σκάφεσι μικροῖς ἐλάνθανον ἢ ἱστίοις, ὅτε λάβρον εἴη τὸ πνεῦμα, ἐβιάζοντο ἢ κώπαις κατὰ τὸ ῥεῦμα, ζεῦξαι μὲν οὐκ ἐδύνατο, πλατὺν ὄντα καὶ πάνυ ῥοώδη, φρούρια δὲ ἀντὶ γεφύρας αὐτῷ δύο περιθεὶς ἀπήρτησε καλῳδίοις δοκοὺς μακρὰς ἐξ ἑκατέρου φρουρίου καὶ ἐς τὸ πλάτος τοῦ ποταμοῦ μεθῆκεν, ἐχούσας ἐμ-

399 πεπηγότα πυκνὰ ξίφη τε καὶ ἀκόντια. αἱ δ᾿ ὑπὸ τοῦ ῥοῦ, τοῖς ξίφεσι καὶ τοῖς ἀκοντίοις ἐμπίπτοντος, αἰεὶ περιστρεφόμεναι οὔτε διανηχομένους οὔτ᾿ ἐπιπλέον-

400 τας οὔτε ὑποδύνοντας εἴων λαθεῖν. τοῦτο δ᾿ ἦν, οὗ μάλιστα ὁ Σκιπίων ἐπεθύμει, μηδενὸς αὐτοῖς ἐπιμιγνυ-μένου μηδ᾿ εἰσιόντος ἀγνοεῖν αὐτούς, ὅ τι γίγνοιτο ἔξω· οὕτω γὰρ ἀπορήσειν ἀγορᾶς τε καὶ μηχανῆς πάσης.

401   92. Ὡς δὲ ἡτοίμαστο πάντα καὶ καταπέλται μὲν ἐπέκειντο τοῖς πύργοις ὀξυβελεῖς τε καὶ λιθοβόλοι, ταῖς δ᾿ ἐπάλξεσιν παρέκειντο λίθοι καὶ βέλη καὶ ἀκόντια, τὰ δὲ φρούρια τοξόται καὶ σφενδονῆται κατ-εῖχον, ἀγγέλους μὲν ἐπέστησε πυκνοὺς κατὰ τὸ ἐπι-τείχισμα πᾶν, οἳ νυκτός τε καὶ ἡμέρας ἔμελλον ἄλλοι παρ᾿ ἄλλων τὸν λόγον ἐκδεχόμενοι μηνύσειν αὐτῷ τὰ

402 γιγνόμενα, κατὰ δὲ πύργον ἐκέλευσεν, εἴ τι γίγνοιτο, σημεῖον ἐκ πρώτου τοῦ πονοῦντος αἴρεσθαι καὶ τὸ

91. In this way, it seems to me, Scipio was the first com-   398
mander to invest a city that was not attempting to avoid
battle. The river Dorius, which flowed beside the stockade
surrounding the city, was proving very useful to the inhabitants of Numantia for bringing in supplies and transporting men. Some were avoiding detection by diving or using
small boats, others were forcing their way through in sail-
ing boats whenever the wind was strong, or in rowing
boats when going downstream. Because of its breadth and
strong current Scipio was unable to bridge the river, but
instead of a bridge he established a blockhouse on each
bank to which he roped long beams and pushed them out
across the river. They were fitted with swords and short   399
spears which, when hit by the current, kept the beams
rotating. This made it impossible for the Numantines to
remain undetected as they tried to swim across, or go by
boat or dive underwater. The result, which was just what   400
Scipio wanted, was that nobody could have any dealings
with them, nobody could get into the city, and they would
have no idea of what was happening outside. In this way
they would find themselves short of supplies and all equipment.

92. When everything was ready, with the catapults, bal-   401
listae, and onagers in position on the towers, the stones,
bolts, and javelins on the parapet, and the archers and
slingers holding the forts, Scipio stationed a large number
of messengers along the whole length of the besieging
stockade to pass word from each other and keep him informed of what was happening. He gave orders to each   402
tower that in the event of any activity, they were to raise a
signal at the first sign of trouble; all should then do the

αὐτὸ πάντας ἐπαίρειν, ὅταν τὸν ἀρξάμενον θεάσων-
ται, ἵνα τὸ μὲν κίνημα παρὰ τοῦ σημείου θᾶσσον
403 ἐπιγιγνώσκοι, τὸ δὲ ἀκριβὲς παρὰ τῶν ἀγγέλων. τῆς
δὲ στρατιᾶς οὔσης σὺν τοῖς ἐπιχωρίοις ἐς ἑξακισμυ-
ρίους, τὸ μὲν ἥμισυ διετέτακτο αὐτῷ τειχοφυλακεῖν
καὶ ἐς τὰ ἀναγκαῖα, εἴ πη δεήσειε, μεταχωρεῖν, δισμύριοι δὲ τειχομαχήσειν ἔμελλον, ὅτε χρεία γένοιτο,
404 καὶ τούτοις ἐφεδρεύειν ἕτεροι μύριοι. χωρίον δὲ καὶ
τούτων ἑκάστοις διετέτακτο· καὶ μεταπηδᾶν, εἰ μὴ κε-
λεύσειεν, οὐκ ἐξῆν. ἐς δὲ τὸ τεταγμένον εὐθὺς ἀνεπήδων, ὅτε τι σημεῖον ἐπιχειρήσεως ἐπαρθείη.

405   93. Οὕτω μὲν τῷ Σκιπίωνι πάντα ἀκριβῶς διετέ-
τακτο· οἱ δὲ Νομαντῖνοι πολλάκις μὲν τοῖς φυλάσ-
σουσιν ἐπεχείρουν, ἄλλοτε ἄλλῃ κατὰ μέρη, ταχεῖα
δ' αὐτίκα καὶ καταπληκτικὴ τῶν ἀμυνομένων ἡ ὄψις
406 ἦν, σημείων τε ὑψηλῶν πανταχόθεν αἰρομένων καὶ
ἀγγέλων διαθεόντων καὶ τῶν τειχομάχων ἀθρόως
ἀναπηδώντων ἐς τὰ τείχη σαλπικτῶν τε κατὰ πάντα
πύργον ἐξοτρυνόντων, ὥστε τὸν κύκλον ὅλον εὐθὺς
ἅπασιν εἶναι φοβερώτατον, ἐς πεντήκοντα σταδίους
ἐπέχοντα ἐν περιόδῳ, καὶ τόνδε τὸν κύκλον ὁ Σκιπίων
ἑκάστης ἡμέρας τε καὶ νυκτὸς ἐπισκοπῶν περιῄει.

407   94. Ὁ μὲν δὴ τοὺς πολεμίους ὧδε συγκλήσας οὐκ
ἐς πολὺ ἀρκέσειν ἐνόμιζεν, οὔτε τροφῆς ἔτι προσιού-
σης σφίσιν οὔτε ὅπλων οὔτ' ἐπικουρίας· Ῥητογένης
δέ, ἀνὴρ Νομαντῖνος, ᾧ Καραύνιος ἐπίκλησις ἦν, ἄριστος ἐς ἀρετὴν Νομαντίνων, πέντε πείσας φίλους,
σὺν παισὶν ἄλλοις τοσοῖσδε καὶ ἵπποις τοσοῖσδε ἐν

same as soon as they saw the first one, so that he would learn quickly of the disturbance from the signals, and get the details from the messengers. Including the native 403 troops, Scipio's army numbered about sixty thousand. Half of them he assigned to protect the stockade and in emergencies to move anywhere they were required; twenty thousand were to carry out the actual fighting on the walls, as the need arose; and a further ten thousand he kept in reserve. Every man in these divisions was given a position 404 and not allowed to change it unless ordered to; he was to move swiftly into his assigned position immediately, whenever the signal for attack was raised.

93. Such were the detailed arrangements made by 405 Scipio. The Numantines launched frequent piecemeal attacks on the besiegers at different times in different places, but as soon as they did, the swift response of the 406 defenders was a frighteneing sight, with signals being raised high in all quarters, messengers running back and forth, those designated as wall fighters leaping en masse to their position on the walls, trumpets urging people to action on each tower. The effect of the whole encirclement, which stretched to some fifty stades all the way round, was immediately terrifying to anyone. Scipio made a tour of inspection around this perimeter every day and night.

94. Having bottled up the enemy in this manner, he 407 thought they could not hold out for long, as no supplies were getting through any more, no weapons, no reinforcements. But the bravest of the Numantines, a man called Rhetogenes, surnamed Caraunius, persuaded five of his associates to join him with the same number of servants and horses and secretly cross the space between the

νυκτὶ συννεφεῖ διῆλθε λαθὼν τὸ μεταίχμιον, κλίμακα
408 φέρων πτυκτήν· καὶ φθάσας ἐς τὸ περιτείχισμα ἀνε-
πήδησεν αὐτός τε καὶ οἱ φίλοι καὶ τοὺς ἑκατέρωθεν
φύλακας ἀνελόντες τοὺς μὲν θεράποντας ἀπέπεμψαν
ὀπίσω, τοὺς δ' ἵππους διὰ τῆς κλίμακος ἀναγαγόντες
ἐξίππευσαν ἐς τὰς Ἀρουακῶν πόλεις σὺν ἱκετηρίαις,
δεόμενοι Νομαντίνοις συγγενέσιν οὖσιν ἐπικουρεῖν.
409 τῶν δ' Ἀρουακῶν οἱ μὲν οὐδ' ὑπήκουον αὐτῶν, ἀλλ'
εὐθὺς ἀπέπεμπον δεδιότες, Λουτία δὲ πόλις ἦν εὐδαί-
μων, τριακοσίους σταδίους ἀφεστῶσα ἀπὸ Νομαντίνων, ἧς οἱ μὲν νέοι περὶ τοὺς Νομαντίνους ἐσπου-
δάκεσαν καὶ τὴν πόλιν ἐς συμμαχίαν ἐνῆγον, οἱ
410 πρεσβύτεροι δ' ἐμήνυσαν κρύφα τῷ Σκιπίωνι. καὶ ὁ
Σκιπίων ὀγδόης ὥρας πυθόμενος ἐξήλαυνεν αὐτίκα
σὺν εὐζώνοις ὅτι πλείστοις καὶ ἅμα ἔῳ τὴν Λουτίαν
φρουρᾷ περιλαβὼν ἐξῄτει τῶν ἐξάρχων τοὺς νέους.[39]
ἐπεὶ δ' ἐξωρμηκέναι τῆς πόλεως αὐτοὺς ἔλεγον, ἐκήρυξε διαρπάσειν τὴν πόλιν, εἰ μὴ τοὺς ἄνδρας παρα-
411 λάβοι. οἱ μὲν δὴ δείσαντες προσῆγον αὐτούς, ἐς
τετρακοσίους γενομένους· ὁ δὲ τὰς χεῖρας αὐτῶν ἐκ-
τεμὼν ἀνέστησε τὴν φρουρὰν καὶ διαδραμὼν αὖθις
ἅμ' ἔῳ τῆς ἐπιούσης παρῆν ἐς τὸ στρατόπεδον.

412   95. Νομαντῖνοι δὲ κάμνοντες ὑπὸ λιμοῦ πέντε ἄνδρας ἔπεμπον ἐς τὸν Σκιπίωνα, οἷς εἴρητο μαθεῖν, εἰ
μετριοπαθῶς σφίσι χρήσεται παραδοῦσιν αὐτούς.
Αὔαρος δὲ αὐτῶν ἡγούμενος πολλὰ μὲν περὶ τῆς
προαιρέσεως καὶ ἀνδρείας τῶν Νομαντίνων ἐσεμνο-
λόγησε καὶ ἐπεῖπεν, ὡς οὐδὲ νῦν ἁμάρτοιεν, ὑπὲρ

armies on a cloudy night, bringing a folding gangway with them. He arrived first at the stockade and scrambled over it, and he and his associates then killed the guards on either side of them. They sent the servants back, led the horses up over the gangway and rode off to the towns of the Arevaci as suppliants to beg them to help their relatives in Numantia. Some of the Arevaci would not even listen to them, but dismissed them immediately out of fear. In the wealthy town of Lutia, however, which was three hundred stades from Numantia, the young men took the side of the Numantines, and urged their town to give them military assistance, but the older men secretly informed Scipio of this. He got the news at the eighth hour and immediately set off with as many light-armed troops as possible. By dawn he was surrounding Lutia with guards and demanded that the leaders surrender the young men. When they said that the youths had left town, he made an announcement that he would sack the town, if he did not get the men. The Lutians duly delivered them up out of fear; there were about four hundred of them. Scipio had their hands cut off, withdrew his guards and hurrying on his way, by dawn of the following day was back in his camp.

95. As the Numantines were suffering from famine, they sent five men to Scipio with instructions to ask him whether he would treat them with moderation if they surrendered. Avarus, their leader, spoke gravely at length about the principles and courage of the Numantine people, and added that even now they were not in the wrong, but were reduced to suffering such a degree of misery for

408

409

410

411

412

---

39 ἐξῄτει τῶν ἐξάρχων τοὺς νέους Goukowsky: ᾔτει τοὺς ἐξάρχους τῶν νέων VM

APPIAN

παίδων καὶ γυναικῶν καὶ ἐλευθερίας πατρίου κακοπα-
413 θοῦντες ἐς τοσόνδε κακοῦ. "Διὸ καὶ μάλιστα," εἶπεν,
"Ὦ Σκιπίων, ἄξιόν ἐστι σέ, τοσῆσδε ἀρετῆς γέμοντα,
φείσασθαι γένους εὐψύχου τε καὶ ἀνδρικοῦ καὶ προ-
τεῖναι τὰ φιλανθρωπότερα τῶν κακῶν ἡμῖν, ἃ καὶ δυ-
νησόμεθα ἐνεγκεῖν, ἄρτι πειρώμενοι μεταβολῆς. ὡς
οὐκ ἐφ' ἡμῖν ἔτι ἐστίν, ἀλλ' ἐπὶ σοὶ τὴν πόλιν ἢ παραλαβεῖν, εἰ τὰ μέτρια κελεύοις, ἢ μαχομένην ὑπερι-
414 δεῖν ἀπολέσθαι." ὁ μὲν Αὖαρος ὧδε εἶπεν, ὁ δὲ Σκιπίων (ᾔσθετο γὰρ παρὰ τῶν αἰχμαλώτων τὰ ἔνδον)
ἔφη δεῖν αὐτοὺς ἐγχειρίσαι τὰ κατὰ σφᾶς καὶ σὺν
415 ὅπλοις παραδοῦναι τὴν πόλιν. ὧν ἀπαγγελθέντων οἱ
Νομαντῖνοι, χαλεποὶ καὶ τέως ὄντες ὀργὴν ὑπ' ἐλευθερίας ἀκράτου καὶ ἀηθείας ἐπιταγμάτων, τότε καὶ
μᾶλλον ὑπὸ τῶν συμφορῶν ἠγριωμένοι τε καὶ ἀλ-
λόκοτοι γεγονότες, τὸν Αὖαρον καὶ τοὺς σὺν αὐτῷ
πέντε πρέσβεις ἀπέκτειναν ὡς κακῶν ἀγγέλους καὶ τὸ
σφέτερον ἀσφαλὲς ἴσως διῳκημένους παρὰ τῷ Σκιπίωνι.

416   96. Μετὰ δ' οὐ πολὺ πάντων αὐτοὺς τῶν ἐδεστῶν
ἐπιλιπόντων, οὐ καρπὸν ἔχοντες, οὐ πρόβατον, οὐ
πόαν, πρῶτα μέν, ὥσπερ τινὲς ἐν πολέμων ἀνάγκαις,
δέρματα ἕψοντες ἐλιχμῶντο, ἐπιλιπόντων δ' αὐτοὺς
καὶ τῶν δερμάτων ἐσαρκοφάγουν ἕψοντες τὰ ἀνθρώ-
πεια, πρῶτα μὲν τὰ τῶν ἀποθνησκόντων κοπτόμενα
ἐν μαγειρείοις, ἐπὶ δ' ἐκείνοις τῶν νοσούντων κατεφρόνουν, καὶ τοὺς ἀσθενεστέρους ἐβιάζοντο οἱ δυνα-
417 τώτεροι. κακῶν τε οὐδὲν αὐτοῖς ἀπῆν, ἠγριωμένοις

294

the sake of their children, wives, and ancestral freedom. "For this reason in particular, Scipio," he said, "it is worthy 413 of you, a man loaded with such great distinctions, to spare a brave and manly people, and extend to us more humane treatment than our present troubles: given our recent reversal of fortune, we will be able to endure this. So, it is no longer up to us, but to you, whether you receive the surrender of the town by issuing moderate orders, or oversee its destruction in battle." These were the words of 414 Avarus, but Scipio, who knew from prisoners the situation in the city, said they must put their fate in his hands and surrender the city and their weapons. The Numantines 415 had been awkwardly ill-tempered even before this—unrestricted as they were in their freedom and not used to taking orders—and now, when they were told of Scipio's response, their disastrous situation made them even more savage and surly, and they killed Avarus and the five envoys for bringing bad news, and perhaps for making private arrangements with Scipio to secure their own safety.

96. Not much later, when there was nothing edible left, 416 and they had no agricultural produce, no animals, no grass, as some do when faced with the necessities of war, they first turned to licking boiled hides. But these too ran out and they began to cook and eat human flesh, at first cutting up in the kitchens the bodies of those who had died, but then, showing disdain for the sick, the stronger began to do violence to the weaker. They were afflicted by 417 every calamity, their minds brutalized by what they were

μὲν τὰς ψυχὰς ὑπὸ τῶν τροφῶν, τεθηριωμένοις δὲ τὰ
σώματα ὑπὸ λιμοῦ καὶ λοιμοῦ καὶ κόμης καὶ χρόνου.
418 οὕτω δ᾽ ἔχοντες αὐτοὺς ἐπέτρεπον τῷ Σκιπίωνι. ὁ δ᾽
ἐκέλευεν αὐτοὺς τῆς μὲν ἡμέρας ἐκείνης συνενεγκεῖν
τὰ ὅπλα, ἔνθα συνέταξε, τῆς δ᾽ ἐπιούσης προσελθεῖν
ἐς ἕτερον χωρίον. οἱ δ᾽ ὑπερεβάλοντο τὴν ἡμέραν,
ὁμολογήσαντες, ὅτι πολλοὶ τῆς ἐλευθερίας ἔτι ἔχον-
ται καὶ ἐθέλουσιν αὐτοὺς ἐξαγαγεῖν τοῦ βίου. τὴν οὖν
ἡμέραν ᾔτουν ἐς τοῦ θανάτου τὴν διάθεσιν.

419   97. Τοσόσδε ἔρως ἐλευθερίας καὶ ἀνδραγαθίας ἦν
ἐν πόλει βαρβάρῳ τε καὶ σμικρᾷ. ἐς γὰρ ὀκτακισχιλίους ἐπ᾽ εἰρήνης γενόμενοι οἷα μὲν καὶ ὅσα Ῥωμαίους ἔδρασαν, οἵας δὲ συνθήκας αὐτοῖς ἔθεντο ἐπὶ
ἴσῃ καὶ ὁμοίᾳ, οὐδέσι ταῦτα[40] συνθέσθαι Ῥωμαίων
ὑποστάντων, οἷον δὲ ὄντα τὸν τελευταῖον στρατηγόν,
ἐξ μυριάσιν αὐτοὺς περικαθήμενον, προυκαλέσαντο
420 πολλάκις ἐς μάχην. ὁ δὲ ἦν ἄρα στρατηγικώτερος
αὐτῶν, ἐς χεῖρας οὐκ ἰὼν θηρίοις, ἀλλὰ τῷ λιμῷ σφᾶς
κατεργαζόμενος, ἀμάχῳ κακῷ, ᾧ δὴ καὶ μόνῳ ληφθῆ-
ναί τε δυνατὸν ἦν ἄρα Νομαντίνους καὶ ἐλήφθησαν
421 μόνῳ. ἐμοὶ μὲν δὴ ταῦτα περὶ Νομαντίνων εἰπεῖν
ἐπῆλθεν, ἐς τὴν ὀλιγότητα αὐτῶν καὶ φερεπονίαν
ἀφορῶντι καὶ ἔργα πολλὰ καὶ χρόνον, ὅσον διεκαρ-
422 τέρησαν· οἱ δὲ πρῶτα μὲν αὐτούς, οἱ βουλόμενοι, διεχρῶντο, ἕτερος ἑτέρως· οἱ λοιποὶ δ᾽ ἐξῄεσαν τρίτης
ἡμέρας ἐς τὸ δεδομένον χωρίον, δυσόρατοί τε καὶ ἀλ-
λόκοτοι πάμπαν ὀφθῆναι, οἷς τὰ μὲν σώματα ἦν
ἀκάθαρτα καὶ τριχῶν καὶ ὀνύχων καὶ ῥύπου μεστά,

eating, their bodies made wild by hunger, disease, long
hair, and the ravages of time. Finding themselves in such
a situation, they surrendered to Scipio. He specified a   418
place for them to bring their weapons on that same day,
and told them to gather at another place the next day. But
they allowed the day to pass, declaring that many of them
still clung to freedom and wanted to take their own lives.
So they asked for the day to prepare their death.

97. That is how much they loved liberty and courage in   419
this small barbarian town. With a peacetime population of
about eight thousand men, they had achieved many and
extraordinary things against the Romans. How often they
had made agreements with them on fair and equal terms,
when the Romans made no such agreements with anyone
else. And how often they had challenged to battle the great
general Rome had sent as its last commander, who had
surrounded them with sixty thousand men. But he had   420
proved too good a general for them, refusing to engage
with wild beasts, instead reducing them by that irresistable
hardship, hunger. This was the only possible way to capture Numantia, and to be sure, it was by hunger alone that
it was taken. These are the things it occurred to me to say   421
about the Numantines, as I reflected on how few they
were, how ready for hardship, how great their deeds and
how long they held out. First of all, those who wanted to,   422
took their own lives in different ways. Then the rest left
the city on the third day and went to the place specified,
an altogether strange sight and difficult to look at. Physically they were filthy with long hair and nails and covered

40 ταὐτὰ Goukowsky: ταῦτα VM

APPIAN

ὀδώδεσαν δὲ χαλεπώτατον, καὶ ἐσθὴς αὐτοῖς ἐπέκειτο
423 πιναρὰ καὶ ἥδε καὶ οὐχ ἧσσον δυσώδης. ἐφαίνοντο
δὲ τοῖς πολεμίοις ἐλεεινοὶ μὲν ἀπὸ τῶνδε, φοβεροὶ δ᾽
ἀπὸ τῶν βλεμμάτων· ἔτι γὰρ αὐτοὺς ἐνεώρων ἔκ τε
ὀργῆς καὶ λύπης καὶ πόνου καὶ συνειδότος ἀλληλο-
φαγίας.

424   98. Ἐπιλεξάμενος δ᾽ αὐτῶν πεντήκοντα ὁ Σκιπίων
ἐς θρίαμβον, τοὺς λοιποὺς ἀπέδοτο καὶ τὴν πόλιν
κατέσκαψεν, δύο μὲν τάσδε πόλεις δυσμαχωτάτας
425 ἑλὼν στρατηγὸς ὅδε Ῥωμαίων, Καρχηδόνα μὲν αὐτῶν
Ῥωμαίων ψηφισαμένων διὰ μέγεθος πόλεώς τε καὶ
ἀρχῆς καὶ εὐκαιρίαν γῆς καὶ θαλάσσης, Νομαντίαν
δὲ σμικράν τε καὶ ὀλιγάνθρωπον, οὔπω τι Ῥωμαίων
426 περὶ αὐτῆς ἐγνωκότων, αὐτός, εἴτε συμφέρειν Ῥωμαίοις ἡγούμενος, εἴτε ἄκρος ὢν ὀργὴν καὶ φιλόνει-
κος ἐς τὰ λαμβανόμενα, εἶθ᾽, ὡς ἔνιοι νομίζουσι, τὴν
δόξαν ἡγούμενος διώνυμον ἐπὶ τοῖς μεγάλοις γίγνεσθαι κακοῖς. καλοῦσι γοῦν αὐτὸν οἱ Ῥωμαῖοι μέχρι
νῦν, ἀπὸ τῶν συμφορῶν, ἃς ἐπέθηκεν ταῖς πόλεσιν,
427 Ἀφρικανόν τε καὶ Νομαντῖνον. τότε δὲ τὴν γῆν τὴν
Νομαντίνων τοῖς ἐγγὺς οἰκοῦσι διελὼν καὶ ταῖς ἄλλαις πόλεσι χρηματίσας καί, εἴ τι ἦν ὕποπτον, ἐπι-
πλήξας τε καὶ ζημιώσας χρήμασιν ἀπέπλευσεν ἐπ᾽
οἴκου.

428   99. Ῥωμαῖοι δέ, ὡς ἔθος, ἐς τὰ προσειλημμένα τῆς
Ἰβηρίας ἔπεμψαν ἀπὸ τῆς βουλῆς ἄνδρας δέκα τοὺς
καταστησομένους αὐτὰ εἰς εἰρήνην, ὅσα Σκιπίων τε
ἔλαβε καὶ Βροῦτος πρὸ τοῦ Σκιπίωνος ὑπηγάγετο ἢ

in dirt, they smelled terrible, and the clothes they wore were also unwashed and equally foul smelling. For these 423 reasons they appeared pitiable to their enemy, but there was also something frightening in their eyes: for they still looked at the Romans from a position of anger, grief, hardship, and guilt about their cannibalism.

98. Scipio picked out fifty of them for his triumph, sold 424 the rest and razed the city to the ground. So it was that this Roman general destroyed two such impregnable cities. First, Carthage. The Romans themselves voted to do 425 this because of the size of the city and its empire, and its advantageous position by land and sea. Then, Numantia. This was a small place with a small population, about which the Romans had made no decision at the time. Scipio acted unilaterally here, either because he thought 426 it was to Rome's advantage, or because he was of fierce disposition and vindictive toward captives; or again, as some think, because he believed that the sort of glory that merits two titles comes from causing great misfortunes. At any rate, it is certainly the case that to this very day the Romans call him "Africanus" and "Numantinus" from the disasters he inflicted on these cities. At the time, having 427 divided the territory of Numantia among its neighbors, and conducted business in the other cities, where, if he found anything suspicious, he issued reprimands and imposed fines, Scipio sailed for home.

99. As was standard practice, Rome sent a commission 428 of ten senators to the newly acquired territories in Iberia to establish a peacetime administration for the lands captured by Scipio, and brought over to Rome or reduced by

429 ἐχειρώσατο. χρόνῳ δ᾽ ὕστερον ἀποστάσεων ἄλλων ἐν
Ἰβηρίᾳ γενομένων Καλπούρνιος Πείσων στρατηγὸς
430 ᾑρέθη. καὶ αὐτὸν διεδέξατο μὲν Σέρουιος Γάλβας,
Κίμβρων δ᾽ ἐπιστρατευόντων τῇ Ἰταλίᾳ καὶ Σικελίας
πολεμουμένης τὸν δεύτερον δουλικὸν πόλεμον στρατιὰν μὲν ἐς Ἰβηρίαν οὐκ ἔπεμπον ὑπ᾽ ἀσχολίας,
πρέσβεις δ᾽ ἀπέστελλον, οἳ τὸν πόλεμον ἔμελλον, ὅπῃ
431 δύναιντο, καταθήσεσθαι. Κίμβρων δ᾽ ἐξελαθέντων Τίτος Δείδιος ἐπελθὼν Ἀρουακῶν μὲν ἔκτεινεν ἐς δισμυρίους, Τερμησὸν δέ, μεγάλην πόλιν αἰεὶ δυσπειθῆ
Ῥωμαίοις γενομένην, ἐξ ἐρυμνοῦ κατήγαγεν ἐς τὸ
432 πεδίον καὶ ἐκέλευσεν οἰκεῖν ἀτειχίστους. Κολένδαν δὲ
προσκαθίσας ἐνάτῳ μηνὶ παρέλαβεν ἐγχειρίσασαν
ἑαυτὴν καὶ τοὺς Κολενδέας ἅπαντας μετὰ παίδων καὶ
γυναικῶν ἀπέδοτο.

433 100. Πόλιν δ᾽ ἑτέραν τῆς Κολένδης πλησίον ᾤκουν
μιγάδες Κελτιβήρων, οὓς Μᾶρκος Μάριος συμμαχή-
σαντας αὐτῷ κατὰ Λυσιτανῶν, τῆς βουλῆς ἐπιτρεπούσης, ᾤκίκει πρὸ πέντε ἐνιαυτῶν. ἐλῄστευον δ᾽ ἐξ
434 ἀπορίας οὗτοι· καὶ κρίνας αὐτοὺς ὁ Δείδιος ἀνελεῖν,
συνθεμένων αὐτῷ τῶν δέκα πρέσβεων ἔτι παρόντων,
ἔφη τοῖς ἐπιφανέσιν αὐτῶν ἐθέλειν τὴν Κολενδέων
435 χώραν αὐτοῖς προσορίσαι πενομένοις. ἀσπαζομένους

---

[88] Appian is referring to the command in Farther Spain. L.
Calpurnius Piso Frugi was killed in battle, according to Cicero
(*Verr.* 2.4.56). Servius Sulpicius Galba (consul 108) was praetor
in or before 111.

Brutus before him. Later on, other revolts broke out in   429
Iberia, and Calpurnius Piso was chosen to take command;
Servius Galba succeeded him.[88] During the invasion of   430
Italy by the Cimbri and the Second Slave War in Sicily,
Rome was too preoccupied to send an army to Iberia, but
dispatched legates to settle the hostilities as best they
could.[89] When the Cimbri had been driven off, Titus Did-   431
ius went to Iberia, killed twenty thousand of the Arevaci
and resettled Termes, a large town that had always been
slow to obey Rome, moving it from its steep location down
into the plain and ordering the inhabitants not to build city
walls.[90] He also besieged Colenda and took possession of   432
it when it surrendered after eight months. He sold the
entire population into slavery, women and children included.

100. Another town near Colenda was inhabited by a   433
mixed population of Celtiberians, whom Marcus Marius
had employed as allies against the Lusitanians and had
settled there five years before, with the approval of the
senate.[91] They were now engaging in banditry because of
poverty. Didius decided to destroy them—the ten com-   434
missioners who were still there agreed with him—and so
he told the leading citizens that because they were impov-
erished, he was willing to assign the land of Colenda to

[89] The Cimbri were a threat on Rome's northern frontier from
113, when they first defeated a Roman army, until they were
defeated by Marius in 101 at the battle of Vercellae. The Second
Slave War lasted from 104 to 100.

[90] Titus Didius was consul in 98 and assigned the governorship of Nearer Spain.

[91] It is not clear who this Marius was, but Appian dates his
foundation of this settlement to 102.

APPIAN

δὲ ὁρῶν ἐκέλευεν, τῷ δήμῳ ταῦτα μετενεγκόντας,
ἥκειν μετὰ γυναικῶν καὶ παίδων τὴν χώραν μεριουμέ-
νους. ἐπεὶ δ' ἀφίκοντο, προσέταξε τοὺς στρατιώτας ἐκ
τοῦ χάρακος ἐξελθεῖν καὶ τοὺς ἐνεδρευομένους εἴσω
παρελθεῖν ὡς ἀπογραψόμενος αὐτῶν ἔνδον τὸ πλῆθος,
ἐν μέρει μὲν ἀνδρῶν, ἐν μέρει δὲ παίδων καὶ γυναικῶν, ἵν' ἐπιγνοίη, πόσην χώραν αὐτοῖς δέοι διελεῖν.
436 ὡς δὲ παρῆλθον ἐς τὴν τάφρον καὶ τὸ χαράκωμα,
περιστήσας αὐτοῖς τὸν στρατὸν ὁ Δείδιος ἔκτεινε
πάντας. καὶ ἐπὶ τοῖσδε Δείδιος μὲν καὶ ἐθριάμβευσεν,
πάλιν δὲ τῶν Κελτιβήρων ἀποστάντων Φλάκκος ἐπι-
437 πεμφθεὶς ἔκτεινε δισμυρίους. ἐν δὲ Βελγήδῃ πόλει ὁ
μὲν δῆμος ἐς ἀπόστασιν ὁρμῶν τὴν βουλὴν ὀκνοῦ-
σαν ἐνέπρησεν αὐτῷ βουλευτηρίῳ, ὁ δὲ Φλάκκος
ἐπελθὼν ἔκτεινε τοὺς αἰτίους.

438   101. Τοσάδε μὲν εὗρον ἄξια λόγου Ῥωμαίοις ἐς
τότε πρὸς Ἴβηρας αὐτοὺς γενόμενα· χρόνῳ δ' ὕστερον στασιαζόντων ἐν Ῥώμῃ Σύλλα τε καὶ Κίννα καὶ
ἐς ἐμφυλίους πολέμους καὶ στρατόπεδα κατὰ τῆς πατρίδος διῃρημένων Κόιντος Σερτώριος, ἐκ τῆς Κίννα
439 στάσεως αἱρεθεὶς τῆς Ἰβηρίας ἄρχειν, Ἰβηρίαν τε
αὐτὴν ἐπανέστησε Ῥωμαίοις καὶ πολὺν στρατὸν
ἀγείρας καὶ βουλὴν τῶν ἰδίων φίλων ἐς μίμημα τῆς

92 C. Valerius Flaccus was consul in 93 and sent to Nearer
Spain either in that year or in the next.

them. Seeing they were pleased at this, he ordered them   435
to communicate the news to the people at large, and come
with their wives and children to divide up the land. On
their arrival, he ordered his troops to vacate the encampment and told the victims of his ambush to enter it; this
was, he said, so that he could register their number inside,
men in their turn, women and children in theirs, and decide how much land he would need to distribute to them.
When they had entered inside the ditch and palisade,   436
Didius positioned his troops round them and killed them
all. For this Didius was even awarded a triumph. Another
revolt of the Celtiberians saw Flaccus sent out to the command and he killed twenty thousand of them.[92] In the   437
town of Belgida the people were enthusiastic for revolt
and when their senate hesitated, they set fire to them
along with the senate building, but Flaccus arrived and
killed the guilty parties.

101. These, then, are the events I have found worthy   438
of record in the story of Rome's relations with the Iberians
up to that point. Later, when Sulla and Cinna were engaged in faction fighting at Rome and had divided the
country into opposing camps for the purpose of civil war,
Quintus Sertorius, a member of Cinna's faction, was appointed to the command in Iberia, which he then brought   439
into revolt against Rome.[93] He collected a large army, appointed a council of his own adherents in imitation of the

[93] Sertorius was praetor in 83 and appointed governor of
Nearer Spain. He was expelled in 81 and went to Africa, but he
returned in 80, on the invitation of the Lusitanians, and set up his
own government in exile, which defied Rome until he was killed
in 73.

συγκλήτου καταλέξας ἤλαυνεν ἐς Ῥώμην ἐπὶ τόλμης
καὶ φρονήματος λαμπροῦ, καὶ τἄλλα ὧν ἐς θρασύ-
440 τητα περιώνυμος, ὥστε τὴν βουλὴν δείσασαν ἑλέ-
σθαι τοὺς παρὰ σφίσιν ἐπὶ μεγίστης τότε δόξης
στρατηγούς, Καικίλιόν τε Μέτελλον μετὰ πολλοῦ
στρατοῦ καὶ Γναῖον Πομπήιον ἐπ' ἐκείνῳ μεθ' ἑτέρου
στρατοῦ, ἵνα τὸν πόλεμον, ὅπῃ δύναιντο, ἐξωθοῖεν ἐκ
τῆς Ἰταλίας ἐν διχοστασίᾳ τότε μάλιστα οὔσης.
441 ἀλλὰ Σερτώριον μὲν τῶν στασιωτῶν τις αὐτοῦ Περ-
πέρνας ἀνελὼν ἑαυτὸν ἐπὶ Σερτωρίῳ στρατηγὸν ἀπέφηνε τῆς ἀποστάσεως, Περπέρναν δ' ἔκτεινε μάχῃ
Πομπήιος, καὶ ὁ πόλεμος ὅδε, θορυβήσας δὴ τῷ
φόβῳ μάλιστα Ῥωμαίους, διελύθη. τὸ δ' ἀκριβὲς
αὐτοῦ δηλώσει τὰ περὶ Σύλλαν ἐμφύλια.

442 102. Μετὰ δὲ τὸν Σύλλα θάνατον Γάιος Καῖσαρ
αἱρεθεὶς Ἰβηρίας στρατηγεῖν, ὥστε καὶ πολεμεῖν, οἷς
δεήσειεν, ὅσα τῶν Ἰβήρων ἐσαλεύετο ἢ Ῥωμαίοις ἔτι
443 ἔλειπεν, πολέμῳ συνηνάγκασεν πάντα ὑπακούειν. καί
τινα αὖθις ἀφιστάμενα Ἰούλιος Καῖσαρ, ὁ τοῦ Γαίου
444 παῖς, ὁ Σεβαστὸς ἐπίκλην, ἐχειρώσατο. καὶ ἐξ ἐκείνου

---

94 Q. Caecilius Metellus Pius was consul in 80 and governor
of Farther Spain from 79 to 71. He was joined in Spain from 77
to 71 by Gnaeus Pompey, who was still only twenty-nine years old
at the time of this proconsular command in Spain.

Roman senate and marched against Rome with daring and sparkling determination; he was a man with a wide reputation for general audacity. The senate took fright and appointed the most distinguished generals in Rome at the time, sending first Caecilius Metellus with a large army, and after him Gnaeus Pompey with another army, to do whatever they could to keep the war away from Italy, so badly divided, as it was then, by civil discord.[94] But one of his own party, Perperna, killed Sertorius and declared himself Sertorius' successor as commander of the revolt; and Pompey killed Perperna in battle, thus bringing to an end this war that had so frightened the Romans.[95] My coverage of the civil wars dealing with Sulla will give a detailed account of it.

102. After the death of Sulla, Gaius Caesar was chosen to command in Iberia and wage war wherever it was needed.[96] All Iberians who were wavering or had still not come under Rome's control, he subjected to her will by force. Further revolts were subdued by Gaius' son, Octavius Caesar, called Augustus. It was from this time, I

[95] M. Perperna had reached the praetorship in about 82. According to Plutarch (*Sert.* 27.1–3), he was captured in battle and then executed by Pompey.

[96] Appian's chronology is vague and compressed. Sulla died in 79, and C. Julius Caesar's first service in Spain was as quaestor in Farther Spain in 69 under the governor Antistius Vetus. Praetor in 62, Caesar received the governorship of Farther Spain, where he campaigned widely. In 49 he conducted a rapid campaign against Pompeian forces in Spain, and he completed their destruction in 45 at the battle of Munda.

440

441

442

443
444

μοι δοκοῦσι Ῥωμαῖοι τὴν Ἰβηρίαν, ἣν δὴ νῦν Ἰσπα-
νίαν καλοῦσιν, ἐς τρία διαιρεῖν καὶ στρατηγοὺς ἐπιπέμπειν, ἐτησίους μὲν ἐς τὰ δύο ἡ βουλή, τὸν δὲ
τρίτον βασιλεύς, ἐφ᾽ ὅσον δοκιμάσειεν.

believe, that Rome divided Iberia, which they now call Hispania, into three parts, to which they send governors, the senate on an annual basis to two of them, the emperor to the third, for as long as he chooses.[97]

[97] From 26 to 19 Augustus completed the conquest of Spain. In the west, a largely new province of Lusitania was formed. Nearer Spain was renamed Tarraconensis. Both were under the emperor's direct control. From 27 the senate appointed the governor of Farther Spain, now renamed Baetica.

VII

ἈΝΝΙΒΑΙΚΗ[1]

1. Ὅσα δὲ Ἀννίβας ὁ Καρχηδόνιος ἐξ Ἰβηρίας ἐς Ἰταλίαν ἐσβαλὼν ἑκκαίδεκα ἔτεσιν, οἷς ἐπέμεινε πολεμῶν, ἔδρασέν τε καὶ ἔπαθεν ὑπὸ Ῥωμαίων, ἕως αὐτὸν Καρχηδόνιοί τε κινδυνεύοντες περὶ τῇ πόλει ἐπὶ τὰ σφέτερα μετεπέμψαντο καὶ Ῥωμαῖοι τῆς Ἰταλίας
2 ἐξήλασαν, ἥδε ἡ γραφὴ δηλοῖ. ἥ τις δὲ τῷ Ἀννίβᾳ γέγονε τῆς ἐσβολῆς αἰτία τε ἀληθὴς καὶ πρόφασις ἐς τὸ φανερόν, ἀκριβέστατα μὲν ἐν τῇ Ἰβηρικῇ συγγραφῇ δεδήλωται, συγγράψω δὲ καὶ νῦν ὅσον εἰς ἀνάμνησιν.

3 2. Ἀμίλχαρ, ᾧ Βάρκας ἐπίκλησις ἦν, Ἀννίβου τοῦδε πατήρ, ἐστρατήγει Καρχηδονίων ἐν Σικελίᾳ, ὅτε Ῥωμαῖοι καὶ Καρχηδόνιοι περὶ αὐτῆς ἀλλήλοις ἐπολέμουν. δόξας δὲ πρᾶξαι κακῶς ὑπὸ τῶν ἐχθρῶν ἐδιώκετο καὶ δεδιὼς ἔπραξεν ἐς τοὺς Νομάδας αἱρε-
4 θῆναι στρατηγὸς πρὸ τῶν εὐθυνῶν. γενόμενος δὲ χρήσιμος ἐν τῷδε καὶ τὴν στρατιὰν θεραπεύσας ἁρπαγαῖς καὶ δωρεαῖς ἤγαγεν ἄνευ τοῦ κοινοῦ Καρχη-

---

[1] Ἀππιανοῦ ῥωμαϊκῶν Ἀννιβαϊκή V: Ἀννιβιακή Goukowsky

BOOK VII

THE HANNIBALIC BOOK

1. This book sets out all that Hannibal the Carthaginian did to, and experienced at the hands of, the Romans in the sixteen years during which he remained at war against them, from the time when he invaded Italy from Iberia, until the Carthaginians, with Carthage itself in danger, recalled him to protect their own interests, and the Romans expelled him from Italy. I have explained in great 2 detail in the Iberian book[1] what Hannibal's real reason was for the invasion, and the pretext he presented publicly, but I will describe them again here in enough detail to remind the reader.

2. Hamilcar, who had the surname Barca, father of our 3 Hannibal, was in command of the Carthaginian forces in Sicily, when Rome and Carthage were at war with each other over it. Believed by his enemies to have performed badly, he was indicted, but fearing the outcome, got himself appointed commander against the Numidians before he was audited. He performed well in this role, and having 4 courted the army's favor with plunder and gifts, he led it

[1] *Ib.* 4.15–13.52.

δονίων ἐπὶ Γάδειρα καὶ ἐπέρασε τὸν πορθμὸν ἐς Ἰβηρίαν, ὅθεν λάφυρα πολλὰ διέπεμπεν ἐς Καρχηδόνα,
θεραπεύων τὸ πλῆθος, εἰ δύναιτο μὴ χαλεπαίνειν
5 αὐτῷ τῆς στρατηγίας τῆς ἐν Σικελίᾳ. χώραν δ' αὐτοῦ
κατακτωμένου πολλὴν κλέος τε μέγα ἦν καὶ Καρχηδονίοις ἐπιθυμία πάσης Ἰβηρίας ὡς εὐμαροῦς ἔργου.
6 Ζακανθαῖοι δὲ καὶ ὅσοι ἄλλοι Ἕλληνες ἐν Ἰβηρίᾳ,
καταφεύγουσιν ἐπὶ Ῥωμαίους, καὶ γίγνεται Καρχηδονίοις ὅρος Ἰβηρίας, μὴ διαβαίνειν τὸν Ἴβηρα
ποταμόν· καὶ τόδε ταῖς Ῥωμαίων καὶ Καρχηδονίων
7 σπονδαῖς ἐνεγράφη. ἐπὶ δὲ τούτῳ Βάρκας μέν, τὴν
ὑπὸ Καρχηδονίοις Ἰβηρίαν καθιστάμενος, ἔν τινι
μάχῃ πεσὼν ἀποθνήσκει, καὶ στρατηγὸς Ἀσρούβας
ἐπ' αὐτῷ γίγνεται, ὃς ἐκήδευε τῷ Βάρκᾳ. καὶ τόνδε
μὲν κτείνει θεράπων ἐν κυνηγεσίοις, οὗ τὸν δεσπότην
ἀνῃρήκει.

8   3. Τρίτος δ' ἐπὶ τοῖσδε στρατηγὸς Ἰβήρων ὑπὸ τῆς
στρατιᾶς ἀποδείκνυται, φιλοπόλεμος καὶ συνετὸς εἶναι δοκῶν, Ἀννίβας ὅδε, Βάρκα μὲν υἱὸς ὤν, Ἀσρούβου δὲ τῆς γυναικὸς ἀδελφός, νέος δὲ κομιδῇ καὶ ὡς
μειράκιον ἔτι τῷ πατρὶ καὶ τῷ κηδεστῇ συνών. καὶ ὁ
δῆμος ὁ Καρχηδονίων αὐτῷ τὴν στρατηγίαν ἐπεψή-
9 φισεν. οὕτω μὲν Ἀννίβας, περὶ οὗ τάδε συγγράφω,
γίγνεται στρατηγὸς Καρχηδονίων ἐπὶ Ἴβηρσι· τῶν
δ' ἐχθρῶν τῶν Βάρκα τε καὶ Ἀσρούβου τοὺς φίλους
τοὺς ἐκείνων διωκόντων καὶ Ἀννίβου τοῦδε καταφρο-
νούντων ὡς ἔτι νέου, ἀρχὴν εἶναι τοῦθ' ὁ Ἀννίβας ἐφ'
ἑαυτὸν ἡγούμενος καὶ νομίζων οἱ τὸ ἀσφαλὲς ἐκ τῶν

against Gadeira without the authority of the Carthaginian senate, and crossed the straits to Iberia. From here he sent large quantities of plunder back to Carthage to conciliate the people, and, if possible, end their anger with him over his Sicilian command. He won great glory for the extensive 5 territories he won, and Carthage developed a desire to acquire the whole of Iberia, which they thought would be an easy undertaking. But Saguntum and the other Greeks 6 in Iberia turn for refuge to Rome, and a limit is set for the Carthaginians in Iberia, requiring them not to cross the river Ebro. This stipulation was included in the treaty between Rome and Carthage. Later, having been put in command of Carthaginian Iberia, Barca falls in battle and dies, 7 and is succeeded as general by Hasdrubal, who was his son-in-law. While Hasdrubal was out hunting, a slave, whose master he had put to death, kills him.

3. Subsequently, our Hannibal is chosen by the army 8 to be the third commander in Iberia, as he had a reputation for being warlike and wise. He was the son of Barca and the brother of Hasdrubal's wife, and very young, and while still a youth had lived with his father and brother-in-law. The Carthaginian people voted to confirm his election as general. This is how Hannibal, the subject of this book, 9 comes to be commander of the Carthaginians against the Iberians. When the enemies of Barca and Hasdrubal prosecuted the associates of these men, treating our Hannibal with contempt because they thought he was still young, Hannibal regarded this as the beginning of a move against himself, and believing that his own security was best pre-

τῆς πατρίδος φόβων περιέσεσθαι, ἐς πόλεμον αὐτοὺς
10 μέγαν ἐμβαλεῖν ἐπενόει. ὑπολαβὼν δ᾽, ὥσπερ ἦν, τὸ
Ῥωμαίοις ἐπιχειρῆσαι χρόνιόν τε Καρχηδονίοις ἔσεσθαι καὶ μεγάλην αὑτῷ δόξαν, εἰ καὶ τύχοι πταίσας,
τό γε ἐγχείρημα οἴσειν, λεγόμενος δὲ καὶ ὑπὸ τοῦ
πατρὸς ἐπὶ βωμῶν ἔτι παῖς ὁρκωθῆναι Ῥωμαίοις ἐπι-
βουλεύων οὔ ποτ᾽ ἐκλείψειν, ἐπενόει παρὰ τὰς σπονδὰς τὸν Ἴβηρα διαβῆναι καὶ παρεσκεύαζέ τινας ἐς
11 πρόφασιν κατηγορεῖν Ζακανθαίων. γράφων τε ταῦτα
συνεχῶς ἐς Καρχηδόνα καὶ προστιθείς, ὅτι Ῥωμαῖοι
κρύφα τὴν Ἰβηρίαν αὐτῶν ἀφιστᾶσιν, ἔτυχε παρὰ
12 Καρχηδονίων πράσσειν, ὅ τι δοκιμάσειεν. ὁ μὲν δὴ
τὸν Ἴβηρα διαβὰς τὴν Ζακανθαίων πόλιν ἡβηδὸν
διέφθειρε, Ῥωμαίοις δὲ καὶ Καρχηδονίοις ἐπὶ τῷδε
ἐλέλυντο αἱ σπονδαὶ αἱ γενόμεναι αὐτοῖς μετὰ τὸν
πόλεμον τὸν ἐν Σικελίᾳ.

13 4. Ἀννίβας δὲ ὅσα μὲν αὐτὸς καὶ οἱ μετ᾽ αὐτὸν
ἄλλοι Καρχηδονίων τε καὶ Ῥωμαίων στρατηγοὶ περὶ
Ἰβηρίαν ἔπραξαν, ἡ Ἰβηρικὴ γραφὴ δηλοῖ· ἐπιλεξάμενος δὲ Κελτιβήρων τε καὶ Λιβύων καὶ ἑτέρων ἐθνῶν
ὅτι πλείστους καὶ τὰ ἐν Ἰβηρίᾳ παραδοὺς Ἀσρούβᾳ
τῷ ἀδελφῷ τὰ Πυρηναῖα ὄρη διέβαινεν ἐς τὴν Κελτικὴν τὴν νῦν λεγομένην Γαλατίαν, ἄγων πεζοὺς ἐνα-
κισμυρίους καὶ ἱππέας ἐς δισχιλίοις ἐπὶ μυρίοις καὶ
14 ἐλέφαντας ἑπτὰ καὶ τριάκοντα. Γαλατῶν δὲ τοὺς μὲν
ὠνούμενος, τοὺς δὲ πείθων, τοὺς δὲ καὶ βιαζόμενος
15 διώδευε τὴν χώραν. ἐλθὼν δ᾽ ἐπὶ τὰ Ἄλπεια ὄρη καὶ

served by the fears of his countrymen, he made plans to
involve them in a great war. Assuming, correctly, that at-   10
tacking Rome would occupy Carthage for a long time, and
that the undertaking would bring him great glory, even if
it should happen to fail—it was also said that his father had
made him swear, when he was still a boy, never to stop
plotting against Rome—he planned to break the treaty
and cross the Ebro. To provide a pretext, he suborned
some men to make accusations against Saguntum. By   11
regularly including these reports in his dispatches to Carthage, and adding that the Romans were secretly trying to
get Iberia to revolt from them, he obtained permission
to take whatever action he thought suitable. And so he   12
crossed the Ebro and destroyed the city of Saguntum and
all its adult population, in the process breaking the treaty
made between Rome and Carthage after the war in Sicily.[2]

4. My Iberian book recounts the whole story of what   13
Hannibal himself, and after him, what the other Carthaginian and Roman generals did in Iberia. Collecting as
large a force as possible of Celtiberians, Africans, and
other peoples, he handed the management of Iberia to his
brother Hasdrubal, and crossed the Pyrenees into Celtic
territory, now called Gaul, with an army of ninety thousand infantry, about twenty thousand cavalry, and thirty-
seven elephants. By paying off some of the Gauls, and   14
persuading or using violence against others, he made his
way through their country. Even when he came to the   15

[2] For Appian's incorrect positioning of Saguntum north of the
river Ebro, in order to make any Carthaginian attack on the city
automatically a breach of the agreement not to cross the Ebro,
see *Ib.* 7.25.

μηδεμίαν μήτε δίοδον μήτε ἄνοδον εὑρών (ἀπόκρημνα
γάρ ἐστιν ἰσχυρῶς) ἐπέβαινε κἀκείνοις ὑπὸ τόλμης,
κακοπαθῶν χιόνος τε πολλῆς οὔσης καὶ κρύους, τὴν
μὲν ὕλην τέμνων τε καὶ κατακαίων, τὴν δὲ τέφραν
σβεννὺς ὕδατι καὶ ὄξει καὶ τὴν πέτραν ἐκ τοῦδε
ψαφαρὰν γιγνομένην σφύραις σιδηραῖς θραύων καὶ
ὁδὸν ποιῶν,² ᾗ καὶ νῦν ἐστιν ἐπὶ τῶν ὀρῶν ἐντριβὴς
16   καὶ καλεῖται δίοδος Ἀννίβου. τῶν δὲ τροφῶν αὐτὸν
ἐπιλειπουσῶν ἠπείγετο μέν, ἔτι λανθάνων, ὅτι καὶ
πάρεστιν ἐς τὴν Ἰταλίαν, ἕκτῳ δὲ μόλις ἀπὸ τῆς ἐξ
Ἰβήρων ἀναστάσεως μηνί, πλείστους ἀποβαλών, ἐς
τὸ πεδίον ἐκ τῶν ὀρῶν κατέβαινεν καὶ μικρὸν ἀνα-
παύσας προσέβαλλε Ταυρασίᾳ, πόλει Κελτικῇ.

17   5. Κατὰ κράτος δ' αὐτὴν ἐξελὼν τοὺς μὲν αἰχμαλώτους ἔσφαξεν ἐς κατάπληξιν τῆς ἄλλης Κελτικῆς,
ἐπὶ δὲ ποταμὸν Ἠριδανόν, τὸν νῦν Πάδον λεγόμενον,
ἐλθών, ἔνθα Ῥωμαῖοι Κελτοῖς τοῖς καλουμένοις Βοιοῖς
18   ἐπολέμουν, ἐστρατοπέδευσεν. ὁ δ' ὕπατος ὁ Ῥωμαίων
Πούπλιος Κορνήλιος Σκιπίων, Καρχηδονίοις ἐν Ἰβηρίᾳ πολεμῶν, ἐπεὶ τῆς εἰσβολῆς Ἀννίβου τῆς ἐς τὴν
Ἰταλίαν ἐπύθετο, τὸν ἀδελφὸν καὶ ὅδε Γναῖον Κορνήλιον Σκιπίωνα ἐπὶ τοῖς ἐν Ἰβηρίᾳ πράγμασι καταλιπὼν διέπλευσεν ἐς Τυρρηνίαν, ὅθεν ὁδεύων τε καὶ
συμμάχους, ὅσους δύναιτο, ἀγείρων ἔφθασεν ἐπὶ τὸν
19   Πάδον Ἀννίβαν. καὶ Μάλλιον μὲν καὶ Ἀτίλιον, οἳ τοῖς
Βοιοῖς ἐπολέμουν, ἐς Ῥώμην ἔπεμψεν, ὡς οὐ δέον

---

² ὁδὸν ποιῶν Musgrave: ὁδοποιῶν VM Suda

Alps, although he could find no route through or over them—they are extremely steep—he still had the daring to set about climbing them. Suffering badly from deep snow and freezing temperatures, he cut down wood, burned it and doused the ashes with water and vinegar, thus making the rock brittle. This he then broke up with iron sledgehammers and made a road, which is still used as a track over the mountains, and is called Hannibal's pass. With his food supply running out, he hurried on still 16 unobserved, even when he actually gets to Italy. Scarcely six months after setting out from Iberia, and with heavy losses, he came down from the mountains into the plain, and after a short rest attacked the Celtic town of Taurasia.

5. This he took by storm and slaughtered the prisoners 17 as a way of terrifying the other Celts. He made camp when he reached the river Eridanus, which is now called the Po, a region where the Romans were at war with a Celtic people called the Boii. When he heard of Hannibal's inva- 18 sion of Italy, the Roman consul Publius Cornelius Scipio, who was campaigning against the Carthaginians in Iberia, left his brother Gnaeus Cornelius Scipio in charge of affairs in Iberia, just as Hannibal had done, and sailed to Etruria.[3] Setting out from here and collecting as many allies as he could on the way, he got to the Po before Hannibal, and sent Manlius and Atilius, who were con- 19 ducting operations against the Boii, back to Rome, since

[3] For Appian's earlier account of the Scipio brothers, P. Cornelius Scipio (consul 218) and Cn. Cornelius Scipio Calvus (consul 222), see *Ib.* 14.54–17.64.

αὐτοὺς ἔτι στρατηγεῖν ὑπάτου παρόντος, αὐτὸς δὲ τὸν
στρατὸν παραλαβὼν ἐς μάχην ἐξέτασσεν πρὸς Ἀννί-
20 βαν. καὶ γενομένης ἀκροβολίας τε καὶ ἱππομαχίας οἱ
Ῥωμαῖοι, κυκλωθέντες ὑπὸ τῶν Λιβύων, ἔφευγον ἐς
τὸ στρατόπεδον καὶ νυκτὸς ἐπιγενομένης ἐς Πλακεν-
τίαν ἀνεχώρουν, ἀσφαλῶς τετειχισμένην, τὸν Πάδον
ἐπὶ γεφυρῶν περάσαντές τε καὶ λύσαντες τὰς γεφύρας.

21 6. Τὸν μὲν οὖν ποταμὸν καὶ ὁ Ἀννίβας ζεύξας
ἐπέρα, τὸ δ᾽ ἔργον εὐθὺς τόδε, πρῶτον ἢ δεύτερον ἐπὶ
τῇ τῶν Ἀλπείων ὀρῶν διαβάσει, παρὰ τοῖς ἐπέκεινα
Κελτῶν ἐξῆρε τὸν Ἀννίβαν ὡς ἄμαχον στρατηγὸν
καὶ τύχῃ λαμπρᾷ χρώμενον. ὁ δ᾽, ὡς ἐν βαρβάροις τε
καὶ τεθηπόσιν αὐτὸν καὶ δι᾽ ἄμφω δυναμένοις ἀπατᾶ-
σθαι, τὴν ἐσθῆτα καὶ τὴν κόμην ἐνήλλασσε συνεχῶς
22 ἐσκευασμέναις ‹. . .›[3] ἐπινοίαις· καὶ αὐτὸν οἱ Κελτοὶ
περιόντα τὰ ἔθνη πρεσβύτην ὁρῶντες, εἶτα νέον, εἶτα
μεσαιπόλιον καὶ συνεχῶς ἕτερον ἐξ ἑτέρου, θαυμάζον-
23 τες ἐδόκουν θειοτέρας φύσεως λαχεῖν. Σεμπρώνιος δ᾽,
ὁ ἕτερος ὕπατος, ἐν Σικελίᾳ τότε ὢν καὶ πυθόμενος,
διέπλευσε πρὸς τὸν Σκιπίωνα καὶ τεσσαράκοντα σταδίους αὐτοῦ διασχὼν ἐστρατοπέδευσε· καὶ τῆς ἐπιού-
24 σης ἔμελλον ἅπαντες ἐς μάχην ἥξειν. ποταμὸς δ᾽ ἦν
ἐν μέσῳ Τρεβίας, ὃν Ῥωμαῖοι πρὸ ἕω, χειμερίου τε
τῆς τροπῆς οὔσης καὶ ὑετοῦ καὶ κρύους, ἐπέρων βρε-

3 ante ἐπινοίαις lac. ind. Goukowsky; ἐσκευασμέναις V M;
ἐσκευασμένος Hermann

it was not fitting for them to continue in command with a consul present.[4] He himself took over the army and drew it up for battle with Hannibal. There was skirmishing and 20 a cavalry engagement, but when surrounded by the Africans the Romans escaped to their camp. At nightfall, they retreated to the strongly fortified town of Placentia, having crossed the Po by bridge, and then destroyed the bridges.

6. Hannibal too, however, bridged the river and made 21 his way across. This exploit, coming more or less straight after his crossing of the Alps, immediately raised Hannibal in the estimation of the Celts in the area, who saw him as a general both invincible and strikingly lucky. Finding himself among barbarians, and men in awe of him, whom he thought could be deceived on both counts, he took to 22 changing his clothes and hair continually with prearranged plans.[5] For when the Celts saw him moving among their peoples now an old man, now young, now middle-aged, and constantly changing from one to the other, they were amazed and regarded him as partly godlike in nature. Sempronius, the other consul,[6] was at the time in Sicily, 23 but when he learned of what happened, he sailed straight to Scipio and encamped forty stades from him. The intention was that they would all go into battle the next day. Between the two armies lay the river Trebia which the 24 Romans crossed before dawn by wading up to their chest in water, although it was the time of the winter solstice,

[4] L. Manlius Vulso and C. Atilius Serranus were praetors in 218.   [5] There may be a lacuna in the text here: the Greek as it stands does not make easy sense.

[6] Tib. Sempronius Longus, consul with Cn. Cornelius Scipio in 218.

χόμενοι μέχρι τῶν μαστῶν. Ἀννίβας δὲ καὶ ἐς δευτέραν ὥραν ἀνέπαυσε τὴν στρατιὰν καὶ τότε ἐξῆγε.

25   7. Παράταξις δ' ἦν ἑκατέρων ‹. . .› τὰ κέρατα κατ-
εῖχον, ἀμφὶ τὴν φάλαγγα τῶν πεζῶν. Ἀννίβας δὲ τοῖς
μὲν ἱππεῦσιν ἀντέταξε τοὺς ἐλέφαντας, τῇ δὲ φάλαγγι
τοὺς πεζούς· τοὺς δ' ἱππέας ἐκέλευσεν ὀπίσω τῶν ἐλε-
26   φάντων ἀτρεμεῖν, ἕως αὐτός τι σημήνῃ. γενομένων δ'
ἐν χερσὶ πάντων οἱ μὲν Ῥωμαίων ἵπποι τοὺς ἐλέφαντας, οὐ φέροντες αὐτῶν οὔτε τὴν ὄψιν οὔτε τὴν ὀδμήν,
ἔφευγον· οἱ δὲ πεζοί, καίπερ ὑπὸ τοῦ κρύους καὶ τοῦ
ποταμοῦ καὶ τῆς ἀγρυπνίας τετρυμένοι τε καὶ μαλα-
κοὶ ὄντες, ὅμως ὑπὸ τόλμης τοῖς θηρίοις ἐπεπήδων
καὶ ἐτίτρωσκον αὐτὰ καί τινων καὶ τὰ νεῦρα ὑπέκο-
27   πτον καὶ τοὺς πεζοὺς ἐνέκλινον ἤδη. θεασάμενος δ' ὁ
Ἀννίβας ἐσήμηνε τὴν ἵππον κυκλοῦσθαι τοὺς πολεμίους. ἐσκεδασμένων δ' ἄρτι τῶν Ῥωμαϊκῶν ἱππέων
διὰ τὰ θηρία καὶ τῶν πεζῶν μόνων τε ὄντων καὶ κακοπαθούντων καὶ δεδιότων τὴν περικύκλωσιν φυγὴ
28   πανταχόθεν ἦν ἐς τὰ στρατόπεδα. καὶ ἀπώλλυντο οἱ
μὲν ὑπὸ τῶν ἱππέων, καταλαμβανόντων ἅτε πεζούς,
οἱ δ' ὑπὸ τοῦ ποταμοῦ παραφέροντος· τοῦ γὰρ ἡλίου
τὴν χιόνα τήξαντος ὁ ποταμὸς ἐρρύη μέγας, καὶ οὔτε
στῆναι διὰ τὸ βάθος οὔτε νεῖν διὰ τὰ ὅπλα ἐδύναντο.
29   Σκιπίων δὲ αὐτοῖς ἑπόμενος καὶ παρακαλῶν ὀλίγου
μὲν ἐδέησε τρωθεὶς διαφθαρῆναι, μόλις δ' ἐς Κρεμῶνα
30   διεσώθη φερόμενος. ἐπίνειον δὲ ἦν τι βραχὺ Πλακεν-

and the weather was wet and cold. Hannibal rested his army until the second hour and then led them out to battle.

7. The battle line of each side was ‹arranged as follows: the Roman cavalry?›[7] held the wings, on either side of the infantry phalanx. Hannibal stationed his elephants opposite the Roman cavalry and his infantry facing the Roman phalanx; he ordered his cavalry to hold position behind the elephants until he himself gave the signal. When everyone joined battle, the Roman horses could not stand the sight or smell of the elephants, and fled, but the infantry, although distressed and weakened by the cold, their soaking in the river and lack of sleep, still bravely attacked these animals and wounded them, in some cases cutting their hamstring; and they were already causing the Carthaginian line to yield. When Hannibal saw this he signaled his cavalry to circle round behind the enemy. As the Roman cavalry had just been scattered because of the elephants, the infantry were left on their own and found themselves struggling. Fearing encirclement, they fled in all sectors back to their camp. Some died overtaken by the cavalry, as you would expect of men on foot, others carried off by the river. For, as the sun had melted the snow, this was now a swollen torrent, and they could not stand up because the water was too deep, and they could not swim because of their armor. Scipio followed and tried to rally them, but was wounded and narrowly missed being killed. He was rescued with considerable difficulty and taken to Cremona. There was a small naval depot belonging to

25

26

27

28

29

30

[7] There is a lacuna in the text at this point, but it should contain something as suggested.

APPIAN

τίας, ᾧ προσβαλὼν ὁ Ἀννίβας ἀπώλεσε τετρακοσίους
καὶ αὐτὸς ἐτρώθη. καὶ ἀπὸ τοῦδε πάντες ἐχείμαζον,
Σκιπίων μὲν ἐν Κρεμῶνι καὶ Πλακεντίᾳ, Ἀννίβας δὲ
περὶ Πάδον.

31   8. Οἱ δ᾽ ἐν ἄστει Ῥωμαῖοι, πυθόμενοι καὶ τρίτον
ἤδη πταίοντες περὶ Πάδον (ἥττηντο γὰρ δὴ καὶ ὑπὸ
Βοιῶν πρὸ Ἀννίβου), στρατιάν τε παρ᾽ αὐτῶν ἄλλην
κατέλεγον, σὺν τοῖς οὖσι περὶ τὸν Πάδον ὡς εἶναι
τρισκαίδεκα τέλη, καὶ τοῖς συμμάχοις ἑτέραν διπλα-
σίονα ταύτης ἐπήγγελλον. ἤδη δ᾽ αὐτοῖς τὸ τέλος εἶχε
32   πεζοὺς πεντακισχιλίους καὶ ἱππέας τριακοσίους. καὶ
τούτων τοὺς μὲν ἐς Ἰβηρίαν ἔπεμπον, τοὺς δ᾽ ἐς Σαρδόνα, κἀκείνην πολεμουμένην, τοὺς δ᾽ ἐς Σικελίαν· τὰ
πλέονα δ᾽ ἦγον ἐπὶ τὸν Ἀννίβαν οἱ μετὰ Σκιπίωνα καὶ
Σεμπρώνιον αἱρεθέντες ὕπατοι, Σερουίλιός τε Γναῖος
33   καὶ Γάιος Φλαμίνιος. ὧν ὁ μὲν Σερουίλιος, ἐπὶ τὸν
Πάδον ἐπειχθείς, τὴν στρατηγίαν ἐκδέχεται παρὰ τοῦ
Σκιπίωνος (ὁ δὲ Σκιπίων, ἀνθύπατος αἱρεθείς, ἐς Ἰβηρίαν διέπλευσεν), Φλαμίνιος δὲ τρισμυρίοις τε πεζοῖς
καὶ τρισχιλίοις ἱππεῦσι τὴν ἐντὸς Ἀπεννίνων ὀρῶν
Ἰταλίαν ἐφύλασσεν, ἣν καὶ μόνην ἄν τις εἴποι κυρίως
34   Ἰταλίαν. τὰ γὰρ Ἀπεννῖνα κατέρχεται μὲν ἐκ μέσων
τῶν Ἀλπείων ἐπὶ θάλασσαν, ἔστι δ᾽ αὐτῶν τὰ μὲν ἐπὶ
δεξιὰ πάντα καθαρῶς Ἰταλία, τὰ δ᾽ ἐπὶ θάτερα, ἐς τὸν
Ἰόνιον φθάνοντα, νῦν μέν ἐστι καὶ ταῦτ᾽ Ἰταλία [ὅτι
καὶ Τυρρηνία νῦν Ἰταλία],[4] οἰκοῦσι δ᾽ αὐτῶν τὰ μὲν

[4] ὅτι καὶ Τυρρηνία νῦν Ἰταλία del. Viereck-Roos

Placentia which Hannibal attacked, but he lost four hundred men and was wounded himself. After this, all parties went into winter quarters, Scipio in Cremona and Placentia, Hannibal on the Po.

8. When news got through to the city of Rome itself— this was now the third defeat they had suffered in the Po region, having already been beaten by the Boii before Hannibal's arrival—they recruited another citizen army. Along with those on the Po, they now had thirteen legions, and they demanded another contingent twice that number from the allies. In that period, a legion had five thousand infantry and three hundred cavalry. They sent some of these to Iberia, others to Sardinia, where there was also fighting, and others to Sicily. But the majority were directed against Hannibal under the command of the next consuls chosen after Scipio and Sempronius, Gnaeus Servilius and Gaius Flaminius.[8] Servilius made straight for the Po, where he took over the command from Scipio, who had been made proconsul and sailed for Iberia, while Flaminius with thirty thousand infantry and three thousand cavalry, guarded the part of Italy to the west of the Apennine mountains, which is the only part that can really be called Italy. The Apennines stretch from the middle of the Alps down to the Mediterranean. Everything to the right of them is Italy proper, although the territory on the other side extending to the Ionian sea is now also called Italy [just as Etruria is now called Italy]. Part of the region is

31

32

33

34

8 Cn. Servilius Geminus and C. Flaminius, the consuls of 217.

Ἕλληνες, ἀμφὶ τὴν Ἰόνιον ἀκτήν, τὰ δὲ λοιπὰ Κελτοί, ὅσοι τῇ Ῥώμῃ τὸ πρῶτον ἐπιθέμενοι τὴν πόλιν
35 ἐνέπρησαν. ὅτε γὰρ αὐτοὺς ἐξελαύνων Κάμιλλος
ἐδίωκε μέχρι τῶν Ἀπεννίνων ὀρῶν, ἐμοὶ δοκοῦσιν
ὑπερβάντες αὐτά, ἀντὶ ἠθῶν τῶν ἰδίων, παρὰ τὸν
Ἰόνιον οἰκῆσαι· καὶ τὸ μέρος τῆς χώρας ἔτι νῦν οὕτω
καλοῦσιν, Ἰταλίαν Γαλατικήν.

36 9. Ῥωμαῖοι μὲν δὴ μεγάλοις στρατοῖς ἐς πολλὰ
ὁμοῦ διῄρηντο· Ἀννίβας δὲ τούτων αἰσθόμενος ἅμα
τῷ ἦρι τοὺς ἄλλους λαθὼν ἐδῄου τὴν Τυρρηνίαν καὶ
37 προύβαινεν ἐς τὸ μέρος τὸ ἐπὶ Ῥώμης. οἱ δὲ πλησι-
άζοντος αὐτοῦ πάνυ ἔδεισαν, οὐ παρούσης σφίσιν
ἀξιομάχου δυνάμεως. ἐστράτευον δὲ ὅμως ἐκ τῶν
ὑπολοίπων ὀκτακισχιλίους καὶ Κεντήνιον αὐτοῖς, τινὰ
τῶν ἐπιφανῶν ἰδιωτῶν, οὐδεμιᾶς ἀρχῆς παρούσης,
ἐπέστησάν τε καὶ ἐξέπεμπον ἐς Ὀμβρικοὺς ἐς τὴν
Πλειστίνην λίμνην, τὰ στενὰ προληψόμενον, ᾗ συν-
38 τομώτατόν ἐστιν ἐπὶ τὴν Ῥώμην. ἐν δὲ τούτῳ καὶ
Φλαμίνιος ὁ τοῖς τρισμυρίοις τὴν ἐντὸς Ἰταλίαν φυ-
λάσσων, αἰσθόμενος τῆς σπουδῆς Ἀννίβου, μετέβαινεν ὀξέως, οὐ διαναπαύων τὴν στρατιάν· δέει τε περὶ
τῆς πόλεως καὶ αὐτὸς ὢν ἀπειροπόλεμός τε καὶ ἐς τὴν

---

9 M. Furius Camillus, the famous fourth-century dictator, was
closely involved in securing the departure of the Gauls who
sacked Rome in 387.

10 Little is known about C. Centenius. Livy (22.8.1) and Cor-

inhabited by Greeks, along the Ionian shore, and the rest by Celts, who in the early days attacked Rome and burned the city. When Camillus drove them off and pursued them 35 to the Apennines, I believe they crossed the mountains and settled by the Ionian sea, instead of returning to their own homes.[9] Even now that part of the country is still called Gallic Italy.

9. The Romans, then, had divided their numerous 36 forces for many simultaneous operations. Hannibal realized this, and at the beginning of spring, avoiding detection he ravaged Etruria and advanced into the region of Rome itself. The inhabitants became very afraid at his 37 approach, as they had no military resources to match him. Nevertheless they enlisted eight thousand men from those who were left available, and, as there were no regular magistrates present, placed Centenius in command of them, a private citizen of high social rank.[10] He was dispatched to Umbria to the Plestine lake, to occupy the passes there that provide the quickest route to Rome.[11] Meanwhile, Flaminius was guarding the interior of It- 38 aly with his thirty thousand troops. When he learned of Hannibal's rapid advance, however, he too moved his position quickly without letting his army rest. Out of fear for the safety of the city, and although he himself lacked military experience and had only been elected to political

nelius Nepos (*Hann.* 4.3) indicate that he had reached the praetorship, but Appian's description of him is very vague.

[11] It is not clear what lake or marsh Appian is referring to, but Plestia (mod. Colfiorito) is located in the hills (at 2,500 feet above sea level) on the border with the Marche, some thirty-seven miles east of Perugia.

ἀρχὴν ἀπὸ δοξοκοπίας ᾑρημένος ἠπείγετο Ἀννίβᾳ
συμπλεκῆναι.

39   10. Ὁ δὲ αἰσθόμενος αὐτοῦ τῆς τε ὁρμῆς καὶ ἀπει-
ρίας ὄρος μέν τι καὶ λίμνην προυβάλετο πρὸ ἑαυτοῦ,
ψιλοὺς δὲ καὶ ἱππέας ἐς φάραγγα ἀποκρύψας ἐστρα-
40 τοπέδευεν. καὶ αὐτὸν ὁ Φλαμίνιος κατιδὼν ἅμα ἔῳ
σμικρὸν μέν τι διέτριψε, τὸν στρατὸν ἀναπαύων ἐξ
ὁδοιπορίας καὶ χαρακοποιούμενος, μετὰ δὲ τοῦτο ἐξῆ-
γεν εὐθὺς ἐπὶ τὴν μάχην αὐτοὺς, ὄντας[5] ὑπ' ἀγρυ-
41 πνίας καὶ κόπου. τῆς δ' ἐνέδρας ἐκφανείσης, ἐν μέσῳ
ληφθεὶς τοῦ τε ὄρους καὶ τῆς λίμνης καὶ τῶν ἐχθρῶν,
42 αὐτός τε ἀνῃρέθη καὶ σὺν αὐτῷ δισμύριοι. τοὺς δὲ
λοιποὺς ἔτι μυρίους ἔς τινα κώμην ὀχυρὰν συμφυγόντας Μαάρβαλ, ὁ ὑποστράτηγος Ἀννίβου, μεγίστην
καὶ ὅδε ἐπὶ στρατηγίᾳ δόξαν ἔχων, οὐ δυνάμενος
ἑλεῖν εὐχερῶς οὐδ' ἀξιῶν ἀπεγνωκόσι μάχεσθαι,
ἔπεισε τὰ ὅπλα ἀποθέσθαι, συνθέμενος ἀπολύσειν,
ὅπῃ θέλοιεν. ὡς δὲ ἀπέθεντο, λαβὼν ἦγεν αὐτοὺς
43 πρὸς τὸν Ἀννίβαν γυμνούς. ὁ δ' οὐ φάμενος εἶναι
κύριον χωρὶς αὐτοῦ ταῦτα συνθέσθαι τὸν Μαάρβαλ,
τοὺς μὲν ἐκ τῶν συμμάχων φιλανθρωπευσάμενος
ἀπέλυσεν ἐς τὰ ἑαυτῶν, θηρεύων τῇ φιλανθρωπίᾳ τὰς
44 πόλεις, ὅσοι δὲ Ῥωμαίων ἦσαν, εἶχε δήσας. τὴν δὲ
λείαν τοῖς συστρατεύουσι Κελτοῖς ἀποδόμενος, ἵνα
καὶ τούσδε θεραπεύσειε τῷ κέρδει, προύβαινεν ἐς τὸ

---

[5] τὴν μάχην αὐτοὺς, ὄντας V Gaillard; τὴν μάχην, αὔους
ὄντας Viereck-Roos

office by courting popular favor, he rushed to engage Hannibal.[12]

10. Hannibal was aware of his rash inexperience and made camp with a mountain and a lake[13] to the front of his position, but hid some light-armed troops and cavalry in a ravine. At dawn, Flaminius saw him, but delayed for a short time to rest his army after their march and the building of the palisade. He then led them straight into battle, although they were suffering from lack of sleep and too much work. When the ambush was sprung, Flaminius himself was caught between the mountain, the lake and the enemy, and was killed, along with twenty thousand of his men. The remaining ten thousand fled to a strongly fortified village, where Maharbal, Hannibal's second-in-command, also a man of the highest military reputation, persuaded them to lay down their weapons, as it would be no easy task to capture the village and he did not think it worth fighting against desperate men. When he agreed to release them and let them go wherever they wanted, they put their weapons aside, and he took them to Hannibal unarmed. Hannibal said that Maharbal did not have the authority to make such an agreement without his approval, but he treated the Roman allies among them courteously and released them to their homes, trying to win over their towns with his kindness; the Romans, however, he kept in irons. He distributed the booty to the Celts serving with him, to cultivate their loyalty too with mate-

39

40

41

42

43

44

---

[12] Other sources report that he entered office at Ariminum (mod. Rimini), failed to take the auspices at Rome, and neglected evil omens.

[13] Lake Trasimene, after which the ensuing battle is named.

πρόσθεν, αἰσθομένου μὲν ἤδη τῶν γιγνομένων τοῦ
περὶ Πάδον στρατηγοῦ Σερουιλίου καὶ τετρακισμυ-
ρίοις ἐπὶ Τυρρηνίας ἐπειγομένου, Κεντηνίου δὲ ἤδη
τοῖς ὀκτακισχιλίοις τὰ στενὰ προειληφότος.

45   11. Ἀννίβας δέ, ἐπειδὴ τήν τε λίμνην εἶδε τὴν
Πλειστίνην καὶ τὸ ὄρος τὸ ὑπὲρ αὐτὴν καὶ τὸν Κεντήνιον ἐν μέσῳ κρατοῦντα τῆς διόδου, τοὺς ἡγεμόνας
46   τῶν ὁδῶν ἐξήταζεν, εἴ τις εἴη περίοδος. οὐδεμίαν δὲ
φαμένων εἶναι τρίβον, ἀλλὰ ἀπόκρημνα πάντα καὶ
φαραγγώδη δι᾽ αὐτῶν ὅμως ἔπεμπε τοὺς ψιλοὺς
νύκτωρ τὸ ὄρος περιέναι, καὶ Μαάρβαλ μετ᾽ αὐτῶν.
τεκμηράμενος δ᾽, ὅτε δύναιντο περιελθεῖν, προσέ-
47   βαλλε τῷ Κεντηνίῳ κατὰ μέτωπον. καὶ συνεστώτων
ἑκατέρων πάνυ προθύμως, ὁ Μαάρβαλ ἐκ κορυφῆς
ἄνωθεν ὤφθη τε καὶ ἠλάλαξεν. Ῥωμαίων δ᾽ εὐθὺς ἦν
φυγὴ καὶ φόνος κεκυκλωμένων, καὶ τρισχίλιοι μὲν
ἔπεσον, ὀκτακόσιοι δ᾽ ἐλήφθησαν· οἱ δὲ λοιποὶ μόλις
48   διέφυγον. πυθόμενοι δ᾽ οἱ ἐν ἄστει καὶ δείσαντες, μὴ
εὐθὺς ἐπὶ τὴν πόλιν ὁ Ἀννίβας ἔλθοι, τό τε τεῖχος
ἐπλήρουν λίθων καὶ τοὺς γέροντας ὥπλιζον, ὅπλων
μὲν ἀποροῦντες, τὰ δὲ λάφυρα ἐκ τῶν ἱερῶν κατα-
φέροντες, ἃ ἐκ πολέμων ἄλλων κόσμος αὐτοῖς περι-
έκειτο· δικτάτορά τε, ὡς ἐν κινδύνῳ, Φάβιον εἵλοντο
Μάξιμον.

49   12. Ἀννίβας δέ, θεοῦ παράγοντος αὐτόν, ἐπὶ τὸν
Ἰόνιον αὖθις ἐτράπη καὶ τὴν παράλιον ὁδεύων ἐπόρ-

---

[14] Q. Fabius Maximus Verrucosus, consul five times between

rial gain, and then he continued his advance. Servilius, in command on the Po, and now aware of what had happened, rushed to Etruria with forty thousand men, while Centenius had already occupied the previously mentioned passes with his eight thousand men.

11. When Hannibal saw the Plestine lake and the 45 mountain above it, and Centenius in between controlling the pass, he asked the guides if there was any way around it. In spite of them saying there was no track and that the 46 whole area was steep and filled with ravines, Hannibal sent in his light-armed troops to circle around behind the mountain at night, under the command of Maharbal. When, according to his estimation, they had been able to make their way around, he attacked Centenius head on. With the two sides locked in fierce combat, Maharbal ap- 47 peared on the ridge above and raised a war cry. The Romans immediately fled, and being surrounded, there was a massacre: three thousand were killed and eight hundred captured. The rest just about succeeded in escaping. As 48 soon as they got news of this in Rome, the fear arose that Hannibal would immediately move against the city, so they piled stones on the walls and armed the old men. Since they were short of weapons, they took down and used the spoils from previous wars with which they had adorned the temples. As was their practice when in danger, they chose a dictator, Fabius Maximus.[14]

12. A god led Hannibal astray, however, and he turned 49 back to the Ionian sea, where he devastated the coast on

233 and 209, developed his famous policy of not engaging Hannibal in pitched battle, for which he was called Cunctator ("the Delayer").

50 θει λείαν τε περιήλαυνε πολλήν. Σερουίλιος δ᾿ ὕπατος
ἀντιπαριὼν αὐτῷ κατῆρεν εἰς Ἀρίμινον, ἀπέχων Ἀννίβου μίαν ἡμέραν· ἔνθα τὴν στρατιὰν συνεῖχε καὶ
τοὺς ἔτι φίλους Κελτῶν ἀνεθάρρυνεν, ἕως ἀφικόμενος
Φάβιος Μάξιμος ὁ δικτάτωρ Σερουίλιον μὲν ἐς
Ῥώμην ἔπεμπεν, ὡς οὔτε ὕπατον οὔτε στρατηγὸν
ἔτι ὄντα δικτάτορος ᾑρημένου, αὐτὸς δὲ τῷ Ἀννίβᾳ
παρακολουθῶν ἐς μὲν χεῖρας οὐκ ᾔει, πολλάκις ἐκείνου προκαλουμένου, πολιορκεῖν δ᾿ οὐδένα εἴα, παραφυ-
51 λάσσων καὶ ἐπικείμενος. ὁ δὲ τῆς χώρας ἐξανηλω-
μένης τροφῶν ἠπόρει καὶ αὐτὴν αὖθις περιιὼν
ἑκάστης ἡμέρας ἐξέτασσε, προκαλούμενος ἐς μάχην·
Φάβιος δ᾿ οὐ συνεπλέκετο, καταγινώσκοντος αὐτοῦ
Μινουκίου Ῥούφου, ὃς ἵππαρχος μὲν ἦν αὐτῷ, ἔγραφε
δ᾿ ἐς Ῥώμην τοῖς φίλοις, ὡς ὀκνοίη Φάβιος ὑπὸ δει-
52 λίας. διαδραμόντος δ᾿ ἐς Ῥώμην ἐπὶ θυσίας τινὰς τοῦ
Φαβίου ὁ Μινούκιος ἡγούμενος τοῦ στρατοῦ συν-
επλέκη τινὰ μάχην τῷ Ἀννίβᾳ καὶ δόξας πλέον ἔχειν
θρασύτερον ἐς Ῥώμην ἐπέστελλε τῇ βουλῇ, τὸν Φάβιον αἰτιώμενος οὐκ ἐθέλοντα νικῆσαι. καὶ ἡ βουλή,
ἐπανεληλυθότος ἐς τὸ στρατόπεδον ἤδη τοῦ Φαβίου,
ἴσον ἰσχύειν αὐτῷ τὸν ἵππαρχον ἀπέφηνεν.
53   13. Οἱ μὲν δὴ μερισάμενοι τὴν στρατιὰν πλησίον
ἀλλήλων ἐστρατοπέδευον καὶ τῆς γνώμης ἑκάτερος

---

15 M. Minucius Rufus, consul in 221.

16 Polybius (3.103.4) interprets this to mean that there were
twin dictators, Livy (22.25–26) simply that the dictator and the

his march, and collected a great deal of booty. The consul 50
Servilius followed a route parallel to him, and came down
to Ariminum, one day's journey separating him from
Hannibal. He based his army here and set about encouraging the Celts who remained allies of Rome, until the
dictator Fabius Maximus arrived and sent him to Rome,
as he was no longer either consul or general, now that a
dictator had been appointed. Fabius himself shadowed
Hannibal, but refused to join battle, although often challenged to do so, and by pressing him hard and keeping a
close watch on him, he prevented him from laying siege
to any town. With the country exhausted, Hannibal was 51
running out of supplies and traversed it again, arraying his
army each day to challenge Fabius to battle. But, while
Fabius would not engage, his master of horse, Minucius
Rufus, began to criticize him and wrote to his associates
in Rome accusing him of hesitating out of cowardice.[15]
When Fabius had to rush off to Rome to perform some 52
sacrificial ceremonies, Minucius took command of the
army and fought an engagement with Hannibal. Thinking
that he had come out on top, he wrote rather recklessly to
the senate in Rome, accusing Fabius of not wanting to
defeat Hannibal. As soon as Fabius was back in camp, the
senate declared that the master of horse should have the
same power as him.[16]

13. At any rate, they divided up the army and camped 53
near each other; and they both stuck to their own opinion,

master of horse had equal power. The idea of twin dictators can
scarcely be right, as the whole point of the dictatorship was its
singularity.

329

εἴχοντο τῆς ἑαυτοῦ, Φάβιος μὲν ἐκτρύχειν Ἀννίβαν τῷ χρόνῳ καὶ πειρᾶσθαι μηδὲν ὑπ' αὐτοῦ παθεῖν, ὁ
54 δὲ Μινούκιος μάχῃ διακριθῆναι. συνιόντος δ' ἐς μάχην τοῦ Μινουκίου Φάβιος, τὸ μέλλον ἔσεσθαι προορῶν, ἐν μέσῳ τὴν στρατιὰν ἀτρεμοῦσαν ἔστησε τὴν ἑαυτοῦ καὶ τοὺς τοῦ Μινουκίου τραπέντας ἀνελάμβα-
55 νεν, τοὺς δ' Ἀννίβου διώκοντας ἀπεκρούετο. καὶ Φάβιος μὲν ὧδε τὴν συμφορὰν ἐπεκούφισε τῷ Μινουκίῳ, οὐδὲν ἐπιμηνίσας τῆς διαβολῆς· ὁ δὲ Μινούκιος αὐτοῦ καταγνοὺς ἀπειρίαν ἀπέθετο τὴν ἀρχὴν καὶ τὸ μέρος τοῦ στρατοῦ παρέδωκε τῷ Φαβίῳ, ἡγουμένῳ πρὸς ἄν-
56 δρα τεχνίτην μάχης ἕνα καιρὸν εἶναι τὴν ἀνάγκην. οὗ δὴ καὶ ὁ Σεβαστὸς ὕστερον πολλάκις ἐμέμνητο, οὐκ ὢν εὐχερὴς οὐδ' οὗτος ἐς μάχας τόλμῃ μᾶλλον ἢ τέ-
57 χνῃ χρῆσθαι. Φάβιος μὲν οὖν αὖθις ὁμοίως ἐφύλασσε τὸν Ἀννίβαν καὶ τὴν χώραν πορθεῖν ἐκώλυεν, οὐ συμπλεκόμενος αὐτοῦ τῷ στρατῷ παντί, τοῖς δ' ἀποσκιδναμένοις μόνοις ἐπιτιθέμενος καὶ σαφῶς εἰδὼς ἀπορήσοντα τροφῶν αὐτίκα τὸν Ἀννίβαν.

58   14. Στενῆς δὲ διόδου πλησιαζούσης, ὁ μὲν Ἀννίβας αὐτὴν οὐ προείδετο, Φάβιος δὲ προπέμψας τετρακισχιλίους κατέλαβε καὶ τοῖς λοιποῖς αὐτὸς ἐπὶ θάτερα
59 ἐστρατοπέδευεν ἐπὶ λόφου καρτεροῦ. ὁ δὲ Ἀννίβας, ὡς ᾔσθετο ληφθεὶς ἐν μέσῳ Φαβίου τε καὶ τῶν στενῶν φυλασσομένων, ἔδεισε μὲν ὡς οὔ ποτε πρότερον· οὐ γὰρ εἶχε διέξοδον, ἀλλὰ πάντα ἦν ἀπόκρημνα καὶ δύσβατα, οὐδ' ἤλπιζε Φάβιον ἢ τοὺς ἐπὶ τῶν στενῶν βιάσεσθαι διὰ τὴν τῶν χωρίων ὀχυρότητα.

Fabius in wanting to wear Hannibal down over time and seek to avoid being harmed by him, Minucius looking for a decisive engagement. When Minucius did join battle, 54 Fabius saw beforehand what was going to happen and stationed his own troops in the open, but holding position, with the result that when Minucius' troops were put to flight he was able to take them in and beat off Hannibal's pursuing forces. In this way Fabius minimized the effect 55 of Minucius' defeat, showing no resentment at his slanders. And recognizing his own inexperience, Minucius resigned his command and transferred his part of the army to Fabius, who believed that the only right time to engage a brilliant military commander is when there is no other option. In later times, Augustus often made reference to 56 this, another person who was less keen to go into battle than to employ daring and skill. So Fabius again kept 57 watch on Hannibal as before, and prevented him from pillaging the country by not coming to grips with the whole Carthaginian army, but only attacking stragglers, as he knew well that Hannibal would soon be short of supplies.

14. Fabius now sent forward four thousand men and 58 occupied a narrow pass they were approaching, which Hannibal did not know about; with the rest of his force he himself pitched camp in a strong position on a hill on the other side of Hannibal. When Hannibal realized he had 59 been caught between Fabius and the pass, which was now guarded, Hannibal was more afraid than he had ever been before. For he had no way out, the whole surrounding terrain being precipitous and impassable. Nor had he any hope of forcing his way past Fabius or those at the pass, as

60 ὧδε δὲ ἔχων ἀπορίας τοὺς μὲν αἰχμαλώτους, ἐς πεντακισχιλίους ὄντας, κατέσφαξεν, ἵνα μὴ ἐν τῷ κινδύνῳ
νεωτερίσειαν, βοῦς δὲ ὅσας εἶχεν ἐν τῷ στρατοπέδῳ
(πολὺ δὲ πλῆθος ἦν), τοῖς κέρασιν αὐτῶν δᾷδας περι-
έθηκε καὶ νυκτὸς ἐπιγενομένης τὰς δᾷδας ἐξάψας τὸ
λοιπὸν ἐν τῷ στρατοπέδῳ πῦρ ἔσβεσεν καὶ σιγὴν
βαθεῖαν ἔχειν παρήγγειλε, τοῖς δ' εὐτολμοτάτοις τῶν
νέων ἐκέλευσε τὰς βοῦς ἐλαύνειν μετὰ σπουδῆς ἄνω
πρὸς τὰ ἀπόκρημνα, ἃ ἦν ἐν μέσῳ τοῦ τε Φαβίου καὶ
61 τῶν στενῶν. αἱ δ', ὑπό τε τῶν ἐλαυνόντων ἐπειγόμεναι
καὶ τοῦ πυρὸς ἐκκαίοντος αὐτάς, ἀνεπήδων ἐπὶ τοὺς
κρημνοὺς ἀφειδῶς καὶ βιαίως, εἶτα κατέπιπτον καὶ
αὖθις ἀνεπήδων.

62 15. Ῥωμαῖοι δὲ οἱ ἑκατέρωθεν, ὁρῶντες ἐν μὲν τῷ
Ἀννίβου στρατοπέδῳ σιγὴν καὶ σκότον, ἐν δὲ τοῖς
ὄρεσι πῦρ πολὺ καὶ ποικίλον, οὐκ ἔχοντες ὡς ἐν νυκτὶ
τὸ γινόμενον ἀκριβῶς ἐπινοῆσαι, ὁ μὲν Φάβιος εἴκα-
ζεν εἶναί τι στρατήγημα τοῦτο Ἀννίβου καὶ συνεῖναι
μὴ δυνάμενος ἀτρέμα συνεῖχε τὴν στρατιάν, τὴν νύ-
63 κτα ὑφορώμενος· οἱ δ' ἐν τοῖς στενοῖς ὑπέλαβον, ἅπερ
ἤθελεν ὁ Ἀννίβας, φεύγειν αὐτὸν ὡς ἐν ἀπόροις, ἄνω
διὰ τῶν κρημνῶν βιαζόμενον, καὶ μετεπήδων ἐπὶ τὴν
φαντασίαν τοῦ πυρὸς καταθέοντες, ὡς ἐκεῖ ληψόμενοι
64 τὸν Ἀννίβαν κακοπαθοῦντα. ὁ δέ, ὡς εἶδε καταβάντας
αὐτοὺς ἐκ τῶν στενῶν, διέδραμεν ἐς αὐτὰ τοῖς ταχυ-
τάτοις ἄνευ φωτὸς μετὰ σιωπῆς, ἵνα διαλάθοι, καταλαβὼν δὲ αὐτὰ καὶ κρατυνάμενος ἐσήμηνε τῇ σάλ-
πιγγι· καὶ τὸ στρατόπεδον ἀντεβόησεν αὐτῷ, καὶ πῦρ

their positions were too strong. Finding himself in such   60
dire straits, he first slaughtered all his prisoners, about five
thousand of them, to make sure they did not use the dangerous situation to plot against him. He then tied torches
to the horns of the large number of cattle he had in the
camp. When night fell, he lit the torches, but otherwise
put out the other camp fires and ordered complete silence.
The most daring of his young troops he told to drive the
cattle quickly up into steep ground between Fabius and
the pass. Singed by the torches and driven on by the herd-   61
ers, the cattle spared no effort in wildly running up the
cliff, falling over and jumping up again.

15. From both their positions, the Romans observed   62
that there was no light or noise in Hannibal's camp, but a
great deal of torchlight scattered on the mountain. In the
dark, they could not see exactly what was happening, but
Fabius guessed that Hannibal was up to some trick. Not
being able to find out, however, and suspicious of the dark,
he held his army in position. The troops in the pass, on the   63
other hand, assumed, as Hannibal wanted them to, that
in view of his precarious situation he was trying to escape
by forcing his way up the cliffs. So they left their post
and ran down to what appeared to be torch light, in the
expectation that they would catch Hannibal there in
serious difficulty. But as soon as he saw them coming down   64
from the pass, he made straight for it with his swiftest
troops, in silence and in the dark, to avoid detection.
Having taken the pass and reinforced the position, he signaled the news with a trumpet blast, and the soldiers in
the camp shouted in response and suddenly lit their fires.

65 αἰφνίδιον ἐξέφηναν. Ῥωμαῖοι μὲν δὴ τότε ᾔσθοντο
τῆς ἀπάτης, ὁ δὲ στρατὸς ὁ ἄλλος Ἀννίβου καὶ οἱ τὰς
βοῦς ἐλαύνοντες ἐπὶ τὰ στενὰ ἀδεῶς διέδραμον. καὶ

66 αὐτοὺς συναγαγὼν ἀπῆρεν ἐς τὸ πρόσω. οὕτω μὲν ἐξ
ἀέλπτου τότε ὁ Ἀννίβας αὐτός τε περιῆν καὶ τὸν
στρατὸν περιέσωζε καὶ ἐς Γερωνίαν τῆς Ἰαπυγίας
ἐπειχθείς, ἣ σίτου πλήρης ἦν, ἐξεῖλεν αὐτὴν καὶ ἐν
ἀφθόνοις ἀδεῶς ἐχείμαζεν·

67 16. Ὁ δὲ Φάβιος, καὶ τότε τῆς αὐτῆς γνώμης ἐχό-
μενος, εἵπετο καὶ τῆς Γερωνίας ἀποσχὼν δέκα σταδίους ἐστρατοπέδευεν, λαβὼν ἐν μέσῳ ποταμὸν Αὔφι-

68 δον. ληγόντων δ᾽ αὐτῷ τῶν ἓξ μηνῶν, ἐφ᾽ οὓς αἱροῦνται
Ῥωμαῖοι τοὺς δικτάτορας, οἱ μὲν ὕπατοι Σερουίλιός
τε καὶ Ἀτίλιος ἐπὶ τὰς ἑαυτῶν ἀρχὰς ἐπανῆεσαν καὶ
ἦλθον ἐπὶ τὸ στρατόπεδον, καὶ ὁ Φάβιος ἐς Ῥώμην

69 ἀπήει. γίγνονται δέ τινες ἐν τῷδε τῷ χειμῶνι Ἀννίβᾳ
καὶ Ῥωμαίοις ἀκροβολισμοὶ συνεχεῖς ἐς ἀλλήλους·
καὶ τὰ Ῥωμαίων ἐπικυδέστερα καὶ εὐθαρσέστερα ἦν.

70 ὁ δ᾽ Ἀννίβας ἐπέστελλε μὲν αἰεὶ τὰ γιγνόμενα Καρχηδονίοις ὑπερεπαίρων, τότε δὲ ἀπολωλότων αὐτῷ

71 πολλῶν ἠπόρει καὶ στρατιὰν ᾔτει καὶ χρήματα. οἱ δ᾽
ἐχθροί, πάντα ἐπισκώπτοντες τὰ Ἀννίβου, καὶ τότε
ὑπεκρίνοντο ἀπορεῖν, ὅτι τῶν νικώντων οὐκ αἰτούντων
χρήματα, ἀλλὰ πεμπόντων ἐς τὰς πατρίδας ὁ Ἀννίβας αἰτοίη, λέγων νικᾶν. οἷς οἱ Καρχηδόνιοι πεισθέν-

72 τες οὔτε στρατιὰν ἔπεμπον οὔτε χρήματα. καὶ ὁ Ἀν-

That is when the Romans realized they had been tricked. 65
The rest of Hannibal's army and those who were herding
the cattle now made their way safely through the pass, and
when he had reunited them, he continued his advance.
This was how, contrary to expectations, Hannibal himself 66
survived and saved his army at that time. He then pushed
on to Geronia in Iapygia,[17] where there was plenty of
grain, captured it and went into safe and well supplied
winter quarters.

16. Fabius, who continued to pursue the same tactics 67
as before, followed him, camping ten stades from Geronia,
and keeping the river Aufidus[18] between them. But the six 68
months' term for which the Romans appoint dictators was
now coming to an end, and the consuls Servilius and
Atilius resumed their office and came to the camp, while
Fabius returned to Rome.[19] During the winter, skirmish- 69
ing between Hannibal and the Romans was continuous,
and the Romans were more successful and spirited. But 70
Hannibal, having greatly exaggerated his achievements in
his reports back to Carthage, now that he had suffered
heavy losses and was in trouble, asked for reinforcements
and money. His enemies, who mocked everything he did, 71
on this occasion too replied that they could not understand
how Hannibal, who claimed to be winning, was asking for
money, when victorious generals do not ask for money, but
send it home. The Carthaginians were persuaded by these
arguments and refused to send either money or men. In 72

---

[17] Apulia.   [18] The modern Ofanto, the biggest river in
Apulia.   [19] Gaius Flaminius, the consul killed at the battle
of Lake Trasimene, was replaced by M. Atilius Regulus, who had
already been consul, in 227.

νίβας ταῦτ᾽ ὀδυρόμενος ἔγραφεν ἐς Ἰβηρίαν Ἀσρούβᾳ
τῷ ἀδελφῷ, παρακαλῶν αὐτὸν ἀρχομένου θέρους
μεθ᾽ ὅσης δύναιτο στρατιᾶς καὶ χρημάτων ἐσβαλεῖν
ἐς τὴν Ἰταλίαν καὶ πορθεῖν αὐτῆς τὰ ἐπέκεινα, ἵνα
δῃῶτο πᾶσα καὶ Ῥωμαῖοι κάμνοιεν ὑπ᾽ αὐτῶν ἑκατέρωθεν.

73   17. Καὶ τάδε μὲν ἦν περὶ Ἀννίβαν, Ῥωμαῖοι δέ, τῷ
τε μεγέθει τῆς ἥττης τῆς Φλαμινίου καὶ Κεντηνίου
περιαλγοῦντες ὡς ἀνάξια σφῶν καὶ παράλογα καὶ
ἀθρόα παθόντες καὶ τὸν πόλεμον ὅλως οὐ φέροντες
ἔνδον ὄντα παρ᾽ ἑαυτοῖς, ἄλλα τε κατέλεγον ἐκ Ῥώμης
τέλη στρατιωτῶν τέσσαρα μετ᾽ ὀργῆς ἐπὶ τὸν Ἀννίβαν καὶ τοὺς συμμάχους πανταχόθεν ἤγειρον ἐς Ἰα-
74   πυγίαν. ὑπάτους τε αἱροῦνται ἐκ μὲν δόξης πολεμικῆς
Λεύκιον Αἰμίλιον, τὸν Ἰλλυριοῖς πολεμήσαντα, ἐκ δὲ
δημοκοπίας Τερέντιον Οὐάρρωνα, πολλὰ αὐτοῖς ἐκ
75   τῆς συνήθους δοξοκοπίας ὑπισχνούμενον. καὶ αὐτοὺς
παραπέμποντες ἐξιόντας ἐδέοντο κρῖναι τὸν πόλεμον
μάχῃ καὶ μὴ τὴν πόλιν ἐκτρύχειν χρόνῳ τε καὶ στρα-
τείαις συνεχέσι καὶ εἰσφοραῖς καὶ λιμῷ καὶ ἀργίᾳ τῆς
76   γῆς δῃουμένης. οἱ δέ, τὴν στρατιὰν τὴν ἐν Ἰαπυγίᾳ
προσλαβόντες καὶ τὸ σύμπαν ἔχοντες πεζοὺς μὲν
ἑπτακισμυρίους, ἱππέας δ᾽ ἑξακισχιλίους, ἐστρατοπέδευον ἀμφὶ κώμῃ τινὶ καλουμένῃ Κάνναις. καὶ ὁ Ἀν-
77   νίβας αὐτοῖς ἀντεστρατοπέδευε. φύσει δ᾽ ὢν φιλοπόλεμος ὁ Ἀννίβας καὶ οὔ ποτε φέρων ἀργίαν, τότε
μάλιστα τῆς ἀπορίας αὐτὸν ἐνοχλούσης, ἐξέτασσε
συνεχῶς ἐς μάχην, δεδιώς, μὴ οἱ μισθοφόροι μετά-

protest, Hannibal wrote to his brother Hasdrubal in Iberia, urging him to invade Italy at the beginning of summer with whatever forces and money he could raise, and ravage the other end of the country, so that the whole land would be devastated and the Romans exhausted by their attack from both ends of Italy.

17. This was the state of Hannibal's affairs. As for the 73 Romans, they were deeply affected by the scale of the defeat suffered by Flaminius and Centenius: such unexpected and numerous setbacks were unworthy of Rome, and they regarded it as intolerable that the war was within their own territory. In their anger at Hannibal they recruited four more legions from the city, and gathered the allies from all quarters in Iapygia. They elect as consuls 74 Lucius Aemilius, who had campaigned against the Illyrians, because of his military reputation, and Terentius Varro, because he offered them all the usual populist promises.[20] The people sent them off begging them as 75 they left to decide the war in battle, and not wear the city out over time with continuous military service and taxes and hunger and unemployment on the land, ravaged as it was. The consuls took command of the army in Iapygia— 76 it numbered in total seventy thousand infantry and six thousand cavalry—and made camp near a village called Cannae, where Hannibal also camped, opposite them. Hannibal was by nature pugnacious and never able to 77 abide inactivity, especially now when troubled by lack of supplies. So he kept on drawing up his army for battle, afraid that his mercenaries might desert because they had

[20] C. Terentius Varro, L. Aemilius Paullus, the consuls of 216.

θοιντο διὰ τὴν ἀμισθίαν ἢ σκεδασθεῖεν ἐπὶ συλλογὴν
ἀγορᾶς. καὶ ὁ μὲν οὕτω προυκαλεῖτο τοὺς πολεμίους.

78 18. Γνώμη δὲ τῶν ὑπάτων ἦν, Αἰμιλίου μέν, ὑπομένειν ἐκτρύχοντας Ἀννίβαν, οὐ δυνησόμενον ἀντέχειν
ἐπὶ πολὺ διὰ τὴν ἀπορίαν, μηδὲ διὰ χειρὸς ἔρχεσθαι
γεγυμνασμένῳ πολέμοις καὶ εὐτυχίαις ἀνδρὶ καὶ
στρατῷ, Τερεντίου δ᾽, οἷα δημοκόπου, μνημονεύειν ὧν
ὁ δῆμος ἐξιοῦσιν ἐνετέλλετο, καὶ κρῖναι τὴν μάχην
79 ὀξέως. τούτοιν Αἰμιλίῳ μὲν προσετίθετο Σερουίλιος, ὁ
πέρυσιν ὕπατος ἔτι παρών, Τερεντίῳ δέ, ὅσοι τε ἀπὸ
βουλῆς καὶ τῶν καλουμένων ἱππέων ἡγοῦντο τῆς
80 στρατιᾶς. ἀντεχόντων δ᾽ ἔτι τῶν ἑτέρων ὁ Ἀννίβας
τοῖς χορτολογοῦσιν αὐτῶν ἢ ξυλευομένοις ἐπιτιθέμενος ὑπεκρίνετο ἡττᾶσθαι καὶ περὶ ἐσχάτην ποτὲ φυ-
81 λακὴν ἐκίνει τὸ πλῆθος ὡς ἀναζευγνύς. ὁ δὲ Τερέντιος
ἰδὼν ἐξῆγε τὴν στρατιὰν ὡς ἐπὶ φεύγοντα τὸν Ἀννί-
82 βαν, ἀπαγορεύοντος αὐτῷ καὶ τότε τοῦ Αἰμιλίου. ὡς
δ᾽ οὐκ ἔπειθεν, οἰωνίζετο ὁ Αἰμίλιος ἐφ᾽ ἑαυτοῦ, καθάπερ εἰώθασιν, καὶ πέμψας ὁδεύοντι ἤδη τῷ Τερεντίῳ
τὴν ἡμέραν ἀπαίσιον ἔλεγεν εἶναι. ὁ δ᾽ ἐπανῄει μέν,
αἰδούμενος οἰωνοῖς ἀπειθῆσαι, τὰς δὲ κόμας ἐν ὄψει
τῆς στρατιᾶς ἐτίλλετο καὶ χαλεπῶς ἔφερεν ὡς τὴν
νίκην ἀφῃρημένος ὑπὸ ζηλοτυπίας τοῦ συνάρχου, καὶ
τὸ πλῆθος αὐτῷ συνηγανάκτει.

83 19. Ἀννίβου δ᾽, ἐπεὶ τῆς πείρας ἐξέπιπτεν, αὐτίκα
εἰς τὸ στρατόπεδον ἐπανελθόντος καὶ τὴν ὑπόκρισιν
ἐκφήναντος, οὐδὲ τοῦτ᾽ ἐδίδασκε τὸν Τερέντιον πάνθ᾽
ὑπονοεῖν τὰ Ἀννίβου, ἀλλ᾽, ὡς εἶχεν, ἐν τοῖς ὅπλοις

not been paid, or scatter in their search for food. So he kept on challenging the enemy in this way.

18. As for the views of the consuls, Aemilius argued for wearing Hannibal out by waiting, as he would not be able to hold out for long given his lack of supplies, rather than closing with a general and an army well used to military success. On the other hand, as was to be expected from a demagogue, Terentius recalled what the people had ordered them to do as they left the city, and was for deciding the war quickly in battle. Of the two of them, Aemilius enjoyed the support of Servilius, the consul of the previous year, who was still there, but Terentius of all the senatorial and so-called equestrian army officers. While the two sides were still arguing, Hannibal attacked the Romans out foraging for wood and provisions, and, pretending to be getting the worst of it, mobilized the whole army at about the last watch of the day, as if he had broken camp. Terentius saw this and began to lead his army out with the intention of pursuing Hannibal in his flight. Aemilius tried, on this occasion too, to dissuade him, but when he failed to do so, he took the omens on his own initiative, as is the Roman custom, and sent word to Terentius, who was already under way, that the day was not auspicious. Terentius came back, afraid to disregard the omens, but in full sight of the army he tore his hair out in exasperation at being robbed of victory by the jealousy of his colleague. The soldiers shared his annoyance.

19. At the failure of his venture, Hannibal immediately returned to his camp thus revealing the pretense of his actions, but not even this taught Terentius to treat everything Hannibal did with suspicion. Indeed, still in armor,

78

79

80

81

82

83

ἐς τὸ στρατήγιον ἐσδραμών, παρόντων ἔτι τῶν τε ἀπὸ
βουλῆς καὶ ταξιάρχων καὶ χιλιάρχων, ἠτιᾶτο περὶ
τῶν οἰωνῶν τὸν Αἰμίλιον προφασίσασθαι καὶ νίκην
φανερὰν ἀφελέσθαι τὴν πόλιν, ὀκνοῦντα ὑπὸ δειλίας
84 ἢ οἱ φθονοῦντα διὰ ζηλοτυπίαν. οὕτω δ' αὐτοῦ βοῶν-
τος ὑπὸ ὀργῆς ἡ στρατιὰ περιεστῶσα τὴν σκηνὴν
ἐπήκουε, καὶ τὸν Αἰμίλιον ἐβλασφήμουν. ὁ δὲ πολλὰ
μὲν εἶπεν τοῖς ἔνδον συμφέροντα μάτην, Τερεντίῳ δὲ
πλὴν Σερουιλίου τῶν ἄλλων συντιθεμένων εἶξε. καὶ
τῆς ἐπιούσης ἐξέτασσεν αὐτὸς ἡγούμενος· παρεχώρει
85 γὰρ ὁ Τερέντιος. Ἀννίβας δ' ἤσθετο· καὶ τότε μὲν οὐκ
ἐπεξῆλθεν (οὐ γάρ πω πρὸς μάχην διετέτακτο), τῇ δ'
ἐπιούσῃ κατέβαινον ἐς τὸ πεδίον ἑκάτεροι, Ῥωμαῖοι
μὲν ἐς τρία τεταγμένοι, μικρὸν ἀπ' ἀλλήλων διεστῶ-
τες, καὶ μέρος ἕκαστον αὐτῶν εἶχε τοὺς πεζοὺς ἐν
86 μέσῳ, τοὺς δὲ ψιλοὺς καὶ ἱππέας ἑκατέρωθεν. στρατηγοὶ δ' ἐφειστήκεσαν τῷ μέσῳ μὲν Αἰμίλιος, τῷ δὲ
λαιῷ Σερουίλιος, Τερέντιος δὲ τοῖς ἐπὶ δεξιά, χιλίους
ἀμφ' αὐτὸν ἕκαστος ἔχων ἱππέας ἐπειλεγμένους ἐπικουρεῖν, ὅπῃ τι πονοίη. οὕτω μὲν ἐτάξαντο Ῥωμαῖοι·
87 20. Ὁ δ' Ἀννίβας πρῶτα μέν, εἰδὼς περὶ μεσημβρίαν εὗρον ζοφώδη τὸν χῶρον ἐξ ἔθους ἐπιπνέοντα,
προύλαβεν, ὅπῃ κατὰ νώτου τὸ πνεῦμα ἔμελλεν ἕξειν·
ἔπειτ' ἐς ὄρος περίφυτον καὶ φαραγγῶδες ἱππέας προ-
ενήδρευσεν καὶ ψιλούς, οἷς εἴρητο, ὅταν αἱ φάλαγγες
ἔργων ἔχωνται καὶ τὸ πνεῦμα ἐπίῃ, κατόπιν γίγνε-
88 σθαι τῶν πολεμίων. ἄνδρας τε πεντακοσίους Κελτίβηρας ἐπὶ τοῖς μακροῖς ξίφεσιν ὑπὸ τοῖς χιτῶσιν

he stormed into the praetorium and, in the continued presence of senators, centurions, and tribunes, accused Aemilius of using the omens as an excuse to rob the city of certain victory, either dithering out of cowardice, or because he had a jealous sense of resentment against him. The soldiers were standing around outside the tent listening to him shouting angrily like this, and they began to abuse Aemilius. Although Aemilius had much to say that was to the advantage of those inside, it had no effect, and when everyone else except Servilius sided with Terentius, Aemilius gave in. The following day, he drew his army up in battle order. He took command himself, Terentius having made way for him. Hannibal observed what was happening, but on this occasion did not leave the camp, as he had not completed his battle preparations. Next day, however, both sides came down onto the flat. The Romans deployed in three divisions, with a small gap between them, each division with the infantry in the middle and skirmishers and cavalry on the wings. Aemilius commanded in the center, Servilius on the left wing, Terentius on the right, and each commander had with him one thousand elite cavalry to offer assistance wherever trouble might develop. Such was the Roman battle order.

20. For his part, Hannibal, aware that a blinding east wind usually blew across the region at about midday, first of all took up position beforehand where he would have the wind at his back. Then, on a hill covered with vegetation and gullies, he laid an ambush of cavalry and skirmishers, whom he ordered to attack the enemy's rear when the battle lines had engaged and the wind began to blow. He armed five hundred Celtiberians with short swords, in addition to their standard long swords, to be

84

85

86

87

88

ἄλλα ξίφη βραχύτερα περιέζωσεν, οἷς ἔμελλεν αὐτός,
89 ὅτε δέοι χρῆσθαι, σημαίνειν. σύμπασαν δὲ τὴν στρατιὰν κἀκεῖνος ἐς τρία διῄρει καὶ τοὺς ἱππέας τοῖς
κέρασιν ἐπέτασσεν ἐκ μεγάλων διαστημάτων, εἰ δύ-
90 ναιντο κυκλώσασθαι τοὺς πολεμίους. ἐπέστησε δὲ
τῷ μὲν δεξιῷ Μάγωνα τὸν ἀδελφόν, τῷ δὲ ἑτέρῳ τὸν
ἀδελφιδοῦν Ἄννωνα· τὸ δὲ μέσον αὐτὸς εἶχεν κατὰ
91 δόξαν Αἰμιλίου τῆς ἐμπειρίας. δισχίλιοί τε ἱππεῖς
ἐπίλεκτοι παρέθεον αὐτῷ, καὶ Μαάρβαλ, ἑτέρους
ἔχων χιλίους, ἐφήδρευεν, ὅπῃ τι πονούμενον ἴδοι. καὶ
τάδε πράσσων ἐς δευτέραν παρέτεινεν ὥραν, ἵνα τὸ
πνεῦμα θᾶσσον ἐπέλθοι.

92   21. Γενομένων δὲ πάντων εὐτρεπῶν ἑκατέροις οἱ
στρατηγοὶ διέθεον παρακαλοῦντες αὐτοὺς καὶ ὑπεμίμνησκον οἱ μὲν γονέων τε καὶ παίδων καὶ γυναικῶν
καὶ τῆς προγεγενημένης ἥττης, ὡς ἐν τῇδε τῇ μάχῃ
περὶ σωτηρίας κριθησομένους, ὁ δ᾿ Ἀννίβας τῶν τε
προγεγονότων ἐπὶ τοῖσδε τοῖς ἀνδράσι κατορθω-
93 μάτων καὶ ὡς αἰσχρὸν ἡττᾶσθαι τῶν ἡττημένων. ἐπεὶ
δ᾿ αἵ τε σάλπιγγες ἤχησαν καὶ αἱ φάλαγγες ἐβόη-
σαν, πρῶτον μὲν αὐτῶν οἱ τοξόται καὶ σφενδονῆται
καὶ λιθοβόλοι προδραμόντες ἐς τὸ μέσον ἀλλήλων
κατῆρχον, μετὰ δὲ τούτους αἱ φάλαγγες ἐχώρουν ἐπὶ
τὸ ἔργον, φόνος τε καὶ πόνος ἦν πολὺς ἐκθύμως ἀγω-
94 νιζομένων ἑκατέρων. ἐν ᾧ σημαίνει μὲν ὁ Ἀννίβας
τοῖς ἱππεῦσι κυκλοῦσθαι τὰ κέρατα τῶν ἐχθρῶν, οἱ δὲ
τῶν Ῥωμαίων ἱππεῖς ὀλιγώτεροι τῶν πολεμίων ὄντες
ἀντιπαρῆγον αὐτοῖς καὶ τὴν τάξιν ἐκτείναντες ἐπὶ λε-

worn under their cloaks and used when he himself gave
the signal. Like the Romans, Hannibal also divided his   89
whole army into three sections, and stationed his cavalry
on the wings, but stretched them out far to see if they
could outflank the enemy. He put his brother Mago in   90
command of the right wing, his nephew Hanno on the left,
while he himself commanded the center to counter the
reputation of Aemilius' experience. Two thousand select   91
cavalry accompanied him and Maharbal held another one
thousand in reserve to help wherever he saw troops in
difficulty. With these arrangements in place, Hannibal delayed until the second watch so that the wind would arrive
sooner.

21. When everything was ready on both sides, the gen-   92
erals went through the ranks encouraging the men. The
Romans were reminded of their parents, children and
wives and the defeat they had already suffered; this battle,
they were told, would decide their security. Hannibal recalled the successes they had already enjoyed against
these very men, and said it would be shameful to be defeated by a defeated army. When the trumpets sounded   93
and the ranks let out a roar, first to advance to the middle
and engage with each other were the archers, slingers and
stone throwers, and then the phalanxes got down to work.
There was much slaughter and pain as both sides fought
fiercely. Meanwhile, Hannibal signals his cavalry to circle 94
around the enemy wings. The Roman cavalry, although
outnumbered by the enemy, countered this movement by

πτὸν ἠγωνίζοντο ὅμως ὑπὸ προθυμίας, καὶ μάλισθ᾽ οἱ
95 τὸ λαιὸν ἔχοντες ἐπὶ τῇ θαλάσσῃ. Ἀννίβας δὲ καὶ
Μαάρβαλ ὁμοῦ τοὺς περὶ σφᾶς ἐπῆγον ἀπλέτῳ
⟨κραυγῇ⟩[6] καὶ βαρβαρικῇ, νομίσαντες ἐκπλήξειν
τοὺς ἐναντίους. οἱ δὲ καὶ τούτους εὐσταθῶς καὶ ἀκα-
ταπλήκτως ὑπέμενον.

96   22. Διαπιπτούσης δὲ καὶ τῆσδε τῆς πείρας ὁ Ἀννίβας τὸ σημεῖον ἐπῆρε τοῖς Κελτίβηρσι τοῖς πεντακο-
σίοις· οἱ δὲ τῆς τάξεως ἐκδραμόντες ἐς τοὺς Ῥωμαίους
μετετίθεντο καὶ τὰς ἀσπίδας αὐτοῖς καὶ τὰ δόρατα καὶ
97 τὰ ξίφη τὰ φανερὰ ὤρεγον ὥσπερ αὐτομολοῦντες. καὶ
ὁ Σερουίλιος αὐτοὺς ἐπαινέσας τὰ μὲν ὅπλα αὐτῶν
αὐτίκα παρεῖλεν, ἐν δὲ μόνοις, ὡς ᾤετο, τοῖς χιτῶσιν
ἔστησεν ὀπίσω. οὐ γὰρ ἐδοκίμαζε καταδεῖν αὐτομόλους ἐν ὄψει πολεμίων οὐδ᾽ ὑπώπτευεν, ἐν χιτῶσι
98 μόνοις ὁρῶν, οὐδὲ καιρὸς ἦν ἐν τοσῷδε πόνῳ. σπεῖραι
δ᾽ ἕτεραι Λιβύων προσεποιήσαντο φεύγειν ἄχρι τῶν
ὁρῶν, ἀναλαλάξαι μέγα. σύμβολον δ᾽ ἦν ἡ βοὴ
τοῖς ἐν ταῖς φάραγξι κεκρυμμένοις ἀναστρέφειν ἐς
99 τοὺς διώκοντας. καὶ εὐθὺς οἵ τε ψιλοὶ καὶ ἱππεῖς ἐκ
τῆς ἐνέδρας ἐξεφαίνοντο, καὶ τὸ πνεῦμα κατέβαινε
πολὺ καὶ ζοφῶδες, ἐς τὰς Ῥωμαίων ὄψεις μετὰ κο-
νιορτοῦ φερόμενον· ὃ καὶ μάλιστα αὐτοὺς ἐκώλυε
100 προορᾶν τοὺς πολεμίους. τά τε βέλη Ῥωμαίοις μὲν
πάντα ἀμβλύτερα διὰ τὴν ἀντίπνοιαν ἦν, τοῖς δ᾽
ἐχθροῖς ἐπιτυχῆ, τοῦ πνεύματος τὴν βολὴν συνωθοῦν-

---

[6] κραυγῇ add. Schweig.

thinning their line and stretching it out; they still fought with spirit, especially those on the left toward the sea. Hannibal and Maharbal together now introduced to the battle the cavalry they had kept in their immediate company. Although they yelled loudly in barbarian fashion, thinking this would cause panic in the men facing them, against these too the Romans stood their ground calmly and undaunted.   95

22. When this attack also failed, Hannibal signaled the five hundred Celtiberians. They now abandoned their own ranks and ran over to the Roman side, and, as if they were intending to desert, held out their shields and spears and the swords that were visible. Servilius complemented them, and immediately removed their weapons, sending them to the rear wearing just their cloaks, so he imagined. For he did not think it was good policy to put deserters in chains in full sight of the enemy: he was not suspicious of them, as he could see they were just wearing cloaks, and it was not the right time to do so in the middle of such a struggle. Some African units now pretended to flee to the hills, crying out loudly with a shout that was the signal for those hidden in the gullies to turn on the pursuers. Immediately, the light-armed troops and cavalry appeared out of their ambush and the wind came down strong and blinding, blowing dust into the eyes of the Romans. This made it particularly difficult for them to see the enemy from any distance. Their missiles, too, were less effective into the wind, while those of the enemy hit their mark, the wind behind them helping their throw. The Romans, un-   96   97   98   99   100

τος. οἳ δὲ οὔτε ἐκκλίνειν αὐτὰ προορῶντες οὔτ' ἀφιέναι καλῶς δυνάμενοι σφίσι τε αὐτοῖς περιπταίοντες ἤδη ποικίλως ἐθορυβοῦντο.

101   23. Τότε δὴ τὸν καιρὸν ὁρῶντες τὸν ἐπηγγελμένον σφίσιν οἱ πεντακόσιοι, τὰ ξίφη τὰ βραχύτερα ἐκ τῶν κόλπων ἐπισπάσαντες, πρώτους ἀνήρουν, ὧν ἦσαν ὀπίσω, μετὰ δ' ἐκείνους, ἁρπάσαντες αὐτῶν τὰ ξίφη τὰ μείζω καὶ τὰς ἀσπίδας καὶ τὰ δόρατα, πᾶσιν ἐνέπιπτον καὶ μετεπήδων ἀφειδῶς· καὶ φόνον εἰργάζοντο

102   πλεῖστον οὗτοι μάλιστα, ἅτε πάντων ὄντες ὀπίσω. τό τε κακὸν ἤδη πολὺ τοῖς Ῥωμαίοις καὶ ποικίλον ἦν, πονουμένοις μὲν ὑπὸ τῶν ἐναντίων, κεκυκλωμένοις δ' ὑπὸ τῆς ἐνέδρας, ἀναιρουμένοις δ' ὑπὸ τῶν ἀναμεμιγμένων. οὐδ' ἐπιστρέψαι πρὸς αὐτοὺς ἐδύναντο διὰ τοὺς ἐπικειμένους σφίσιν ἐκ μετώπου· οὐδ' ἐπεγίγνωσκον ἔτι αὐτοὺς εὐμαρῶς, Ῥωμαϊκὰς ἀσπίδας ἔχον-

103   τας. ὑπὲρ ἅπαντα δ' αὐτοὺς ὁ κονιορτὸς ἠνώχλει, καὶ οὐκ εἶχον οὐδ' εἰκάσαι τὸ συμβαῖνον, ἀλλ' οἷον ἐν θορύβῳ καὶ φόβῳ πάντα πλείω νομίζοντες εἶναι καὶ τὰς ἐνέδρας οὐ τοσαύτας οὐδὲ τοὺς πεντακοσίους εἰδότες, ὅτι ἦσαν πεντακόσιοι, ἀλλὰ ὅλον σφῶν τὸ στρατόπεδον ὑπὸ ἱππέων καὶ αὐτομόλων ἡγούμενοι

104   κεκυκλῶσθαι, τραπέντες ἔφευγον ἀκόσμως, πρῶτοι μὲν οἱ ἐπὶ τοῦ δεξιοῦ, καὶ ὁ Τερέντιος αὐτοῖς ἐξῆρχε τῆς φυγῆς, μετὰ δ' ἐκείνους οἱ τὸ λαιὸν ἔχοντες, ὧν ὁ Σερουίλιος ἡγούμενος πρὸς τὸν Αἰμίλιον διέδραμεν· καὶ περὶ αὐτοὺς ἦν, ὅσον ἄριστον ἱππέων τε καὶ πεζῶν, ἀμφὶ τοὺς μυρίους.

able to dodge the missiles they could not see, or release their own missiles effectively, began to stumble around against each other, thrown into confusion in different ways.

23. At this point, the five hundred Celtiberians saw the opportunity they had been told of, and drawing the short swords from the folds of their tunic, killed the first men they encountered in front of them, then taking the longer swords, shields and spears of these men, fell on all the others, mercilessly bounding from one person to the next. They caused particularly wide slaughter as they were right at the back of the whole battlefield. The Romans were now in a very bad way, and on several counts: they were struggling against those facing them, they were surrounded as a result of the ambush, and they were being killed by the enemy mixed in with their own men. They could not turn their attention to these latter because of the pressure on them at the front; indeed, it was not easy to recognize them any more, as they had Roman shields. Above all, it was the dust that was disorienting them, making it impossible even to guess what was happening. But, as usually happens in confused and frightening situations, their fear led them to believe that their situation was worse than it really was: they did not know the ambush was smaller than they thought, or that the five hundred were in fact five hundred, but believed that their whole force was surrounded by cavalry and deserters. So they turned and fled in disorder, those on the right first, with Terentius leading the flight, and after them those on the left: here their commanding officer, Servilius, ran over to join Aemilius; and gathered around them were about ten thousand of the bravest among the infantry and cavalry.

101

102

103

104

105 24. Καταθορόντες δ᾽ ἀπὸ τῶν ἵππων οἱ στρατηγοὶ
καὶ μετ᾽ αὐτούς, ὅσοι ἄλλοι ἦσαν ἐπὶ ἵππων, ἐπεζο-
μάχουν τοῖς ἱππεῦσιν τοῖς Ἀννίβου κεκυκλωμένοι. καὶ
πολλὰ μὲν ἐξ ἐμπειρίας σὺν εὐψυχίᾳ καὶ ἀπονοίᾳ
λαμπρὰ ἔδρασαν, ἐμπίπτοντες σὺν ὀργῇ τοῖς πολεμίοις, πανταχόθεν δ᾽ ἀνῃροῦντο, περιτρέχοντος αὐτοὺς
τοῦ Ἀννίβου καὶ τοὺς ἰδίους ὀτὲ μὲν ἐξοτρύνοντος καὶ
παρακαλοῦντος τὸ λείψανον τῆς νίκης ἐκπονῆσαι, ὀτὲ
δ᾽ ἐπιπλήσσοντός τε καὶ ὀνειδίζοντος, εἰ τὸ πλῆθος
106 νενικηκότες ὀλίγων οὐ περιέσονται. Ῥωμαῖοι δ᾽, ἕως
μὲν αὐτοῖς ὁ Αἰμίλιος καὶ ὁ Σερουίλιος περιῆσαν,
πολλὰ δρῶντές τε καὶ πάσχοντες ὅμως ὑπέμενον ἐν
τάξει· ἐπεὶ δ᾽ ἔπεσον αὐτῶν οἱ στρατηγοί, διὰ μέσων
βιαζόμενοι τῶν ἐχθρῶν μάλα καρτερῶς κατὰ μέρη
107 διέφευγον, οἳ μέν, ἔνθαπερ οἱ πρὸ αὐτῶν ἐπεφεύγε-
σαν, ἐς τὰ στρατόπεδα δύο ὄντα· καὶ σύμπαντες οἵδε
ἐγένοντο ἀμφὶ τοὺς μυρίους καὶ πεντακισχιλίους, οἷς
ὁ Ἀννίβας φυλακὴν ἐπέστησε· οἳ δὲ ἐς Κάννας, περὶ
δισχιλίους, καὶ παρέδωκαν ἑαυτοὺς οἵδε οἱ δισχίλιοι
τῷ Ἀννίβᾳ. ὀλίγοι δ᾽ ἐς Κανύσιον διέδρασαν, καὶ οἱ
λοιποὶ κατὰ μέρος ἐσκεδάσθησαν ἀνὰ τὰς ὕλας.

108 25. Τοῦτο τέλος ἦν τῆς ἐπὶ Κάνναις Ἀννίβου τε καὶ
Ῥωμαίων μάχης, ἀρξαμένης μὲν ὑπὲρ ὥραν δευτέραν,
ληξάσης δὲ πρὸ δύο τῆς νυκτὸς ὡρῶν, οὔσης δ᾽ ἔτι
109 νῦν ἀοιδίμου Ῥωμαίοις ἐπὶ συμφορᾷ· ἀπέθανον γὰρ
αὐτῶν ἐν ταῖσδε ταῖς ὥραις πεντακισμύριοι, καὶ ζών-
των ἐλήφθη πολὺ πλῆθος ἀπό τε τῆς βουλῆς πολλοὶ
παρόντες ἐτελεύτησαν, καὶ ἐπ᾽ αὐτοῖς ταξίαρχοί τε

24. The generals and, after them, any other mounted 105
men jumped down from their horses and fought on foot,
surrounded by Hannibal's cavalry. And, although in their
furious attack on the enemy they performed many brilliant
deeds, driven by experience allied to courage and desperation, they met their death on all sides, Hannibal cir-
cling around them. His own men at one moment he was
encouraging and urging to finish off the last remaining
element of the victory, at another he was rebuking and
admonishing for being unable to overcome a small number when they had defeated the main body of the enemy.
As long as Aemilius and Servilius survived, the Romans 106
held their ranks, inflicting and taking heavy casualties. But
when their generals were killed, they forced their way
resolutely through the middle of the enemy lines and escaped in groups. Some made their way to the two camps 107
where those who had earlier fled had taken refuge—in
total there were about fifteen thousand of these and
Hannibal immediately stationed a guard on them. Others,
about two thousand of them, fled to Cannae and surrendered to Hannibal. A few got through to Canusium, and
the rest were scattered in groups in the woods.

25. Such was the end of the battle at Cannae between 108
Hannibal and Rome. It started after the second hour and
finished two hours before dark, and to this day remains a
notorious disaster for Romans. For in those few hours fifty 109
thousand of them died, and of the survivors a great number were taken prisoner. Many senators present were
killed, all the military tribunes and centurions, and the

πάντες καὶ λοχαγοὶ καὶ τῶν στρατηγῶν αὐτῶν οἱ ἄριστοι δύο. ὁ δὲ φαυλότατός τε καὶ τῶν συμφορῶν

110 αἴτιος ἀρχομένης τῆς τροπῆς ἐπεφεύγει. καὶ Ῥωμαῖοι δύο ἔτεσιν ἤδη περὶ τὴν Ἰταλίαν Ἀννίβᾳ πολεμοῦντες ἀπολωλέκεσαν ἀνδρῶν ἰδίων τε καὶ συμμάχων ἐς δέκα μυριάδας.

111 26. Ἀννίβας δὲ νίκην ἀρίστην τε καὶ σπάνιον ἐξενεγκάμενος ἡμέρας μιᾶς στρατηγήμασι τέσσαρσι, τοῦ τε πνεύματος τῇ φορᾷ καὶ τοῖς ὑποκριθεῖσιν αὐτομολεῖν καὶ τοῖς προσποιηθεῖσι φεύγειν καὶ τοῖς ἐν μέσαις ταῖς φάραγξι κεκρυμμένοις, εὐθὺς ἀπὸ τοῦ ἔργου τοὺς πεσόντας ἐπῄει, θεώμενος δὲ τῶν φίλων τοὺς ἀρίστους ἀνῃρημένους ᾤμωξε καὶ δακρύσας εἶ-

112 πεν οὐ χρῄζειν ἑτέρας τοιᾶσδε νίκης. ὃ καὶ Πύρρον φασὶν εἰπεῖν πρὸ αὐτοῦ, τὸν Ἠπείρου βασιλέα, Ῥωμαίων κἀκεῖνον ἐν Ἰταλίᾳ κρατοῦντα σὺν ὁμοίᾳ ζη-

113 μίᾳ. τῶν δὲ φυγόντων ἐκ τῆς μάχης οἱ μὲν ἐν τῷ μείζονι στρατοπέδῳ στρατηγὸν αὐτῶν ἑσπέρας ἑλόμενοι Πούπλιον Σεμπρώνιον ἐβιάσαντο τοὺς Ἀννίβου φύλακας, ὕπνου καὶ κόπου πλήρεις ὄντας, καὶ διέδραμον ἐς Κανύσιον περὶ μέσας νύκτας ἀμφὶ τοὺς μυρίους, οἱ δ' ἐν τῷ βραχυτέρῳ πεντακισχίλιοι τῆς ἐπιού-

114 σης ἡμέρας ἐλήφθησαν ὑπὸ τοῦ Ἀννίβου. Τερέντιος δὲ στρατὸν ἀγείρας τοὺς διερριμμένους ἐπειρᾶτο παραθαρρύνειν καὶ στρατηγὸν αὐτοῖς ἐπιστήσας τῶν χιλιάρχων τινὰ Σκιπίωνα ἐς Ῥώμην διέδραμεν.

115 27. Ἡ δὲ πόλις, ἀπαγγελθείσης τῆς συμφορᾶς, οἱ μὲν ἐν ταῖς ὁδοῖς ἐθρήνουν τε τοὺς οἰκείους ἀνακαλοῦ-

two bravest of their generals. The most useless of them, however, and the one responsible for the disaster, escaped at the beginning of the rout. In two years of campaigning against Hannibal throughout Italy, the Romans had now lost, of both citizens and allies, about one hundred thousand men. 110

26. Hannibal won this rare and magnificent victory by using four subterfuges in one day: the direction of the wind, the false desertion, the pretended flight, and the men hidden in the middle of the gullies. Immediately after the battle, he went to inspect the dead, and seeing the best of his associates killed, he cried aloud, and in tears said that he did not want another victory like this. On an earlier occasion, Pyrrhus, the king of Epirus, is supposed to have said the same when he too defeated the Romans in Italy at a similar cost. In the evening, the Romans who had fled from the battle to the larger camp, chose Publius Sempronius[21] as their commander and forced their way past Hannibal's guarding troops, who were sleepy and exhausted. They got through to Canusium around midnight, but the five thousand in the smaller camp were captured by Hannibal next day. Terentius tried to lift the spirits of the army by encouraging the downcast men, and then, leaving Scipio,[22] one of the military tribunes, in charge, he hurried off to Rome. 111 112 113 114

27. When news of the calamity got to Rome, the men grieved for their relatives, calling out their names, and 115

[21] P. Sempronius Tuditanus was a military tribune and later, in 204, a consul.

[22] P. Cornelius Scipio Africanus (consul 205, 194), the eventual victor over Hannibal at the battle of Zama in 202.

ντες καὶ σφᾶς ὡς αὐτίκα ἁλωσομένους ὠλοφύροντο,
αἱ δὲ γυναῖκες ἱκέτευον ἐν τοῖς ἱεροῖς μετὰ τῶν τέκνων
λῆξαί ποτε τὰς συμφορὰς τῇ πόλει, οἱ δ᾽ ἄρχοντες
θυσίαις τε καὶ εὐχαῖς ἱλάσκοντο τοὺς θεούς, εἴ τι
116 μήνιμα ἐνοχλεῖ, κορεσθῆναι τοῖς γεγονόσιν. ἡ δὲ
βουλὴ Κόιντον μὲν Φάβιον, τὸν συγγραφέα τῶνδε
τῶν ἔργων, ἐς Δελφοὺς ἔπεμπε χρησόμενον περὶ τῶν
παρόντων, δούλους δὲ ἐς ὀκτακισχιλίους τῶν δεσπο-
τῶν ἐπιδόντων ἠλευθέρου ὅπλα τε καὶ τόξα τοὺς ἐν
ἄστει πάντας ἐργάζεσθαι παρεσκεύαζε καὶ συμμά-
117 χους καὶ ὥς τινας συνέλεγεν. Κλαύδιόν τε Μάρκελλον, μέλλοντα πλεῖν ἐς Σικελίαν, ἐς τὸν Ἀννίβου
πόλεμον μετέφερεν. ὃ δὲ τὸν μὲν στόλον ἐμερίσατο τῷ
συνάρχῳ Φουρίῳ καὶ τὸ μέρος ἔπεμψεν ἐς τὴν Σικελίαν, αὐτὸς δὲ τοὺς δούλους ἄγων καὶ ὅσους ἄλλους ἐδύνατο τῶν πολιτῶν ἢ συμμάχων, γενομένους
ἅπαντας ἐς μυρίους πεζοὺς καὶ δισχιλίους ἱππέας, ἐς
τὸ Τεανὸν παρῆλθε καί, ὅ τι πράξειν ὁ Ἀννίβας μέλ-
λοι, παρεφύλασσεν.

118   28. Ἀννίβου δὲ δόντος τοῖς αἰχμαλώτοις ἐς Ῥώμην
πρεσβεύσασθαι περὶ σφῶν, εἰ θέλοιεν αὐτοὺς οἱ ἐν
ἄστει λύσασθαι χρημάτων, καὶ τοὺς αἱρεθέντας ὑπ᾽
αὐτῶν τρεῖς, ὧν ἡγεῖτο Γναῖος Σεμπρώνιος, ὁρκώσαν-
τος ἐς αὐτὸν ἐπανήξειν, οἱ μὲν οἰκεῖοι τῶν ἁλόντων,

---

23 Q. Fabius Pictor wrote, in Greek, the first history of Rome.
24 M. Claudius Marcellus was one of Rome's greatest generals
in the second century. Praetor for the second time in 216, he had

bemoaned their own fate, assuming they would soon be made prisoners themselves. The women with their children went as suppliants to the temples to beg that the city would eventually stop suffering disasters. The magistrates sought to appease the gods with sacrifices and by praying that, if they had some cause for their anger, they would be satisfied with what had happened. The senate sent Quintus Fabius,[23] who wrote a history of these events, to consult the Delphic oracle about the situation, and, with the approval of their owners, freed some eight thousand slaves. They made everyone in the city contribute to the production of arms and bows, and, even in this situation, began to collect some allies. They also transferred Claudius Marcellus, who was about to sail for Sicily, to the Hannibalic War.[24] He divided the fleet with his colleague Furius,[25] and sent part of it to Sicily. He himself took the slaves and as many other citizens and allies as he could find—all told they were about ten thousand infantry and two thousand cavalry—and went to Teanum, to watch closely what Hannibal would do next.

28. Hannibal allowed the prisoners to send representatives to Rome to negotiate for them, in case the citizens were willing to pay a ransom for them, but made the three-man delegation they chose, with Gnaeus Sempronius[26] as leader, swear an oath to return to him. The relatives of the

116

117

118

already been consul in 222, and would be again on four more occasions.

[25] M. Furius Philus (consul 223), who received life-threatening wounds in a raid on Africa, according to Livy (23.21.2).

[26] It is not known who this Sempronius was.

περιστάντες τὸ βουλευτήριον, ἐπηγγέλλοντο λύσε-
σθαι τοὺς οἰκείους ἕκαστος ἰδίοις χρήμασι καὶ παρεκάλουν τὴν βουλὴν τοῦτο σφίσιν ἐπιτρέψαι, καὶ ὁ
119 δῆμος αὐτοῖς συνεδάκρυε καὶ συνεδεῖτο. τῶν δὲ βου-
λευτῶν οἱ μὲν οὐκ ἠξίουν ἐπὶ τοσαῖσδε συμφοραῖς
ἄλλους τοσούσδε βλαβῆναι τὴν πόλιν οὐδὲ δούλους
μὲν ἐλευθεροῦν, τοὺς δὲ ἐλευθέρους ὑπερορᾶν, οἱ δ᾽
οὐκ ᾤοντο δεῖν αὐτοὺς ἐθίζειν τῷδε τῷ ἐλέῳ φεύγειν,
ἀλλ᾽ ἢ νικᾶν μαχομένους ἢ ἀποθνήσκειν, ὡς οὐκ ὂν
120 οὐδ᾽ ὑπὸ τῶν οἰκείων ἐλεεῖσθαι τὸν φυγόντα. πολλῶν
δὲ παραδειγμάτων ἐς ἑκάτερα λεχθέντων οὐκ ἐπέτρεψεν ἡ βουλὴ τοῖς συγγενέσι λύσασθαι τοὺς αἰχμαλώτους, ἡγουμένη, πολλῶν σφίσιν ἔτι κινδύνων
ἐπόντων, οὐ συνοίσειν ἐς τὸ μέλλον τὴν ἐν τῷ παρόντι φιλανθρωπίαν, τὸ δ᾽ ἀπάνθρωπον, εἰ καὶ σκυ-
θρωπὸν εἴη, πρός τε τὰ μέλλοντα χρήσιμον ἔσεσθαι
καὶ ἐν τῷ παρόντι καταπλήξειν Ἀννίβαν τῷ τολ-
121 μήματι. Σεμπρώνιος οὖν καὶ οἱ σὺν αὐτῷ δύο τῶν
αἰχμαλώτων πρὸς Ἀννίβαν ἐπανήεσαν. ὁ δ᾽ ἔστι μὲν
οὓς ἀπέδοτο τῶν αἰχμαλώτων, ἔστι δ᾽ οὓς ὑπ᾽ ὀργῆς
ἀνῄρει καὶ τοῖς σώμασι τὸν ποταμὸν ἐγεφύρου καὶ
122 ἐπέρα. ὅσοι δ᾽ ἦσαν ἀπὸ τῆς βουλῆς ἢ ἄλλως ἐπιφανεῖς, μονομαχεῖν αὐτοὺς ὑπὸ θεαταῖς τοῖς Λίβυσιν
ἠνάγκασεν, πατέρας τε υἱοῖς καὶ ἀδελφοὺς ἀδελφοῖς,
οὐδὲν ἐκλείπων ὑπεροψίας ὠμῆς.

123   29. Μετὰ δὲ τοῦτο ἐπιὼν τὰ ὑπὸ Ῥωμαίοις ἐλυμαίνετο καὶ Πετηλίνοις μηχανήματα προσῆγεν. οἱ δ᾽ ὀλίγοι μὲν ἦσαν, ὑπὸ δὲ τόλμης μετὰ τῶν γυναικῶν

prisoners gathered around the senate house and all declared themselves ready to ransom their own family members with their own money; they appealed to the senate to allow them to do this, the people adding their own tearful support for this request. Some senators thought that in the 119
wake of such disasters, the city should not lose so many additional men, or free slaves while at the same time showing no concern for free men. Others said that they should not allow such a display of pity to accustom men to the idea of fleeing in battle: they should either conquer or die fighting in the knowledge that there would be no pity for the man who fled, even from his own family. After many 120
arguments had been produced by both sides, the senate decided not to allow relatives to ransom the prisoners. Their thinking was that, with many dangers still threatening the state, a kind heart now would not work to their future advantage, while a hard heart, even if distressful, would be useful in future, and in the present circumstances would astonish Hannibal by its audacity. So Sem- 121
pronius and his two fellow prisoner delegates returned to Hannibal. Some of the prisoners Hannibal sold into slavery, others he executed out of spite and used their bodies to make a bridge and cross the river. Senators and other- 122
wise distinguished prisoners he forced to fight in single combat watched by his Africans; father against son, brother against brother, there was no form of cruel humiliation he left untried.

29. Hannibal next invaded and laid waste the land of 123
Rome's subjects, and brought up his siege engines against the town of Petilia. It was only a small town, but the defenders, including the women, made brave sorties against

ἐπεξέθεον αὐτῷ καὶ πολλὰ καὶ γενναῖα ἔδρων τάς τε
μηχανὰς αὐτοῦ συνεχῶς ἐνεπίμπρασαν, οὐχ ἧσσον
124 αὐτοῖς τῶν γυναικῶν ἀνδριζομένων. ὀλιγώτεροι δὲ γι-
γνόμενοι καθ' ἕκαστον ἔργον ἐκακοπάθουν μάλιστα
ὑπὸ λιμοῦ· καὶ ὁ Ἀννίβας αἰσθανόμενος περιετείχι-
125 σεν αὐτοὺς καὶ Ἄννωνα ἐπέστησε τῇ πολιορκίᾳ. οἳ δ',
ἐπιτείνοντος αὐτοῖς τοῦ κακοῦ, πρῶτα μὲν τοὺς ἀχρεί-
ους σφῶν ἐς μάχας ἐξέβαλον ἐς τὸ μεσοτείχιον καὶ
κτιννυμένους ὑπὸ τοῦ Ἄννωνος ἐφεώρων ἀλύπως ὡς
126 εὐμοιρότερον ἀποθνήσκοντας. τῷ δ' αὐτῷ λόγῳ καὶ οἱ
λοιποὶ πάμπαν ἀποροῦντες ἐξέδραμον ἐπὶ τοὺς πολεμίους καὶ πολλὰ μὲν καὶ γενναῖα καὶ τότε ἔδρασαν,
ὑπὸ δὲ ἀτροφίας καὶ ἀσθενείας σωμάτων οὐδ' ὑπο-
στρέψαι δυνάμενοι διεφθάρησαν ἅπαντες ὑπὸ τῶν
Λιβύων. καὶ τὴν πόλιν εἷλεν ὁ Ἄννων, ἐκφυγόντων
καὶ ὡς ἀπ' αὐτῆς ὀλίγων τῶν δραμεῖν δυνηθέντων.
127 τούτους διερριμμένους οἱ Ῥωμαῖοι σπουδῇ συνῆγον
καὶ γενομένους ἐς ὀκτακοσίους κατήγαγόν τε καὶ
συνῴκισαν μετὰ τόνδε τὸν πόλεμον αὖθις εἰς τὴν πατρίδα, ἀγάμενοι τῆς τε περὶ σφᾶς εὐνοίας καὶ τοῦ
παραδόξου τῆς προθυμίας.
128   30. Τῶν δὲ Κελτιβήρων ἱππέων, οἳ ἐμισθοφόρουν
Ἀννίβᾳ, λαμπρῶς ἀγωνιζομένων, ὅσοι Ῥωμαίων
ἐστρατήγουν ἐν Ἰβηρίᾳ, τοιούσδε ἑτέρους τὰς πόλεις
τὰς ὑπὸ σφίσιν αἰτήσαντες εἰς ἀντίπαλον ἐκείνων
ἔπεμψαν ἐς τὴν Ἰταλίαν, οἳ τοῖς ὁμοεθνέσιν, ὅτε πλησίον Ἀννίβου στρατοπεδεύοιεν, ἀναμιγνύμενοι μετέ-
129 πειθον αὐτούς. καὶ πολλῶν μετατιθεμένων τε καὶ

him. Among their many noble deeds they kept on setting fire to his siege engines, the women displaying the same courage as the men. But with each engagement their num-   124
bers dwindled and they began to suffer terribly from hunger. When he noticed this, Hannibal built a stockade around the town and put Hanno in charge of the siege. The plight of the defenders continued to get worse, and   125
they now took those unable to fight and removed them outside the walls, where they watched Hanno kill them, and did so without grief as they thought they were dying a more fortunate death. On the same line of reasoning,   126
when their situation had become completely desperate, those who were left made a sortie against the enemy, and after fighting long and bravely on this occasion too, and unable even to drag their weak and starved bodies back to the town, they were all killed by the Africans. Hanno took the town, but even so a few who were still capable of running escaped. The Romans took care to gather about eight   127
hundred of these stragglers, and after the war took them back and resettled them in their own homeland, admiring their loyalty to Rome and extraordinary spirit.

30. To counterbalance the Celtiberian cavalry serving   128
as mercenaries with Hannibal, who were proving to be brilliant fighters, the Roman governors in Iberia demanded the same number from the towns under their control and sent them to Italy. Here, when camping near Hannibal, they would mix with their Celtiberian countrymen and try to persuade them to change sides. Many of   129
them did go over to the Roman side, or deserted or ran

αὐτομολούντων ἢ ἀποδιδρασκόντων οὐδὲ τὸ λοιπὸν
ἦν ἔτι τῷ Ἀννίβᾳ πιστόν, ὑποπτευόμενόν τε ὑπ᾽ ἐκείνου καὶ ὑποπτεύοντες αὐτόν. κάκιον οὖν ἔπρασσεν ὁ
Ἀννίβας τὸ ἀπὸ τοῦδε.

130   31. Ἀργύριππα δ᾽ ἐστὶ πόλις ἐν τῇ Δαυνίᾳ, ἣν
Διομήδης ὁ Ἀργεῖος λέγεται κτίσαι. καί τις ἔκγονος
εἶναι τοῦ Διομήδους νομιζόμενος, Δάσιος, ἀνὴρ εὐμε-
τάβολός τε τὸ φρόνημα καὶ οὐ Διομήδους ἄξιος, Ῥωμαίων περὶ Κάννας τὴν μεγάλην ἧτταν ἡττημένων,
ἀπέστησε τὴν πατρίδα πρὸς τοὺς Λίβυας ἀπὸ Ῥω-
131   μαίων. τότε δ᾽ αὖ δυσπραγοῦντος Ἀννίβου ἔλαθεν ἐς
Ῥώμην διιππεύσας καὶ ἐπὶ τὴν βουλὴν ἐπαχθεὶς
ἔφη δύνασθαι τὸ ἁμάρτημα ἰάσασθαι καὶ μεταβαλεῖν
αὖθις ἐς Ῥωμαίους τὴν πόλιν. οἱ δ᾽ ὀλίγου μὲν αὐτὸν
132   καὶ διέφθειραν, ἐξέβαλον δ᾽ εὐθὺς ἐκ τῆς πόλεως. ὁ
δὲ καὶ τούσδε καὶ τὸν Ἀννίβαν δεδιὼς ἠλᾶτο ἀνὰ τὴν
χώραν, καὶ ὁ μὲν Ἀννίβας αὐτοῦ τὴν γυναῖκα καὶ τὰ
τέκνα ζῶντας ἔκαυσε, τὰ δ᾽ Ἀργύριππα ἑτέρων ἐνδόν-
των εἷλε Φάβιος Μάξιμος νυκτὸς καὶ κτείνας ὅσους
εὗρε Λιβύων, φρουρὰν ἐπέστησε τῇ πόλει.

133   32. Τάραντα δὲ φρουρουμένην ὑπὸ Ῥωμαίων Κονωνεὺς ὧδε προέδωκε. κυνηγετεῖν εἴθιστο ὁ Κονωνεὺς
καὶ φέρων αἰεί τι τῷ φρουράρχῳ Ἰουνίῳ⁷ συνήθης ἐκ

---

⁷ Ἰουνίῳ VM Gaillard: Λιβίῳ edd.

---

[27] Argurippa is modern Arpi, five miles north of Foggia in
Apulia. After his exploits as one of the great Achaean heroes in

away, with the result that Hannibal could no longer even trust the ones who stayed: he was suspicious of them and they were suspicious of him. It was from this time, then, that things began to go downhill for Hannibal.

31. There is a town in Daunia called Argurippa, which is said to have been founded by Diomedes.[27] A certain Dasios, supposedly a descendant of Diomedes, but of unstable disposition and not worthy of him, brought Argurippa over from the Roman side to the African after the great defeat of Rome at Cannae. But at this moment, with Hannibal's fortunes now in decline, he rode undetected to Rome and, on being introduced to the senate, said that he could correct his mistake and bring the town back to the Roman side. The Romans very nearly put him to death, and expelled him immediately from the city. Now, afraid both of Hannibal and the Romans, he wandered around the country. Hannibal burned his wife and children alive, while others betrayed Argurippa, and Fabius Maximus took possession of it at night, killed all the Africans he found and stationed a garrison in the town.

32. The city of Tarentum, which was garrisoned by Rome, was betrayed by a man called Cononeus in the following way. Cononeus used to go hunting regularly, and he would always bring something back for the garrison commander, Iunius.[28] As a result, they had become ac-

130

131

132

133

the Trojan War, Diomedes is said to have settled in Italy with king Daunus. [28] Most editors follow Schweighäuser in emending the manuscripts' reading "Iunius" to "Livius," which is the name of the garrison commander reported by Polybius (8.24–36) and Livy (26.39.1). But Appian may have been following another textual tradition.

τοῦδε ἐγεγένητο, ὡς δ᾽ ἐν πολεμουμένῃ χώρᾳ νυκτὸς
ἔφη δεῖν κυνηγετεῖν καὶ νυκτὸς φέρειν τὰ λαμβανό-
134 μενα. νυκτὸς οὖν αὐτῷ τῶν πυλῶν ἀνοιγομένων, συνθέμενος Ἀννίβᾳ καὶ στρατιώτας λαβών, τοὺς μὲν
ἔκρυψεν ἐν λόχμῃ τινὶ πλησίον, τοὺς δ᾽ ἐπακολουθεῖν
ἐκέλευσεν ἑαυτῷ δι᾽ ὀλίγου, τοὺς δὲ σὺν αὐτῷ προσιέναι, θώρακας ἔνδοθεν ὑπεζωσμένους καὶ ξίφη, τὰ δ᾽
135 ἐκτὸς ὡς ἂν ἐς κυνηγέτας ἐσκευασμένους. κάπρον τε
αὐτοῖς ἐπὶ ξύλων ἐπιθεὶς ἧκε νυκτὸς ἐπὶ τὰς πύλας,
καὶ τῶν φυλάκων, ὥσπερ ἔθος ἦν, ἀνοιξάντων, οἱ
μὲν συνεισελθόντες αὐτῷ τοὺς ἀνοίξαντας αὐτίκα διεχρῶντο, οἱ δ᾽ ἑπόμενοι κατὰ σπουδὴν συνεισέπιπτον
ἐκείνοις καὶ τοὺς ἀπὸ τῆς λόχμης ἐδέχοντο καὶ τὰς
136 πύλας ἀνεῴγνυον τῷ Ἀννίβᾳ. ὁ δ᾽ εἴσω παρελθὼν τῆς
μὲν ἄλλης πόλεως εὐθὺς ἐκράτει καὶ τοὺς Ταραντίνους ἑταιρισάμενος τὴν ἄκραν ἔτι φρουρουμένην ἐπολιόρκει.

137   33. Ὧδε μὲν Κονωνεὺς Τάραντα προέδωκε· Ῥωμαῖοι δ᾽, ὅσοι τὴν ἀκρόπολιν εἶχον, ἐς μὲν πεντακισχιλίους ἦσαν, καὶ αὐτοῖς Ταραντίνων τέ τινες προσ-
εχώρουν, καὶ ὁ τῆς ἐν Μεταποντίῳ φρουρᾶς ἡγεμὼν
τὸ ἥμισυ τῆς φρουρᾶς ἔχων ἦλθε, βελῶν τε καὶ ὀρ-
γάνων πολλῶν εὐπόρουν, ὡς ἀπὸ τείχους εὐμαρῶς
138 ἀμύνεσθαι τὸν Ἀννίβαν. εὐπόρει δὲ καὶ ὁ Ἀννίβας.
πύργους τε οὖν καὶ καταπέλτας ἐπάγων καὶ χελώνας
ἔνια διέσειε καὶ δρεπάνοις ἀπὸ κάλων ἐπάλξεις τε
139 κατέσυρε καὶ τὸ τεῖχος ἀπεγύμνου. οἱ δὲ λίθους μὲν
ἐπὶ τὰς μηχανὰς ἀφιέντες πολλὰ συνέτριβον, βρό-

quainted. With the countryside in a state of war, he said it was necessary to go hunting at night, and bring back what he caught at night. Since the gates were, therefore, opened   134 for him at night, he made an agreement with Hannibal to take his soldiers, hide some of them in a copse nearby, order others to follow him at a short distance, and others again to accompany him, dressed outwardly as hunters, but wearing breastplates and swords underneath. Putting   135 a wild boar on poles for them one night, he came to the gates, which the guards opened, as usual. Those with him immediately killed those who opened the gates; the ones following behind quickly rushed in with them, let in the troops from the copse and held the gates open for Hannibal. Once he had entered the town, he immediately took   136 possession of the rest of it, and after making friendly overtures to the Tarentines, he laid siege to the citadel which still had a Roman garrison.

33. This was how Cononeus betrayed Tarentum. The   137 Romans holding the citadel numbered about five thousand. A certain number of Tarentines came to help them, while the garrison commander at Metapontum also arrived with half his force. The Romans had a good supply of missiles and machines, and thought they would easily drive Hannibal off from the walls. But Hannibal was also   138 well equipped. Bringing up siege towers, catapults and sheds, he shook the wall in places, pulled down the battlements with hooks tied to ropes and stripped the wall of its defenses. The defenders threw rocks at the siege engines,   139 shattering some of them, pulled the hooks away with

χοις δὲ τὰ δρέπανα περιέσπων καὶ πολλάκις ἐκθέον-
τες ἄφνω συνετάρασσον ἀεί τι καὶ κτείναντες ἐπανῆε-
140 σαν. ὡς δὲ καὶ πνεῦμά ποτε λάβρον ἐθεάσαντο, οἱ
μὲν ἀπὸ τοῦ τείχους δᾷδας ἡμμένας καὶ στυππίον καὶ
πίσσαν αὐτοῦ τοῖς μηχανήμασιν ἐπερρίπτουν, οἱ δὲ
141 καὶ ἐκδραμόντες ὑπέθηκαν. ἀπογνοὺς οὖν ὁ Ἀννίβας
τῆσδε τῆς πείρας περιετείχισε τὴν ἀκρόπολιν⁸ χωρίς
γε τοῦ πρὸς θαλάσσῃ μέρους· οὐ γὰρ ἦν καὶ τοῦτο
δυνατόν. καὶ παραδοὺς Ἄννωνι τὴν πολιορκίαν εἰς
Ἰάπυγας ἀνεχώρει.

142   34. Λιμένες δ᾽ εἰσὶ τοῖς Ταραντίνοις πρὸς βορρᾶν
ἄνεμον ἐκ πελάγους ἐσπλέοντι διὰ ἰσθμοῦ, καὶ τὸν
ἰσθμὸν ἀπέκλειον γεφύραις, ὧν τότε κρατοῦντες οἱ
Ῥωμαίων φρουροὶ σφίσι μὲν ἐδέχοντο τὴν ἀγορὰν ἐκ
θαλάσσης, Ταραντίνοις δ᾽ ἐκώλυον ἐσκομίζεσθαι.
143 ὅθεν ἠπόρουν ἀγορᾶς οἱ Ταραντίνοι, ἕως ἐπελθὼν
αὐτοῖς ὁ Ἀννίβας ἐδίδαξε λεωφόρον ὁδόν, ἣ διὰ μέ-
σης τῆς πόλεως ἔφερεν ἀπὸ τῶν λιμένων ἐπὶ τὴν
νότιον θάλασσαν, ὀρύξαντας ἰσθμὸν ἕτερον ποιήσα-
144 σθαι. καὶ οἱ μὲν οὕτω πράξαντες εἶχόν τε ἀγορὰν καὶ
τριήρεσι τοὺς Ῥωμαίων φρουρούς, ναῦς οὐκ ἔχοντας,
ὑπὸ τὸ τεῖχος ἔβλαπτον, ὅτε μὴ χειμὼν εἴη μάλιστα,
καὶ τὴν ἀγορὰν τὴν καταπλέουσαν ἐκείνοις ἀφη-
145 ροῦντο· οἱ δ᾽ ἠπόρουν. καὶ νυκτὸς αὐτοῖς Θουρίων
σῖτόν τε ναυσὶ πεμπόντων καὶ τριήρεις ἐς φυλακὴν
τῶν νεῶν οἱ Ταραντῖνοι καὶ οἱ σὺν αὐτοῖς Λίβυες πυθόμενοι καὶ λοχήσαντες ἔλαβον αὐτῷ τε σίτῳ καὶ

nooses, and made frequent sorties, regularly causing sudden consternation and returning after inflicting casualties. On one occasion, observing that there was a strong wind, 140 some of the Romans threw down burning torches, flax and pitch from the wall onto Hannibal's siege engines, while others ran out and set fire to them from underneath. This 141 caused Hannibal to despair of the attempt and throw a wall around the citadel, apart from the area on the sea side, where it was not possible. He put Hanno in charge of the siege and retired to Iapygia.

34. The Tarentines have harbors that lie to the north as 142 you sail in from the sea through narrows. They used to close off the narrows with booms, but at this time, the Roman garrison controlled the booms, enabling them to supply themselves by sea and prevent the Tarentines from doing so. For this reason, the latter began to run short of 143 food, until, that is, Hannibal arrived and showed them how to construct another narrow channel, by digging out a wide street that ran through the middle of the city from the harbor to the sea on the south side. With this work 144 they secured their food supply and, except in particularly stormy weather, used their triremes to sail right up under the walls and molest the Roman garrison, who had no ships of their own. With the Tarentines depriving them of the food being brought to them by sea, it was the Romans who began to run short of supplies. When the people of 145 Thurii sent grain transports to them one night with triremes as protection, the Tarentines and the Africans in league with them learned of the plan and, laying an ambush, captured the whole expedition, grain, crews and all.

---

8 πόλιν VM: ἀκρόπολιν Viereck-Roos

146 αὐτοῖς ἀνδράσιν ἁπάσας. πρεσβευομένων δὲ θαμινὰ
τῶν Θουρίων καὶ ἀξιούντων λύσασθαι τοὺς εἰλημμένους οἱ Ταραντῖνοι τοὺς φοιτῶντας αὐτῶν μετέπειθον
ἐς Ἀννίβαν. καὶ ὁ Ἀννίβας, ὅσους εἶχε Θουρίων αἰχμαλώτους, εὐθὺς ἀπέλυεν. οἳ δέ, τοὺς οἰκείους σφῶν
147 βιασάμενοι, τὰς πύλας Ἄννωνι ἀνέῳξαν. καὶ Θούριοι
μέν, Ῥωμαίοις Τάραντα περιποιούμενοι, ἔλαθον οὕτως
ὑπὸ Καρχηδονίοις αὐτοὶ γενόμενοι· ἡ δ' ἐν τῇ πόλει
φρουρὰ Ῥωμαίων εἰς Βρεντέσιον λαθοῦσα διέπλευσεν.

148 35. Μεταποντῖνοι δ', ἐξ οὗ σφῶν ὁ φρούραρχος τὸ
ἥμισυ τῆς φρουρᾶς ἄγων ἐς Τάραντα ᾤχετο, τοὺς
λοιποὺς ὀλίγους γενομένους ἀπέκτειναν καὶ Ἀννίβᾳ
149 προσέθεντο. προσέθετο δὲ καὶ ἡ μεταξὺ Μεταποντί-
νων τε καὶ Θουρίων[9] Ἡράκλεια, δέει μᾶλλον ἢ γνώμῃ.
150 καὶ πάλιν ἦν ἐπικυδέστερα τὰ Ἀννίβου. τοῦ δ' ἑξῆς
ἔτους καὶ Λευκανῶν τινες ἀπέστησαν ἀπὸ Ῥωμαίων·
οἷς Σεμπρώνιος Γράκχος ἀνθύπατος ἐπελθὼν ἐπολέ-
151 μει. Λευκανὸς δέ τις ἐκ τῶν ἔτι Ῥωμαίοις ἐμμενόντων,
Φλάυιος, φίλος ὢν καὶ ξένος Γράκχου, προδιδοὺς
αὐτὸν ἔπεισεν ἔς τι χωρίον ἐλθόντα συνθέσθαι Λευκανῶν τοῖς στρατηγοῖς, ὡς μετανοοῦσι καὶ δοῦναι καὶ
λαβεῖν πίστεις. ὁ δ' οὐδὲν ὑποτοπήσας εἵπετο μεθ'
152 ἱππέων τριάκοντα. Νομάδων δὲ πολλῶν αὐτὸν ἐξ ἐνέδρας κυκλωσαμένων ὁ μὲν Φλάυιος ἐξίππευσεν ἐς
ἐκείνους, ὁ δὲ Γράκχος συνεὶς τῆς προδοσίας καθή-

[9] Θουρίων Schweig.: Ταραντίνων VM

Seeking the ransom of those taken prisoner, the Thurians   146
sent a number of delegations, but the Tarentines persuaded their negotiators to go over to Hannibal's side.
Hannibal immediately released all the Thurian prisoners
he had taken, and they forced their own families to open
the gates of Thurii to Hanno. So the people of Thurii, in   147
seeking to secure Tarentum for Rome, themselves unin-
tentionally fell under Carthaginian rule in this way. The
Roman garrison in the town sailed away unnoticed to
Brundisium.

35. The people of Metapontum, after their garrison   148
commander had gone off to Tarentum with half his garrison force, killed the few who remained, and went over
to Hannibal's side. Heracleia, too, which is located be-   149
tween Metapontum and Thurii, defected to Hannibal,
more out of fear than conviction. So Hannibal began to
enjoy more success again. In the following year some Lu-   150
canians also revolted from Rome, and Sempronius Gracchus went off as proconsul to campaign against them.[29]
One of the Lucanians who were still on Rome's side, a man   151
called Flavius, an associate and guest-friend of Gracchus,
betrayed him by persuading him to go to a particular place
to make an agreement and exchange pledges with the
Lucanian generals who were supposedly changing their
mind. Sempronius suspected nothing and followed along
with thirty cavalrymen, but was ambushed by a large num-   152
ber of Numidians who surrounded him. When Flavius
rode over to them, Sempronius knew he had been be-

[29] Tib. Sempronius Gracchus, consul in 215 and 213, was the
grand-uncle of the famous Gracchan brothers. The ambush in
which he was killed occurred in 212.

λατο μετὰ τῶν ἱππέων καὶ πολλὰ καὶ γενναῖα δρῶν
κατεκόπη μετὰ πάντων πλὴν τριῶν, οὓς μόνους εἷλεν
ὁ Ἀννίβας, πολλὴν ποιησάμενος σπουδὴν λαβεῖν
ζῶντα Ῥωμαίων τὸν ἀνθύπατον. αἰσχρῶς δ᾽ αὐτὸν
ἐνηδρευμένον ἀγάμενος ὅμως τῆς τελευταίας ἀρετῆς
ἔθαψεν καὶ τὰ ὀστᾶ Ῥωμαίοις ἔπεμψεν.

153   36. Καὶ ἀπὸ τοῦδε αὐτὸς μὲν ἐν Ἰάπυξιν ἐθέριζεν
καὶ σῖτον πολὺν ἐσώρευεν, Ῥωμαίων δ᾽ ἐπιθέσθαι
Καπυαίοις ἐγνωκότων ἔπεμπεν Ἄννωνα μετὰ χιλίων
πεζῶν καὶ χιλίων ἱππέων ἐσδραμεῖν νυκτὸς ἐς Κα-
154   πύην. καὶ ὁ μὲν ἐσέδραμε Ῥωμαίους λαθών, οἱ δὲ
ἡμέρας γενομένης, ὡς πλέονας εἶδον ἐπὶ τῶν τειχῶν,
τὸ συμβὰν ἔγνωσαν καὶ τῆς μὲν πόλεως εὐθὺς ἀνεχώρουν, τὰ δὲ θέρη τὰ Καπυαίων καὶ τῶν ἄλλων
155   Καμπανῶν προκατελάμβανον. ὀδυρομένοις δὲ περὶ
τοῦδε τοῖς Καμπανοῖς ὁ Ἀννίβας ἔφη πολὺν ἔχειν
σῖτον ἐν Ἰαπυγίᾳ καὶ πέμποντας ἐκέλευεν λαμβάνειν,
ὁσάκις θέλοιεν. οἱ δ᾽ οὐχ ὑποζύγια μόνον οὐδ᾽ ἄνδρας, ἀλλὰ καὶ γύναια καὶ παιδία ἔπεμπον ἀχθο-
156   φορήσοντα τοῦ σίτου· καὶ γὰρ ἐθάρρουν τῇ διόδῳ,
μετελθόντος ἐς αὐτὴν ἐξ Ἰαπύγων Ἀννίβου καὶ παρὰ
τὸν Κάλωρα ποταμὸν στρατοπεδεύοντος πλησίον Βε-
νεβενδέων, οὓς μόνους ἐδεδοίκεσαν, Ῥωμαίοις ἔτι
συμμάχους ὄντας. τότε δ᾽ Ἀννίβου παρόντος ἁπάντων
κατεφρόνουν.

157   37. Συνέβη δ᾽ Ἀννίβαν μέν, καλοῦντος αὐτὸν Ἄννωνος, ἐς Λευκανοὺς διελθεῖν, τὰ πολλὰ τῆς κατα-
σκευῆς ἐν τῷ περὶ Βενεβενδὸν στρατοπέδῳ μετ᾽

trayed, and jumping from his horse along with his men, was cut down after a long and brave fight. All died with him except three, the only ones Hannibal was able to capture, although he tried very hard to take the Roman proconsul alive. He had trapped Sempronius dishonorably, but Hannibal nevertheless admired his courage at the end and, after giving him a funeral, sent his bones to Rome.

36. After this, he himself spent the summer in Iapygia, 153 where he stored up a great supply of grain. When the Romans decided to attack Capua, he sent Hanno with a thousand infantry and a thousand cavalry to make their way swiftly into the city by night. This they succeeded in 154 doing undetected until daybreak when the Romans saw more men on the walls and realized what had happened. The Romans immediately withdrew from the city and began to harvest the crops of Capua and the rest of Campania before the inhabitants could do so. When the Campa- 155 nians complained about this to Hannibal, he said he had a big store of grain in Iapygia, and told them to send men to help themselves as often as they wanted. They did not just send transport animals and men to collect the loads of grain, but women and children too. For they had no fear 156 about the journey, as Hannibal had moved his base there from Iapygia, and was encamped beside the river Calor, near Beneventum, the only place they feared, as it remained an ally of Rome. But now, with Hannibal in the vicinity, they could ignore everyone.

37. As it turned out, however, at Hanno's request, 157 Hannibal went across to Lucania, leaving most of his baggage in the camp at Beneventum with only a small force

158 ὀλίγης φρουρᾶς καταλιπόντα, δυοῖν δὲ Ῥωμαίοις
στρατηγούντοιν, Κλαυδίου τε καὶ Ἀππίου,[10] τὸν ἕτερον αὐτοῖν πυθόμενον ἐπιδραμεῖν τοῖς Καμπανοῖς,
διαφέρουσι τὰ θέρη, καὶ πολλοὺς μὲν οἷα ἀπαρα-
σκεύους διαφθεῖραι καὶ τὸν σῖτον Βενεβενδεῦσι δοῦναι, λαβεῖν δὲ καὶ τὸ στρατόπεδον Ἀννίβου καὶ τὴν
ἐν αὐτῷ παρασκευὴν ἁρπάσαι καὶ Καπύην, ἔτι ὄντος
ἐν Λευκανοῖς Ἀννίβου, περιταφρεῦσαί τε καὶ ἐπὶ τῇ
159 τάφρῳ περιτειχίσαι πᾶσαν ἐν κύκλῳ. καὶ τοῦδε τοῦ
περιτειχίσματος ἐκτὸς ἄλλο ποιήσαντες οἱ στρατηγοὶ
τὸ μέσον εἶχον ἀντὶ στρατοπέδου. ἐπάλξεις δ' ἦσαν
αὐτοῖς αἱ μὲν ἐς Καπναίους πολιορκουμένους, αἱ δ' ἐς
τοὺς ἔξωθεν ἐπιόντας ἐπεστραμμέναι, ἥ τε ὄψις ἦν
160 πόλεως μεγάλης, σμικροτέραν ἐχούσης ἐν μέσῳ. τὸ
δ' ἀπὸ τοῦ περιτειχίσματος ἐς τὴν Καπύην διάστημα
δισστάδιον ἦν μάλιστα· ἐν ᾧ πολλαὶ ἐγίγνοντο πεῖραι
καὶ συμβολαὶ καθ' ἑκάστην ἡμέραν, πολλὰ δὲ ὡς ἐν
θεάτρῳ μεσοτειχίῳ μονομάχια, προκαλουμένων ἀλ-
161 λήλους τῶν ἀρίστων. καί τις Καπναῖος, Ταυρέας,
Ῥωμαίων ἐν μονομαχίῳ Κλαύδιον Ἄσελλον περιφεύ-
γων ὑπεχώρει, μέχρι τοῖς Καπναίων τείχεσιν ὁ Ἄσελ-
λος ἐγκύρσας καὶ τὸν ἵππον οὐ δυνάμενος ἐκ τῆς
ῥύμης ἐπιστρέψαι διὰ τῶν πολεμίων πυλῶν ἐς τὴν
Καπύην ἐσήλατο σὺν ὁρμῇ καὶ διιππεύσας τὴν πόλιν

[10] Κλαυδίου τε καὶ Ἀππίου Goukowsky: Κλαυδίου τε καὶ
Ἀννίου VM: ὑπάτοιν, Φουλβίου τε Φλάκκου καὶ Κλαυδίου
Ἀππίου Schweig.

to guard it. In command of the Roman army were Claudius 158
and Appius.[30] When the latter heard of the situation, he
attacked the Campanians transporting the crops and killed
many of them, unprepared as they were, and gave the
grain to the Beneventines. He also captured Hannibal's
camp and seized the equipment in it, and, as Hannibal
remained in Lucania, dug a ditch around Capua with a
wall above it surrounding the entire city. Outside this sur- 159
rounding wall the generals built another wall, and used
the space in between as a camp. Some of the battlements
were aligned against the besieged Capuans, others against
those attacking from outside: it looked like a big town with
a smaller one inside it. The distance between the sur- 160
rounding wall and Capua itself was about two stades, and,
with the best fighters challenging each other, many trials
of strength, many engagements took place there every day,
and many single combats, as if in a walled amphitheater.
In one single combat, a certain Capuan, called Taureas, 161
trying to escape his Roman opponent, Claudius Asellus,
continued to fall back, until Asellus reached the walls of
Capua, and unable to turn his horse from the route of its
charge, leaped at speed through the enemy gates into
Capua itself, galloped right through the whole city and

[30] On the assumption that Appian must have been referring
to the consuls of 212, Q. Fulvius Flaccus and Ap. Claudius Pulcher, editors have generally emended the text accordingly. But
the text says nothing about the consuls. I have adopted Goukowsky's reading and his explanation that Appian has somehow
confused the consul Appius Claudius and a propraetor, C.
Claudius Nero, active at Capua according to Livy (25.22.7,
26.5.8).

ὅλην κατὰ τὰς ἑτέρας ἐξέδραμεν ἐς τοὺς ἐπὶ θάτερα
Ῥωμαίους.

162   38. Καὶ ὁ μὲν οὕτως παραβόλως διεσώζετο, Ἀννίβας δέ, τῆς χρείας ψευσθείς, ἐφ᾽ ἣν ἐς Λευκανοὺς
μετεκέκλητο, ἀνέστρεφεν ἐς Καπύην, μέγα ποιούμενος μὴ περιιδεῖν πόλιν μεγάλην καὶ εὔκαιρον ὑπὸ
163   Ῥωμαίοις γενομένην. προσβαλὼν δὲ τῷ περιτειχίσματι καὶ μηδὲν δυνηθεὶς μηδ᾽ ἐπινοῶν, ὅπως ἂν ἐς
τὴν πόλιν ἐσπέμψειεν ἢ σῖτον ἢ στρατιάν, οὐδενὸς
οὐδ᾽ ἀπ᾽ ἐκείνων αὐτῷ συμβαλεῖν δυναμένου διὰ τὴν
ἐπιτείχισιν πάντῃ περιλαμβάνουσαν, ἐπὶ τὴν Ῥώμην
ἠπείγετο παντὶ τῷ στρατῷ, πυνθανόμενος μὲν κἀκεί-
νους ὑπὸ λιμοῦ πιέζεσθαι, ἐλπίζων δὲ τοὺς στρατηγοὺς αὐτῶν ἀπὸ Καπύης ἀναστήσειν ἢ αὐτός τι Κα-
164   πύης μεῖζον ἐργάσεσθαι. συντόνῳ δὲ σπουδῇ διελθὼν
ἔθνη πολλὰ καὶ πολέμια, τῶν μὲν οὐ δυνηθέντων
αὐτὸν ἐπισχεῖν, τῶν δὲ οὐδ᾽ ἐς πεῖραν ἐλθεῖν ὑποστάντων, ἀπὸ δύο καὶ τριάκοντα σταδίων τῆς Ῥώμης
ἐστρατοπέδευσεν ἐπὶ τοῦ Ἀνίηνος ποταμοῦ.

165   39. Καὶ ἡ πόλις ἐθορυβήθη θόρυβον οἷον οὐ πρότερον, οἰκεῖον μὲν οὐδὲν ἔχοντες ἱκανόν (ὃ γὰρ εἶχον, ἐν
Καμπανίᾳ τότε ἦν), πολεμίου δὲ στρατοῦ τοσοῦδε
σφίσιν ἐπιστάντος ἄφνω καὶ στρατηγοῦ δι᾽ ἀρετὴν
166   καὶ εὐτυχίαν ἀμάχου. ὅμως δ᾽ ἐκ τῶν παρόντων οἱ μὲν
δυνάμενοι φέρειν ὅπλα τὰς πύλας ἐφύλασσον, οἱ δὲ
γέροντες ἐς τὸ τεῖχος ἀνεπήδων, γύναια δὲ καὶ παιδία
λίθους καὶ βέλη παρέφερον· οἱ δ᾽ ἐκ τῶν ἀγρῶν
συνέθεον ἐς τὸ ἄστυ δρόμῳ. βοῆς δὲ παμμιγοῦς καὶ

came tearing out the other gates to the Roman lines on the other side.

38. He thus saved himself in an extraordinary manner. Hannibal, having failed to deal with the crisis that had called him to Lucania, now returned to Capua, regarding it of great importance not to allow a large and strategically situated town to come under Roman control. He attacked the surrounding wall, but could do nothing, and was unable to devise a way of getting either grain or men into the city. And since nobody from the inside could make contact with him, being completely surrounded by the siege wall, he hurried against Rome with his whole army. He had learned that the Romans too were pressed by hunger, and he hoped either to get their generals to lift the siege of Capua, or to have a success himself that would be more important than relieving Capua. Moving at extreme speed through large tracts of enemy territory—some were unable to hold him up, others did not even try—he made camp beside the river Anio, thirty two stades from Rome.

39. The city suffered higher levels of agitation than ever before. With no adequate force of their own (what they had was in Campania at the time), they suddenly had to face a strong hostile army and a general of irresistible courage and good fortune. Nevertheless, from the resources they did have, those capable of bearing arms guarded the gates, the old men sprang into position on the walls, the women and children brought up stones and missiles, and those in the fields ran together into the city. The whole place was full of all sorts of shouting, complaints,

162

163

164

165

166

θρήνων καὶ εὐχῶν καὶ παρακελεύσεων πρὸς ἀλλήλους
πάντα μεστὰ ἦν. εἰσὶν δ' αὐτῶν, οἳ τὴν γέφυραν τὴν
167 ἐπὶ τοῦ Ἀνιῆνος ἐκδραμόντες ἔκοπτον. μικρὸν δέ τι
πολίχνιον Ῥωμαῖοί ποτε ἐπιτειχίζοντες Αἰκανοῖς Ἄλβην ἀπὸ τῆς αὐτῶν μητροπόλεως ἐκάλεσαν· σὺν
χρόνῳ δ' ἐπισύροντες ἢ διαφθείροντες ἢ ἐς τὴν Ἀλ-
168 βανῶν σύγκρισιν Ἀλβησέας αὐτοὺς καλοῦσιν. τούτων τότε τῶν Ἀλβησέων ἐς Ῥώμην δισχίλιοι δρόμῳ
διέθεον, τοῦ κινδύνου μετασχεῖν, καὶ ἅμα ἀφικνοῦντο
169 καὶ ὡπλίζοντο καὶ τὰς πύλας ἐφρούρουν. τοσῇδε προ-
θυμίᾳ βραχὺ πολίχνιον ἐκ τοσῶνδε ἀποικιῶν ἐχρή-
σατο μόνη, οἷόν τι καὶ Ἀθηναίοις ἐς Μαραθῶνα μικρὰ πόλις, ἡ Πλαταιέων, ἔδραμε τοῦ τότε κινδύνου
μετασχεῖν.

170 40. Τῶν δὲ στρατηγῶν Ἄππιος[11] μὲν Καπύῃ παρ-
έμενε, κἀκεῖνος ἐπειγόμενος[12] ἑλεῖν Καπύην, Κλαύδιος[13] δὲ [Φλάκκος][14] ἑτέραις ὁδοῖς ἐπειχθεὶς ἀλήκτῳ
τάχει ἀντεστρατοπέδευσε τῷ Ἀννίβᾳ, μέσον ἔχων τὸν
171 Ἀνιῆνα. τῷ δ' Ἀννίβᾳ τὴν γέφυραν εὑρόντι λελυμένην
καὶ τὸν Κλαύδιον ἀντικαθήμενον ἔδοξε τὰς πηγὰς τοῦ
172 ποταμοῦ περιοδεῦσαι. καὶ ὁ μὲν Κλαύδιος ἀντιπαρώ-
δευεν, ὁ δὲ καὶ ὡς ἐνήδρευε, Νομάδας ἱππέας ὑπολιπών, οἳ τῶν στρατῶν ἀναστάντων τὸν Ἀνιῆνα ἐπέρασαν καὶ τὰ Ῥωμαίων ἐδῄουν, μέχρι παρὰ τὴν πόλιν

---

11 Ἄννιος VM; Ἄππιος edd.   12 ἡγούμενος VM: ἐπειγόμενος Goukowsky   13 Κλαύδιος hic et deinceps VM:
Φούλβιος Viereck-Roos   14 Φλάκκος del. Goukowsky

prayers and mutual encouragement. Some of them rushed
out and cut down the bridge over the river Anio. The   167
Romans had once fortified a small town against the Aequi
and called it Alba after their mother city.[31] Over the course
of time, out of carelessness or philological corruption or
to distinguish them from the Albani, they call them Albenses. Two thousand of these Albenses now rushed to   168
Rome to share the danger, and no sooner had they arrived
than they were given weapons and took up guard duty at
the gates. Such was the enthusiasm this one small town   169
displayed, alone out of so many colonies, just as the small
state of Plataea had rushed to Marathon to help the Athe-
nians and share the danger they then faced.

40. Of the Roman generals, Appius stayed at Capua, as   170
he too was eager to capture it, while Claudius,[32] making
a rapid and unbroken march along an alternative route,
camped opposite Hannibal with the Anio in between
them. When he found that the bridge had been destroyed   171
and that Claudius was facing him on the other side, Hannibal decided to go around the sources of the river. Although 172
Claudius kept pace with him on the other bank, even so
Hannibal set a trap for him, by leaving some Numidian
cavalry behind, who, when the armies had broken camp,
crossed the Anio and ravaged the territory of Rome. They

[31] Appian is referring to Alba Fucens, named after Alba
Longa.

[32] The manuscripts continue to refer to Annius and Claudius.
To avoid confusion, I translate the emended text, but Appian may
simply have got the names wrong.

APPIAN

αὐτὴν γενόμενοι καὶ φοβήσαντες ἐπέστρεψαν ἐς Ἀν-
173 νίβαν· οὕτω γὰρ αὐτοῖς παρήγγελτο. αὐτὸς δ', ἐπεὶ
τάς τε πηγὰς τοῦ ποταμοῦ περιῆλθεν καὶ ὁδὸς ἦν ἐς
τὸ ἄστυ οὐ πολλή, λέγεται μὲν νυκτὸς σὺν τρισὶν
ὑπασπισταῖς λαθὼν κατασκέψασθαι τὸ ἄστυ καὶ τὴν
τῆς δυνάμεως ἐρημίαν καὶ θόρυβον τὸν ἐπέχοντα
ἰδεῖν, ἀναστρέψαι δ' ἐς Καπύην, εἴτε θεοῦ παράγοντος
αὐτὸν αἰεὶ ὡς καὶ τότε, εἴτε τὴν τῆς πόλεως ἀρετὴν
καὶ τύχην δείσας, εἴτε, ὡς αὐτὸς τοῖς ἐσβαλεῖν προ-
τρέπουσιν ἔλεγεν, οὐκ ἐθέλων τὸν πόλεμον ἐκλῦσαι
δέει Καρχηδονίων, ἵνα μὴ καὶ τὴν στρατηγίαν αὐτὸς
ἀποθοῖτο· οὐ γὰρ ὅ γε σὺν Κλαυδίῳ στρατὸς ἦν αὐτῷ
174 πάμπαν ἀξιόμαχος. ὁ δὲ Κλαύδιος ἀναστρέφοντι
παρείπετο, κωλύων τε προνομεύειν καὶ φυλασσόμενος
μηδὲν ἐξ ἐνέδρας παθεῖν.

175   41. Ὁ δ' ἐπιτηρήσας νύκτα ἀσέληνον καὶ χωρίον,
ἐν ᾧ Κλαύδιος ἑσπέρας τεῖχος μὲν οὐκ ἔφθανεν
ἐγεῖραι, τάφρον δ' ὀρυξάμενος καὶ διαστήματα ἀντὶ
πυλῶν καταλιπὼν καὶ τὸ χῶμα προβαλὼν ἀντὶ τείχους ἡσύχαζεν, ἔς τε λόφον ὑπερκείμενον αὐτοῦ καρ-
176 τερὸν ἔπεμψε λαθὼν ἱππέας, οἷς εἴρητο ἡσυχάζειν,
ἕως οἱ Ῥωμαῖοι τὸν λόφον ὡς ἔρημον ἀνδρῶν κατα-
λαμβάνωσι, τοῖς δ' ἐλέφασι τοὺς Ἰνδοὺς ἐπιβήσας
ἐκέλευσεν ἐς τὸ τοῦ Κλαυδίου στρατόπεδον ἐσβιάζε-
σθαι διά τε τῶν διαστημάτων καὶ διὰ τῶν χωμάτων,
177 ὡς δύναιντο. σαλπικτὰς δὲ αὐτοῖς καὶ βυκανητάς
τινας ἐξ ὀλίγου διαστήματος ἕπεσθαι κελεύσας προσ-

went as far as the city itself, causing alarm, but then returned to Hannibal as he had ordered. When he made his   173
way round the springs of the river, and was only a short
distance from Rome, he is said to have reconnoitered the
city himself at night with three escorts. Although he is
supposed to have observed how weak the Roman forces
were and how confused the situation was in the city, he
still returned to Capua. He did this either because a god
led him away from the city on this occasion, as always, or
because he feared the courage and good fortune of the
citizens, or because, as he himself said to those urging him
to attack, he did not want to finish the war as he was afraid
that the Carthaginians might force him to resign his command. For it is certainly the case that the army under
Claudius' command was no match at all for him. Claudius   174
shadowed Hannibal as he retreated, preventing him from
foraging, and making sure to avoid trouble from an ambush.

41. Hannibal waited for a moonless night, one on   175
which Claudius occupied a position where evening arrived
before he had time to build a proper wall, but suspended
work for the day after digging a ditch, leaving gaps in it
instead of gates, and banking up earth in front of it instead
of building a wall. Without being detected, Hannibal sent
some cavalry to occupy a strategically strong hill overlook-
ing Claudius' camp, with orders to maintain silence until   176
the Romans moved to take possession of the hill in the
belief that it was unoccupied. Hannibal then ordered his
mahouts to mount their elephants and force their way into
Claudius' camp as best they could over the mounds of
earth and through the gaps in the trench. He also ordered   177
some trumpeters and buglers to follow a short distance

ἔταξεν, ὅταν ἔνδον γένωνται, τοὺς μὲν θόρυβον πολὺν
ἐγείρειν περιθέοντας, ἵνα πολλοὶ δόξωσιν εἶναι, τοὺς
δὲ ῥωμαΐζοντας βοᾶν, ὅτι Κλαύδιος, ὁ Ῥωμαίων
στρατηγός, κελεύει τὸ στρατόπεδον ἐκλιπόντας ἐπὶ
178 τὸν ἐγγὺς λόφον ἀναπηδᾶν. τόδε μὲν ἦν τὸ στρατήγημα τοῦ Ἀννίβου, καὶ τούτων τὰ μὲν πρῶτα πάντα
κατὰ νοῦν ἀπήντησεν· οἵ τε γὰρ ἐλέφαντες ἐσῆλθον
τοὺς φύλακας καταπατήσαντες, καὶ οἱ σαλπικταὶ
τὸ αὑτῶν ἐποίουν, καὶ ὁ θόρυβος Ῥωμαίοις ἐξ εὐνῆς
ἀνισταμένοις ἐν μελαίνῃ νυκτὶ ἀδόκητος ἐμπεσὼν
ἐπιφοβώτατος ἦν, τῶν τε ῥωμαϊζόντων ἀκούοντες, ὅτι
παρήγγελται φεύγειν ἐς τὸν λόφον, περὶ τοῦτ᾽ ἐγίγνοντο.

179 42. Κλαύδιος δ᾽ αἰεί τινα προσδοκῶν ἐνέδραν καὶ
τοῦτο ὑποπτεύων ἐν ἅπασι τοῖς Ἀννίβου, εἴθ᾽ ὑπ᾽
οἰκείας τότε συνέσεως, εἴτε θεολήπτῳ γνώμῃ προσπε-
σών, εἴτε παρὰ αἰχμαλώτου τὰ ἀκριβέστατα μαθών,
τοὺς χιλιάρχους ὀξέως ἐπέστησε ταῖς εἰς τὸν λόφον
ἀγούσαις ὁδοῖς, κωλύειν τοὺς δι᾽ αὐτῶν φερομένους
καὶ μεταδιδάσκειν, ὅτι τοῦτ᾽ οὐχ ὁ στρατηγὸς Ῥω-
180 μαίων, ἀλλ᾽ Ἀννίβας ἐκήρυξεν ἐνεδρεύων. αὐτὸς δὲ
τοῖς χώμασι φυλακὰς ἀκριβεῖς ἐπιστήσας, μή τις
ἔφοδος ἔξωθεν ἄλλη γένοιτο, ἐβοηδρόμει μεθ᾽ ἑτέρων
ἀνὰ τὸ στρατόπεδον, ἅπαντα ἔχειν ἀσφαλῶς καὶ ὀλίγους τοὺς μετὰ τῶν ἐλεφάντων ἐσελθόντας εἶναι.
181 δᾷδάς τε ἧπτε καὶ πῦρ πανταχόθεν ἤγειρε, καὶ κατα-
φανὴς ἦν ἡ τῶν ἐσελθόντων ὀλιγότης, ὥστε αὐτῶν
πάνυ καταφρονήσαντες οἱ Ῥωμαῖοι, ἐς ὀργὴν ἐκ τοῦ

behind them with instructions that, when they were inside the camp, some of them were to run around making a great deal of noise, in order to give the impression that there was a large number of them, and others were to shout out in Latin that the Roman general Claudius had given orders to abandon the camp and rush up to a position on the hill nearby. This was Hannibal's ploy, and the first part of it went entirely according to plan. The elephants trampled the guards and got into the camp and the trumpeters followed their orders. The unexpected disturbance that greeted the Romans as they clambered out of bed in the black night was extremely alarming, and when they heard an order in Latin to escape to the hill, they set about obeying it. 178

42. But Claudius was constantly on the lookout for one of Hannibal's tricks, and suspected one in everything he did. On this occasion, benefiting either from his own native intelligence, or from divinely inspired judgment or because he had learned the details from a prisoner, he quickly stationed his military tribunes on the roads leading to the hill to stop the men rushing along them, and to give them the correct information that it was not the Roman general, but Hannibal, who had issued the order as a trap. Claudius himself then put the earth mounds under close guard in case another attack came from outside, and went around the camp with others, shouting out that everything was secure and that there was only a small number of intruders with the elephants. He had torches lit and fires kindled everywhere, and it was clear how few had broken in. The result was that the Romans were completely contemptuous of them, and moving from fear to 179 180 181

πρὶν δέους μεταβαλόντες, εὐμαρῶς οἷα ψιλοὺς καὶ
182 ὀλίγους διέφθειραν. οἱ δ᾽ ἐλέφαντες, οὐκ ἔχοντες εὐ-
ρύχωρον οὐδὲν ἐς ἀναστροφήν, εἰλούμενοι περὶ σκηνὰς καὶ φάτνας, ἐβάλλοντο πρὸς ἁπάντων ἐπιτυχῶς
διὰ τὴν στενότητα τοῦ χωρίου καὶ τὸ μέγεθος τῶν
σωμάτων, μέχρι περιαλγοῦντές τε καὶ ἀγανακτοῦντες
καὶ ἐπιδραμεῖν ἐς τοὺς πολεμίους οὐκ ἔχοντες τοὺς
ἐπιβάτας σφῶν ἀπεσείοντο καὶ κατεπάτουν σὺν ὀργῇ
καὶ βοῇ πάνυ ἠγριωμένοι καὶ ἐξεπήδων ἐκ τοῦ στρα-
183 τοπέδου. Κλαύδιος μὲν δὴ [Φλάκκος],[15] εὐσταθῶς καὶ
εὐμηχάνως αἰφνιδίῳ συνενεχθεὶς ἐνέδρᾳ, περιῆν τοῦ
Ἀννίβου καὶ τὸν στρατὸν περιέσῳζεν αἰεὶ πεφρικότα
τὰς Ἀννίβου μηχανάς·
43. Ὁ δ᾽ Ἀννίβας, ἐπεὶ τῆς πείρας ἀπέτυχεν, ἐς
Λευκανοὺς διελθὼν ἐχείμαζε καὶ ἐπὶ τρυφῆς ἦν οὐ
συνήθους· ἐρωμένην τε εἶχεν ἄγριος ἀνήρ. καὶ εὐθὺς
184 αὐτῷ κατ᾽ ὀλίγον ἐτρέπετο πάντα. Κλαύδιος δ᾽ ἐς Καπύην πρὸς τὸν συστράτηγον ἐπανῄει, καὶ τοῖς Καπυαίοις προσέβαλλον ἄμφω καρτερῶς, ἐπειγόμενοι χει-
185 μῶνος ἑλεῖν τὴν πόλιν, ἕως Ἀννίβας ἠρεμεῖ. Καπυαῖοι
δέ, τῶν τροφῶν σφᾶς ἐπιλειπουσῶν καὶ οὐδαμόθεν
ἄλλων ἐπεισαγομένων, ἐνεχείρισαν ἑαυτοὺς τοῖς
στρατηγοῖς· ἐνεχείρισαν δὲ καὶ ὅσοι Λιβύων αὐτοὺς
ἐφρούρουν, αὐτοῖς στρατηγοῖς, Ἄννωνι ἑτέρῳ καὶ
186 Βωτᾷ. Ῥωμαῖοι δὲ τῇ μὲν πόλει φρουρὰν ἐπέστησαν
καὶ ὅσους εὗρον αὐτομολοῦντας, χεῖρας αὐτῶν ἀπέτε-

15 Φλάκκος del. Goukowsky

outrage, easily killed such a small group of light-armed men. As the elephants did not have enough room to turn around and were getting tangled in the tents and stalls, and because the place was so narrow and the elephants so big, those shooting at them easily hit their target. Eventually, in pain and frustration, and unable to attack their enemy, the elephants threw off their riders, trampled them with angry roars, and ran from the camp, completely out of control. It was, then, with this display of steadfastness and clear thinking that Claudius survived his encounter with Hannibal's unexpected trap, and saved his army, which had always been afraid of the tricks Hannibal devised. 182 183

43. When his venture failed to work, Hannibal went off to winter quarters in Lucania where, fierce though he was, he indulged himself in unaccustomed luxury, and took a lover. Immediately his luck took a slow turn for the worse. Claudius returned to Capua to join his fellow general, and together they energetically pressed the attack on the town, trying hard to capture it in the winter, while Hannibal remained inactive. When their food supply ran out and there was nowhere they could get any more from, the Capuans surrendered to the Roman generals, also handing over all the African garrison troops along with their commanders, Hanno (another one)[33] and Bostar. The Romans put their own garrison in the town and cut the hands off any deserters they found; they sent the dis- 184 185 186

[33] That is, not Hannibal's nephew, who has been featuring prominently in the story so far.

μον· Λιβύων δὲ τοὺς μὲν ἐπιφανεῖς ἐς Ῥώμην ἔπεμ-
187 ψαν, τοὺς δὲ λοιποὺς ἀπέδοντο. καὶ Καπυαίων αὐτῶν
τοὺς μὲν αἰτίους μάλιστα τῆς ἀποστάσεως ἀπέκτειναν, τῶν δ' ἄλλων τὴν γῆν ἀφείλοντο μόνον. εὔφορος
δ' ἐστὶν ἐς σῖτον ἡ περὶ τὴν Καπύην πᾶσα· πεδιὰς
γάρ ἐστιν.

188   44. Καπύη μὲν δὴ πάλιν ἐς Ῥωμαίους ἐπανῆκτο,
καὶ μέγα τοῦτο Λιβύων ἐς τὴν Ἰταλίαν πλεονέκτημα
περιῄρητο· ἐν δὲ Βρυττίοις, οἳ μέρος εἰσὶ τῆς Ἰταλίας,
ἀνὴρ ἐκ πόλεως Τισίας φρουρουμένης ὑπὸ τῶν Λιβύων, ἐθίσας αἰεί τι λήζεσθαι καὶ φέρειν τῷ φρουράρχῳ καὶ παρὰ τοῦτο αὐτῷ συνήθης ἐς πάντα γεγονὼς καὶ σχεδὸν συστράτηγος, ἤλγει τῶν φρουρῶν ἐς
189 τὴν πατρίδα ὑβριζόντων. συνθέμενος οὖν τῷ Ῥωμαίων στρατηγῷ καὶ πιστὰ δοὺς καὶ λαβὼν ἑκάστοτέ
τινας ὡς αἰχμαλώτους ἐσῆγεν ἐς τὴν ἄκραν καὶ τὰ
ὅπλα αὐτῶν ἐσέφερεν ὡς σκῦλα. ἐπεὶ δὲ πλέονες ἐγένοντο, ἐξέλυσεν αὐτοὺς καὶ ὥπλισε καὶ τὴν Λιβύων
φρουρὰν ἀνεῖλε καὶ παρὰ Ῥωμαίων ἄλλην ἐσηγά-
190 γετο. Ἀννίβου δὲ οὐ πολὺ ὕστερον παροδεύοντος
αὐτοὺς οἱ μὲν φρουροὶ καταπλαγέντες ὑπὸ τοῦ δέους
ἐξέφυγον ἐς Ῥήγιον, οἱ δὲ Τισιᾶται παρέδωκαν
αὐτοὺς τῷ Ἀννίβᾳ. καὶ ὁ Ἀννίβας τοὺς μὲν αἰτίους
τῆς ἀποστάσεως ἔκαυσε, τῇ δὲ πόλει φρουρὰν ἐπέστησεν ἄλλην.

191   45. Ἰαπύγων δ' ἐν πόλει Σαλαπίᾳ, Λιβύων ὑπηκόῳ,
δύο ἤστην ἄνδρε τῶν μὲν ἄλλων γένει καὶ πλούτῳ καὶ
δυνάμει διαφέροντε, ἀλλήλοιν δ' ἐκ πολλοῦ διαφόρω.

tinguished Africans to Rome and sold the rest into slavery; and of the Capuans themselves, those who had been particularly responsible for the insurrection, they executed, but merely confiscated the land of the others. For the whole area around Capua is flat, and good for growing grain. 187

44. So Capua returned to Roman rule and the Africans were deprived of this important advantage in the fight for Italy. Meanwhile in Bruttium, which is a part of Italy, there was a man from the town of Tisia, which had a garrison of Africans, who was in the habit of carrying out bandit raids, but who would always give the garrison commander something, and as a result had become a close associate of his in all matters and virtually joint commander. He was, however, angered by the insulting behavior of the garrison toward his hometown, and so, after exchanging mutual pledges with the Roman general, came to an agreement, by which he would from time to time bring into the citadel certain men he had captured supposedly as prisoners, along with their weapons supposedly as booty. When there were enough of them he released and armed them, and killed the African garrison, replacing it with one of Romans. But not long after, when Hannibal was marching past the town, the garrison troops were struck with fear and fled to Rhegium, and the inhabitants of Tisia surrendered to Hannibal. He burned at the stake those who had caused the defection, and stationed another garrison in the town. 188 189 190

45. In the Iapygian town of Salapia, which was under African control, there were two men who stood out from the rest by reason of birth, wealth and power, but who had 191

τούτοιν Δάσιος μὲν τὰ Λιβύων ᾑρεῖτο, Βλάτιος δὲ τὰ
192 Ῥωμαίων. ἕως μὲν οὖν ἤκμαζεν τὰ Ἀννίβου, ἐφ᾽ ἡσυχίας ἦν ὁ Βλάτιος· ἐπεὶ δὲ ἠγείρετο τὰ Ῥωμαίων καὶ
τὰ πολλὰ τῆς ἐσφετερισμένης ἀρχῆς ἀνελάμβανον,
ἔπειθεν ὁ Βλάτιος τὸν ἐχθρὸν ὑπὲρ τῆς πατρίδος
αὐτῷ συμφρονῆσαι μόνης, μή τι πάθοι, Ῥωμαίων
193 αὐτὴν βίᾳ λαβόντων, ἀνήκεστον. ὁ δ᾽ ὑποκρινάμενος
συντίθεσθαι κατεμήνυσε τοῦτ᾽ Ἀννίβᾳ. καὶ ἐδίκαζεν
αὐτοῖς ὁ Ἀννίβας, Δασίου μὲν κατηγοροῦντος, Βλατίου δ᾽ ἀπολογουμένου καὶ συκοφαντεῖσθαι διὰ τὴν
ἔχθραν λέγοντος· ὃ καὶ τέως ἄρα προορῶν ἐτόλμησεν
ἐχθρῷ προσενεγκεῖν λόγον τοιόνδε, ὡς ἀπίστῳ κατη-
194 γόρῳ διὰ τὴν ἔχθραν ἐσομένῳ. Ἀννίβας δ᾽ οὔτε ἀπορ-
ρῖψαι τὸ ἔργον οὔτε τῷ παρ᾽ ἐχθροῦ πιστεῦσαι ῥᾳδίως ἀξιῶν μεθίστατο αὐτοὺς ὡς σκεψόμενος ἐφ᾽
ἑαυτοῦ. στενῆς δὲ τῆς ἐξόδου πάμπαν οὔσης ὁ
Βλάτιος ἔφη τῷ Δασίῳ, τοὺς ἄλλους λαθών· "Οὐ σώ-
σεις, ὦ ἀγαθέ, τὴν πατρίδα;" ὁ δὲ καὶ τοῦτ᾽ εὐθὺς
ἐκβοήσας ἐμήνυεν.

195   46. Καὶ ὁ Βλάτιος οἰκτισάμενος τότε μάλιστα ἀξι-
οπίστως εἶπεν, ὡς ἐπιβουλεύοιτο ὑπ᾽ ἐχθροῦ τεχνίτου.
"Τοῦτο δ᾽," ἔφη, "Τὸ νῦν ἐπιβούλευμα καὶ τῆς πρότε-
196 ρον ἀμφιλογίας, εἴ τις ἦν, ῥύσεταί με. τίς γὰρ ἂν ἢ
πρότερον ἐχθρῷ περὶ τοιῶνδε διεπίστευσεν ἢ νῦν, εἰ
καὶ τέως ἐπεπλάνητο, ἀπίστῳ καὶ κατηγόρῳ περὶ
ἐκεῖνα γεγενημένῳ, κινδυνεύων ἔτι καὶ κρινόμενος καὶ

been at odds with each other for a long time, since Dasius
favored the Africans, and Blatius the Romans. As long as   192
Hannibal was doing well, Blatius kept quiet, but when
Rome's fortunes improved and they began to recover most
of the power they had lost, Blatius set about persuading
his enemy to come to an agreement with him, simply for
the sake of their home town, so that if Rome took it by
force, it would not suffer a ruinous fate. Dasius pretended   193
to go along with this, but informed Hannibal. With Hannibal adjudicating between them, Dasius acted as prosecu-
tor and Blatius presented his defense, maintaining that he
was being denounced out of personal animosity. It was
probably because Blatius had foreseen this all along that
he dared to make such a proposal to an enemy in the first
place, knowing that because of the personal hostility involved the accusation would lack credibility. Hannibal   194
thought it unwise to dismiss the matter out of hand or trust
the word of a personal enemy, so he sent them off with the
intention of investigating the matter himself. As the way
out was through a very narrow corridor, Blatius said to
Dasius quietly so that no one else could hear, "So, my good
friend, don't you want to save our hometown?," which
Dasius immediately repeated in a loud voice, thus letting
Hannibal know.

46. At this, Blatius very convincingly grumbled that he   195
was the target of a plot by an artful enemy. "This present
plot," he said, "will surely dispel the previous suspicion
about me, if indeed there was any. For who would speak   196
in confidence to an enemy about these things in the first
place? Or, even if he was misguided for a time, who would
now, when he was still in danger, on trial and denying the
charges, dare to repeat what he said to a person who was

ἀρνούμενος αὖθις ἂν τὰ δεύτερα ταῦτ᾽ ἐθάρρησεν εἰπεῖν, καὶ μάλιστ᾽ ἐν τῷ δικαστηρίῳ, πολλῶν μὲν
ἀκοῦσαι δυναμένων, τοῦ δὲ κατηγόρου καὶ τόδε μέλ-
197 λοντος εὐθὺς ὁμοίως ἐρεῖν; εἰ δὲ δὴ καὶ ἐγεγένητο,"
ἔφη, "Χρηστὸς ἐξαίφνης καὶ φίλος, τί μοι συλλαβεῖν
ὑπὲρ τῆς πατρίδος ἔτι δυνατὸς ἦν; τί δ᾽ ἂν ἐδεόμην
198 ἐγὼ μηδὲν ἐπικουρεῖν δυναμένου;" ἅ μοι δοκεῖ προϊ-
δὼν πάλιν ὁ Βλάτιος ψιθύρως ἐντυχεῖν τῷ Δασίῳ καὶ
ἐς ἀπιστίαν αὐτὸν ἐμβαλεῖν μείζονα, ἐπαγαγέσθαι δ᾽
ἐκ τοῦδε καὶ Ἀννίβαν ἐς ἀπιστίαν τῶν πρότερον εἰρη-
199 μένων. οὐ μὴν οὐδ᾽ ἐκφυγὼν τὴν δίκην ὁ Βλάτιος ἀφίστατο μὴ μεταπείθειν τὸν ἐχθρόν, καταφρονῶν ἄρα
ὡς ἐς πάντα γεγονότος ἀπίστου. ὁ δὲ αὖθις ὑπεκρίνετο συντίθεσθαι καὶ τὴν ἐπίνοιαν τῆς ἀποστάσεως
200 ᾔτει μαθεῖν. ὁ δὲ οὐδὲν ὀκνήσας ἔφη· "Διαδραμοῦμαι
μὲν ἐπί τι τῶν στρατοπέδων ἐγὼ τῶν Ῥωμαϊκῶν," μη-
νύσας αὐτῷ τὸ πάνυ πορρωτάτω, "Καὶ στρατιὰν ἄξω
λαβών· ἔστι γάρ μοι φίλος ὁ στρατηγὸς ἐκείνου τοῦ
στρατοῦ· σὺ δ᾽ ὑπομένειν μοι δεῦρο καὶ τὰ ἔνδον ἐπι-
τηρεῖν."

201 47. Ὁ μὲν εἶπεν οὕτω καὶ εὐθὺς ἐξέδραμε, λαθὼν
Δάσιον, οὐκ ἐς ἐκεῖνο τὸ στρατόπεδον, ἀλλὰ ἐς
Ῥώμην, ὁδὸν ἐλάσσονα. καὶ δοὺς τῇ βουλῇ τὸν υἱὸν
ὅμηρον ἱππέας ᾔτει χιλίους, μεθ᾽ ὧν ἠπείγετο κατὰ
202 σπουδήν, τὸ μέλλον ἔσεσθαι προορώμενος. ὁ δὲ Δάσιος ταῖς ἐπιούσαις ἡμέραις τὸν ἐχθρὸν οὐχ ὁρῶν,
εἴκασεν αὐτὸν ἐγχειρεῖν τοῖς ἐγνωσμένοις ὡς ἤδη πι-
στεύοντα αὐτῷ. νομίσας οὖν ἐς ἐκεῖνο τῷ ὄντι τὸ πορ-

untrustworthy and had already accused him on this score, and particularly in court, in the hearing of many, and with his accuser prepared immediately to relay this too, as he had done before? Even if the man had suddenly become 197 obligingly friendly," he continued, "how would he still be able to help me on behalf of our hometown? Why would I ask for help from someone who could not give it?" In my 198 opinion, Blatius had foreseen all this beforehand, and had repeated his words in a whisper to Dasius with the intention of discrediting him all the more, and of getting Hannibal to disbelieve the previous accusations. Even after his 199 acquittal, Blatius did not stop trying to get his enemy to change his allegiance, in spite of regarding him with contempt as somebody who had become completely untrustworthy. Dasius again pretended to go along with him and asked to know what was planned for the revolt. Without 200 hesitating Blatius replied: "I myself will hurry over to one of the Roman camps"—he mentioned the one that was by far the furthest away—"where I will collect a force to bring here. For the commanding officer of that army is a friend of mine. You wait for me here and keep an eye on what is happening in the town."

47. With these words he hurried off, but Dasius failed 201 to notice that he went, not to the camp he had mentioned, but to Rome, which was a shorter journey. Here he gave his son as a hostage to the senate, asked for a thousand cavalry and rushed back eagerly with them in anticipation of the outcome. Seeing nothing of his enemy in the follow- 202 ing days, Dasius supposed that Blatius now trusted him and was carrying out what they had decided. So, believing

ρωτέρω στρατόπεδον αὐτὸν οἴχεσθαι διέδραμεν πρὸς
Ἀννίβαν, καταφρονῶν, ὅτι φθάσει ἐκεῖνον ἐπανελθών,
"Καὶ νῦν μέν," ἔφη, "Παραδώσω σοι τὸν Βλάτιον ἐπ'
203   αὐτοφώρῳ στρατιὰν ἐπάγοντα τῇ πόλει." καὶ τὸ γε-
γονὸς ἐκθέμενος καὶ λαβών τινας ἐπανῆγεν ἐς τὴν
πατρίδα μετὰ σπουδῆς ὡς οὔπω τοῦ Βλατίου πλησι-
άζοντος. ὁ δ' ἔνδον τε ἦν ἄρτι καὶ τὴν φρουρὰν τὴν
Λιβύων ὀλίγην οὖσαν ἀνελὼν ἐφύλασσε μηδένα παρελθεῖν καὶ πύλας τὰς μὲν ἄλλας ἐκεκλείκει, τὰς δ' ἐς
204   τὴν ἐπάνοδον Δασίου μόνας εἴασεν ἀνεῷχθαι. καὶ τὸ
κατ' ἐκείνας μέρος ἅπαν εἶχεν ἀνυπόπτως· τὰ δ' ἐντὸς
ἐξετετάφρευτο καὶ διείληπτο, ὡς μὴ δύνασθαι τοὺς
ἐμπεσόντας ἐς ὅλην διαδραμεῖν. Δάσιος δέ, ἐπεὶ τὰς
πύλας εἶδεν ἀνεῳγμένας, ἤσθη νομίσας προλαβεῖν
205   τὸν ἐχθρὸν καὶ ἐσήλατο γεγηθώς. ὁ δ' ἐπικλείσας διέφθειρεν αὐτόν τε καὶ τοὺς ἐσδραμόντας, ὠθουμένους
ἐν στενῷ καὶ διαδρομὴν διὰ τὰς τάφρους οὐκ ἔχοντας. ὀλίγοι δ' αὐτῶν διὰ τοῦ τείχους ἐξαλόμενοι διέφυγον.

206   48. Καὶ Βλάτιος μὲν οὕτω περιῆν Δασίου, τρὶς
ἀντενεδρεύων, Φούλβιος δέ, Ῥωμαίων ὕπατος, Ἑρδο-
νίαν ἐπολιόρκει· καὶ αὐτὸν Ἀννίβας ἔλαθεν ἑσπέρας
ἐγγὺς γενόμενος καὶ ἀπεῖπε πυρὰ μὴ καίειν καὶ σιω-
207   πὴν παρήγγειλε. περὶ δὲ ἕω, γενομένης ὁμοῦ τι καὶ
ὁμίχλης, τοὺς μὲν ἱππέας ἔπεμψεν ἐπιχειρεῖν τῷ Ῥω-

---

34 The two consuls of 211 were Q. Fulvius Centumalus Maximus and P. Sulpicius Galba Maximus. After his consular com-

that Blatius had in fact gone to the further camp, Dasius
rushed off to Hannibal, presuming that he would get back
to Salapia before Blatius. "Now," he said, "I am going to
hand Blatius to you caught red-handed leading an army
against the town." Having explained what had been hap- 203
pening, he took some men and hurried back to his hometown, assuming that Blatius was not yet in the vicinity. But
the latter had just got back into the town and killed the
small African garrison, and was taking care to prevent
anyone entering. He left open only the gates on Dasius'
return route, and closed all the others. So, with regard to 204
these gates, everything looked unsuspicious. On the inside, however, trenches had been dug at intervals to prevent attacking forces from being able to run straight
through the whole town. When he saw the gates were
open, Dasius was delighted, believing he had forestalled
his enemy, and he enjoyed sweeping into the town. But 205
Blatius closed the gates and killed both him and those who
had come running in, and who were constrained in a narrow place and unable to make their way through the
ditches. A few escaped by jumping down from the walls.

48. This was how Blatius got the better of Dasius, three 206
times devising ways to counter his schemes. Meanwhile,
when the Roman consul Fulvius was besieging Erdonia,[34]
Hannibal approached him undetected one evening, having given orders that no fires were to be lit, and that silence
was to be observed. Around daybreak, when it was also 207
somewhat foggy, he ordered his cavalry to attack the Ro-

mand in Spain in 211, Fulvius was given proconsular command
in 210. Erdonia is modern Odona in Puglia.

μαίων στρατοπέδῳ, καὶ αὐτοὺς ἠμύνοντο ἐκεῖνοι, σὺν
θορύβῳ μὲν ὡς ἀπ' εὐνῆς, σὺν θάρσει δὲ οἷα ὀλίγους
208 ποθὲν αὐτοῖς ἐπιφανέντας. ὁ δ' Ἀννίβας ἐπὶ θάτερα
τῷ πεζῷ τὴν πόλιν περιῄει, κατασκεπτόμενος ἅμα καὶ
τοὺς ἔνδον ἐπελπίζων, ἕως ἐπῆλθεν τοῖς Ῥωμαίοις ἐν
τῇ περιόδῳ, εἴτε προϊδόμενος, εἴτε κατὰ συντυχίαν
209 κυκλούμενος αὐτούς. οἱ δ' ἔπιπτον ἤδη λάβρως καὶ
ἀθρόως, ἀμφίβολοι γεγονότες· καὶ ἀπέθανον αὐτῶν ἐς
ὀκτακισχιλίους καὶ ὁ ὕπατος αὐτὸς ὁ Φούλβιος. οἱ
λοιποὶ δ' ἔς τι χῶμα πρὸ τοῦ στρατοπέδου ἀναθορόν-
τες αὐτό τε διέσωσαν γενναίως ἀμυνόμενοι καὶ τὸν
Ἀννίβαν ἐκώλυσαν λαβεῖν τὸ στρατόπεδον.

210   49. Μετὰ δὲ τοῦτο Ῥωμαῖοι μὲν τὴν Ἰαπύγων ἀποστάντων ἐδῄουν, Ἀννίβας δὲ τὴν Καμπανῶν, ἐς Ῥωμαίους μεταθεμένων χωρὶς Ἀτέλλης μόνης. καὶ Ἀτελ-
λαίους μετῴκιζεν ἐς Θουρίους, ἵνα μὴ τῷ Βρυττίων
211 καὶ Λευκανῶν καὶ Ἰαπύγων ἐνοχλοῖντο πολέμῳ. καὶ
Ῥωμαῖοι τοὺς ἐκ Νουκερίας ἐκπεσόντας ἐν Ἀτέλλῃ
μετῴκιζον ἔς τε τὴν Ἀννίβου ἔτι ὑπήκοον ἐσβαλόντες
Αὐλωνίαν τε εἷλον καὶ τὴν Βρυττίων γῆν ἐπέτρεχον
καὶ Τάραντα, φρουρουμένην ὑπὸ Καρθάλωνος, ἐκ γῆς
212 καὶ θαλάσσης ἐπολιόρκουν. ὁ δὲ Καρθάλων ὀλίγων
Καρχηδονίων παρόντων Βρυττίους ἐς τὴν φρουρὰν
προσέλαβεν. τῶν δὲ Βρυττίων ὁ φρούραρχος ἤρα γυναικός, ἧς ἀδελφὸς ὑπὸ Ῥωμαίοις στρατευόμενος
ἔπραξεν διὰ τῆς ἀδελφῆς τὸν φρούραρχον ἐνδοῦναι

man camp. The Romans beat them off, in some confusion as they had just woken up, but fought confidently in the belief that there were only a few of them who had suddenly appeared out of nowhere. Hannibal circled round 208 with his infantry to the other side of the town to reconnoiter the situation and at the same time to encourage the inhabitants. On his way round, he came across the Romans, either by design or by chance, and surrounded them. Attacked on both sides, they fell fast and in large 209 numbers, about eight thousand of them, including the consul himself Fulvius.[35] The rest jumped up onto a mound in front of the camp which they saved by bravely defending themselves, and they prevented Hannibal from capturing the camp.

49. After this the Romans ravaged the land of the Ia- 210 pygians, who were in revolt from them, and Hannibal the land of the Campanians, who, apart from Atella alone, had gone over to the Roman side. Hannibal resettled the Atellians in Thurii to protect them from being troubled by the war in Bruttium, Lucania and Iapygia; and the Romans 211 resettled the Nucerian exiles in Atella, and attacked the land still subject to Hannibal. They captured Aulonia, overran the territory of the Brutii and laid siege by land and sea to Tarentum, whose garrison was under the command of Carthalo. Having only a few Carthaginians, Car- 212 thalo enrolled Brutii in the garrison. But the commander of the Bruttian garrison troops was in love with a woman whose brother was serving with the Romans. The latter arranged through his sister for the Bruttian commander

[35] The year was 210, when Fulvius was no longer consul, but proconsul, an easy mistake to make.

Ῥωμαίοις, ἐπάγουσι τὰς μηχανάς, ᾗ τοῦ τείχους
213 αὐτὸς ἐφρούρει. Τάραντα μὲν δὴ Ῥωμαῖοι τόνδε τὸν
τρόπον ἀνέλαβον, εὔκαιρον ἐς πολέμους χωρίον καὶ
κατὰ γῆν καὶ κατὰ θάλασσαν·

50. Ἀννίβας δ᾽ ἐπειγόμενος ἐς αὐτήν, ὡς ἔμαθεν
εἰλημμένην, παρῆλθεν ἀχθόμενος ἐς Θουρίους κἀκεῖ-
θεν ἐς Βενουσίαν, ἔνθα αὐτῷ Κλαύδιός τε Μάρκελλος,
ὁ Σικελίαν ἑλών, πέμπτον ὑπατεύων τότε, καὶ Τίτος
Κρισπῖνος ἀντιστρατοπεδεύοντες οὐκ ἐτόλμων ἄρχειν
214 μάχης. λείαν δέ τινα ὑπὸ Νομάδων ἀγομένην Μάρκελλος ἰδὼν καὶ δόξας ὀλίγους εἶναι τοὺς ἄγοντας
ἐπέδραμεν αὐτοῖς μετὰ τριακοσίων ἱππέων σὺν κατα-
φρονήσει καὶ πρῶτος ἡγεῖτο, θυμικὸς ὢν ἐς μάχας
215 καὶ παρακινδυνευτικὸς αἰεί. ἄφνω δὲ πολλῶν τῶν Λιβύων φανέντων καὶ πανταχόθεν αὐτῷ προσπεσόντων
οἱ μὲν οὐραγοῦντες Ῥωμαίων πρῶτοι φυγῆς ἦρχον, ὁ
δὲ Μάρκελλος ὡς ἑπομένων αὐτῶν ἐμάχετο γενναίως,
216 μέχρι κατακοντισθεὶς ἀπέθανε. καὶ αὐτοῦ τῷ σώματι
ὁ Ἀννίβας ἐπιστάς, ὡς εἶδε τὰ τραύματα πάντα ἐπὶ
τῶν στέρνων, ἐπήνεσε μὲν ὡς στρατιώτην, ἐπέσκωψε
217 δὲ ὡς στρατηγόν. καὶ τὸν δακτύλιον αὐτοῦ περιελὼν
τὸ μὲν σῶμα ἔκαυσε λαμπρῶς καὶ τὰ ὀστᾶ τῷ παιδὶ
προσέπεμψεν ἐς τὸ Ῥωμαίων στρατόπεδον·

218 51. Σαλαπίνοις δὲ μηνίων εὐθὺς ἐτύπωσεν ἐπιστολὴν τῇ σφραγῖδι Μαρκέλλου, πρὶν αἰσθέσθαι
πολλοὺς περὶ τοῦ θανάτου, καὶ αὐτόμολον ἄνδρα
Ῥωμαῖον ἔπεμψε φέρειν δηλοῦντα, ὅτι στρατιὰ Μαρκέλλου κατόπιν ἔρχοιτο καὶ ὁ Μάρκελλος αὐτὴν ὑπο-

to surrender to the Romans, who brought their siege engines up to the section of the wall that he himself was
guarding. This was how the Romans took Tarentum, a   213
place well positioned for war both by land and sea.

50. Hannibal was hurrying there when he heard it had
been captured, and, bitterly disappointed, turned to Thurii and from there to Venusia. Here he was opposed by
Claudius Marcellus, the conqueror of Sicily and now consul for the fifth time, and Titus Crispinus.[36] They did not
dare to initiate battle, but when Marcellus saw what he   214
thought was a small number of Numidians carrying away
some plunder, he overconfidently attacked them with
three hundred cavalry. He led the attack from the front,
as he was always spirited in battle and scorned danger. But   215
suddenly large numbers of Africans appeared and attacked him from all sides, and while the Roman rearguard
were the first to take to flight, Marcellus himself, assuming
they were following, fought nobly, until he was killed by a
missile. When Hannibal stood over the body and saw the   216
wounds all over his chest, he praised him as a soldier, but
mocked him as a general. He took the ring off his finger,   217
cremated his body with full honors, and sent his bones to
his son in the Roman camp.

51. Hannibal was angry with the people of Salapia, and,   218
before news of Marcellus' death had become generally
known, he immediately wrote them a letter, sealed with
Marcellus' signet ring, and sent a Roman deserter to deliver it and tell them that Marcellus' army was following
behind, and that Marcellus had given orders for them to

[36] M. Claudius Marcellus and T. Quinctius Crispinus were
consuls in 208.

219 δέξασθαι κελεύοι. ἄρτι δ᾽ εἰλήφεσαν Κρισπίνου
γράμματα περιπέμψαντος ἐς ἅπαντας, ὅτι τῆς Μαρκέλλου σφραγῖδος Ἀννίβας κεκρατήκοι. τὸν οὖν ἄγγελον, ἵνα μὴ παραμένων ἐπιγνοίη τὰ γιγνόμενα,
ἀπέπεμψαν ὑποσχόμενοι τὰ προστασσόμενα ποιήσειν, αὐτοὶ δ᾽ ὁπλισάμενοι τὴν ἐνέδραν ἐπὶ τῶν τει-
220 χῶν ἀνέμενον. καὶ προσιόντος τοῦ Ἀννίβου μετὰ
Νομάδων, οὓς Ῥωμαϊκοῖς ὅπλοις ἐσκεύασεν, τὰς μὲν
πύλας ἐκ μηχανήματος ἀνέσπασαν ὡς δὴ Μαρκέλλου
προσιόντος ἀσμενίζοντες, εἰσδεξάμενοι δ᾽, ὅσων εὐμαρῶς κρατήσειν ἔμελλον, αὖθις ἐκ τοῦ μηχανήματος
αὐτὰς ἐπικαθῆκαν καὶ τοὺς μὲν ἐσελθόντας ἔκτειναν,
τοὺς δ᾽ ἔξω τῶν τειχῶν ἔτι περιεστῶτας ἄνωθεν ἔβαλ-
λόν τε καὶ κατετίτρωσκον. καὶ δευτέρας τῆσδε πείρας
ὁ Ἀννίβας ἐπὶ τῇ πόλει σφαλεὶς ἀπεχώρει.

221   52. Ἐν τούτῳ δὲ καὶ Ἀσρούβας, ὁ ἀδελφὸς Ἀννίβου, τὴν στρατιάν, ἣν ἐξενάγησεν ἐν τοῖς Κελτίβηρσιν, ἔχων, διέβαινεν ἐς τὴν Ἰταλίαν καὶ Κελτῶν φι-
λίως αὐτὸν δεχομένων τὰ Ἄλπεια ὄρη, ὡδοποιημένα
πρότερον ὑπὸ Ἀννίβου, διώδευε δύο μησίν, ὅσα τέως
Ἀννίβας ἐξ διῆλθεν, ἐσέβαλλέν τε ἐς Τυρρηνίαν,
ἄγων πεζοὺς μὲν τετρακισμυρίους ἐπὶ ὀκτακισχιλίοις,
ἱππέας δὲ ὀκτακισχιλίους καὶ ἐλέφαντας πεντεκαίδεκα, καὶ γράμματα πρὸς τὸν ἀδελφὸν ἔπεμπε, δη-
222 λῶν, ὅτι παρείη. τούτων δὲ τῶν γραμμάτων ὑπὸ Ῥωμαίων ἁλόντων οἱ ὕπατοι Σαλινάτωρ καὶ Νέρων,
μαθόντες αὐτοῦ τὸ πλῆθος τῆς στρατιᾶς ἀπὸ τῶν
γραμμάτων, συνῆλθον ἐς ταὐτὸ πάσαις ταῖς δυνάμε-

admit his troops. But the Salapians had just received a 219
letter from Crispinus, who had sent a circular round to
everyone with the information that Hannibal had gotten
hold of Marcellus' signet ring. Not wanting the messenger
to stay and find out what was happening, they sent him off,
promising to follow the orders they had been given, but
in fact arming themselves and waiting in ambush on the
walls. When Hannibal approached with some Numidians, 220
whom he had equipped with Roman weapons, the Salapians winched up the gates as if they were welcoming Marcellus' arrival. They let in as many as they thought they
could easily overcome, and then used the winches again
to close the gates. They killed those who had got in, and
wounded those who were still milling around outside the
walls, by throwing missiles on them from above. After this
second failure to capture the city, Hannibal withdrew.

52. While this was happening, Hannibal's brother Has- 221
drubal took the army he had recruited among the Celtiberians, and set out for Italy. He crossed the Alps along
the route Hannibal had opened, but as the Celts wel-
comed him warmly, it took him only two months where
Hannibal had previously taken six. He entered Etruria at
the head of forty-eight thousand infantry, eight thousand
cavalry and fifteen elephants, and sent a letter to his
brother to inform him of his arrival. But the letter was 222
intercepted by the Romans, and learning from it the size
of his army, the consuls, Salinator and Nero, united all
their troops into one army and camped opposite him near

σιν καὶ ἀντεστρατοπέδευσαν αὐτῷ περὶ πόλιν Σήνας.
223 ὃ δ' οὔπω μάχεσθαι κεκρικώς, ἀλλὰ τῷ ἀδελφῷ συνελθεῖν ἐπειγόμενος ὑπεχώρει καὶ νυκτὸς ἀναζεύξας
περὶ ἕλη καὶ τέλματα καὶ ποταμὸν οὐκ εὔπορον
ἠλᾶτο, μέχρι φανείσης ἡμέρας οἱ Ῥωμαῖοι, καταλα-
βόντες αὐτοὺς διερριμμένους τε καὶ κεκμηκότας ὑπὸ
ἀγρυπνίας καὶ κόπου, πλείστους μὲν αὐτῶν ἅμα τοῖς
ταξιάρχοις συντασσομένους ἔτι καὶ συνιόντας διέφθειραν καὶ αὐτὸν ἐπ' ἐκείνοις Ἀσρούβαν, πλείστους
δ' αἰχμαλώτους ἔλαβον καὶ μεγάλου δέους ἀπήλλα-
ξαν τὴν Ἰταλίαν, ἀμάχου ἂν σφίσι τοῦ Ἀννίβου γενομένου, εἰ καὶ τήνδε τὴν στρατιὰν προσέλαβεν.

224   53. Θεὸς δέ μοι δοκεῖ τόδε Ῥωμαίοις ἀντιδοῦναι τῆς
ἐπὶ Κάνναις ἀτυχίας, οὐ πόρρω τε ἐπ' ἐκείνῃ καὶ ἰσο-
στάσιόν πως ἐκείνῃ γενόμενον· στρατηγοί τε γὰρ οἱ
ἑκατέρων ἀπώλοντο, καὶ στρατοῦ πλῆθος ἐγγυτάτω
μάλιστα ἐπ' ἴσης, καὶ τὰ αἰχμάλωτα πολλὰ γενέσθαι
καὶ τοῖσδε κἀκείνοις συνηνέχθη, στρατοπέδων τε καὶ
παρασκευῆς τῆς ἀλλήλων δαψιλοὺς ἐκράτουν ἑκάτεροι. οὕτω παραλλὰξ ἡ πόλις εὐτυχιῶν καὶ συμφορῶν
ἐπειρᾶτο. Κελτιβήρων δ' ὅσοι διέφυγον ἐκ τοῦ κακοῦ,
οἳ μὲν ἐς τὰ οἰκεῖα, οἳ δ' ἐς Ἀννίβαν ἐχώρουν.

225   54. Ὁ δ', ἐπί τε τῷ ἀδελφῷ καὶ στρατιᾷ τοσῇδε δι'
ἀπειρίαν ὁδῶν αἰφνίδιον ἀπολωλυίᾳ δυσφορῶν καὶ

[37] C. Claudius Nero and M. Livius Salinator were the consuls
of 207. Sena, modern Senigallia, is on the Adriatic coast, about
fifteen miles north of Ancona.

the town of Sena.[37] Hasdrubal had decided not to join 223
battle yet, but to press on and link up with his brother, and
so he withdrew. Breaking camp at night, he got lost among
swamps and marshes and an unfordable river, until at daybreak the Romans caught up with them. The Carthaginians were scattered and exhausted by lack of sleep and
hard work, and the Romans killed most of them, along
with their officers, while they were still assembling and
being drawn up for battle. They killed Hasdrubal too, and
took a large number of prisoners, thus freeing Italy of its
great fear that Hannibal would have become invincible if
he had been reinforced by this army.[38]

53. It seems to me that a god compensated the Romans 224
in this way for the misfortune at Cannae, for the battle
happened not long after Cannae and paralleled it in certain ways. The generals on both sides were killed and very
nearly the same number of men; it is also the case that
many prisoners were captured on both occasions, and
each side took possession of the other's camp along with
large quantities of matériel. So it was that Rome experienced triumph and disaster in turn. Of the Celtiberians
who escaped the disaster, some made their way home,
others to Hannibal.

54. Hannibal himself was depressed by his brother's 225
death and the sudden destruction of such a large army
brought about by ignorance of the roads. Now in the four-

---

[38] This is known as the battle of the Metaurus River, described
in much greater (and very different) detail by Polybius (11.1–3)
and Livy (27.43–51). The site of the battle is not known, but the
river flows into the sea near the town of Fano.

τεσσαρεσκαιδέκατον ἔτος ἔχων ἐν πόνοις ἀτρύτοις, ἐξ
οὗ Ῥωμαίοις ἐν Ἰταλίᾳ διεπολέμει, πάντων τε ὧν
εἰλήφει πρότερον, ἐκπεπτωκώς, ἐς Βρυττίους, ὅπερ
αὐτῷ λοιπὸν ἔθνος ὑπήκοον ἦν, ἀνεχώρει καὶ ἡσύχαζεν ὡς ἑτέρας δυνάμεως ἀφιξομένης ἀπὸ Καρχηδό-
226 νος. οἱ δ' ἔπεμψαν μὲν αὐτῷ ναῦς ἑκατὸν στρογγύλας,
ἐφ' ὧν σῖτός τε ἦν καὶ στρατιὰ καὶ χρήματα, οὐδενὸς
δ' ἐρετικοῦ παραπέμποντος αὐτὰς ἄνεμος ἐς Σαρδόνα
κατήνεγκεν, καὶ ὁ τῆς Σαρδόνος στρατηγὸς ἐπιπλεύ-
σας μακραῖς ναυσὶν κατέδυσε μὲν αὐτῶν εἴκοσιν,
ἑξήκοντα δ' ἔλαβεν, αἱ δὲ λοιπαὶ διέφυγον ἐς Καρχη-
227 δόνα. καὶ ὁ Ἀννίβας ἔτι μᾶλλον ἀπορούμενός τε καὶ
τὰ παρὰ Καρχηδονίων ἀπεγνωκώς, οὐδὲ Μάγωνος
αὐτῷ τι, τοῦ ξενολογοῦντος ἐν Κελτοῖς καὶ Λίγυσιν,
ἐπιπέμποντος, ἀλλὰ τὸ μέλλον ἔσεσθαι περιορωμέ-
νου, συνιδών, ὅτι μένειν ἐπὶ πλεῖον οὐ δυνήσεται,
αὐτῶν ἤδη Βρυττίων ὡς ἀλλοτρίων ὅσον οὔπω γενη-
σομένων κατεφρόνει καὶ ἐσφορὰς ἐπέβαλλεν αὐτοῖς
πάνυ πολλὰς τάς τε ὀχυρὰς τῶν πόλεων μετῴκιζεν ἐς
τὰ πεδινά, ὡς βουλευούσας ἀπόστασιν, πολλούς τε
τῶν ἀνδρῶν αἰτιώμενος διέφθειρεν, ἵνα τὰς περιουσίας αὐτῶν σφετερίζοιτο.

228 55. Καὶ ὁ μὲν ἐν τούτοις ἦν, ἐν δὲ Ῥώμῃ γίγνονται
μὲν ὕπατοι Λικίνιός τε Κράσσος καὶ Πόπλιος Σκιπίων, ὁ λαβὼν Ἰβηρίαν· τούτων δὲ Κράσσος μὲν
ἀντεστρατοπέδευσεν Ἀννίβᾳ περὶ Ἰαπυγίαν, Σκιπίων
δὲ τὸν δῆμον ἐδίδασκεν οὔ ποτε Καρχηδονίους οὐδ'
Ἀννίβαν ἀποστήσεσθαι σφίσιν ἐνοχλοῦντας ἀμφὶ

teenth year of unremitting toil since he had begun his campaigns against the Romans in Italy, he had lost all his previous gains. He withdrew to the Brutii, the only people still subject to him, and remained inactive, awaiting the arrival of a new expedition from Carthage. While they did 226 send him one hundred merchant ships carrying grain, troops and money, there were no rowers in the convoy, and the wind forced them to Sardinia, where the praetor attacked them with warships, sank twenty and captured six; the rest escaped to Carthage. So, Hannibal was now in 227 even greater difficulty and gave up hope of getting help from Carthage. Nor did Mago send him any assistance: he was recruiting mercenaries among the Celts and Ligurians, but was waiting to see what would happen. Hannibal, realizing that he would not be able to stay for long, began to treat the Brutii with contempt, as they would soon be total strangers to him: he imposed very heavy taxes on them and, on the grounds that they were planning revolt, he resettled their strong towns in the plains, and making accusations against many of their men, executed them, so that he could appropriate their assets.

55. That was Hannibal's situation. In Rome, Licinius 228 Crassus and Publius Scipio, the conqueror of Iberia, become consuls.[39] Of these, Crassus took up position opposite Hannibal in Iapygia, while Scipio explained to the people that they would never stop the Carthaginians or

[39] P. Cornelius Scipio Africanus and P. Licinius Crassus Dives were the consuls of 205. Scipio's exploits in Spain are treated by Appian at length in *Ib.* 18.68–38.154.

APPIAN

τὴν Ἰταλίαν, εἰ μὴ Ῥωμαίων στρατὸς ἐς Λιβύην δι-
229 έλθοι καὶ κίνδυνον αὐτοῖς ἐπιστήσειεν οἰκεῖον. λι-
παρήσας τε πάνυ καρτερῶς καὶ πείσας ὀκνοῦντας
ᾑρέθη στρατηγὸς αὐτὸς ἐς Λιβύην καὶ διέπλευσεν
230 εὐθὺς ἐς Σικελίαν. ἔνθα στρατὸν ἀγείρας τε καὶ
γυμνάσας ἐπέπλευσε Λοκροῖς ἄφνω τοῖς ἐν Ἰταλίᾳ,
φρουρουμένοις ὑπὸ Ἀννίβου· καὶ τὴν φρουρὰν κατα-
σφάξας τε καὶ παραδοὺς Πλημινίῳ τὴν πόλιν αὐτὸς
231 ἐς Λιβύην διέπλευσεν. Πλημίνιος δέ, οὐδεμίαν ὕβριν
ἢ ἀσέλγειαν ἢ ὠμότητα ἐς τοὺς Λοκροὺς ἐκλιπών,
ἐσύλησε λήγων καὶ τὸ τῆς Φερσεφόνης ἱερόν. καὶ
τόνδε μὲν Ῥωμαῖοι μετὰ τῶν συναμαρτόντων αὐτῷ
φίλων διέφθειραν ἐν τῷ δεσμωτηρίῳ καὶ τὰς περιουσίας αὐτῶν ἔδοσαν Λοκροῖς ἐς τὸν θησαυρὸν τῆς
θεοῦ φέρειν· ὅσα τε ἄλλα ἐδύναντο τῶν ἀπολωλότων
ἀνευρόντες, τὸ λεῖπον ἐκ τοῦ κοινοῦ σφῶν ταμιείου τῇ
θεῷ προσέθεσαν.

232   56. Τοῦ δ' αὐτοῦ χρόνου Κωνσεντίαν τε, μεγάλην
πόλιν Βρυττίων, καὶ ἄλλας ἓξ ἐπ' αὐτῇ περιέσπασεν
233 ἀπὸ Ἀννίβου Κράσσος. καὶ γιγνομένων ἐν Ῥώμῃ σημείων ἐκ Διὸς φοβερῶν οἱ μὲν τὰ Σιβύλλεια ἐπισκε-
πτόμενοι δέκα ἄνδρες ἔφασαν ἐξ οὐρανοῦ τι ἐς Πεσι-
νοῦντα τῆς Φρυγίας, ἔνθα σέβουσιν οἱ Φρύγες θεῶν
μητέρα, πεσεῖσθαι τῶνδε τῶν ἡμερῶν καὶ δεῖν αὐτὸ
ἐς τὴν Ῥώμην ἐνεχθῆναι. μετ' οὐ πολὺ δὲ πεσεῖν τε
προσηγγέλθη καὶ ἐς Ῥώμην ἐκομίσθη τὸ βρέτας. καὶ

40 The main task of the *decemviri sacris faciundis* (ten-man
commission for doing sacred things—it was later increased to

Hannibal troubling them in Italy, unless a Roman army went to Africa and put them in danger in their own territory. By persistently and obstinately pressing his case, and winning over waverers, he was himself appointed to the command in Africa, and sailed immediately to Sicily. Here he collected an army, trained it, and suddenly moved against Italian Locri, which was garrisoned by Hannibal. He killed the garrison, handed over the city to Pleminius, and set off across to Africa. There was no violence, insolence, or cruelty that Pleminius failed to inflict on the Locrians, and he even ended up robbing the temple of Persephone. The Romans executed him and his fellow criminals in prison, and granted their assets to the Locrians to deposit in the treasury of the goddess. Having recovered all they could of what had been taken, they paid the remainder to the goddess from their own public treasury.

56. In the same period, Crassus succeeded in detaching from Hannibal Consentia, a large town in Bruttium, and six others as well. At Rome, when alarming omens arrived from Zeus, the ten-man board for examining the Sibylline Books said that in the coming days something would fall from heaven at Pessinus in Phrygia, where the Phrygians worship the mother of the gods, and that it should be brought to Rome.[40] Not long after, it was reported that an image had indeed fallen, and it was brought to Rome. And to the present day, they still celebrate the anniversary of its original conveyance to the city as a fes-

229

230

231

232

233

fifteen) was the care and interpretation of the Sibylline Books, a set of discursive Greek oracles dating, so legend recorded, from Rome's regal period.

τὴν ἡμέραν ἑορτάζουσι καὶ νῦν μητρὶ θεῶν, ᾗ τότε
234 ἐκομίσθη. λέγεται δὲ τὴν ναῦν, ἣ ἔφερεν αὐτό, ἰλύι
τοῦ ποταμοῦ τοῦ Τιβέριος ἐνσχεθεῖσαν οὐδεμιᾷ μηχανῇ σαλεύεσθαι, μέχρι τῶν μάντεων προειπόντων
ἕψεσθαι μόνως, εἰ γυνὴ καθαρεύουσα ξένων ἀνδρῶν
ἑλκύσειεν, Κλαυδίαν Κόινταν, μοιχείας ἔγκλημα
ἔχουσαν ἔτι ἄκριτον καὶ δι᾽ ἀσωτίαν ἐς αὐτὸ πιθανω-
τάτην οὖσαν, ἐπιθειάσαι τε πολλὰ περὶ τῆς ἀναμαρ-
τησίας καὶ ἀναδήσασθαι τῇ μίτρᾳ τὸ σκάφος. καὶ ἡ
235 θεὸς ἕσπετο. Κλαυδία μὲν δὴ ἐξ αἰσχίστης δόξης ἐς
ἀρίστην μετέβαλεν, Ῥωμαίοις δὲ καὶ πρὸ τῆς Κλαυ-
δίας ἐκέλευε τὰ Σιβύλλεια διὰ τοῦ παρὰ σφίσιν ἀρί-
236 στου τὸ βρέτας ἐκ Φρυγίας μεταγαγεῖν. καὶ τὸν ἄριστον ἐν τῷ τότε σφίσι δοκοῦντα εἶναι, Σκιπίωνα τὸν
Νασικᾶν ἐπίκλην, ἐπεπόμφεσαν, υἱὸν μὲν ὄντα Γναίου
Σκιπίωνος τοῦ στρατηγήσαντος ἐν Ἰβηρίᾳ καὶ ἐν
αὐτῇ πεσόντος, ἀνεψιὸν δὲ Σκιπίωνος τοῦ Καρχηδονίους ἀφελομένου τὴν ἡγεμονίαν καὶ πρώτου κληθέν-
τος Ἀφρικανοῦ.

237 57. Ὧδε μὲν ἡ θεὸς ἐς Ῥώμην δι᾽ ἀνδρῶν καὶ γυναικῶν ἀρίστων ἀφικνεῖτο· ἐν δὲ Λιβύῃ Καρχηδονίων
συνεχῶς ὑπὸ τοῦδε τοῦ Σκιπίωνος ἡττωμένων, ὅσοι
Βρυττίων ταῦτ᾽ ἐγίγνωσκον, ἀφίσταντο ἀπὸ τοῦ Ἀννίβου καὶ τὰς φρουρὰς οἱ μὲν ἔκτεινον, οἱ δ᾽ ἐξέβαλ-
238 λον. οἱ δὲ οὐδέτερα τούτων δυνάμενοι λάθρᾳ πρὸς τὴν

---

41 The Megalesia, the festival to which Appian refers, in honor
of the Anatolian goddess Cybele, was celebrated at Rome in early
April.

tival dedicated to the mother of the gods.[41] The story goes 234
that the ship on which it was being carried stuck fast in the
mud of the river Tiber, and they could find no way to pull
it free. Eventually, the seers declared that the ship would
only follow if a woman who had never committed adultery
pulled it. Claudia Quinta was a woman who had a still
untried charge of adultery against her—her profligate lifestyle made it a very credible charge—but vehemently pro-
testing her innocence, she tied the boat to her belt, and
the goddess followed. Claudia, of course, now exchanged 235
her most shameful reputation for a most honorable one.[42]
Before Claudia's intervention, the Sibylline Books had ordered the Romans to send the best man among them to
bring the image of the goddess back from Phrygia. So they 236
had sent the man judged to be the best among them at that
time, Scipio surnamed Nasica, son of the Gnaeus Scipio
who had commanded in Iberia and had fallen in battle
there, and cousin of the first Scipio to have the name
Africanus, who deprived the Carthaginians of their dominance.[43]

57. So it was that the goddess arrived in Rome by the 237
agency of their best man and best woman. In Africa, the
Carthaginians were suffering repeated defeats at the
hands of this Scipio, and the Brutii who learned of this
revolted from Hannibal, some of them killing their garrisons, others driving them out. Those who were not in a 238

[42] Livy (29.14) refers only fleetingly to her earlier dubious
reputation.

[43] P. Cornelius Scipio Nasica reached the consulship in 191.
His father (Cn. Cornelius Scipio Calvus) and his uncle (P. Corne-
lius Scipio, father of Africanus) had died in Spain in 211: see
Appian's account in *Ib.* 14.53–17.74.

σύγκλητον ἐπρέσβευον, τὴν μὲν ἀνάγκην αὐτῶν καὶ
239 τὴν προαίρεσιν ὑποδεικνύοντες. Ἀννίβας δὲ ἐς μὲν
Πετηλίαν ἔνοπλος παρῆλθεν, οὐκέτι Πετηλίνων ἐχόντων αὐτήν· ἐκβαλὼν γὰρ αὐτοὺς ἐδεδώκει Βρυττίοις.
ᾐτιᾶτο δ᾽, ὅτι ἐπρέσβευσαν ἐς Ῥώμην, ἀρνουμένων δ᾽
240 ἐκείνων ὑπεκρίνετο πιστεύειν. "Ἵνα δ᾽," ἔφη, "Μηδ᾽
ὑπονοῆσθε," τοὺς μὲν δυνατοὺς παρέδωκε τοῖς Νομά-
σιν κεχωρισμένως τηρεῖν αὐτῶν ἕκαστον, τοῦ δὲ πλήθους τὰ ὅπλα παρείλετο, τοὺς δὲ δούλους καθοπλίσας
ἐπέστησε τῇ πόλει φύλακας. καὶ τούτοις ὅμοια τὰς
241 ἄλλας πόλεις ἐπιὼν ἐποίει. Θουρίων δὲ τρισχιλίους
Καρχηδονίοις μάλιστα εὔνους ἐξελόμενος καὶ πεντακοσίους ἄλλους ἀπὸ τῶν ἀγρῶν τὰ λοιπὰ τῇ στρατιᾷ
242 διαρπάζειν ἔδωκε. καὶ τῆς πόλεως ἐγκρατῆ φρουρὰν
καταλιπὼν ἐς Κρότωνα τοὺς τρισχιλίους καὶ πεντακοσίους μετῴκιζε, τὴν πόλιν εὔκαιρον ἡγούμενος εἶναι καὶ ταμιεῖον αὐτὴν ἑαυτῷ καὶ ὁρμητήριον ἐπὶ τὰς
ἄλλας τιθέμενος.

243   58. Καρχηδονίων δ᾽ αὐτὸν μετακαλούντων κατὰ
σπουδὴν ἐπικουρεῖν κινδυνευούσῃ τῇ πατρίδι ὑπὸ
Σκιπίωνος καὶ τὸν ναύαρχον Ἀσρούβαν ἐπ᾽ αὐτόν,
ἵνα μὴ βραδύνειε, πεμψάντων ἤχθετο μέν, τῆς Καρχηδονίων ἐς τοὺς ἄρχοντας ἀπιστίας τε καὶ ἀχαρι-
στίας ἐς πεῖραν ἐρχόμενος διὰ μακροῦ, καὶ τὴν αἰτίαν
ἐδεδοίκει τοῦ τοσοῦδε πολέμου πρῶτος ἐμβαλὼν ἐν
Ἰβηρίᾳ, ἐγνώκει δ᾽ ὑπ᾽ ἀνάγκης ὅμως ἕπεσθαι καὶ
ναῦς εἰργάζετο πολλάς, εὐξύλου τῆς Ἰταλίας οὔσης.

position to do either secretly sent embassies to the senate to make clear their difficult situation and their preference for Rome. Hannibal now came in force to Petelia, which 239 was no longer inhabited by the Petelians, as he had driven them out and given the town to some Brutii.[44] He accused the Brutii of sending a diplomatic mission to Rome, but pretended to believe them when they denied it. Their leading citizens, however, he handed over to the Numidians to guard each of them separately, "So that there is no 240 reason even to suspect you," he said. The ordinary people he disarmed, but he gave weapons to the slaves and set them to guard the town. He also went round the other towns and followed a similar procedure. Making an excep- 241 tion of three thousand Thurians who were particularly well disposed to Carthage, and five hundred others from the countryside, he plundered the belongings of the rest and gave them to his soldiers. Leaving a strong garrison in 242 the town, he resettled these three thousand five hundred in Croton, which he regarded as strategically located: he made it his depot and base for operations against the other towns.

58. When the Carthaginians urgently summoned 243 Hannibal to come to the aid of his country now threatened by Scipio, and sent their admiral, Hasdrubal, to him to make sure he did not delay, he complained about the suspicious and ungrateful treatment of its leaders by Carthage, which he had experienced over a long period. He was also afraid he would be blamed for causing this great war by initiating the attack in Iberia, but decided, nevertheless, he had no option but to obey and set about building many ships, Italy having a rich supply of wood.

[44] Petelia is modern Strongoli in Calabria.

244 τῶν δ' ἔτι ὑπηκόων οἱ πόλεων ὡς ἀλλοτρίων καταφρονῶν ἔγνω διαρπάσαι πάσας καὶ τὴν στρατιὰν
πλουτίσας εὔνουν ἐς τὰς ἐν Καρχηδόνι συκοφαντίας
245 ἐπαγαγέσθαι. αἰδούμενός τε αὐτὸς παρασπονδεῖν
Ἀσρούβαν τὸν ναύαρχον ἐπὶ προφάσει περιέπεμπε,
τοὺς φρουροῦντας ὀψόμενον. ὁ δὲ εἰς ἑκάστην πόλιν
εἰσιὼν ἐκέλευε τοῖς ἐνοικοῦσιν αὐτούς τε καὶ δούλους
αὐτῶν, ὅσα δύναιντο, λαβόντας ἐκ τῶν πόλεων μεθ-
246 ίστασθαι καὶ τὰ λοιπὰ διήρπαζε. τούτων ἔνιοι πυνθανόμενοι, πρὶν τὸν Ἀσρούβαν ἥκειν, τοῖς φρουροῖς
ἐπετίθεντο, καὶ συνέβαινεν ὅπου μὲν κρατεῖν τὰς
πόλεις, ὅπου δὲ τοὺς φρουρούς, σφαγή τε ποικίλη καὶ
γυναικῶν ὕβρις καὶ παρθένων ἀπαγωγαὶ καὶ πάντα,
ὅσα ἐν πόλεσιν ἑαλωκυίαις, ἐγίγνοντο.

247 59. Αὐτὸς δὲ ὁ Ἀννίβας τοὺς συστρατευομένους οἱ
τῶν Ἰταλῶν εἰδὼς εὖ γεγυμνασμένους ἔπειθε πολλαῖς
ὑποσχέσεσιν ἐς τὴν Λιβύην αὑτῷ συστρατεῦσαι. καὶ
τούτων οἱ μὲν τὰ ἡμαρτημένα σφίσιν ἐς τὰς πατρίδας
δεδιότες εἵποντο, φεύγοντες τὴν οἰκείαν ἑκόντες, οἱ δὲ
248 οὐδὲν ἁμαρτόντες ᾤκνουν. ἀθροίσας οὖν τούσδε τοὺς
ὑπομένειν ἀξιοῦντας ὡς δή τι λέξων αὐτοῖς ἢ χαριού-
μενος τῶν γεγονότων ἢ περὶ τοῦ μέλλοντος ἐπισκή-
ψων περιέστησε τὴν στρατιὰν ὡπλισμένην ἄφνω καὶ
προσέταξε τοῖς ἰδίοις ἀνδράποδα ἐξ αὐτῶν, ὅσα
249 θέλουσιν, ἐπιλέξασθαι. ὡς δὲ οἱ μὲν ἐπελέξαντο, οἱ δὲ
ᾐδοῦντο συστρατιώτας πολλὰ συνειργασμένους σφίσιν ἀνδραποδίσασθαι, τοὺς λοιποὺς κατηκόντισεν
ἅπαντας, τοῦ μὴ τοιούσδε ἄνδρας ποτὲ Ῥωμαίοις

Disdainfully treating the towns that still remained subject   244
to him as aliens, he decided to plunder them all, and by
making the soldiers rich, to win their favor to his side in
the chicanery he would face at Carthage. He was ashamed   245
personally to break his word, however, and sent his admiral Hasdrubal around the towns, supposedly to inspect the
garrisons. On entering each town, Hasdrubal told the inhabitants to take what they and their slaves could carry,
and move elsewhere: anything left he plundered. Some   246
heard about this before Hasdrubal's arrival, and attacked
the garrisons. Whether the towns prevailed, as in some
places, or the garrisons, as in others, there was widespread
slaughter, women were raped and girls kidnapped, along
with all the usual things that happen in captured towns.

59. Hannibal himself knew that his allied troops from   247
Italy were well trained, and he set about persuading them
with lavish promises to serve with him back in Africa.
Some, who were afraid because of the crimes they had
committed against their country, agreed to follow him and
willingly leave their homeland for exile, while others who
had done no wrong hesitated. So, gathering together those   248
who chose to stay, as if he was going to address them, or
reward them for past services or give instructions about
the future, he suddenly surrounded them with armed
troops, and told his men to choose out from the gathering
those they would like to have as slaves. Some made their   249
choice, others were ashamed to enslave their fellow soldiers with whom they had fought side by side on so many
occasions. The remaining Italians were shot down, so that
such good men should never be of service to the Romans.

γενέσθαι χρησίμους· ἐπικατέσφαξε δ' αὐτοῖς καὶ ἵππους ἐς τετρακισχιλίους καὶ πλῆθος ὑποζυγίων, οὐ
δυνάμενος ἐς Λιβύην ἐπάγεσθαι.

250   60. Μετὰ δὲ τοῦτ' ἐς τὰς ναῦς τὸ πλῆθος ἐμβιβάσας
τὸ πνεῦμα ἀνέμενεν, ὀλίγους ἐς φυλακὴν ἐπὶ τῆς γῆς
καταλιπών. οἱ δὲ Πετηλῖνοι καὶ σὺν αὐτοῖς ἕτεροι
Ἰταλοὶ ἐπέθεντο καί τινας αὐτῶν κατασφάξαντες ἀπέ-
251   δρασαν. Ἀννίβας δ' ἐπὶ Λιβύης ἀνήγετο, ἑκκαίδεκα
ἔτεσιν ὁμαλῶς πορθήσας τε τὴν Ἰταλίαν καὶ τοὺς
ἄνδρας ἐμπλήσας κακῶν μυρίων καὶ ἐς κίνδυνον
ἔσχατον πολλάκις συναγαγὼν τοῖς τε ὑπηκόοις αὐτοῦ
καὶ συμμάχοις ἐνυβρίσας ὡς πολεμίοις· ἅτε γὰρ καὶ
τέως αὐτοῖς οὐκ ἐπ' εὐνοίᾳ μᾶλλον ἢ χρείᾳ χρώμενος,
οὐδὲν ἔχων ἔτι πρὸς αὐτῶν ὠφελεῖσθαι, κατεφρόνη-
σεν ὡς πολεμίων.

252   61. Ἀννίβου δ' ἀποπλεύσαντος ἡ βουλὴ τοῖς μὲν
ἄλλοις ἔθνεσι τῆς Ἰταλίας, ὅσοι μετέθεντο πρὸς ἐκεῖνον, συνέγνω τῶν γεγονότων καὶ ἀμνηστίαν ἐψηφίσατο, Βρυττίων δὲ μόνων, οἳ μέχρι τέλους αὐτῷ προ-
θυμότατοι γεγένηντο, χώραν τε πολλὴν ἀφείλετο καὶ
253   ὅπλα, εἴ τινα ἦν ἔτι χωρὶς ὧν Ἀννίβας ἀφῄρητο· ἔς
τε τὸ μέλλον ἀπεῖπεν αὐτοῖς μὴ στρατεύεσθαι ὡς οὐδ'
ἐλευθέροις οὖσιν, ὑπηρέτας δὲ τοῖς τε ὑπάτοις καὶ
στρατηγοῖς, τοῖς ἐς τὰς τῶν ἐθνῶν ἡγεμονίας ἀπιοῦ-
σιν, ἐς τὰς δημοσίας ὑπηρεσίας οἷα θεράποντας ἀκο-
λουθεῖν. τοῦτο τὸ τέλος ἦν Ἀννίβου τῆς ἐς τὴν
Ἰταλίαν γενομένης ἐσβολῆς.

In addition to the men, he also slaughtered about four thousand horses and a large number of transport animals, which they could not bring back to Africa.

60. Hannibal then embarked the main body and waited 250 for the wind, leaving a few on the land as a rearguard. The Petelians along with other Italians attacked and killed some of them and then ran off. So Hannibal set sail for 251 Africa. For sixteen consecutive years he had devastated Italy, inflicting countless miseries on the people and repeatedly driving them to the very edge of disaster. His allies and subjects he now insulted as if they were the enemy. For he had only used them before because he had to, not because he liked them, and now, with nothing more to be gained from them, he treated them like the enemy with contempt.

61. On Hannibal's departure, the senate pardoned all 252 the Italian peoples who had gone over to his side, and voted an amnesty for past events, with the exception only of the Brutii, who had remained his keenest supporters right up to the end. The senate confiscated much of their land and any weapons they still had, not taken by Hannibal. For the future, they were forbidden from serving in 253 the Roman army, as they were not even free men, and they were made to accompany consuls and praetors going to their provinces, to help them, like servants, in carrying out their public duties. So ended Hannibal's invasion of Italy.